The Princeton Review®

Cracking the GRE® Mathematics Subject Test

THE STAFF OF THE PRINCETON REVIEW

FOURTH EDITION

RANDOM HOUSE, INC.
NEW YORK

Penguin
Random
House

PrincetonReview.com

The Princeton Review, Inc.
24 Prime Parkway, Suite 201
Natick, MA 01760
E-mail: editorialsupport@review.com

Published in the United States by Random House LLC, New York
and simultaneously in Canada by Random House of Canada Limited, Toronto.

A Penguin Random House Company.

ISBN: 978-0-375-42972-9
ISSN: 1541-4957

Editor: Rebecca Lessem
Production Editor: Meave Shelton
Production Coordinator: Mary Kinzel

Printed in the United States of America on partially recycled
paper.

20   19   18   17   16   15   14   13

Fourth Edition

Editorial

Rob Franek, Senior VP, Publisher
Casey Cornelius, VP Content Development
Mary Beth Garrick, Director of Production
Selena Coppock, Managing Editor
Calvin Cato, Editor
Colleen Day, Editor
Aaron Riccio, Editor
Meave Shelton, Editor
Orion McBean, Editorial Assistant

Random House Publishing Team

Tom Russell, Publisher
Alison Stoltzfus, Publishing Manager
Dawn Ryan, Associate Managing Editor
Ellen Reed, Production Manager
Kristin Lindner, Production Supervisor
Andrea Lau, Designer

CONTENTS

Preface

WHAT IS ETS?

The General and Subject Graduate Record Examinations (GRE®) are created and administered by Educational Testing Service, Inc., a private, nonprofit corporation located in Princeton, New Jersey. ETS sounds like a scholarly organization, but in truth it's a business that's devoted to churning out standardized tests that are inflicted on you from your high-school years onward (remember the SAT?). If you need to contact ETS:

Address:	GRE-ETS
	P.O. Box 6000
	Princeton, NJ 08541-6000
Phone:	609-771-7670 or toll-free 866-473-4373
	Monday–Friday 8:00 A.M.– 7:45 P.M. EST (except for U.S. Holidays)
Fax:	610-290-8975
E-mail:	use form provided at **www.ets.org/gre**

WHAT IS THE PRINCETON REVIEW?

The Princeton Review is a test-preparation company based in New York City. We analyze actual standardized tests and use them to develop techniques for test taking. We find the tests' weaknesses, quirks, and patterns, and we pass this information on to you. After reading this book, you'll be far better prepared to tackle ETS's tests!

WHAT'S THE GRE MATH SUBJECT TEST AND WHY DO I NEED TO TAKE IT?

The GRE® Subject Test in Mathematics is taken by students who are applying for admission (or a fellowship) to study mathematics at the graduate level. It's offered three times a year—in April, October, and November. Graduate school admissions committees consider your GRE Subject Test score in addition to your undergraduate record (GPA, institution, courses taken, letters of recommendation, etc.) in making their decision about your application to graduate school.

The GRE Math Subject Test consists of about 66 multiple-choice questions that are intended to assess the knowledge and skills you've developed as an undergraduate math major. The time limit is 2 hours and 50 minutes (so you have about 2.5 minutes per question, but I didn't need to tell *you* that). Each question is followed by five choices—A through E—and your job, of course, is to choose the one right answer and bubble it in on a separate answer sheet in #2 lead pencil. No notes, books, calculators, or scratch paper are permitted. (All scratchwork is done directly in the exam booklet itself.) Protractors and slide rules are also prohibited, so be sure to leave these handy items at home.

HOW'S THE TEST SCORED, AND HOW WELL DO I NEED TO DO?

The computer that scores your answer sheet awards you 1 point for each correct answer but subtracts 1/4 of a point for each wrong answer; the net result is called your *raw score*. (Since there is a penalty for a wrong answer, there's little to be gained by randomly guessing on a question you know nothing about, but if you're able to eliminate one or more answer choices, then it's a good strategy to guess among the remaining choices.) Your raw score is then converted to a *scaled score*, which is then reported to you. Officially, the score range is 200 to 990, but the very lowest scaled score given (something you want to avoid, by the way) may be much higher than 200. The scaled score is meant to equate your performance with that of others who have taken the test over the previous three years, so that scores from different administrations of the test can be compared. The answer to the natural question, *"How well do I need to do?"* depends on many factors. You can check with the admissions offices of the graduate schools to which you're planning to apply to see if they release average scores of the students they accepted the previous year. Generally, scoring above an 800 puts you in the top quarter of test takers, and would be considered a very good score. Finally, be aware that applying for a fellowship is more competitive than "just" applying for graduate admission, so you'll typically need a higher score to be granted a fellowship.

WHAT TOPICS DOES THE TEST COVER?

The content of the GRE Subject Test in Mathematics includes:

- Precalculus (algebra, trigonometry)

- Calculus I (limits, derivatives, integrals, etc., for functions of one variable)

- Calculus II (multivariable calculus)

- Differential equations

- Linear algebra

- Abstract algebra and number theory

- Additional topics such as:

  - Set theory

  - Probability and statistics

  - Combinatorics

  - Real analysis

  - Topology

  - Complex variables

About half of the questions on the test are in calculus and differential equations; another roughly 25 percent are in algebra (precalculus, linear algebra, abstract algebra, and number theory). The remaining questions cover the additional topics.

Remember: You're being tested on what you learned as an undergraduate. The questions are *not* like those on a Ph.D. qualifying exam you might take as a graduate student. Also, because mathematics curricula vary from institution to institution, the questions are intended to cover material most undergraduates are likely to have studied. Therefore, specialized knowledge in, say, a new subfield of abstract algebra (no pun intended) isn't going to be on the test. Furthermore, you don't have to get every question right to get the maximum score. (In fact, if your raw score is 2/3 of the maximum raw score, your scaled score will generally put you in the top 25 percent.)

HOW CAN I PREPARE FOR THIS TEST?

Naturally, it's important to be familiar with the topics—to know definitions, statements of important theorems, and techniques for solving the most common problems. Then you must practice applying what you've learned to answering questions like those you'll see on the test, many of which can look rather unconventional. This book is designed to review virtually all of the content areas covered on the test. Each chapter (except the last) is followed by sample multiple-choice questions, and perhaps even more important, answers and explanations are provided for every example and question in this book. You'll learn as much—if not more—from actively reading the solutions as you will from reading the text and examples. Finally, a full-length practice test is provided, with a complete explanation for every question. The difficulty level of the examples and questions in this book is at or slightly above GRE level, so if you have the time and motivation to attack these questions and learn from the solutions, you should feel confident that you will do your very best on the real thing.

Here's an important strategy: Don't linger over any one question. Go through the exam and answer the questions on the topics you know well, leaving the tough ones for later when you make another pass. All the questions are worth the same amount, so you don't want to run out of time and not get to questions you could have answered because you spent too much time agonizing over a few difficult ones. No one is expected to answer all of them, so maximize the number you get right.

WHERE CAN I GET MORE INFORMATION ABOUT THE TEST?

On the Internet, go to www.gre.org and click on Subject Tests. This Web site provides valuable information about the GRE Subject Tests including test descriptions, test dates, test fees, and complete registration information. It should answer all your questions about the administration of the test.

Everyone who registers for one of the GRE Subject Tests will be sent—free of charge—a subject test practice book, published by ETS. Each book contains information about the specific subject test for which you have registered, and includes a sample, full-length practice test. You can also download the practice book for free from the GRE Web site.

I wish you all the best as you prepare for the GRE Math Subject Test. Good luck!

—*Steve Leduc*

Precalculus

INTRODUCTION

In this first chapter, we'll review topics such as functions, graphs, polynomial equations, logarithms, and trigonometry, which are commonly tested on the GRE Math Subject Test. We will assume that you're comfortable with the laws of exponents and radicals as well as with basic arithmetic operations involving real numbers, complex numbers, and general algebraic expressions.

FUNCTIONS

Functions constitute a very important notion in mathematics, and the definition of a function becomes increasingly sophisticated as your mathematical education progresses. Basically, a **function** is a rule that assigns to each element of one set (the **domain**) exactly one element of another set (the **range**). A function f with domain A and range B is denoted by

$$f: A \to B$$

If f assigns to the element x of A the element y of B, we say that f **maps** x to y, and write either

$$y = f(x) \quad \text{or} \quad x \overset{f}{\mapsto} y$$

and call y the **image** of x. It is common to refer to "the function $f(x)$," especially when there's a formula for $f(x)$, even though it's actually f that's the function; $f(x)$ is the image of x.

Example 1.1 Consider the real-valued function f, defined by the equation

$$f(x) = -\sqrt{\frac{x+1}{|2x-1|}}$$

(a) Determine the largest subset of **R** that can serve as the domain of f.

(b) A point x_0 in the domain of f is called a *fixed point* of f if $f(x_0) = x_0$. This function f has exactly one rational fixed point. What is it?

Solution:

(a) First, the expression in the denominator cannot equal 0, so $x = \frac{1}{2}$ has to be excluded from the domain. Next, the fraction under the square root sign must be nonnegative. Since the denominator is positive for all $x \neq \frac{1}{2}$, we need only ensure that the numerator is nonnegative; thus, it must be true that $x \geq -1$. Therefore, the domain of f is equal to $[-1, \frac{1}{2}) \cup (\frac{1}{2}, \infty)$.

(b) To determine the fixed points of f, we need to solve the equation $f(x) = x$. Because of the presence of the absolute value sign, this leads to the two equations

$$\frac{x+1}{2x-1} = x^2 \quad \text{or} \quad \frac{x+1}{1-2x} = x^2$$

which are equivalent to the equations:

$$2x^3 - x^2 - x - 1 = 0 \quad \text{or} \quad 2x^3 - x^2 + x + 1 = 0$$

By the Rational Roots theorem (see the section on roots of polynomial equations on page 18), the only possible rational roots of these equations are ± 1 or $\pm\frac{1}{2}$. We can disregard $x = \frac{1}{2}$, because it's not in the domain of f, and simply check the remaining three possible rational roots. None of them satisfies the first equation, but $x = -\frac{1}{2}$ satisfies the second. Therefore, the function f has $x = -\frac{1}{2}$ is a fixed point, as this calculation shows:

$$f\left(-\frac{1}{2}\right) = -\sqrt{\frac{-\frac{1}{2}+1}{\left|2\left(-\frac{1}{2}\right)-1\right|}} = -\sqrt{\frac{\frac{1}{2}}{2}} = -\sqrt{\frac{1}{4}} = -\frac{1}{2}$$

COMPOSITION OF FUNCTIONS

Functions can be added, subtracted, multiplied, and divided, but another way to combine functions is to compose them. For example, let f and g be functions such that the domain of g contains the range of f. Then we could take some element, x, in the domain of f, substitute it into f, then take the result and substitute it into g. This kind of substitution of one function into another is the basic idea of the composition of functions. For example, if $f: A \rightarrow B$ and $g: B \rightarrow C$, then the **composite** function $g \circ f$ (read "g of f" or "g circle f") is defined as follows:

$$(g \circ f)(x) = g(f(x))$$

Be careful to distinguish $g \circ f$ from $f \circ g$, which would be defined by the equation:

$$(f \circ g)(x) = f(g(x))$$

The compositions $g \circ f$ and $f \circ g$ are rarely the same. For example, if $f(x) = x^2$ and $g(x) = x + 7$, then:

$$(g \circ f)(x) = g(x^2) = x^2 + 7 \qquad \text{but} \qquad (f \circ g)(x) = f(x + 7) = (x + 7)^2$$

It's also important to remember to work from right to left when applying the functions in a composition; the notation $g \circ f$ tells you to apply f first, then g.

Example 1.2 Consider functions f and g such that $(f \circ g)(x) = \sqrt{x^2 + 1} - 1$. If $g(x) = x^2 + 1$, then what's the value of $f(4)$?

Solution: Since $f(x^2 + 1) = \sqrt{x^2 + 1} - 1$, we know that $f(x) = \sqrt{x} - 1$. Therefore, $f(4) = \sqrt{4} - 1 = 1$.

Example 1.3 Let f and g be real-valued functions defined on the entire real line such that $f(x) = g(x^2 - 1)$ and $g(x) = x - 1$. Find all values of x such that:

$$(f \circ g)(x) = (g \circ f)(x)$$

Solution: First, we'll simplify each side of the equation. Since

$$(f \circ g)(x) = f(g(x)) = f(x - 1) = g[(x - 1)^2 - 1] = g(x^2 - 2x) = x^2 - 2x - 1$$

and

$$(g \circ f)(x) = g(f(x)) = f(x) - 1 = g(x^2 - 1) - 1 = [(x^2 - 1) - 1] - 1 = x^2 - 3$$

we need to solve the equation $x^2 - 2x - 1 = x^2 - 3$. Subtracting the x^2-term from each side leaves $-2x - 1 = -3$, so $x = 1$.

INVERSE FUNCTIONS

A function $f\colon A \to B$ is said to be **one-to-one** (or **injective**) if no two elements in A are mapped by f to the same element in B. That is, f is one-to-one if $x_1 \neq x_2$ implies $f(x_1) \neq f(x_2)$. For example, the function $f\colon \mathbf{R} \to \mathbf{R}$, defined by $f(x) = x^3$ is one-to-one, but the function $g\colon \mathbf{R} \to \mathbf{R}$ defined by $g(x) = x^2$ is not (because, for instance, both -2 and 2 are mapped by g to 4; but if the domain of g were restricted to, say, just the nonnegative reals, then g would be one-to-one). A function $f\colon A \to B$ is said to be **onto** (or **surjective**) if every element in B is the image of some element in A. For example, the function $f\colon \mathbf{R} \to \mathbf{R}$ defined by $f(x) = x^3$ is onto, but the function $g\colon \mathbf{R} \to \mathbf{R}$ defined by $g(x) = x^2$ is not (because -4 is in the range of g, but there's no element in $\mathbf{R}$ mapped by g to -4; but if the range of g were restricted to just the nonnegative reals, then g would be onto). If $f\colon A \to B$ is both one-to-one and onto, it is said to be **bijective**, and it's guaranteed that for every element y in B there is one, and only one, element x in A such that $f(x) = y$. So, we can define another function, $f^{-1}\colon B \to A$, as follows:

$$f^{-1}(y) = x \quad \text{iff} \quad f(x) = y$$

The function f^{-1} is called the **inverse** of f. It's important not to interpret the superscript "–1" as an exponent; in this context, it's not. The function f^{-1} is usually very different from $\dfrac{1}{f}$, the reciprocal of f, which is defined by the equation:

$$\left(\frac{1}{f}\right)(x) = \frac{1}{f(x)} \quad \text{(as long as } f(x) \neq 0)$$

By definition, then, both of the following equations will always hold for a bijective function $f: A \to B$ and its inverse, $f^{-1}: B \to A$:

$$f^{-1}(f(x)) = x \quad \text{for every } x \text{ in } A$$

and

$$f(f^{-1}(y)) = y \quad \text{for every } y \text{ in } B$$

If you're given an equation in the form $y = f(x)$, the way to determine a formula for f^{-1} is simply to interchange x and y in the given equation, then solve for y.

Example 1.4   Define f by the equation $f(x) = x^3 + x - 4$. Given that this function has a well-defined inverse, determine the value of $f^{-1}(-2)$.

Solution: Actually finding a formula for $f^{-1}(x)$ would be quite difficult here, but we don't need to. If $a = f^{-1}(-2)$, then by definition, $f(a) = -2$. So we simply need to find the value of a such that $f(a) = -2$:

$$f(a) = -2 \quad \Rightarrow \quad a^3 + a - 4 \; = -2 \quad \Rightarrow \quad a^3 + a = 2$$

By inspection, we can see that $a = 1$, so $f^{-1}(-2) = 1$.

Example 1.5   Let A be the open interval $(-1, 1)$ and define a bijective function f on A by the equation:

$$f(x) = \frac{x}{1 - x^2}$$

Find a formula for $f^{-1}(x)$ that works for every real x.

Solution: Given the equation $y = \dfrac{x}{1 - x^2}$, we interchange x and y and solve for y:

$$x = \frac{y}{1 - y^2}$$

$$xy^2 + y - x = 0$$

$$y = \frac{-1 \pm \sqrt{1 + 4x^2}}{2x} \quad (*)$$

There are two problems with the form of this result. The first problem is that it specifies two functions because of the ±. The second is that $x = 0$ is excluded from the domain of this function (because of the $2x$ in the denominator); but since 0 is in the range of f [because $f(0) = 0$], it *must* be in the domain of f^{-1}. Let's start by solving the first problem. Notice that $\sqrt{1+4x^2} > \sqrt{4x^2} = 2|x|$, so if we use the form of (*) with the minus sign, then

$$x > 0 \quad \Rightarrow \quad -1 - \sqrt{1+4x^2} < -2x \quad \Rightarrow \quad \frac{-1-\sqrt{1+4x^2}}{2x} < -1$$

and

$$x < 0 \quad \Rightarrow \quad -1 - \sqrt{1+4x^2} < 2x \quad \Rightarrow \quad \frac{-1-\sqrt{1+4x^2}}{2x} > 1$$

both of which contradict the fact that the range of f^{-1} must be the domain of f, $A = (-1, 1)$. Therefore, we only consider the plus sign in (*). To solve the second problem—that is, to rewrite the equation for f^{-1} in a form that does not exclude $x = 0$—we rationalize the numerator:

$$y = \frac{-1+\sqrt{1+4x^2}}{2x} \cdot \frac{-1-\sqrt{1+4x^2}}{-1-\sqrt{1+4x^2}}$$

$$= \frac{1-(1+4x^2)}{-2x(1+\sqrt{1+4x^2})}$$

$$f^{-1}(x) = \frac{2x}{1+\sqrt{1+4x^2}}$$

GRAPHS IN THE *XY*-PLANE

If the domain and range of a function are subsets of the real numbers, then the function can be graphed in the *xy*-plane. The **graph** of f consists of all points (x, y) in the plane such that $y = f(x)$. A graph is said to be **symmetric with respect to the *y*-axis** if, whenever (x, y) is on the graph, $(-x, y)$ is also. A graph is said to be **symmetric with respect to the origin** if, whenever (x, y) is on the graph, $(-x, -y)$ is also. The graph of $y = f(x)$ and the graph of its inverse function $y = f^{-1}(x)$ are **symmetric with respect to the line *y* = *x***, since if (x, y) lies on one of the graphs, then (y, x) lies on the other.

Any equation that involves two variables can be sketched in the plane: The graph simply consists of all points (x, y) that satisfy the equation. In some cases, the resulting graph may not be the graph of a function. The **vertical-line test** says that a given graph is not the graph of a function if there are two (or more) points that lie on the same vertical line; this would be a violation of the definition of a function, which says that for every value of the **independent variable** (from the domain), a function assigns *exactly one* value to the **dependent variable** (from the range). A graph is said to be **symmetric with respect to the *x*-axis** if, whenever (x, y) is on the graph, $(x, -y)$ is also. The *x*-coordinate (**abscissa**) of a point at which a graph crosses the *x*-axis is called an ***x*-intercept**, and the *y*-coordinate (**ordinate**) of a point at which a graph crosses the *y*-axis is called a ***y*-intercept**.

Example 1.6   Sketch the graph of the function:

$$y = \begin{cases} \sqrt{1-x^2} & \text{if } -1 \le x < 0 \\ |x-1| & \text{if } x \ge 0 \end{cases}$$

Solution: The equation $y = \sqrt{1-x^2}$ (for $-1 \le x < 0$) describes the section of the unit circle that exists in the second quadrant, and the graph of the equation $y = |x-1|$ is the graph of $y = |x|$ moved 1 unit to the right:

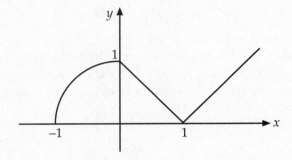

Example 1.7   Sketch the graph of the function

$$y = \begin{cases} 2-x^2 & \text{if } -2 \le x \le 1 \\ [x] & \text{if } x > 1 \end{cases}$$

where $[x]$ is the greatest integer $\le x$.

Solution: We can get the graph of the equation $y = 2 - x^2$ by inverting the graph of the basic parabola $y = x^2$, and then translating upward by 2 units to get $y = -x^2 + 2$. The graph of the greatest integer function, $y = [x]$, has a break at each integer n, since for every x such that $n - 1 \le x < n$, the value of $[x]$ is $n - 1$, but at $x = n$, the value of $[x]$ jumps to n. This is an example of a step function.

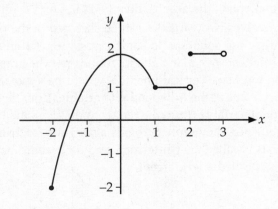

ANALYTIC GEOMETRY

Analytic geometry centers on the interplay between algebra and geometry. In this section, we'll review lines, parabolas, circles, ellipses, and hyperbolas in the xy-plane. All of these curves fall under a common heading: They are **conic sections** and have as their universal equation the general second-degree equation in x and y:

$$Ax^2 + Bxy + Cy^2 + Dx + Ey + F = 0$$

The identity of the graph depends on the values of the coefficients. If the curve is not a straight line or circle, then its symmetry axis (or axes) will not be parallel to one of the coordinate axes if $B \neq 0$, but the coordinate axes can be rotated to simplify the equation of the curve and place the axis of the conic parallel to one of the coordinate axes.

LINES

The equation for a straight line in the x-y plane is

$$ax + by + c = 0$$

in which a and b are not both 0. If the line is not vertical, then the equation of the line with slope m passing through the point (x_1, y_1) can be written as:

$$y - y_1 = m(x - x_1)$$

This is called the **point-slope formula**. Recall that if (x_1, y_1) and (x_2, y_2) are any two points on a nonvertical line, then the **slope** is defined as:

$$m = \frac{\Delta y}{\Delta x} = \frac{y_2 - y_1}{x_2 - x_1}$$

We do not define the slope of a vertical line. If two nonvertical lines have the same slope, then they're parallel (or overlapping), and if the product of the slopes of two nonvertical lines is equal to -1, then they're perpendicular.

PARABOLAS

Let F be a given fixed point and D a given fixed line that doesn't contain F. By definition, a **parabola** is the set of points in the plane containing F and D that are equidistant from the point F (the **focus**) and the line D (the **directrix**). The **axis** of a parabola is the line through the focus and perpendicular to the directrix. The **vertex** of a parabola is the turning point, the point on the parabola's axis that's midway between the focus and the directrix. The standard equations of the parabolas with vertex at the origin and axis either the x- or y-axis are:

$$y = \pm\frac{1}{4p}x^2 \quad \text{or} \quad x = \pm\frac{1}{4p}y^2$$

The following diagrams summarize the basic characteristics of these standard parabolas. The axis of the top two parabolas is the y-axis; the bottom two parabolas have the x-axis as their axis.

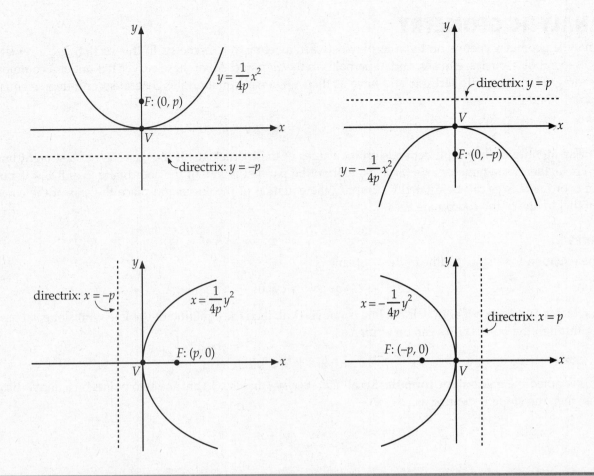

Example 1.8   Find the focus of the parabola $y = x^2$ and determine the length of the *latus rectum*, which is the line segment with endpoints on the parabola that passes through the focus, perpendicular to the axis (or, equivalently, parallel to the directrix).

Solution: The equation $y = x^2$ fits the form $y = (\dfrac{1}{4p})x^2$ if $p = \dfrac{1}{4}$. Therefore, the focus of this parabola is the point $F: (0, p) = (0, \dfrac{1}{4})$. Now, let A and B be the endpoints of the chord that passes through the focus and is perpendicular to the parabola's axis (which is the y-axis in this case). The coordinates of A and B must be $(-x, p)$ and (x, p), respectively.

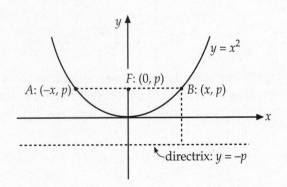

Since the (vertical) distance from B to the directrix is $p - (-p) = 2p$, the distance from B to F must also be $2p$. The distance from A to F must also be $2p$, so the length of the segment AB must be $2p + 2p = 4p$. Because $p = \dfrac{1}{4}$ for this parabola, the length of the latus rectum—the focal width—equals 1.

CIRCLES

A **circle** is the set of points in the plane that are all at a constant, positive distance from a given fixed point. This constant distance is called the **radius**, and the given fixed point is the **center**. The standard equation of the circle with radius a, centered at the origin is

$$x^2 + y^2 = a^2$$

or, equivalently,

$$\frac{x^2}{a^2} + \frac{y^2}{a^2} = 1$$

If the center is at the point (h, k), then we can replace x by $x - h$ and y by $y - k$ and write:

$$(x - h)^2 + (y - k)^2 = a^2 \quad \text{or} \quad \frac{(x-h)^2}{a^2} + \frac{(y-k)^2}{a^2} = 1$$

Example 1.9 A circle has A: $(-2, -3)$ and B: $(6, 1)$ as the endpoints of a diameter.
(a) Where does this circle cross the y-axis?
(b) Where does the line tangent to this circle at the point B cross the y-axis?

Solution:

(a) The midpoint of the diameter $\overline{AB}$ is the center of the circle:

$$C = \left(\frac{-2+6}{2}, \frac{-3+1}{2} \right) = (2, -1)$$

The radius a of the circle is equal to the distance from C to either A or B. Computing BC, we find that:

$$a = \sqrt{(6-2)^2 + [1-(-1)]^2} = \sqrt{20} \quad \Rightarrow \quad a^2 = 20$$

Therefore, the equation for this circle is:

$$(x - 2)^2 + (y + 1)^2 = 20$$

To find the points where the circle crosses the y-axis, we set x equal to 0 and solve for y:

$$(0 - 2)^2 + (y + 1)^2 = 20 \quad \Rightarrow \quad (y + 1)^2 = 16 \quad \Rightarrow \quad y = 3, -5$$

Thus, the circle crosses the y-axis at the points $(0, 3)$ and $(0, -5)$.

(b) Let L denote the tangent line for which we're looking. Then L must be perpendicular to the radius $\overline{BC}$. Because the slope of $\overline{BC}$ is

$$m_{BC} = \frac{1-(-1)}{6-2} = \frac{1}{2}$$

the slope of L must be the negative reciprocal, -2. Since $m_L = -2$ and L passes through the point B: (6, 1), the equation of the line is

$$y - 1 = -2(x - 6)$$

which we can write as $y = -2x + 13$. When $x = 0$, the value of y is 13, so L crosses the y-axis at the point (0, 13).

ELLIPSES

By definition, an **ellipse** is the set of points in the plane such that the sum of the distances from every point on the ellipse to two given fixed points (the **foci**) is a constant. (And to avoid a degenerate case, the constant sum must be greater than the distance between the foci.) The standard equation of an ellipse centered at the origin—with axes parallel to the coordinate axes—is:

$$\frac{x^2}{a^2} + \frac{y^2}{b^2} = 1$$

The longer symmetry axis of the ellipse is called the **major axis** (on which the foci are located), and the shorter one is the **minor axis**. The endpoints of the major axis are called the **vertices**. The **eccentricity** of an ellipse is a number (denoted e) between 0 and 1 that measures its "flatness." The closer e is to zero, the more the ellipse resembles a perfect circle; as e increases to 1, the ellipse flattens out.

By comparing the standard equations for the circle and the ellipse, we notice that the only difference is

that while the x^2- and y^2-terms always have identical positive coefficients for a circle, these terms have dif-

ferent positive coefficients for an ellipse. Therefore, a circle can be transformed into an ellipse (or vice ver-

sa) by changing the scale on one of the axes. For example, we can turn the circle $\frac{x^2}{a^2} + \frac{y^2}{a^2} = 1$ into the ellipse $\frac{x^2}{a^2} + \frac{y^2}{b^2} = 1$ by replacing every point (x, y) on the circle by the point $(x, \frac{by}{a})$.

The following diagrams summarize the basic characteristics of the ellipse, where the cases $a > b$ and $a < b$ are considered separately.

$\frac{x^2}{a^2} + \frac{y^2}{b^2} = 1$, $a > b$

foci: $(\pm c, 0)$, where $c = \sqrt{a^2 - b^2}$

vertices: $(\pm a, 0)$

major axis length = $2a$

minor axis length = $2b$

eccentricity: $e = \dfrac{c}{a}$

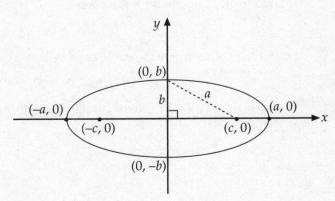

$\dfrac{x^2}{a^2} + \dfrac{y^2}{b^2} = 1,\ a < b$

foci: $(0, \pm c)$, where $c = \sqrt{b^2 - a^2}$

vertices: $(0, \pm b)$

major axis length $= 2b$

minor axis length $= 2a$

eccentricity: $e = \dfrac{c}{b}$

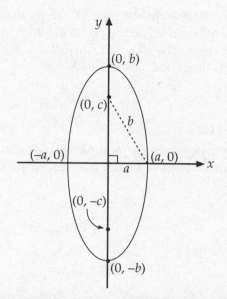

Example 1.10 The sum of the distances from every point on an ellipse to the points $(\pm 2, 0)$ is equal to 8. Find the positive value of x such that the point $(x, 3)$ is on this ellipse.

Solution: Since the foci are on the x-axis and their midpoint (which is the center of the ellipse) is the origin, the equation of the ellipse has the form

$$\frac{x^2}{a^2} + \frac{y^2}{b^2} = 1$$

where $a > b$. In this case, the sum of the distances from every point on the ellipse to the foci is equal to $2a$. Since $2a = 8$, we have $a = 4$. So the fact that $c = 2$ tells us that:

$$b = \sqrt{a^2 - c^2} = \sqrt{4^2 - 2^2} = 2\sqrt{3}$$

So the equation of the ellipse is:

$$\frac{x^2}{16} + \frac{y^2}{12} = 1$$

Substituting $y = 3$, we solve for x:

$$\frac{x^2}{16} + \frac{3^2}{12} = 1 \quad \Rightarrow \quad \frac{x^2}{16} = \frac{1}{4} \quad \Rightarrow \quad x^2 = 4 \quad \Rightarrow \quad x = \pm 2$$

Since the question asks for the positive value of x, the answer is $x = 2$.

HYPERBOLAS

By definition, a **hyperbola** is the set of points in the plane such that the difference between the distances from every point on the hyperbola to two fixed points (the **foci**) is a constant. (And to avoid a degenerate case, the constant difference must be smaller than the distance between the foci.) Unlike a parabola, circle, or ellipse, a hyperbola is not a single curve; instead, it consists of two separate curves called **branches**. A hyperbola is also different from these other curves in that it has **asymptotes**, which are lines that its branches approach but never touch, as the magnitudes of x and y increase.

The line that contains the foci is called the **focal axis**; the midpoint of the segment joining the foci is the **center** of the hyperbola; and the points at which the branches of the hyperbola intersect the focal axis are called the **vertices**. The standard equations of the hyperbolas centered at the origin with either the x- or the y-axis as their focal axis are:

$$\frac{x^2}{a^2} - \frac{y^2}{b^2} = 1 \quad \text{or} \quad \frac{y^2}{b^2} - \frac{x^2}{a^2} = 1$$

The diagrams below summarize the basic characteristics of these standard hyperbolas. Notice that the hyperbolas of the first family do not intersect the y-axis, and those of the second family do not intersect the x-axis.

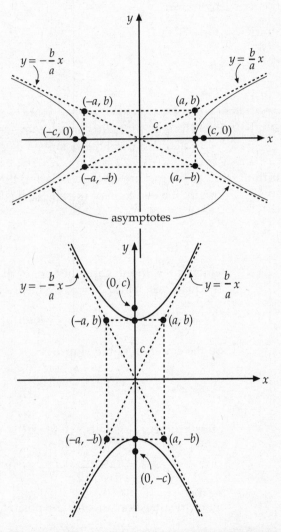

$$\frac{x^2}{a^2} - \frac{y^2}{b^2} = 1$$

foci: $(\pm c, 0)$, where $c = \sqrt{a^2 + b^2}$

vertices: $(\pm a, 0)$

asymptotes: $y = \pm\dfrac{b}{a}x$

$$\frac{y^2}{b^2} - \frac{x^2}{a^2} = 1$$

foci: $(0, \pm c)$, where $c = \sqrt{a^2 + b^2}$

vertices: $(0, \pm b)$

asymptotes: $y = \pm\dfrac{b}{a}x$

Example 1.11 The foci of a hyperbola are at $(\pm 3, 0)$, and the difference between the distances from every point on the hyperbola to the foci is 2. What's the equation of this hyperbola?

Solution: Since the foci are on the x-axis and their midpoint (the center of the hyperbola) is the origin, the equation of the hyperbola has the form:

$$\frac{x^2}{a^2} - \frac{y^2}{b^2} = 1$$

The vertices of this hyperbola are $(\pm a, 0)$. The difference between the distances from the vertex $(a, 0)$ to the two foci, $(-c, 0)$ and $(c, 0)$, is $[a - (-c)] - (c - a) = 2a$. Because we're told that this equals 2, we know that $a = 1$. Finally, since $c = \sqrt{a^2 + b^2}$, we can solve for b:

$$b = \sqrt{c^2 - a^2} = \sqrt{3^2 - 1^2} = 2\sqrt{2}$$

Therefore, the equation of this hyperbola is:

$$x^2 - \frac{y^2}{8} = 1$$

POLYNOMIAL EQUATIONS

A polynomial in the variable x is an expression of the form $a_n x^n + a_{n-1} x^{n-1} + \cdots + a_1 x + a_0$, where n is a nonnegative integer and the coefficients a_i are constants. If $a_n \neq 0$, the integer n is called the **degree** of the polynomial and a_n is called the **leading coefficient**. (No degree is defined for 0, the zero polynomial.) A polynomial of degree 2 is called a **quadratic** polynomial, and the roots of the quadratic equation

$$ax^2 + bx + c = 0$$

are given by the well-known **quadratic formula**:

$$x = \frac{-b \pm \sqrt{b^2 - 4ac}}{2a}$$

The quantity under the square root sign, $\Delta = b^2 - 4ac$, is called the **discriminant** of the polynomial; it determines the nature of the roots. If $\Delta > 0$, the equation has two distinct real roots; if $\Delta < 0$, the roots are distinct complex conjugates; and if $\Delta = 0$, the equation has exactly one (double) root. In this section, we'll also look at more general polynomial equations.

THE DIVISION ALGORITHM, REMAINDER THEOREM, AND FACTOR THEOREM

Let $p(x)$ and $d(x)$ be polynomials. If $d(x)$ is not identically zero, the **division algorithm** guarantees that dividing $p(x)$ by $d(x)$ gives unique polynomials $q(x)$ and $r(x)$, such that

$$p(x) = q(x)d(x) + r(x)$$

where either $r(x)$ is identically zero or the degree of $r(x)$ is less than the degree of $d(x)$. The polynomial $q(x)$ is called the **quotient**, and $r(x)$ is the **remainder**. In particular, assume that the degree of $p(x)$ is at least 1, and let $d(x) = x - k$, a polynomial of degree 1. If $p(x)$ is divided by $x - k$, we get

$$p(x) = q(x) \bullet (x - k) + r$$

where r is a constant. Substituting $x = k$ into this equation gives us $p(k) = r$, which says that when $p(x)$ is divided by $x - k$, the remainder is $p(k)$. This is the **Remainder theorem**. From this, we can conclude that $x = k$ is a root of the polynomial equation $p(x) = 0$ if and only if $x - k$ is a factor of $p(x)$; this is the **Factor theorem**.

THE FUNDAMENTAL THEOREM OF ALGEBRA AND ROOTS OF POLYNOMIAL EQUATIONS

The **Fundamental Theorem of Algebra** states that every polynomial equation

$$a_n x^n + a_{n-1} x^{n-1} + \cdots + a_1 x + a_0 = 0 \quad (*)$$

of degree $n \geq 1$ has at least one root (real or complex). By using the division algorithm repeatedly, every polynomial of degree $n \geq 1$ can be written as the product of unique, linear (degree 1) factors,

$$a_n x^n + a_{n-1} x^{n-1} + \cdots + a_1 x + a_0 = a_n (x - k_1)(x - k_2) \cdots (x - k_n)$$

where each k_i is a constant (real or complex). If the factor $x - k_i$ appears on the right-hand side exactly m_i times, then $x - k_i$ is a factor of multiplicity m_i, and the polynomial equation (*) has $x = k_i$ as a root of **multiplicity** m_i. So every degree n polynomial equation has exactly n roots, where a root of multiplicity m_i is counted m_i times.

Let $p(x)$ be a polynomial of degree $n \geq 1$, with real coefficients. There are several results that restrict the possibilities when searching for the roots of the polynomial equation $p(x) = 0$.

The Root Location Theorem

If $p(x)$ is a real polynomial, and real numbers a and b can be found such that $p(a) < 0$ and $p(b) > 0$, then there must be at least one value of x between a and b such that $p(x) = 0$. (This is a consequence of the Intermediate Value theorem, which you'll see in Chapter 2.)

The Rational Roots Theorem

If the coefficients of

$$p(x) = a_n x^n + a_{n-1} x^{n-1} + \cdots + a_1 x + a_0$$

are integers, then the **Rational Roots theorem** says that if the equation $p(x) = 0$ has any rational roots, then, when expressed in lowest terms, they must be of the form $x = \dfrac{s}{t}$, where s is a factor of the constant term (a_0) and t is a factor of the leading coefficient (a_n).

The Conjugate Radical Roots Theorem

If the coefficients of

$$p(x) = a_n x^n + a_{n-1} x^{n-1} + \cdots + a_1 x + a_0$$

are rational, then the **Conjugate Radical Roots theorem** states that if the equation $p(x) = 0$ has a root of the form $x = s + t\sqrt{u}$ (where $\sqrt{u}$ is irrational), then the equation must also have the conjugate radical, $x = s - t\sqrt{u}$, as a root. That is, irrational roots of rational-coefficient polynomial equations must occur in conjugate radical pairs.

The Complex Conjugate Roots Theorem

If the coefficients of

$$p(x) = a_n x^n + a_{n-1} x^{n-1} + \cdots + a_1 x + a_0$$

are real, then the **Complex Conjugate Roots theorem** states that if the equation $p(x) = 0$ has a complex root of the form $x = s + ti$, then the equation must also have the complex conjugate, $x = s - ti$, as a root. That is, complex roots of real-coefficient polynomial equations must occur in complex conjugate pairs.

SUM AND PRODUCT OF THE ROOTS

For the polynomial equation

$$a_n x^n + a_{n-1} x^{n-1} + \cdots + a_1 x + a_0 = 0 \ (a_n \neq 0)$$

the sum and product of the n roots can be written in terms of the coefficients, as follows:

$$\text{sum of the roots} = -\frac{a_{n-1}}{a_n}$$

$$\text{product of the roots} = (-1)^n \frac{a_0}{a_n}$$

In particular, if the polynomial is **monic** (which means that the leading coefficient, a_n, is equal to 1), then the sum of the roots is $-a_{n-1}$, and the product of the roots is $(-1)^n a_0$.

Example 1.12   Find the monic cubic polynomial $p(x)$ that has real coefficients such that the equation $p(x) = 0$ has 1 and $2 - i$ as roots.

Solution: Since $p(x)$ is a real polynomial, the fact that $2 - i$ is a root implies that the complex conjugate, $2 + i$, is also a root. So both $x - (2 - i)$ and $x - (2 + i)$ are factors of $p(x)$. And since 1 is a root, $p(x)$ also has $x - 1$ as a factor. Since $p(x)$ is monic and has a degree of 3, it must be true that $p(x)$ is the product of these linear factors:

$$p(x) = [x - (2 - i)][x - (2 + i)][x - 1]$$

$$= [(x - 2) + i][(x - 2) - i][x - 1]$$

$$= [(x^2 - 4x + 4) - (-1)][x - 1]$$

$$= (x^2 - 4x + 5)(x - 1)$$

$$= x^3 - 5x^2 + 9x - 5$$

Example 1.13   For the equation $x^2 + bx + c = 0$, the sum of the roots is 3, and the sum of the squares of the roots is 1. Find the numerical value of c.

Solution: First, notice that if r_1 and r_2 are the roots of the quadratic equation $x^2 + bx + c = 0$, then the sum of the roots is $-b$ and the product of the roots is c, so the sum of the squares of the roots is:

$$r_1^2 + r_2^2 = (r_1 + r_2)^2 - 2r_1 r_2 = (-b)^2 - 2c = b^2 - 2c$$

So for this question, we have $-b = 3$ and $b^2 - 2c = 1$. Since $b = -3$, the second equation becomes $(-3)^2 - 2c = 1$, which gives $c = 4$.

Example 1.14   The equation $3x^4 - 7x^3 + 5x^2 - 7x + 2 = 0$ has exactly two rational roots, both of which are positive. Find the larger of these two roots.

Solution: Since this polynomial has integer coefficients, we can apply the Rational Roots theorem to determine the set of possible rational roots. The factors of the constant term, $a_0 = 2$, are ± 1 and ± 2, and the factors of the leading coefficient, $a_4 = 3$, are ± 1 and ± 3, which means that the rational roots are among the following:

$$\pm 1, \pm \frac{1}{3}, \pm 2, \pm \frac{2}{3}$$

Since we're told that the equation has exactly two positive rational roots, we only need to consider the four possibilities 1, $\frac{1}{3}$, 2, and $\frac{2}{3}$. Substituting each of these into the polynomial, we find that $x = \frac{1}{3}$ and $x = 2$ satisfy the equation. The larger of these roots is 2, and that is our answer.

LOGARITHMS

Logarithms are exponents. Given the equation $b^y = x$, the exponent is y, which means that the logarithm is y. More precisely, we'd say that y is the **logarithm** base b of x, and write $y = \log_b x$. The laws of logarithms follow directly from the corresponding laws of exponents. In the equations below, b is a positive number that's not equal to 1.

- $\log_b x = y$ means $b^y = x$

- The function $y = \log_b x$ is the inverse of the exponential function $y = b^x$. The domain of the function $f(x) = \log_b x$ is $x > 0$, and the range is the set of all real numbers. If $b > 1$, the function is increasing (see the diagram below); if $0 < b < 1$, the function is decreasing.

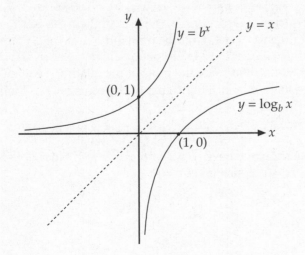

- $\log_b(x_1 x_2) = \log_b x_1 + \log_b x_2$

- $\log_b \dfrac{x_1}{x_2} = \log_b x_1 - \log_b x_2$

- $\log_b(x^a) = a \log_b x$

- $b^{\log_b x} = x$

- $(\log_b a)(\log_a x) = \log_b x$ (this is the **change-of-base formula**, with $a \neq 1$)

The two most important bases for logarithms are $b = 10$ [because we use a base-10 (decimal) number system] and $b = e$, where e is an irrational constant, approximately equal to 2.718. The selection of this seemingly unusual number is based on considerations in calculus (which we'll review in the next chapter) and is so important that the function $f(x) = \log_e x$ is called the **natural logarithm function**.

On the GRE Math Subject Test, the "e" is understood, so log x means $\log_e x$. It's important to be aware of this, since in many precalculus and calculus texts—and on calculators—log x denotes $\log_{10} x$ and the abbreviation for $\log_e x$ is ln x.

Example 1.15 Solve for x: $4^x = 2^x + 3$

Solution: Since $4^x = (2^2)^x = 2^{2x} = (2^x)^2$, the equation is equivalent to $(2^x)^2 - 2^x - 3 = 0$, which is quadratic in 2^x. The quadratic formula gives:

$$2^x = \frac{1 \pm \sqrt{13}}{2}$$

Since 2^x cannot be negative, we have to disregard the negative value on the right-hand side and conclude that:

$$2^x = \frac{1 + \sqrt{13}}{2}$$

Therefore, $x = \log_2 \dfrac{1 + \sqrt{13}}{2} = \log_2(1 + \sqrt{13}) - 1$.

Example 1.16 If $x^2 + y^2 = 14xy$, then $\log[k(x + y)] = \frac{1}{2}(\log x + \log y)$ for some constant k. Find the value of k.

Solution: Adding $2xy$ to both sides of the first equation gives $(x + y)^2 = 16xy$, which is equivalent to $[\frac{1}{4}(x + y)]^2 = xy$. Taking the log of both sides of this equation gives:

$$2\log[\tfrac{1}{4}(x + y)] = \log x + \log y \;\Rightarrow\; \log\left[\tfrac{1}{4}(x + y)\right] = \tfrac{1}{2}(\log x + \log y)$$

Therefore, $k = \dfrac{1}{4}$.

Example 1.17   Simplify $[\log_{xy}(x^y)][1 + \log_x y]$.

Solution: Since $1 = \log_x x$, the second factor, $1 + \log_x y$, is equal to:

$$\log_x x + \log_x y = \log_x xy$$

Applying the change-of-base formula, $(\log_a b)(\log_b c) = \log_a c$, we find that:

$$[\log_x xy]\,[\log_{xy}(x^y)] = \log_x(x^y) = y$$

TRIGONOMETRY

Although trigonometry began as the study of triangles, the usefulness of the trigonometric functions now extends far beyond this simple geometric form. We'll begin our study by reviewing the definitions of the trig functions, first with acute angles in right triangles and then with arbitrary angles and real numbers.

TRIG FUNCTIONS OF ACUTE ANGLES

The classical definitions of the six trig functions—sine, cosine, tangent, cosecant, secant, and cotangent—use the lengths of the sides of a right triangle. In the figure below, triangle ABC is a right triangle with its right angle at C. The lengths of the legs BC and AC are denoted a and b, respectively, and the length of the hypotenuse AB is denoted c.

$$\sin A = \frac{\text{opp}}{\text{hyp}} = \frac{a}{c} \qquad \csc A = \frac{\text{hyp}}{\text{opp}} = \frac{c}{a}$$

$$\cos A = \frac{\text{adj}}{\text{hyp}} = \frac{b}{c} \qquad \sec A = \frac{\text{hyp}}{\text{adj}} = \frac{c}{b}$$

$$\tan A = \frac{\text{opp}}{\text{adj}} = \frac{a}{b} \qquad \cot A = \frac{\text{adj}}{\text{opp}} = \frac{b}{a}$$

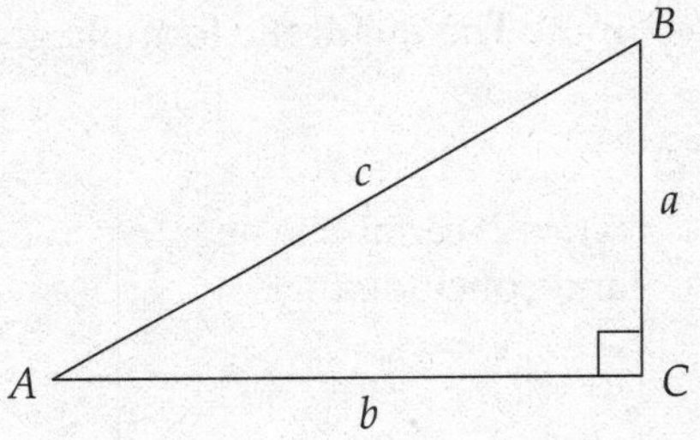

Angles A and B are complementary (that is, the sum of their measures is 90°), and notice that $\sin A = \cos B$. That is, the sine of B's complement (namely, A) is $\cos B$, which is where the name "cosine" comes from (complement's sine). The same is true for the other pairs of cofunctions—tangent and cotangent, secant and cosecant. You'll also notice certain reciprocal relationships among the functions. Cosecant is the reciprocal of sine, secant is the reciprocal of cosine, and cotangent is the reciprocal of tangent. Finally, all of the trig functions can be written in terms of sine and cosine: The reciprocal relationships take care of secant and cosecant, and it's easy to see that tangent is the ratio of sine to cosine, and cotangent is the ratio of cosine to sine.

Two special right triangles allow us to determine the numerical values of the trig functions of the angles 30°, 45°, and 60°.

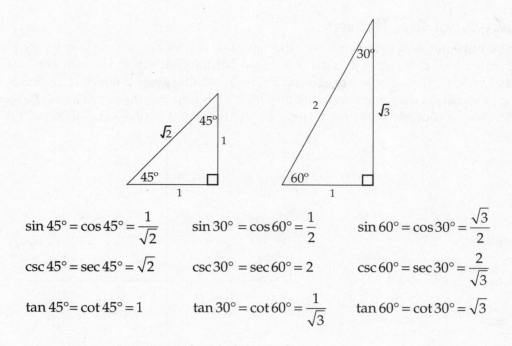

$$\sin 45° = \cos 45° = \frac{1}{\sqrt{2}} \qquad \sin 30° = \cos 60° = \frac{1}{2} \qquad \sin 60° = \cos 30° = \frac{\sqrt{3}}{2}$$

$$\csc 45° = \sec 45° = \sqrt{2} \qquad \csc 30° = \sec 60° = 2 \qquad \csc 60° = \sec 30° = \frac{2}{\sqrt{3}}$$

$$\tan 45° = \cot 45° = 1 \qquad \tan 30° = \cot 60° = \frac{1}{\sqrt{3}} \qquad \tan 60° = \cot 30° = \sqrt{3}$$

TRIG FUNCTIONS OF ARBITRARY ANGLES

The definitions above work only for acute angles (that is, ones whose measures are between 0° and 90°), but they can be extended to any size angle. In the xy-plane, consider the ray along the positive x-axis whose initial point is the origin, O. This ray can be rotated in the plane either clockwise or counterclockwise any number of degrees to form an angle, θ, with the positive x-axis as its initial side. By convention, counter-clockwise rotation results in a positive angle, and clockwise rotation gives a negative angle. Choose any point P: (x, y)—except the origin—on the terminal side of the angle and let r be the distance from O to P. Then the values of the six trig functions of θ are as follows:

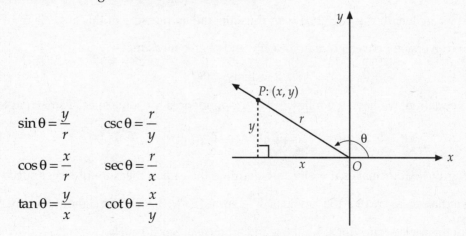

$$\sin \theta = \frac{y}{r} \qquad \csc \theta = \frac{r}{y}$$

$$\cos \theta = \frac{x}{r} \qquad \sec \theta = \frac{r}{x}$$

$$\tan \theta = \frac{y}{x} \qquad \cot \theta = \frac{x}{y}$$

If the terminal side of θ coincides with one of the coordinate axes, either x or y will be zero, and exactly two of the trig functions (tan, csc, sec, or cot) will be undefined. For example, if $\theta = 90°$, then at every point P on the terminal side, the value of x is zero, so $\tan \theta$ and $\sec \theta$ are undefined. Notice also that the trig functions of arbitrary angles can be positive, negative, or zero. Since r is always positive, the sign of each trig function depends on the sign of x or y (or both). For example, if the terminal side of θ lies in the second quadrant—as it does in the illustration above—then x is negative and y is positive. So $\sin \theta$ and $\csc \theta$ will be positive, but the values of the other four trig functions of θ will be negative.

TRIG FUNCTIONS OF REAL NUMBERS

An alternate but equivalent definition of the trig functions utilizes the unit circle in the xy-plane. This circle has a radius of 1, is centered at the origin, and has the equation $x^2 + y^2 = 1$. Let θ be any real number and measure the arc of length $|\theta|$ along the circle, starting at the point A: $(1, 0)$. If θ is positive, travel along the circle in the counterclockwise direction; if θ is negative, measure a length $|\theta|$ clockwise. If P: (x, y) denotes the endpoint of the arc, then the trig functions of θ are defined as follows.

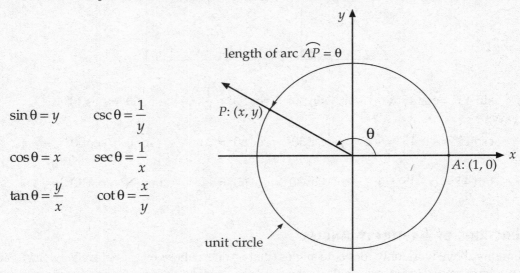

$$\sin \theta = y \qquad \csc \theta = \frac{1}{y}$$

$$\cos \theta = x \qquad \sec \theta = \frac{1}{x}$$

$$\tan \theta = \frac{y}{x} \qquad \cot \theta = \frac{x}{y}$$

These definitions are the same as those preceding if we interpret θ as the radian measure of the central angle. Recall that if the central angle in a circle of radius r subtends an arc of length s, then the radian measure of the angle is defined as $\frac{s}{r}$. In particular, if the central angle measures $180°$, it subtends half the circle, and its arc length is $s = \frac{1}{2}(2\pi r) = \pi r$; thus, the radian measure of this angle is $\theta = \frac{s}{r} = \frac{\pi r}{r} = \pi$. This gives the conversion between radian measure and degree measure:

$$\pi \text{ radians} = 180°$$

Using this equation, we have the following correspondences for some special small angles:

$$\frac{\pi}{6} \leftrightarrow 30° \qquad \frac{\pi}{4} \leftrightarrow 45° \qquad \frac{\pi}{3} \leftrightarrow 60° \qquad \frac{\pi}{2} \leftrightarrow 90°$$

Memorizing these four makes it easier to determine the radian measure of larger special angles; for example, the radian measure of a $150°$ angle is $\frac{5\pi}{6}$, since $150° = 5(30°)$. Throughout the remainder of this chapter and in the review questions, we'll use radian measure exclusively.

TRIG IDENTITIES AND FORMULAS

In this section, we'll give you a list of some of the most important trig identities and formulas; these are equations that involve trig functions that hold true for *any* values of the argument(s) for which both sides are defined. All of these identities can be proved using the definitions given above. Remember that for any number k except -1, the notation $\sin^k x$ denotes $(\sin x)^k$; the same is true for the other trig functions.

Fundamental Identities

$$\tan\theta = \frac{\sin\theta}{\cos\theta} \qquad \cot\theta = \frac{\cos\theta}{\sin\theta} \qquad \csc\theta = \frac{1}{\sin\theta} \qquad \sec\theta = \frac{1}{\cos\theta}$$

Opposite-Angle Identities

$$\sin(-\theta) = -\sin\theta \qquad \cos(-\theta) = \cos\theta$$

(These identities say that sine is an odd function and cosine is an even function.)

Pythagorean Identities

$$\sin^2\theta + \cos^2\theta = 1 \qquad 1 + \tan^2\theta = \sec^2\theta \qquad 1 + \cot^2\theta = \csc^2\theta$$

Addition and Subtraction Formulas

$$\sin(\alpha + \beta) = \sin\alpha\cos\beta + \cos\alpha\sin\beta \qquad \cos(\alpha + \beta) = \cos\alpha\cos\beta - \sin\alpha\sin\beta$$

$$\sin(\alpha - \beta) = \sin\alpha\cos\beta - \cos\alpha\sin\beta \qquad \cos(\alpha - \beta) = \cos\alpha\cos\beta + \sin\alpha\sin\beta$$

$$\tan(\alpha + \beta) = \frac{\tan\alpha + \tan\beta}{1 - \tan\alpha\tan\beta}$$

$$\tan(\alpha - \beta) = \frac{\tan\alpha - \tan\beta}{1 + \tan\alpha\tan\beta}$$

Double-Angle Formulas

$$\sin 2\theta = 2\sin\theta\cos\theta$$

$$\cos 2\theta = \cos^2\theta - \sin^2\theta = 1 - 2\sin^2\theta = 2\cos^2\theta - 1$$

$$\tan 2\theta = \frac{2\tan\theta}{1 - \tan^2\theta}$$

Complementary-Angle (Reduction) Formulas

$$\sin\left(\frac{\pi}{2} - \theta\right) = \cos\theta \qquad \cos\left(\frac{\pi}{2} - \theta\right) = \sin\theta$$

Half-Angle Formulas

$$\sin\frac{\theta}{2} = \pm\sqrt{\frac{1 - \cos\theta}{2}} \qquad \cos\frac{\theta}{2} = \pm\sqrt{\frac{1 + \cos\theta}{2}} \qquad \tan\frac{\theta}{2} = \frac{\sin\theta}{1 + \cos\theta}$$

Example 1.18 What is the exact value of $\tan\dfrac{\pi}{12}$?

Solution: Since $\dfrac{\pi}{12} = \dfrac{\pi}{3} - \dfrac{\pi}{4}$, we can use the formula for $\tan(\alpha - \beta)$ to find that:

$$\tan\frac{\pi}{12} = \tan\left(\frac{\pi}{3} - \frac{\pi}{4}\right) = \frac{\tan\dfrac{\pi}{3} - \tan\dfrac{\pi}{4}}{1 + \tan\dfrac{\pi}{3}\tan\dfrac{\pi}{4}}$$

$$= \frac{\sqrt{3} - 1}{1 + \sqrt{3}}$$

$$= \frac{\sqrt{3} - 1}{1 + \sqrt{3}} \cdot \frac{1 - \sqrt{3}}{1 - \sqrt{3}}$$

$$= \frac{-1 + 2\sqrt{3} - 3}{1 - 3}$$

$$= 2 - \sqrt{3}$$

Another way to get this result would be to notice that $\dfrac{\pi}{12} = \dfrac{1}{2}\left(\dfrac{\pi}{6}\right)$, so the half-angle formula for tangent gives:

$$\tan\frac{\pi}{12} = \tan\frac{1}{2}\left(\frac{\pi}{6}\right) = \frac{\sin\dfrac{\pi}{6}}{1 + \cos\dfrac{\pi}{6}}$$

$$= \frac{\dfrac{1}{2}}{1 + \dfrac{\sqrt{3}}{2}}$$

$$= \frac{1}{2 + \sqrt{3}}$$

$$= \frac{1}{2 + \sqrt{3}} \cdot \frac{2 - \sqrt{3}}{2 - \sqrt{3}}$$

$$= 2 - \sqrt{3}$$

Example 1.19 If $\sin\theta = \dfrac{1}{3}$, what's the value of $\sec 2\theta$?

Solution: We first find the value of $\cos 2\theta$:

$$\cos 2\theta = 1 - 2\sin^2\theta = 1 - 2\left(\frac{1}{3}\right)^2 = \frac{7}{9}$$

Therefore, since secant is the reciprocal of cosine,

$$\sec 2\theta = \frac{1}{\cos 2\theta} = \frac{1}{\dfrac{7}{9}} = \frac{9}{7}$$

PERIODICITY OF THE TRIG FUNCTIONS

A function f is said to be **periodic** if a constant k exists, such that $f(x + k) = f(x)$ for all x (such that both x and $x + k$ are in the domain of f). It's clear from the definitions that all of the trig functions are periodic with $k = 2\pi$, since 2π corresponds to one complete rotation, so the terminal side of $\theta + 2\pi$ coincides with the terminal side of θ. However, it turns out that $k = \pi$ also works for the tangent and cotangent functions. Therefore, these two functions are said to be periodic with their **period**—the smallest positive value of k, such that $f(x + k) = f(x)$ always holds—equal to π; the other four trig functions are periodic with period 2π.

GRAPHS OF THE TRIG FUNCTIONS

From the definitions, we can determine the domain and range of each of the six trig functions.

- The functions $\sin x$ and $\cos x$ are defined for every real x, and the range of each of these functions is the set of y such that $|y| \geq 1$; that is, the closed interval $[-1, 1]$.

- The function $\csc x$ is defined for all values of x for which $\sin x \neq 0$, that is, for all x except multiples of π; the range of this function consists of all y such that $|y| \geq 1$.

- The function $\sec x$ is defined for all values of x for which $\cos x \neq 0$, that is, for all x except odd multiples of $\frac{1}{2}\pi$; the range of this function consists of all y such that $|y| \geq 1$.

- The function $\tan x$ is defined for all values of x for which $\cos x \neq 0$, that is, for all x except odd multiples of $\frac{1}{2}\pi$; the range of this function consists of all real numbers y.

- The function $\cot x$ is defined for all values of x for which $\sin x \neq 0$, that is, for all x except multiples of π; the range of this function also consists of all real y.

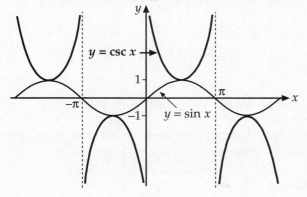

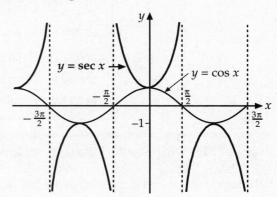

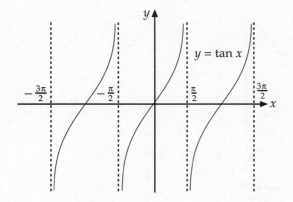

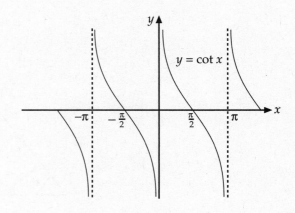

THE INVERSE TRIG FUNCTIONS

Suppose we wanted to find all real numbers x such that $\sin x = \dfrac{1}{2}$. We could immediately choose $x = \dfrac{\pi}{6}$ or $x = \dfrac{5\pi}{6}$, but there are infinitely many values of x that satisfy this equation (each equal to one of the aforementioned values, plus or minus any multiple of 2π). The function $\sin x$ is not one-to-one, because for every value of y in the range of $\sin x$, there's more than one x, such that $\sin x = y$. So, if we want to define an inverse function for sine, we must first restrict the domain of $\sin x$ to obtain a one-to-one function. The standard way to do this is to define a new function, denoted $\text{Sin } x$, that's identical to $\sin x$ except that its domain is restricted to the closed interval $\left[-\dfrac{\pi}{2}, \dfrac{\pi}{2}\right]$. This function *is* one-to-one (and onto), so it has a well-defined inverse, which is denoted by $\sin^{-1}x$ or $\arcsin x$. [Remember that $\sin^{-1}x$ is *not* the same as $(\sin x)^{-1}$. The former is the notation for a number whose sine is x; the latter is the reciprocal of $\sin x$.] Therefore, $\arcsin x$ is the unique number (or angle) between $\dfrac{-\pi}{2}$ and $\dfrac{\pi}{2}$ (inclusive), whose sine is x.

Similar methods are used to define the inverses of the other trig functions; for simplicity, we have recorded all the results in the following table:

Function	Domain	Range
$\arcsin x$	$|x| \le 1$	$\left[-\frac{\pi}{2}, \frac{\pi}{2}\right]$
$\arccos x$	$|x| \le 1$	$[0, \pi]$
$\arctan x$	all x	$\left(-\frac{\pi}{2}, \frac{\pi}{2}\right)$
$\text{arccsc } x$	$|x| \ge 1$	$\left[-\frac{\pi}{2}, \frac{\pi}{2}\right]$ except 0
$\text{arcsec } x$	$|x| \ge 1$	$[0, \pi]$ except $\frac{\pi}{2}$
$\text{arccot } x$	all x	$(0, \pi)$

Example 1.20   Express the following in simplest form, in terms of x: $\sin(2 \arctan x)$

Solution: If $\theta = \arctan x$, then, as the following diagram shows:

$$\sin \theta = \frac{x}{\sqrt{x^2 + 1}} \quad \text{and} \quad \cos \theta = \frac{1}{\sqrt{x^2 + 1}}$$

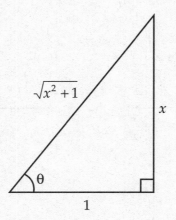

Therefore, $\sin(2 \arctan x) = \sin 2\theta = 2\sin\theta\cos\theta$

$$= 2 \cdot \frac{x}{\sqrt{x^2+1}} \cdot \frac{1}{\sqrt{x^2+1}}$$

$$= \frac{2x}{x^2+1}$$

Example 1.21   Evaluate: $\arccos \dfrac{2}{\sqrt{5}} + \arccos \dfrac{3}{\sqrt{10}}$

Solution: Let $\alpha = \arccos \dfrac{2}{\sqrt{5}}$; then $\cos\alpha = \dfrac{2}{\sqrt{5}}$, and:

$$\sin\alpha = \sqrt{1 - \cos^2\alpha} = \sqrt{1 - \left(\frac{2}{\sqrt{5}}\right)^2} = \sqrt{1 - \frac{4}{5}} = \frac{1}{\sqrt{5}}$$

Next, let $\beta = \arccos \dfrac{3}{\sqrt{10}}$; then $\cos\beta = \dfrac{3}{\sqrt{10}}$, and:

$$\sin\beta = \sqrt{1 - \cos^2\beta} = \sqrt{1 - \left(\frac{3}{\sqrt{10}}\right)^2} = \sqrt{1 - \frac{9}{10}} = \frac{1}{\sqrt{10}}$$

In order to evaluate $\alpha + \beta$, we will first determine $\sin(\alpha + \beta)$:

$$\sin(\alpha + \beta) = \sin\alpha\cos\beta + \cos\alpha\sin\beta$$

$$= \frac{1}{\sqrt{5}}\frac{3}{\sqrt{10}} + \frac{2}{\sqrt{5}}\frac{1}{\sqrt{10}}$$

$$= \frac{1}{\sqrt{2}}$$

Since both $\dfrac{2}{\sqrt{5}}$ and $\dfrac{3}{\sqrt{10}}$ are greater than $\dfrac{1}{\sqrt{2}}$, both $\alpha = \arccos \dfrac{2}{\sqrt{5}}$ and $\beta = \arccos \dfrac{3}{\sqrt{10}}$ are less than $\dfrac{\pi}{4}$. This means that their sum is less than $\dfrac{\pi}{2}$, so the fact that $\sin(\alpha + \beta) = \dfrac{1}{\sqrt{2}}$ tells us that $\alpha + \beta = \arcsin \dfrac{1}{\sqrt{2}} = \dfrac{\pi}{4}$.

CHAPTER 1 REVIEW QUESTIONS

Complete the following review questions using the techniques outlined in this chapter. Then, see Chapter 8 for answers and explanations.

1. Find the sum of the roots of the equation $\sqrt{x-1} + \sqrt{2x-1} = x$.

    (A) 1   (B) 2   (C) 4   (D) 5   (E) 6

2. Determine the set of positive values of x that satisfy the following inequality:

    $$\frac{1}{x} - \frac{1}{x-1} > \frac{1}{x-2}$$

    (A) $(0, 1) \cup (\sqrt{2}, 2)$ (B) $(0, \frac{1}{2}) \cup (1, 2)$ (C) $(\frac{1}{2}, 1) \cup (\sqrt{2}, 2\sqrt{2})$

    (D) $(0, \sqrt{2}) \cup (\frac{3}{2}, 2)$ (E) $(1, \sqrt{2}) \cup (2, 2\sqrt{2})$

3. Solve for x: $|x+1| - |x| + 2|x-1| = 2x - 1$

    (A) $x = -\frac{1}{2}, 1$ (B) $x = -\frac{1}{2}, 2$ (C) $x = 1, 2$ (D) $x = -\frac{1}{2}, 1, 2$ (E) $x \geq 1$

4. Let f be a function such that $f(n + 1) = 1 - [f(n)]^2$ for all nonnegative integers n. Which of the following correctly expresses $f(n + 2)$ in terms of $f(n)$?

    (A) $2[f(n)]^2$ (B) $2f(n) - 2[f(n)]^2$ · (C) $2f(n) + 2[f(n)]^2$
    (D) $2[f(n)]^2 - [f(n)]^4$ (E) $2[f(n)]^2 + [f(n)]^4$

5. Let f be a real-valued function whose inverse is given by the equation:

    $$f^{-1}(x) = x(1 + x^2) + (1 - x^2)$$

    What's the value of $f(f^{-1}(f(2)))$?

    (A) –2   (B) –1   (C) 1   (D) 2   (E) 7

6. Let f, g, and h be real-valued functions defined for all positive x such that:

$$(f \circ g)(x) = (g \circ h)(x)$$

handwritten: $\sqrt{x} + 1 = \sqrt{h(x)}$

If $f(x) = x + 1$ and $g(x) = \sqrt{x}$, what is $h(x)$?

handwritten: $(\sqrt{x}+1)^2 = h(x)$

(A) $x^2 - 1$ (B) $\sqrt{x-1}$ (C) $\sqrt{x} + 2$ (D) $x\sqrt{x} + 1$ (E) $1 + (\sqrt{x}+2)\sqrt{x}$

handwritten: $x+1+2\sqrt{x}$

---

7. What's the equation of all points in the xy-plane that are equidistant from the points $(-1, 4)$ and $(5, -2)$?

handwritten: $(2,1)$

(A) $2x - y = 3$ (B) $x - y = 1$ (C) $x + y = 3$

(D) $y = x^2 - 4x + 1$ (E) $(x - 2)^2 + (y - 1)^2 = 18$

handwritten: $(-1,-2)$

---

8. Which of the following best describes the graph of the equation $x^2 + y^2 - 2x + 4y + 5 = 0$ in the xy-plane?

(A) circle (B) parabola (C) ellipse (D) line (E) point

---

9. Let C be the curve in the xy-plane described by the equation $x^2 + 4y^2 = 16$. If every point (x, y) on C is replaced by the point $(\frac{1}{2}x, y)$, what is the area enclosed by the resulting curve?

handwritten: 8π

(A) 8 (B) 4π (C) 16 (D) 8π (E) 16π

---

10. Every point on the parabola $y = \sqrt{2x - 1}$ is equidistant from the y-axis and which of the following points?

handwritten: $y^2 = 2x - 1$

(A) $(\frac{1}{2}, 0)$ (B) $(1, 0)$ (C) $(\frac{3}{2}, 0)$ (D) $(2, 0)$ (E) $(\frac{5}{2}, 0)$

---

11. One of the foci of the hyperbola $y^2 = \left(\dfrac{x}{a}\right)^2 + 1$ is the point $(0, \sqrt{2})$. Find a.

(A) $\dfrac{1}{2\sqrt{2}}$ (B) $\dfrac{1}{\sqrt{2}}$ (C) $\dfrac{1}{2}$ (D) 1 (E) $\sqrt{3}$

---

12. Which one of the following polynomials $p(x)$ has the property that $\sqrt{3} - \sqrt{2}$ is a root of the equation $p(x) = 0$?

handwritten: $z^2 = 5 - 2\sqrt{6}$ $z^4 = 49 - 20\sqrt{6}$

(A) $2x^2 + 6x + 3$ (B) $x^3 - 2x + 6$ (C) $x^4 + 2x^2 - 3$ (D) $x^4 - 10x^2 + 1$ (E) $x^4 - 5x^2 + 6$

13. When the polynomial $p(x)$ is divided by $x - 1$, it leaves a remainder of 1, and when $p(x)$ is divided by $x + 1$, it leaves a remainder of -1. Find the remainder when $p(x)$ is divided by $x^2 - 1$.

   (A) -1 (B) 0 (C) x (D) $-x$ (E) $2x$

---

14. Given that $p(x)$ is a real polynomial of degree ≤ 4 such that one can find five distinct solutions to the equation $p(x) = 5$, what is the value of $p(5)$?

   (A) 0 (B) 1 (C) 4 (D) 5
   (E) Cannot be determined from the information given

---

15. If the roots of the equation $x^2 + Bx + 1 = 0$ are the squares of the roots of the equation $x^2 + bx + 1 = 0$, which of the following expresses B in terms of b?

   (A) $2 - b^2$ (B) $1 - b^2$ (C) $b^2 - 1$ (D) b^2 (E) $b^2 - 2$

---

16. Find the largest value of b such that $1 + bi$ satisfies the equation

$$x^3 - 3x^2 + 6x - 4 = 0$$

given that *every* root of this equation has the form $1 + bi$ (where b is real).

   (A) 1 (B) $\sqrt{2}$ (C) $\sqrt{3}$ (D) 2 (E) 3

---

17. If a and x are positive numbers and $A = a^2$, express the following in its simplest form in terms of x:

$$a^{(\log_a x) + (\log_A x)}$$

   (A) $2x$ (B) x^2 (C) $\sqrt{x}$ (D) x^3 (E) $x\sqrt{x}$

---

18. What are the roots of the following equation?

$$(\log x)^2 = 2 \log x$$

   (A) $1, e^{-2}$ (B) $1, \sqrt{e}$ (C) $1, e^2$ (D) all $x > 0$ (E) all real x

---

19. The hyperbolic sine function, denoted sinh, is defined by the equation:

$$\sinh x = \frac{e^x - e^{-x}}{2}$$

Find a formula for $\sinh^{-1} x$.

(A) $\log(1 - \sqrt{x^2 + 1})$ (B) $\log(1 + \sqrt{x^2 + 1})$ (C) $\log(x - \sqrt{x^2 + 1})$

(D) $\log(x + \sqrt{x^2 + 1})$ (E) $\log(\sqrt{x^2 + 1} - x)$

---

20. The hyperbolic cosine function, denoted cosh, is defined by the equation:

$$\frac{e^x + e^{-x}}{2}$$

If the hyperbolic tangent function, tanh, is defined by

$$\tanh x = \frac{\sinh x}{\cosh x}$$

find a formula for $\tanh^{-1} x$.

(A) $\dfrac{1}{2}\log\dfrac{x-1}{x+1}$ (B) $\log\dfrac{\frac{1}{2}x-1}{\frac{1}{2}x+1}$ (C) $\log\dfrac{1+\frac{1}{2}x}{1-\frac{1}{2}x}$ (D) $\dfrac{1}{2}\log\dfrac{x+1}{x-1}$ (E) $\dfrac{1}{2}\log\dfrac{1+x}{1-x}$

---

21. Let x be the real number such that $\sin(\sin x) = \dfrac{1}{2}$ and $2 < x < 3$. What's the value of $\cos(-\sin x)$?

(A) $-\sqrt{1-\left(\dfrac{\pi}{6}\right)^2}$ (B) $\sqrt{1-\left(\dfrac{\pi}{3}\right)^2}$ (C) $\sqrt{1-\left(\dfrac{\pi}{6}\right)^2}$ (D) $-\dfrac{\sqrt{3}}{2}$ (E) $\dfrac{\sqrt{3}}{2}$

---

22. Which one of the following is in the domain of the function $f(x) = \log(\sin x)$? (You may use the fact that 1111 is just slightly greater than $353.64 \times \pi$.)

(A) 11   (B) 111   (C) 1111   (D) 11,111   (E) None of these

---

23. Simplify $\tan(2 \arcsin \frac{1}{3})$.

(A) $\dfrac{2\sqrt{2}}{9}$ (B) $\dfrac{\sqrt{2}}{3}$ (C) $\dfrac{3}{4}$ (D) $\dfrac{4\sqrt{2}}{7}$ (E) $\dfrac{6}{5}$

---

24. Simplify $\sqrt{\csc^2\left(\text{arccot}\dfrac{\pi}{4}\right)-1}$.

(A) −1   (B) 1   (C) $\dfrac{\pi^2}{16}$ (D) $\dfrac{\pi}{4}$ (E) $\dfrac{\sqrt{\pi}}{2}$

---

25. Determine the exact value of the sum arctan 1 + arctan 2 + arctan 3.

(A) $\dfrac{\pi}{2}$ (B) π (C) $\dfrac{3\pi}{2}$ (D) $\dfrac{\pi}{4}-1$ (E) $\dfrac{\pi}{2}-1$

Calculus I

INTRODUCTION

A full fifty percent of the questions on the GRE Math Subject Test involve calculus, which includes differential equations. We'll review single-variable calculus in this chapter, multivariable calculus in Chapter 3, and differential equations in Chapter 4.

LIMITS OF SEQUENCES

Let's begin our review of limits by looking at the limit of a **sequence**. Although a sequence is formally defined as a function that's defined on the set of positive integers, we usually think of a sequence as an infinite, ordered list of terms:

$$x_1, x_2, x_3, \ldots$$

For now, we'll restrict the values of the terms to real numbers. We say that a sequence, (x_n), approaches (or has) a **limit**, L, if for every $\varepsilon > 0$, no matter how small, there's an integer, N, such that the difference between x_n and L is less than ε for every $n > N$. If a value of L exists that satisfies this criterion, then we say the sequence is **convergent**, and that it **converges** to L; this is written $x_n \to L$ or $\lim x_n = L$. If there's no real number L with this property, that is, if the limit does not exist, the sequence is said to be **divergent**.

For example, let's consider the sequence (x_n), where $x_n = \dfrac{(2n-1)}{n}$. The first few terms of this sequence are $x_1 = 1$, $x_2 = \dfrac{3}{2}$, $x_3 = \dfrac{5}{3}$, ... If we rewrite this equation for x_n as $x_n = 2 - \left(\dfrac{1}{n}\right)$, it's clear that as n increases, the quantity $\dfrac{1}{n}$ decreases to zero, so the terms x_n should approach a limit of 2. We prove this conjecture as follows: Let $\varepsilon > 0$ be given. Then, if $N > \dfrac{1}{\varepsilon}$, every term x_n with $n > N$ will be within ε of 2; thus, the limit of this sequence is indeed equal to 2.

There are two types of divergent sequences that are often described as though they have a limit:

1. If, for any choice of $M > 0$ (no matter how large), we have $x_n > M$ for every n greater than some N (which will, in general, depend on M), then we say that the sequence **diverges to infinity** (∞) and write $x_n \to \infty$, or $\lim x_n = \infty$, even though ∞ doesn't denote a real number. For example, the sequence (x_n) with $x_n = 2n - 1$ diverges to ∞.

2. If, for any choice of $M > 0$ (no matter how large), we have $x_n < -M$ for every n greater than some N (which will, in general, depend on M), then we say that the sequence **diverges to minus infinity** and write $x_n \to -\infty$ or $\lim x_n = -\infty$. As an example, the sequence (x_n) with $x_n = 2n - n^2$ diverges to $-\infty$.

Of course, there are divergent sequences that don't fall into either of these two latter categories. For example, the sequence (x_n) with $x_n = (-1)^n$ diverges; the terms simply oscillate between -1 and 1, so the sequence doesn't approach a unique limiting value.

One more important definition: A sequence (x_n) is said to be **monotonic** if it's **increasing** ($x_n \le x_{n+1}$ for every n from some point on) or **decreasing** ($x_n \ge x_{n+1}$ for every n from some point on). The sequences $(2 - \dfrac{1}{n})$ and $(2n - 1)$ are increasing, and $(2n - n^2)$ is decreasing, but $((-1)^n)$ is not monotonic because it oscillates.

Some of the most useful rules about convergent sequences are summarized below:

1. Every convergent sequence is **bounded**; that is, there exists a positive number, M, such that the absolute value of every term of the sequence is no greater than M. [The converse of this statement is not true; for example, the sequence (x_n) with $x_n = (-1)^n$ is bounded, but not convergent.]

2. If a sequence is monotonic and bounded, then it's convergent.

3. If k is a constant, and (a_n) converges to A, then $(ka_n) \to kA$.

4. If (a_n) converges to A and (b_n) converges to B, then

$$(a_n + b_n) \to A + B,$$
$$(a_n - b_n) \to A - B,$$
$$(a_n b_n) \to AB, \text{ and}$$
$$\left(\frac{a_n}{b_n}\right) \to \frac{A}{B} \text{ (assuming that } B \ne 0).$$

5. (a) If k is a positive constant, then $\left(\dfrac{1}{n^k}\right) \to 0$.

   (b) If $|k| > 1$, then $\left(\dfrac{1}{k^n}\right) \to 0$.

6. Assume that (a_n) and (c_n) are sequences that converge to the same limit, L. If (b_n) is a sequence such that $a_n \le b_n \le c_n$ for every $n > N$, then (b_n) also converges to L. This is sometimes called the **Sandwich** (or **Squeeze**) **theorem**, since the terms of the sequence (b_n) are sandwiched between those of (a_n) and (c_n).

7. If $a_n = f(n)$, then the sequence (a_n) converges to L if $f(x)$ converges to L as $x \to \infty$ (which may be decided using L'Hôpital's rule).

Rule 7 is included in the list for completeness, but we'll postpone illustrating its use until we've reviewed L'Hôpital's rule (later in this chapter).

Example 2.1   In each case, show that the sequence (x_n) is convergent:

(a) $x_n = \dfrac{4n^3 - n^2 + 5n}{2n^3 + 6n^2 - 11}$

(b) $x_n = \sqrt{n+k} - \sqrt{n}$ (k is a constant)

(c) $x_n = \dfrac{1 \cdot 3 \cdot 5 \cdots (2n-1)}{2 \cdot 4 \cdot 6 \cdots (2n)}$

(d) $x_n = (-1)^n \left(\dfrac{1}{n^2} \right)$

(e) $x_n = (\cos n^n) e^{-n}$

Solution:

(a) Dividing both the numerator and denominator of the expression for x_n by n^3 and applying rules 4 and 5, we see that this sequence converges to 2:

$$x_n = \frac{4n^3 - n^2 + 5n}{2n^3 + 6n^2 - 11} = \frac{4 - \dfrac{1}{n} + \dfrac{5}{n^2}}{2 + \dfrac{6}{n} - \dfrac{11}{n^3}} \to \frac{4 - 0 + 0}{2 + 0 - 0} = 2$$

(b) Notice that if k is negative, then the sequence will start with the first integer, n, that's greater than or equal to $-k$ (otherwise $\sqrt{n+k}$ would not be real). A sequence can start at any n, and neither its convergence nor its limit will be affected. We can rewrite the terms x_n as follows:

$$x_n = \left(\sqrt{n+k} - \sqrt{n} \right) \cdot \frac{\sqrt{n+k} + \sqrt{n}}{\sqrt{n+k} + \sqrt{n}} = \frac{k}{\sqrt{n+k} + \sqrt{n}}$$

Now, for all $n \ge -k$, we have $\sqrt{n+k} + \sqrt{n} \ge \sqrt{n}$, so $x_n = \dfrac{k}{\sqrt{n+k} + \sqrt{n}} \le \dfrac{k}{\sqrt{n}}$. Because the sequence $\left(\dfrac{1}{\sqrt{n}} \right)$ converges to zero (rule 5a, with $k = \dfrac{1}{2}$), the sequence $\dfrac{k}{\sqrt{n}}$ converges to zero (rule 3). Now apply the Sandwich theorem (rule 6), with the sequence (a_n) every term of which equals zero, and the sequence (c_n) with $c_n = \dfrac{k}{\sqrt{n}}$. Since $a_n \le x_n \le c_n$ for every $n \ge -k$, we know that the sequence (x_n) also converges to zero.

(c) The first few terms of this sequence are $x_1 = \frac{1}{2}$, $x_2 = \left(\frac{1}{2}\right)\left(\frac{3}{4}\right) = \frac{3}{8}$, $x_3 = \left(\frac{1}{2}\right)\left(\frac{3}{4}\right)\left(\frac{5}{6}\right) = \frac{15}{48}$, ... Since $x_{n+1} = x_n \cdot [(2n+1)/(2n+2)]$ and $[(2n+1)/(2n+2)] < 1$, we see that $x_{n+1} < x_n$, so the sequence is decreasing; and because all the terms are positive, the sequence is bounded below by zero. Since the sequence is monotonic and bounded, rule 2 assures us that it converges.

(d) The sequence (c_n), with $c_n = \frac{1}{n^2}$, converges to zero (rule 5a, with $k = 2$), so the sequence (a_n) with $a_n = \frac{-1}{n^2}$ also converges to zero (rule 3). Since $a_n \leq x_n \leq c_n$ for every n, the sandwich theorem tells us that the sequence (x_n) also converges to zero. This example shows us that an oscillating sequence may converge.

(e) The sequence $(\cos n^n)$ diverges, but as we'll see, the sequence (x_n) converges. The sequence (c_n) with $c_n = e^{-n}$ converges to zero (rule 5b, with $k = e$), so the sequence (a_n) with $a_n = -e^{-n}$ also converges to zero (rule 3). Since $a_n \leq x_n \leq c_n$ for every n (because $-1 \leq \cos n^n \leq 1$), the sandwich theorem tells us that the sequence (x_n) also converges to zero.

LIMITS OF FUNCTIONS

Let f be a real-valued function whose domain is a subset of the real line. We need a way to talk about the behavior of f near a point $x = a$, which may or may not be in the domain of f. Let (x_n) be a sequence (whose terms *are* in the domain of f) that converges to a; if the sequence $(f(x_n))$ converges to a limit, L, then we write either $\lim_{x \to a} f(x) = L$ or $f(x) \to L$ as $x \to a$, and call L the **limit** of $f(x)$ as x approaches a.

This is the general definition of the limit of the function f, but there are two other types of limits for functions that are very useful. If every term of the convergent sequence (x_n) used above is less than a, then we say that x approaches a **from below** (or **from the left**), and write $x \to a-$. If, for every such sequence (x_n), the sequence $(f(x_n))$ approaches a limit l, then we call l the **left-hand limit** of $f(x)$ as x approaches a, and write $\lim_{x \to a-} f(x) = l$.

On the other hand, if every term of the sequence (x_n) is greater than a, we say that x approaches a **from above** (or **from the right**), and write $x \to a+$. If, for every such sequence (x_n), the sequence $(f(x_n))$ approaches a limit r, then we call r the **right-hand limit** of $f(x)$ as x approaches a, and write $\lim_{x \to a+} f(x) = r$.

In order for f to have a limit as x approaches a, the left-hand limit and the right-hand limit must both exist and they must be identical. If this is the case, the common value of these limits is *the* limit of $f(x)$ as x approaches a.

Let's look at an example. Consider the function g given by:

$$g(x) = \begin{cases} x+1 \text{ if } x < 1 \\ x+2 \text{ if } x \geq 1 \end{cases}$$

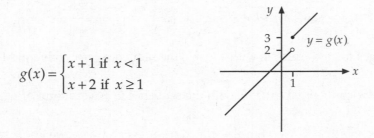

Then, as its graph shows:

$$\lim_{x \to 1-} g(x) = 2 \qquad \text{but} \qquad \lim_{x \to 1+} g(x) = 3$$

Since the left-hand limit at 1 is not equal to the right-hand limit at 1, the limit of $g(x)$ as x approaches 1 does not exist.

An equivalent definition of the limit of a function does not involve sequences explicitly. To say that $\lim_{x \to a} f(x) = L$ means that, given any $\varepsilon > 0$ (no matter how small), we can always find a positive number such that:

$$0 < |x - a| < \delta \;\Rightarrow\; |f(x) - L| < \varepsilon$$

This is the (in)famous ε–δ definition of a limit. It says that we can make $f(x)$ as close as we like to L, as long as we take x close enough to a.

When working with limits of functions, the following rules are often used:

1. $\lim_{x \to a} x = a$, $\lim_{x \to a} k = k$ (for any constant k), and $\lim_{x \to a} x^n = a^n$.

2. If $\lim_{x \to a} f(x) = L_1$ and $\lim_{x \to a} g(x) = L_2$, then

    $$\lim_{x \to a} [f(x) + g(x)] = L_1 + L_2$$

    $$\lim_{x \to a} [f(x) - g(x)] = L_1 - L_2$$

    $$\lim_{x \to a} [f(x)g(x)] = L_1 L_2$$

    $$\lim_{x \to a} \left[\frac{f(x)}{g(x)} \right] = \frac{L_1}{L_2} \text{ (assuming that } L_2 \neq 0).$$

3. To say that $\lim_{x \to a} f(x) = L$ means that for every sequence (x_n) converging to a, the sequence $(f(x_n))$ converges to L.

4. Assume that $\lim_{x \to a} f(x) = L$ and $\lim_{x \to a} h(x) = L$. If there is a positive number δ such that $f(x) \leq g(x) \leq h(x)$ for all x satisfying $0 < |x - a| < \delta$, then $\lim_{x \to a} g(x) = L$. This, again, is the Sandwich (or Squeeze) theorem.

Example 2.2   Evaluate each of the following limits:

(a) $\lim_{x \to 1} \dfrac{x-1}{\sqrt{x}+1}$ (b) $\lim_{x \to 1} \dfrac{x-1}{\sqrt{x}-1}$ (c) $\lim_{x \to 1-} \dfrac{x-1}{|x-1|}$ (d) $\lim_{x \to 1-}[x-1]$

[In (d), the symbol $[x - 1]$ denotes the greatest integer $\leq x - 1$.]

Solution:

(a) Since $\lim_{x \to 1}(x - 1) = \lim_{x \to 1} x - \lim_{x \to 1} 1 = 1 - 1 = 0$, and $\lim_{x \to 1}(\sqrt{x} + 1) =$

$\lim_{x \to 1} \sqrt{x} + \lim_{x \to 1} 1 = \sqrt{1} + 1 = 2$, we have $\lim_{x \to 1} \dfrac{x-1}{\sqrt{x}+1} = \dfrac{0}{2} = 0$.

(b) Since $\lim_{x \to 1}(x - 1) = 0$ and $\lim_{x \to 1}(\sqrt{x} - 1) = \sqrt{1} - 1 = 0$, we must first algebraically manipulate the

given expression to find the limit:

$$\lim_{x \to 1} \frac{x-1}{\sqrt{x}-1} = \lim_{x \to 1} \frac{(\sqrt{x}+1)(\sqrt{x}-1)}{\sqrt{x}-1} = \lim_{x \to 1-}(\sqrt{x}+1) = \sqrt{1}+1 = 2$$

(c) Since we're approaching 1 from below, we notice that for every $x < 1$, the value of $x - 1$ is negative, so:

$$\lim_{x \to 1^-} \frac{x-1}{|x-1|} = \lim_{x \to 1^-} \left\{ \frac{x-1}{-(x-1)} \right\} = \lim_{x \to 1^-}(-1) = -1$$

(d) For every value of x such that $0 \le x < 1$, we have $-1 \le x - 1 < 0$, so $[x - 1] = -1$. Therefore:

$$\lim_{x \to 1^-}[x-1] = \lim_{x \to 1^-}(-1) = -1$$

LIMITS OF FUNCTIONS AS $x \to \pm\infty$

We can also look at the behavior of a function $f(x)$ as x increases (or decreases) without bound. To mimic the ε–δ definition given above, we say that $f(x) \to M$ as $x \to \infty$ if, for every $\varepsilon > 0$ (no matter how small), we can find a positive number δ such that $x > \delta$ implies $|f(x) - M| < \varepsilon$. On the other hand, we say that $f(x) \to m$ as $x \to -\infty$ if, for every $\varepsilon > 0$ (no matter how small), we can find a negative number δ, such that $x < \delta$ implies $|f(x) - m| < \varepsilon$.

Example 2.3 Find the value of each of these limits (if they exist):

(a) $\lim\limits_{x \to \infty} \dfrac{2x^2 - x + 1}{x^2 + 4}$ (b) $\lim\limits_{x \to \infty} \dfrac{2x^2 - x + 1}{x^3 + 4}$ (c) $\lim\limits_{x \to -\infty}(\arctan x)$ (d) $\lim\limits_{x \to 0} \dfrac{1}{x}$

Solution:

(a) Dividing the numerator and denominator by x^2 gives us:

$$\lim_{x \to \infty} \frac{2x^2 - x + 1}{x^2 + 4} = \lim_{x \to \infty} \frac{2 - \dfrac{1}{x} + \dfrac{1}{x^2}}{1 + \dfrac{4}{x^2}} = \frac{2 - 0 + 0}{1 + 0} = 2$$

This tells us that the graph of $y = \dfrac{2x^2 - x + 1}{x^2 + 4}$ would have $y = 2$ as a horizontal asymptote.

(b) Dividing the numerator and denominator by x^3 gives us:

$$\lim_{x \to \infty} \frac{2x^2 - x + 1}{x^3 + 4} = \lim_{x \to \infty} \frac{\dfrac{2}{x} - \dfrac{1}{x^2} + \dfrac{1}{x^3}}{1 + \dfrac{4}{x^3}} = \frac{0 - 0 + 0}{1 + 0} = 0$$

This tells us that the graph of $y = \dfrac{2x^2 - x + 1}{x^3 + 4}$ would have $y = 0$ (the x-axis) as a horizontal asymptote.

(c) We know, from the graph of $y = \arctan x$, that $\lim\limits_{x \to -\infty} (\arctan x) = \dfrac{-\pi}{2}$:

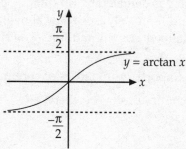

(d) As the graph below shows, we can write $\lim\limits_{x \to 0-} \left(\dfrac{1}{x}\right) = -\infty$ and $\lim\limits_{x \to 0+} \left(\dfrac{1}{x}\right) = \infty$; but $\lim\limits_{x \to 0} \left(\dfrac{1}{x}\right)$ does not exist, not only because the left- and right-hand limits are not the same, but also because they're both infinite!

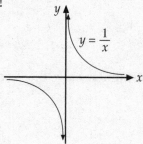

CONTINUOUS FUNCTIONS

Intuitively, a real-valued function f is continuous if the graph of the equation $y = f(x)$ contains no breaks. To make this more precise, we say that a function f is **continuous at** a if $\lim\limits_{x \to a} f(x) = f(a)$.

Notice that this definition involves checking three things. First, f must be defined at $x = a$, so that $f(a)$ actually exists; second, the limit of $f(x)$ as x approaches a must exist (and be finite); and third, this limit must be equal to the value of f at $x = a$. If f is continuous at every point in its domain, then we simply say that f is continuous.

Let's look at some examples. The functions whose graphs are shown below are continuous at all points except at $x = 1$, but the reason that f fails to be continuous at $x = 1$ is different in each case.

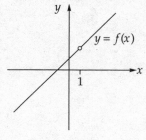

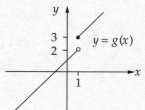

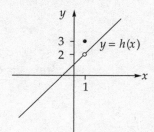

$$f(x) = \frac{x^2 - 1}{x - 1}$$

$$g(x) = \begin{cases} x+1 & \text{if } x < 1 \\ x+2 & \text{if } x \geq 1 \end{cases}$$

$$h(x) = \begin{cases} x+1 & \text{if } x \neq 1 \\ 3 & \text{if } x = 1 \end{cases}$$

The function f is discontinuous at $x = 1$ because f is not defined at this point. The function g is discontinuous at $x = 1$ because, even though g is defined at $x = 1$, $\lim_{x \to 1} g(x)$ does not exist (since the left-hand limit at 1 is not equal to the right-hand limit at 1, as we saw above). Finally, the function h is discontinuous at $x = 1$ because, although h is defined at $x = 1$ and $\lim_{x \to 1} h(x)$ exists (it's equal to 2), the value of h at $x = 1$ is 3, so $\lim_{x \to 1} h(x) \neq h(1)$.

The list below summarizes some important properties of continuous functions.

1. The following functions are continuous everywhere:

   Every constant function, $f(x) = k$

   Every polynomial function, $f(x) = a_n x^n + a_{n-1} x^{n-1} + \cdots + a_1 x + a_0$

   Every exponential function, $f(x) = k^x$ (with $k > 0$)

2. The following functions are continuous everywhere they're defined:

   Every function of the form $f(x) = x^r$, where r is a rational number

   The logarithm function, $f(x) = \log x$

   The trig functions

3. If the functions f and g are both continuous at a, then each of the following functions is also continuous at a:

   $f + g$

   $f - g$

   fg

   $\dfrac{f}{g}$ (provided that $g(a) \neq 0$)

4. If f is continuous at a and g is continuous at $f(a)$, then the composite function $g \circ f$ is continuous at $x = a$.

Example 2.4   What value must we choose for k so that the function

$$f(x) = \begin{cases} \dfrac{x^3 - 8}{x - 2} & \text{if } x \neq 2 \\ k & \text{if } x = 2 \end{cases}$$

is continuous everywhere?

Solution: Regardless of the value of k, this function is continuous for every $x \neq 2$ since, for all such x, $f(x)$ is the quotient of two polynomials (which are everywhere continuous), where the polynomial in the denominator is never equal to zero. So the question is, *What should* k *be for this function to be continuous at* x = 2? By definition, f is continuous at 2 if $\lim_{x \to 2} f(x) = f(2)$, which gives us:

$$\lim_{x \to 2} \frac{x^3 - 8}{x - 2} = k$$

$$\lim_{x \to 2} \frac{(x - 2)(x^2 + 2x + 4)}{x - 2} = k$$

$$\lim_{x \to 2}(x^2 + 2x + 4) = k$$

$$2^2 + 2 \bullet 2 + 4 = k$$

$$12 = k$$

Example 2.5   Let f be the function defined on the interval $I = (0, 1)$ as follows:

$$f(x) = \begin{cases} 0 & \text{if } x \text{ is irrational} \\ \dfrac{1}{n} & \text{if } x = \dfrac{m}{n} \text{ (in lowest terms, } m \text{ and } n \text{ are integers with } n > 0) \end{cases}$$

Show that f is continuous at every irrational point in I and discontinuous at every rational point in I.

Solution: Let a be an irrational number in I, and let $\varepsilon > 0$ be given. We want to show that there exists a positive number δ such that:

$$|x - a| < \delta \quad \Rightarrow \quad f(x) < \varepsilon$$

Choose a positive integer q such that $\dfrac{1}{q}$ is less than ε. Then, in any open interval centered at a and contained within I, there are fewer than $1 + 2 + \cdots + (q - 1) = \dfrac{q(q-1)}{2}$ positive rational numbers less than 1 and of the form $\dfrac{m}{n}$, where m and n are positive integers and n is less than q. From this finite list of rational numbers, choose the one—call it r—that's closest to a, and let $\delta = |r - a|$. Then, within the open interval $(a - r, a + r)$, the value of $f(x)$ will be less than $\dfrac{1}{q}$, so $f(x)$ will certainly be less than ε. This establishes that f is continuous at every irrational a in I.

To show that f is discontinuous at every rational a in I, choose an arbitrary rational number $a = \dfrac{p}{q}$ in this interval, where p and q are positive integers and $\dfrac{p}{q}$ is in lowest terms. If we can find a sequence (x_n) that converges to a such that the sequence $(f(x_n))$ does not converge to $f(a)$, then we will have established that f is not continuous at a. To do this, simply consider the sequence (x_n) where $x_n = a - \dfrac{1}{n\sqrt{2}}$. For every integer n greater than

$\dfrac{1}{a\sqrt{2}}$, the terms of the sequence are in $(0, 1)$ and increase monotonically to a. Since every term of this sequence is irrational, the value of $f(x_n)$ is 0 for every n, which means that the sequence $(f(x_n))$ converges trivially to 0. Since $(f(x_n)) \to 0$ but $f(a) = \dfrac{1}{q} \neq 0$, we conclude that f is not continuous at a.

THEOREMS CONCERNING CONTINUOUS FUNCTIONS

There are several important theorems of calculus in which continuity plays a central role. In each of these theorems, continuity of a real-valued function on a closed interval of the real line is an *essential* hypothesis; that is, if the function is not continuous on a closed interval, then none of the statements below is necessarily true. If f is defined on a closed interval $[a, b]$, then continuity at the left-hand endpoint, a, means that $\lim_{x \to a+} f(x) = f(a)$, and continuity of f at the right-hand endpoint, b, means that $\lim_{x \to b-} f(x) = f(b)$.

The Extreme Value theorem: If f is a function that's continuous on a closed interval $[a, b]$, then f attains an absolute minimum value, m, at some point $c \in [a, b]$, and an absolute maximum value, M, at some point $d \in [a, b]$. That is, there exist points c and d in $[a, b]$ such that $f(c) \leq f(x) \leq f(d)$ holds true for every $x \in [a, b]$.

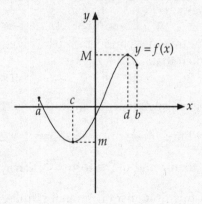

Bolzano's theorem: If f is a function that's continuous on a closed interval $[a, b]$ such that $f(a)$ and $f(b)$ have opposite signs, then there's a point c between a and b such that $f(c) = 0$.

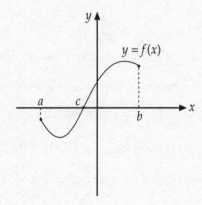

Bolzano's theorem is generalized in the following theorem:

The Intermediate Value theorem: Let f be a function that's continuous on a closed interval $[a, b]$. Let m be the absolute minimum value of f on $[a, b]$, and let M be the absolute maximum value of f on $[a, b]$. Then, for every number Y such that $m \leq Y \leq M$, there is at least one value of $c \in [a, b]$ such that $f(c) = Y$.

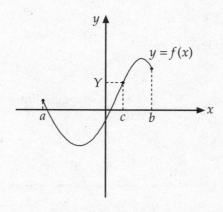

Example 2.6   Prove or give a counterexample to the following statement:

If f is continuous on the interval $[0, 1]$ and if $0 \leq f(x) \leq 1$ for every $x \in [0, 1]$, then there exists a point $c \in [0, 1]$ such that $f(c) = c$.

Solution: The statement is true, and in fact it has a name: **Brouwer's fixed-point theorem**. If $f(0) = 0$ or if $f(1) = 1$, then the conclusion is immediate, so in what follows, we'll assume that $0 < f(0) \leq 1$ and $0 \leq f(1) < 1$. If we define a new function g by the equation $g(x) = f(x) - x$, then g is continuous on $[0, 1]$. The value of g at 0 is equal to $f(0)$, which is positive, and the value of g at 1 is $f(1) - 1$, which is negative. By Bolzano's theorem, there must be a point $c \in [a, b]$ such that $g(c) = 0$. This last equation means that $f(c) - c = 0$ or, equivalently, $f(c) = c$.

THE DERIVATIVE

For a real-valued function f of a single real variable, the **derivative** of f is the function f' whose value at x is

$$f'(x) = \lim_{h \to 0} \frac{f(x+h) - f(x)}{h}$$

if this limit exists. Geometrically, the difference quotient, $[f(x + h) - f(x)]/h$, gives the slope of the secant line through the points $(x, f(x))$ and $(x + h, f(x + h))$. If the limit above exists, then as $h \to 0$, this secant line becomes the tangent line to the graph of f at the point $(x, f(x))$:

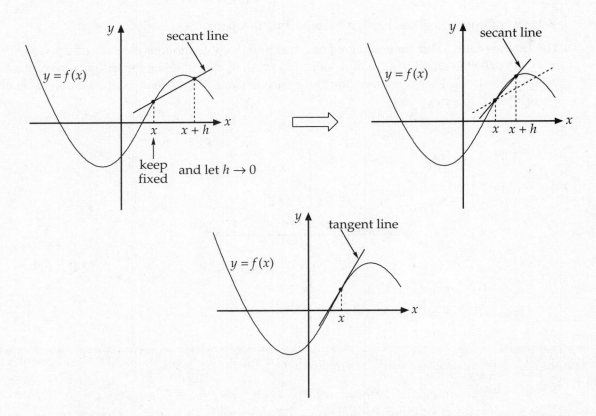

The value of the derivative, $f'(x)$, gives the slope of the tangent line, which is, by definition, the slope of the curve at x.

To illustrate this definition, consider the function $f(x) = x^2$. Its derivative is found in this way:

$$f'(x) = \lim_{h \to 0} \frac{f(x+h) - f(x)}{h}$$

$$= \lim_{h \to 0} \frac{(x+h)^2 - x^2}{h}$$

$$= \lim_{h \to 0} \frac{h(2x+h)}{h}$$

$$= \lim_{h \to 0} (2x + h)$$

$$= 2x$$

This tells us, for example, that the slope of the tangent line to the curve $y = x^2$, at the point where $x = 1$, is $f'(1) = 2 \cdot 1 = 2$, so the equation of this tangent line is $y = 2x - 1$.

Not all functions have derivatives. For example, the absolute-value function, $f(x) = |x|$, is not differentiable at $x = 0$, because the limit

$$\lim_{h \to 0} \frac{|0 + h| - |0|}{h} = \lim_{h \to 0} \frac{|h|}{h}$$

does not exist (since the left-hand limit is –1, but the right-hand limit is +1). Loosely speaking, a continuous function will fail to have a derivative at a point where its graph has a sharp corner (like the absolute-value function) or a cusp; that is, functions with derivatives have *smooth* graphs.

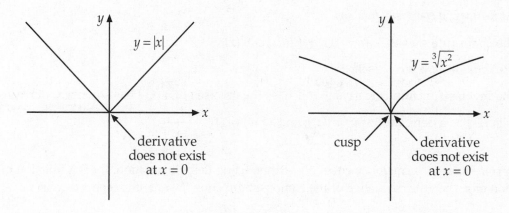

derivative
does not exist
at $x = 0$

cusp

derivative
does not exist
at $x = 0$

Other examples of functions that do not have derivatives can be given by exploiting the following important fact about differentiability: If f is not continuous at a, then f is not differentiable at a. For example, the function f whose value at every rational point on the real line is 0 and whose value at every irrational point is 1, is continuous nowhere, so it's differentiable nowhere. It's important to notice that the examples illustrated above show us that the converse of the fact given above about differentiability and continuity is not true: The functions $y = |x|$ and $y = \sqrt[3]{x^2}$ are continuous at $x = 0$, but they're not differentiable there. So differentiability implies continuity, but continuity by itself doesn't guarantee differentiability.

We've used a prime to denote the derivative of a function. Another very common notation for derivatives of functions is called **Leibniz notation**. The difference quotient used in the definition of the derivative is a change in f divided by a change in x; that is, we can write:

$$f'(x) = \lim_{\Delta x \to 0} \frac{f(x + \Delta x) - f(x)}{\Delta x} = \lim_{\Delta x \to 0} \frac{\Delta f}{\Delta x} = \frac{df}{dx}$$

Therefore, the derivative of f with respect to x can be written either as $f'(x)$ or, in Leibniz notation, as df/dx. We think of the symbol d/dx as the differentiation operator; that is, it says to differentiate whatever follows it. For example $(d/dx)(x^2) = 2x$. The prime notation and the Leibniz notation for derivatives can be used interchangeably.

When we want to find the derivative of a function, we usually use a table of standard derivatives and rules that make the computation easy, rather than going back to the definition every time. Following is a list of rules, all of which can be proved directly from the definition of a derivative. These rules must be memorized for the GRE Math Subject Test.

1. *Derivative of a sum*

    The derivative of a sum is the sum of the derivatives: $(f+g)'(x) = f'(x) + g'(x)$

2. *Derivative of a constant times a function:* $(kf)'(x) = kf'(x)$

3. *Derivative of a product*

    The **product rule** says that: $(fg)'(x) = f(x)g'(x) + f'(x)g(x)$

4. *Derivative of a quotient*

    The **quotient rule** says that: $\left(\dfrac{f}{g}\right)'(x) = \dfrac{g(x)f'(x) - f(x)g'(x)}{[g(x)]^2}$

5. *Derivative of a composite function*

   The **chain rule** says that: $(f \circ u)'(x) = f'(u(x)) \cdot u'(x)$

6. *Derivative of an inverse function*

   The **inverse-function rule** says that if f^{-1} is the inverse of f, and f has a nonzero derivative at x_0, then f^{-1} has a derivative at $y_0 = f(x_0)$, and $(f^{-1})'(y_0) = \dfrac{1}{f'(x_0)}$.

The chain rule is easy to remember when it's written using Leibniz notation. If f is a function of u and u is a function of x, then the derivative of the composite function, $f \circ u$, with respect to x, is:

$$\frac{df}{dx} = \frac{df}{du}\frac{du}{dx}$$

This equation makes it look like the du's cancel out of the fractions, even though the expressions in this equation aren't fractions. The rule for differentiating an inverse function is also easy to remember in Leibniz notation. If the derivative of $y = f(x)$ is written dy/dx and the derivative of the inverse function, $x = g(y)$, is written dx/dy, then

$$\frac{dx}{dy} = \frac{1}{\dfrac{dy}{dx}}$$

which looks like a simple identity if we think of the derivatives as simple fractions.

Of all of these rules, the chain rule is arguably the most widely used, and we can write it in an alternative (and more compact) form. In Leibniz notation, the chain rule is

$$\frac{d}{dx}[f(u(x))] = \frac{df}{du} \cdot \frac{du}{dx}$$

which we can simplify, using the notation of **differentials**. To illustrate this, consider the function $u(x) = x^2$, whose derivative is $du/dx = 2x$. If we move the dx to the right-hand side of this equation—as if du/dx were a fraction with numerator du and denominator dx—we get $du = 2x\,dx$. This says that du, the differential of u, is equal to $2x$ times dx, the differential of x. A principal use of differentials is in providing us with a simpler way of writing derivative formulas. For example, it's easy to show that the derivative of x^k (where k is a constant) is equal to kx^{k-1}. So, if u is a differentiable function of x, then the chain rule tells us that the derivative of u^k is $ku^{k-1}(du/dx)$. Rather than writing $d(u^k)/dx = (ku^{k-1})(du/dx)$, we can use differentials and write $d(u^k) = ku^{k-1}du$, which means the same thing.

In the list below, k is any constant, a is any positive constant, and u is any differentiable function.

$$d(k) = 0$$

$$d(u^k) = ku^{k-1}du$$

$$d(e^u) = e^u du$$

$$d(a^u) = (\log a)a^u du$$

$$d(\log u) = \frac{1}{u}du$$

$$d(\log_a u) = \frac{1}{(u\log a)}du \; (a \neq 1)$$

$$d(\sin u) = \cos u \; du$$

$$d(\cos u) = -\sin u \; du$$

$$d(\tan u) = \sec^2 u \; du$$

$$d(\cot u) = -\csc^2 u \; du$$

$$d(\sec u) = \sec u \tan u \; du$$

$$d(\csc u) = -\csc u \cot u \; du$$

$$d(\arcsin u) = \frac{du}{\sqrt{1-u^2}}$$

$$d(\arctan u) = \frac{du}{1+u^2}$$

Example 2.7   Find the derivative of each of the following:

(a) $f(x) = x^3 e^{-x^3} - x - 3$ (b) $g(x) = \dfrac{\log(\sin^2 x)}{\cos x}$ (c) $h(x) = \arctan\sqrt{x}$

Solution:

(a) $f'(x) = x^3(-3x^2 e^{-x^3}) + 3x^2 e^{-x^3} - 1 = 3x^2 e^{-x^3}(1-x^3) - 1$

(b) $g'(x) = \dfrac{(\cos x)\dfrac{2\sin x \cos x}{\sin^2 x} - (-\sin x)\log(\sin^2 x)}{\cos^2 x} = \dfrac{2\cos^2 x + \sin^2 x \log(\sin^2 x)}{\cos^2 x \sin x}$

(c) $h'(x) = \dfrac{\dfrac{1}{2\sqrt{x}}}{1+(\sqrt{x})^2} = \dfrac{1}{2\sqrt{x}(1+x)}$

Example 2.8   What's the equation of the normal line through the origin to the curve
$y = (x^4 - 1)^3 \log(x+1)$?

Solution: First, we'll need to find the slope of the line tangent to the curve at the indicated point; the normal line's slope will then be the opposite reciprocal of the tangent line's slope. Since

$y' = (x^4 - 1)^3 \dfrac{1}{x+1} + 3(x^4 - 1)^2 \cdot 4x^3 \cdot \log(x+1)$, the slope of the line tangent to the curve at the point where $x = 0$ is $y'(0) = -1$, which tells us that the slope of the normal line is 1.

The equation of the line with slope 1 through the origin is $y = x$.

LINEAR APPROXIMATIONS USING DIFFERENTIALS

Let f be a continuous function such that $f'(a) \neq 0$. The line tangent to the curve $y = f(x)$ at $x = a$ provides a good approximation of the graph of f near $x = a$.

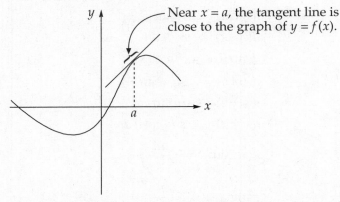

Near $x = a$, the tangent line is close to the graph of $y = f(x)$.

So, if we want to figure out the value of f at a point b close to a, we can instead find the value of y at b on the tangent line; this result will be a good approximation, and its accuracy will improve as b moves closer to a.

The equation of the line tangent to the graph of $y = f(x)$ at the point $x = a$ is $y = f(a) + f'(a)(x - a)$, so $f(b)$ will be approximately equal to $f(a) + f'(a)(b - a)$.

The equation of the line tangent at $x = a$ can be written as $y - f(a) = f'(a)(x - a)$. If we think of $y - f(a)$ as Δy, and $x - a$ as Δx, then we have $\Delta y = f'(a)\Delta x$ as the equation of the tangent line. In the limit as x approaches a, this equation becomes $dy = f'(a)dx$ which contains the differentials dy and dx, and illustrates the Leibniz notation, $dy/dx = f'$.

Example 2.9	What's an approximate value for $e^{0.1}$?

Solution: If we let $f(x) = e^x$, then we want the value of $f(b)$, where $b = 0.1$. Since $f(a)$, where $a = 0$, is easy to compute, and since b is close to a, we'll use the tangent line to the graph of $y = f(x)$ at $x = a$ to approximate the value of $f(b)$. Since $f'(x) = e^x$, we know that $f'(a) = f'(0) = e^0 = 1$, so we have:

$$dy = f'(0)dx \;\;\Rightarrow\;\; dy = 1 \cdot dx \;\;\Rightarrow\;\; dy = dx \;\;\Rightarrow\;\; \Delta y \approx \Delta x$$

Because $\Delta x = b - a = 0.1 - 0 = 0.1$, this result tells us that $\Delta y \approx 0.1$. Finally, since y at $a = 0$ is $e^0 = 1$, we know that y at b is approximately $1 + \Delta y = 1.1$. (By the way, a calculator would tell you that $e^{0.1} \approx 1.105$, so our approximation of 1.1 is pretty good.)

Implicit Differentiation

An equation of the form $y = f(x)$ defines y as an explicit function of x, since the dependent variable, y, appears all by itself on one side of the equation, and the formula for computing it involves only the independent variable, x. But sometimes an equation that mixes the variables x and y can define a function. For example, the equation $x^2y + y = 2$ defines y as a function of x, since for every value of x, there is exactly one value of y that satisfies the equation. In this case, we could solve for y explicitly and get $y = 2/(x^2 + 1)$, and the derivative of this function can be determined as we've done before.

But the equation $x^2y^5 + y = 2$ is a different story. This fifth-degree equation cannot be solved for y explicitly in terms of x. Nevertheless, if we plot every point (x, y) that satisfies the equation, we'd get a curve that's the graph of a function of x. Even though we can't solve for y in terms of x, we can still figure out the derivative of this function by using a technique called **implicit differentiation**. In implicit differentiation, we differentiate both sides of the equation with respect to x, remembering that y is a function of x. This means that every time we differentiate an expression involving y, the chain rule requires that we multiply by y', and then solve for y'. For this equation, we'd find that:

$$x^2y^5 + y = 2$$
$$(x^2 \cdot 5y^4y' + 2xy^5) + y' = 0$$
$$y'(5x^2y^4 + 1) = -2xy^5$$
$$y' = -\frac{2xy^5}{5x^2y^4 + 1}$$

Using this formula for the derivative, we can find the slope of the curve at any point.

The **Implicit Function theorem** tells us precisely when an equation of the form $f(x, y) = c$ (where c is a constant) actually defines y as a function of x, so that the formula we'd derive for y' using implicit differentiation gives a result that makes sense. This theorem involves *partial derivatives* (which we'll review in the next chapter), but for the sake of completeness, we'll state it here. The implicit function theorem states that, if $P_0 = (x_0, y_0)$ satisfies the equation $f(x, y) = c$ and both partial derivatives f_x and f_y are continuous in a neighborhood of P_0, then if the value of f_y is not zero at P_0, there exists a unique differentiable function, $y = g(x)$, that satisfies both the original equation, $f(x, y) = c$, and $y_0 = g(x_0)$. Furthermore, the derivative of this function is given by the equation $y' = \dfrac{-f_x}{f_y}$.

Higher-Order Derivatives

If we differentiate a function $y = f(x)$, we generally get another function, $y = f'(x)$. If we then differentiate this function—that is, find the derivative of the derivative—we'll get another function, $y = f''(x)$, called the **second derivative** of f. The process can continue: The derivative of the second derivative gives f''', the **third derivative** of f, and so on. These higher-order derivatives can be used to give important information about the graph of a function and to classify critical points (as we'll see in the next section), as well as to determine the Taylor polynomials and Taylor series of a function, topics we'll review in the last section of this chapter.

In Leibniz notation, the second derivative of $y = y(x)$ is d^2y/dx^2, the third derivative is d^3y/dx^3, and so on.

> **Example 2.10** What's the second derivative of the function $f(x) = \log(\log x)$?

Solution: We begin by finding the first derivative, $f'(x) = \dfrac{\dfrac{1}{x}}{\log x} = \dfrac{1}{x \log x} = (x \log x)^{-1}$,

then we differentiate again to get the second derivative:

$$f''(x) = -(x \log x)^{-2}[x \cdot \frac{1}{x} + \log x] = -\frac{1 + \log x}{(x \log x)^2}$$

CURVE SKETCHING

The first and second derivatives of a function $y = f(x)$ can provide us with valuable information about the shape of the graph, if we keep the following geometric facts in mind.

PROPERTIES OF THE FIRST DERIVATIVE

- At a point where $f'(x) > 0$, the slope is positive, so the function is increasing.

- At a point where $f'(x) < 0$, the slope is negative, so the function is decreasing.

- At a point where $f'(x) = 0$, the slope is zero, so the function has a horizontal tangent line. This point is called a **critical** (or **stationary**) **point** of f, and often signifies a turning point.

- At a point where $f'(x)$ does not exist, the function could have a vertical tangent line, or it might not be differentiable at that point. This point is also called a **critical** point of f and can sometimes signify a turning point for a function.

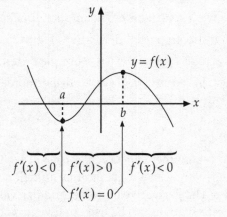

f is decreasing for $x < a$
f has a critical point at $x = a$
f is increasing for $a < x < b$
f has a critical point at $x = b$
f is decreasing for $x > b$

PROPERTIES OF THE SECOND DERIVATIVE

- At a point where $f''(x) > 0$, the curve is **concave up** (or **convex**), which means that the curve lies *above* its tangent line.

- At a point where $f''(x) < 0$, the curve is **concave down** (or just **concave**), which means that the curve lies *below* its tangent line.

- An **inflection point** is a point on a curve where the second derivative changes sign; thus, the curve is concave up on one side of an inflection point and concave down on the other side. In order for the curve $y = f(x)$ to have an inflection point at a point x in the domain of f, $f''(x)$ must equal 0 or $f''(x)$ must be undefined. (This condition is not sufficient, however.)

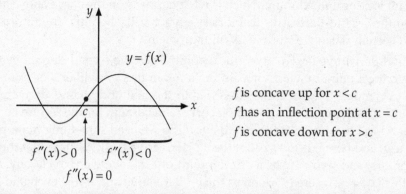

f is concave up for $x < c$

f has an inflection point at $x = c$

f is concave down for $x > c$

Example 2.11   Sketch the curve $y = x^2(x - 2)^2$.

Solution: We'll begin by finding the first derivative, and then we'll determine where it's zero and where it's positive and negative. By the product rule, we have:

$$y' = x^2 \cdot 2(x - 2) + (x - 2)^2 \cdot 2x$$
$$= 2x(x - 2)[x + (x - 2)]$$
$$= 4x(x - 1)(x - 2)$$

Setting this equal to zero, we see that critical points occur at $x = 0$, 1, and 2. For $x < 0$, the sign of y' is negative, so the curve is decreasing; for $0 < x < 1$, the sign of y' is positive, so the curve is increasing; for $1 < x < 2$, the sign of y' is negative, so the curve is decreasing; and for $x > 2$, the sign of y' is positive, so the curve is increasing.

Now, for the second derivative: Since $y' = 4(x^3 - 3x^2 + 2x)$, we find that:

$$y'' = 4(3x^2 - 6x + 2)$$

Setting this equal to zero, the quadratic formula tells us that $y'' = 0$ when:

$$x = \frac{-(-6) \pm \sqrt{(-6)^2 - 4 \cdot 3 \cdot 2}}{2 \cdot 3} = 1 \pm \frac{1}{\sqrt{3}}$$

Since y'' changes sign at each of these values of x, these are indeed inflection points. Finally, we figure out the y-coordinates of the critical points and the inflection points (and a couple of other arbitrary points if needed) and use the information about the signs of the first and second derivatives to make a sketch of the curve:

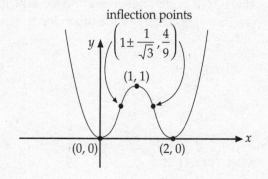

The curve in this example illustrates what the second derivative can tell us about the nature of the critical points. If the second derivative is positive at a critical point, then the critical point is a **local minimum**. You can see this on the curve on page 53, at the points where $x = 0$ and $x = 2$ (where this curve actually has **absolute minima**). On the other hand, if the second derivative is negative at a critical point, then the critical point is a **local maximum**, which is what happens on the curve above at the point where $x = 1$. This is called the **second-derivative test** for classifying critical points, an important tool that we'll also use in the next section when we study max/min problems.

What if the second derivative is zero at a critical point? Then the second-derivative test tells us nothing conclusive; the critical point may be a maximum, a minimum, or neither. For example, consider the curves $y = x^4$, $y = -x^4$, and $y = x^3$; for these curves, both the first and second derivatives equal zero at $x = 0$. But the point $(0, 0)$ is a minimum for the first curve, a maximum for the second curve, and neither a local minimum nor a local maximum for the third curve. So we need something more powerful than the second-derivative test, and here it is (let's call it the nth**-derivative test**): Assume that the function $f(x)$ has derivatives of all orders, and let $x = x_0$ be a critical point of f that we want to classify. Find the smallest integer n such that $f^{(n)}(x_0) \neq 0$, where $f^{(n)}$ denotes the nth derivative of f. If n is even and $f^{(n)}(x_0) > 0$, then f has a local minimum at x_0; if n is even and $f^{(n)}(x_0) < 0$, then f has a local maximum at x_0 (you can see that these two statements include the second-derivative test as a special case); if n is odd, then f has neither a local minimum nor a local maximum at x_0.

THEOREMS CONCERNING DIFFERENTIABLE FUNCTIONS

Earlier in this chapter, we stated several theorems that concern continuous functions. Here, we'll give two important theorems about differentiable functions.

> **Rolle's Theorem:** Assume that f is continuous on a closed interval $[a, b]$, with $f(a) = f(b)$, and that f is differentiable at every point in (a, b). If this is true, there's at least one point c in (a, b) at which $f'(c) = 0$.

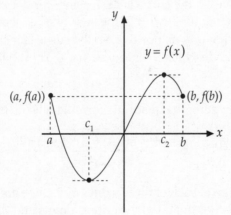

Therefore, there must be at least one point c between a and b at which the graph of $y = f(x)$ has a horizontal tangent line. Rolle's theorem is a special case of the following theorem.

The Mean-Value theorem (for derivatives): Assume that f is continuous on a closed interval $[a, b]$ and differentiable at every point in (a, b). Then there's at least one point c in (a, b), such that:

$$f'(c) = \frac{f(b) - f(a)}{b - a}$$

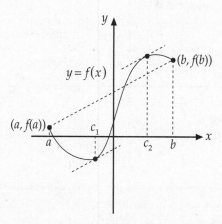

The Mean-Value theorem guarantees that there's at least one point c between a and b at which the slope of the line tangent at c is equal to the slope of the secant line (or chord) joining the points $(a, f(a))$ and $(b, f(b))$. This theorem can be used to prove several other important results, such as:

1. If f is continuous on an interval I, and $f'(x) = 0$, then $f(x)$ is constant on I.

2. If $f'(x)$ is positive on an interval I, then f is increasing on this interval; similarly, if $f'(x)$ is negative on I, then it's decreasing.

MAX/MIN PROBLEMS

From our work with curve sketching, we know that the maximum or minimum values of a function may be found by determining its critical points. Let's clarify this: Assume that a real-valued function f is continuous on an interval I of the real line. If there's a point c in this interval such that $f(c) \leq f(x)$ for all x in some subinterval of I that contains c, then we call $f(c)$ a **local minimum** of f; if $f(c) \leq f(x)$ for *all* x in I, then we call $f(x)$ an **absolute minimum** of f on I. Likewise, if there's a point c in I such that $f(c) \geq f(x)$ for all x in some subinterval of I containing c, then we call $f(c)$ a **local maximum** of f; if $f(c) \geq f(x)$ for *all* x in I, then we call $f(c)$ an **absolute maximum** of f on I. If $f(c)$ is a local minimum or maximum for a function, we say that $f(c)$ is an **extremum**. Of course, the question is, *How do we find a point c that makes f(c) an extremum?* If $f(c)$ is an extremum of f, then $f'(c) = 0$ or $f'(c)$ fails to exist. If we locate an extremum, we may be able to use the second-derivative test to classify it as a local minimum or a local maximum; remember that:

$$f'(c) = 0 \text{ and } f''(c) > 0 \quad \Rightarrow \quad f(c) \text{ is a local minimum}$$
$$f'(c) = 0 \text{ and } f''(c) < 0 \quad \Rightarrow \quad f(c) \text{ is a local maximum}$$

Furthermore, if f is defined on a *closed* interval, then the Extreme Value theorem guarantees that f will actually attain an absolute minimum and an absolute maximum on this interval. There are three possibilities for the location of the absolute extrema on a closed interval: An absolute extremum will occur at a point c such that $f'(c) = 0$, $f'(c)$ fails to exist, or at an endpoint of the interval.

$$y = f(x)$$
on the interval $[a, b]$

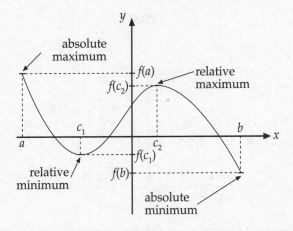

Example 2.12   The sum of two nonnegative numbers, x and y, is 12. What's the largest possible product of x^2 and y? What's the smallest?

Solution: Since $x + y = 12$, we know that $y = 12 - x$; and because x and y are nonnegative, it must be true that $0 \le x \le 12$. Therefore, we first want to maximize the function $f(x) = x^2(12 - x) = 12x^2 - x^3$ on the closed interval $[0, 12]$. To do this, we first set f' equal to zero to find the critical points:

$$f(x) = 12x^2 - x^3 \quad \Rightarrow \quad f'(x) = 24x - 3x^2 \overset{\text{set}}{=} 0$$
$$3x(8 - x) = 0$$
$$x = 0,\ 8$$

Let's use the second-derivative test to classify these points. Since $f''(x) = 24 - 6x$, we have $f''(0) = 24 > 0$. This means that f has a minimum at $x = 0$; and $f''(8) = -24 < 0$, so f has a maximum at $x = 8$. Because we're finding the extreme values of f on a closed interval, we must check the endpoints; at either $x = 0$ or $x = 12$, the value of f is 0, so these are the absolute minima, and $f(8) = 8^2 \cdot 4 = 256$ is the absolute maximum of f on $[0, 12]$.

Example 2.13   A rectangle in the fourth quadrant of the xy-plane has adjacent sides on the coordinate axes. If the vertex opposite the origin is on the curve $y = \log x$, what's the maximum area this rectangle can have?

Solution: The value of $\log x$ is negative on the interval $(0, 1)$, so the area of the rectangle is $A(x) = x(-\log x) = -x \log x$.

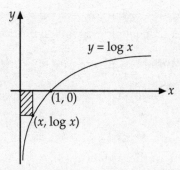

To find the maximum value of the function A on this interval, we take its derivative, set it equal to zero, and solve:

$$A(x) = -x \log x \quad \Rightarrow \quad A'(x) = -(1 + \log x) \overset{\text{set}}{=} 0$$

$$\log x = -1$$

$$x = e^{-1} = \frac{1}{e}$$

(Notice that $0 < \dfrac{1}{e} < 1$.) The second-derivative test verifies that this critical point does indeed give a maximum:

$$A''(x) = -\frac{1}{x} \quad \Rightarrow \quad A''\left(\frac{1}{e}\right) = -e < 0$$

Therefore, the maximum area of the rectangle is $A\left(\dfrac{1}{e}\right) = -\left(\dfrac{1}{e}\right) \log\left(\dfrac{1}{e}\right) = \dfrac{1}{e}$.

RELATED RATES

The derivative of a function $f(x)$ gives the rate of change of f with respect to x. So, if the variable t represents time, the derivative of a function $f(t)$ tells us how f changes with time. For example, consider a spherical balloon that's being inflated. How fast does its volume change? Let's see. The volume of a sphere of radius r is given by the formula $V(r) = \dfrac{4}{3}\pi r^3$; differentiating this equation with respect to time, we find that, using Leibniz notation:

$$\frac{dV}{dt} = 4\pi r^2 \frac{dr}{dt}$$

So, the rate at which V changes depends on the sphere's radius and how fast the radius is changing. This equation illustrates the concept of **related rates**: V depends on r, and the rate at which V changes is related to the rate at which r changes.

Example 2.14   A ladder of length 5 m is leaning against a vertical wall. The base of the ladder is then pulled away from the wall at a rate of $\frac{1}{2}$ m/s. At the moment at which the base of the ladder is 3 m from the wall, how fast is the top of the ladder sliding down the wall?

Solution: First, let's draw a picture of the situation:

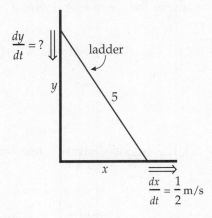

By the Pythagorean theorem, we know that $x^2 + y^2 = 5^2$. Differentiating both sides of this equation with respect to time, we find that:

$$2x\frac{dx}{dt} + 2y\frac{dy}{dt} = 0$$

$$\frac{dy}{dt} = -\frac{x}{y}\frac{dx}{dt}$$

This tells us how the rate at which the top of the ladder is sliding down the wall, dy/dt, is related to the rate at which the base of the ladder is being pulled away from the wall, dx/dt. Now, when $x = 3$ m, we know that $y = 4$ m, so the equation above gives us:

$$\frac{dy}{dt} = -\frac{x}{y}\frac{dx}{dt} = -\frac{3\text{ m}}{4\text{ m}} \cdot \frac{1}{2}\text{ m/s} = -\frac{3}{8}\text{ m/s}$$

Since the distance y is decreasing with time (because the top of the ladder is sliding down the wall), we expect its rate of change to be negative, and the calculation above confirms this. So we can say that, at the moment at which the base of the ladder is 3 m from the wall, the top of the ladder is sliding down at a rate of $\frac{3}{8}$ m/s.

INDEFINITE INTEGRATION (ANTIDIFFERENTIATION)

An **indefinite integral** of a function $f(x)$ is a function $F(x)$ whose derivative is $f(x)$. For this reason, indefinite integration is also known as **antidifferentiation**. For example, the function $F(x) = x^3 + 4$ is an indefinite integral (or **antiderivative**—the terms are interchangeable) of $f(x) = 3x^2$. Indefinite integrals are not unique; because the derivative of a constant vanishes, any function of the form $F(x) = x^3 + c$, where c is a constant, is an indefinite integral of $f(x) = 3x^2$. (We call c the **constant of integration**.) In fact, we can conclude that if $F(x)$ and $G(x)$ are antiderivatives of a given function $f(x)$, then $F(x)$ and $G(x)$ can only differ by a constant. The notation for an indefinite integral of $f(x)$ is

$$\int f(x)\,dx$$

where $\int(\cdots)\,dx$ is regarded as a single object. The function being integrated, $f(x)$, is called the **integrand**, and the dx, the differential of x, specifies the variable of integration; this means that $\int f(x)\,dx$ denotes an antiderivative of f with respect to x, while $\int f(t)\,dt$ is an antiderivative of f with respect to t.

For example, since the derivative of x^n is nx^{n-1} and the derivative of $\log x$ is $\dfrac{1}{x}$, we know that:

$$\int x^n\,dx = \begin{cases} \frac{1}{n+1}x^{n+1} + c & \text{if } n \neq -1 \\ \log|x| + c & \text{if } n = -1 \end{cases}$$

Example 2.15   The function $F(x)$ is the antiderivative of $f(x) = 6\sqrt{x} + \sin x - 1$ and satisfies $F(0) = 3$. What's $F(x)$?

Solution: Since the derivative of a sum is equal to the sum of the derivatives (from the derivative rules), it's also true that the integral of a sum is equal to the sum of the integrals. Therefore,

$$\begin{aligned} F(x) &= \int (6\sqrt{x} + \sin x - 1)\,dx \\ &= \int 6\sqrt{x}\,dx + \int \sin x\,dx + \int (-1)\,dx \\ &= 4x^{3/2} - \cos x - x + c \end{aligned}$$

Now we use the condition $F(0) = 3$ to figure out the constant of integration:

$$F(0) = 3 \quad \Rightarrow \quad c = 4 \quad \Rightarrow \quad F(x) = 4x^{3/2} - \cos x - x + 4$$

TECHNIQUES OF INTEGRATION

Integration by Substitution

The most widely used differentiation formula is the chain rule, and the most widely used antidifferentiation technique is based on the reverse of this formula—**integration by substitution**. The differential dx, which is part of the symbol for an indefinite integral, is especially helpful for handling this technique. To illustrate differentials again, notice that if $u(x) = x^3 + 4$, then, using Leibniz notation, $du/dx = 3x^2$. If we move the dx to the right-hand side (thinking of du/dx as if it were a fraction), we get the equation $du = 3x^2\,dx$, which says that the differential of u is equal to $3x^2$ times the differential of x; this means the same as $du/dx = 3x^2$.

Let's see how integration by substitution works by figuring out $\int x^2(x^3+4)^5 dx$.

The technique is easy to describe: Let the variable u stand for some expression in the integral; if its differential, du, (or a scalar multiple of it) is left over in the integrand, we'll be done. In this case, we'll let $u = x^3 + 4$; since $du = 3x^2\, dx$, we can write

$$\int x^2(x^3+4)^5 dx = \int u^5 \cdot \tfrac{1}{3} du$$
$$= \tfrac{1}{3}\int u^5 du$$
$$= \tfrac{1}{3}\left(\tfrac{1}{6}u^6\right)+c$$
$$= \tfrac{1}{18}(x^3+4)^6 + c$$

The trick to integration by substitution is in choosing the right u in the integrand. Although it seems like a process of trial-and-error, with practice this choice gets easier.

Here's a list of integration formulas (that you should memorize for the exam). We've used u as the variable of integration, so, if u is a (differentiable) function of x, each entry can be used in an integration-by-substitution solution:

$$\int k\, du = ku + c$$

$$\int u^k du = \begin{cases} \frac{1}{k+1}u^{k+1}+c & (\text{if } k \neq -1) \\ \log|u|+c & (\text{if } k = -1) \end{cases}$$

$$\int e^u du = e^u + c$$

$$\int a^u du = \tfrac{1}{\log a}a^u + c \quad (\text{if } a > 0)$$

$$\int \sin u\, du = -\cos u + c$$

$$\int \cos u\, du = \sin u + c$$

$$\int \sec^2 u\, du = \tan u + c$$

$$\int \csc^2 u\, du = -\cot u + c$$

$$\int \sec u \tan u\, du = \sec u + c$$

$$\int \csc u \cot u\, du = -\csc u + c$$

$$\int \frac{du}{\sqrt{1-u^2}} = \arcsin u + c$$

$$\int \frac{du}{1+u^2} = \arctan u + c$$

Example 2.16   Evaluate each of the following integrals:

(a) $\int \tan x \, dx$ (b) $\displaystyle\int \frac{x \, dx}{x^4 + 2x^2 + 2}$ (c) $\int \sin^2 x \, dx$

Solution:

(a) First, we write $\tan x$ as $(\sin x)/(\cos x)$. Now, if we let $u = \cos x$, then $du = -\sin x \, dx$, and:

$$\int \tan x \, dx = \int \frac{\sin x}{\cos x} \, dx = \int \frac{-du}{u} = -\log|u| + c = -\log|\cos x| + c$$

(b) The denominator of the integrand is equal to $(x^2 + 1)^2 + 1$. If we let $u = x^2 + 1$, then $du = 2x \, dx$, and the given integral becomes:

$$\int \frac{x \, dx}{x^4 + 2x^2 + 2} = \int \frac{x \, dx}{(x^2 + 1)^2 + 1} = \int \frac{\frac{1}{2} \, du}{u^2 + 1} = \tfrac{1}{2}\arctan u + c = \tfrac{1}{2}\arctan(x^2 + 1) + c$$

(c) The double-angle formula for the cosine function says $\cos 2x = 1 - 2\sin^2 x$; solving this for $\sin^2 x$ gives $\sin^2 x = \dfrac{1}{2}(1 - \cos 2x)$. Therefore,

$$\int \sin^2 x \, dx = \tfrac{1}{2}\int (1 - \cos 2x)\,dx = \tfrac{1}{2}\int dx - \tfrac{1}{2}\int \cos 2x \, dx$$

In this last integral, let $u = 2x$, so $du = 2 \, dx$. This gives us:

$$\int \sin^2 x \, dx = \tfrac{1}{2}\int dx - \tfrac{1}{2}\int \cos 2x \, dx$$
$$= \tfrac{1}{2}x - \tfrac{1}{2}\int \cos u \bullet \tfrac{1}{2} du$$
$$= \tfrac{1}{2}x - \tfrac{1}{4}\sin u + c$$
$$= \tfrac{1}{2}x - \tfrac{1}{4}\sin 2x + c$$

Integration by Parts

This integration technique is simply the reverse of the product rule for differentiation. The differential of the product of the functions u and v is

$$d(uv) = u \, dv + v \, du$$

which is equivalent to the equation $u \, dv = d(uv) - v \, du$. Therefore,

$$\int u \, dv = uv - \int v \, du$$

This is the formula for **integration by parts**. To illustrate, let's evaluate this integral:

$$\int x \log x \, dx$$

Any attempt at integration by substitution will be in vain, but, if we let $u = \log x$ and $dv = x\,dx$, then we can write $du = \dfrac{1}{x}\,dx$ and $v = \dfrac{1}{2}x^2$, and the integration by parts formula gives us:

$$\int x \log x \, dx = (\log x)(\tfrac{1}{2}x^2) - \int (\tfrac{1}{2}x^2)\left(\frac{1}{x}\right) dx$$
$$= \tfrac{1}{2}x^2 \log x - \tfrac{1}{2}\int x \, dx$$
$$= \tfrac{1}{2}x^2 \log x - \tfrac{1}{2}(\tfrac{1}{2}x^2) + c$$
$$= (\tfrac{1}{2}x^2)(\log x - \tfrac{1}{2}) + c$$

The secret to integration by parts is in choosing which part of the integrand to call u and which part to call dv so that the resulting integral is easier to figure out than the original integral. For example, if we had chosen $u = x$ and $dv = \log x\, dx$ for the integral above, finding v would have been just as difficult as evaluating the given integral.

Trig Substitutions

Integrals that contain the expressions $\sqrt{a^2 - u^2}$, $\sqrt{a^2 + u^2}$, or $\sqrt{u^2 - a^2}$, where a is a positive constant, can be simplified by making a change of variable that involves a trigonometric function. For example, if we're given an integral that contains the expression $\sqrt{a^2 - u^2}$, we can make the change of variable $u = a \sin \theta$, to get:

$$\sqrt{a^2 - u^2} = \sqrt{a^2 - (a \sin \theta)^2} = \sqrt{a^2(1 - \sin^2 \theta)} = \sqrt{a^2 \cos^2 \theta} = a \cos \theta$$

The square root sign disappears, and that's the point; each of the trig substitutions uses a Pythagorean identity to eliminate the square root. What substitution should we make in each of the three cases?

If the integrand contains	Make this substitution
$\sqrt{a^2 - u^2}$	$u = a \sin \theta$ (and $du = a \cos \theta \, d\theta$)
$\sqrt{a^2 + u^2}$	$u = a \tan \theta$ (and $du = a \sec^2\theta \, d\theta$)
$\sqrt{u^2 - a^2}$	$u = a \sec \theta$ (and $du = a \sec \theta \tan \theta \, d\theta$)

Let's try this out by evaluating the integral:

$$\int \frac{1}{x^2 \sqrt{x^2 + 1}} \, dx$$

If we were to attempt a basic substitution, like letting $u = x^2 + 1$, we wouldn't have $du = 2x\,dx$ left over in the integrand. Instead, we let $x = \tan \theta$, $dx = \sec^2\theta\,d\theta$ and transform the integral into:

$$\int \frac{1}{x^2\sqrt{x^2+1}}\,dx = \int \frac{1}{\tan^2\theta\sqrt{(\tan\theta)^2+1}}(\sec^2\theta\,d\theta)$$
$$= \int \frac{\sec\theta}{\tan^2\theta}\,d\theta$$
$$= \int \frac{\cos\theta}{\sin^2\theta}\,d\theta$$

To evaluate this last integral, we let $u = \sin\theta$, $du = \cos\theta\, d\theta$, which gives us:

$$\int \frac{\cos\theta}{\sin^2\theta}\, d\theta = \int \frac{1}{u^2}\, du = -\frac{1}{u} + c = -\frac{1}{\sin\theta} + c = -\csc\theta + c$$

Now, all that we have to do is rewrite this final result in terms of our original variable, x. In the right triangle below, $\tan\theta = \dfrac{x}{1} = x$; this triangle is an illustration of our original substitution, $x = \tan\theta$:

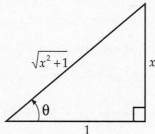

Since the triangle tells us that $\csc\theta = \dfrac{\sqrt{x^2+1}}{x}$, we can now write:

$$\int \frac{1}{x^2\sqrt{x^2+1}}\, dx = -\frac{\sqrt{x^2+1}}{x} + c$$

The Method of Partial Fractions

If the integrand is a rational function of x, that is, if it's equal to $\dfrac{P(x)}{Q(x)}$, where P and Q are polynomials (with deg P < deg Q), we can often evaluate the integral by first expressing $\dfrac{P(x)}{Q(x)}$ as a sum of simpler rational functions that are susceptible to quick integration. For example, let's figure out this integral:

$$\int \frac{1}{x^4 - x^2}\, dx$$

Our first step is to factor the denominator,

$$\frac{1}{x^4 - x^2} = \frac{1}{x^2(x^2-1)} = \frac{1}{x^2(x+1)(x-1)}$$

and then we express this as the sum

$$\frac{1}{x^2(x+1)(x-1)} = \frac{A}{x} + \frac{B}{x^2} + \frac{C}{x+1} + \frac{D}{x-1}$$

which is called the **partial-fraction decomposition**. Notice that every term of the form $(ax + b)^n$ in the denominator on the left is represented on the right, and if n is greater than 1, there'll be n corresponding partial fractions, with denominators $(ax + b)$, $(ax + b)^2$, ..., up to $(ax + b)^n$.

If the original rational function includes an irreducible quadratic factor—for example, $x^2 + 1$ in the denominator—then the partial-fraction decomposition will have a polynomial of degree one for the numerator of the term with the irreducible quadratic denominator:

$$\frac{1}{x(x^2+1)} = \frac{A}{x} + \frac{Bx+C}{x^2+1}$$

Now, we need to figure out the values of the constants $A, B, C,$ and D. One way, of course, is to multiply both sides by $x^2(x^2 - 1)$, which will clear all the fractions. We would then simplify the right-hand side and equate coefficients of like terms. This process will always work, but the algebra can get unwieldy. Here's a better approach: If we multiply both sides of the equation by $(x - 1)$, we get:

$$\frac{1}{x^2(x+1)} = \frac{A(x-1)}{x} + \frac{B(x-1)}{x^2} + \frac{C(x-1)}{x+1} + D$$

Since this is an identity, it must hold true for every value of x for which both sides are defined; in particular, it must be true for $x = 1$. Notice that substituting $x = 1$ into this equation immediately gives us $D = \frac{1}{2}$. Let's now multiply both sides of the partial-fraction decomposition by $(x + 1)$:

$$\frac{1}{x^2(x-1)} = \frac{A(x+1)}{x} + \frac{B(x+1)}{x^2} + C + \frac{D(x+1)}{x-1}$$

Substituting $x = -1$ gives us $C = -\frac{1}{2}$. Next, multiplying both sides of the decomposition by x^2 gives

$$\frac{1}{(x+1)(x-1)} = Ax + B + \frac{Cx^2}{x+1} + \frac{Dx^2}{x-1}$$

so substituting $x = 0$ tells us that $B = -1$. At this point, we have:

$$\frac{1}{x^2(x+1)(x-1)} = \frac{A}{x} + \frac{-1}{x^2} + \frac{-\frac{1}{2}}{x+1} + \frac{\frac{1}{2}}{x-1}$$

To find A, just substitute any value for x (except 0, 1, or –1); let's use $x = 2$

$$\frac{1}{12} = \frac{A}{2} + \frac{-1}{4} + \frac{-1}{6} + \frac{1}{2} \quad \Rightarrow \quad A = 0$$

and finally we are able to write:

$$\int \frac{1}{x^4 - x^2}\, dx = \int \left(\frac{-1}{x^2} + \frac{-\frac{1}{2}}{x+1} + \frac{\frac{1}{2}}{x-1} \right) dx$$

$$= \frac{1}{x} - \tfrac{1}{2}\log|x+1| + \tfrac{1}{2}\log|x-1| + c$$

$$= \frac{1}{x} + \log\sqrt{\frac{x-1}{x+1}} + c$$

DEFINITE INTEGRATION

The geometric motivation for the derivative is finding the slope of the line tangent to a curve. The motivation for the other principal idea of calculus, the integral, is finding the area *under* a curve. Following is a graph of the function $f(x) = 9 - x^2$, from $x = 0$ to $x = 3$. What's the area bounded by this curve and the x-axis?

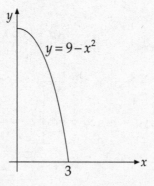

Well, we know the formulas for finding the areas of shapes like rectangles and triangles, whose sides are straight lines. But what about regions that have curved boundaries? One way to determine their area is to approximate, using a collection of narrow rectangular strips:

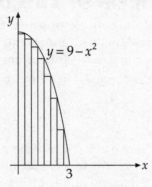

Let's imagine that we have n rectangular strips, each of which has a base of width of $\dfrac{3}{n}$. We'll take the height of each rectangle to be the value of $f(x)$ at the right-hand endpoint of the rectangle's base. Since the formula for the area of a rectangle is base $\times$ height, the sum of the areas of these rectangles is:

$$S_n = \frac{3}{n}\left[9-\left(\frac{3}{n}\right)^2\right]+\frac{3}{n}\left[9-\left(\frac{3\bullet 2}{n}\right)^2\right]+\cdots+\frac{3}{n}\left[9-\left(\frac{3(n-1)}{n}\right)^2\right]+\frac{3}{n}\left[9-\left(\frac{3n}{n}\right)^2\right]$$

This sum, S_n, which is called a **Riemann sum**, is close to, but slightly less than, the area under the curve. But if we increase n, the little triangular-shaped wedges that the rectangles don't account for will get smaller and smaller, and in the limit as $n\to\infty$, the total area of these wedges decreases to zero. This means that the limit of the sum shown above will give us the exact area under the curve. Let's see what this limit is. Simplifying the expression above, we find that

$$S_n = \frac{3}{n}\left[9-\left(\frac{3}{n}\right)^2\right]+\frac{3}{n}\left[9-\left(\frac{3\bullet 2}{n}\right)^2\right]+\cdots+\frac{3}{n}\left[9-\left(\frac{3(n-1)}{n}\right)^2\right]+\frac{3}{n}\left[9-\left(\frac{3n}{n}\right)^2\right]$$

$$= n\left(\frac{3}{n}\bullet 9\right)-\frac{3}{n}\left(\frac{3}{n}\right)^2[1^2+2^2+\cdots+(n-1)^2+n^2]$$

$$= 27-\frac{27}{n^3}[1^2+2^2+\cdots+(n-1)^2+n^2]$$

$$= 27-\frac{27}{n^3}\left[\frac{n(n+1)(2n+1)}{6}\right]$$

$$= 27-\frac{27}{6}\left[\frac{2n^3+3n^2+n}{n^3}\right]$$

where we've used the formula

$$1^2 + 2^2 + \cdots + n^2 = \frac{n(n+1)(2n+1)}{6}$$

which may be proved by mathematical induction. We now take the limit:

$$\text{exact area under curve} = \lim_{n \to \infty} S_n = \lim_{n \to \infty}\left[27 - \frac{27}{6}\left(\frac{2n^3 + 3n^2 + n}{n^3}\right)\right]$$

$$= 27 - \frac{27}{6} \cdot 2$$

$$= 18$$

THE FUNDAMENTAL THEOREM OF CALCULUS

The calculation we just finished was quite a chore. Fortunately, there's a much easier way to figure out the area under a curve. The method is based on the **fundamental theorem of calculus**, which links the apparently unrelated concepts of the slope of a curve and the area under it.

The area bounded by the x-axis and the curve $y = f(x)$, from $x = a$ to $x = b$, is denoted by

$$\int_a^b f(x)\,dx$$

which is called the **definite integral of f from a to b**. The numbers a and b are called the **limits of integration**. The fundamental theorem of calculus tells us that the definite integral of f can be computed by first determining an indefinite integral (antiderivative) of f. Let $f(x)$ be a continuous function on the interval $[a, b]$, and let $F(x)$ be an antiderivative of $f(x)$; then:

$$\int_a^b f(x)\,dx = F(b) - F(a)$$

The expression $F(b) - F(a)$ is written more compactly as $F(x)\Big]_a^b$, so this equation becomes:

$$\int_a^b f(x)\,dx = F(x)\Big]_a^b$$

Let's use this result to figure out the area we calculated above. Since $f(x) = 9 - x^2$, we can easily determine an indefinite integral: $F(x) = 9x - \frac{1}{3}x^3$. Therefore,

$$\int_0^3 (9 - x^2)\,dx = 9x - \tfrac{1}{3}x^3\Big]_0^3$$

$$= \left[9 \cdot 3 - \tfrac{1}{3} \cdot 3^3\right] - \left[9 \cdot 0 - \tfrac{1}{3} \cdot 0^3\right]$$

$$= 18$$

just as we found before. Notice that we don't need to bother adding a constant of integration to $F(x)$ when evaluating a definite integral, since it'll just cancel out when we perform the subtraction $F(b) - F(a)$. The fundamental theorem of calculus is usually given in two parts; one is the result above, the other makes explicit that differentiation and integration are inverse operations. It says that if $f(t)$ is a continuous function on $[a, b]$, then for any x in this interval:

$$\frac{d}{dx}\int_a^x f(t)\,dt = f(x)$$

The letter t in the expression on the left is known as a *dummy variable*, because any letter could be used in its place, and the meaning of the formula wouldn't change. It's considered bad form to have the same variable in the integrand and in the limits of integration, so we simply changed the x in $f(x)$ and dx to t to avoid this.

The definite integral $\int_a^b f(x)\,dx$ gives the total *algebraic* area bounded by the curve $y = f(x)$, the vertical lines $x = a$ and $x = b$, and the x-axis; this means that areas above the x-axis are counted as positive and those below the x-axis are negative. If we want to calculate the actual geometric area, we need to add the opposite of any negative algebraic area to the positive algebraic area.

The following rules are often used in dealing with definite integrals:

1. $\int_b^a f(x)\,dx = -\int_a^b f(x)\,dx$

   This says that reversing the limits of integration changes the sign of the integral. Notice that if $a = b$, then this rule implies:

   $\int_a^a f(x)\,dx = 0$

2. $\int_a^c f(x)\,dx = \int_a^b f(x)\,dx + \int_b^c f(x)\,dx$

   This says that the integral from a to c is equal to the integral from a to b plus the integral from b to c.

3. $\int_a^b kf(x)\,dx = k\int_a^b f(x)\,dx$ (where k is a constant)

   This says that the integral of kf is equal to k times the integral of f, so a constant may be moved outside the integral sign.

4. $\int_a^b [f(x) \pm g(x)]\,dx = \int_a^b f(x)\,dx \pm \int_a^b g(x)\,dx$

   The integral of a sum (or difference) is equal to the sum (or difference) of the integrals.

5. If $f(x) \le g(x)$ for all $x \in [a, b]$, then $\int_a^b f(x)\,dx \le \int_a^b g(x)\,dx$

   This says that if one function is always greater than another function over a defined interval, then the integral is also greater.

Example 2.17   Find the area of the region bounded by the x-axis, the line $x = 4$, and the curve $y = \sqrt{x}$.

Solution: The area is equal to:

$$\int_0^4 \sqrt{x}\,dx = \int_0^4 x^{1/2}\,dx = \tfrac{2}{3} x^{3/2} \Big]_0^4 = \tfrac{2}{3}(4^{3/2}) = \tfrac{16}{3}$$

Example 2.18   Simplify the following:

$$\frac{d}{dx}\int_x^{x^2}\frac{t}{\log t}\,dt$$

Solution: Let $f(t)=\dfrac{t}{\log t}$, and let $F(t)$ be an antiderivative of $f(t)$. Then:

$$\int_x^{x^2}\frac{t}{\log t}\,dt = F(t)\Big]_x^{x^2} = F(x^2)-F(x)$$

So, by the chain rule:

$$\frac{d}{dx}\int_x^{x^2}\frac{t}{\log t}\,dt = \frac{d}{dx}\Big[F(x^2)-F(x)\Big] = F'(x^2)\bullet 2x - F'(x)$$

Now, since $F'(t)=f(t)=\dfrac{t}{\log t}$, we find that:

$$\frac{d}{dx}\int_x^{x^2}\frac{t}{\log t}\,dt = F'(x^2)\bullet 2x - F'(x)$$

$$= 2x\bullet f(x^2)-f(x)$$

$$= 2x\frac{x^2}{\log(x^2)}-\frac{x}{\log x}$$

$$= \frac{x^3-x}{\log x}$$

The method used to solve this example can be used to show that, in general,

$$\frac{d}{dx}\int_{a(x)}^{b(x)}f(t)\,dt = f(b(x))\bullet b'(x)-f(a(x))\bullet a'(x)$$

THE AVERAGE VALUE OF A FUNCTION

Let f be a function that's continuous on a closed interval $[a, b]$. Then, according to the **mean-value theorem for integrals**, there's at least one point c between a and b, such that:

$$\int_a^b f(x)\,dx = f(c)(b-a)$$

What this says geometrically is that there's a point c such that the area of the rectangle whose base is $b - a$ and whose height is $f(c)$ is equal to the area under the curve from a to b.

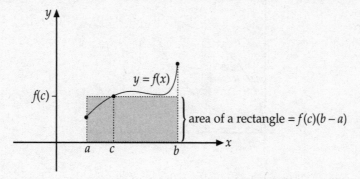

The value $f(c)$ is the **average value** of the function $f(x)$ on the interval $[a, b]$.

Finding the Area Between Two Curves

What's the area, A, of the region bounded by the curves $y = x^2$ and $y = \sqrt{x}$?

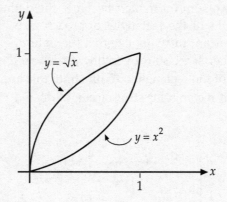

It's easy to see that this area is equal to the area under the curve $y = \sqrt{x}$ minus the area under the curve $y = x^2$, from $x = 0$ to $x = 1$; that is:

$$A = \int_0^1 (\sqrt{x})\, dx - \int_0^1 (x^2)\, dx = \int_0^1 (\sqrt{x} - x^2)\, dx$$

Another way to answer this question is to construct a typical rectangular strip of width Δx within this region; its height is $\sqrt{x} - x^2$, so its area is $(\sqrt{x} - x^2)\Delta x$.

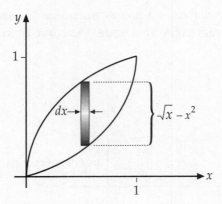

When we add the areas of all these strips (calling the sum S), and pass to the limit as the widths of the rectangles approach zero, we get

$$S = \Sigma(\sqrt{x} - x^2)\Delta x \to \int_0^1 (\sqrt{x} - x^2)\,dx$$

as before. Notice that the Riemann sum on the left becomes the definite integral on the right once we pass to the limit, where the widths of the rectangles approach zero. (In fact, the integral sign itself is simply an elongated S, which is meant to symbolize that the limit of a *sum* is being computed.) We can abbreviate this method even further, if we start by letting dx denote the width of the rectangle, and add up—that is, integrate—the areas of the rectangles. To illustrate this approach in a slightly different way, imagine constructing a horizontal rectangular strip of height dy and width $\sqrt{y} - y^2$—and thus, area of $(\sqrt{y} - y^2)\,dy$—within the region:

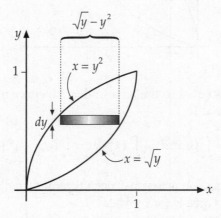

Allowing this strip to sweep through the region, by integrating from $y = 0$ up to $y = 1$, will give us the region's total area

$$A = \int_0^1 (\sqrt{y} - y^2)\,dy$$

which is the same as the integral given earlier in the variable x (since x and y are just dummy variables). The value of A is:

$$A = \int_0^1 (\sqrt{y} - y^2)\,dy = \frac{2}{3}y^{3/2} - \frac{1}{3}y^3 \Big]_0^1 = \frac{1}{3}$$

Example 2.19 Find the area of the region in the first quadrant, bounded by the curves $y = x^3$ and $y = 4x$.

Solution: These curves intersect at $x = -2$, 0, and 2, so the area of the region in the first quadrant, between the curves is equal to:

$$A = \int_0^2 (4x - x^3)\,dx = 2x^2 - \tfrac{1}{4}x^4 \Big]_0^2 = 8 - 4 = 4$$

We could also compute this area by integrating with respect to y, as follows:

$$A = \int_0^8 (\sqrt[3]{y} - \tfrac{1}{4}y)\,dy = \tfrac{3}{4}y^{4/3} - \tfrac{1}{8}y^2 \Big]_0^8 = 12 - 8 = 4$$

POLAR COORDINATES

So far, we've been exclusively using **rectangular** (or **Cartesian**) coordinates, x and y, to describe curves in the plane. But some curves are more easily described in terms of a different set of coordinates. The most common alternative is the pair of **polar coordinates**, r and θ. For a given point P in the plane, the coordinate r gives the distance between P and the origin (O), and the coordinate θ gives the angle that the ray OP makes with the positive x-axis:

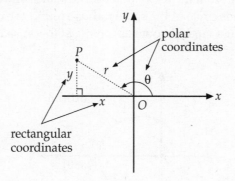

As usual, a positive value for θ implies a counterclockwise rotation from the positive x-axis, and a negative value of θ indicates a clockwise rotation. While the value of r is usually taken to be positive, we can include negative values of r by agreeing that the coordinates (r, θ) refer to the same point as the coordinates $(-r, \theta + \pi)$.

For example, the point in the plane whose rectangular coordinates are $(x, y) = (1, 1)$ can be expressed in polar coordinates as $(r, \theta) = (\sqrt{2}, \frac{\pi}{4})$ or $(-\sqrt{2}, \frac{5\pi}{4})$. From the figure above, we can write down the equations that relate Cartesian coordinates and polar coordinates:

$$x = r\cos\theta \qquad r = \sqrt{x^2 + y^2}$$

$$y = r\sin\theta \qquad \tan\theta = \frac{y}{x}\ (\text{if } x \neq 0)$$

In rectangular coordinates, the equation of the unit circle is $x^2 + y^2 = 1$, but in polar coordinates, the equation of the unit circle is much simpler: it's $r = 1$. Other circles also have simpler equations when they're expressed in polar coordinates:

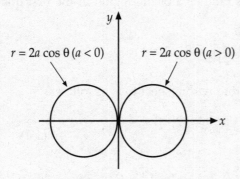

circles centered at $(a, 0)$ and tangent to the y-axis at the origin, with diameters of length $2|a|$

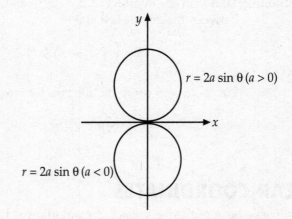

circles centered at $(0, a)$ and tangent to the x-axis at the origin, with diameters of length $2|a|$

But not only circles can benefit from the use of polar coordinates. If we take a circle of radius a centered at the point $(a, 0)$, and roll another circle of the same radius around the circumference of the first, a point on the rolling circle will trace out a curve known as a *cardioid* (because of its heart shape):

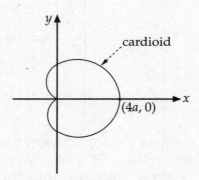

The equation for the cardioid in rectangular coordinates is a complicated, fourth-degree equation in both x and y, but in polar coordinates, the equation is much simpler:

$$r = 2a(1 + \cos \theta)$$

The area of a region bounded by a curve expressed in polar coordinates can also be found by integration. Instead of constructing thin rectangles in the region (as we do when we integrate with respect to x or y), we instead construct narrow circular sectors of angle $d\theta$ and length r. The area of a sector like this is given by the formula $\frac{1}{2} r^2 d\theta$, so if the region is described by the polar equation $r = r(\theta)$ from $\theta = \alpha$ to $\theta = \beta$, then the enclosed area is given by the equation:

$$A = \int_{\alpha}^{\beta} \tfrac{1}{2} r^2 d\theta$$

Example 2.20   Find the area enclosed by the cardioid $r = 2a(1 + \cos\theta)$.

Solution: The complete cardioid is traced out as θ increases from 0 to 2π, so the area enclosed by the cardioid is equal to:

$$A = \int_\alpha^\beta \tfrac{1}{2} r^2 d\theta = \int_0^{2\pi} \tfrac{1}{2}[2a(1+\cos\theta)]^2 \, d\theta$$

$$= 2a^2 \int_0^{2\pi}(1 + 2\cos\theta + \cos^2\theta)\, d\theta$$

$$= 2a^2 \int_0^{2\pi}[1 + 2\cos\theta + \tfrac{1}{2}(1 + \cos 2\theta)]\, d\theta$$

$$= 2a^2[\theta + 2\sin\theta + \tfrac{1}{2}\theta + \tfrac{1}{4}\sin 2\theta]_0^{2\pi}$$

$$= 6\pi a^2$$

VOLUMES OF SOLIDS OF REVOLUTION

Imagine that we have a portion of a curve, $y = f(x)$ from $x = a$ to $x = b$, in the x-y plane, and we revolve it around a straight line—the x-axis, for example:

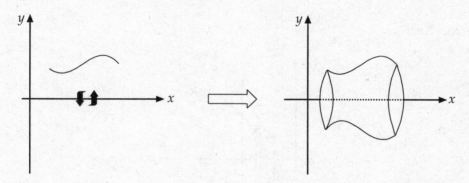

The result is called a **solid of revolution**. In this section, we'll develop techniques for finding the volumes of solids of revolution.

As we've done before, let's construct a narrow rectangle of base width dx and height $f(x)$, sitting under the curve. When this rectangle is revolved around the x-axis, we get a disk whose radius is $f(x)$ and whose height is dx. The volume of this disk is $dV = \pi\big[f(x)\big]^2 dx$, so the total volume of the solid is:

$$V = \int_a^b dV = \int_a^b \pi[f(x)]^2\, dx$$

If the curve is revolved around a vertical line (such as the y-axis), then horizontal disks are used. If the curve can be solved for x in terms of y, $x = g(y)$, the formula above becomes:

$$V = \int_c^d \pi[g(y)]^2\, dy$$

These equations illustrate the **disk method** for finding the volume of a solid of revolution.

Sometimes the region between two curves is revolved around an axis, and a gap is created between the solid and the axis. A rectangle within the rotated region will become a disk with a hole in it—also known as a washer. If the rectangle is vertical and extends from the curve $y = g(x)$ up to the curve $y = f(x)$, then when it's rotated around the x-axis, it will result in a washer with volume equal to

$$dV = \pi\left\{\left[f(x)\right]^2 - \left[g(x)\right]^2\right\}dx$$

which gives us:

$$V = \int_a^b \pi\left\{[f(x)]^2 - [g(x)]^2\right\}dx$$

Similarly, if the region is revolved around a vertical axis, we'll get horizontal washers and the formula above will involve the variable y. This is the **washer method** for finding the volume of a solid of revolution.

Example 2.21   What's the volume of the solid of revolution generated in each case?
(a) The portion of the curve $y = x^2$ from $x = 1$ to $x = 2$ is revolved around the x-axis.
(b) The region bounded by the curve $x = y^2 + 3$ and $x = 4y$ is revolved around the y-axis.

Solution:

(a) In this case,

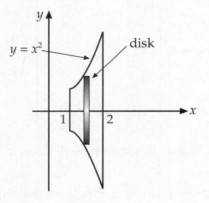

we can use the disk method:

$$V = \int_1^2 \pi[(x^2)]^2\,dx = \pi\int_1^2 x^4\,dx = \pi\left[\tfrac{1}{5}x^5\right]_1^2 = \tfrac{31}{5}\pi$$

(b) First, by setting $y^2 + 3$ equal to $4y$, we can determine that the two curves intersect at the points (4, 1) and (12, 3). We'll use washers that are perpendicular to the y-axis to find the volume of the solid we'd get by revolving the region between the two curves around the y-axis.

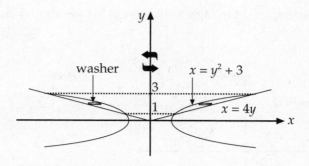

The curve $x = y^2 + 3$ is the "inside" curve and the line $x = 4y$ is the "outside" curve (that is, for $1 \leq y \leq 3$, the curve $x = y^2 + 3$ is closer to the y-axis than is the line $x = 4y$), so the washer method gives us:

$$V = \int_c^d \pi \left\{ [f(y)]^2 - [g(y)]^2 \right\} dy$$

$$= \int_1^3 \pi [(4y)^2 - (y^2 + 3)^2] \, dy$$

$$= \pi \int_1^3 [10y^2 - y^4 - 9] \, dy$$

$$= \pi \left[\tfrac{10}{3} y^3 - \tfrac{1}{5} y^5 - 9y \right]_1^3$$

$$= \pi \left[\left(\tfrac{10}{3} \cdot 3^3 - \tfrac{1}{5} \cdot 3^5 - 9 \cdot 3 \right) - \left(\tfrac{10}{3} \cdot 1^3 - \tfrac{1}{5} \cdot 1^5 - 9 \cdot 1 \right) \right]$$

$$= \tfrac{304}{15} \pi$$

ARC LENGTH

The length of a smooth curve (also called an arc) can also be found by integration. To establish the formula we need, let's consider the portion of the curve $y = f(x)$ from (a, c) to (b, d):

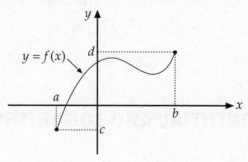

We can construct a differential right triangle with sides of lengths dx and dy, and hypotenuse ds along the curve:

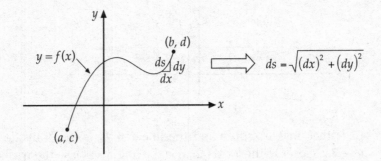

By adding up—that is, by integrating—the contributions ds, we get the following formula for s, the length of the curve:

$$s = \int ds = \int \sqrt{(dx)^2 + (dy)^2} = \int_a^b \sqrt{1 + \left(\frac{dy}{dx}\right)^2}\, dx \quad \text{or} \quad \int_c^d \sqrt{\left(\frac{dx}{dy}\right)^2 + 1}\, dy$$

Example 2.22   What's the length of the curve $y = \sqrt{x^3}$, from $x = 0$ to $x = 28$?

Solution: Using the formula above, we find that:

$$s = \int_a^b \sqrt{1 + (y')^2}\, dx = \int_0^{28} \sqrt{1 + \left(\tfrac{3}{2} x^{1/2}\right)^2}\, dx$$

$$= \int_0^{28} \sqrt{1 + \tfrac{9}{4} x}\, dx$$

$$= \tfrac{4}{9} \cdot \tfrac{2}{3} \left[\left(1 + \tfrac{9}{4} x\right)^{3/2}\right]_0^{28}$$

$$= \tfrac{8}{27} \left[64^{3/2} - 1\right]$$

$$= \tfrac{4088}{27}$$

THE NATURAL EXPONENTIAL AND LOGARITHM FUNCTIONS

Although we've already included the functions e^x and $\log x$ in the tables of differentials and integrals, we also want to include some other important information about these functions and the choice of the base, e.

The function e^x arises from the attempt to find a nonzero function that equals its own derivative. The derivative of every exponential function of the form $f(x) = a^x$ (with a positive) is equal to a multiple of itself, as the following calculation shows:

$$f'(x) = \lim_{h \to 0} \frac{f(x+h) - f(x)}{h} = \lim_{h \to 0} \frac{a^{x+h} - a^x}{h} = a^x \cdot \left(\lim_{h \to 0} \frac{a^h - 1}{h}\right)$$

If we can find the value of a that makes the expression in parentheses equal to 1, we will have satisfied the equation $f'(x) = f(x)$. This value of a is denoted by e. To obtain a numerical value for e, we notice that, by definition,

$$\lim_{h \to 0} \frac{e^h - 1}{h} = 1$$

so for small values of h, we can write:

$$e^h - 1 \approx h \quad \Rightarrow \quad e^h \approx 1 + h \quad \Rightarrow \quad e \approx (1 + h)^{1/h}$$

If we replace h by $\frac{1}{n}$, then

$$e \approx \left(1 + \frac{1}{n}\right)^n$$

and the approximation gets better as n gets larger. In fact, the number e is often *defined* as:

$$e = \lim_{n \to \infty} \left(1 + \frac{1}{n}\right)^n$$

We can now approximate e as closely as we wish; to 15 decimal places, the value of e is:

$$e = 2.718281828459045 \ldots$$

This real number is not only irrational, but it's also transcendental, which means that no polynomial with integer coefficients has e as a zero. Although the number looks messy, it's specifically chosen to provide the equation $f'(x) = f(x)$ with the simplest possible solution. Also notice that, of all the exponential functions ($f(x) = a^x$), only when $a = e$ will the slope of this curve at $x = 0$ be equal to 1. For these reasons, the function $f(x) = e^x$ is called the **natural exponential** function.

The **natural logarithm** function, $f(x) = \log_e x = \log x$, is the inverse of the natural exponential function. The most important property of the natural logarithm function is that it provides an antiderivative of the function $g(x) = \frac{1}{x}$. We can prove this easily. If $y = \log x$, then $x = e^y$; these two equations are equivalent. If we differentiate the equation $x = e^y$ implicitly with respect to x, we get:

$$1 = e^y \frac{dy}{dx} \quad \Rightarrow \quad \frac{dy}{dx} = \frac{1}{e^y} = \frac{1}{x}$$

It's also useful to know that, because of the fundamental theorem of calculus and the fact that $\log 1 = 0$, the expression $\log x$ can be written as:

$$\log x = \int_1^x \frac{1}{t} dt$$

In fact, $\log x$ can be defined by this equation from the start, and all the properties of the logarithm, and of its inverse function, $f(x) = e^x$, can then be derived.

Example 2.23 What's the value of this limit if $a > 0$?

$$\lim_{x \to 0} \frac{a^x - 1}{x}$$

Solution: We notice that this looks like the definition of a derivative. If we let $f(x) = a^x$, then the derivative of f at $x = 0$ is

$$f'(0) = \lim_{h \to 0} \frac{f(0+h) - f(0)}{h} = \lim_{h \to 0} \frac{a^h - 1}{h}$$

which (except for the choice of the dummy variable) is exactly the same as the limit for which we're looking. Since $f(x) = a^x = e^{x \log a}$, we know that

$$f'(0) = e^{x \log a} \cdot \log a \Big|_{x=0} = \log a$$

and this is our answer. (Note: the value of a derivative of f at a point $x = a$ can be written either as $f'(a)$ or $f'|_{x=a}$.)

Example 2.24 Let A denote the area of the region bounded by the curve $y = \dfrac{1}{x}$, the x-axis, and the vertical lines $x = 1$ and $x = a$ (where $a > 1$). In terms of A, what's the area of the region bounded by the curve $y = \dfrac{1}{x}$, the x-axis, and the vertical lines $x = a^2$ and $x = a^3$?

Solution: The area we're trying to find can be expressed as the definite integral

$$\int_{a^2}^{a^3} \frac{1}{x} \, dx$$

which we can simplify as follows:

$$\int_{a^2}^{a^3} \frac{1}{x} \, dx = \log x \Big]_{a^2}^{a^3} = \log a^3 - \log a^2 = 3 \log a - 2 \log a = \log a$$

The information we're given about A allows us to write

$$A = \int_{1}^{a} \frac{1}{x} \, dx$$

so $A = \log a$. Therefore, the area we're trying to find is also equal to A.

Example 2.25   What's the derivative of the function $f(x) = x^{\sqrt{x}}$?

Solution: The differentiation formula

$$\frac{d}{dx}(x^k) = kx^{k-1}$$

only works when the expression in the exponent is a constant. For the function we're given, however, the expression in the exponent is not a constant, so this differentiation formula cannot be used. Instead we use the fact that $u^v = e^{v \log u}$ to rewrite $f(x)$ as

$$f(x) = x^{\sqrt{x}} = e^{\sqrt{x} \log x}$$

and then apply the differentiation formula $d(e^u) = e^u du$, to find that:

$$f(x) = x^{\sqrt{x}} \quad \Rightarrow \quad f(x) = e^{\sqrt{x} \log x} \quad \Rightarrow \quad f'(x) = e^{\sqrt{x} \log x} \cdot \frac{d}{dx}(\sqrt{x} \log x)$$

$$= e^{\sqrt{x} \log x} \cdot \left(\sqrt{x} \cdot \frac{1}{x} + \log x \cdot \frac{1}{2\sqrt{x}} \right)$$

$$= \frac{x^{\sqrt{x}}}{\sqrt{x}} \left(1 + \frac{\log x}{2} \right)$$

L'HÔPITAL'S RULE

The list of rules for dealing with limits (given in the first section of this chapter) mentioned **L'Hôpital's rule**, and we'll now discuss it. L'Hôpital's rule provides us with one of the most useful techniques for evaluating limits.

Let's start by reconsidering Example 2.2(b) from page 39:

$$\lim_{x \to 1} \frac{x-1}{\sqrt{x}-1}$$

If we attempt to substitute $x = 1$ into this expression, we get the meaningless fraction $\frac{0}{0}$; this is called an **indeterminate form**, since it has no unique value. L'Hôpital's rule gives us an easy way to handle this situation; it says that if $f(x)$ and $g(x)$ are functions that are differentiable in an open interval, I, containing a (except possibly at a itself) such that $g'(x) \neq 0$ for all $x \neq a$ in I, and $f(a) = g(a) = 0$, then

$$\lim_{x \to a} \frac{f(x)}{g(x)} = \lim_{x \to a} \frac{f'(x)}{g'(x)} \quad (*)$$

provided that the limit on the right exists. Applying this rule to the limit problem above, we'd differentiate the numerator and denominator (separately!) and find

$$\lim_{x \to 1} \frac{x-1}{\sqrt{x}-1} = \lim_{x \to 1} \frac{1}{\frac{1}{2\sqrt{x}}} = \frac{1}{\frac{1}{2 \cdot 1}} = 2$$

just as we did earlier. The statement of L'Hôpital's rule remains valid if "$x \to a$" is replaced by either the left-hand limit "$x \to a-$" or the right-hand limit "$x \to a+$." It also applies when "$x \to a$" is replaced by

"$x \to \infty$" or "$x \to -\infty$." Furthermore, the rule can take care of the indeterminate form $\frac{\infty}{\infty}$, which arises when both $f(x)$ and $g(x)$ become infinite, as $x \to a$. And finally, the statement of (*) is still valid even when the right-hand side of (*) is $+\infty$. L'Hôpital's rule is truly powerful!

Example 2.26 Find each of the following limits:

(a) $\lim\limits_{x\to0} \dfrac{\sin 4x}{x}$ (b) $\lim\limits_{x\to1} \dfrac{\sqrt{x}-1}{\sqrt[3]{x}-1}$ (c) $\lim\limits_{x\to0} \dfrac{x^2}{1-\cos x}$

(d) $\lim\limits_{x\to\infty} \dfrac{1}{x(\frac{\pi}{2}-\arctan x)}$ (e) $\lim\limits_{x\to1+} x^{1/(x^2-1)}$

Solution:

(a) This limit gives us the indeterminate form $\frac{0}{0}$, so we apply L'Hôpital's rule:

$$\lim_{x\to0} \frac{\sin 4x}{x} = \lim_{x\to0} \frac{4\cos 4x}{1} = \frac{4\cos 0}{1} = \frac{4}{1} = 4$$

(b) This problem also gives the indeterminate form $\frac{0}{0}$, and we find that:

$$\lim_{x\to1} \frac{\sqrt{x}-1}{\sqrt[3]{x}-1} = \lim_{x\to1} \frac{x^{1/2}-1}{x^{1/3}-1} = \lim_{x\to1} \frac{\frac{1}{2}x^{-1/2}}{\frac{1}{3}x^{-2/3}} = \frac{\frac{1}{2}\cdot 1^{-1/2}}{\frac{1}{3}\cdot 1^{-2/3}} = \frac{\frac{1}{2}}{\frac{1}{3}} = \frac{3}{2}$$

(c) Once again, we have the indeterminate form $\frac{0}{0}$; applying L'Hôpital's rule gives us:

$$\lim_{x\to0} \frac{x^2}{1-\cos x} = \lim_{x\to0} \frac{2x}{\sin x}$$

But notice that the limit on the right-hand side is also of the form $\frac{0}{0}$, so we simply apply L'Hôpital's rule again:

$$\lim_{x\to0} \frac{2x}{\sin x} = \frac{2}{\cos x} = \lim_{x\to0} \frac{2x}{\cos x} = \frac{2}{1} = 2$$

(d) The expression in the denominator gives us $\infty \cdot 0$, which is another indeterminate form, but we can easily turn this into a $\frac{0}{0}$ indeterminate form, as follows

$$\lim_{x\to\infty} \frac{1}{x(\frac{\pi}{2}-\arctan x)} = \lim_{x\to\infty} \frac{\frac{1}{x}}{\frac{\pi}{2}-\arctan x}$$

and then apply L'Hôpital's rule:

$$\lim_{x\to\infty} \frac{\frac{1}{x}}{\frac{\pi}{2}-\arctan x} = \lim_{x\to\infty} \frac{\frac{-1}{x^2}}{\frac{-1}{1+x^2}} = \lim_{x\to\infty} \frac{1+x^2}{x^2}$$

Now at this point, we could apply L'Hôpital's rule again, but it's easier to simply notice that:

$$\lim_{x \to \infty} \frac{1+x^2}{x^2} = \lim_{x \to \infty} \left(\frac{1}{x^2} + 1 \right) = 0 + 1 = 1$$

(e) This limit problem gives rise to the indeterminate form 1^∞. When faced with a limit of an expression like $[f(x)]^{g(x)}$ that gives any of the indeterminate forms 1^∞, ∞^0, or 0^0, the trick is first to figure out the limit of $\log[f(x)]^{g(x)} = g(x) \log f(x)$. In this case, we would let $y = x^{1/(x^2-1)}$, so $\log y = (\log x)/(x^2 - 1)$. The limit of $\log y$ as $x \to 1+$ gives us the familiar $\dfrac{0}{0}$ indeterminate form, and L'Hôpital's rule tells us that:

$$\lim_{x \to 1+} \frac{\log x}{x^2 - 1} = \lim_{x \to 1+} \frac{\frac{1}{x}}{2x} = \frac{1}{2}$$

Therefore, since $\log y$ approaches $\dfrac{1}{2}$, y approaches $e^{1/2} = \sqrt{e}$.

Example 2.27   What's the limit of the sequence (a_n), where

$$a_n = \frac{(\log n)^2}{\sqrt{n}} \, ?$$

Solution: Remember rule 7, given near the beginning of this chapter on page 37:

If $a_n = f(n)$, then the sequence (a_n) converges to L if and only if $f(x)$ converges to L as $x \to \infty$ (which may be decided using L'Hôpital's rule).

Therefore, we determine the value of:

$$\lim_{x \to \infty} \frac{(\log x)^2}{\sqrt{x}}$$

Since this limit is of the indeterminate form $\dfrac{\infty}{\infty}$, we apply L'Hôpital's rule:

$$\lim_{x \to \infty} \frac{(\log x)^2}{\sqrt{x}} = \lim_{x \to \infty} \frac{2(\log x) \cdot x^{-1}}{\frac{1}{2} x^{-1/2}} = \lim_{x \to \infty} \frac{4 \log x}{x^{1/2}}$$

But the limit on the right is also of the form $\dfrac{\infty}{\infty}$, so we apply L'Hôpital's rule again:

$$\lim_{x \to \infty} \frac{4 \log x}{x^{1/2}} = \lim_{x \to \infty} \frac{4x^{-1}}{\frac{1}{2} x^{-1/2}} = \lim_{x \to \infty} \frac{8}{x^{1/2}} = 0$$

IMPROPER INTEGRALS

Up to now, the only definite integrals we've looked at have been integrals over a bounded interval, $[a, b]$. But we will now begin to work with **improper integrals**, one type of which are integrals over unbounded intervals, of the form $[a, \infty)$, $(-\infty, b]$, or $(-\infty, \infty)$. The definition of such an integral is easy to give. For example,

$$\int_a^\infty f(x)\,dx = \lim_{b\to\infty} \int_a^b f(x)\,dx$$

provided that the limit on the right exists; if it does, then we say that the integral **converges**. Similarly, we define:

$$\int_{-\infty}^b f(x)\,dx = \lim_{a\to-\infty} \int_a^b f(x)\,dx$$

For an improper integral over the entire real line, $(-\infty, \infty)$, we agree that, if both

$$\int_{-\infty}^c f(x)\,dx \quad \text{and} \quad \int_c^\infty f(x)\,dx$$

converge for some number c, then $\int_{-\infty}^\infty f(x)\,dx$ converges, and $\int_{-\infty}^\infty f(x)\,dx = \int_{-\infty}^c f(x)\,dx + \int_c^\infty f(x)\,dx$.

For example, let's determine the value of:

$$\int_0^\infty \frac{2}{1+x^2}\,dx$$

By definition, we would write:

$$\int_0^\infty \frac{2}{1+x^2}\,dx = \lim_{b\to\infty} \int_0^b \frac{2}{1+x^2}\,dx = \lim_{b\to\infty}\Big[2\arctan x\Big]_0^b$$

$$= 2\lim_{b\to\infty}[\arctan b]$$

$$= 2\left(\frac{\pi}{2}\right)$$

$$= \pi$$

As an example of a divergent improper integral, notice that:

$$\int_1^\infty \frac{1}{x}\,dx = \lim_{b\to\infty} \int_1^b \frac{1}{x}\,dx = \lim_{b\to\infty}\Big[\log x\Big]_1^b = \lim_{b\to\infty}[\log b] = \infty$$

This type of integral is called *improper* because one or both of the limits of integration are infinite; these are sometimes referred to as *improper integrals of the first kind*. Another type of integral that's also called improper has finite limits of integration but the integrand becomes infinite at one or both of the limits of integration or at a point between them. (These are *improper integrals of the second kind*.) For example,

$$\int_0^1 \frac{1}{\sqrt{1-x^2}}\,dx$$

is an improper integral (of the second kind) because the integrand, $1/\sqrt{1-x^2}$, goes to infinity as $x \to 1$, the upper limit of integration. This kind of improper integral is also defined as a limit; in this case, we would write:

$$\int_0^1 \frac{1}{\sqrt{1-x^2}}\,dx = \lim_{b\to1} \int_0^b \frac{1}{\sqrt{1-x^2}}\,dx = \lim_{b\to1}\Big[\arcsin x\Big]_0^b = \lim_{b\to1}[\arcsin b] = \frac{\pi}{2}$$

Example 2.28   Evaluate each of the following improper integrals:

$$\text{(a)} \int_0^\infty \frac{e^{-\sqrt{x}}}{\sqrt{x}}\,dx \qquad \text{(b)} \int_e^\infty \frac{dx}{x\log x} \qquad \text{(c)} \int_0^3 \frac{x}{(x^2-1)^{2/3}}\,dx$$

Solution:

(a) This integral is improper for two reasons; not only is one of the limits of integration infinite, but the integrand itself becomes infinite at the lower limit of integration. (We might call this an improper integral of the third kind!) First, let's find an antiderivative of the integrand. By letting $u = \sqrt{x}$ so that $du = dx/2\sqrt{x}$, we find that:

$$\int \frac{e^{-\sqrt{x}}}{\sqrt{x}}\,dx = \int 2e^{-u}\,du = -2e^{-u} = -2e^{-\sqrt{x}} = \frac{-2}{e^{\sqrt{x}}}$$

Therefore,

$$\int_0^\infty \frac{e^{-\sqrt{x}}}{\sqrt{x}}\,dx = \lim_{\substack{b\to\infty \\ a\to 0+}} \int_a^b \frac{e^{-\sqrt{x}}}{\sqrt{x}}\,dx = \lim_{\substack{b\to\infty \\ a\to 0+}} \left[\frac{-2}{e^{\sqrt{x}}}\right]_a^b = -2 \cdot \lim_{\substack{b\to\infty \\ a\to 0+}} \left[\frac{1}{e^{\sqrt{b}}} - \frac{1}{e^{\sqrt{a}}}\right] = -2 \cdot \left[0 - \frac{1}{1}\right] = 2$$

(b) By making the substitution $u = \log x$, $du = dx/x$, we find that

$$\int \frac{dx}{x\log x} = \int \frac{du}{u} = \log u = \log(\log x)$$

which gives us:

$$\int_e^\infty \frac{dx}{x\log x} = \lim_{b\to\infty} \int_e^b \frac{dx}{x\log x} = \lim_{b\to\infty} \left[\log(\log x)\right]_e^b = \lim_{b\to\infty}\left[\log(\log b)\right] = \infty$$

This improper integral diverges to infinity.

(c) The integrand goes to infinity at $x = 1$, a point within the domain of integration, $[0, 3]$. Therefore, we write the given integral as the sum

$$\int_0^3 \frac{x}{(x^2-1)^{2/3}}\,dx = \int_0^1 \frac{x}{(x^2-1)^{2/3}}\,dx + \int_1^3 \frac{x}{(x^2-1)^{2/3}}\,dx$$

and attempt to evaluate each of the two integrals on the right, which are improper at a limit of integration. First, let's substitute $u = x^2 - 1$, $du = 2x\,dx$ to find:

$$\int \frac{x}{(x^2-1)^{2/3}}\,dx = \int \frac{\frac{1}{2}\,du}{u^{2/3}} = \tfrac{3}{2}u^{1/3} = \tfrac{3}{2}(x^2-1)^{1/3}$$

Therefore,

$$\int_0^1 \frac{x}{(x^2-1)^{2/3}}\,dx = \lim_{b\to 1^-}\left[\tfrac{3}{2}(x^2-1)^{1/3}\right]_0^b = \tfrac{3}{2}\cdot\lim_{b\to 1^-}\left[(b^2-1)^{1/3}-(-1)\right] = \tfrac{3}{2}[0+1] = \tfrac{3}{2}$$

and

$$\int_1^3 \frac{x}{(x^2-1)^{2/3}}\,dx = \lim_{a\to 1^+}\left[\tfrac{3}{2}(x^2-1)^{1/3}\right]_a^3 = \tfrac{3}{2}\cdot\lim_{a\to 1^+}\left[(3^2-1)^{1/3}-(a^2-1)^{1/3}\right] = \tfrac{3}{2}[2-0] = 3$$

Since both of these integrals converge, we can conclude that the original improper integral converges, and:

$$\int_0^3 \frac{x}{(x^2-1)^{2/3}}\,dx = \int_0^1 \frac{x}{(x^2-1)^{2/3}}\,dx + \int_1^3 \frac{x}{(x^2-1)^{2/3}}\,dx = \tfrac{3}{2}+3 = \tfrac{9}{2}$$

INFINITE SERIES

If we're given a sequence $(a_n) = a_1, a_2, a_3, \ldots$, then

$$\sum_{n=1}^{\infty} a_n = a_1 + a_2 + a_3 + \cdots$$

is called an **infinite series**. We know how to add a finite number of terms, but how do we find the sum of infinitely many? The answer is to form a sequence associated with the series, the sequence (s_n) of its **partial sums**:

$$s_1 = a_1$$
$$s_2 = a_1 + a_2$$
$$s_3 = a_1 + a_2 + a_3$$
$$\vdots$$
$$s_n = a_1 + a_2 + \cdots + a_n$$
$$\vdots$$

If the sequence of partial sums converges to a finite limit, S, then we say the infinite series **converges** to S; otherwise, the series is said to **diverge**.

Let's look at an example; consider the series:

$$\sum_{n=1}^{\infty}\left(\tfrac{1}{2}\right)^n$$

The first few terms of its corresponding sequence of partial sums are

$$\tfrac{1}{2},\ \tfrac{1}{2}+\tfrac{1}{4},\ \tfrac{1}{2}+\tfrac{1}{4}+\tfrac{1}{8},\ \ldots = \tfrac{1}{2},\ \tfrac{3}{4},\ \tfrac{7}{8},\ \ldots$$

which seem to be tending to 1. We can prove this by using the formula

$$1 + x + x^2 + \cdots + x^n = \frac{1-x^{n+1}}{1-x}$$

which holds for every x not equal to 1. (If x does equal 1, the sum on the left is just equal to $n + 1$.) In this case, then, the nth term of the sequence of the series' partial sums is:

$$s_n = \tfrac{1}{2} + \left(\tfrac{1}{2}\right)^2 + \cdots + \left(\tfrac{1}{2}\right)^n = \frac{1 - \left(\tfrac{1}{2}\right)^{n+1}}{1 - \left(\tfrac{1}{2}\right)} - 1 = 2\left[1 - \left(\tfrac{1}{2}\right)^{n+1}\right] - 1 = 1 - \tfrac{1}{2^n}$$

Since $\dfrac{1}{2^n} \to 0$ as $n \to \infty$, we see that $s_n \to 1$. Therefore,

$$\sum_{n=1}^{\infty} \left(\tfrac{1}{2}\right)^n = 1$$

If r is a constant, then the series $\sum r^n$ is called a **geometric series**, and it can be shown that this series converges if and only if $|r| < 1$. If this is the case, the following formula holds true for $r \neq 0$:

$$\sum_{n=0}^{\infty} r^n = \frac{1}{1-r}$$

Notice that this series starts at $n = 0$. A series can start at any value of the index n, with no effect on its convergence. However, the *sum* of a convergent series depends on which terms are included.

The geometric series is one of the few series for which we can compute the value of its sum by a simple formula; this won't be the case for most series. Instead, we'll only be concerned with whether a series converges and, for this purpose, we need tests for convergence. The list below gives some of the most common and useful convergence tests for infinite series.

1. If the terms a_n of the series $\sum a_n$ do not approach zero as $n \to \infty$, then the series cannot converge.

This does not imply that if the terms a_n do approach 0, then the series converges. This statement is not true, as the following important example illustrates. Let $a_n = \dfrac{1}{n}$. Then, although $a_n \to 0$, the series

$$\sum_{n=1}^{\infty} \frac{1}{n} = 1 + \frac{1}{2} + \frac{1}{3} + \cdots$$

which is called the **harmonic series**, can be shown to diverge: $\sum \dfrac{1}{n} = \infty$.

2. If $\sum a_n$ converges, then $\sum k a_n$ converges to $k \sum a_n$ for every constant k. If $\sum a_n$ diverges, then $\sum k a_n$ diverges for every constant $k \neq 0$.

3. If $\sum a_n$ and $\sum b_n$ both converge, then the series $\sum (a_n + b_n)$ converges, and:

$$\sum (a_n + b_n) = \sum a_n + \sum b_n$$

4. The series $\sum \dfrac{1}{n^p}$ (called the *p*-series) converges for every $p > 1$ and diverges for every $p \leq 1$.

5. **The comparison test.** Assume that $0 \leq a_n \leq b_n$ for all $n > N$. Then:

$$\sum b_n \text{ converges} \implies \sum a_n \text{ converges}$$

$$\sum a_n \text{ diverges} \implies \sum b_n \text{ diverges}$$

6. **The ratio test.** Given a series $\sum a_n$ of nonnegative terms, form the limit:

$$\lim_{n \to \infty} \frac{a_{n+1}}{a_n} = L$$

Then:

$$L < 1 \implies \sum a_n \text{ converges}$$
$$L > 1 \implies \sum a_n \text{ diverges}$$

(Note: If $L = 1$, then this test is inconclusive.)

7. **The root test.** Given a series $\sum a_n$ of nonnegative terms, form the limit:

$$\lim_{n \to \infty} \sqrt[n]{a_n} = L$$

Then:

$$L < 1 \implies \sum a_n \text{ converges}$$
$$L > 1 \implies \sum a_n \text{ diverges}$$

(Note: If $L = 1$, then this test is inconclusive.)

8. **The integral test.** If $f(x)$ is a positive, monotonically decreasing function for $x \geq 1$, such that $f(n) = a_n$ for every positive integer n, then:

$$\sum_{n=1}^{\infty} a_n \text{ converges} \iff \int_1^{\infty} f(x)\,dx \text{ converges}$$

Example 2.29   Which of the following series converge, and which diverge?

(a) $\displaystyle\sum_{n=1}^{\infty} \frac{\sin^2 n}{n^3 + n}$

(b) $\displaystyle\sum_{n=0}^{\infty} \frac{1}{\sqrt{n+3}}$

(c) $\displaystyle\sum_{n=1}^{\infty} \frac{n^{2000}}{n!}$

(d) $\displaystyle\sum_{n=1}^{\infty} \frac{n^3}{(\log 3)^n}$

(e) $\displaystyle\sum_{n=1}^{\infty} \frac{\log n}{n^2}$

Solution:

(a) Notice that, for every $n \geq 1$, we have:

$$\frac{\sin^2 n}{n^3 + n} \leq \frac{1}{n^3 + n} \leq \frac{1}{n^3}$$

Since the series $\displaystyle\sum_{n=1}^{\infty} \frac{1}{n^3}$ converges (it's the p-series with $p = 3$), this series converges, by the comparison test.

(b) The following inequality is true for every $n > 1$:

$$\frac{1}{\sqrt{n+3}} > \frac{1}{2\sqrt{n}}$$

Since the series $\displaystyle\sum \frac{1}{2\sqrt{n}}$ diverges (it's a nonzero multiple of the p-series, with $p = \frac{1}{2}$), this series diverges by the comparison test.

(c) Let's apply the ratio test:

$$\lim_{n \to \infty} \frac{a_{n+1}}{a_n} = \lim_{n \to \infty}\left[\frac{(n+1)^{2000}}{(n+1)!} \cdot \frac{n!}{n^{2000}}\right] = \lim_{n \to \infty}\left[\left(\frac{n+1}{n}\right)^{2000} \cdot \frac{1}{n+1}\right] = 1 \cdot 0 = 0$$

Since the value of this limit is less than 1, the ratio test tells us that the series converges.

(d) Here, we apply the root test:

$$\lim_{n \to \infty} \sqrt[n]{a_n} = \lim_{n \to \infty} \sqrt[n]{\frac{n^3}{(\log 3)^n}} = \lim_{n \to \infty} \frac{n^{3/n}}{\log 3} = \frac{1}{\log 3} \cdot \lim_{n \to \infty} n^{3/n}$$

In order to figure out $\displaystyle\lim_{n \to \infty} n^{3/n}$, we first find $\displaystyle\lim_{x \to \infty} x^{3/x}$ using L'Hôpital's rule. Letting $y = x^{3/x}$, we have $\log y = \left(\dfrac{3}{x}\right) \log x$, and:

$$\lim_{x \to \infty} (\log y) = \lim_{x \to \infty} \frac{3 \log x}{x} = \lim_{x \to \infty} \frac{\frac{3}{x}}{1} = 0 \quad \Rightarrow \quad \lim_{x \to \infty} y = e^0 = 1 \quad \Rightarrow \quad \lim_{x \to \infty} x^{3/x} = 1$$

Therefore,

$$\lim_{n \to \infty} \sqrt[n]{a_n} = \frac{1}{\log 3} \cdot \lim_{n \to \infty} n^{3/n} = \frac{1}{\log 3} \cdot 1 = \frac{1}{\log 3} < 1$$

so the series converges.

(e) We'll apply the integral test here; this means we must investigate the convergence of the improper integral:

$$\int_1^{\infty} \frac{\log x}{x^2}\, dx$$

Let's use integration by parts, with $u = \log x$, $du = \left(\dfrac{1}{x}\right) dx$, $dv = dx/x^2$, and $v = -\dfrac{1}{x}$:

$$\int \frac{\log x}{x^2}\, dx = -\frac{\log x}{x} - \int \frac{-1}{x^2}\, dx = -\frac{\log x + 1}{x}$$

Therefore,

$$\int_1^\infty \frac{\log x}{x^2}\,dx = \lim_{b\to\infty}\int_1^b \frac{\log x}{x^2}\,dx = \lim_{b\to\infty}\left[-\frac{\log x + 1}{x}\right]_1^b = \lim_{b\to\infty}\left[1 - \frac{\log b + 1}{b}\right]$$

But, by L'Hôpital's rule,

$$\lim_{b\to\infty}\frac{\log b + 1}{b} = \lim_{b\to\infty}\frac{\frac{1}{b}}{1} = 0$$

so the improper integral converges (to 1). The integral test now assures us that the series will converge, too.

ALTERNATING SERIES

Convergence tests 5 through 8 apply only to series whose terms are all nonnegative. But what if some of the terms are negative? One important type of series, which contains infinitely many negative terms, is the **alternating series**

$$\sum_{n=1}^\infty (-1)^{n+1} a_n$$

in which each a_n is nonnegative. The series is called *alternating* since the terms alternate in sign. Loosely speaking, alternating series have a better chance of converging to a finite sum, since the negative summands help offset the positive ones. The convergence test for an alternating series is simple:

9. **The alternating series test.** The alternating series $\sum_{n=1}^\infty (-1)^{n+1} a_n$ (with $a_n \geq 0$ for all n) will converge provided that the terms a_n decrease monotonically, with a limit of zero.

Notice that the condition "a_n decrease monotonically to 0" is not sufficient to ensure that a general series $\sum a_n$ converges [remember rule 1 above], but it *is* sufficient to guarantee that an alternating series $\sum (-1)^{n+1} a_n$ converges.

Given a series $\sum a_n$, some or all of whose terms a_n may be negative, we can form the series $\sum |a_n|$, all of whose terms are clearly nonnegative. If this latter series converges, then we say the original series **converges absolutely**. If the original series converges but the latter does not, then we say the original series **converges conditionally**. Because convergence tests 5 through 8 apply only to series of nonnegative terms, the following rule is especially helpful for deciding the convergence of series that may contain infinitely many negative terms, but which aren't necessarily alternating:

10. Every absolutely convergent series is convergent.

Notice how helpful rule 10 is in the following example: If we let

$$a_n = \begin{cases} \dfrac{1}{n^2} & \text{if } n \text{ is not prime} \\[2mm] -\dfrac{1}{n^2} & \text{if } n \text{ is prime} \end{cases}$$

then does the series $\sum_{n=2}^\infty a_n$ converge or diverge? Although this series contains infinitely many negative terms (because there are infinitely many primes), it is not alternating, so the alternating series test cannot be applied. However, since the series $\sum \frac{1}{n^2}$ is convergent (it's the p-series with $p = 2$), our series is absolutely convergent, and so, by rule 10, it's convergent.

POWER SERIES

A **power series in** x is an infinite series whose terms are $a_n x^n$, where each a_n is a constant:

$$\sum_{n=0}^{\infty} a_n x^n = a_0 + a_1 x + a_2 x^2 + a_3 x^3 + \cdots$$

You can think of a power series as a polynomial of infinite degree, but since it's actually an infinite series, the definitions and convergence tests we've studied will apply here. A power series is useful only if it converges, so we'll first determine the values of x for which the series is convergent. Since some of the terms may be negative, we'll find those values of x for which the series is absolutely convergent. According to the ratio test, the series will converge absolutely if:

$$\lim_{n \to \infty} \left| \frac{a_{n+1} x^{n+1}}{a_n x^n} \right| = |x| \cdot \lim_{n \to \infty} \left| \frac{a_{n+1}}{a_n} \right| < 1$$

Let $L = \lim_{n \to \infty} \left| \frac{a_{n+1}}{a_n} \right|$, where we'll allow $L = \infty$. If $L = 0$, then the power series converges absolutely for all x; if $L = \infty$, then the power series converges only for $x = 0$; and if L is positive and finite, then the power series converges absolutely for $|x| < \frac{1}{L}$ and diverges for $|x| > \frac{1}{L}$. The set of all values of x for which the series converges is called the **interval of convergence**, and we now see that every power series in x falls into one of three categories:

1. The power series converges absolutely for all x in the interval $(-R, R)$ and diverges for all x such that $|x| > R$, for some positive number R called the **radius of convergence**. The value of R is equal to $\frac{1}{L}$, where L is defined as above. (The power series may also converge at one or both endpoints of the interval—that is, at $x = \pm R$—but this must be checked on a case-by-case basis.)

2. The power series converges absolutely for all x; the interval of convergence is $(-\infty, \infty)$, and we say that the radius of convergence is ∞.

3. The power series converges only for $x = 0$, so the radius of convergence is 0.

Example 2.30   What's the interval of convergence for this power series?

$$2x + x^2 + \frac{8}{9} x^3 + x^4 + \cdots = \sum_{n=1}^{\infty} \frac{2^n}{n^2} x^n$$

Solution: According to the ratio test, the series will converge absolutely if:

$$\lim_{n \to \infty} \left| \frac{2^{n+1} x^{n+1}}{(n+1)^2} \cdot \frac{n^2}{2^n x^n} \right| = |x| \cdot \lim_{n \to \infty} \left| 2 \cdot \left(\frac{n}{n+1} \right)^2 \right| = 2|x| < 1 \quad \Rightarrow \quad |x| < \tfrac{1}{2}$$

We'll now check convergence at the endpoints of the interval $(-\frac{1}{2}, \frac{1}{2})$. When $x = \frac{1}{2}$, the series becomes

$$\sum_{n=1}^{\infty} \frac{2^n}{n^2}\left(\tfrac{1}{2}\right)^n = \sum_{n=1}^{\infty} \frac{1}{n^2}$$

which converges (it's the p-series, with $p = 2$). Therefore, the interval of convergence also includes the point $x = \frac{1}{2}$. Now, at $x = -\frac{1}{2}$, the series becomes

$$\sum_{n=1}^{\infty} \frac{2^n}{n^2}\left(-\tfrac{1}{2}\right)^n = \sum_{n=1}^{\infty} (-1)^n \frac{1}{n^2}$$

which also converges (because it's an alternating series whose terms are decreasing and approach zero). So we conclude that the interval of convergence of the power series is the closed interval $[-\frac{1}{2}, \frac{1}{2}]$.

FUNCTIONS DEFINED BY POWER SERIES

A function of x can be defined by a power series; in fact, this is where power series are most used. Let $\sum_{n=0}^{\infty} a_n x^n$ be a power series in x, and define a function f by:

$$f(x) = \sum_{n=0}^{\infty} a_n x^n$$

Notice that, in order for the function to be well defined, the domain of f must be a subset of the interval of convergence of the power series, so that the series actually converges. We'll now list a few very important facts about functions defined by power series.

Within the interval of convergence of the power series,

1. The function f is continuous, differentiable, and integrable.

2. The power series can be differentiated term by term, and the resulting power series gives the derivative of f; that is:

$$f(x) = \sum_{n=0}^{\infty} a_n x^n \quad \Rightarrow \quad f'(x) = \sum_{n=0}^{\infty} \frac{d}{dx}(a_n x^n) = \sum_{n=1}^{\infty} n a_n x^{n-1}$$

3. The power series can be integrated term by term, and the resulting power series gives an integral of f; that is:

$$f(x) = \sum_{n=0}^{\infty} a_n x^n \quad \Rightarrow \quad \int_0^x f(t)\,dt = \sum_{n=0}^{\infty} \left(\int_0^x a_n t^n \, dt \right) = \sum_{n=0}^{\infty} \frac{a_n}{n+1} x^{n+1}$$

Example 2.31   We know that the geometric series

$$1 + x + x^2 + \cdots = \sum_{n=0}^{\infty} x^n = \frac{1}{1-x}$$

converges for $|x| < 1$. Use this series to find a power series expansion for
(a) $g(x) = \log(1 - x)$,
(b) $h(x) = x/(1 - x)^2$, and
(c) $k(x) = \arctan x$.

Solution:

(a) Once we realize that $\log(1 - x)$ is an integral of $-1/(1 - x)$, we can write:

$$-\frac{1}{1-x} = \sum_{n=0}^{\infty} (-1)x^n \quad \Rightarrow \quad \log(1-x) = \sum_{n=0}^{\infty} \frac{-1}{n+1} x^{n+1} = \sum_{n=1}^{\infty} \frac{-1}{n} x^n$$

(b) Now, for $h(x)$, we know that $1/(1 - x)^2$ is the derivative of $1/(1 - x)$, so:

$$\frac{1}{1-x} = \sum_{n=0}^{\infty} x^n \quad \Rightarrow \quad \frac{1}{(1-x)^2} = \sum_{n=1}^{\infty} n x^{n-1}$$

Multiplying this series by x gives us the power series for $x/(1 - x)^2$:

$$\frac{1}{(1-x)^2} = \sum_{n=1}^{\infty} n x^{n-1} \quad \Rightarrow \quad \frac{x}{(1-x)^2} = \sum_{n=1}^{\infty} n x^n$$

(c) We want to use the fact that $\arctan x$ is an integral of $1/(1 + x^2)$. So, first, we'll take the power series expansion of $1/(1 - x)$ and replace x with $-x$; this gives us:

$$\frac{1}{1-x} = \sum_{n=0}^{\infty} x^n \quad \Rightarrow \quad \frac{1}{1-(-x)} = \sum_{n=0}^{\infty} (-x)^n \quad \Rightarrow \quad \frac{1}{1+x} = \sum_{n=0}^{\infty} (-1)^n x^n$$

Next, we replace x by x^2

$$\frac{1}{1+x} = \sum_{n=0}^{\infty} (-1)^n x^n \quad \Rightarrow \quad \frac{1}{1+x^2} = \sum_{n=0}^{\infty} (-1)^n x^{2n}$$

and then integrate term by term:

$$\frac{1}{1+x^2} = \sum_{n=0}^{\infty} (-1)^n x^{2n} \quad \Rightarrow \quad \arctan x = \sum_{n=0}^{\infty} \frac{(-1)^n}{2n+1} x^{2n+1}$$

Notice that in part (c), we found the power series for $1/(1 + x^2)$ from the power series for $1/(1 + x)$ by replacing x with x^2. In general, we can get the power series for $f[g(x)]$ from the power series for $f(x)$ by replacing x with $g(x)$. Other operations that are permitted on power series include adding, subtracting, multiplying, and dividing two power series or multiplying a power series by a polynomial [as we did in part (b), when we multiplied the power series for $1/(1 - x)^2$ by x to get the power series for $x/(1 - x)^2$].

TAYLOR SERIES

We'll complete our study of power series by learning how to generate the power series for a given function. Let's assume that a function f has a power series expansion of the form:

$$f(x) = \sum_{n=0}^{\infty} a_n x^n = a_0 + a_1 x + a_2 x^2 + a_3 x^3 + \cdots$$

Substituting $x = 0$, we immediately get $a_0 = f(0)$. But what are the values of the other coefficients: a_1, a_2, etc.? Well, differentiating the equation above gives us $f'(x) = a_1 + 2a_2 x + 3a_3 x^2 + \cdots$. If we now substitute $x = 0$, we get $a_1 = f'(0)$. Differentiating again gives us $f''(x) = 2a_2 + 2 \cdot 3a_3 x + \cdots$, so $a_2 = \frac{1}{2} f''(0)$. Continuing like this, we can figure out that the following formula gives us every coefficient, a_n:

$$a_n = \frac{f^{(n)}(0)}{n!}$$

These numbers are called the **Taylor coefficients** of f, the power series

$$f(x) = \sum_{n=0}^{\infty} \frac{f^{(n)}(0)}{n!} x^n$$

is called the **Taylor series** of f and, if $f(x)$ can be represented by a power series, then this is it.

Example 2.32   Find the power series expansions for e^x and $\sin x$.

Solution: If $f(x) = e^x$, then $f^{(n)}(x) = e^x$ for every n, so:

$$a_n = \frac{f^{(n)}(0)}{n!} = \frac{e^0}{n!} = \frac{1}{n!}$$

Therefore, the power series for e^x is:

$$e^x = \sum_{n=0}^{\infty} \frac{1}{n!} x^n = 1 + x + \frac{x^2}{2!} + \frac{x^3}{3!} + \cdots$$

As for $\sin x$, we have

$$f(x) = \sin x \quad \Rightarrow \quad f(0) = 0 \quad \Rightarrow \quad a_0 = 0$$

$$f'(x) = \cos x \quad \Rightarrow \quad f'(0) = 1 \quad \Rightarrow \quad a_1 = \frac{1}{1!} = 1$$

$$f''(x) = -\sin x \quad \Rightarrow \quad f''(0) = 0 \quad \Rightarrow \quad a_2 = 0$$

$$f'''(x) = -\cos x \quad \Rightarrow \quad f'''(0) = -1 \quad \Rightarrow \quad a_3 = -\frac{1}{3!}$$

$$\vdots$$

and the cycle repeats for the higher-order derivatives. Therefore, every a_n with an even n is equal to 0, leaving only the coefficients a_n with an odd n; we conclude that:

$$\sin x = \sum_{n=0}^{\infty} \frac{(-1)^n}{(2n+1)!} x^{2n+1} = x - \frac{x^3}{3!} + \frac{x^5}{5!} - \cdots$$

The Taylor series we found in the preceding example belong to a list that you should memorize for the test; these are the Taylor series for some of the most common functions encountered in calculus:

$$\frac{1}{1-x} = 1 + x + x^2 + x^3 + \cdots = \sum_{n=0}^{\infty} x^n \qquad \text{valid for } -1 < x < 1$$

$$\frac{1}{1+x} = 1 - x + x^2 - x^3 + \cdots = \sum_{n=0}^{\infty} (-1)^n x^n \qquad \text{valid for } -1 < x < 1$$

$$\log(1+x) = x - \frac{x^2}{2} + \frac{x^3}{3} - \cdots = \sum_{n=1}^{\infty} \frac{(-1)^{n+1}}{n} x^n \qquad \text{valid for } -1 < x \le 1$$

$$e^x = 1 + x + \frac{x^2}{2!} + \frac{x^3}{3!} + \cdots = \sum_{n=0}^{\infty} \frac{1}{n!} x^n \qquad \text{valid for all } x$$

$$\sin x = x - \frac{x^3}{3!} + \frac{x^5}{5!} - \cdots = \sum_{n=0}^{\infty} \frac{(-1)^n}{(2n+1)!} x^{2n+1} \qquad \text{valid for all } x$$

$$\cos x = 1 - \frac{x^2}{2!} + \frac{x^4}{4!} - \cdots = \sum_{n=0}^{\infty} \frac{(-1)^n}{(2n)!} x^{2n} \qquad \text{valid for all } x$$

TAYLOR POLYNOMIALS

If we truncate a Taylor series, we obtain a **Taylor polynomial**, which can be used to give us an approximation of the value of the Taylor series' function at some x in its interval of convergence. For example, let's use the Taylor series for e^x to obtain an approximation of $\sqrt{e}$. If we choose the first four terms of the series, we get the cubic polynomial:

$$e^x \approx 1 + x + \frac{x^2}{2!} + \frac{x^3}{3!}$$

Therefore,

$$\sqrt{e} = e^{1/2} \approx 1 + \tfrac{1}{2} + \frac{\left(\tfrac{1}{2}\right)^2}{2!} + \frac{\left(\tfrac{1}{2}\right)^3}{3!} = 1 + \tfrac{1}{2} + \tfrac{1}{8} + \tfrac{1}{48} = 1\tfrac{31}{48} \approx 1.646$$

(A calculator would tell you that, to three decimal places, $\sqrt{e} \approx 1.649$, so our approximation is pretty good.) The error we incur in approximating the value of $f(x)$ by the nth-degree Taylor polynomial

$$P_n(x) = f(0) + \frac{f'(0)}{1!} x + \frac{f''(0)}{2!} x^2 + \cdots + \frac{f^{(n)}(0)}{n!} x^n$$

is exactly equal to

$$f(x) - P_n(x) = \frac{f^{(n+1)}(c)}{(n+1)!} x^{n+1}$$

where c is some number between 0 and x. This form of the *remainder* (as it's called) can be used to find an upper bound on the error. Also, if the expression above is positive, then we know the approximation is too low, and if the error is negative, then the approximation is too high. Let's figure out a bound for the error in our estimation of $\sqrt{e}$. Since we approximated $\sqrt{e}$ with the Taylor polynomial of degree $n = 3$, the exact error is equal to

$$\frac{f^{(4)}(c)}{4!}x^4 = \frac{e^c}{24}\left(\frac{1}{2}\right)^4$$

for some number c between 0 and $\frac{1}{2}$. Since $e = 2.718... < 4$, we know, for example, that for $0 < c < \frac{1}{2}$, the value of e^c certainly satisfies $1 < e^c < 2$. Therefore, we can be assured that the error is less than:

$$\frac{2}{24}\left(\frac{1}{2}\right)^4 = \frac{1}{192} \approx 0.0052$$

Using the values given above (our approximation, $\sqrt{e} \approx 1.646$, and the exact value to three decimal places, $\sqrt{e} \approx 1.649$), we can see that our approximation is too low by about 0.003, which is indeed within the bound established in the calculation above.

One final note. The power series we've studied have been series in x; that is, the terms contain powers of x. However, we can also obtain a series expansion for a function in powers of $(x - a)$, that is, a series of the form:

$$\sum_{n=0}^{\infty} a_n (x-a)^n$$

In this case, we'd find the Taylor coefficients from the formula:

$$a_n = \frac{f^{(n)}(a)}{n!}$$

When $a = 0$, we obtain the Taylor series in powers of x, which is sometimes referred to as the *Maclaurin series*, although this old-fashioned terminology is going out of style.

If we use a Taylor polynomial in powers of $(x - a)$ to approximate the value of a function at a point x within the interval of convergence of its Taylor series, then the error is

$$f(x) - P_n(x) = \frac{f^{(n+1)}(c)}{(n+1)!}(x-a)^{n+1}$$

where c is some number between a and x.

CHAPTER 2 REVIEW QUESTIONS

Complete the following review questions using the techniques outlined in this chapter. Then, see Chapter 8 for answers and explanations.

1. Consider the sequence (x_n) whose terms are given by the formula

    $$x_n = \frac{(\cos n\pi)(\sin^2 n)}{\sqrt[e]{n}}$$

    for each integer $n \geq 1$. Given that this sequence converges, what is its limit?

    (A) 0   (B) 1   (C) $\log 2$ (D) $\sqrt[e]{2}$ (E) $\sqrt[e]{e}$

---

2. Let (x_n) be the sequence with $x_1 = 2$ and $x_n = \sqrt{5x_{n-1} + 6}$ for every integer $n \geq 2$. Given that this sequence converges, what is its limit?

    (A) 4   (B) 6   (C) 8   (D) 10   (E) 16

    $x^2 = 5x + 6$

---

3. Let $[x]$ denote the greatest integer $\leq x$. If n is a positive integer, then

    $$\lim_{x \to -n-} \left(|x| - [x]\right) - \lim_{x \to n-} \left(|x| - [x]\right) = \ ?$$

    $n - (-n-1) -$
    $2n+1 - (1)$ $\left(n - (n-1)\right)$

    (A) –2   (B) 0   (C) 2   (D) $2n - 1$ (E) $2n$

---

4. Evaluate the following limit:

    $$\lim_{x \to 0} \frac{\arcsin x - x}{x^3}$$

    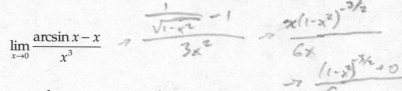

    (A) 0   (B) $\frac{1}{6}$ (C) $\frac{1}{3}$ (D) $\frac{1}{2}$ (E) 1

---

5. The curve whose equation is

    $$2x^2 + 3x - 2xy - y = 6$$

    has two asymptotes. Identify these lines.

    $2x^2 + 3x - y(2x+1) = 0$
    $y = \frac{2x^2 + 3x}{2x+1}$

    (A) $x = -1$ and $y = -2$ (B) $x = -2$ and $y = 1$ (C) $x = -\frac{1}{2}$ and $y = x$

    (D) $x = -\frac{1}{2}$ and $y = x + 1$ (E) $x = \frac{1}{2}$ and $y = 1 - x$

---

6. If the function

$$f(x) = \begin{cases} \dfrac{x^2 - 6x + 8}{x^3 - 2x^2 + 2x - 4} & \text{if } x \neq 2 \\ k & \text{if } x = 2 \end{cases}$$

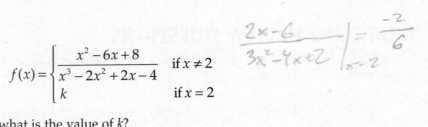

is continuous everywhere, what is the value of k?

(A) 1   (B) $\dfrac{1}{2}$ (C) $\dfrac{1}{8}$ (D) $-\dfrac{1}{3}$ (E) -1

7. Evaluate the following limit:

$$\lim_{x \to 0} \left[\frac{1}{x^2} \int_0^x \frac{t + t^2}{1 + \sin t} \, dt \right]$$

(A) $\dfrac{1}{2\pi}$ (B) $\dfrac{1}{\pi}$ (C) $\dfrac{1}{2}$ (D) 1   (E) $\dfrac{\pi}{2}$

8. Determine the domain of the following function:

$$f(x) = \arcsin(\log \sqrt{x})$$

$$\hookrightarrow -1 \leq \log \sqrt{x} \leq 1$$

(A) $[0, \dfrac{1}{e^2}]$ (B) $[\dfrac{1}{e^2}, 1]$ (C) $[e, e^2]$ (D) $[\dfrac{1}{e^2}, e^2]$ (E) $[1, e^2]$

9. Evaluate the derivative of the following function at $x = e$:

$$f(x) = \arcsin(\log \sqrt{x})$$

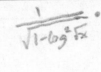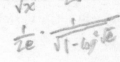

(A) $\dfrac{1}{e\sqrt{3}}$ (B) $\dfrac{e}{\sqrt{2}}$ (C) $\dfrac{\pi e}{2}$ (D) $\sqrt{2e}$ (E) $\dfrac{3e}{\sqrt{2}}$

10. For what values of m and b will the following function have a derivative for every x?

$$f(x) = \begin{cases} x^2 + x - 3 & \text{if } x \leq 1 \\ mx + b & \text{if } x > 1 \end{cases}$$

$f(1) = -1$

$f'(1) = 3$

(A) $m = 3, b = -2$ (B) $m = -2, b = -3$ (C) $m = 1, b = -4$

(D) $m = -2, b = 1$ (E) $m = 3, b = -4$

11. If $f(x)$ is a function that's differentiable everywhere, what is the value of this limit?

$$\lim_{h \to 0} \frac{f(x+3h^2)-f(x-h^2)}{2h^2}$$

(A) $4f'(x)$　　　　(B) $2f'(x)$　　　　(C) $f'(x)$　　　　(D) $\frac{1}{2}f'(x)$

(E) The limit does not exist.

---

12. What is the equation of the tangent line to the curve $y = x^3 - 3x^2 + 4x$ at the curve's inflection point?

(A) $y = 2x - 3$　　(B) $y = x - 1$　　(C) $y = x + 1$　　(D) $y = 3x - 2$　　(E) $x + y = 1$

---

13. What is the slope of the tangent line to the curve $xy(x + y) = x + y^4$ at the point $(1, 1)$?

(A) 2　　　　(B) 1　　　　(C) 0　　　　(D) –1　　　　(E) –2

---

14. If $f(x) = 2|x-1| + (x-1)^2$, what is the value of $f'(0)$?

(A) 4　　　　(B) 2　　　　(C) 0　　　　(D) –2　　　　(E) –4

---

15. If

$$f(x) = \frac{e^x \arccos x}{\cos x}$$

then the slope of the line tangent to the graph of f at its y-intercept is

(A) $-\dfrac{\pi}{2}$　　(B) –1　　(C) $\dfrac{\pi}{2}-1$　　(D) 1　　(E) $\dfrac{\pi}{2}+1$

---

16. Let $y = \dfrac{1}{\sqrt{x^3+1}}$. If x increases from 2 to 2.09, which of the following most closely approximates the change in y?

(A) 0.08　　(B) 0.04　　(C) –0.02　　(D) –0.06　　(E) –0.09

---

17. If $f(1) = 1$ and $f'(1) = -1$, then the value of $\dfrac{d}{dx}\left[\dfrac{f(x^3)}{xf(x^2)}\right]$ at $x = 1$ is equal to

(A) 1　　(B) 0　　(C) –1　　(D) –2　　(E) –3

18. If n is a positive integer, what is the value of the nth derivative of $f(x) = \dfrac{1}{1-2x}$ at $x = -\dfrac{1}{2}$?

(A) $\dfrac{1}{2}(n^n)$ (B) $\dfrac{1}{2}(n!)$ (C) $\dfrac{1}{2}n$ (D) n (E) $\dfrac{n^n}{n!}$

19. Let $f(x)$ be continuous on a bounded interval, $[a, b]$, where $a \neq b$, such that $f(a) = 1$ and $f(b) = 3$, and $f'(x)$ exists for every x in (a, b). What does the Mean-Value theorem say about f?

(A) There exists a number c in the interval (a, b) such that $f'(c) = 0$.
(B) There exists a number c in the interval (a, b) such that $f(c) = 0$.
(C) There exists a number c in the interval (a, b) such that $f'(c) = 2$.
(D) There exists a number c in the interval (a, b) such that $f'(c) = 2(b-a)$.
(E) There exists a number c in the interval (a, b) such that $(b-a)f'(c) = 2$.

20. What is the maximum area of a rectangle inscribed in a semicircle of radius a?

(A) $\dfrac{\sqrt{2}}{2}a^2$ (B) $\dfrac{\sqrt{3}}{2}a^2$ (C) a^2 (D) $\dfrac{\pi}{2\sqrt{2}}a^2$ (E) $a^2\sqrt{2}$

21. The following function is defined for all positive x:

$$f(x) = \int_x^{2x} \frac{\sin t}{t}\, dt$$

At what value of x on the interval $(0, \dfrac{3\pi}{2})$ does this function attain a local maximum?

(A) $\dfrac{\pi}{6}$ (B) $\dfrac{\pi}{3}$ (C) $\dfrac{\pi}{2}$ (D) π (E) $\dfrac{2\pi}{3}$

22. Let $f(x) = x^k e^{-x}$, where k is a positive constant. For $x > 0$, what is the maximum value attained by f?

(A) $\left(\dfrac{e}{k}\right)^k$ (B) $\sqrt[k]{\dfrac{e}{k^k}}$ (C) $\dfrac{(\log k)^k}{k}$ (D) $\left(\dfrac{e}{\log k}\right)^k$ (E) $\left(\dfrac{k}{e}\right)^k$

23. The radius of a circle is decreasing at a rate of 0.5 cm per second. At what rate, in cm^2/sec, is the circle's area decreasing when the radius is 4 cm?

(A) 4π (B) 2π (C) π (D) $\dfrac{1}{2}\pi$ (E) $\dfrac{1}{4}\pi$

24. The function $f(x) = \int_{e^x}^{e^{2x}} t \log t\, dt$ has an absolute minimum at $x = 0$, and a local maximum at $x =$

(A) $-\log 4$ (B) $-\log 2$ (C) $\log 2$ (D) 1 (E) $\log 4$

25. Evaluate the following integral:

$$\int_{-1}^{0} x^2(x+1)^3\,dx$$

(A) $-\dfrac{7}{20}$ (B) $-\dfrac{1}{60}$ (C) $\dfrac{2}{15}$ (D) $\dfrac{1}{60}$ (E) $\dfrac{7}{20}$

26. If $[x]$ denotes the greatest integer $\leq x$, then $\int_{0}^{\frac{7}{2}} [x]\,dx =$

(A) $\dfrac{5}{2}$ (B) $\dfrac{7}{2}$ (C) $\dfrac{9}{2}$ (D) $\dfrac{17}{2}$ (E) $\dfrac{37}{2}$

27. If

$$f(x) = \begin{cases} -2(x+1) & \text{if } x \leq 0 \\ k(1-x^2) & \text{if } x > 0 \end{cases}$$

then the value of k for which $\int_{-1}^{1} f(x)\,dx = 1$ is

(A) -1 (B) 0 (C) 1 (D) 2 (E) 3

28. Integrate $\displaystyle\int \frac{x^2\,dx}{\sqrt{1-x^2}}$.

(A) $\dfrac{1}{2}\left(\arcsin x - \sqrt{1-x^2}\right)+c$ (B) $\dfrac{1}{2}\left(\arcsin x + x\sqrt{1-x^2}\right)+c$ (C) $\dfrac{1}{2}\left(x\arcsin x - \sqrt{1-x^2}\right)+c$

(D) $\dfrac{1}{2}\left(\arcsin x - x\sqrt{1-x^2}\right)+c$ (E) $\dfrac{1}{2}\left(x\arcsin x + \sqrt{1-x^2}\right)+c$

29. What is the area of the region in the first quadrant bounded by the curve $y = x \arctan x$ and the line $x = 1$?

(A) $\dfrac{\pi-4}{4}$ (B) $\dfrac{\pi-2}{4}$ (C) $\dfrac{\pi}{4}$ (D) $\dfrac{\pi+2}{4}$ (E) $\dfrac{\pi+4}{4}$

30. Simplify the following:

$$\exp\int_{3}^{5} \frac{dx}{x^2-3x+2}$$

[Note: Recall that $\exp x$ is a standard, alternate notation for e^x.]

(A) $\dfrac{3}{8}$ (B) $\dfrac{2}{3}$ (C) $\dfrac{4}{3}$ (D) $\dfrac{3}{2}$ (E) $\dfrac{5}{3}$

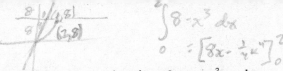

31. Calculate the area of the region in the first quadrant bounded by the graphs of $y = 8x$, $y = x^3$, and $y = 8$.

   (A) 12   (B) 8   (C) 6   (D) $\dfrac{16}{3}$ (E) 4

32. Which of the following expressions gives the area of the region bounded by the two circles pictured below?

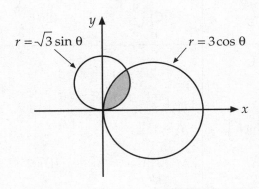

   (A) $\int_0^{\frac{\pi}{2}} \frac{1}{2}\left[(\sqrt{3}\sin\theta)^2 - (3\cos\theta)^2\right] d\theta$

   (B) $\int_0^{\frac{\pi}{6}} \frac{1}{2}(3\cos\theta)^2\, d\theta + \int_{\frac{\pi}{6}}^{\frac{\pi}{2}} \frac{1}{2}(\sqrt{3}\sin\theta)^2\, d\theta$

   (C) $\int_0^{\frac{\pi}{6}} \frac{1}{2}(\sqrt{3}\sin\theta)^2\, d\theta + \int_{\frac{\pi}{6}}^{\frac{\pi}{2}} \frac{1}{2}(3\cos\theta)^2\, d\theta$

   (D) $\int_0^{\frac{\pi}{3}} \frac{1}{2}(3\cos\theta)^2\, d\theta + \int_{\frac{\pi}{3}}^{\frac{\pi}{2}} \frac{1}{2}(\sqrt{3}\sin\theta)^2\, d\theta$

   (E) $\int_0^{\frac{\pi}{3}} \frac{1}{2}(\sqrt{3}\sin\theta)^2\, d\theta + \int_{\frac{\pi}{3}}^{\frac{\pi}{2}} \frac{1}{2}(3\cos\theta)^2\, d\theta$

33. Let a and b be positive numbers. The region in the second quadrant bounded by the graphs of $y = ax^2$ and $y = -bx$ is revolved around the x-axis. Which of the following relationships between a and b would imply that the volume of this solid of revolution is a constant, independent of a and b?

   (A) $b^4 = 2a^5$ (B) $b^3 = 2a^5$ (C) $b^5 = 2a^3$ (D) $b^4 = 2a^2$ (E) $b^2 = 2a^3$

34. The region bounded by the graphs of $y = x^2$ and $y = 6 - |x|$ is revolved around the y-axis. What is the volume of the generated solid?

   (A) $\dfrac{32}{3}\pi$ (B) 9π (C) 8π (D) $\dfrac{20}{3}\pi$ (E) $\dfrac{16}{3}\pi$

35. Calculate the length of the portion of the hypocycloid $x^{2/3} + y^{2/3} = 1$ in the first quadrant from the point $\left(\dfrac{1}{8}, \dfrac{3\sqrt{3}}{8}\right)$, to the point $(1, 0)$.

(A) $\dfrac{9}{8}$ (B) $\dfrac{3\sqrt{2}}{4}$ (C) 1 (D) $\dfrac{5\sqrt{2}}{8}$ (E) $\dfrac{\sqrt{3}}{2}$

---

36. What positive value of a satisfies the following equation?

$$\int_e^{ae} \frac{dx}{x \int_a^{ax} \frac{dy}{y}} = 1$$

(A) $\dfrac{1}{e}$ (B) $\sqrt[e]{e}$ (C) $\sqrt{e}$ (D) e (E) e^2

---

37. Evaluate the following limit:

$$\lim_{x \to 0} (\cos x)^{\cot^2 x}$$

(A) $\dfrac{1}{2}$ (B) $\dfrac{1}{\sqrt{e}}$ (C) $\dfrac{\sqrt{e}}{2}$ (D) 1 (E) $\sqrt{e}$

---

38. Let n be a number for which the improper integral

$$\int_e^{\infty} \frac{dx}{x(\log x)^n}$$

converges. Determine the value of the integral.

(A) $\dfrac{1}{n+1}$ (B) $\dfrac{1}{n}$ (C) $\dfrac{1}{n-1}$ (D) $\dfrac{\log n}{n+1}$ (E) $\dfrac{\log n}{n-1}$

---

39. Find the positive value of a that satisfies the equation:

$$\int_0^a \frac{dx}{\sqrt{a^2 - x^2}} = \int_0^a \frac{x\,dx}{\sqrt{a^2 - x^2}}$$

(A) $\dfrac{2\sqrt{2}}{\pi}$ (B) 1 (C) $\dfrac{\pi}{2\sqrt{2}}$ (D) $\sqrt{2}$ (E) $\dfrac{\pi}{2}$

40. Which of the following improper integrals converge?

   I. $\int_{-\infty}^{\infty} \frac{dx}{(x^2+1)^2}$

   II. $\int_{1}^{\infty} xe^{-x}\, dx$

   III. $\int_{0}^{2} \frac{dx}{(2-x)^2}$

   (A) I only   (B) I and II only   (C) II only

   (D) I and III only   (E) II and III only

---

41. Which of the following infinite series converge?

   I. $\sum_{n=1}^{\infty} \frac{\cos^4(\arctan n)}{n\sqrt[4]{n}}$

   II. $\sum_{n=2}^{\infty} \frac{1}{n\log n}$

   III. $\sum_{n=0}^{\infty} \frac{(n+1)^3}{5(n+2)(n+3)(n+4)}$

   (A) I only   (B) I and II only   (C) II only

   (D) I and III only   (E) II and III only

---

42. Find the smallest value of b that makes the following statement true:

   If $0 \le a < b$, then the series $\sum_{n=1}^{\infty} \frac{(n!)^2 a^n}{(2n)!}$ converges.

   (A) 1   (B) $2\log 2$ (C) 2   (D) $\sqrt{2}$ (E) 4

---

43. Evaluate the following limit:

$$\lim_{n\to\infty} \sum_{k=1}^{n} \left[\frac{k}{n^2} - \frac{k^2}{n^3} \right]$$

   (A) $\frac{2}{3}$ (B) $\frac{1}{2}$ (C) $\frac{1}{3}$ (D) $\frac{1}{6}$ (E) $\frac{1}{12}$

44. Which of the following statements are true?

I. If $a_n \geq 0$ for every n, then: $\displaystyle\sum_{n=1}^{\infty} a_n$ converges $\Rightarrow$ $\displaystyle\sum_{n=1}^{\infty} \sqrt{a_n}$ converges.

II. If $a_n \geq 0$ for every n, then: $\displaystyle\sum_{n=1}^{\infty} na_n$ converges $\Rightarrow$ $\displaystyle\sum_{n=1}^{\infty} a_n$ converges.

III. If $a_n \geq 0$ and $a_{n+1} \leq a_n$ for every n, then: $\displaystyle\sum_{n=1}^{\infty} a_n^2$ converges $\Rightarrow$ $\displaystyle\sum_{n=1}^{\infty} (-1)^n a_n$ converges.

(A) I and II only   (B) I and III only   (C) II only

(D) II and III only   (E) III only

---

45. If $-1 < x < 1$, then $\displaystyle\sum_{n=1}^{\infty} nx^{2n} =$

(A) $\dfrac{x^3}{(1-x)^2}$ (B) $\dfrac{x^2}{(1-x^2)^2}$ (C) $\dfrac{x}{(1+x^2)^2}$

(D) $\dfrac{x^3}{(1+x)^2}$ (E) $\dfrac{x^2}{(1+x^2)^2}$

---

46. The smallest positive integer x for which the power series $\displaystyle\sum_{n=1}^{\infty} \frac{n!(2n)!}{(3n)!} x^n$ does *not* converge is

(A) 4   (B) 6   (C) 7   (D) 8   (E) 9

---

47. In the Taylor series expansion (in powers of x) of the function $f(x) = e^{x^2 - x}$, what is the coefficient of x^3?

(A) -7 (B) $-\dfrac{3}{2}$ (C) $-\dfrac{7}{6}$ (D) $\dfrac{7}{6}$ (E) $\dfrac{3}{2}$

---

48. If k_i $(i = 0, 1, 2, 3, 4)$ are constants such that $x^4 = k_0 + k_1(x+1) + k_2(x+1)^2 + k_3(x+1)^3 + k_4(x+1)^4$ is an identity in x, what is the value of k_3?

(A) -4 (B) -3 (C) -2 (D) 3   (E) 4

49. If the function $f(x) = e^x$ is expanded in powers of x, what is the minimum number of terms of the Taylor series that must be used to ensure that the resulting polynomial will approximate $\sqrt[5]{e}$ to within 10^{-6}?

(A) 3   (B) 4   (C) 5   (D) 6   (E) 7

---

50. There is exactly one value of the constant k such that

$$\lim_{x \to 0} \frac{(e^{x^2} - x^2 - 1)(\cos x - 1)}{x^k}$$

is finite and nonzero. What is this value of k, and what is the limit, L?

(A) $k = 4, L = -\dfrac{1}{2}$ (B) $k = 6, L = \dfrac{1}{4}$ (C) $k = 4, L = 1$

(D) $k = 6, L = -\dfrac{1}{4}$ (E) $k = 4, L = \dfrac{1}{2}$

Calculus II

INTRODUCTION

In the previous chapter, we reviewed the calculus of functions of one independent variable. In this chapter, we'll study the calculus of functions of two or more independent variables. We'll begin by reviewing the analytic geometry of euclidean **3-space** ($\mathbf{R}^3$), then move on to topics that involve the differentiation of functions of several variables, and finish up by introducing topics that involve the integration of functions of several variables.

ANALYTIC GEOMETRY OF R³

If we construct a third copy of the real line and place it perpendicular to the *x-y* plane so that all the origins coincide, we have the geometric representation of three-dimensional space, R^3 ("R-three"). This third line is called the **z-axis**, and any point P in this three-dimensional space is uniquely specified by its three coordinates, as an ordered triple.

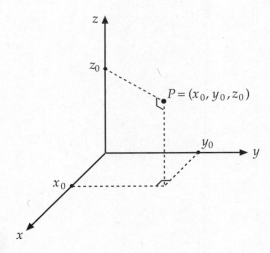

Just as the x- and y-axes partition the plane into $2^2 = 4$ quadrants, the x-, y-, and z-axes partition space (sometimes called ***xyz*-space**) into $2^3 = 8$ **octants**. The octant in which all three coordinates are positive is called the **first octant**; there is no universal agreement on how the other seven octants are numbered. As in the figure above, the first octant is almost always the one that's presented face-on when we view xyz-space.

The unit vectors $\hat{\mathbf{i}}$ and $\hat{\mathbf{j}}$ which point in the $+x$ and $+y$ directions, respectively, are now joined by a third unit vector, $\hat{\mathbf{k}}$, which points in the $+z$ direction. So in 3-space, we have

$$\hat{\mathbf{i}} = (1, 0, 0), \quad \hat{\mathbf{j}} = (0, 1, 0), \quad \hat{\mathbf{k}} = (0, 0, 1)$$

and any vector in 3-space can be written in terms of these three unit vectors:

$$\mathbf{v} = (x, y, z) \quad \Leftrightarrow \quad \mathbf{v} = x\hat{\mathbf{i}} + y\hat{\mathbf{j}} + z\hat{\mathbf{k}}$$

When a vector is written like this—that is, in terms of its components—the **magnitude** (or **norm**) of the vector, which is its length, is given by:

$$v = |\mathbf{v}| = \|\mathbf{v}\| = \sqrt{x^2 + y^2 + z^2}$$

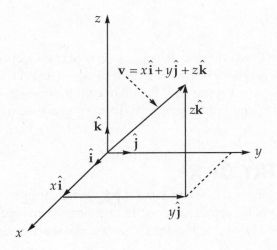

The operations of vector addition, vector subtraction, and scalar multiplication are also easy to perform. If $\mathbf{v}_1 = (x_1, y_1, z_1)$ and $\mathbf{v}_2 = (x_2, y_2, z_2)$, then

$$\mathbf{v}_1 + \mathbf{v}_2 = (x_1 + x_2, y_1 + y_2, z_1 + z_2)$$

$$\mathbf{v}_1 - \mathbf{v}_2 = \mathbf{v}_1 + (-\mathbf{v}_2) = (x_1, y_1, z_1) + (-x_2, -y_2, -z_2)$$
$$= (x_1 - x_2, y_1 - y_2, z_1 - z_2)$$

$$a\mathbf{v}_1 = (ax_1, ay_1, az_1)$$

where a is a scalar (that is, a number). The distance between two points, $P_1 = (x_1, y_1, z_1)$ and $P_2 = (x_2, y_2, z_2)$, is the length of the vector, $\mathbf{v} = P_1 P_2$, that connects them:

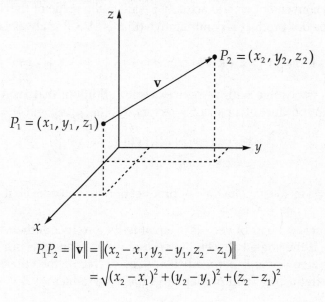

$$P_1 P_2 = \|\mathbf{v}\| = \|(x_2 - x_1, y_2 - y_1, z_2 - z_1)\|$$
$$= \sqrt{(x_2 - x_1)^2 + (y_2 - y_1)^2 + (z_2 - z_1)^2}$$

THE DOT PRODUCT

One way to multiply two vectors is to form their **dot product**. The dot product of two vectors, **A** and **B**, is defined as

$$\mathbf{A} \cdot \mathbf{B} = AB\cos\theta$$

where θ is the angle between them. Particularly, notice that the dot product of two vectors is a *scalar*; for this reason, the dot product is also called the **scalar product**. The dot product has a variety of uses. For example, consider the vector **projection** of **B** onto **A**, which is denoted $\mathbf{proj_A B}$:

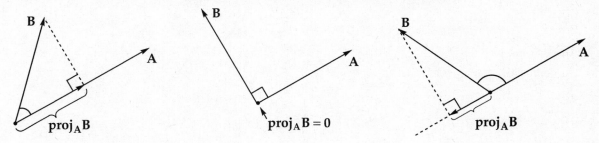

If $0 \leq \theta \leq 90°$, then the **scalar projection** of **B** onto **A**, $\text{proj}_A B$, is the magnitude of the vector projection; if $90° < \theta \leq 180°$, then $\text{proj}_A B$ is equal to the negative of the magnitude of the vector projection. In all cases (assuming only that $\mathbf{A} \neq \mathbf{0}$), we have $\text{proj}_A B = B \cos \theta$, so:

$$\mathbf{proj_A B} = (\text{proj}_A B)\hat{\mathbf{A}} = (\text{proj}_A B)\frac{\mathbf{A}}{A}$$

This equation can be rewritten neatly using the dot product. Since it's clear from the definition that the dot product of a vector with itself gives the square of its magnitude, $\mathbf{A} \bullet \mathbf{A} = A^2$, and since $\text{proj}_A B = B \cos \theta = (\mathbf{A} \bullet \mathbf{B})/A$, we can write:

$$\mathbf{proj_A B} = \frac{\mathbf{A} \bullet \mathbf{B}}{\mathbf{A} \bullet \mathbf{A}}\mathbf{A}$$

All we need now is a convenient way to actually calculate the value of the dot product. Well, we notice that, by definition, the dot product is commutative (that is, $\mathbf{A} \bullet \mathbf{B}$ is always equal to $\mathbf{B} \bullet \mathbf{A}$) and that:

$$\hat{\mathbf{i}} \bullet \hat{\mathbf{i}} = \hat{\mathbf{j}} \bullet \hat{\mathbf{j}} = \hat{\mathbf{k}} \bullet \hat{\mathbf{k}} = 1 \quad \text{and} \quad \hat{\mathbf{i}} \bullet \hat{\mathbf{j}} = \hat{\mathbf{j}} \bullet \hat{\mathbf{k}} = \hat{\mathbf{k}} \bullet \hat{\mathbf{i}} = 0$$

The dot product is also associative with respect to vector addition; that is, $\mathbf{A} \bullet (\mathbf{B} + \mathbf{C}) = (\mathbf{A} \bullet \mathbf{B}) + (\mathbf{A} \bullet \mathbf{C})$. Therefore, the dot product of a pair of 3-vectors, $\mathbf{A} = (a_1, a_2, a_3)$ and $\mathbf{B} = (b_1, b_2, b_3)$, is equal to:

$$\mathbf{A} \bullet \mathbf{B} = (a_1\hat{\mathbf{i}} + a_2\hat{\mathbf{j}} + a_3\hat{\mathbf{k}}) \bullet (b_1\hat{\mathbf{i}} + b_2\hat{\mathbf{j}} + b_3\hat{\mathbf{k}})$$
$$= a_1 b_1 + a_2 b_2 + a_3 b_3$$

This simple formula allows us to evaluate the dot product of two vectors even if we don't know the angle between them.

Because the dot product of a pair of vectors is equal to the product of their lengths and the cosine of the angle between them, if the angle between the vectors is 90°, then their dot product will be equal to zero. If we agree that the zero vector is perpendicular to every vector, then the converse is also true. This gives us one of the most frequently used properties of the dot product:

$$\mathbf{A} \perp \mathbf{B} \quad \Leftrightarrow \quad \mathbf{A} \bullet \mathbf{B} = 0$$

THE CROSS PRODUCT

The other principal way to multiply two vectors is to form their **cross product**. The cross product of two vectors, **A** and **B**, is defined as the vector that's perpendicular to the plane containing **A** and **B** (in accordance with the right-hand rule, which we'll explain shortly), and whose magnitude is

$$\mathbf{A} \times \mathbf{B} = AB \sin \theta$$

where θ is the angle between them. The magnitude of the cross product is equal to the area of the parallelogram determined by vectors **A** and **B**:

$$\|\mathbf{A} \times \mathbf{B}\| = \text{area of parallelogram}$$

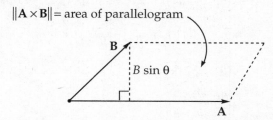

Since the cross product of two vectors is a vector, the cross product is also called the **vector product**.

To figure out the direction of the cross product, we use the **right-hand rule**. To understand this rule, first remember that any two vectors in space (neither of which is a scalar multiple of the other) determine a unique plane; the question is, *Which of the two directions perpendicular to this plane is the direction of the cross product?* Let the vectors **A** and **B** share the same initial point, and imagine placing the wrist of your right hand at this initial point, with your fingers pointing in the direction of vector **A** and your palm facing **B**. If you close your hand, curling your fingers inward (toward **B**), then your thumb will point in the direction of **A** × **B**. This shows that, unlike the dot product, the cross product is *anticommutative*; that is, **B** × **A** is always equal to –(**A** × **B**).

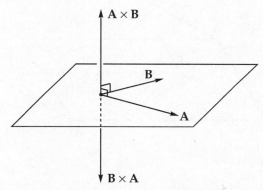

One of the most common uses of the cross product is in figuring out a vector normal to a plane. Since, by definition the cross product of two vectors is perpendicular (normal) to the plane that defines them, all we need is a convenient way to calculate the cross product of two vectors. To do this, we notice that $\hat{\mathbf{i}} \times \hat{\mathbf{i}} = \hat{\mathbf{j}} \times \hat{\mathbf{j}} = \hat{\mathbf{k}} \times \hat{\mathbf{k}} = \mathbf{0}$ and that:

$$\hat{\mathbf{i}} \times \hat{\mathbf{j}} = \hat{\mathbf{k}} = -(\hat{\mathbf{j}} \times \hat{\mathbf{i}})$$

$$\hat{\mathbf{j}} \times \hat{\mathbf{k}} = \hat{\mathbf{i}} = -(\hat{\mathbf{k}} \times \hat{\mathbf{j}})$$

$$\hat{\mathbf{k}} \times \hat{\mathbf{i}} = \hat{\mathbf{j}} = -(\hat{\mathbf{i}} \times \hat{\mathbf{k}})$$

[We use the diagram on the previous page as follows: The cross product of any vector into the next vector (following the arrow) gives the third vector, and the cross product of any vector into the previous one (that is, going against the arrow) gives the *opposite* of the third vector.] Next, the cross product is associative with respect to vector addition; that is, $\mathbf{A} \times (\mathbf{B} + \mathbf{C}) = (\mathbf{A} \times \mathbf{B}) + (\mathbf{A} \times \mathbf{C})$. So, the cross product of a pair of 3-vectors, $\mathbf{A} = (a_1, a_2, a_3)$ and $\mathbf{B} = (b_1, b_2, b_3)$, is equal to

$$
\begin{aligned}
\mathbf{A} \times \mathbf{B} &= (a_1\hat{\mathbf{i}} + a_2\hat{\mathbf{j}} + a_3\hat{\mathbf{k}}) \times (b_1\hat{\mathbf{i}} + b_2\hat{\mathbf{j}} + b_3\hat{\mathbf{k}}) \\
&= (a_2 b_3 - a_3 b_2)\hat{\mathbf{i}} + (a_3 b_1 - a_1 b_3)\hat{\mathbf{j}} + (a_1 b_2 - a_2 b_1)\hat{\mathbf{k}} \\
&= \begin{vmatrix} a_2 & a_3 \\ b_2 & b_3 \end{vmatrix}\hat{\mathbf{i}} - \begin{vmatrix} a_1 & a_3 \\ b_1 & b_3 \end{vmatrix}\hat{\mathbf{j}} + \begin{vmatrix} a_1 & a_2 \\ b_1 & b_2 \end{vmatrix}\hat{\mathbf{k}} \\
&= \begin{vmatrix} \hat{\mathbf{i}} & \hat{\mathbf{j}} & \hat{\mathbf{k}} \\ a_1 & a_2 & a_3 \\ b_1 & b_2 & b_3 \end{vmatrix}
\end{aligned}
$$

where the last two equations use the determinant of a matrix, which makes the formula easier to remember.

THE TRIPLE SCALAR PRODUCT

One of the higher-order products of vectors is the **triple scalar product**, $(\mathbf{A} \times \mathbf{B}) \bullet \mathbf{C}$. The absolute value of this product is the volume of the parallelepiped formed by the vectors $\mathbf{A}$, $\mathbf{B}$, and $\mathbf{C}$:

$$|(\mathbf{A} \times \mathbf{B}) \bullet \mathbf{C}| = \text{volume of parallelepiped}$$

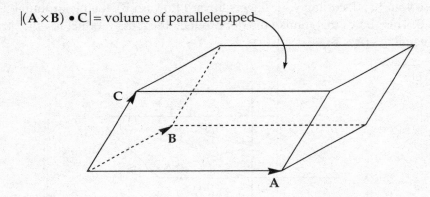

It can be shown that:

$$(\mathbf{A} \times \mathbf{B}) \bullet \mathbf{C} = \begin{vmatrix} a_1 & a_2 & a_3 \\ b_1 & b_2 & b_3 \\ c_1 & c_2 & c_3 \end{vmatrix}$$

Example 3.1   Let $\mathbf{A} = -\hat{\mathbf{i}} + \hat{\mathbf{k}}$ and $\mathbf{B} = \hat{\mathbf{i}} - 2\hat{\mathbf{j}} + 2\hat{\mathbf{k}}$.

(a) What's the magnitude of the vector $5\mathbf{A} - \mathbf{B}$?

(b) Find a vector whose $\hat{\mathbf{j}}$ component is 6, and is orthogonal to both $\mathbf{A}$ and $\mathbf{B}$.

(c) Find a vector whose magnitude is 6, and is orthogonal to both $\mathbf{A}$ and $\mathbf{B}$.

Solution:

(a) Since

$$5\mathbf{A} - \mathbf{B} = 5(-1, 0, 1) - (1, -2, 2) = (-5, 0, 5) - (1, -2, 2) = (-6, 2, 3)$$

we find that:

$$\|5\mathbf{A} - \mathbf{B}\| = \|(-6, 2, 3)\| = \sqrt{(-6)^2 + 2^2 + 3^2} = 7$$

(b) Let $\mathbf{C} = (c_1, 6, c_3)$ be the vector we're looking for. If $\mathbf{C}$ is to be orthogonal (that is, perpendicular) to both $\mathbf{A}$ and $\mathbf{B}$, then its dot product with both $\mathbf{A}$ and $\mathbf{B}$ must be equal to zero. This gives us two equations:

$$\mathbf{A} \cdot \mathbf{C} = 0 \;\Rightarrow\; (-1, 0, 1) \cdot (c_1, 6, c_3) = 0 \;\Rightarrow\; -c_1 + c_3 = 0$$
$$\mathbf{B} \cdot \mathbf{C} = 0 \;\Rightarrow\; (1, -2, 2) \cdot (c_1, 6, c_3) = 0 \;\Rightarrow\; c_1 - 12 + 2c_3 = 0$$

Solving these simultaneous equations gives us $c_1 = c_3 = 4$, so the vector $\mathbf{C}$ is $(4, 6, 4) = 4\hat{\mathbf{i}} + 6\hat{\mathbf{j}} + 4\hat{\mathbf{k}}$.

(c) Trying the approach we used in part (b) would not be as simple here. Instead, we'll use the fact that $\mathbf{A} \times \mathbf{B}$ is automatically orthogonal to both $\mathbf{A}$ and $\mathbf{B}$, and start by figuring out the cross product:

$$\mathbf{A} \times \mathbf{B} = \begin{vmatrix} \hat{\mathbf{i}} & \hat{\mathbf{j}} & \hat{\mathbf{k}} \\ -1 & 0 & 1 \\ 1 & -2 & 2 \end{vmatrix} = [0 - (-2)]\hat{\mathbf{i}} - (-2 - 1)\hat{\mathbf{j}} + (2 - 0)\hat{\mathbf{k}} = 2\hat{\mathbf{i}} + 3\hat{\mathbf{j}} + 2\hat{\mathbf{k}}$$

Since any scalar multiple of this vector will also be orthogonal to both $\mathbf{A}$ and $\mathbf{B}$, all we need is to find a scalar multiple of $\mathbf{A} \times \mathbf{B}$ that has magnitude 6. Let $\mathbf{D} = \mathbf{A} \times \mathbf{B} = (2, 3, 2)$. Since $\dfrac{\mathbf{D}}{D}$ is a unit vector (magnitude = 1), the vector

$$6\hat{\mathbf{D}} = 6\frac{\mathbf{D}}{D} = 6\frac{(2, 3, 2)}{\sqrt{2^2 + 3^2 + 2^2}} = \tfrac{6}{\sqrt{17}}(2, 3, 2) = \tfrac{6}{\sqrt{17}}(2\hat{\mathbf{i}} + 3\hat{\mathbf{j}} + 2\hat{\mathbf{k}})$$

has magnitude 6 and thus satisfies the conditions of the problem.

LINES IN 3-SPACE

A line in the plane is determined once we know its slope and a point through which the line passes. Similarly, a line in 3-space is determined once we know a point, $P_0 = (x_0, y_0, z_0)$, on the line and a vector, $\mathbf{v} = (v_1, v_2, v_3)$, that's parallel to the line; $\mathbf{v}$ tells us the line's direction. As the figure below shows, a point $P = (x, y, z)$ will lie on line L if and only if $\mathbf{P_0P} = (x - x_0, y - y_0, z - z_0)$, the vector from P_0 to P, is a scalar multiple of $\mathbf{v}$:

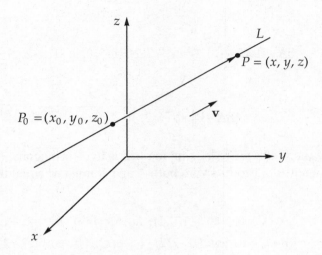

That is, $P = (x, y, z)$ is on L if and only if

$$(x - x_0, y - y_0, z - z_0) = t\mathbf{v} = t(v_1, v_2, v_3)$$

which is equivalent to the three **parametric equations**:

$$L: \begin{cases} x = x_0 + tv_1 \\ y = y_0 + tv_2 \\ z = z_0 + tv_3 \end{cases}$$

We can also eliminate the parameter, t, from this set of equations and write the equation of L in the form:

$$\frac{x - x_0}{v_1} = \frac{y - y_0}{v_2} = \frac{z - z_0}{v_3}$$

If any *one* of the components v_1, v_2, or v_3 is equal to zero, then the fraction containing that component is simply omitted from the equation. These equations are the **symmetric equations** of the line.

Example 3.2 Where does the line that passes through the points $P = (-3, -1, 2)$ and $Q = (5, 8, 4)$ pierce the xy-plane?

Solution: The line is parallel to the vector

$$\mathbf{PQ} = (5, 8, 4) - (-3, -1, 2) = (8, 9, 2)$$

so the parametric equations for the line are:

$$x = -3 + 8t, \quad y = -1 + 9t, \quad z = 2 + 2t$$

The line will intersect the x-y plane when $z = 0$. The value of t that makes z equal to 0 is $t = -1$. For this t, the values of x and y are $x = -3 + 8(-1) = -11$ and $y = -1 + 9(-1) = -10$, so the line crosses the x-y plane at the point $(-11, -10, 0)$.

PLANES IN 3-SPACE

A plane in 3-space can be determined once we know a point, $P_0 = (x_0, y_0, z_0)$, on the plane and a vector, $\mathbf{n} = (n_1, n_2, n_3)$, that is perpendicular (normal) to the plane; $\mathbf{n}$ tells us the plane's orientation in space. As the figure below shows, a point $P = (x, y, z)$ will lie on the plane if and only if $\mathbf{P_0P}$, the vector from P_0 to P, is normal to $\mathbf{n}$:

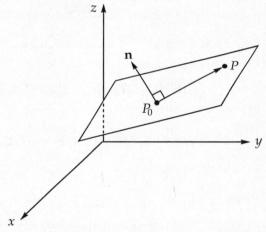

That is, $P = (x, y, z)$ is on the plane if and only if the dot product of $\mathbf{P_0P}$ and $\mathbf{n}$ is zero:

$$(x - x_0, y - y_0, z - z_0) \bullet (n_1, n_2, n_3) = 0$$

which can be rewritten as

$$n_1(x - x_0) + n_2(y - y_0) + n_3(z - z_0) = 0$$

or, more simply, as

$$n_1 x + n_2 y + n_3 z = d$$

where $d = n_1 x_0 + n_2 y_0 + n_3 z_0$. It's important to notice that *the coefficients of x, y, and z in the equation of the plane are the components of a vector normal to the plane.*

Planes that are parallel to one of the coordinate planes have particularly simple equations. Any plane parallel to the x-y plane must have $\hat{\mathbf{k}} = (0, 0, 1)$ as a normal vector, so the equation of such a plane must have the form $z = z_0$. Similarly, any plane parallel to the x-z plane has $y = y_0$ as its equation, and any plane parallel to the y-z plane has $x = x_0$ as its equation. The three planes $x = x_0$, $y = y_0$, and $z = z_0$ intersect in the point $P = (x_0, y_0, z_0)$, as shown on the following page.

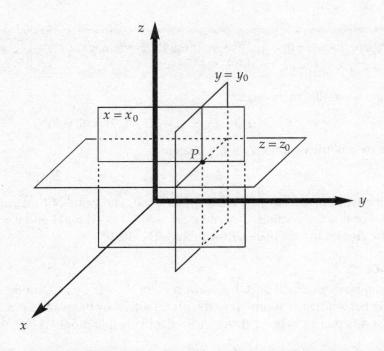

Example 3.3 Find the equation of the plane that contains the points $A = (4, 1, 2)$, $B = (1, 5, 4)$, and $C = (-3, 2, 6)$.

Solution: The vectors

$$\mathbf{AB} = (1, 5, 4) - (4, 1, 2) = (-3, 4, 2)$$

and

$$\mathbf{AC} = (-3, 2, 6) - (4, 1, 2) = (-7, 1, 4)$$

lie in the plane, so their cross product,

$$\mathbf{AB} \times \mathbf{AC} = \begin{vmatrix} \hat{\mathbf{i}} & \hat{\mathbf{j}} & \hat{\mathbf{k}} \\ -3 & 4 & 2 \\ -7 & 1 & 4 \end{vmatrix} = (16 - 2)\hat{\mathbf{i}} - (-12 + 14)\hat{\mathbf{j}} + (-3 + 28)\hat{\mathbf{k}} = 14\hat{\mathbf{i}} - 2\hat{\mathbf{j}} + 25\hat{\mathbf{k}}$$

gives a vector normal to the plane. Since $\mathbf{n} = (14, -2, 25)$ is normal to the plane, the equation of the plane must have the form $14x - 2y + 25z = d$, for some constant d. Substituting the coordinates of any of the three points into this equation will give us the value of d. Using $A = (4, 1, 2)$, we find that $d = 14(4) - 2(1) + 25(2) = 104$. Therefore, the equation of the plane that contains A, B, and C is $14x - 2y + 25z = 104$. (The coordinates of B and C also satisfy this equation, which verifies it.)

CYLINDERS

In the x-y plane, the graph of the equation $x^2 + y^2 = 1$ is a circle. In 3-space, this equation would describe a right circular cylinder, which has circular cross sections parallel to the x-y plane. Because the variable z is missing from the equation, it can assume any value, as the figure below illustrates.

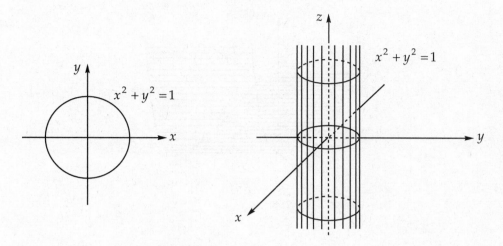

In general, given a curve, C, a **cylinder** is a surface in 3-space generated by moving a line along C so that it is always parallel to a given line, L (called the **generator**). The lines that make up the surface of the cylinder are called **elements**. The figure below shows a cylinder generated by a line perpendicular to the x-y plane along a curve C in the x-y plane whose equation is $f(x, y) = 0$:

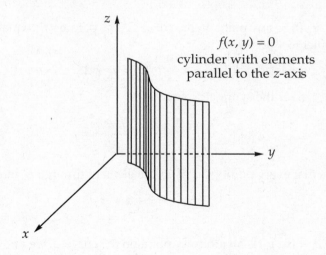

$f(x, y) = 0$
cylinder with elements
parallel to the z-axis

As the example of the right circular cylinder illustrates, an equation that is missing one of the variables x, y, or z represents a cylinder whose generator is parallel to the axis of the missing variable. For example, the equation $y^2 + 9z^2 = 1$ describes an elliptic cylinder whose elements are parallel to the x-axis, and, pictured below, $z = x^2$ is a parabolic cylinder with elements parallel to the y-axis.

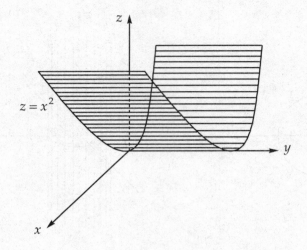

Example 3.4   Let C be the curve $x = y^2$ in the xy-plane, and let **v** be the vector $(-1, 2, 1)$. What's the equation of the cylinder generated by a line moving along C in such a way that it's always parallel to **v**?

Solution: Let $P_0 = (x_0, y_0, 0)$ be any point on the curve C. The parametric equations of the line through P_0 and parallel to **v** are:

$$x = x_0 - t, \quad y = y_0 + 2t, \quad z = t$$

Eliminating t gives the symmetric equations:

$$\frac{x - x_0}{-1} = \frac{y - y_0}{2} = z$$

This tells us that every point (x, y, z) on the element through P_0 must satisfy the equations:

$$x + z = x_0$$
$$y - 2z = y_0$$

Now, since $P_0 = (x_0, y_0)$ is an arbitrary point on the curve C, we know that $x_0 = y_0^2$; substituting the pair of equations displayed above into this last equation gives

$$x + z = (y - 2z)^2$$

as the equation of the cylinder.

SURFACES OF REVOLUTION

In the previous chapter, we learned how to figure out the volume of a solid of revolution, obtained by rotating a curve in the x-y plane around a horizontal or vertical line. In this section, we will show how to find equations for surfaces of revolution in 3-space.

Let's consider the curve $z = y^2$ in the yz-plane; what would be the equation of the surface we'd get if this curve were revolved around the z-axis? Let $P_0 = (0, y_0, z_0)$, with $y_0 > 0$ be a point on the curve.

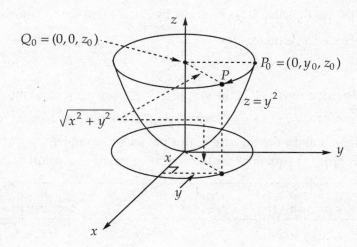

Referring to the figure above, we notice that as the point P_0 revolves around the z-axis (that is, as we revolve the curve around the z-axis), it generates a circle of radius y_0 centered at Q_0 in the plane $z = z_0$. A point P, at height z_0 above the xy-plane, will lie on the surface of revolution if $Q_0 P$ is equal to $Q_0 P_0$; that is, if the distance from P to the z-axis is also equal to y_0. Since the distance from P to the z-axis is $\sqrt{x^2 + y^2}$, the point $P = (x, y, z_0)$ will lie on the surface if $\sqrt{x^2 + y^2}$ is equal to $\pm\, y_0$. (We include the $\pm$ here because y_0 could be negative.) Now, since $z_0 = y_0^2$, we can conclude that $P = (x, y, z_0)$ will lie on the surface if:

$$z_0 = \left(\pm\sqrt{x^2 + y^2}\right)^2$$

This will be true for any height $z_0 \geq 0$. So if we replace y by $\pm\sqrt{x^2 + y^2}$ in the equation of the curve, we'll get the equation of the surface of revolution:

$$z = y^2 \qquad \text{becomes} \qquad z = \left(\pm\sqrt{x^2 + y^2}\right)^2$$

which we can rewrite as $z = x^2 + y^2$. In general, if we take the curve $f(y, z) = 0$ in the y-z plane and revolve it around the z-axis, the equation of the surface we generate is $f(\pm\sqrt{x^2 + y^2}, z) = 0$, where we use $\pm$ to account for the possibility that y may be negative (this can be eliminated by squaring the resulting equation).

What if we revolved this same curve around the y-axis? Let $Q_0 = (0, y_0, 0)$ and, as before, let $P_0 = (0, y_0, z_0)$ be a point on the curve. As P_0 revolves around the y-axis, it generates a circle of radius $Q_0P_0 = z_0$ in the plane $y = y_0$, centered at Q_0. So a point $P = (x, y_0, z)$ will lie on the surface of revolution if Q_0P is equal to Q_0P_0; that is, if the distance from P to the y-axis is also equal to z_0. Since the distance from P to the y-axis is $\sqrt{x^2 + z^2}$, the point $P = (x, y_0, z)$ will lie on the surface if $\sqrt{x^2 + z^2}$ is equal to z_0. Since this will be true for any y_0, the result is that if we replace z by $\sqrt{x^2 + z^2}$ in the equation of the curve, we'll get the equation of the surface of revolution:

$$z = y^2 \qquad \text{becomes} \qquad \sqrt{x^2 + z^2} = y^2$$

In general, if we take the curve $f(y, z) = 0$ in the y-z plane and revolve it around the y-axis, the equation of the surface we generate is $f(y, \pm\sqrt{x^2 + z^2}) = 0$, where we include the $\pm$ to account for the possibility that z may be negative (although that's not the case in this particular example).

The table below lists how the equations for the various surfaces of revolution are found.

If the curve	is revolved around the	then replace	by	to get surface of revolution
$f(x,y) = 0$	x-axis	y	$\pm\sqrt{y^2 + z^2}$	$f(x, \pm\sqrt{y^2 + z^2}) = 0$
	y-axis	x	$\pm\sqrt{x^2 + z^2}$	$f(\pm\sqrt{x^2 + z^2}, y) = 0$
$f(x,z) = 0$	x-axis	z	$\pm\sqrt{y^2 + z^2}$	$f(x, \pm\sqrt{y^2 + z^2}) = 0$
	z-axis	x	$\pm\sqrt{x^2 + y^2}$	$f(\pm\sqrt{x^2 + y^2}, z) = 0$
$f(y,z) = 0$	y-axis	z	$\pm\sqrt{x^2 + z^2}$	$f(y, \pm\sqrt{x^2 + z^2}) = 0$
	z-axis	y	$\pm\sqrt{x^2 + y^2}$	$f(\pm\sqrt{x^2 + y^2}, z) = 0$

Example 3.5 If the ellipse $x^2 + (\frac{1}{9})x^2 = 1$ in the xz-plane, is revolved around the z-axis, what's the equation of the resulting ellipsoid surface?

Solution: Using the table above, we replace x by $\pm\sqrt{x^2 + y^2}$ in the equation of the curve to obtain the equation of the surface of revolution. This gives us:

$$\left(\pm\sqrt{x^2 + y^2}\right)^2 + \tfrac{1}{9}z^2 = 1 \quad \Rightarrow \quad x^2 + y^2 + \tfrac{1}{9}z^2 = 1$$

LEVEL CURVES AND LEVEL SURFACES

The graph of a function $z = f(x, y)$ is the set of all points (x, y, z) in three-dimensional space that satisfy the equation. It is often difficult to sketch these graphs, since they may have peaks, valleys, and other features that aren't easy to illustrate on a flat sheet of paper. A simple way to provide some kind of representation of the graph of the function $z = f(x, y)$ is to draw some of its **level curves**; these lie flat in the x-y plane.

If c is a constant, then $f(x, y) = c$ is called the **level curve of height** c of the function $z = f(x, y)$. Therefore, a level curve is the set of all points (x, y) in the x-y plane where the function assumes a given, constant value. Geometrically, we imagine slicing through the surface with the horizontal plane $z = c$; in general, the intersection of this plane with the surface will be a curve, called a **contour curve**. Projecting this curve perpendicularly onto the x-y plane gives the level curve of height c.

Let's look at an example. The graph of the function $z = f(x, y) = x^2 + y^2$ was shown on page 117; it's the surface of revolution we get by revolving the curve $z = y^2$ around the z-axis. This surface is called a *circular paraboloid* because its cross sections perpendicular to the z-axis are circles, and its cross sections perpendicular to the xy-plane are parabolas. The level curves of this function are described by the equation $x^2 + y^2 = c$, where c is a positive constant. (Of course, if $c = 0$, then the level curve is just a point; the origin.) These curves are circles centered at the origin, which are easy to sketch:

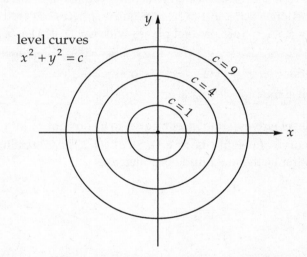

How do you use level curves to reconstruct the actual graph of the function? By imagining that the level curve of height c is actually *at* height c above the x-y plane. (If c is negative, imagine the curve to be $|-c|$ units below the x-y plane.) So, for the level curves pictured above, we would imagine the circle $x^2 + y^2 = 1$ lifted a distance of 1 unit; the circle $x^2 + y^2 = 4$ lifted up by 4 units; and so on, so that these elevated level curves form the surface. Now it isn't difficult to picture the paraboloid in 3-space, as on the following page.

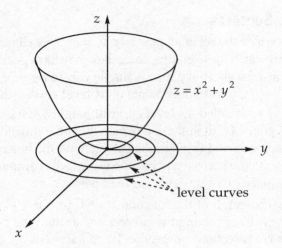

$$z = x^2 + y^2$$

level curves

If $w = f(x, y, z)$ is a function of three independent variables, we would need a space of four dimensions for its graph, which is clearly hopeless. In this case, we have no choice but to sketch its **level surfaces**. If c is a constant, then $f(x, y, z) = c$ is a level surface on which the value of w is always equal to c. For example, the level surfaces of the function $w = x^2 + y^2 + z^2$ are concentric spheres centered at the origin, and the level surfaces of the function $w = x + y + z$ are parallel planes with $\mathbf{n} = (1, 1, 1)$ as a normal.

Example 3.6 The equation $x^2 + \frac{1}{9}y^2 - z^2 = 1$ describes a surface called a *hyperboloid of one sheet*. Sketch some of its level curves.

Solution: To find the level curves, simply set z equal to a constant, c. In this case, then, the equation of the level curve of height c is $x^2 + \frac{1}{9}y^2 = c^2 + 1$. These are ellipses centered at the origin that grow larger as the magnitude of c increases.

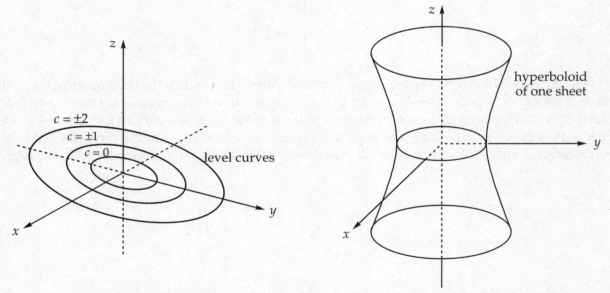

$c = \pm 2$
$c = \pm 1$
$c = 0$
level curves

hyperboloid of one sheet

Also notice here that the level curve of height $-c$ is the same as the level curve of height c. This means that the surface extends both above and below the xy-plane, and, in fact, the xy-plane cuts the surface into symmetrical halves. Cross sections parallel to the xy-plane are ellipses, while cross sections perpendicular to the xy-plane are hyperbolas.

CYLINDRICAL COORDINATES

In 3-space, **cylindrical coordinates** are nothing more than the polar coordinates r and θ in the x-y plane, along with the usual (cartesian) z-coordinate. To find the cylindrical coordinates of a point $P = (x, y, z)$ in 3-space, we drop a perpendicular from P to the xy-plane, and let Q be the foot of this segment. (Of course, if P is already in the xy-plane, then $Q = P$.) Now, by definition, if (r, θ) are polar coordinates of Q, then (r, θ, z) are cylindrical coordinates of P.

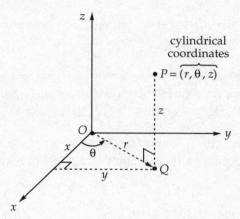

The name *cylindrical* comes from the fact that the surface described by the equation $r = c$ (where c is a nonzero constant) is a right circular cylinder in space. The surface $\theta = c$ (where c is a nonzero constant) is a plane through the origin and perpendicular to the xy-plane and, of course, the surface $z = c$ (where c is a constant) is simply a horizontal plane (that is, parallel to the xy-plane).

SPHERICAL COORDINATES

To find the **spherical coordinates** of a point P in 3-space, we once again drop a perpendicular from P to the x-y plane, and let Q be the foot of this segment. Then we draw line segments from the origin, O, to both P and Q. The spherical coordinates of the point P are (ρ, ϕ, θ), where ρ is the distance OP, ϕ is the angle that the segment OP makes with the positive z-axis, and θ is the angle that the segment OQ makes with the positive x-axis (the same as the cylindrical coordinate θ).

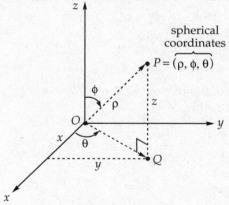

The equations that relate cartesian coordinates to spherical coordinates can be derived from the figure above. Since $\angle OPQ = \phi$, we have $z = \rho \cos \phi$ and $OQ = r = \rho \sin \phi$; this equation tells us that:

$$x = r \cos \theta = \rho \sin \phi \cos \theta \quad \text{and} \quad y = r \sin \theta = \rho \sin \phi \sin \theta$$

The name *spherical* comes from the fact that the coordinate surface described by the equation $\rho = c$ (where c is a positive constant) is a sphere of radius c, centered at the origin. The coordinate surface $\phi = c$ (where c is a positive constant) is generally a cone centered on the z-axis, with vertex angle $2c$. (The surface $\phi = 0$ is just the positive z-axis, $\phi = \dfrac{\pi}{2}$ is the xy-plane, and $\phi = \pi$ is the negative z-axis.) And, just as with cylindrical coordinates, the surface $\theta = c$ (where c is a nonzero constant) is a plane through the origin and perpendicular to the x-y plane.

Example 3.7	Let S be the sphere that's tangent to the xz-plane and whose center is $C = (0, 1, 0)$. Write the equation of S in spherical coordinates.

Solution: Since S is centered at $(0, 1, 0)$ and tangent to the xz-plane, the radius of the sphere must be 1. In cartesian coordinates, the equation of the sphere with center (x_0, y_0, z_0) and radius a is

$$(x - x_0)^2 + (y - y_0)^2 + (z - z_0)^2 = a^2$$

so the cartesian equation for S is

$$x^2 + (y - 1)^2 + z^2 = 1$$

which we can rewrite as $x^2 + y^2 + z^2 - 2y = 0$. Because $x^2 + y^2 + z^2 = \rho^2$ and $y = \rho \sin \phi \sin \theta$, the equation for S in spherical coordinates is:

$$\rho^2 - 2\rho \sin \phi \sin \theta = 0$$

Factoring gives $\rho(\rho - 2\sin \phi \sin \theta) = 0$, so either $\rho = 0$ or $\rho = 2 \sin \phi \sin \theta$. Since the latter equation includes the former one, we can conclude that the equation for S in spherical coordinates is $\rho = 2 \sin \phi \sin \theta$.

PARTIAL DERIVATIVES

Let $f(x, y)$ be a function of two variables. Keep y constant, and consider the limit:

$$\lim_{h \to 0} \frac{f(x+h, y) - f(x, y)}{h}$$

If this limit exists, its value is the derivative of f with respect to x at (x, y); it's called the **partial derivative of f with respect to x**, and is denoted by:

$$\frac{\partial f}{\partial x}(x, y) \quad \text{or} \quad f_x(x, y)$$

Similarly, we can keep x constant and consider:

$$\lim_{k \to 0} \frac{f(x, y+k) - f(x,y)}{k}$$

If this limit exists, it's called the **partial derivative of f with respect to y**, and denoted by

$$\frac{\partial f}{\partial y}(x,y) \quad \text{or} \quad f_y(x,y)$$

To determine the partial derivative of $f(x, y)$ with respect to, say, x, we treat y as if it were a constant and apply the usual differentiation rules. For example, consider the function:

$$f(x,y) = 2x^3 y + x \sin y$$

Its partial derivatives with respect to x and y are:

$$f_x = 6x^2 y + \sin y \qquad \text{and} \qquad f_y = 2x^3 + x \cos y$$

Although we've introduced the idea of a partial derivative for a function of two variables, we can also find partial derivatives of a function of three or more variables, and the rule is the same: Treat every variable—except the one you're differentiating with respect to—as a constant and apply the usual differentiation rules. So, for example, if

$$g(w,x,y,z) = x^2 e^{2w} - wyz^3 + 8x - 1$$

then:

$$g_w = 2x^2 e^{2w} - yz^3, \quad g_x = 2xe^{2w} + 8, \quad g_y = -wz^3, \quad \text{and} \quad g_z = -3wyz^2$$

GEOMETRIC INTERPRETATION OF f_x AND f_y

For a function $f(x, y)$ of two variables, what do the partial derivatives f_x and f_y represent geometrically? Remember that for a function of one variable, the derivative is the slope of the line tangent to the curve. When we want to take a partial derivative of $f(x, y)$, we treat one of the variables as a constant. In effect, we consider f as a function of one variable, so the value of the derivative should again be the slope of the line tangent to a curve. Let's look at this a little more closely. To form f_x, we treat y as a constant (let's call it y_0), so the graph of the function $z = f(x, y_0)$ is a curve: It's the intersection of the surface $z = f(x, y)$ with the plane $y = y_0$. The partial derivative of f with respect to x gives the slope of the line tangent to this curve. Similarly, the partial derivative with respect to y gives the slope of the tangent line to the curve $z = f(x_0, y)$, which is the intersection of the surface $z = f(x, y)$ with the plane $x = x_0$.

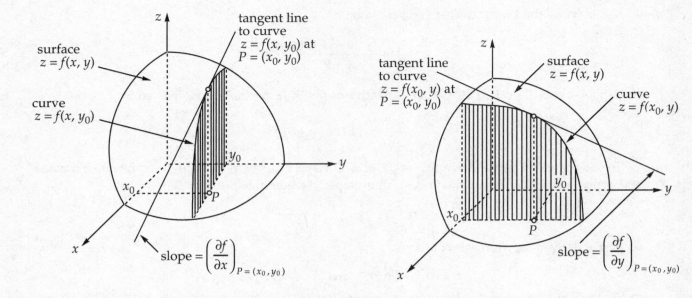

Example 3.8 What's the equation of the line tangent to the intersection of the surface $z = \arctan xy$ with the plane $x = 2$, at the point $(2, \frac{1}{2}, \frac{\pi}{4})$?

Solution: Since x is held constant, the slope of the tangent line we're looking for is equal to the value of the partial derivative $(\partial/\partial y)(\arctan xy)$ at $(x_0, y_0) = (2, \frac{1}{2})$:

$$\frac{\partial}{\partial y}(\arctan xy) = \frac{x}{1 + (xy)^2} \implies \text{slope} = \left[\frac{x}{1 + (xy)^2}\right]_{(2, \frac{1}{2})} = 1$$

Since the tangent line is in the plane $x = 2$, this calculation shows that the line is parallel to the vector $\mathbf{v} = (0, 1, 1)$, so we can write the equation of the tangent line in parametric form, as follows:

$$x = 2, \, y = \frac{1}{2} + t, \, z = \frac{\pi}{4} + t$$

HIGHER-ORDER PARTIAL DERIVATIVES

A partial derivative of a function of two or more variables is itself a function, so it may be differentiated with respect to any of the variables. For example, after finding f_x and f_y for a function $f(x, y)$, we may differentiate the derivatives with respect to either x or y. The derivative of f_x with respect to x is denoted:

$$\frac{\partial^2 f}{\partial x^2} \quad \text{or} \quad f_{xx}$$

and the derivative of f_y with respect to y is denoted:

$$\frac{\partial^2 f}{\partial y^2} \quad \text{or} \quad f_{yy}$$

The second-order **mixed** partials—which are the derivatives of f_x with respect to y, and of f_y with respect to x—are denoted, respectively:

$$\frac{\partial^2 f}{\partial y \partial x} = f_{xy} \quad \text{and} \quad \frac{\partial^2 f}{\partial x \partial y} = f_{yx}$$

For almost all commonly encountered functions, these mixed partials are continuous, which ensures that they're identical; that is, $f_{xy} = f_{yx}$, so the order in which the derivatives are taken doesn't matter. To illustrate, let's consider the function:

$$f(x, y) = y \log(4x + y^2)$$

Its first-order partial derivatives are

$$f_x = \frac{4y}{4x + y^2} \quad \text{and} \quad f_y = \frac{2y^2}{4x + y^2} + \log(4x + y^2)$$

and the second-order mixed partial derivatives of f are identical, since

$$f_{xy} = (f_x)_y = \frac{\partial}{\partial y}\left(\frac{4y}{4x + y^2}\right) = \frac{4(4x - y^2)}{(4x + y^2)^2}$$

and:

$$f_{yx} = (f_y)_x = \frac{\partial}{\partial x}\left[\frac{2y^2}{4x + y^2} + \log(4x + y^2)\right]$$

$$= -\frac{8y^2}{(4x + y^2)^2} + \frac{4}{4x + y^2}$$

$$= \frac{4(4x - y^2)}{(4x + y^2)^2}$$

We can also form partial derivatives of orders higher than two; f_{xxy} or f_{yxy}, for example. Just remember that the order in which the derivatives are taken is specified differently in our two notations for a partial derivative. When using the Leibniz "fraction" notation, we look at the denominator and read the variables from right to left; but when using the subscript notation, we read the subscripts from left to right. For example, if we differentiate $f(x, y)$ first with respect to x, then we differentiate the result with respect to x, and then finish by differentiating the result with respect to y, the resulting third-order partial derivative would be written as either:

$$\frac{\partial^3 f}{\partial y \partial x \partial x} \quad \text{or} \quad f_{xxy}$$

Notice that by invoking the equality of mixed partials, f_{xxy} is equal to f_{xyx} or to f_{yxx}.

THE TANGENT PLANE TO A SURFACE

Just as the derivative of a function of one variable can be used to find the equation of a tangent line to a curve, the partial derivatives of a function of two variables can be used to find the equation of a tangent plane to a surface. Let $z = f(x, y)$ be the equation of a surface in 3-space, and let f_x and f_y denote, as usual, the first partial derivatives of f. Then the equation of the tangent plane to the surface at $P = (x_0, y_0, z_0)$ is

$$z - z_0 = f_x\big|_P \bullet (x - x_0) + f_y\big|_P \bullet (y - y_0)$$

assuming that f_x and f_y aren't both equal to zero at P. The equation of a surface can also be given in the form $f(x, y, z) = c$, for some constant c. The difference is that z is not written explicitly in terms of x and y, as is the case if the surface is described by an equation of the form $z = f(x, y)$. To take care of this situation, simply use the equation $f(x, y, z) = c$ to find $\dfrac{\partial z}{\partial x}$ and $\dfrac{\partial z}{\partial y}$ by implicit differentiation; the equation of the tangent plane to the surface at the point $P = (x_0, y_0, z_0)$ is

$$z - z_0 = \frac{\partial z}{\partial x}\bigg|_P \bullet (x - x_0) + \frac{\partial z}{\partial y}\bigg|_P \bullet (y - y_0)$$

assuming once again that $\dfrac{\partial z}{\partial x}$ and $\dfrac{\partial z}{\partial y}$ don't both equal zero at P.

Example 3.9   Find the equation of the tangent plane to the surface

$$x^2z - y^3z^5 + xy = 9$$

at the point $P = (1, 2, -1)$.

Solution: Since the equation of this surface is given in the form $f(x, y, z) = c$, we use implicit differentiation to find the partial derivatives. First, we hold y fixed and differentiate implicitly with respect to x to find $\dfrac{\partial z}{\partial x}$:

$$x^2z - y^3z^5 + xy = 9$$

$$\left(x^2 \frac{\partial z}{\partial x} + 2xz\right) - 5y^3z^4 \frac{\partial z}{\partial x} + y = 0$$

$$\frac{\partial z}{\partial x} = \frac{-2xz - y}{x^2 - 5y^3z^4}$$

Next, we hold x fixed and differentiate implicitly with respect to y to find $\dfrac{\partial z}{\partial y}$:

$$x^2z - y^3z^5 + xy = 9$$

$$x^2 \frac{\partial z}{\partial y} - \left(5y^3z^4 \frac{\partial z}{\partial y} + 3y^2z^5\right) + x = 0$$

$$\frac{\partial z}{\partial y} = \frac{3y^2z^5 - x}{x^2 - 5y^3z^4}$$

Evaluating each of these at the point $P = (1, 2, -1)$ gives

$$\left.\frac{\partial z}{\partial x}\right|_P = \left.\frac{-2xz - y}{x^2 - 5y^3 z^4}\right|_{(1,2,-1)} = \frac{-2(1)(-1) - 2}{1^2 - 5(2^3)(-1)^4} = 0$$

and

$$\left.\frac{\partial z}{\partial y}\right|_P = \left.\frac{3y^2 z^5 - x}{x^2 - 5y^3 z^4}\right|_{(1,2,-1)} = \frac{3(2^2)(-1)^5 - 1}{1^2 - 5(2^3)(-1)^4} = \frac{1}{3}$$

so the equation of the tangent plane at P is $z + 1 = \dfrac{1}{3}(y - 2)$, or, equivalently:

$$y - 3z = 5$$

LINEAR APPROXIMATIONS

The equation of the tangent plane to a surface $z = f(x, y)$ at a point $P_0 = (x_0, y_0)$ provides a first-order (linear) approximation of the value of z at points near P_0. To be more specific, let's say we wanted to evaluate f at a point $P_1 = (x_1, y_1)$ that's close to P_0. Since P_1 is close to P_0, the value of z at P_1 on the tangent plane is close to the value of z at P_1 on the surface. So, if $z_1 = f(x_1, y_1)$, we can use the equation of the tangent plane at P_0 to say that:

$$z_1 \approx z_0 + f_x\big|_P \cdot (x - x_0) + f_y\big|_P \cdot (y - y_0)$$

Example 3.10   What's an approximate value for this expression?

$$(1.1) \log [4(0.05) + (1.1)^2]$$

Solution: If we let $f(x, y) = y \log (4x + y^2)$, then we're being asked to approximate the value of $f(0.05, 1.1)$. Notice that the point $P_1 = (0.05, 1.1)$ is very close to the point $P_0 = (0, 1)$, at which the exact value of f is easy to calculate: $z_0 = f(x_0, y_0) = 1 \log (0 + 1^2) = 0$. So, if we figure out the equation of the plane tangent to the surface $z = f(x, y)$ at the point P_0, then the value of f at P_1 will be approximately equal to the value of z at P_1 on the tangent plane. Earlier in this section, we found the first-order partial derivatives of $f(x, y)$; they are:

$$f_x = \frac{4y}{4x + y^2} \quad \text{and} \quad f_y = \frac{2y^2}{4x + y^2} + \log(4x + y^2)$$

Evaluating each of these at the point P_0 gives

$$f_x\big|_{P_0} = \left.\frac{4y}{4x + y^2}\right|_{(0,1)} = 4 \quad \text{and} \quad f_y\big|_{P_0} = \left[\frac{2y^2}{4x + y^2} + \log(4x + y^2)\right]_{(0,1)} = 2$$

so the equation of the tangent plane to the surface at P_0 is $z - 0 = 4(x - 0) + 2(y - 1)$ or, more simply:

$$z = 4x + 2y - 2$$

Since $P_1 = (0.05, 1.1)$ is close to $P_0 = (0, 1)$, the value of z at P_1 on the tangent plane,

$$z = 4(0.05) + 2(1.1) - 2 = 0.4$$

should give a close approximation to the value of z at P_1 on the surface. [Note: A calculator would tell you that $(1.1) \log [4(0.05) + (1.1)^2] \approx 0.378$, so our approximation of 0.4 is pretty good.]

THE CHAIN RULE FOR PARTIAL DERIVATIVES

In the previous chapter, we used the chain rule to differentiate composite functions: If f is a function of u, and u is a function of x, then we find the derivative of f with respect to x from the equation:

$$\frac{df}{dx} = \frac{df}{du}\frac{du}{dx}$$

For functions of a single variable, this is the only form of the chain rule we need. But in the case of functions of more than one variable, there are many different forms of the chain rule; which one to apply depends on how many variables there are and how they're interrelated. Here we'll describe a method that you can use to differentiate a composite function in any situation.

As our first illustration of this method, let's say that we're given a function $z = F(u, v)$ with $u = f(x, y)$ and $v = g(x, y)$. Notice that z depends on the variables u and v, and these variables in turn depend on x and y; so ultimately, z depends on x and y. We call z the **dependent variable**, u and v the **intermediate variables**, and x and y the **independent variables**. Therefore, you could be asked to find the derivative of z with respect to x or to y.

The first step is to sketch a diagram of the situation by drawing an arrow from the dependent variable to every intermediate variable, and one from every intermediate variable to every independent variable. Our diagram would look like this:

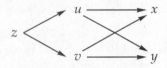

Think of each arrow as meaning *depends on*. So, for example, the arrow pointing from z to u means that z depends on u—since $z = F(u, v)$, and the arrow from v to y means that v depends on y—since $v = g(x, y)$. Now, let's say we are asked to find the derivative of z with respect to x. To answer this question, we use the diagram to find every path from z to x. Each path will give us a product of derivatives, one derivative for each arrow, and then we add up the products for every path. In this case, there are two paths from z to x; one going through u and one going through v. The path $z \to u \to x$ contains two arrows; the arrow $z \to u$ gives us the derivative $\dfrac{\partial z}{\partial u}$, and the arrow $u \to x$ gives us the derivative $\dfrac{\partial u}{\partial x}$. (Notice that we have to use partial derivatives here because z depends on more than one variable, as does u.) So, the double-arrow path $z \to u \to x$ gives us two derivatives, which we multiply to give:

$$\frac{\partial z}{\partial u}\frac{\partial u}{\partial x}$$

In the same way, the other path from z to x, the double-arrow path $z \to v \to x$, gives us:

$$\frac{\partial z}{\partial v} \frac{\partial v}{\partial x}$$

Therefore, the derivative of z with respect to x is the sum of all possible paths from z to x:

$$\frac{\partial z}{\partial x} = \frac{\partial z}{\partial u} \frac{\partial u}{\partial x} + \frac{\partial z}{\partial v} \frac{\partial v}{\partial x}$$

You can imagine how things can get messy. For example, let's say we were given $z = F(u, v, y)$, where $u = f(v, x)$ and $v = g(x, y)$. The diagram we'd draw to depict the complicated dependencies in this situation would look like this:

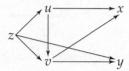

Now, let's find the derivative of z with respect to y. First, we need to find all the paths that connect z to y. There are three: the one-arrow path $z \to y$; the two-arrow path $z \to v \to y$; and the three-arrow path $z \to u \to v \to y$. Since there are three paths from z to y, we know that the expression for $\frac{\partial z}{\partial y}$ will consist of three terms, one for each path:

$$\frac{\partial z}{\partial y} = \frac{\partial z}{\partial y} + \frac{\partial z}{\partial v} \frac{\partial v}{\partial y} + \frac{\partial z}{\partial u} \frac{\partial u}{\partial v} \frac{\partial v}{\partial y}$$

One of the drawbacks of the partial-derivative Leibniz notation is apparent here. Notice that the equation above has $\frac{\partial z}{\partial y}$ on the left-hand side *and* on the right-hand side, and it seems like we could cancel them out (which would leave us with no answer to our question, "What's $\frac{\partial z}{\partial y}$?"). But the problem is that $\frac{\partial z}{\partial y}$ on the left-hand side means *the derivative of the composite function with respect to y* (that is, the derivative of z with respect to y taking any dependency of u and v on y into account, which is the derivative we're looking for), while the $\frac{\partial z}{\partial y}$ on the right-hand side means *the derivative of z with respect to y, holding u and v constant*. There's a way to remove the ambiguity: We write the variables being held constant as subscripts on each partial derivative. While at first this might seem superfluous—after all, that's how we figure out partial derivatives, by keeping all the variables constant except the one we're differentiating with respect to—this example shows that it's not. So, using this more careful notation, the equation for $\frac{\partial z}{\partial y}$ would be written like this:

$$\left(\frac{\partial z}{\partial y} \right)_x = \left(\frac{\partial z}{\partial y} \right)_{u,v} + \left(\frac{\partial z}{\partial v} \right)_{u,y} \left(\frac{\partial v}{\partial y} \right)_x + \left(\frac{\partial z}{\partial u} \right)_{v,y} \left(\frac{\partial u}{\partial v} \right)_x \left(\frac{\partial v}{\partial y} \right)_x$$

It looks bad, but it resolves all possible ambiguities.

Example 3.11 Let $z = F(u, w, x)$, where $u = f(x, y)$ and $w = g(x, y)$.

(a) Find a general expression for $\dfrac{\partial z}{\partial x}$.

(b) Verify your answer to (a) if $F(u, w, x) = w^3 - 2ux$, $f(x, y) = 4xy - x + 1$, and $g(x, y) = y + xy^2$.

Solution:

(a) First draw a diagram:

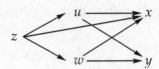

In order to find $\dfrac{\partial z}{\partial x}$, we find all paths from z to x. Since there are three such paths, $z \to x$, $z \to u \to x$, and $z \to w \to x$, we get the following three terms:

$$\frac{\partial z}{\partial x} = \frac{\partial z}{\partial x} + \frac{\partial z}{\partial u}\frac{\partial u}{\partial x} + \frac{\partial z}{\partial w}\frac{\partial w}{\partial x}$$

To resolve the ambiguities of these partial derivatives, we can write

$$\left(\frac{\partial z}{\partial x}\right)_y = \left(\frac{\partial z}{\partial x}\right)_{u,w} + \left(\frac{\partial z}{\partial u}\right)_{w,x}\left(\frac{\partial u}{\partial x}\right)_y + \left(\frac{\partial z}{\partial w}\right)_{u,x}\left(\frac{\partial w}{\partial x}\right)_y$$

or, by labeling the arrows with the names of the functions,

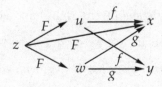

we can also write:

$$\left(\frac{\partial z}{\partial x}\right)_y = \left(\frac{\partial F}{\partial x}\right)_{u,w} + \left(\frac{\partial F}{\partial u}\right)_{w,x}\frac{\partial f}{\partial x} + \left(\frac{\partial F}{\partial w}\right)_{u,x}\frac{\partial g}{\partial x}$$

(b) First, we use the formulas given and write z explicitly in terms of the independent variables x and y:

$$z = F(u, w, x)$$
$$= w^3 - 2ux$$
$$= (y + xy^2)^3 - 2(4xy - x + 1)x$$
$$= (y + xy^2)^3 - 8x^2y + 2x^2 - 2x$$

From this, it's easy to determine $\dfrac{\partial z}{\partial x}$:

$$\frac{\partial z}{\partial x} = 3(y + xy^2)^2(y^2) - 16xy + 4x - 2$$

Now, we can check that our formula from part (a) gives the same result:

$$\left(\frac{\partial F}{\partial x}\right)_{u,w} + \left(\frac{\partial F}{\partial u}\right)_{w,x}\frac{\partial f}{\partial x} + \left(\frac{\partial F}{\partial w}\right)_{u,x}\frac{\partial g}{\partial x} = (-2u) + (-2x)(4y - 1) + (3w^2)(y^2)$$

$$= -2(4xy - x + 1) - 2x(4y - 1) + 3y^2(y + xy^2)^2$$

$$= -16xy + 4x - 2 + 3y^2(y + xy^2)^2$$

Example 3.12   Let $w = f(x, y, z) = yz^2 - x$, where x, y, and z are the following functions of t: $x(t) = t^2$, $y(t) = 2t - 3$, and $z(t) = 1 - t$. Find $\dfrac{dw}{dt}$ at $t = 1$.

Solution: Our schematic of the variables in this case is

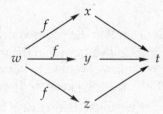

so we can write:

$$\frac{dw}{dt} = \frac{\partial f}{\partial x}\frac{dx}{dt} + \frac{\partial f}{\partial y}\frac{dy}{dt} + \frac{\partial f}{\partial z}\frac{dz}{dt}$$

This gives us:

$$\frac{dw}{dt} = (-1)(2t) + (z^2)(2) + (2yz)(-1)$$

$$= (-2t) + 2(1 - t)^2 - 2(2t - 3)(1 - t)$$

Therefore:

$$\left.\frac{dw}{dt}\right|_{t=1} = \left[(-2t) + 2(1 - t)^2 - 2(2t - 3)(1 - t)\right]\Big|_{t=1} = -2$$

DIRECTIONAL DERIVATIVES AND THE GRADIENT

Consider the surface $z = f(x, y)$, and let $P = (x_0, y_0)$ be a point in the domain of f. What if we were asked to find the value of the derivative of f at P? The derivative should tell us how z changes as we move away from P, but a moment's reflection tells us that the rate at which z changes depends on the direction in which we want to move.

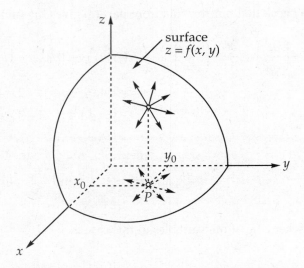

For example, if we move away from P in the positive x direction, then we know the rate of change of z will be the value of f_x at P, and if we move from P in the positive y direction, then the rate of change of z will be the value of f_y at P. But what if we wanted to know how z changes if we move from P in some other direction? We need a way to figure out a general **directional derivative**.

The easiest way to determine a directional derivative is to first form the following vector, whose components are the first-order partial derivatives of f:

$$\left(\frac{\partial f}{\partial x}\right)\hat{\mathbf{i}} + \left(\frac{\partial f}{\partial y}\right)\hat{\mathbf{j}} = \left(\frac{\partial f}{\partial x}, \frac{\partial f}{\partial y}\right)$$

This vector is called the **gradient** of f, and is denoted either by grad f, or more commonly by ∇f (the symbol ∇ is pronounced **del**). The rate of change of f at the point P in the direction of $\mathbf{u}$ (where $\mathbf{u}$ is a vector whose initial point is P) is denoted $D_{\mathbf{u}}f|_P$ and is called the directional derivative of f at P in the direction of $\mathbf{u}$. It's found by evaluating the dot product of the gradient of f at P and the **unit** vector, $\hat{\mathbf{u}}$:

$$D_{\mathbf{u}}f\big|_p = \nabla f\big|_p \bullet \hat{\mathbf{u}}$$

This equation verifies that f_x is just the derivative of f in the $+x$ direction (that is, in the direction $\hat{\mathbf{i}}$), and f_y is the derivative of f in the $+y$ direction (that is, in the direction $\hat{\mathbf{j}}$), since

$$D_{\mathbf{i}}f\big|_p = \nabla f\big|_p \bullet \hat{\mathbf{i}} = (f_x, f_y)\big|_p \bullet (1,0) = f_x\big|_p \quad \text{and} \quad D_{\mathbf{j}}f\big|_p = \nabla f\big|_p \bullet \hat{\mathbf{j}} = (f_x, f_y)\big|_p \bullet (0,1) = f_y\big|_p$$

but the real power of the equation is that it tells us how f will change as we move in *any* direction.

Example 3.13   Let $f(x, y) = \sqrt{81 - x^2 - y^2}$. Find the rate of change of f as we move from the point $P = (1, 4)$ in the direction toward the point $Q = (4, 8)$.

Solution: We want to move in the direction of the vector $\mathbf{u} = \mathbf{PQ} = (4 - 1, 8 - 4) = (3, 4)$. Because this vector has magnitude 5, the unit vector in this direction is $\hat{\mathbf{u}} = (\frac{3}{5}, \frac{4}{5})$. Since the gradient of f is

$$\nabla f = (f_x, f_y) = \left(\frac{-x}{\sqrt{81 - x^2 - y^2}}, \frac{-y}{\sqrt{81 - x^2 - y^2}} \right)$$

our equation for the directional derivative tells us that:

$$D_{\mathbf{u}} f \big|_P = \nabla f \big|_P \bullet \hat{\mathbf{u}} = \left(\frac{-x}{\sqrt{81 - x^2 - y^2}}, \frac{-y}{\sqrt{81 - x^2 - y^2}} \right)\Bigg|_{(1,4)} \bullet (\tfrac{3}{5}, \tfrac{4}{5})$$

$$= (-\tfrac{1}{8}, -\tfrac{1}{2}) \bullet (\tfrac{3}{5}, \tfrac{4}{5})$$

$$= -\tfrac{19}{40}$$

Since $D_{\mathbf{u}} f \big|_P = -\tfrac{19}{40}$, the line that's tangent to the surface at the point $P = (1, 4)$ and parallel to the vector $\mathbf{PQ}$ will descend by $\tfrac{19}{40}$ of a unit as we move from P one unit in the direction $\hat{\mathbf{u}}$.

Now, let's take a closer look at the equation for calculating a directional derivative:

$$D_{\mathbf{u}} f \big|_P = \nabla f \big|_P \bullet \hat{\mathbf{u}}$$

Let θ be the angle between the vectors $\nabla f \big|_P$ and $\hat{\mathbf{u}}$; by definition of the dot product, we can write

$$D_{\mathbf{u}} f \big|_P = \nabla f \big|_P \bullet \hat{\mathbf{u}} = \left\| \nabla f \big|_P \right\| \bullet \|\hat{\mathbf{u}}\| \cos \theta = \left\| \nabla f \big|_P \right\| \bullet \cos \theta$$

since $\|\hat{\mathbf{u}}\| = 1$. The maximum value of $\cos \theta$ is 1, which occurs when $\theta = 0$, so the maximum directional derivative is $\left\| \nabla f \big|_P \right\|$, which occurs when $\hat{\mathbf{u}}$ points in the same direction as $\nabla f \big|_P$. This property of the gradient is important enough to repeat:

The vector ∇f points in the direction in which f increases most rapidly, and the magnitude of ∇f gives the maximum rate of increase.

It's also easy to see that the vector $-\nabla f$ points in the direction in which f *decreases* most rapidly, and the negative of the magnitude of f gives the maximum rate of decrease.

So far, we have discussed directional derivatives and the gradient of functions of two variables, but these ideas carry over to functions of three or more variables. For example, given a function $f(x, y, z)$, its gradient is the vector

$$\nabla f = \frac{\partial f}{\partial x} \hat{\mathbf{i}} + \frac{\partial f}{\partial y} \hat{\mathbf{j}} + \frac{\partial f}{\partial z} \hat{\mathbf{k}} = (f_x, f_y, f_z)$$

and the formula for the directional derivatives of f is exactly the same as before. By looking at functions of three variables, we can derive another important property of the gradient.

Let $f(x, y, z)$ be a given function, and let $P = (x_0, y_0, z_0)$ be a point on the level surface $f(x, y, z) = c$. Since the value of f doesn't change on the surface, the directional derivative of f at P should equal zero no matter in what direction we move . That is, if $\hat{u}$ is any vector tangent to the level surface at P, then $\nabla = 0$. So, according to our formula for the directional derivative, the dot product of the vector ∇f with any vector $\hat{u}$ tangent to the surface is equal to zero. This tells us that ∇f is perpendicular to every tangent vector at P, which means ∇f is perpendicular to the tangent plane at P. In other words:

> For a function $f(x, y, z)$, the vector $\nabla f|_P$ is perpendicular (normal) to the level surface of f that contains P.

By similar reasoning, we can also conclude that:

> For a function $f(x, y)$, the vector $\nabla f|_P$ is perpendicular (normal) to the level curve of f that contains P.

Since the vector $\nabla f|_P = \left(f_x|_P, f_y|_P, f_z|_P \right)$ is normal to the level surface—and, therefore, to the tangent plane—of $f(x, y, z)$ that contains P, we can write the equation of the tangent plane as follows:

$$f_x|_P \bullet (x - x_0) + f_y|_P \bullet (y - y_0) + f_z|_P \bullet (z - z_0) = 0$$

Notice that every surface whose equation is given in the form $z = f(x, y)$ can be rewritten as $f(x, y) - z = 0$, which is a level surface of the function $g(x, y, z) = f(x, y) - z$, whose gradient is $\nabla g = (f_x, f_y, -1)$. So, the equation of the tangent plane to the level surface $g(x, y, z) = 0$ is

$$f_x|_P \bullet (x - x_0) + f_y|_P \bullet (y - y_0) - (z - z_0) = 0$$

which is equivalent to the equation of the tangent plane to the surface $z = f(x, y)$ that we gave earlier.

Example 3.14   Use the gradient to find the equation of the tangent plane to the surface $x^2 z - y^3 z^5 + xy = 9$, at the point $P = (1, 2, -1)$.

Solution: If $f(x, y, z) = x^2 z - y^3 z^5 + xy$, then the given equation represents the level surface of f that contains the point P. Since the gradient of f is

$$\nabla f = (f_x, f_y, f_z) = (2xz + y, -3y^2 z^5 + x, x^2 - 5y^3 z^4)$$

the vector $\nabla f|_P = \nabla f|_{(1,2,-1)} = (0, 13, -39)$ is normal to the tangent plane at P. Therefore, the equation of the tangent plane is

$$0(x - 1) + 13(y - 2) - 39(z + 1) = 0$$

which simplifies to $y - 3z = 5$. Compare this solution to the one given for Example 3.9.

MAX/MIN PROBLEMS

We can locate points at which a function of one variable, $f(x)$, attains a local maximum or minimum value by first finding its critical points (the points at which $f'(x) = 0$ or $f'(x)$ is undefined). Once we find the critical points, we use the second-derivative test to classify them. Remember that if $x = x_0$ is a critical point of $f(x)$, then $f''(x_0) < 0$ means that f has a local maximum at $x = x_0$, and $f''(x_0) > 0$ means that f has a local minimum at $x = x_0$. (If $f''(x_0) = 0$, then the test is inconclusive: f could have a local maximum, a local minimum, or neither, at $x = x_0$.) We now want to extend these ideas to maximize or minimize a function of two variables.

Let's assume that we're given a function $f(x, y)$ and asked to find its extreme values. If f has a maximum (or minimum) at $P_0 = (x_0, y_0)$, then the curve $z = f(x, y_0)$ has a maximum (or minimum) at $x = x_0$, so $\frac{\partial f}{\partial x} = 0$ at $x = x_0$; it will also be true that the curve $z = f(x_0, y)$ has a maximum (or minimum) at $y = y_0$, so $\frac{\partial f}{\partial y} = 0$ at $y = y_0$. Therefore, we say that P_0 is a critical point of $f(x, y)$ if the first partial derivatives of f are both equal to zero there:

$$P_0 \text{ is a critical point of } f(x, y) \text{ if: } \left(\frac{\partial f}{\partial x}\right)_{P_0} = 0 \ \text{ and } \ \left(\frac{\partial f}{\partial y}\right)_{P_0} = 0$$

In the one-variable case, a critical point doesn't have to be the location of a maximum or a minimum; perhaps the simplest example of this is the function $f(x) = x^3$. Although its derivative equals zero at $x = 0$, the point $(0, 0)$ is neither a local maximum nor a local minimum; it's an inflection point. The same kind of behavior can be exhibited by a function of two variables.

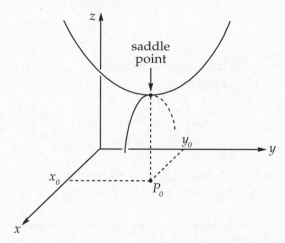

For example, if, at $P_0 = (x_0, y_0)$, the curve $z = f(x, y_0)$ has a maximum at $x = x_0$, but the curve $z = f(x_0, y)$ has a minimum at $y = y_0$ (or vice versa), then we say that $f(x, y)$ has a **saddle point** at P_0. Although P_0 is a critical point, a saddle point is neither a local maximum nor a local minimum for the function.

Here's the **second-derivative test** for classifying a critical point, $P_0 = (x_0, y_0)$, of a function $f(x, y)$. Let Δ be the determinant of the following 2-by-2 matrix, which contains the second partial derivatives of f, evaluated at P_0:

$$\Delta = \det \begin{bmatrix} f_{xx} & f_{xy} \\ f_{yx} & f_{yy} \end{bmatrix}_{P_0} = f_{xx}(P_0)f_{yy}(P_0) - [f_{xy}(P_0)]^2$$

(This matrix is called the **Hessian matrix** of $f(x, y)$, and its determinant, Δ, is called the **Hessian** of f. We're assuming that the mixed second partials of f are continuous at P_0, so $f_{xy} = f_{yx}$.) Then the following statements hold:

If $\Delta > 0$ and $f_{xx}(P_0) < 0$, then f attains a local maximum at P_0.

If $\Delta > 0$ and $f_{xx}(P_0) > 0$, then f attains a local minimum at P_0.

If $\Delta < 0$, then f has a saddle point at P_0.

If $\Delta = 0$, then no conclusion can be drawn (any of these behaviors is possible).

Example 3.15 Locate and classify the critical points of the function:

$$f(x, y) = x^2 + y^3 - 6xy$$

Solution: The first step is to find f_x and f_y and set both equal to zero:

$$f_x = 2x - 6y = 0$$
$$f_y = 3y^2 - 6x = 0$$

From the first equation, we see that $x = 3y$, and substituting this into the second equation gives us:

$$3y^2 - 6(3y) = 0$$
$$y^2 - 6y = 0$$
$$y(y - 6) = 0$$
$$y = 0, 6$$

Therefore, the function has two critical points, $P_1 = (0, 0)$ and $P_2 = (18, 6)$. To classify them, we figure out the Hessian of f:

$$\Delta = \det \begin{bmatrix} f_{xx} & f_{xy} \\ f_{yx} & f_{yy} \end{bmatrix} = \det \begin{bmatrix} 2 & -6 \\ -6 & 6y \end{bmatrix} = 12y - 36$$

The value of Δ at $P_1 = (0, 0)$ is $12(0) - 36 = -36$; since $\Delta < 0$, P_1 is a saddle point. The value of Δ at $P_2 = (18, 6)$ is $12(6) - 36 = 36$; since $\Delta > 0$ and $f_{xx} = 2 > 0$, the point P_2 is a minimum.

Example 3.16 Let S be the closed square region:

$$S = \{(x, y): 0 \le x \le 2 \text{ and } 0 \le y \le 2\}$$

Determine the absolute minimum and maximum values on S of the function:

$$f(x,y) = x^2 + 4xy - y^2 - 5x$$

Solution: In the last chapter, we learned that every continuous function on a closed interval attains both an absolute maximum and an absolute minimum value; these values can be assumed either at critical points or at the endpoints of the interval. This example illustrates the corresponding property for functions of two variables. Since S is closed (because it contains its boundaries) and bounded (because it's a subset of a circular region of finite radius), any continuous function defined on S is guaranteed to attain an absolute maximum and an absolute minimum value, and these values may occur either at critical points or at points on the boundary of S. So our first step is to find the critical points. Setting both f_x and f_y equal to zero gives us:

$$f_x = 2x + 4y - 5 = 0$$
$$f_y = 4x - 2y = 0$$

Solving this pair of simultaneous equations yields the critical point, $P = (\frac{1}{2}, 1)$, which is in the interior of the square S. The value of f at P is $f(\frac{1}{2}, 1) = -\frac{5}{4}$. We don't need to classify this critical point because now we'll examine the behavior of f on the boundaries of S. Along the left edge of the square, x is always equal to 0, so $f(x, y) = f(0, y) = -y^2$. On the closed interval $0 \leq y \leq 2$, this function has an absolute maximum at $y = 0$ (where its value is 0), and an absolute minimum at $y = 2$ (where its value is –4). Next, along the top edge, y is always equal to 2, so $f(x, y) = f(x, 2) = x^2 + 3x - 4$. This function has a critical point at $x = \frac{-3}{2}$, which is on the top edge, but not withinin S, so we just evaluate the function at the endpoints of the top edge: $f(0, 2) = -4$, and $f(2, 2) = 6$. Along the right edge, x is always equal to 2, so $f(x, y) = f(2, y) = -6 + 8y - y^2$. This function has a critical point at $y = 4$, which is not in S, so we just evaluate the function at the endpoints of the right edge: $f(2, 0) = -6$, and $f(2, 2) = 6$. Finally, along the bottom edge, y is always equal to 0, so $f(x, y) = f(x, 0) = x^2 - 5x$. This function has a critical point at $x = \frac{5}{2}$, which is not in S, so we just evaluate the function at the endpoints of the bottom edge: $f(0, 0) = 0$, and $f(2, 0) = -6$. We can now say that the absolute maximum value of f on S is 6, attained at the point (2, 2), and the absolute minimum value of f on S is –6, attained at the point (2, 0). [By the way, the second-derivative test tells us that the critical point $P = (\frac{1}{2}, 1)$ is a saddle point.]

MAX/MIN PROBLEMS WITH A CONSTRAINT

Often, a question will ask us to maximize or minimize a function subject to a constraint. For example, "What is the maximum value of the function $f(x, y) = xy$ subject to the constraint $x^2 + y^2 = 1$?" The constraint equation limits the possible choices of x and y, so the question really asks, "For all pairs (x, y) such that $x^2 + y^2 = 1$, which pair(s) maximize the value of $f(x, y) = xy$?" One way to solve this problem is to use the constraint equation to rewrite the function to be maximized or minimized in terms of just one variable, and then proceed as we did in the one-variable case. For example, solving this constraint equation for y gives us:

$$y = \pm\sqrt{1 - x^2}$$

Let's ignore the minus sign for the moment, and substitute $y = \sqrt{1 - x^2}$ into $f(x, y) = xy$:

$$g(x) = f(x, \sqrt{1 - x^2}) = x\sqrt{1 - x^2}, \text{ for } -1 \leq x \leq 1$$

To maximize g, we first set its derivative equal to zero and solve for x:

$$g'(x) = \frac{-x^2}{\sqrt{1-x^2}} + \sqrt{1-x^2} = 0$$

$$-x^2 + (1-x^2) = 0$$

$$x = \pm\frac{1}{\sqrt{2}}$$

(Had we used $y = -\sqrt{1-x^2}$, we would have found the same critical values of x.) Since $g(x) = 0$ at both endpoints of the closed interval $-1 \leq x \leq 1$, we can say that $g(x)$ attains a maximum value of $\frac{1}{2}$ at $x = \frac{1}{\sqrt{2}}$ and a minimum value of $-\frac{1}{2}$ at $x = -\frac{1}{\sqrt{2}}$. Since $y = \pm\sqrt{1-x^2}$, we see that there are four critical points:

$$P_1 = \left(\frac{1}{\sqrt{2}}, \frac{1}{\sqrt{2}}\right), \; P_2 = \left(-\frac{1}{\sqrt{2}}, \frac{1}{\sqrt{2}}\right), \; P_3 = \left(\frac{1}{\sqrt{2}}, -\frac{1}{\sqrt{2}}\right), \; P_4 = \left(-\frac{1}{\sqrt{2}}, -\frac{1}{\sqrt{2}}\right)$$

We can now conclude that, subject to the given constraint, the function f attains a maximum value of $\frac{1}{2}$ at P_1 and P_4 and a minimum value of $-\frac{1}{2}$ at P_2 and P_3.

THE LAGRANGE MULTIPLIER METHOD

Another method of maximizing or minimizing a function subject to a constraint, and one that's especially useful if the constraint equation cannot be easily solved for one of the variables, is known as the **Lagrange multiplier method**. Let's assume that we're asked to find the extreme values of $f(x, y)$ subject to the constraint $g(x, y) = c$ (where c is a constant). If M is an extreme value of f—attained at the point $P = (x_0, y_0)$—then the level curve $f(x, y) = M$ and the curve $g(x, y) = c$ share the same tangent line at P.

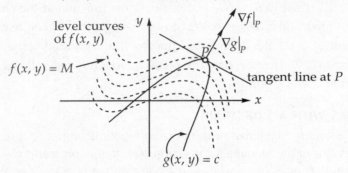

Now, because these curves share the tangent line at P, they also share the normal line at P. Since the vector ∇f is normal to the curve $f(x, y) = M$ and the vector ∇g is normal to the curve $g(x, y) = c$, one of these vectors must be a scalar multiple of the other; that is,

$$\nabla f = \lambda \nabla g$$

for some scalar assuming that $\nabla g \neq 0$. The scalar λ is called the **Lagrange multiplier**. Its value is unimportant; it only serves to help us figure out the critical point P.

Example 3.17 Use the Lagrange multiplier method to determine the extreme values of the function $f(x, y) = xy$, subject to the constraint $x^2 + y^2 = 1$.

Solution: Since the constraint is $x^2 + y^2 = 1$, we set $g(x, y)$ equal to $x^2 + y^2$. The equation $\nabla f = \lambda \nabla g$ becomes

$$(y, x) = \lambda(2x, 2y)$$

which is equivalent to the pair of equations

$$y = \lambda \cdot 2x$$
$$x = \lambda \cdot 2y$$

Since the first equation says that $\lambda = \dfrac{y}{2x}$ and the second equation says that $\lambda = \dfrac{x}{2y}$, we know that $\dfrac{y}{2x} = \dfrac{x}{2y}$, so $x^2 = y^2$. (We're assuming here that neither x nor y is 0; if x or y were equal to zero, then the value of the function f would be zero. We'll see that 0 is neither a maximum nor a minimum value after we find the critical points.) Substituting this into the constraint, $x^2 + y^2 = 1$, gives us $x^2 + x^2 = 1$, so $x = \pm\dfrac{1}{\sqrt{2}}$. Therefore $y = \pm\dfrac{1}{\sqrt{2}}$, and we have four critical points:

$$P_1 = \left(\frac{1}{\sqrt{2}}, \frac{1}{\sqrt{2}}\right), \; P_2 = \left(-\frac{1}{\sqrt{2}}, \frac{1}{\sqrt{2}}\right),$$

$$P_3 = \left(\frac{1}{\sqrt{2}}, -\frac{1}{\sqrt{2}}\right), \; P_4 = \left(-\frac{1}{\sqrt{2}}, -\frac{1}{\sqrt{2}}\right)$$

We can now conclude that, subject to the given constraint, the function f attains a maximum value of $\dfrac{1}{2}$ at P_1 and P_4, and a minimum value of $-\dfrac{1}{2}$ at P_2 and P_3, just as we found on the previous page.

LINE INTEGRALS

When we integrate a function $f(x)$ of one variable from, say, $x = a$ to $x = b$, we can interpret the integration as taking place over the path on the x-axis from a to b, and the value of the integral as giving the area bounded by the curve $y = f(x)$ over this path, $[a, b]$:

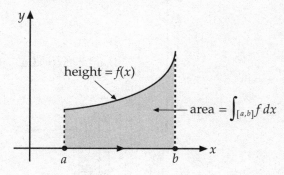

But we can also integrate functions over other paths, not just straight-line paths along the x-axis. The result is called a **curve**, **contour**, or **path integral**, or, most commonly, a **line integral** (even though the path does not need to be a straight line).

LINE INTEGRALS WITH RESPECT TO ARC LENGTH

To see how these integrals can be defined, let's begin by considering a function $f(x, y)$ and a smooth curve, C, in the x-y plane. [A curve given parametrically by the vector equation $\mathbf{r} = \mathbf{r}(t) = ((x(t), y(t))$ is said to be **smooth** if the derivative $\mathbf{r}'(t)$ is continuous and nonzero. To say that C is **piecewise smooth** means that it's composed of a finite number of smooth curves joined at consecutive endpoints.] Imagine breaking C into n tiny segments, of arc length Δs_i.

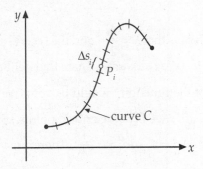

On each of these tiny pieces, choose any point $P_i = (x_i, y_i)$, then multiply $f(x_i, y_i)$—the value of the function at P_i—by the length Δs_i, and form the following sum:

$$\sum_{i=1}^{n} f(x_i, y_i) \Delta s_i$$

If the value of this sum approaches a finite, limiting value as $n \to \infty$, then the result is called the **line integral of f along C with respect to arc length**, and is written as:

$$\int_C f \, ds$$

What does the value of this integral mean geometrically? It's the area of the region whose base is the curve C and whose height above each point (x, y) is given by the value of the function, $f(x, y)$. That is, it's the area of the vertical curtain or fence (portion of the vertical cylinder) whose base is C and whose height at each point (x, y) is $f(x, y)$:

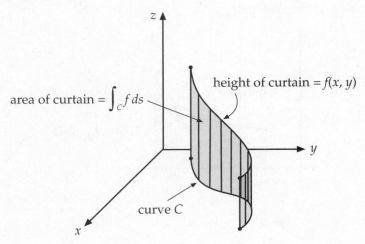

To actually evaluate this line integral, first parameterize the curve C:

$$C = \begin{cases} x = x(t) \\ y = y(t) \end{cases} \quad \text{for } a \le t \le b \quad (\text{or } a \xrightarrow{t} b)$$

We consider the curve C to be **directed**; that is, we think of the curve as being traced in a definite direction, which we call the **positive** direction. By writing $a \xrightarrow{t} b$ in the parameterization, we're saying that the parameter t runs *from a to b*, so $A = (x(a), y(a))$ is the **initial point** and $B = (x(b), y(b))$ is the **final point** of the curve, which gives C a positive direction. Now, since $(ds)^2 = (dx)^2 + (dy)^2$, we can write

$$\frac{ds}{dt} = \pm\sqrt{\left(\frac{dx}{dt}\right)^2 + \left(\frac{dy}{dt}\right)^2} = \pm\sqrt{[x'(t)]^2 + [y'(t)]^2}$$

where we use the $+$ sign if the parameter t increases in the positive direction on C and the $-$ sign if t decreases in the positive direction on C. We then have:

$$\int_C f\, ds = \int_a^b f(x(t), y(t)) \frac{ds}{dt}\, dt$$

Example 3.18 Determine the value of the line integral of the function $f(x, y) = x + y^2$ over the quarter circle $x^2 + y^2 = 4$ in the first quadrant, from $(2, 0)$ to $(0, 2)$.

Solution: First we parameterize the curve. Since C is directed counterclockwise, we can write:

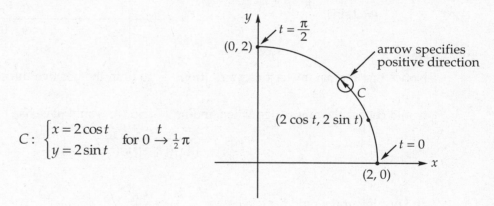

$$C: \begin{cases} x = 2\cos t \\ y = 2\sin t \end{cases} \quad \text{for } 0 \xrightarrow{t} \tfrac{1}{2}\pi$$

Next, we use the parameterization to find $\dfrac{ds}{dt}$:

$$\frac{ds}{dt} = +\sqrt{[x'(t)]^2 + [y'(t)]^2}$$
$$= \sqrt{(-2\sin t)^2 + (2\cos t)^2}$$
$$= 2$$

where we choose the + sign, since in our parameterization, t increases (from 0 to $\frac{\pi}{2}$) in the positive direction on C. This gives us:

$$\int_C f \, ds = \int_a^b f(x(t), y(t)) \cdot \frac{ds}{dt} \, dt$$

$$= \int_0^{\pi/2} (2\cos t + 4\sin^2 t) \cdot 2 \, dt$$

$$= 4\int_0^{\pi/2} (\cos t + 2\sin^2 t) \, dt$$

$$= 4\left[\sin t + t - \tfrac{1}{2}\sin 2t \right]_0^{\pi/2}$$

$$= 2(2 + \pi)$$

Let's see what the value of this line integral would have been if we had traversed the curve C in the opposite direction; that is, if we had chosen the positive direction for C to be clockwise, from (0, 2) to (2, 0). In this case, we could parameterize the curve as follows:

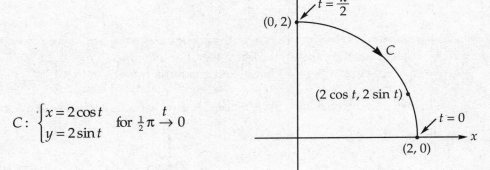

$$C: \begin{cases} x = 2\cos t \\ y = 2\sin t \end{cases} \text{ for } \tfrac{1}{2}\pi \xrightarrow{t} 0$$

Notice that the parameter t *decreases* (from $\frac{\pi}{2}$ to 0) in the positive direction on C, so we would choose the minus sign when finding $\frac{ds}{dt}$. So we would have had

$$\frac{ds}{dt} = -\sqrt{[x'(t)]^2 + [y'(t)]^2}$$

$$= -2$$

and our integral would have been

$$\int_C f \, ds = \int_a^b f(x(t), y(t)) \cdot \frac{ds}{dt} \, dt$$

$$= \int_{\pi/2}^0 (2\cos t + 4\sin^2 t) \cdot (-2) \, dt$$

$$= -\int_{\pi/2}^0 (2\cos t + 4\sin^2 t) \cdot 2 \, dt$$

$$= 4\int_0^{\pi/2} (\cos t + 2\sin^2 t) \, dt$$

$$= 2(2 + \pi)$$

just as we found before. This illustrates an important property of line integrals with respect to arc length: *The value of $\int_C f \, ds$ does not depend on the orientation or parameterization of C.*

Line integrals with respect to arc length can also be easily defined over curves in 3-space. If $f(x, y, z)$ is a function defined on a smooth curve

$$C: \begin{cases} x = x(t) \\ y = y(t) \quad \text{for } a \xrightarrow{t} b \\ z = z(t) \end{cases}$$

then

$$\int_C f \, ds = \int_a^b f(x(t), y(t), z(t)) \frac{ds}{dt} \, dt$$

where

$$\frac{ds}{dt} = \pm \sqrt{\left(\frac{dx}{dt}\right)^2 + \left(\frac{dy}{dt}\right)^2 + \left(\frac{dz}{dt}\right)^2}$$

In this case, one interpretation of the value of the line integral involves thinking of C as a curved wire and $f(x, y, z)$ as its linear density (mass per unit length); $\int_C f \, ds$ then gives the total mass of the wire.

THE LINE INTEGRAL OF A VECTOR FIELD

Now, we'll look at another kind of line integral: the line integral of a vector field. We'll define this line integral in two dimensions; the generalization to three dimensions follows as easily as it did in the case of a line integral with respect to arc length.

A **vector field** is a vector-valued function. Let D be a region of the x-y plane on which a pair of continuous functions, $M(x, y)$ and $N(x, y)$, are both defined. Then the function, **F**, that assigns to each point (x, y) in D the vector

$$\mathbf{F}(x, y) = M(x, y)\hat{\mathbf{i}} + N(x, y)\hat{\mathbf{j}} = \big(M(x, y), N(x, y)\big)$$

is a continuous vector field on D. Now, if C is an oriented, piecewise smooth curve in D, we want to define the line integral of **F** along C. Let

$$\mathbf{r}(t) = x(t)\hat{\mathbf{i}} + y(t)\hat{\mathbf{j}} = \big(x(t), y(t)\big), \quad \text{for } a \xrightarrow{t} b$$

be a parameterization of the curve C. Then the line integral of the vector field **F** along C is defined as:

$$\int_C \mathbf{F} \cdot d\mathbf{r} = \int_a^b \mathbf{F}(\mathbf{r}(t)) \cdot \mathbf{r}'(t) \, dt$$

What's the interpretation of the value of this integral? Consider **F** a force field, and imagine a particle moving along the curve C. Along each infinitesimal piece—specified by the vector $d\mathbf{r}$—of the curve C, the field **F** is approximately constant, so the work, dW, done by **F** as the particle undergoes the displacement $d\mathbf{r}$ is equal to the dot product $\mathbf{F} \cdot d\mathbf{r}$.

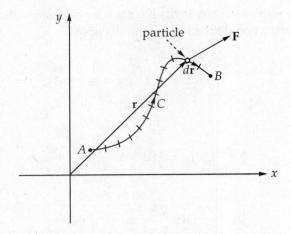

Adding up (that is, integrating) all these contributions gives the total work done by **F** as the particle moves along the entire curve:

$$W = \int_C dW = \int_C \mathbf{F} \bullet d\mathbf{r}$$

To actually evaluate this integral, we proceed as before. First we parameterize the curve,

$$\mathbf{r}(t) = x(t)\hat{\mathbf{i}} + y(t)\hat{\mathbf{j}} = \big(x(t), y(t)\big), \quad \text{for } a \xrightarrow{t} b$$

then we substitute, to write everything in terms of t:

$$
\begin{aligned}
\int_C \mathbf{F} \bullet d\mathbf{r} &= \int_a^b \mathbf{F}(\mathbf{r}(t)) \bullet \mathbf{r}'(t)\,dt \\
&= \int_a^b \mathbf{F}\big(x(t), y(t)\big) \bullet \big(x'(t), y'(t)\big)\,dt \\
&= \int_a^b \big(M(x(t), y(t)),\ N(x(t), y(t))\big) \bullet \big(x'(t), y'(t)\big)\,dt \\
&= \int_a^b \Big[M\big(x(t), y(t)\big)x'(t) + N\big(x(t), y(t)\big)y'(t)\Big]\,dt
\end{aligned}
$$

Since $dx = x'(t)dt$ and $dy = y'(t)dt$, the last equation is also commonly written in the abbreviated form:

$$\int_C \mathbf{F} \bullet d\mathbf{r} = \int_C M\,dx + N\,dy$$

Example 3.19   Evaluate the line integral

$$\int_C (7y^3 - x)\, dx + (x^2 + 2y - 1)\, dy$$

(a) if C is the portion of the parabola $y = x^2$ from $(0, 0)$ to $(1, 1)$;

(b) if C is the straight-line path from $(0, 0)$ to $(1, 1)$.

Solution:

(a)   We can parameterize the curve as follows:

$$C: \begin{cases} x = t \\ y = t^2 \end{cases} \text{ for } 0 \xrightarrow{t} 1$$

With this parameterization, we have $dx = dt$ and $dy = 2t\, dt$, so:

$$\int_C (7y^3 - x)\, dx + (x^2 + 2y - 1)\, dy = \int_0^1 \left(7(t^2)^3 - t\right) dt + \left(t^2 + 2t^2 - 1\right) \cdot 2t\, dt$$

$$= \int_0^1 (7t^6 + 6t^3 - 3t)\, dt$$

$$= t^7 + \tfrac{3}{2}t^4 - \tfrac{3}{2}t^2 \Big]_0^1$$

$$= 1$$

(b)   We can parameterize the curve as follows:

$$C: \begin{cases} x = t \\ y = t \end{cases} \text{ for } 0 \xrightarrow{t} 1$$

With this parameterization, we have $dx = dt$ and $dy = dt$, so:

$$\int_C (7y^3 - x)\, dx + (x^2 + 2y - 1)\, dy = \int_0^1 \left(7t^3 - t\right) dt + \left(t^2 + 2t - 1\right) dt$$

$$= \int_0^1 (7t^3 + t^2 + t - 1)\, dt$$

$$= \tfrac{7}{4}t^4 + \tfrac{1}{3}t^3 + \tfrac{1}{2}t^2 - t \Big]_0^1$$

$$= \tfrac{19}{12}$$

This example shows that, for a given vector field **F**, the value of $\int_C \mathbf{F} \cdot d\mathbf{r}$ depends, in general, not just on the endpoints of C, but also on the choice of the path.

Example 3.20   Evaluate the line integral

$$\int_C y^2 \, dx + (2xy - 1) \, dy$$

along each of the paths from $A = (2, 0)$ to $B = (0, 2)$ shown in this figure:

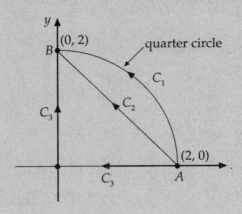

Solution:

(a)   We can parameterize the circular arc C_1 as we did earlier:

$$C_1 : \begin{cases} x = 2\cos t \\ y = 2\sin t \end{cases} \text{ for } 0 \xrightarrow{t} \tfrac{1}{2}\pi$$

Since $dx = (-2 \sin t) \, dt$ and $dy = (2 \cos t) \, dt$, the line integral along C_1 becomes:

$$\int_{C_1} y^2 \, dx + (2xy - 1) \, dy = \int_0^{\pi/2} (4\sin^2 t)(-2\sin t \, dt) + (8\cos t \sin t - 1)(2\cos t \, dt)$$

$$= \int_0^{\pi/2} \left[-8(1 - \cos^2 t)\sin t + (16\cos^2 t \sin t - 2\cos t) \right] dt$$

$$= 8\cos t - 8\cos^3 t - 2\sin t \Big]_0^{\pi/2}$$

$$= -2$$

(b)   We can parameterize the straight line C_2 as follows:

$$C_2 : \begin{cases} x = 2 - t \\ y = t \end{cases} \text{ for } 0 \xrightarrow{t} 2$$

Because we now have $dx = -dt$ and $dy = dt$, the line integral along C_2 is:

$$\int_{C_2} y^2 \, dx + (2xy-1) \, dy = \int_0^2 (t^2)(-dt) + [2(2-t)t - 1] \, dt$$

$$= \int_0^2 (-3t^2 + 4t - 1) \, dt$$

$$= -t^3 + 2t^2 - t \Big]_0^2$$

$$= -2$$

(c) The path C_3 is a piecewise smooth curve, composed of two smooth curves that meet at a corner. The first, which we'll call $C_{3\text{-}1}$, is the straight-line path along the x-axis from A to the origin; the second, $C_{3\text{-}2}$, is the straight-line path along the y-axis from the origin to B. The line integral along C_3 is the sum of the line integrals along these two paths, which we can parameterize as follows:

$$C_{3\text{-}1}: \begin{cases} x = t \\ y = 0 \end{cases} \text{ for } 2 \xrightarrow{t} 0 \quad \text{ and } \quad C_{3\text{-}2}: \begin{cases} x = 0 \\ y = t \end{cases} \text{ for } 0 \xrightarrow{t} 2$$

Along $C_{3\text{-}1}$, we have $dx = dt$ and $dy = 0$; along $C_{3\text{-}2}$, we have $dx = 0$ and $dy = dt$, so:

$$\int_{C_3} y^2 \, dx + (2xy-1) \, dy = \int_{C_{3\text{-}1}} y^2 \, dx + (2xy-1) \, dy + \int_{C_{3\text{-}2}} y^2 \, dx + (2xy-1) \, dy$$

$$= 0 + \int_0^2 (-1) \, dt$$

$$= -t \Big]_0^2$$

$$= -2$$

Notice that although we had a different path in each part, all three of these line integrals had the same value. We might guess that—unlike the line integral in Example 3.19—the line integral from A to B in this example *doesn't* depend on the choice of path. This guess would turn out to be correct, and in the next section, we'll learn why.

THE FUNDAMENTAL THEOREM OF CALCULUS FOR LINE INTEGRALS

Simply put, the reason that the line integral in Example 3.20 did not depend on the choice of the path was because the vector field we were integrating,

$$\mathbf{F}(x,y) = M \, dx + N \, dy = y^2 \, dx + (2xy - 1) \, dy$$

is a **gradient field**. That is, $\mathbf{F}$ is equal to the gradient of a *scalar field* (that is, of a real-valued function). In this case, it's easy to see that $\mathbf{F}$ is equal to ∇f where

$$f(x, y) = xy^2 - y$$

(we could also add any constant to this function and not change the fact that $\mathbf{F} = \nabla f$). A function f, such that $\mathbf{F} = \nabla f$, is called a **potential** for $\mathbf{F}$. The **Fundamental theorem of calculus for line integrals** says that the line integral of a gradient field depends only on the endpoints of the path, not the choice of the path. More precisely, it says that if C is any piecewise smooth curve oriented from the initial point A to the final point B, and f is a continuously differentiable function defined on C, then:

$$\int_C \nabla f \cdot d\mathbf{r} = f(B) - f(A)$$

Notice the similarity between this equation and the corresponding equation for the Fundamental theorem of calculus we reviewed in the last chapter:

$$\int_a^b \frac{df}{dx}\,dx = f(b) - f(a)$$

Using the Fundamental theorem, we could evaluate the line integral of Example 3.20 very easily. Notice that every path in that example connected the initial point, $A = (2, 0)$, to the final point, $B = (0, 2)$; so, because $\mathbf{F} = \nabla f$, where we can take $f(x, y) = xy^2 - y$, we have

$$\oint_c y^2\,dx + (2xy - 1)\,dy = \int_{A=(2,0)}^{B=(0,2)} \nabla(xy^2 - y) \bullet d\mathbf{r}$$

$$= \left[xy^2 - y \right]_{(2,0)}^{(0,2)}$$

$$= (0 - 2) - (0 - 0)$$

$$= -2$$

which is the value we obtained for every path in that example. A vector field $\mathbf{F}$ that has the property that the value of $\oint_C \mathbf{F} \bullet d\mathbf{r}$ depends only on the initial and final points of C (but not on the choice of the path C), is called **conservative**. So, if $\mathbf{F}$ is a gradient field, then $\mathbf{F}$ is conservative.

But how do we know if $\mathbf{F}$ is a gradient field? Remember that, given $f(x, y)$, its gradient is $\nabla f = (f_x, f_y)$. So, if $\mathbf{F} = (M, N)$ is a gradient field, then $M = f_x$ and $N = f_y$ for some function f. If we were to differentiate M with respect to y, we'd get $M_y = f_{xy}$; and if we were to differentiate N with respect to x, we'd get $N_x = f_{yx}$. Assuming that these mixed partials are continuous, we know they're identical; that is, $f_{xy} = f_{yx}$, so $M_y = N_x$. Therefore, we can say that if $\mathbf{F} = (M, N)$ is the gradient of a scalar field $f(x, y)$, then it must be true that $M_y = N_x$. This condition is *necessary* for $\mathbf{F}$ to be a gradient field, meaning that if $M_y \ne N_x$, then $\mathbf{F}$ is definitely not a gradient field. However, the condition $M_y = N_x$ is not *sufficient* to conclude that $\mathbf{F}$ is a gradient field; an additional, mild hypothesis is required, one that we'll give in the last section.

The path over which a line integral is evaluated can be **closed**; that is, its final point can also be its initial point. When a line integral is taken around a closed curve C, the notation for the integral is changed slightly. To indicate that C is closed, a small circle is drawn on the integral sign, like this:

$$\oint_C \mathbf{F} \bullet d\mathbf{r} \qquad \text{or} \qquad \oint_C M\,dx + N\,dy$$

If $\mathbf{F}$ is a gradient field, the value of this line integral is easy to figure out. Using the Fundamental theorem, we know that:

$$\oint_C \mathbf{F} \bullet d\mathbf{r} = \oint_C \nabla f \bullet d\mathbf{r} = f(B) - f(A)$$

But since the curve is closed, the final point, B, is the same as the initial point, A. Because $A = B$, the right-hand side of the equation above, $f(B) - f(A)$, is equal to zero. Therefore, we can say that *if $\mathbf{F}$ is a gradient field, then $\oint_C \mathbf{F} \bullet d\mathbf{r}$ equals zero for every closed path C.* The converse is also true.

Example 3.21   Let C be the boundary of the square whose vertices are $(0, 0)$, $(2, 0)$, $(2, 2)$, and $(0, 2)$, taken counterclockwise. Evaluate each of the following line integrals around C:

(a) $\displaystyle\oint_C (x + 2y)\,dx + (x - 3y^2)\,dy$

(b) $\displaystyle\oint_C (x + y)\,dx + (x - 3y^2)\,dy$

Solution:

(a)   Notice that $M_y = 2$ and $N_x = 1$; since $M_y \neq N_x$, we know that $(M, N) = (x + 2y, x - 3y^2)$ is not a gradient field, so we can't expect its integral around the closed path, C, simply to be zero. We have to do the calculation (since we can't apply the Fundamental theorem), so we begin by parametrizing the four sides of the square, as shown:

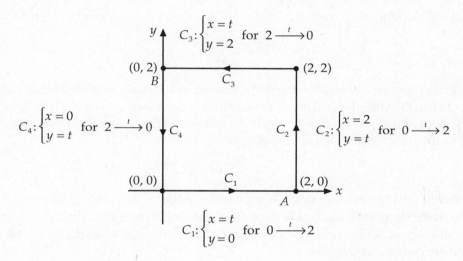

Since $\displaystyle\oint_C = \int_{C_1} + \int_{C_2} + \int_{C_3} + \int_{C_4}$, we have:

$$\oint_C (x + 2y)\,dx + (x - 3y^2)\,dy = \underbrace{\int_0^2 (t)\,dt}_{\text{over } C_1} + \underbrace{\int_0^2 (2 - 3t^2)\,dt}_{\text{over } C_2} + \underbrace{\int_2^0 (t + 4)\,dt}_{\text{over } C_3} + \underbrace{\int_2^0 (-3t^2)\,dt}_{\text{over } C_4}$$

$$= \int_0^2 [t + (2 - 3t^2) - (t + 4) - (-3t^2)]\,dt$$

$$= \int_0^2 (-2)\,dt$$

$$= -4$$

It's worth noting that, if the positive direction of this path C instead had been clockwise, the value of the line integral would have been 4. For line integrals of vector fields, the orientation of the curve is important. Let C be a path (closed or not) with a given orientation; if $-C$ denotes the same path with the opposite orientation, then the following equation is always true:

$$\int_{-C} \mathbf{F} \cdot d\mathbf{r} = -\int_C \mathbf{F} \cdot d\mathbf{r}$$

(b) This part's easy. $(M, N) = (x + y, x - 3y^2)$ is a gradient field (notice that $M_y = N_x = 1$), because it's equal to the gradient of $f(x, y) = \frac{1}{2}x^2 + xy - y^3$. Since C is a closed path, the integral of the gradient field (M, N) around C is zero. No calculation is needed.

DOUBLE INTEGRALS

Given a function of one variable, $f(x)$, and an interval I of the real line, we can form the (single) integral of $f(x)$ over I. The basic interpretation of the value of this integral is the area of the region bounded by I and $y = f(x)$, the graph of the function. By analogy, if we're given a function of two variables, $f(x, y)$, and a region R in the x-y plane, we can form a **double integral** of $f(x, y)$ over R. In this case, the basic interpretation of the value of the integral is the volume of the 3-dimensional region bounded by R and by $z = f(x, y)$, the graph of the function. Here's the intuitive way to define this double integral: We imagine splitting the region R in the x-y plane into n small rectangles. In rectangle number i, whose sides have lengths Δx_i and Δy_i, we choose any point $P_i = (x_i, y_i)$ and evaluate the function f at P_i. Multiplying $f(x_i, y_i)$ by $\Delta A_i = (\Delta x_i)(\Delta y_i)$, the area of the rectangle, gives ΔV_i, the volume of the narrow column whose base is the rectangle and whose height is $f(P_i)$. Adding all these contributions gives the approximate value of the total volume, V, of the solid region bounded by the region R and the surface $z = f(x, y)$:

$$V \approx \sum_{i=1}^{n} f(x_i, y_i) \Delta A_i$$

When we pass to the limit, allowing the number of little rectangles to go to infinity and ensuring that the maximum length of the diagonal of any of these little rectangles goes to zero, if this sum approaches a finite, limiting value, it will give the exact volume, V, of the solid that's bounded by the region R and the surface $z = f(x, y)$. This is written as the double integral of f over R:

$$V = \iint\limits_{R} f(x, y)\, dA$$

As we've seen before with single integrals, the value of this integral gives an algebraic sum if the function being integrated assumes both positive and negative values. That is, V is the algebraic volume of the solid region, where volumes above the xy-plane are counted as positive, and volumes below the xy-plane are counted as negative.

A double integral is evaluated by writing it as a pair of **iterated integrals** whose limits describe the plane region R. For example, let's integrate the function $f(x, y) = y^2 - xy$ over the region R, in the xy-plane bounded by the x-axis, the parabola $y = x^2$, and the line $x = 2$. First, we sketch the region R, as on the next page.

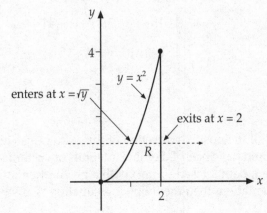

In order to find the value of the double integral

$$\iint\limits_{R} (y^2 - xy)\, dA$$

we first write $dA = dy\, dx$, and then determine the limits on the integrals to describe the region R:

These limits describe x in R These limits describe y in R

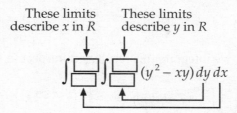

To determine the limits on the inner integral (the one that describes y), fix a value of x in R and construct an imaginary vertical line in the xy-plane at this x. The line enters the region at $y = 0$ and exits at $y = x^2$:

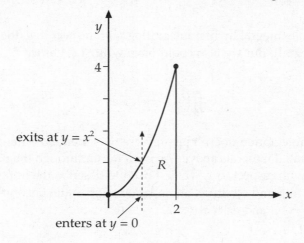

Therefore, the lower limit on the inner integral is $y = 0$, and the upper limit is $y = x^2$:

$$\int \boxed{} \int_{\boxed{y=0}}^{\boxed{y=x^2}} (y^2 - xy)\, dy\, dx$$

The limits on the outer integral are easy to determine, since x goes from 0 to 2:

$$\int_{\boxed{0}}^{\boxed{2}} \int_{\boxed{y=0}}^{\boxed{y=x^2}} (y^2 - xy)\, dy\, dx$$

The limits on the outside integral (which is the first integral sign written) should never contain variables. Now, to evaluate these iterated integrals, you always work from the inside out, so you may find it helpful to insert brackets around the inner integral as follows:

$$\int_0^2 \left[\int_{y=0}^{y=x^2} (y^2 - xy)\, dy \right] dx$$

Since the inner integral is an integration with respect to y (because of the dy), we find that

$$\int_{y=0}^{y=x^2} (y^2 - xy)\,dy = \left[\tfrac{1}{3}y^3 - \tfrac{1}{2}xy^2 \right]_{y=0}^{y=x^2}$$

$$= \left[\tfrac{1}{3}(x^2)^3 - \tfrac{1}{2}x(x^2)^2 \right] - \left[\tfrac{1}{3}(0)^3 - \tfrac{1}{2}x(0)^2 \right]$$

$$= \tfrac{1}{3}x^6 - \tfrac{1}{2}x^5$$

and, to complete the evaluation, we integrate this result with respect to x:

$$\int_0^2 \left[\int_{y=0}^{y=x^2} (y^2 - xy)\,dy \right] dx = \int_0^2 \left(\tfrac{1}{3}x^6 - \tfrac{1}{2}x^5 \right) dx$$

$$= \left[\tfrac{1}{21}x^7 - \tfrac{1}{12}x^6 \right]_0^2$$

$$= \tfrac{16}{21}$$

We computed this double integral by first integrating with respect to y (the inner integral), then with respect to x (the outer integral). But we also could have written dA as $dx\,dy$, and reversed the order of integration:

$$\iint (y^2 - xy)\,dx\,dy$$

Reversing the order of integration doesn't just reverse the inner and outer limits, so we can't use the limits we found for the iterated integrals above. We need to run through the procedure again. This time, since the inner integral is with respect to x, we first need to describe the limits on x, in the region R. To do this, we fix a value of y in R and construct an imaginary horizontal line in the x-y plane at this y. This line enters the region at $x = \sqrt{y}$ and exits at $x = 2$.

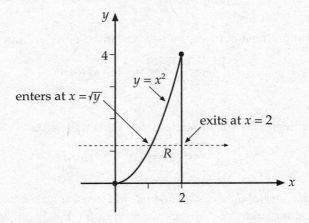

Therefore, the lower limit on the inner integral is $x = \sqrt{y}$ and the upper limit is $x = 2$. Since y goes from 0 to 4 in the region, these are the outer limits. So we have:

$$\int_0^4 \int_{x=\sqrt{y}}^{x=2} (y^2 - xy)\,dx\,dy$$

Let's evaluate this iterated integral. Beginning with the inner integral (as always), we find that:

$$\int_{x=\sqrt{y}}^{x=2} (y^2 - xy)\,dx = \left[xy^2 - \tfrac{1}{2}x^2y \right]_{x=\sqrt{y}}^{x=2}$$

$$= \left[2y^2 - \tfrac{1}{2}(2^2)y \right] - \left[\sqrt{y} \cdot y^2 - \tfrac{1}{2}(\sqrt{y})^2 y \right]$$

$$= \tfrac{5}{2}y^2 - 2y - y^{5/2}$$

The outer integral is then

$$\int_0^4 \left(\tfrac{5}{2}y^2 - 2y - y^{5/2} \right) dy = \left[\tfrac{5}{6}y^3 - y^2 - \tfrac{2}{7}y^{7/2} \right]_0^4$$

$$= \tfrac{5}{6}(4^3) - 4^2 - \tfrac{2}{7}(4^{7/2})$$

$$= \tfrac{16}{21}$$

in agreement with the value we found earlier. The order in which you choose to do the integrations doesn't matter, as long as you properly choose the limits to describe the region R. Often, one order is more difficult—or even impossible—to do; if so, choose the other order!

Example 3.22   What's the value of the double integral

$$\iint_R e^{y^2}\,dy\,dx$$

where R is the triangular region in the xy-plane with vertices $(-2, 2)$, $(0, 0)$, and $(2, 2)$?

Solution: First, we notice that the integral cannot be evaluated in the order in which it's written, because the inner integral,

$$\int e^{y^2}\,dy$$

cannot be expressed in terms of elementary functions. So we must reverse the order of integration and integrate first with respect to x, and then with respect to y. The next step is to sketch the region R, in order to determine the limits on the iterated integrals:

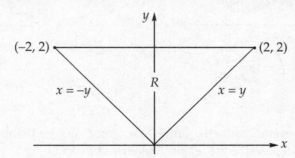

Using the figure, we can write:

$$\iint_R e^{y^2}\,dy\,dx = \int_0^2 \int_{x=-y}^{x=y} e^{y^2}\,dx\,dy$$

$$= \int_0^2 \left[xe^{y^2} \right]_{x=-y}^{x=y} dy$$

$$= \int_0^2 2ye^{y^2}\,dy$$

$$= [e^{y^2}]_0^2$$

$$= e^4 - 1$$

DOUBLE INTEGRALS IN POLAR COORDINATES

As we saw in the last chapter, it is sometimes convenient to make a change of variable when evaluating an integral. Here, we'll look at a common change of variable in computing double integrals, that of changing from the rectangular coordinates x and y to the polar coordinates r and θ. In order to write a double integral in polar coordinates, we need to make two changes. First, we write f in terms of r and θ, by setting $x = r \cos \theta$ and $y = r \sin \theta$. Then, we replace the element of area, $dA = dx\,dy$ (or $dy\,dx$), by $dA = r\,dr\,d\theta$. The reason for the change in the area element dA is easily intuited. When using rectangular coordinates x and y, we imagine the region R partitioned into small pieces formed by constructing lines across R where x and y are constants; this leads to the pieces being rectangles of area $dx\,dy$. If we do the same thing with polar coordinates, we would partition R into small pieces formed by constructing lines across R where r and θ are constants; this leads to the pieces being small curvilinear "rectangles" of area $r\,dr\,d\theta$:

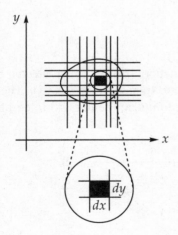 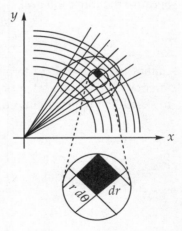

Once these changes are made, the limits that appear on the iterated integrals used to evaluate the double integral should describe the region R in terms of r and θ.

Example 3.23   Use polar coordinates to find the volume of the region bounded below by the interior of the curve $r = 2 \sin 2\theta$ in the first quadrant, and bounded above by the surface $z = x^3 y + x y^3$.

Solution: If R is the region in the first quadrant enclosed by the curve $r = 2 \sin 2\theta$, then the volume we're looking for is:

$$V = \iint_R (x^3 y + x y^3)\, dA = \iint_R x y (x^2 + y^2)\, dA$$

Writing this double integral in polar coordinates gives us:

$$\iint_R x y (x^2 + y^2)\, dA = \iint_R (r \cos\theta)(r \sin\theta)(r^2) \cdot (r\, dr\, d\theta)$$

$$= \iint_R (r^5 \cos\theta \sin\theta)\, dr\, d\theta$$

Next, we place the proper limits on the integrals to describe R; the lower and upper limits on the inner integral are $r = 0$ and $r = 2 \sin 2\theta$, respectively; on the outer integral, they're 0 and $\dfrac{\pi}{2}$. This gives us:

$$\iint_R (r^5 \cos\theta \sin\theta)\, dr\, d\theta = \int_0^{\pi/2} \int_{r=0}^{r=2\sin 2\theta} (r^5 \cos\theta \sin\theta)\, dr\, d\theta$$

$$= \int_0^{\pi/2} \left[\tfrac{1}{6} r^6 \sin\theta \cos\theta \right]_{r=0}^{r=2\sin 2\theta} d\theta$$

$$= \int_0^{\pi/2} \left[\tfrac{1}{6} (2 \sin 2\theta)^6 \sin\theta \cos\theta \right] d\theta$$

$$= \tfrac{2^6}{6} \int_0^{\pi/2} (2 \sin\theta \cos\theta)^6 \sin\theta \cos\theta\, d\theta$$

$$= \tfrac{2^{12}}{6} \int_0^{\pi/2} \sin^7\theta \cos^6\theta \cos\theta\, d\theta$$

$$= \tfrac{2^{12}}{6} \int_0^{\pi/2} \sin^7\theta (1 - \sin^2\theta)^3 \cos\theta\, d\theta$$

$$= \tfrac{2^{12}}{6} \int_0^{\pi/2} (\sin^7\theta - 3\sin^9\theta + 3\sin^{11}\theta - \sin^{13}\theta) \cos\theta\, d\theta$$

$$= \tfrac{2^{12}}{6} \left[\tfrac{1}{8} \sin^8\theta - \tfrac{3}{10} \sin^{10}\theta + \tfrac{1}{4} \sin^{12}\theta - \tfrac{1}{14} \sin^{14}\theta \right]_0^{\pi/2}$$

$$= \tfrac{2^{12}}{6} \left[\tfrac{1}{8} - \tfrac{3}{10} + \tfrac{1}{4} - \tfrac{1}{14} \right]$$

$$= \tfrac{256}{105}$$

GREEN'S THEOREM

Now that we've looked at line integrals and double integrals, we will introduce an equation that connects them. The type of line integral that we'll be using is that of a vector field around a simple closed curve. We know what a closed curve is; a **simple** closed curve is one that doesn't cross itself between its endpoints. A circle, an ellipse, and the boundary of a rectangle are all examples of simple closed curves; a figure-8 is not (it's closed but not simple). Next, we will always assume that the closed curve is oriented; the positive direction of the closed curve is defined as the direction you would have to walk in order to keep the region enclosed by the curve on your *left*. Consider a simple closed curve C enclosing a region R, so that C is the boundary of R. If $M(x, y)$ and $N(x, y)$ are functions that are defined and have continuous partial derivatives both on C and throughout R, then **Green's theorem** says that:

$$\oint_C M\,dx + N\,dy = \iint_R \left(\frac{\partial N}{\partial x} - \frac{\partial M}{\partial y} \right) dA$$

Since these two integrals are identical, if you're asked to evaluate one of them, it might be easier to figure out the other one instead; the answer will be the same.

Here's an example in which your first thought might be to evaluate a double integral, but it may be easier to work out the corresponding line integral. The double integral over R of the function $f(x, y)$ that's identically equal to 1,

$$\iint_R 1 \cdot dA = \iint_R dA$$

gives the area of the region R. If we take $M(x, y) = -y$ and $N(x, y) = x$, then the line integral

$$\frac{1}{2} \oint_C M\,dx + N\,dy = \frac{1}{2} \oint_C -y\,dx + x\,dy$$

will, by Green's theorem, be equal to:

$$\frac{1}{2} \iint_R \left(\frac{\partial N}{\partial x} - \frac{\partial M}{\partial y} \right) dA = \frac{1}{2} \iint_R [1 - (-1)]dA = \frac{1}{2} \iint_R 2\,dA = \iint_R dA$$

So if R is a region of the xy-plane whose boundary, C, is a simple closed curve, then the area of R can be determined by integrating the vector field $\mathbf{F} = (-y, x)$ around C, and multiplying by $\frac{1}{2}$:

$$\text{area of } R = \frac{1}{2} \oint_C -y\,dx + x\,dy$$

It's also easy to see that we could compute the area of R by using either of these two shorter formulas:

$$\text{area of } R = \oint_C -y\,dx = \oint_C x\,dy$$

Example 3.24   Use Green's theorem to find the area enclosed by the ellipse:

$$\frac{x^2}{a^2} + \frac{y^2}{b^2} = 1$$

Solution: We parameterize the ellipse by the equations:

$$\begin{cases} x = a\cos t \\ y = b\sin t \end{cases} \quad \text{for } 0 \overset{t}{\to} 2\pi$$

Green's theorem tells us that the area of R, the region enclosed by this simple closed curve, is:

$$\begin{aligned} \text{area of } R &= \oint_C x\,dy \\ &= \int_0^{2\pi} (a\cos t)(b\cos t\,dt) \\ &= ab\int_0^{2\pi} (\cos^2 t)\,dt \\ &= ab\int_0^{2\pi} \tfrac{1}{2}(1 + \cos 2t)\,dt \\ &= \tfrac{1}{2}ab\left[t + \tfrac{1}{2}\sin 2t\right]_0^{2\pi} \\ &= \pi ab \end{aligned}$$

Notice that if b is equal to a, then the ellipse is actually a circle of radius a, and the expression for the area of the ellipse becomes πa^2, which we know is the area of the circle.

Example 3.25   What's the value of the line integral

$$\oint_C \left(\sin^5(\log(x+1)) + 4y\right)dx + \left(6x - y^3 \arctan\sqrt{e^y}\right)dy$$

if C is the rectangle shown below?

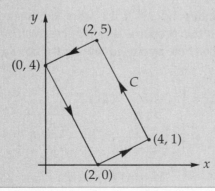

Solution: This line integral would be a nightmare to try to calculate directly, but we don't have to do so. We simply notice that

$$\frac{\partial N}{\partial x} = \frac{\partial}{\partial x}\left(6x - y^3 \arctan\sqrt{e^y}\right) = 6 \quad \text{and} \quad \frac{\partial M}{\partial y} = \frac{\partial}{\partial y}\left(\sin^5(\log(x+1)) + 4y\right) = 4$$

so, by Green's theorem, the given line integral is equal to

$$\iint\limits_R \left(\frac{\partial N}{\partial x} - \frac{\partial M}{\partial y}\right)dA = \iint\limits_R (6-4)\,dA = 2\iint\limits_R dA = 2(\text{area of } R)$$

where R is the rectangular region enclosed by C. The area of the rectangle is equal to $(\sqrt{5})(2\sqrt{5}) = 10$, so the value of the double integral, and thus the given line integral, is $2(10) = 20$.

PATH INDEPENDENCE AND GRADIENT FIELDS

The statement of Green's theorem allows us to complete some unfinished business from the last section. We know that the condition $M_y = N_x$ is necessary for the vector field $\mathbf{F} = (M, N)$ to be a gradient field, that is, for the line integral $\int_C \mathbf{F} \cdot d\mathbf{r}$ to be path independent. The question we left unresolved was, "Is this condition also sufficient to establish that $\mathbf{F}$ is a gradient field?" By itself, the answer is "no," as the following important (and classic) example illustrates. Consider the vector field:

$$\mathbf{F}(x, y) = \left(\frac{-y}{x^2 + y^2}, \frac{x}{x^2 + y^2}\right)$$

This vector field passes the test $M_y = N_x$, since

$$M_y = \frac{\partial}{\partial y}\left(\frac{-y}{x^2+y^2}\right) = \frac{(x^2+y^2)(-1)-(-y)(2y)}{(x^2+y^2)^2} = \frac{y^2-x^2}{(x^2+y^2)^2}$$

and

$$N_x = \frac{\partial}{\partial x}\left(\frac{x}{x^2+y^2}\right) = \frac{(x^2+y^2)(1)-(x)(2x)}{(x^2+y^2)^2} = \frac{y^2-x^2}{(x^2+y^2)^2}.$$

But is the line integral of $\mathbf{F}$ path independent? If it is, then the integral around any closed path would have to be zero. A vector field with this property is called *conservative*. Let's integrate this field $\mathbf{F}$ around the unit circle. We parameterize the circle by the equations $x = \cos t$ and $y = \sin t$, with the parameter t increasing from 0 to 2π. Then:

$$\oint_C \mathbf{F} \cdot d\mathbf{r} = \oint_C (M\,dx + N\,dy)$$
$$= \oint_C \left(\frac{-y}{x^2+y^2}dx + \frac{x}{x^2+y^2}dy\right)$$
$$= \int_0^{2\pi} [(-\sin t)(-\sin t\,dt) + (\cos t)(\cos t\,dt)]$$
$$= 2\pi$$

Since this is not zero, we must conclude that **F** is not conservative.

But if $M_y = N_x$, isn't the integrand of the double integral in Green's theorem equal to zero, which means that the value of the line integral around any closed curve (such as the unit circle) must also be zero? What went wrong in this example? Well, notice that the hypothesis of Green's theorem says that if $M(x, y)$ and $N(x, y)$ are functions that are defined and have continuous partial derivatives both on C and throughout R (the region enclosed by C), then equality of the line integral and double integral is guaranteed. But for the vector field **F** defined above, the functions M and N are *not* defined and continuously differentiable throughout R; the unit circle encloses the origin, and neither M nor N is defined at this point. Since this field **F** does not satisfy the hypothesis of the theorem, it shouldn't be surprising that the conclusion of the theorem doesn't follow either.

To make sure this kind of behavior isn't seen, we can restrict the regions we study to be **convex**, which means that for any pair of points in the region, every point on the line segment joining the pair also lies in R. If R is the interior of the unit circle with the origin excluded, then R is not convex, since, for example, the line segment that joins the points $(-\frac{1}{2}, 0)$ and $(\frac{1}{2}, 0)$ would have to pass through the origin, but this point is excluded from R. A less restrictive condition is to require that the domain of **F** merely be **simply connected**. This means that the interior of every simple closed curve in the domain of **F**—which we're calling R—is contained in R; intuitively, it means that R doesn't contain any holes. Every convex set is simply connected but not every simply connected set is convex, so requiring that the domain of **F** be simply connected is a weaker (and more easily satisfied) condition than requiring that it be convex.

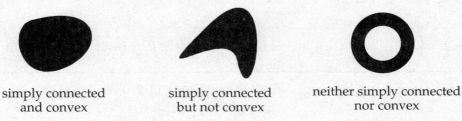

simply connected
and convex

simply connected
but not convex

neither simply connected
nor convex

So, if $\mathbf{F}(x, y) = (M(x, y), N(x, y))$ is a vector field defined and continuously differentiable throughout a simply connected region R of the plane, then all of the following statements about **F** are equivalent:

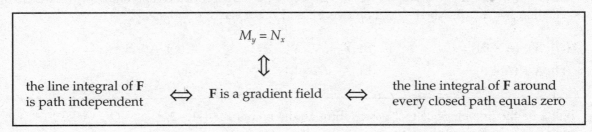

$$M_y = N_x$$

$\Updownarrow$

the line integral of **F** $\Longleftrightarrow$ **F** is a gradient field $\Longleftrightarrow$ the line integral of **F** around
is path independent   every closed path equals zero

CHAPTER 3 REVIEW QUESTIONS

Complete the following review questions using the techniques outlined in this chapter. Then, see Chapter 8 for answers and explanations.

1. Find the angle between the diagonals of the back and left faces of the cube shown below:

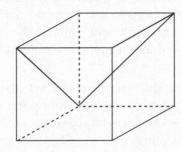

   (A) $60°$ (B) $\cos^{-1}\dfrac{1}{\sqrt{6}}$ (C) $\cos^{-1}\dfrac{1}{3\sqrt{2}}$ (D) $90°$ (E) $120°$

2. If $\hat{\mathbf{i}} = (1, 0, 0)$, $\hat{\mathbf{j}} = (0, 1, 0)$, and $\hat{\mathbf{k}} = (0, 0, 1)$, which one of the following vectors is *not* orthogonal to $\mathbf{v} = 2\hat{\mathbf{i}} - \hat{\mathbf{j}} + 3\hat{\mathbf{k}}$?

   (A) $\hat{\mathbf{i}} - \hat{\mathbf{j}} - \hat{\mathbf{k}}$ (B) $\hat{\mathbf{i}} + 2\hat{\mathbf{j}}$ (C) $3\hat{\mathbf{i}} - 2\hat{\mathbf{k}}$ (D) $\hat{\mathbf{i}} + 3\hat{\mathbf{j}} - \hat{\mathbf{k}}$ (E) $2\hat{\mathbf{i}} + \hat{\mathbf{j}} - \hat{\mathbf{k}}$

3. What's the area of the triangle whose vertices are $(0, 0, 1)$, $(0, 2, 0)$, and $(3, 0, 0)$?

   (A) $\dfrac{8}{3}$ (B) $\dfrac{7}{2}$ (C) 3 (D) 6 (E) 7

4. Given the vector identity $\mathbf{A} \times (\mathbf{B} \times \mathbf{C}) = (\mathbf{A} \bullet \mathbf{C})\mathbf{B} - (\mathbf{A} \bullet \mathbf{B})\mathbf{C}$, which of the following $\mathbf{V}$ satisfies the equation $\mathbf{A} \times \mathbf{V} = \mathbf{B}$, where $\mathbf{A}$ is a unit vector and $\mathbf{B}$ is a vector orthogonal to $\mathbf{A}$?

   (A) $\mathbf{B} + (\mathbf{A} \times \mathbf{B})$ (B) $\mathbf{B} - (\mathbf{A} \times \mathbf{B})$ (C) $\mathbf{A} \times \mathbf{B}$
   (D) $\mathbf{A} + (\mathbf{A} \times \mathbf{B})$ (E) $\mathbf{A} - (\mathbf{A} \times \mathbf{B})$

5. Let L be the line in space that passes through the points $P = (-1, -2, 4)$ and $Q = (4, 2, 1)$. At what point does L intersect the plane $x + y + 2z = 11$?

   (A) $(5, -4, 1)$ (B) $(1, 2, 4)$ (C) $(8, 9, -3)$ (D) $(6, 7, -1)$ (E) $(9, 6, -2)$

6. Let $P = (1, -1, 1)$ and $Q = (-3, 3, 3)$. Find the point R on the line containing P and Q whose distance from P is 3 times its distance from Q, given that R is *not* between P and Q.

   (A) $(-4, 4, \frac{7}{2})$ (B) $(-5, 5, 4)$ (C) $(-\frac{13}{3}, \frac{13}{3}, \frac{11}{3})$
   (D) $(-\frac{15}{2}, \frac{15}{2}, \frac{11}{2})$ (E) $(-9, 9, 6)$

7. If L is the line through the point $A = (3, 2, 1)$ and parallel to the vector $\mathbf{v} = (-2, 1, 3)$, what's the equation of the plane that contains L and the point $B = (-2, 3, 1)$?

(A) $-x + y + z = 6$ (B) $3x - 2y - z = 4$ (C) $x + 6y - 11z = 5$

(D) $x + 5y - z = 12$ (E) $2x + 10y - 19z = 7$

---

8. Find the perpendicular distance from the origin to the plane $x + 2y + 2z = 6$.

(A) 1   (B) $\dfrac{4}{3}$ (C) 2   (D) $\dfrac{8}{3}$ (E) 3

---

9. If the curve $z = f(x)$ in the xz-plane is revolved around the x-axis, which of the following is an equation that describes the resulting surface?

(A) $y^2 + z^2 = |f(x)|$ (B) $z^2 = f(x^2 + y^2)$ (C) $y^2 = f(x^2 + z^2)$

(D) $x^2 + z^2 = [f(x)]^2$ (E) $y^2 + z^2 = [f(x)]^2$

---

10. Which of the following depicts level curves of the surface whose equation in cylindrical coordinates is $z = r^2 \cos 2\theta$?

(A)
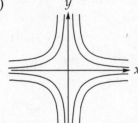

(B)
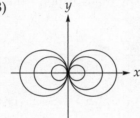

(C)
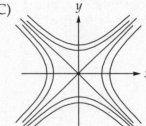

(D)
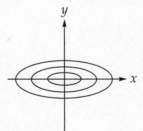

(E)
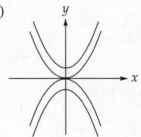

11. Consider the following three functions, each of which is defined for all (x, y) in the plane:

$$f_1(x, y) = \begin{cases} \dfrac{x-y}{x+y} & \text{if } x + y \neq 0 \\ 1 & \text{if } x + y = 0 \end{cases} \quad f_2(x, y) = \begin{cases} \dfrac{xy}{x^2 + y^2} & \text{if } (x, y) \neq (0, 0) \\ 0 & \text{if } (x, y) = (0, 0) \end{cases} \quad f_3(x, y) = \begin{cases} \dfrac{x^3 - y^3}{x^2 + y^2} & \text{if } (x, y) \neq (0, 0) \\ 0 & \text{if } (x, y) = (0, 0) \end{cases}$$

Which of these functions is/are continuous at the origin?

(A) None   (B) f_1 only   (C) f_2 only   (D) f_3 only   (E) All three

---

12. The plane $y = 1$ slices the surface

$$z = \arctan \frac{x+y}{1 - xy}$$

in a curve, C. Find the slope of the tangent line to C at the point where $x = 2$.

(A) –3   (B) –1   (C) $\dfrac{1}{5}$ (D) $\dfrac{1}{3}$ (E) $\dfrac{1}{2}$

---

13. If the variables P, V, and T are related by the equation $PV = nRT$, where n and R are constants, simplify the expression

$$\frac{\partial V}{\partial T} \cdot \frac{\partial T}{\partial P} \cdot \frac{\partial P}{\partial V}$$

(A) –1   (B) 1   (C) $-nR$ (D) nR (E) $\dfrac{1}{nR}$

---

14. Let f be the function defined for all (x, y) as follows:

$$f(x, y) = \begin{cases} xy\dfrac{x^2 - y^2}{x^2 + y^2} & \text{if } (x, y) \neq (0, 0) \\ 0 & \text{if } (x, y) = (0, 0) \end{cases}$$

What is the value of f_{xy} at the point $(0, 0)$?

(A) –1   (B) 0   (C) $\dfrac{1}{2}$ (D) 1   (E) Undefined

---

15. A right circular cylinder has base radius $r = 100$ cm and height $h = 100$ cm. Which of the following best describes how the volume of the cylinder will change if r increases to 101 cm and h decreases to 99 cm?

(A) Volume will decrease by approximately $3\pi(100)^2$ cubic cm
(B) Volume will decrease by approximately $\pi(100)^2$ cubic cm
(C) Volume will increase by approximately $\pi(100)^2$ cubic cm
(D) Volume will increase by approximately $2\pi(100)^2$ cubic cm
(E) Volume will increase by approximately $3\pi(100)^2$ cubic cm

---

16. Let P be the tangent plane to the surface

$$y^2z - 2xz^2 + 3x^2y = 2$$

at the point $Q = (1, 1, 1)$. Which of the following points also lies in P?

(A) $(4, 5, -3)$ (B) $(6, -4, 3)$ (C) $(3, -1, 5)$ (D) $(5, 3, -2)$ (E) $(-2, 4, 2)$

---

17. The equation $x^3z^5 - y^2z^3 - 3xy = 1$ defines an implicit function $z = f(x, y)$. What's the value of $\dfrac{\partial f}{\partial y}$ at the point $(x, y) = (-1, 1)$?

(A) -8 (B) -1 (C) $-\dfrac{1}{8}$ (D) $\dfrac{1}{8}$ (E) 8

---

18. Let f, g, and h be functions of two variables that are differentiable everywhere such that $z = f(x, y)$, where $x = g(u, v)$ and $y = h(u, v)$. When $u = 0$ and $v = 1$, the values of x and y are 2 and 1, respectively. Let P_0 denote the point $(u, v) = (0, 1)$, and let Q_0 denote the point $(x, y) = (2, 1)$. Given the following data,

$$\left.\frac{\partial f}{\partial x}\right|_{Q_0} = 11, \qquad \left.\frac{\partial f}{\partial y}\right|_{Q_0} = -3, \qquad \left.\frac{\partial g}{\partial u}\right|_{P_0} = 1, \qquad \left.\frac{\partial h}{\partial u}\right|_{P_0} = -3, \qquad \left.\frac{\partial g}{\partial v}\right|_{P_0} = \left.\frac{\partial h}{\partial v}\right|_{P_0} = 2$$

what's the value of $\dfrac{\partial z}{\partial v}$ at P_0?

(A) -21 (B) 16 (C) 15 (D) 12 (E) -10

---

19. The temperature at each point (x, y, z) in a room is given by the equation $T(x, y, z) = 9x^2 - 3y^2 + 6xyz$. A fly is currently hovering at the point $(2, 2, 2)$. In the direction of which of the following vectors should the fly move in order to cool off as rapidly as possible?

(A) $-5\hat{\mathbf{i}} - \hat{\mathbf{j}} - 2\hat{\mathbf{k}}$ (B) $-4\hat{\mathbf{i}} - 3\hat{\mathbf{j}} - \hat{\mathbf{k}}$ (C) $3\hat{\mathbf{i}} + \hat{\mathbf{j}} - 6\hat{\mathbf{k}}$ (D) $-2\hat{\mathbf{i}} + 8\hat{\mathbf{j}} - 5\hat{\mathbf{k}}$ (E) $-6\hat{\mathbf{i}} + 4\hat{\mathbf{j}} - 3\hat{\mathbf{k}}$

---

20. Let $f(x, y)$ be a function that is differentiable everywhere. At a certain point P in the xy-plane, the directional derivative of f in the direction of $\hat{\mathbf{i}} - \hat{\mathbf{j}}$ is $\sqrt{2}$ and the directional derivative of f in the direction of $\hat{\mathbf{i}} + \hat{\mathbf{j}}$ is $3\sqrt{2}$. What is the maximum directional derivative of f at P?

(A) $3\sqrt{2}$ (B) $2\sqrt{5}$ (C) $43\sqrt{2}$ (D) 6 (E) 8

---

21. Which of the following vectors is normal to the surface

$$\log(x + y^2 - z^3) = x - 1$$

at the point where $y = 8$ and $z = 4$?

(A) $\hat{\mathbf{i}} - \hat{\mathbf{j}} - 2\hat{\mathbf{k}}$ (B) $2\hat{\mathbf{i}} - 3\hat{\mathbf{j}} + \hat{\mathbf{k}}$ (C) $\hat{\mathbf{i}} + 2\hat{\mathbf{j}}$ (D) $-2\hat{\mathbf{i}} + \hat{\mathbf{j}} + 3\hat{\mathbf{k}}$ (E) $\hat{\mathbf{j}} - 3\hat{\mathbf{k}}$

22. The function $f(x, y) = x^3 + y^3 - 3xy$ has a local minimum at exactly one point, P. What's the value of f at P?

(A) –6   (B) –3   (C) –2   (D) –1   (E) 0

---

23. Find the minimum distance from the origin to the curve $3x^2 + 4xy + 3y^2 = 20$.

(A) 1   (B) $3\sqrt{2}$ (C) 2   (D) $23\sqrt{2}$ (E) $53\sqrt{2}$

---

24. A vertical fence is constructed whose base is the curve $y = x\sqrt{x}$, from $(0, 0)$ to $(1, 1)$, and whose height above each point (x, y) along the curve is $x^3 - y^2 + 27$. Find the area of this fence.

(A) $\frac{1}{9}(5\sqrt{5} - 2)$ (B) $5\sqrt{13} - 6$ (C) $9\sqrt{3}$ (D) $13\sqrt{13} - 8$ (E) 27

---

25. If $\mathbf{F} = (3y - 2x)\,\hat{\mathbf{i}} + (x^2 + y)\,\hat{\mathbf{j}}$, find the value of $\int_C \mathbf{F} \bullet d\mathbf{r}$, where C is the portion of the parabola $y = x^2$, directed from $(-1, 1)$ to the origin.

(A) –1   (B) 0   (C) 1   (D) 2   (E) 3

---

26. Let C be the portion of the astroid $x^{2/3} + y^{2/3} = 1$ from $(1, 0)$ to $(0, 1)$, which can be parameterized by the equations

$$x = \cos^3 t, \quad y = \sin^3 t$$

as t increases from 0 to $\dfrac{\pi}{2}$. Evaluate the integral:

$$\int_C (y \cos xy - 1)\,dx + (1 + x \cos xy)\,dy$$

(A) –2   (B) –1   (C) 1   (D) $\frac{1}{2}\pi - 1$ (E) 2

---

27. Find the volume of the solid in the first octant of xyz-space, bounded below by the coordinate axes and the unit circle, and bounded above by the surface $z = 8xy$.

(A) $\frac{1}{2}$ (B) 1   (C) 2   (D) 4   (E) 8

---

28. Set up, but do not evaluate, a double integral that gives the volume of the solid bounded above by the elliptic paraboloid $z = 1 - (x^2 + \frac{1}{9}y^2)$ and bounded below by the elliptic cone $z = \sqrt{x^2 + \frac{1}{9}y^2} - 1$.

(A) $4\int_0^1 \int_0^3 \left(2 - \sqrt{x^2 + \frac{1}{9}y^2}\right) dy\, dx$

(B) $\int_{-1}^1 \int_{-3\sqrt{1-x^2}}^{3\sqrt{1-x^2}} \left(2 - \frac{3}{2}\sqrt{x^2 + \frac{1}{9}y^2}\right) dy\, dx$

(C) $2\int_0^1 \int_{-3}^3 \left(x^2 - \frac{1}{9}y^2 - \sqrt{x^2 + \frac{1}{9}y^2}\right) dy\, dx$

(D) $2\int_0^1 \int_{-3}^3 \left(2 - x^2 - \frac{1}{9}y^2 - \sqrt{x^2 + \frac{1}{9}y^2}\right) dy\, dx$

(E) $\int_{-1}^1 \int_{-3\sqrt{1-x^2}}^{3\sqrt{1-x^2}} \left(2 - x^2 - \frac{1}{9}y^2 - \sqrt{x^2 + \frac{1}{9}y^2}\right) dy\, dx$

29. If a is a positive number, what's the value of the following double integral?

$$\int_0^{2a} \int_{-\sqrt{2ay-y^2}}^0 \sqrt{x^2 + y^2}\, dx\, dy$$

(A) $\frac{16}{9}a^3$ (B) $\frac{32}{9}a^3$ (C) $\frac{\pi}{2}a^2$ (D) $\frac{8\pi}{3}a^2$ (E) $2a^4$

30. Let C be the boundary of the triangular region, as shown below:

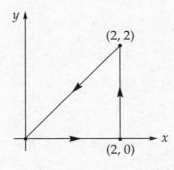

Determine the value of the integral:

$$\int_C (e^{2x} - y)\, dx + (2x + y\sqrt{y})\, dy$$

(A) 2   (B) 4   (C) 6   (D) $e^2 + 2\sqrt{2} - 3$ (E) $e^4 + 2(\sqrt{2} - 1)$

Differential Equations

INTRODUCTION

Simply put, an equation that contains derivatives or differentials is called a **differential equation**. If the equation contains ordinary derivatives only, it's called an **ordinary differential equation** (**ODE**); if it contains partial derivatives, it's a **partial differential equation** (**PDE**). Except for a couple of review questions, our attention will be focused exclusively on ODEs.

The **order** of a differential equation is the order of the highest derivative that appears in the equation. For example, a first-order equation involves the first derivative $\frac{dy}{dx}$, but no second (or higher) derivatives.

In this chapter, we'll examine various types of elementary differential equations and illustrate the methods for solving them.

The simplest types of differential equations are of the form

$$\frac{dy}{dx} = f(x)$$

where f is a given function. Solving for y is easy; just integrate both sides: $y = \int f(x)dx$

This gives the **family** of solutions $y = F(x) + c$ for the differential equation, where c is an arbitrary constant of integration. Solutions to an ordinary differential equation are often called **integral curves**, particularly when they are graphed in the x-y plane. If an **initial condition** is given along with the differential equation, that is, a constraint of the form $y = y_0$ when $x = x_0$, then this information can be used to determine the particular value of c. In this way, one particular solution can be selected from the family of solutions—the one that satisfies both the differential equation and the initial condition.

Example 4.1   Solve the IVP:

$$\left[-x\cos x\right] + \sin x + 1$$

$$\frac{dy}{dx} = x \sin x, \quad y(0) = 1$$

$$1 \quad -\cos x$$

Solution: An IVP is an **initial value problem**, a differential equation accompanied by one (or more) initial conditions. The first step here is to integrate in order to determine y. Using integration by parts, we find that:

$$\int x \sin x \, dx = x(-\cos x) - \int (-\cos x) \, dx = -x \cos x + \sin x + c$$

This tells us that the general solution of the equation $y' = x \sin x$ is:

$$y = -x \cos x + \sin x + c$$

As the final step, apply the initial condition to evaluate the constant, c. When we substitute into the equation above, we see that if $y = 1$ when $x = 0$, then c must equal 1. Therefore, the solution of the given IVP is:

$$y = -x \cos x + \sin x + 1$$

Example 4.2   Show that the integral curves of the differential equation

$$(y - x^3) \, dx + (y^3 + x) \, dy = 0$$

are given by the family $y^4 + 4xy - x^4 = c$.

$$4y^3 \frac{dy}{dx} + 4x \frac{dy}{dx} + 4y 4x^3 = 0$$

$$(y^3 + x)dy + (y - x^3)dx = 0$$

Solution: Apply implicit differentiation to the proposed family of integral curves to find y':

$$y^4 + 4xy - x^4 = c$$

$$4y^3 y' + (4xy' + 4y) - 4x^3 = 0$$

$$y'(y^3 + x) + (y - x^3) = 0$$

$$\frac{dy}{dx}(y^3 + x) + (y - x^3) = 0$$

$$\frac{dy}{dx} = \frac{-(y - x^3)}{y^3 + x}$$

This last equation can then be written in terms of the differentials dx and dy:

$$(y^3 + x)\,dy = -(y - x^3)\,dx \;\Rightarrow\; (y - x^3)\,dx + (y^3 + x)\,dy = 0$$

Notice that the equation $M(x, y)\,dx + N(x, y)\,dy = 0$ is simply an alternate form of the equation:

$$\frac{dy}{dx} = -\frac{M(x, y)}{N(x, y)}$$

SEPARABLE EQUATIONS

A differential equation of the form

$$\frac{dy}{dx} = \frac{f(x)}{g(y)}$$

is called **separable** because its variables can be separated,

$$g(y)\,dy = f(x)dx$$

after which the equation can be solved by a pair of integrations:

$$\int g(y)\,dy = \int f(x)\,dx$$

Example 4.3   Solve the equation:

$$\frac{dy}{dx} = \frac{x(x-2)}{e^y}$$

$e^y\,dy = x^2 - 2x\,dx$

$e^y = \frac{1}{3}x^3 - x^2 + C$

$y = \log\left|\frac{1}{3}x^3 - x^2 + c\right|$

Solution: Separate the variables

$$e^y\,dy = x(x - 2)\,dx$$

then integrate:

$$\int e^y\,dy = \int (x^2 - 2x)\,dx$$

$$e^y = \frac{1}{3}x^3 - x^2 + c$$

You can leave the solution in this form or solve for y:

$$y = \log\left|\frac{1}{3}x^3 - x^2 + c\right|$$

HOMOGENEOUS EQUATIONS

A function of two variables, $f(x, y)$, is said to be **homogeneous of degree** n if there is a constant n such that

$$f(tx, ty) = t^n f(x, y)$$

for all t, x, and y for which both sides are defined. A differential equation of the form

$$M(x, y)\, dx + N(x, y)\, dy = 0$$

is **homogeneous** if M and N are both homogeneous functions of the same degree. To solve homogeneous equations, turn them into separable equations using the substitution $y = xv$.

Example 4.4   Solve the equation:

$$(x^2 + y^2)\, dx - 2xy\, dy = 0$$

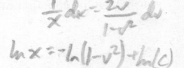

Solution: Notice that the functions $M(x, y) = x^2 + y^2$ and $N(x, y) = -2xy$ are both homogeneous of degree 2; therefore, the differential equation is homogeneous. The substitution $y = xv$ implies that $dy = x\, dv + v\, dx$, and the given equation is transformed into:

$$[x^2 + (xv)^2]\, dx - 2x(xv)(x\, dv + v\, dx) = 0$$

After a little algebra, this becomes the separable equation:

$$\frac{1}{x}\, dx = \frac{2v}{1 - v^2}\, dv$$

Integrating both sides gives $\log x = -\log(1 - v^2) + \log c$, in which we wrote the arbitrary constant of integration as $\log c$ because it makes the next step neater:

$$\log x = \log \frac{c}{1 - v^2} \implies x = \frac{c}{1 - v^2}$$

Finally, to write the solution in terms of the original variables, x and y, we replace v by $\frac{y}{x}$:

$$x = \frac{c}{1 - \left(\dfrac{y}{x}\right)^2} \implies x^2 - y^2 = cx$$

EXACT EQUATIONS

Given a function $f(x, y)$, its **total differential**, df, is defined as:

$$df = \frac{\partial f}{\partial x}\, dx + \frac{\partial f}{\partial y}\, dy$$

This shows that the family of curves $f(x, y) = c$ satisfies the differential equation $df = 0$:

$$\frac{\partial f}{\partial x}\, dx + \frac{\partial f}{\partial y}\, dy = 0$$

So, if there exists a function $f(x, y)$ such that

$$M(x, y) = \frac{\partial f}{\partial x} \quad \text{and} \quad N(x, y) = \frac{\partial f}{\partial y}$$

then $M(x, y)\, dx + N(x, y)\, dy$ is called an **exact differential**, and the equation

$$M(x, y)\, dx + N(x, y)\, dy = 0$$

is said to be an **exact** equation, whose solution is the family $f(x, y) = c$.

How can you tell when a differential equation is exact? Recall that if $f(x, y)$ has continuous second partial derivatives, then $\dfrac{\partial^2 f}{\partial x\, \partial y} = \dfrac{\partial^2 f}{\partial y\, \partial x}$ (that is, the order of differentiation doesn't matter). So, if $\dfrac{\partial f}{\partial x} = M$ and $\dfrac{\partial f}{\partial y} = N$, then:

$$\frac{\partial M}{\partial y} = \frac{\partial N}{\partial x}$$

Not only is this condition necessary for exactness, it also determines exactness.

Example 4.5   Solve the differential equation:

$$(1 - 2xy)\, dx + (4y^3 - x^2)\, dy = 0$$

x − x²y + yᵞ = c

Solution: With $M(x, y) = 1 - 2xy$ and $N(x, y) = 4y^3 - x^2$, we notice that

$$\frac{\partial M}{\partial y} = -2x = \frac{\partial N}{\partial x}$$

so the given functions M and N pass the test for exactness. All that's left to do is to find the function $f(x, y)$, such that $\dfrac{\partial f}{\partial x} = M$ and $\dfrac{\partial f}{\partial y} = N$. The way to accomplish this is to integrate M with respect to x, integrate N with respect to y, and then merge the results:

$$\int M(x, y)\, dx = \int (1 - 2xy)\, dx = x - x^2 y + \text{a function of } y \text{ alone}$$

$$\int N(x, y)\, dy = \int (4y^3 - x^2)\, dy = y^4 - x^2 y + \text{a function of } x \text{ alone}$$

These calculations imply that a function $f(x, y)$ which satisfies both $\dfrac{\partial f}{\partial x} = M = 1 - 2xy$ and $\dfrac{\partial f}{\partial y} = N = 4y^3 - x^2$ is:

$$f(x, y) = x - x^2 y + y^4$$

Therefore, the exact equation we were given is satisfied by the family of curves:

$$x - x^2 y + y^4 = c$$

NONEXACT EQUATIONS AND INTEGRATING FACTORS

Consider the differential equation:

$$(xy + x - 1)\, dx + x^2\, dy = 0 \quad (*)$$

Notice that it isn't exact, since $M_y \ne N_x$:

$$M_y = \frac{\partial}{\partial y}(xy + x - 1) = x \quad \text{but} \quad N_x = \frac{\partial}{\partial x}(x^2) = 2x$$

However, if we multiply both sides of equation (*) by $\mu(x) = \dfrac{1}{x}$, the resulting equivalent equation

$$(y + 1 - x^{-1})\, dx + x\, dy = 0 \quad (**)$$

is exact, as we can check:

$$\frac{\partial \overline{M}}{\partial y} = \frac{\partial}{\partial y}(y + 1 - x^{-1}) = 1 \quad \text{and} \quad \frac{\partial \overline{N}}{\partial x} = \frac{\partial}{\partial x}(x) = 1$$

We can then solve equation (**) by integrating $\overline{M}$ with respect to x, and $\overline{N}$ with respect to y, and merging the results:

$$\int \overline{M}(x, y)\, dx = \int (y + 1 - x^{-1})\, dx = xy + x - \log x + (\text{a function of } y \text{ alone})$$

$$\int \overline{N}(x, y)\, dy = \int x\, dy = xy + (\text{a function of } x \text{ alone})$$

Therefore, a function whose total differential is the left-hand side of (**) is

$$f(x, y) = xy + x - \log x$$

which makes the general solution of (**)—and of the original equation (*)—the family:

$$xy + x - \log x = c$$

The multiplier $\mu(x) = \dfrac{1}{x}$, which transformed the given, nonexact equation into an equivalent, exact equation, is called an **integrating factor**. If a nonexact equation has a solution, then an integrating factor is guaranteed to exist; this doesn't mean it's easy to find it, but we'll take a look at cases where it is easy. Let

$$M(x, y)\, dx + N(x, y)\, dy = 0 \quad (*)$$

be the given nonexact equation, which means $M_y - N_x \ne 0$.

Case 1: *If* $\dfrac{(M_y - N_x)}{N}$ *is a function of x alone, call this function* $\xi(x)$. *Then* $\mu(x) = e^{\int \xi(x)dx}$ *is an integrating factor of (*).*

Case 2: *If* $\dfrac{(M_y - N_x)}{(-M)}$ *is a function of y alone, call this function* $\psi(y)$. *Then* $\mu(y) = e^{\int \psi(y)dy}$ *is an integrating factor of (*).*

Example 4.6 Find the integral curve of

$$\frac{dy}{dx} + \frac{x^2 y}{x^3 + y} = 0$$

that passes through the point $(x_0, y_0) = (1, 1)$.

[handwritten annotations:]
$x^2 y\, dx + (x^3 + y)\, dy = 0$
$x^2 y^3\, dx + (x^3 y^2 + y^3)\, dy = 0$
$\frac{1}{3} x^3 y^3 + \frac{1}{4} y^4 = C$
$C = \frac{7}{12}$
$4 x^3 y^3 + 3 y^4 = 7$

Solution: First, let's rearrange the equation and write it in the form:

$$(x^2 y)\, dx + (x^3 + y)\, dy = 0 \quad (*)$$

This equation is not exact, because $M_y = x^2$, but $N_x = 3x^2$. However, we notice that

$$\frac{M_y - N_x}{-M} = \frac{x^2 - 3x^2}{-x^2 y} = \frac{2}{y}$$

is a function of y alone; call it $\psi(y)$. Therefore,

$$\mu(y) = e^{\int \psi(y)\, dy} = e^{\int (\frac{2}{y})\, dy} = e^{2 \log y} = y^2$$

will be an integrating factor. Multiplying both sides of (*) by $\mu(y) = y^2$ gives the equation

$$(x^2 y^3)\, dx + (x^3 y^2 + y^3)\, dy = 0 \quad (**)$$

which is exact, since:

$$\frac{\partial \overline{M}}{\partial y} = \frac{\partial}{\partial y}(\mu M) = \frac{\partial}{\partial y}(x^2 y^3) = 3x^2 y^2 \quad \text{and} \quad \frac{\partial \overline{N}}{\partial x} = \frac{\partial}{\partial x}(\mu N) = \frac{\partial}{\partial x}(x^3 y^2 + y^3) = 3x^2 y^2$$

By integrating $\overline{M} = x^2 y^3$ with respect to x and $\overline{N} = x^3 y^2 + y^3$ with respect to y, we find that the general solution of (**) is the family

$$\frac{1}{3} x^3 y^3 + \frac{1}{4} y^4 = c$$

so if we seek the specific curve that passes through the point (1, 1), the value of c must be $\frac{7}{12}$. With $c = \frac{7}{12}$, the above equation can be written in the form:

$$4x^3 y^3 + 3y^4 = 7$$

FIRST-ORDER LINEAR EQUATIONS

A **first-order linear equation** is defined as a differential equation of the form:

$$\frac{dy}{dx} + P(x)y = Q(x) \quad (*)$$

The procedure for solving these equations is similar to the one used to solve nonexact equations. Multiplying both sides of the equation by a particular function, an integrating factor, transforms it into an equivalent one that is easy to solve by integration. The integrating factor is:

$$\mu(x) = e^{\int P(x)dx}$$

Once both sides of (*) are multiplied by this function μ,

$$\mu(x)\frac{dy}{dx} + \mu(x)P(x)y = \mu(x)Q(x)$$

the left-hand side is (μy)′, so the equation becomes:

$$\frac{d}{dx}(\mu y) = \mu Q$$

Integrating both sides gives the general solution:

$$y = \frac{1}{\mu}\int (\mu Q)\, dx$$

$e^{3h(x)} = x^3$

Example 4.7   Find the solution of

$$\frac{dy}{dx} = 5x - \frac{3y}{x}$$

such that $y(1) = 2$.

$\frac{dy}{dx} + \left(\frac{3}{x}\right)y = 5x$

$\frac{dy}{dx}x^3 + 3yx^2 = 5x^4$

$\int yx^3 = x^5 + C$

Solution: First, we rearrange the equation to put it in the standard form (*) of a linear equation:

$$\frac{dy}{dx} + \frac{3}{x}y = 5x \qquad y = x^2 + \frac{1}{x^3}$$

Multiplying both sides of this by the integrating factor

$$\mu(x) = e^{\int P(x)dx} = e^{\int \left(\frac{3}{x}\right)dx} = e^{3\log x} = x^3$$

gives the equivalent equation:

$$x^3\frac{dy}{dx} + 3x^2y = 5x^4$$

Notice that the left-hand side is $\left(x^3 y\right)'$, so by integrating both sides, we get:

$$x^3 y = \int \left(5x^4\right) dx$$
$$= x^5 + c$$
$$y = x^2 + cx^{-3}$$

Now, to satisfy the initial condition, $y(1) = 2$, the value of c must be 1. Therefore, the solution to the given IVP is:

$$y = x^2 + x^{-3}$$

HIGHER-ORDER LINEAR EQUATIONS WITH CONSTANT COEFFICIENTS

So far, all the equations we've studied have been first order, which means that they contained only the first derivative, y'. Now, we will turn to higher-order equations. In particular, we'll look at one of the most common (and, fortunately, easily solved) types of higher-order equations—the linear equations with constant coefficients.

The general **second-order linear differential equation with constant coefficients** is

$$ay'' + by' + cy = d(x) \quad (*)$$

where a, b, and c are real constants (and $a \neq 0$). If the right-hand side of this equation is identically zero, that is, if the equation is in the form

$$ay'' + by' + cy = 0 \quad (**)$$

then it's said to be **homogeneous**. (Notice that this definition of the term *homogeneous* is different from the one we gave earlier—this definition is encountered much more frequently.) A standard theorem states that the general solution of the nonhomogeneous equation (*) is given by

$$y = y_h + y_p$$

where y_h is the general solution of the corresponding homogeneous equation (**) and y_p is any particular solution of (*). We will begin our discussion of the nonhomogeneous equation by showing how the homogeneous equation is solved.

Given the equation $ay'' + by' + cy = 0$, we write down its corresponding **auxiliary polynomial** equation

$$am^2 + bm + c = 0$$

by replacing the nth derivative $y^{(n)}$ by m^n. The roots of this polynomial equation determine the solutions of the original differential equation. There are three cases to consider.

Case 1: *If the roots are real and distinct.*
If we denote the roots by m_1 and m_2, then the general solution of the differential equation is:
$$y = c_1 e^{m_1 x} + c_2 e^{m_2 x}$$

Case 2: *If the roots are real and identical.*
If we denote the double root by m_1, then the general solution of the differential equation is:

$$y = c_1 e^{m_1 x} + c_2 x e^{m_1 x}$$

Case 3: *If the roots are not real.*
In this case, the roots are complex conjugates. If we denote them by $m_1 = \alpha + \beta i$ and $m_2 = \alpha - \beta i$, then the general solution of the differential equation is:

$$y = e^{\alpha x}(c_1 \cos \beta x + c_2 \sin \beta x)$$

Example 4.8   Find the general solution of each of the following equations:
(a) $y'' + 4y = 0$ (b) $2y'' + 7y' = 4y$
(c) $y'' + 2y' + y = 0$ (d) $y''' - y'' - 9y' + 9y = 0$

Solution: For each differential equation, we solve the corresponding auxiliary polynomial equation, then use the roots to write down the general solution of the differential equation.

(a)   The corresponding auxiliary polynomial equation is $m^2 + 4 = 0$, whose roots are the complex conjugates $m = \pm 2i$. This example falls into Case 3 with $\alpha = 0$ and $\beta = 2$, so the general solution of the differential equation is:

$$y = e^{0x}(c_1 \cos 2x + c_2 \sin 2x) = c_1 \cos 2x + c_2 \sin 2x$$

(b)   After rewriting this equation in the standard form, $2y'' + 7y' - 4y = 0$, we write its auxiliary polynomial equation, $2m^2 + 7m - 4 = 0$. To solve this, we notice that the polynomial can be factored to give $(2m - 1)(m + 4)$, so the roots are $m_1 = \dfrac{1}{2}$ and $m_2 = -4$. Since this example falls into Case 1, the general solution of the differential equation is:

$$y = c_1 e^{x/2} + c_2 e^{-4x}$$

(c)   Here, the auxiliary polynomial equation is $m^2 + 2m + 1 = 0$, which is equivalent to $(m + 1)^2 = 0$. Therefore, it has $m = -1$ as a double root. This example falls into Case 2, so the general solution of the differential equation is:

$$y = c_1 e^{-x} + c_2 x e^{-x}$$

(d)   This is a *third*-order linear equation with constant coefficients, but the solution method remains the same. The auxiliary polynomial equation is $m^3 - m^2 - 9m + 9 = 0$, which we can solve by factoring:

$$m^3 - m^2 - 9m + 9 = 0$$
$$m^2(m-1) - 9(m-1) = 0$$
$$(m^2 - 9)(m-1) = 0$$
$$(m+3)(m-3)(m-1) = 0$$

This equation has three distinct real roots: $m_1 = -3$, $m_2 = 3$, and $m_3 = 1$, which places it in the category of Case 1 (distinct real roots), so the general solution of this third-order differential equation is:

$$y = c_1 e^{-3x} + c_2 e^{3x} + c_3 e^x$$

Notice that the general solution of the second-order equations contained two arbitrary constants, and the general solution of the third-order equation contained three arbitrary constants. You should expect that the general solution of an nth-order, ordinary differential equation will contain n arbitrary constants (pathological examples not included). You should also expect that the general solution of an nth-order homogeneous equation is the sum of n linearly independent functions.

Example 4.9   Find the general solution of the equation:

$$y'' = x + y$$

Solution: Writing this linear equation in standard form, $y'' - y = x$, we notice immediately that it's not homogeneous, since the right-hand side isn't zero. The general solution of a nonhomogeneous linear equation is $y = y_h + y_p$ where y_h is the general solution of the corresponding homogeneous equation, and y_p is any particular solution of the nonhomogeneous equation.

The corresponding homogeneous equation is $y'' - y = 0$. Since the auxiliary polynomial equation is $m^2 - 1 = 0$ (whose roots are $m = \pm 1$), we know that $y_h = c_1 e^x + c_2 e^{-x}$. By inspection, we see that $y = -x$ is a particular solution of the given nonhomogeneous equation, so we can take $y_p = -x$. Therefore, the general solution of the nonhomogeneous equation is:

$$y = c_1 e^x + c_2 e^{-x} - x$$

The key to finding the solution to this example is noticing the particular solution $y_p = -x$ to the nonhomogeneous equation. If the nonhomogeneous right-hand term isn't complicated, finding a particular solution is usually not too difficult. Fortunately, however, the GRE Math Subject Test is a multiple-choice exam, so you can always test the possible choices to see if they solve the given equation, rather than trying to discover a solution from scratch. Of course, this is true not only for nonhomogeneous linear equations, but for any type of differential equation you encounter on the exam!

CHAPTER 4 REVIEW QUESTIONS

Complete the following review questions using the techniques outlined in this chapter. Then, see Chapter 8 for answers and explanations.

1.   Let $y = f(x)$ be the solution of the equation

$$\frac{dy}{dx} = \frac{x^2}{x^2 + 1}$$

such that $y = 0$ when $x = 0$. What is the value of $f(1)$?

(A) $1 - \log 2$ (B) $1 + \log 2$ (C) 1 (D) $\log 2$ (E) $\frac{1}{4}(4 - \pi)$

2.   A population of bacteria grows at a rate proportional to the number present. After two hours, the population has tripled. After two more hours elapse, the population will have increased by a factor of k. What is the value of k?

(A) 6   (B) 8   (C) 9   (D) 27   (E) 81

3.   Every curve in a certain family, $y = f(x, c)$, has the following property: the area of the region in the first quadrant bounded above by the curve from $(0, 0)$ to (x, y) and bounded below by the x-axis is $\frac{1}{3}$ the area of the rectangle with opposite vertices at $(0, 0)$ and (x, y). Find $f(x, c)$.

(A) cx^3 (B) $cx^3 + x$ (C) $cx^3 - x$ (D) cx^2 (E) $c\sqrt{x}$

4.   Which of the following depicts integral curves of the differential equation $\left(\frac{dy}{dx}\right)^2 = \frac{x}{y}\left(2\frac{dy}{dx} - \frac{x}{y}\right)$?

(A)   (B)   (C)

(D)   (E)

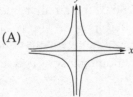

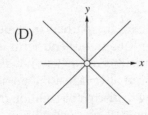

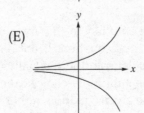

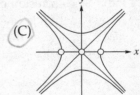

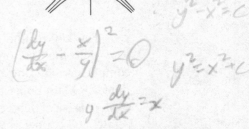

5.   If a is a positive constant, let $y = f(x)$ be the solution of the equation

$$y''' - ay'' + a^2 y' - a^3 y = 0$$

such that $f(0) = 1$, $f'(0) = 0$, and $f''(0) = a^2$. How many positive values of x satisfy the equation $f(x) = 0$?

(A) 0   (B) 1   (C) 2   (D) 3   (E) more than 3

6. Let $g: \mathbf{R} \to \mathbf{R}$ be a differentiable and integrable function. The integral curve of the differential equation

$$[y + g(x)]\, dx + [x - g(y)]\, dy = 0$$

✓ that passes through the point $(1, 1)$ must also pass through which of the following points?

(handwritten: $xy + \int g(x)dx - \int g(y)dy = 0$)
(handwritten: $xy + G(x) - G(y) + c = 1$)

(A) $(0, 0)$ (B) $(2, \frac{1}{2})$ (C) $(\frac{1}{2}, 2)$ (D) $(-1, -1)$ (E) $(0, 1)$

---

7. Let $y = f(x)$ be the solution of the equation

$$\frac{dy}{dx} + \frac{y}{x} = \sin x$$

✓ such that $f(\pi) = 1$. What is the value of $f(\frac{1}{2}\pi)$?

(handwritten: $\mu(x) = e^{\int \frac{1}{x}dx} = x$)
(handwritten: $x\frac{dy}{dx} + y = x\sin x$)
(handwritten: $[xy]' = -x\cos x + \sin x + C$)
(handwritten: $y(\pi) = \frac{\pi + c}{\pi} \quad c = 0$)

(A) $\dfrac{2}{\pi} - 1$ (B) $\dfrac{2}{\pi}$ (C) $\dfrac{2}{\pi} + 1$ (D) $\dfrac{\pi}{2}$ (E) $\dfrac{\pi}{2} + 1$

(handwritten: $y(\frac{\pi}{2}) = \frac{1}{\pi/2}$)

---

8. Let $y = f(x)$ be the solution of the equation

$$\frac{d^4 y}{dx^4} = \frac{d^2 y}{dx^2}$$

✓ such that $f(0) = f'(0) = f''(0) = 0$ and $f'''(0) = -1$. What is $f(x)$?

(handwritten: $\cosh x = \frac{e^x + e^{-x}}{2} \quad |_0 = 1$)
(handwritten: $\sinh x = \frac{e^x - e^{-x}}{2} \quad |_0 = 0$)

(A) $x - \cosh x$ (B) $x - \sinh x$ (C) $x + \cosh x$ (D) $x + \sinh x$ (E) $\cosh x + \sinh x$

---

9. What is the general solution of the differential equation

$$2\frac{d^3 x}{dt^3} + 7\frac{d^2 x}{dt^2} + 3\frac{dx}{dt} = 6?$$

(handwritten: $2m^3 + 7m^2 + 3m = 0 \quad m = 0$)
(handwritten: $2m^2 + 7m + 3 = 0$)
(handwritten: $\frac{-7 \pm 5}{4} \quad -3, -\frac{1}{2}$)

(A) $x = 2t + c_1 e^t + c_2 e^{-t/2} + c_3 e^{-3t}$ (B) $x = 2 + c_1 e^t + c_2 e^{-t/2} + c_3 e^{-3t}$ (C) $x = t^2 + c_1 + c_2 e^{-t/3} + c_3 e^{-2t}$

(D) $x = 2t + c_1 + c_2 e^{-t/3} + c_3 e^{-2t}$ (E) $x = 2t + c_1 + c_2 e^{-t/2} + c_3 e^{-3t}$

---

10. Given that the following differential equation has an integrating factor of the form $\mu(x, y) = x^m y^n$, determine its general solution.

$$(3xy^2 - 5y)\, dx + (2x^2 y - 3x)\, dy = 0$$

(handwritten at left: $3x^5 y^4 - 5x^4 y^3$)
(handwritten: $\frac{1}{2}x^6 y^4 - x^5 y^3 = \frac{1}{2}x^6 y^4 - x^5 y^3$)
(handwritten: $x^4 y^2$)
(handwritten: $2x^6 y^3 - 3x^5 y^3$

(handwritten top right: $x^4 y^2$)
(handwritten: $(3x^{m+1} y^{n+2} - 5x^m y^{n+1})dx$)
(handwritten: $+ (2x^{m+2} y^n - 3x^{m+1} y^n)dy = 0$)

(A) $x^4 y^2 (\frac{1}{2} xy - 1) = c$ (B) $x^4 y^2 (xy - 1) = c$ (C) $x^4 y^2 (2xy - 1) = c$

(D) $x^5 y^3 (\frac{1}{2} xy - 1) = c$ (E) $x^5 y^3 (2xy - 1) = c$

(handwritten: $x^5 y^3 (\frac{1}{2} xy - 1)$)

(handwritten: $(2n + 1 = 6m)$... $3(n+2) = 2(n+2)$)
(handwritten: $n + 1 = 6m$)
(handwritten: $5(n+1) = 3(n+1)$)
(handwritten: $-n + 6 = 6n$)
(handwritten: $n = 2$)
(handwritten: $m = 4$)
(handwritten: $5n + 2 = 3m$)
(handwritten: $3n + 2 = 2m$)

(handwritten right: $3(n+2)x^{m+1} y^{n+1} - 5n+1)x^m y^n$)
(handwritten: $= 2(n+2)x^{m+1} y^{n+1} - 3(n+1)x^m y^n$)

11. At every point (x, y) on a curve in the xy-plane, the slope is equal to:

$$\frac{dy}{dx} = \frac{1 - 2xy}{x^2 + 3y^2 + 1}$$

What is the equation of this curve, given that it passes through the point $(1, 1)$?

(A) $\frac{1}{3}x^3 + 3xy^2 + x + y - xy^2 = \frac{13}{3}$ (B) $xy^2 + y^3 + x - y = 2$

(C) $\frac{1}{3}x^3 + 3xy^2 - x + y + xy^2 = \frac{13}{3}$ (D) $x^2y + y^3 - x + y = 2$

(E) $x^2y^2 + xy^3 + x - y = 1$

12. Find the general solution of the differential equation:

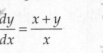

$$\frac{dy}{dx} = \frac{x + y}{x}$$

(A) $e^{y/x} = cx$ (B) $e^{y/x} = cy$ (C) $e^{x/y} = cx$ (D) $e^{x/y} = cy$ (E) $e^{-x/y} = cx$

13. Consider the family F of circles in the xy-plane, $(x - c)^2 + y^2 = c^2$, that are tangent to the y-axis at the origin. Which of the following gives the differential equation that is satisfied by the family of curves orthogonal to F?

(A) $y' = \frac{x}{x - y}$ (B) $y' = \frac{x}{y - x}$ (C) $y' = \frac{xy}{x - y}$ (D) $y' = \frac{2xy}{x^2 - y^2}$ (E) $y' = \frac{2xy}{y^2 - x^2}$

14. Let $g(x, y)$ be the function defined for all x and all nonzero y such that the differential equation

$$(\sin xy)\,dx + g(x, y)\,dy = 0$$

is exact and $g(0, y) = 0$ for all $y \neq 0$. What is $g(x, 1)$?

(A) $\sin x + \cos x - 1$ (B) $x \sin x + \cos x - 1$ (C) $x \sin x - \cos x + 1$

(D) $x \sin x + \cos x$ (E) $\sin x - x \cos x + 1$

15. If $w = f(x, y)$ is a solution of the partial differential equation

$$2\frac{\partial w}{\partial x} - 3\frac{\partial w}{\partial y} = 0$$

then w could equal

(A) $(2x - 3y)^6$ (B) $\sin\left[\log(3x - 2y)\right]$ (C) $e^{\arctan(3x + 2y)}$

(D) $\left[\arccos(2y - 3x)\right]^2$ (E) $\sqrt{2x + 3y}$

Linear Algebra

INTRODUCTION

A **linear equation** in the variables (or unknowns) $x_1, x_2, \ldots, x_n$ is an equation of the form

$$a_1x_1 + a_2x_2 + \ldots + a_nx_n = b$$

where the coefficients $a_1, a_2, \ldots, a_n$ and the term b are constants. A **linear system** is a collection of one or more linear equations for which we seek solutions (values of the unknowns x_i) that satisfy all the equations of the system *simultaneously*. The study of such systems motivates the content of linear algebra.

SOLUTIONS OF LINEAR SYSTEMS

A fundamental fact about linear systems states that:

> No matter how many equations a linear system contains or how many unknowns are involved, there are only three possibilities for the number of solutions:

1. There are no solutions. This means there are no values of the unknowns that satisfy all the equations in the system simultaneously. Such a system is said to be **inconsistent**.

2. There is exactly one solution.

3. There are infinitely many solutions.

A system that has at least one solution is called **consistent**. To illustrate this general result, notice that the first system below has no solutions, the second system has exactly one solution, and the third has infinitely many:

$$x + 2y = 5 \qquad\qquad x + 2y = 5 \qquad\qquad x + 2y = 5$$
$$3x + 6y = 13 \qquad\qquad 3x + 5y = 14 \qquad\qquad 3x + 6y = 15$$

No solutions $\qquad\qquad$ Exactly one solution $\qquad\qquad$ Infinitely many solutions

Consider the graphs of these equations in the x-y plane. The graphs of the equations in the first system are parallel lines with no points in common; although there are infinitely many values of (x, y) that satisfy each equation separately, there are no values of (x, y) that satisfy both equations simultaneously. The graphs of the equations in the second system are lines that intersect in exactly one point; and those of the third are lines that coincide, so every point that lies on the first graph automatically lies on the second, since the equations in this system describe the same line.

When there are three unknowns in the system, the graph of a linear equation is generally a plane in 3-space. But the possibilities for the number of solutions to the system remain the same, because, for example, planes can be parallel or intersect in lines that are parallel (and hence not intersect at all), intersect in exactly one point, or intersect in a line (or plane) and thus have infinitely many intersection points. When there are more than three unknowns in the system, we can no longer envision the graphs, but an algebraic proof can establish the result above.

To find the solutions of a given linear system, we can try various values of the unknowns and hope we stumble upon the correct set. For example, for the system given above,

$$x + 2y = 5$$
$$3x + 5y = 14$$

it isn't difficult to figure out that $x = 3$ and $y = 1$ satisfy both equations, so $(x, y) = (3, 1)$ is the solution to the system. However, what we really want is a step-by-step method that can be applied to any system. The best method for solving a linear system is called **Gaussian elimination**. The idea is simple: Multiply the equations by carefully chosen constants so that upon combining the resulting equations, the variables are eliminated one at a time. Eventually, we'll have just one equation and one unknown, which can be solved immediately. With the value of this unknown in hand, we substitute back into the other equations and solve for the other unknowns one by one.

Let's illustrate Gaussian elimination with the system above. If we multiply the first equation by 3, the system becomes:

$$3x + 6y = 15$$
$$3x + 5y = 14$$

Subtracting the second equation from the first eliminates the variable x and gives $y = 1$. Then, substituting this into either equation gives $x = 3$. Thus, the system has exactly one solution: $(x, y) = (3, 1)$.

In order to simplify the work involved in Gaussian elimination, especially with larger systems, we use rectangular arrays of numbers called matrices. Since matrices have properties of their own and can be studied separately from linear systems, we'll first discuss matrices as objects in their own right and then apply what we've learned to solving systems by Gaussian elimination.

MATRICES AND MATRIX ALGEBRA

A **matrix** is a rectangular array of numbers enclosed in a large pair of parentheses or brackets. The **size** or **dimensions** of a matrix are the number of rows and the number of columns it contains; if there are m rows and n columns, the matrix is said to be m by n, which is written $m \times n$. (The number of rows is always written first.) For example, the matrix A below is 2×3, the matrix B is 3×3, and the matrix C is 4×2:

$$A = \begin{pmatrix} -3 & 0 & 4 \\ 2 & -2 & 5 \end{pmatrix} \qquad B = \begin{pmatrix} 7 & 1 & -2 \\ 0 & 0 & \frac{1}{2} \\ -6 & 3 & 1 \end{pmatrix} \qquad C = \begin{pmatrix} 1 & 9 \\ -4 & 0 \\ 2 & 0 \\ 0 & -8 \end{pmatrix}$$

The numbers that appear in a matrix are its **entries**. The entry in row i and column j is called the (i, j) entry; if the matrix is denoted A, then the (i, j) entry is denoted a_{ij}. For example, for the matrix A given above, $a_{11} = -3$, $a_{21} = 2$, $a_{12} = 0$, $a_{23} = 5$, and so forth. An entry whose column number matches its row number is called a **diagonal** entry. In the matrix B, the diagonal entries are $b_{11} = 7$, $b_{22} = 0$, and $b_{33} = 1$; these entries form the **main diagonal** of B. A matrix that has only zeros above its main diagonal—that is, if every (i, j) entry for which $i < j$ is 0—is said to be **lower triangular**. A matrix that has only zeros below its main diagonal—that is, if every (i, j) entry for which $i > j$ is 0—is called **upper triangular**. For example, the following matrix L is lower triangular and U is upper triangular:

$$L = \begin{pmatrix} 1 & 0 \\ -1 & -2 \end{pmatrix} \qquad U = \begin{pmatrix} 1 & 8 & 0 & 2 \\ 0 & -2 & -3 & 0 \\ 0 & 0 & 0 & 4 \\ 0 & 0 & 0 & 1 \end{pmatrix}$$

A matrix that has as many columns as rows is a **square** matrix. The matrix B above is a 3×3 square matrix; the matrices L and U also happen to be examples of square matrices.

MATRIX OPERATIONS

Matrices can be added, subtracted, multiplied by scalars, and multiplied by each other, with some restrictions. If two matrices are the same size, then they can be added or subtracted; the result is another matrix of the same size as the two that were combined. The rules for addition and subtraction are easy. If $A = (a_{ij})$ and $B = (b_{ij})$ are both $m \times n$ matrices, then their sum, $C = A + B$, is also $m \times n$ and its entries are given by the formula

$$c_{ij} = a_{ij} + b_{ij}$$

and their difference, $D = A - B$, is also $m \times n$ and its entries are given by the equation:

$$d_{ij} = a_{ij} - b_{ij}$$

These equations say that to form the sum (or difference) of two matrices, simply add (or subtract) their corresponding entries.

Any matrix may be multiplied by a number (a scalar). If $A = (a_{ij})$ is an $m \times n$ matrix and k is a scalar, then the **scalar multiple** $S = kA$ is also $m \times n$ and its entries are given by the formula:

$$s_{ij} = ka_{ij}$$

Therefore, to multiply a matrix by a scalar, just multiply every entry of the matrix by that scalar.

A simple but useful operation to perform on a matrix is to form its transpose. The **transpose** of an $m \times n$ matrix A is the $n \times m$ matrix A^T formed by making the rows of A the columns of A^T (an operation that automatically makes the columns of A the rows of A^T). For example, the transpose of the 2×3 matrix

$$A = \begin{pmatrix} -3 & 0 & 4 \\ 2 & -2 & 5 \end{pmatrix}$$

is the 3×2 matrix:

$$A^T = \begin{pmatrix} -3 & 2 \\ 0 & -2 \\ 4 & 5 \end{pmatrix}$$

Clearly, $(A^T)^T = A$. Also notice that the transpose of a row matrix (row vector) is a column matrix (column vector), and vice versa.

The final operation we'll consider here is **matrix multiplication**, which is by far the most important. The motivation for the definition of matrix multiplication is the dot product of vectors. Recall that if $\mathbf{u} = (u_1, u_2, \ldots, u_n)$ and $\mathbf{v} = (v_1, v_2, \ldots, v_n)$ are both n-vectors, then we can form their dot product, which is the scalar:

$$\mathbf{u} \bullet \mathbf{v} = u_1 v_1 + u_2 v_2 + \cdots + u_n v_n$$

Only vectors that have the same number of components can be dotted in this way, a fact that's crucial in the definition of matrix multiplication. If A and B are matrices, then their **product**, AB, is defined only if the number of columns of A equals the number of rows of B. So, if the matrix A is $m \times n$, then B must be $n \times p$ in order for the product AB to be defined. If this is the case, the size of the product matrix AB is $m \times p$, and the (i, j) entry of AB is given by the dot product of row i in A and column j in B, thought of as n-vectors:

$$(i, j) \text{ entry of } AB = (r_i \text{ in } A) \bullet (c_j \text{ in } B)$$

To help remember when matrix multiplication is defined and the size of the product matrix, the following diagram is helpful:

$$\underbrace{A}_{m \times n} \bullet \underbrace{B}_{n \times p} = \underbrace{AB}_{m \times p}$$

Example 5.1   Consider the following four matrices:

$$A = \begin{pmatrix} -3 & 0 & 4 \\ 2 & -2 & 5 \end{pmatrix}, \quad B = \begin{pmatrix} 7 & 1 & -2 \\ 0 & 0 & \frac{1}{2} \\ -6 & 3 & 1 \end{pmatrix},$$

$$C = \begin{pmatrix} 1 & 9 \\ -4 & 0 \\ 2 & -1 \end{pmatrix}, \quad \text{and} \quad D = \begin{pmatrix} -5 & -1 & 4 \\ 3 & 1 & 8 \\ 0 & 2 & 6 \end{pmatrix}$$

(a) Which two of these matrices can be added together? What is their sum?
(b) Compute $A - C^{\mathrm{T}}$.
(c) Which one of the matrix products AB, AC, BA, or CA is *not* defined? Compute the three matrix products that are defined.

Solution:

(a) Only matrices of the same size can be added; therefore only the matrices B and D can be added together. (Of course, any matrix can be added to itself, but the question asked which *two* of the given matrices could be added together.) The sum of B and D is:

$$B + D = \begin{pmatrix} 7 & 1 & -2 \\ 0 & 0 & \frac{1}{2} \\ -6 & 3 & 1 \end{pmatrix} + \begin{pmatrix} -5 & -1 & 4 \\ 3 & 1 & 8 \\ 0 & 2 & 6 \end{pmatrix} = \begin{pmatrix} 2 & 0 & 2 \\ 3 & 1 & \frac{17}{2} \\ -6 & 5 & 7 \end{pmatrix}$$

(b) Because C is 3×2, its transpose is 2×3, the same size as A. Therefore, the expression $A - C^{\mathrm{T}}$ is defined:

$$A - C^{\mathrm{T}} = \begin{pmatrix} -3 & 0 & 4 \\ 2 & -2 & 5 \end{pmatrix} - \begin{pmatrix} 1 & -4 & 2 \\ 9 & 0 & -1 \end{pmatrix} = \begin{pmatrix} -4 & 4 & 2 \\ -7 & -2 & 6 \end{pmatrix}$$

(c) Since A is 2×3, B is 3×3, and C is 3×2, the matrix product BA is the one product from the given list that is not defined, since the number of columns of B (namely, 3) does not equal the number of rows of A (which is 2). We begin with the calculation of the product AB. The $(1, 1)$ entry of AB is equal to the dot product of row 1 of A—which is $(-3, 0, 4)$—and column 1 of B—which is $(7, 0, -6)^{\mathrm{T}}$:

$$(1, 1) \text{ entry of } AB = (-3, 0, 4) \bullet (7, 0, -6) = (-3)(7) + (0)(0) + (4)(-6) = -45$$

The $(1, 2)$ entry of AB is equal to the dot product of row 1 of A and column 2 of B,

$$(1, 2) \text{ entry of } AB = (-3, 0, 4) \bullet (1, 0, 3) = (-3)(1) + (0)(0) + (4)(3) = 9$$

and so forth for the other entries. Completing the calculations gives:

$$AB = \begin{pmatrix} -3 & 0 & 4 \\ 2 & -2 & 5 \end{pmatrix} \begin{pmatrix} 7 & 1 & -2 \\ 0 & 0 & \frac{1}{2} \\ -6 & 3 & 1 \end{pmatrix} = \begin{pmatrix} -45 & 9 & 10 \\ -16 & 17 & 0 \end{pmatrix}$$

We now compute the products AC and CA:

$$AC = \begin{pmatrix} -3 & 0 & 4 \\ 2 & -2 & 5 \end{pmatrix} \begin{pmatrix} 1 & 9 \\ -4 & 0 \\ 2 & -1 \end{pmatrix} = \begin{pmatrix} 5 & -31 \\ 20 & 13 \end{pmatrix}$$

$$CA = \begin{pmatrix} 1 & 9 \\ -4 & 0 \\ 2 & -1 \end{pmatrix} \begin{pmatrix} -3 & 0 & 4 \\ 2 & -2 & 5 \end{pmatrix} = \begin{pmatrix} 15 & -18 & 49 \\ 12 & 0 & -16 \\ -8 & 2 & 3 \end{pmatrix}$$

This example illustrates an important difference between the multiplication of scalars and the multiplication of matrices. If a and b are scalars, then ab always equals ba; we say that multiplication is **commutative**, since the order in which the factors are multiplied is irrelevant. But this is not true for matrix multiplication; that is, it is generally false that $AB = BA$. For example, for the matrices given above, the product AB did not equal BA since BA wasn't even defined. And although the products AC and CA were both defined, they weren't identical; in fact, they weren't even the same size! While one can find examples of matrices A and B for which $AB = BA$ (in which case the matrices are said to **commute**), matrix multiplication is generally **noncommutative**. Matrix multiplication is **associative**, however. That is, if A, B, and C are matrices such that both AB and BC are defined, then $A(BC) = (AB)C$; the order in which the factors are *grouped* doesn't matter (just like for scalars).

IDENTITY MATRICES AND INVERSES

Consider a square matrix I whose (i, j) entry is given by the **Kronecker delta**:

$$\delta_{ij} = \begin{cases} 1 & \text{if } i = j \\ 0 & \text{if } i \neq j \end{cases}$$

Such a matrix has 1's along its main diagonal and 0's elsewhere. It is called an **identity matrix**, since if A is any matrix for which AI is defined, then $AI = A$; similarly, if B is any matrix for which IB is defined, then $IB = B$. Thus, multiplying a compatible matrix by I leaves the matrix unchanged; it's just like multiplying a scalar by the number 1, the identity element for scalar multiplication. In the set of $n \times n$ matrices, the $n \times n$ matrix I_n is the multiplicative identity; that is, $AI_n = I_nA = A$ for any $n \times n$ matrix A.

If the product of two scalars is equal to 1, then each is called the multiplicative inverse of the other; that is, if $ab = 1$, then $b = a^{-1}$ and $a = b^{-1}$. The same can be said for matrices. If $AB = I$, then A is called a left inverse of B, and B is called a right inverse of A. If $AB = I$ and both A and B are square matrices (necessarily of the same size), we can omit the designations "left" and "right" and simply say that A is the **inverse** of B and B is the inverse of A (because it can be shown that if A and B are square with $AB = I$, then $BA = I$ also). In this case, we write $B = A^{-1}$ and $A = B^{-1}$. For example, the inverse of the matrix

$$A = \begin{pmatrix} 1 & 2 \\ 3 & 4 \end{pmatrix}$$

is the matrix

$$A^{-1} = \begin{pmatrix} -2 & 1 \\ \frac{3}{2} & -\frac{1}{2} \end{pmatrix}$$

because

$$AA^{-1} = A^{-1}A = I = \begin{pmatrix} 1 & 0 \\ 0 & 1 \end{pmatrix}$$

as you can check. A square matrix that has an inverse is said to be **invertible**. An example of a matrix that is not invertible is:

$$B = \begin{pmatrix} 0 & 0 \\ 1 & 1 \end{pmatrix}$$

To see why B is noninvertible, notice that if C is any 2×2 matrix, then the product BC can never equal I, because the first row of BC will contain zeros only (as you can verify).

Example 5.2   Consider the matrices:

$$A = \begin{pmatrix} 3 & -1 \\ -5 & 2 \end{pmatrix} \quad \text{and} \quad B = \begin{pmatrix} -4 & 7 \\ 3 & -5 \end{pmatrix}$$

(a) Compute $3A - B$.
(b) What is A^2?
(c) Verify that:

$$A^{-1} = \begin{pmatrix} 2 & 1 \\ 5 & 3 \end{pmatrix} \quad \text{and} \quad B^{-1} = \begin{pmatrix} 5 & 7 \\ 3 & 4 \end{pmatrix}$$

(d) Show that $(AB)^{-1} = B^{-1}A^{-1}$.
(e) The matrix A satisfies the equation $A^2 - 5A + I = 0$, where 0 denotes the 2×2 *zero matrix*. Use this equation to find a formula for A^{-1} in terms of A, and show that the matrix A^{-1} obtained from this formula equals the matrix A^{-1} given in part (c).

Solution:

(a) Multiplying the matrix A by 3, then subtracting B from the result yields:

$$3A - B = 3\begin{pmatrix} 3 & -1 \\ -5 & 2 \end{pmatrix} - \begin{pmatrix} -4 & 7 \\ 3 & -5 \end{pmatrix} = \begin{pmatrix} 9 & -3 \\ -15 & 6 \end{pmatrix} - \begin{pmatrix} -4 & 7 \\ 3 & -5 \end{pmatrix} = \begin{pmatrix} 13 & -10 \\ -18 & 11 \end{pmatrix}$$

(b) The expression A^2 denotes the product AA:

$$A^2 = \begin{pmatrix} 3 & -1 \\ -5 & 2 \end{pmatrix}\begin{pmatrix} 3 & -1 \\ -5 & 2 \end{pmatrix} = \begin{pmatrix} 14 & -5 \\ -25 & 9 \end{pmatrix}$$

(c) The matrices given are the inverses of A and B, since $AA^{-1} = BB^{-1} = I$:

$$AA^{-1} = \begin{pmatrix} 3 & -1 \\ -5 & 2 \end{pmatrix}\begin{pmatrix} 2 & 1 \\ 5 & 3 \end{pmatrix} = \begin{pmatrix} 1 & 0 \\ 0 & 1 \end{pmatrix}$$

$$BB^{-1} = \begin{pmatrix} -4 & 7 \\ 3 & -5 \end{pmatrix}\begin{pmatrix} 5 & 7 \\ 3 & 4 \end{pmatrix} = \begin{pmatrix} 1 & 0 \\ 0 & 1 \end{pmatrix}$$

(d)   First, we figure out the products AB and $B^{-1}A^{-1}$:

$$AB = \begin{pmatrix} 3 & -1 \\ -5 & 2 \end{pmatrix}\begin{pmatrix} -4 & 7 \\ 3 & -5 \end{pmatrix} = \begin{pmatrix} -15 & 26 \\ 26 & -45 \end{pmatrix}$$

$$B^{-1}A^{-1} = \begin{pmatrix} 5 & 7 \\ 3 & 4 \end{pmatrix}\begin{pmatrix} 2 & 1 \\ 5 & 3 \end{pmatrix} = \begin{pmatrix} 45 & 26 \\ 26 & 15 \end{pmatrix}$$

To show that the inverse of AB is $B^{-1}A^{-1}$, we check that $(AB)(B^{-1}A^{-1}) = I$:

$$(AB)(B^{-1}A^{-1}) = \begin{pmatrix} -15 & 26 \\ 26 & -45 \end{pmatrix}\begin{pmatrix} 45 & 26 \\ 26 & 15 \end{pmatrix} = \begin{pmatrix} 1 & 0 \\ 0 & 1 \end{pmatrix}$$

Of course, a numerical verification of this formula isn't really necessary, since we can use associativity of matrix multiplication to conclude that:

$$(AB)(B^{-1}A^{-1}) = A(BB^{-1})A^{-1} = AIA^{-1} = AA^{-1} = I$$

This proof shows that if A and B are *any* invertible matrices of the same size, then their product, AB, is also invertible, and the inverse of the product is equal to the product of the inverses, in the reverse order.

(e)   Starting with the equation $A^2 - 5A + I = 0$, we write:

$$A(A - 5I) + I = 0 \quad \Rightarrow \quad A(A - 5I) = -I \quad \Rightarrow \quad A(5I - A) = I$$

This final equation says that the product of A and $(5I - A)$ gives the identity matrix; by definition, then, $(5I - A)$ must be the inverse of A:

$$A^{-1} = 5I - A$$

To check this formula, we compute

$$5I - A = \begin{pmatrix} 5 & 0 \\ 0 & 5 \end{pmatrix} - \begin{pmatrix} 3 & -1 \\ -5 & 2 \end{pmatrix} = \begin{pmatrix} 2 & 1 \\ 5 & 3 \end{pmatrix}$$

and notice that this does indeed match the matrix A^{-1} given in part (c).

GAUSSIAN ELIMINATION

Now that we have the machinery of matrix algebra at our disposal, we return to the solution of linear systems. To solve the linear system

$$x + 2y = 5$$
$$3x + 5y = 14$$

we take the coefficients of the unknowns and form the **coefficient matrix**

$$\begin{pmatrix} 1 & 2 \\ 3 & 5 \end{pmatrix}$$

and attach the constants that appear on the right-hand sides of the equations as an additional column, producing the **augmented matrix**:

$$\begin{pmatrix} 1 & 2 & 5 \\ 3 & 5 & 14 \end{pmatrix}$$

Now, to eliminate the variable x, for example, we multiply the first row by -3 and add the result to the second row; this operation doesn't change the first row, but it does change the second row:

$$\begin{pmatrix} 1 & 2 & 5 \\ 0 & -1 & -1 \end{pmatrix}$$

The bottom row of this matrix is equivalent to the equation $0x + (-1)y = -1$, from which we immediately get $y = 1$. Plugging $y = 1$ into the equation that corresponds to the top row, $1x + 2y = 5$, gives $x = 3$. Therefore, the solution of the given linear system is $(x, y) = (3, 1)$.

In general, Gaussian elimination proceeds as follows:

Step 1: *Write down the augmented matrix corresponding to the given linear system.*

Step 2: *Perform a series of elementary row operations to **reduce** (transform) the augmented matrix to echelon form. An **elementary row operation** is one of the following:*

1. *Multiplying a row by a nonzero constant.*

2. *Interchanging two rows.*

3. *Adding a multiple of one row to another row.*

*A matrix is said to be in **echelon** form when it is an upper triangular matrix, any zero rows appear at the bottom of the matrix, and the first nonzero entry in any row appears to the right of the first nonzero entry in any higher row. Thus, the goal of this step is to use elementary row operations to produce zeros below the first entry in the first column, then below the second entry in the second column, and so forth.*

Step 3: *Working from the bottom of the echelon matrix upward, evaluate the unknowns using **back-substitution**.*

Example 5.3   Solve the following linear system using Gaussian elimination:

$$\begin{aligned} x &- 2y &+ 3z &= 3 \\ 2x &+ y &- z &= 9 \\ -3x &+ 5y & &= -2 \end{aligned}$$

Solution: The first step is to write down the corresponding augmented matrix:

$$\begin{pmatrix} 1 & -2 & 3 & 3 \\ 2 & 1 & -1 & 9 \\ -3 & 5 & 0 & -2 \end{pmatrix}$$

To get a matrix that has zeros below the first entry in the first column, we perform the following elementary row operations: add –2 times the first row to the second row (abbreviated as $-2\mathbf{r}_1 + \mathbf{r}_2$) and add 3 times the first row to the third row ($3\mathbf{r}_1 + \mathbf{r}_3$):

$$\begin{pmatrix} 1 & -2 & 3 & 3 \\ 2 & 1 & -1 & 9 \\ -3 & 5 & 0 & -2 \end{pmatrix} \xrightarrow[3\mathbf{r}_1+\mathbf{r}_3]{-2\mathbf{r}_1+\mathbf{r}_2} \begin{pmatrix} 1 & -2 & 3 & 3 \\ 0 & 5 & -7 & 3 \\ 0 & -1 & 9 & 7 \end{pmatrix}$$

Next, let's interchange rows 2 and 3 ($\mathbf{r}_2 \leftrightarrow \mathbf{r}_3$):

$$\begin{pmatrix} 1 & -2 & 3 & 3 \\ 0 & 5 & -7 & 3 \\ 0 & -1 & 9 & 7 \end{pmatrix} \xrightarrow{\mathbf{r}_2\leftrightarrow\mathbf{r}_3} \begin{pmatrix} 1 & -2 & 3 & 3 \\ 0 & -1 & 9 & 7 \\ 0 & 5 & -7 & 3 \end{pmatrix}$$

Finally, add 5 times the second row to the third row ($5\mathbf{r}_2 + \mathbf{r}_3$):

$$\begin{pmatrix} 1 & -2 & 3 & 3 \\ 0 & -1 & 9 & 7 \\ 0 & 5 & -7 & 3 \end{pmatrix} \xrightarrow{5\mathbf{r}_2+\mathbf{r}_3} \begin{pmatrix} 1 & -2 & 3 & 3 \\ 0 & -1 & 9 & 7 \\ 0 & 0 & 38 & 38 \end{pmatrix}$$

The matrix is now in echelon form. The bottom row translates to the equation $38z = 38$, so we see that $z = 1$. Working our way up the echelon matrix, the second row corresponds to the equation $-y + 9z = 7$, so substituting $z = 1$, we get $y = 2$. Finally, the top row corresponds to the equation $x - 2y + 3z = 3$; substituting both $z = 1$ and $y = 2$ into this equation yields $x = 4$. Therefore, the solution to the system is $(x, y, z) = (4, 2, 1)$.

Example 5.4   Solve this system using Gaussian elimination:

$$\begin{aligned} x - 2y + 3z &= 3 \\ 2x + y - z &= 9 \\ -3x - 4y + 5z &= -8 \end{aligned}$$

Solution: The corresponding augmented matrix is:

$$\begin{pmatrix} 1 & -2 & 3 & 3 \\ 2 & 1 & -1 & 9 \\ -3 & -4 & 5 & -8 \end{pmatrix}$$

Performing the series of elementary row operations indicated below,

$$\begin{pmatrix} 1 & -2 & 3 & 3 \\ 2 & 1 & -1 & 9 \\ -3 & -4 & 5 & -8 \end{pmatrix} \xrightarrow[3\mathbf{r}_1+\mathbf{r}_3]{-2\mathbf{r}_1+\mathbf{r}_2} \begin{pmatrix} 1 & -2 & 3 & 3 \\ 0 & 5 & -7 & 3 \\ 0 & -10 & 14 & 1 \end{pmatrix} \xrightarrow{2\mathbf{r}_2+\mathbf{r}_3} \begin{pmatrix} 1 & -2 & 3 & 3 \\ 0 & 5 & -7 & 3 \\ 0 & 0 & 0 & 7 \end{pmatrix}$$

we run into a problem. The bottom row of this final matrix corresponds to the equation $0x + 0y + 0z = 7$, which clearly has no solutions! Gaussian elimination stops. This system has no solutions; it is inconsistent.

Example 5.5   Solve the following linear system:

$$\begin{aligned} x &- 2y &+ 3z &= 3 \\ 2x &+ y &- z &= 9 \\ -3x &- 4y &+ 5z &= -15 \end{aligned}$$

Solution: The corresponding augmented matrix is:

$$\begin{pmatrix} 1 & -2 & 3 & 3 \\ 2 & 1 & -1 & 9 \\ -3 & -4 & 5 & -15 \end{pmatrix}$$

Since the coefficient matrix is the same as it was in the previous example, we'd apply the same elementary row operations:

$$\begin{pmatrix} 1 & -2 & 3 & 3 \\ 2 & 1 & -1 & 9 \\ -3 & -4 & 5 & -15 \end{pmatrix} \xrightarrow[3r_1+r_3]{-2r_1+r_2} \begin{pmatrix} 1 & -2 & 3 & 3 \\ 0 & 5 & -7 & 3 \\ 0 & -10 & 14 & -6 \end{pmatrix} \xrightarrow{2r_2+r_3} \begin{pmatrix} 1 & -2 & 3 & 3 \\ 0 & 5 & -7 & 3 \\ 0 & 0 & 0 & 0 \end{pmatrix}$$

The bottom row of the final matrix corresponds to the equation $0x + 0y + 0z = 0$, which places no restriction on the variable z. It therefore become a **free variable**; let's call it t. Substituting $z = t$ into the (equation corresponding to the) second row of the echelon matrix, $5y - 7z = 3$, gives $y = \frac{1}{5}(7t + 3)$. Finally, back-substituting both $z = t$ and $y = \frac{1}{5}(7t + 3)$ into the first row yields $x = \frac{1}{5}(-t + 21)$. Therefore, this system has infinitely many solutions, all of which can be expressed as follows:

$$(x, y, z) = \left(\tfrac{1}{5}(-t+21),\ \tfrac{1}{5}(7t+3),\ t\right) \text{ for any } t \in \mathbf{R}$$

Example 5.6   Solve this linear system:

$$\begin{aligned} x &- 2y &+ 3z &= 0 \\ 2x &+ y &- z &= 0 \\ -3x &- 4y &+ 5z &= 0 \end{aligned}$$

Solution: The corresponding augmented matrix is:

$$\begin{pmatrix} 1 & -2 & 3 & 0 \\ 2 & 1 & -1 & 0 \\ -3 & -4 & 5 & 0 \end{pmatrix}$$

Because the coefficient matrix is the same as it was in the previous two examples, we will apply the same elementary row operations:

$$\begin{pmatrix} 1 & -2 & 3 & 0 \\ 2 & 1 & -1 & 0 \\ -3 & -4 & 5 & 0 \end{pmatrix} \xrightarrow[3r_1+r_3]{-2r_1+r_2} \begin{pmatrix} 1 & -2 & 3 & 0 \\ 0 & 5 & -7 & 0 \\ 0 & -10 & 14 & 0 \end{pmatrix} \xrightarrow{2r_2+r_3} \begin{pmatrix} 1 & -2 & 3 & 0 \\ 0 & 5 & -7 & 0 \\ 0 & 0 & 0 & 0 \end{pmatrix}$$

Once again, we let $z = t$ be the free variable. Substituting $z = t$ into the second row of the echelon matrix, $5y - 7z = 0$, gives $y = \frac{1}{5}(7t)$. Finally, back-substituting both $z = t$ and $y = \frac{1}{5}(7t)$ into the first row yields $x = \frac{1}{5}(-t)$. Therefore, this system also has infinitely many solutions, all of which can be expressed as follows:

$$(x, y, z) = \left(-\tfrac{1}{5}t, \tfrac{7}{5}t, t\right) \text{ for any } t \in \mathbf{R}$$

The preceding two examples illustrate an important general fact about linear systems. The system in Example 5.6 has only 0's on the right-hand side of every equation; such a system is called **homogeneous**. Homogeneous systems are always consistent, because there is always at least one solution, namely, all the unknowns equalling zero (this is called the **trivial** solution). The system in Example 5.5 had the same coefficient matrix, but it was nonhomogeneous. Comparing the general solution of the nonhomogeneous system with the solution of the corresponding homogeneous system reveals their similarity:

Solution to nonhomogeneous system: $(x, y, z) = \left(-\tfrac{1}{5}t, \tfrac{7}{5}t, t\right) + \left(\tfrac{21}{5}, \tfrac{3}{5}, 0\right)$ for any $t \in \mathbf{R}$

Solution to homogeneous system: $(x, y, z) = \left(-\tfrac{1}{5}t, \tfrac{7}{5}t, t\right)$ for any $t \in \mathbf{R}$

In general, every solution of a consistent, nonhomogeneous system can be expressed in the form $\mathbf{x} = \mathbf{x}_h + \mathbf{x}_p$, where $\mathbf{x} = \mathbf{x}_h$ is the general solution of the corresponding homogeneous system, and $\mathbf{x}_p$ is a particular solution of the nonhomogeneous system. Notice the similarity between this theorem and the corresponding theorem for linear differential equations.

In the case illustrated above, $\mathbf{x}_h = \left(-\tfrac{1}{5}t, \tfrac{7}{5}t, t\right)$ and $\mathbf{x}_p = \left(\tfrac{21}{5}, \tfrac{3}{5}, 0\right)$.

Example 5.7   Find all the solutions of the following linear system:

$$\begin{aligned} w &- 2x &&&+ 3z &= -5 \\ 2w &+ x &- y &+ z &&= 2 \\ -w &- 8x &+ 2y &+ 7z &&= -19 \end{aligned}$$

Solution: The corresponding augmented matrix is:

$$\begin{pmatrix} 1 & -2 & 0 & 3 & -5 \\ 2 & 1 & -1 & 1 & 2 \\ -1 & -8 & 2 & 7 & -19 \end{pmatrix}$$

We perform the following elementary row operations to reduce this to echelon form:

$$\begin{pmatrix} 1 & -2 & 0 & 3 & -5 \\ 2 & 1 & -1 & 1 & 2 \\ -1 & -8 & 2 & 7 & -19 \end{pmatrix} \xrightarrow[\substack{-2r_1+r_2 \\ r_1+r_3}]{} \begin{pmatrix} 1 & -2 & 0 & 3 & -5 \\ 0 & 5 & -1 & -5 & 12 \\ 0 & -10 & 2 & 10 & -24 \end{pmatrix}$$

$$\begin{pmatrix} 1 & -2 & 0 & 3 & -5 \\ 0 & 5 & -1 & -5 & 12 \\ 0 & -10 & 2 & 10 & -24 \end{pmatrix} \xrightarrow{2r_2+r_3} \begin{pmatrix} 1 & -2 & 0 & 3 & -5 \\ 0 & 5 & -1 & -5 & 12 \\ 0 & 0 & 0 & 0 & 0 \end{pmatrix}$$

As in the preceding example, we have a zero row, but in this case there are a total of four unknowns. Since there are two nonzero rows in the echelon matrix, there are really only two constraints on the variables, so the other $4 - 2 = 2$ are free. Let's designate y and z as the free variables, denoting y by t_1 and z by t_2. Substituting these into the second row yields

$$5x - t_1 - 5t_2 = 12 \quad \Rightarrow \quad x = \tfrac{1}{5}(t_1 + 5t_2 + 12)$$

and back-substitution into the first row gives:

$$w - 2[\tfrac{1}{5}(t_1 + 5t_2 + 12)] + 3t_2 = -5 \quad \Rightarrow \quad w = \tfrac{1}{5}(2t_1 - 5t_2 - 1)$$

Therefore, all the solutions of the given linear system are given by the equation:

$$(w, x, y, z) = \left(\tfrac{1}{5}(2t_1 - 5t_2 - 1), \ \tfrac{1}{5}(t_1 + 5t_2 + 12), \ t_1, \ t_2\right) \text{ for any } t_1, t_2 \in \mathbf{R}$$

In general, the number of free variables (also called **parameters**) appearing in the solution of a linear system (that possesses infinitely many solutions) is equal to the number of unknowns minus the number of nonzero rows in the echelon form of the augmented matrix.

SOLVING MATRIX EQUATIONS USING A^{-1}

Any linear system can be written in the form $A\mathbf{x} = \mathbf{b}$, where A is the coefficient matrix, $\mathbf{x}$ is the column matrix containing the unknowns, and $\mathbf{b}$ is the column matrix whose entries are the constants on the right-hand sides of the equations in the system. For example, the system of Example 5.3,

$$\begin{array}{rcrcrcr} x & - & 2y & + & 3z & = & 3 \\ 2x & + & y & - & z & = & 9 \\ -3x & + & 5y & & & = & -2 \end{array}$$

can be expressed as the matrix equation $A\mathbf{x} = \mathbf{b}$, where:

$$A = \begin{pmatrix} 1 & -2 & 3 \\ 2 & 1 & -1 \\ -3 & 5 & 0 \end{pmatrix}, \qquad \mathbf{x} = \begin{pmatrix} x \\ y \\ z \end{pmatrix}, \qquad \text{and} \qquad \mathbf{b} = \begin{pmatrix} 3 \\ 9 \\ -2 \end{pmatrix}$$

Since the coefficient matrix A is square, it may be invertible. If A is invertible and we had a way to compute A^{-1}, then we could determine $\mathbf{x}$ by a simple matrix multiplication, $\mathbf{x} = A^{-1}\mathbf{b}$, since:

$$A(A^{-1}\mathbf{b}) = (AA^{-1})\mathbf{b} = I\mathbf{b} = \mathbf{b}$$

Therefore, if A is an invertible square matrix, then the system $A\mathbf{x} = \mathbf{b}$ is consistent for *every* choice of the column matrix $\mathbf{b}$, and the unique solution is given by the product $\mathbf{x} = A^{-1}\mathbf{b}$. Since figuring out A^{-1} is usually more time-consuming than simply using Gaussian elimination to solve the original system, this theorem does not offer an improved method of calculation. But if you do happen to know A^{-1}, then this theorem immediately provides a quick way to find the solution. Notice, for example, that we can use this theorem to conclude that if A is square and invertible, then the homogeneous system $A\mathbf{x} = \mathbf{0}$ has only the trivial solution (since $\mathbf{x} = A^{-1}\mathbf{0} = \mathbf{0}$).

We'll close this section by giving the formula for the inverse of a 2×2 matrix A. The 2×2 matrix

$$A = \begin{pmatrix} a & b \\ c & d \end{pmatrix}$$

is invertible if and only if $ad - bc \neq 0$; in this case, the inverse of the matrix is:

$$A^{-1} = \begin{pmatrix} \frac{d}{ad-bc} & \frac{-b}{ad-bc} \\ \frac{-c}{ad-bc} & \frac{a}{ad-bc} \end{pmatrix} = \frac{1}{ad-bc}\begin{pmatrix} d & -b \\ -c & a \end{pmatrix}$$

You should memorize this result for the GRE Math Subject Test.

Example 5.8   Find the matrix X that satisfies the equation $AX = B$, where:

$$A = \begin{pmatrix} 3 & 4 \\ 5 & 6 \end{pmatrix} \quad \text{and} \quad B = \begin{pmatrix} 28 & 35 & 42 \\ 42 & 53 & 64 \end{pmatrix}$$

Solution: First, we notice that because A is 2×2 and B is 2×3, the matrix X must also be 2×3. Now, if A is invertible, then by multiplying both sides of the equation $AX = B$ by A^{-1} on the left, we'd get:

$$A^{-1}(AX) = A^{-1}(B) \implies (A^{-1}A)X = A^{-1}B \implies X = A^{-1}B$$

Since A is 2×2, we can use the result above to find A^{-1}. Since $ad - bc = (3)(6) - (4)(5) = -2 \neq 0$, A *is* invertible and:

$$A^{-1} = \frac{1}{-2}\begin{pmatrix} 6 & -4 \\ -5 & 3 \end{pmatrix} = \begin{pmatrix} -3 & 2 \\ \frac{5}{2} & -\frac{3}{2} \end{pmatrix}$$

Therefore,

$$X = A^{-1}B = \begin{pmatrix} -3 & 2 \\ \frac{5}{2} & -\frac{3}{2} \end{pmatrix}\begin{pmatrix} 28 & 35 & 42 \\ 42 & 53 & 64 \end{pmatrix} = \begin{pmatrix} 0 & 1 & 2 \\ 7 & 8 & 9 \end{pmatrix}$$

VECTOR SPACES

The general definition of a vector space reads as follows: A **vector space** is a set that is closed with respect to two operations, addition and scalar multiplication. The scalars we'll consider are real numbers, so the resulting structure is called a **real vector space**. The elements of the set are called **vectors**, even when those objects are not of the traditional, directed-line-segment variety.

The x-y plane, referred to as $\mathbf{R}^2$ ("R-two"), is an example of a vector space. Any two vectors in $\mathbf{R}^2$ can be added together (component-wise) and the result is again a vector in $\mathbf{R}^2$. Thus, the set is closed under addition. Furthermore, multiplying a vector in $\mathbf{R}^2$ by a (real) scalar always results in a vector in $\mathbf{R}^2$; this means the set is also closed under scalar multiplication.

$\mathbf{R}^2$ is a rather "big" vector space, however. Much more interesting are proper subsets of $\mathbf{R}^2$ that are themselves vector spaces. For example, consider the line $y = 2x$ in $\mathbf{R}^2$. This subset consists of all vectors, or points, of the form $(x, 2x)$. Adding any two such vectors gives a vector of the same type, since:

$$(x_1, 2x_1) + (x_2, 2x_2) = (x_1 + x_2, 2(x_1 + x_2))$$

Multiplying a vector in this set by a scalar also gives a vector of the same type:

$$k(x, 2x) = (kx, 2(kx))$$

Since this subset is closed under addition and scalar multiplication, it is itself a vector space; it's a **subspace** of $\mathbf{R}^2$.

Now consider the line $y = 2x + 1$; it consists of all vectors or points of the form $(x, 2x + 1)$. This set is *not* a subspace of $\mathbf{R}^2$; in fact, it fails to satisfy both requirements. It's not closed under addition, because, for example, although both $(1, 3)$ and $(2, 5)$ are in this set, their sum, $(3, 8)$, is not. It's also not closed under scalar multiplication since $(1, 3)$ is in the set, but the scalar multiple $2(1, 3) = (2, 6)$ is not.

Because a vector space must be closed under scalar multiplication, every vector space must contain the zero vector. The line $y = 2x + 1$ does not define a subspace of $\mathbf{R}^2$ because, for one thing, it doesn't contain the origin. However, containing the origin doesn't guarantee that a subset is a subspace. Consider, for example, the closed first quadrant of the x-y plane; this is the set of all points (x, y) such that $x \geq 0$ and $y \geq 0$. This subset of $\mathbf{R}^2$ contains the origin, but it's not a subspace, because although it's closed under addition, it's *not* closed under scalar multiplication. For example, multiplying the vector $(1, 2)$ in this subset by the negative scalar $k = -3$ gives the vector $(-3, -6)$, which does not lie in the closed first quadrant.

Example 5.9   Let A be a 3×3 matrix such that the matrix equation

$$A\mathbf{x} = (1, 2, 4)^\mathrm{T}$$

has infinitely many solutions. Does the set of solutions form a subspace of $\mathbf{R}^3$?

Solution: Let $\mathbf{x}_1$ and $\mathbf{x}_2$ be two of the solutions of the given equation. Then $A\mathbf{x}_1 = (1, 2, 4)^\mathrm{T}$ and $A\mathbf{x}_2 = (1, 2, 4)^\mathrm{T}$, so

$$A\mathbf{x}_1 + A\mathbf{x}_2 = (2, 4, 8)^\mathrm{T} \quad \Rightarrow \quad A(\mathbf{x}_1 + \mathbf{x}_2) = (2, 4, 8)^\mathrm{T} \neq (1, 2, 4)^\mathrm{T}$$

which shows that $\mathbf{x}_1 + \mathbf{x}_2$ is *not* a solution of $A\mathbf{x} = (1, 2, 4)^\mathrm{T}$. Since the set of solutions of $A\mathbf{x} = (1, 2, 4)^\mathrm{T}$ is not closed under addition, it is not a vector space. Another way to see that the answer to the question is *no* is simply to notice that the zero vector is not in the solution set, because $\mathbf{x} = \mathbf{0}$ clearly doesn't satisfy the given nonhomogeneous equation. Since every subspace of $\mathbf{R}^3$ must contain the zero vector, the set of solutions to this equation is not a subspace of $\mathbf{R}^3$.

THE NULLSPACE

Let A be an $m \times n$ matrix. The set of all solutions of the homogeneous equation $A\mathbf{x} = \mathbf{0}$ forms a subspace of $\mathbf{R}^n$ called the **nullspace** of A, denoted $N(A)$. That $N(A)$ actually is a subspace follows from the fact that the sum of any two solutions of $A\mathbf{x} = \mathbf{0}$ is itself a solution—so $N(A)$ is closed under addition—and any scalar multiple of a solution is also a solution—so $N(A)$ is also closed under scalar multiplication. In Example 5.6, we found that the solution set of the linear system

$$
\begin{array}{rrrrrrr}
x & - & 2y & + & 3z & = & 0 \\
2x & + & y & - & z & = & 0 \\
-3x & - & 4y & + & 5z & = & 0
\end{array}
$$

is:

$$
\left\{ \left(-\tfrac{1}{5}t, \tfrac{7}{5}t, t \right) : t \in \mathbf{R} \right\}
$$

This is the nullspace of the system's coefficient matrix:

$$
A = \begin{pmatrix} 1 & -2 & 3 \\ 2 & 1 & -1 \\ -3 & -4 & 5 \end{pmatrix}
$$

Example 5.10 What is the nullspace of an invertible matrix?

Solution: If A is invertible, then the only solution of $A\mathbf{x} = \mathbf{0}$ is $\mathbf{x} = \mathbf{0}$. Therefore, the nullspace of an invertible $n \times n$ matrix is the trivial subspace of $\mathbf{R}^n$.

LINEAR COMBINATIONS

Consider a collection of n-vectors, $\mathbf{v}_1, \mathbf{v}_2, \ldots, \mathbf{v}_m$. Any expression of the form

$$
k_1 \mathbf{v}_1 + k_2 \mathbf{v}_2 + \cdots + k_m \mathbf{v}_m
$$

where the coefficients k_i are scalars, is called a **linear combination** of the vectors $\mathbf{v}_i$. The set of *all* linear combinations of the vectors $\mathbf{v}_i$ is called their **span**. For example, consider the vectors $\hat{\mathbf{i}} = (1, 0, 0)$ and $\hat{\mathbf{j}} = (0, 1, 0)$ in $\mathbf{R}^3$. The span of $\hat{\mathbf{i}}$ and $\hat{\mathbf{j}}$ is equal to the xy-plane, since every vector in the xy-plane can be expressed as a linear combination of $\hat{\mathbf{i}}$ and $\hat{\mathbf{j}}$ and vice versa. The vector $\mathbf{v} = (1, 1, 1)$, for example, is not in span $\{ \hat{\mathbf{i}}, \hat{\mathbf{j}} \}$ because no linear combination of $\hat{\mathbf{i}}$ and $\hat{\mathbf{j}}$ could equal $\mathbf{v}$. Notice that the span of any collection of n-vectors is always a subspace of $\mathbf{R}^n$ because it's automatically closed under addition and scalar multiplication; after all, the span contains *all* linear combinations of the vectors in the spanning set.

If all the scalars k_i in the linear combination

$$
k_1 \mathbf{v}_1 + k_2 \mathbf{v}_2 + \cdots + k_m \mathbf{v}_m
$$

are zero, then the result is the zero vector, $\mathbf{0}$. This is called the **trivial** combination. If this is the *only* way the vectors $\mathbf{v}_i$ can be combined to give the zero vector, then the vectors $\mathbf{v}_i$ are said to be **linearly independent**. On the other hand, if

$$
k_1 \mathbf{v}_1 + k_2 \mathbf{v}_2 + \cdots + k_m \mathbf{v}_m = \mathbf{0}
$$

is true for some nontrivial choice of the scalars k_i, then the vectors $\mathbf{v}_i$ are said to be linearly **dependent**. The name arises because in this case at least one of the vectors depends on the others, that is, it can be written as a linear combination of the other vectors in the collection. For example, the vectors $\mathbf{v}_1 = (1, -2, 3)$, $\mathbf{v}_2 = (-1, -4, 9)$, and $\mathbf{v}_3 = (-1, 0, 1)$ are dependent since we can find a nontrivial linear combination that gives $\mathbf{0}$; one such combination is $2\mathbf{v}_1 - \mathbf{v}_2 + 3\mathbf{v}_3$, as you may verify. An equivalent way to show that these three vectors are dependent is to notice that we can write, say, $\mathbf{v}_2$ as a linear combination of $\mathbf{v}_1$ and $\mathbf{v}_3$:

$$\mathbf{v}_2 = 2\mathbf{v}_1 + 3\mathbf{v}_3$$

Because of this, the span of $\mathbf{v}_1$, $\mathbf{v}_2$, and $\mathbf{v}_3$ is the same as the span of just $\mathbf{v}_1$ and $\mathbf{v}_3$. The inclusion of $\mathbf{v}_2$ doesn't enlarge the span; any linear combination of $\mathbf{v}_1$, $\mathbf{v}_2$, and $\mathbf{v}_3$ is already a linear combination of just $\mathbf{v}_1$ and $\mathbf{v}_3$. (In fact, since $\mathbf{v}_1$ can be written in terms of $\mathbf{v}_2$ and $\mathbf{v}_3$, we could just as well leave out $\mathbf{v}_1$ and just keep $\mathbf{v}_2$ and $\mathbf{v}_3$. Or we could keep just $\mathbf{v}_1$ and $\mathbf{v}_2$ and ignore $\mathbf{v}_3$.) Therefore, $\mathrm{span}\{\mathbf{v}_1, \mathbf{v}_2, \mathbf{v}_3\} = \mathrm{span}\{\mathbf{v}_1, \mathbf{v}_2\} = \mathrm{span}\{\mathbf{v}_1, \mathbf{v}_3\} = \mathrm{span}\{\mathbf{v}_2, \mathbf{v}_3\}$. So any one of these two-element sets is a *minimal* spanning set for the space $\mathrm{span}\{\mathbf{v}_1, \mathbf{v}_2, \mathbf{v}_3\}$. A minimal spanning set for a vector space is called a **basis** for the space. In other words, a basis is a collection of vectors from the space that not only span the space but are also linearly independent. A basis is just the right size; it contains enough vectors to span the entire space, but not so many as to include unnecessary (dependent) ones. If B is a finite set and a basis for a space V, then the number of vectors in B is independent of the choice of B; this number is called the **dimension** of V, denoted $\dim V$. If no finite collection of vectors spans V, then V is said to be infinite dimensional and we write $\dim V = \infty$.

Example 5.11 Consider the vectors:

$$\mathbf{v}_1 = (1, -2, 3), \quad \mathbf{v}_2 = (-1, -4, 9), \quad \text{and} \quad \mathbf{v}_3 = (-1, 0, 1)$$

(a) Describe the set $\mathrm{span}\{\mathbf{v}_1, \mathbf{v}_2, \mathbf{v}_3\}$.
(b) Find a basis for P.
(c) What is $\dim P$?

Solution:

(a) The span of $\mathbf{v}_1$, $\mathbf{v}_2$, and $\mathbf{v}_3$ is the set of all linear combinations of these vectors. Since they are 3-vectors, the span is some subspace of $\mathbf{R}^3$. A subspace of $\mathbf{R}^3$ must be one of the following: the trivial subspace ($\{\mathbf{0}\}$), a line through the origin, a plane through the origin, or all of $\mathbf{R}^3$. Because the vectors are not all scalar multiples of a single vector, the span is not a line through the origin (and the span is clearly not the trivial subspace, since we're given nonzero vectors). Therefore, if the three given vectors are linearly independent, then the span will be all of $\mathbf{R}^3$; otherwise, the span will be a plane through the origin.

The vectors are linearly independent if the only scalars k_1, k_2, and k_3 that satisfy $k_1\mathbf{v}_1 + k_2\mathbf{v}_2 + k_3\mathbf{v}_3 = \mathbf{0}$ are $k_1 = k_2 = k_3 = 0$. The equation $k_1\mathbf{v}_1 + k_2\mathbf{v}_2 + k_3\mathbf{v}_3 = \mathbf{0}$ is equivalent to the homogeneous system $A\mathbf{k} = \mathbf{0}$, where $\mathbf{k} = (k_1, k_2, k_3)^\mathrm{T}$ and:

$$A = \begin{pmatrix} 1 & -1 & -1 \\ -2 & -4 & 0 \\ 3 & 9 & 1 \end{pmatrix}$$

Applying Gaussian elimination to the system $A\mathbf{k} = \mathbf{0}$, we get:

$$\begin{pmatrix} 1 & -1 & -1 & 0 \\ -2 & -4 & 0 & 0 \\ 3 & 9 & 1 & 0 \end{pmatrix} \xrightarrow[-3r_1+r_3]{2r_1+r_2} \begin{pmatrix} 1 & -1 & -1 & 0 \\ 0 & -6 & -2 & 0 \\ 0 & 12 & 4 & 0 \end{pmatrix} \xrightarrow{2r_2+r_3} \begin{pmatrix} 1 & -1 & -1 & 0 \\ 0 & -6 & -2 & 0 \\ 0 & 0 & 0 & 0 \end{pmatrix}$$

The bottom row of zeros implies that we can take k_3 as a free variable, so there are infinitely many solutions. Since $k_1 = k_2 = k_3 = 0$ is not the only solution, the vectors $\mathbf{v}_1$, $\mathbf{v}_2$, and $\mathbf{v}_3$ are not linearly independent. We can eliminate, say, $\mathbf{v}_3$ from the original set without altering the span. So, the span of $\mathbf{v}_1$, $\mathbf{v}_2$, and $\mathbf{v}_3$ is identical to the span of $\mathbf{v}_1$ and $\mathbf{v}_2$ alone, which is a plane through the origin. Because $\mathbf{v}_1$ and $\mathbf{v}_2$ lie in this plane, a vector normal to the plane is any nonzero scalar multiple of the cross product:

$$\mathbf{v}_1 \times \mathbf{v}_2 = \begin{vmatrix} \hat{\mathbf{i}} & \hat{\mathbf{j}} & \hat{\mathbf{k}} \\ 1 & -2 & 3 \\ -1 & -4 & 9 \end{vmatrix} = -6\hat{\mathbf{i}} - 12\hat{\mathbf{j}} - 6\hat{\mathbf{k}} = -6(\hat{\mathbf{i}} + 2\hat{\mathbf{j}} + \hat{\mathbf{k}})$$

We can therefore take $\mathbf{N} = (1, 2, 1)$ as a normal vector to the plane, so the equation of the plane is $x + 2y + z = d$, for some constant d. Since the plane must contain the origin (since the span is a subspace, and any subspace must contain the zero vector), the value of d must be 0. The span of $\mathbf{v}_1$, $\mathbf{v}_2$, $\mathbf{v}_3$ is the plane P in $\mathbf{R}^3$ whose equation is $x + 2y + z = 0$.

(b) A basis for P consists of any two of the three vectors $\mathbf{v}_1$, $\mathbf{v}_2$, and $\mathbf{v}_3$.

(c) Since a basis for P contains two vectors, dim $P = 2$.

THE RANK, COLUMN SPACE, AND ROW SPACE OF A MATRIX

We can view the columns of an m × n matrix as vectors in Rm, and the rows of the matrix as vectors in Rn. The maximum number of linearly independent columns is called the column rank of the matrix, and the maximum number of linearly independent rows is called the row rank. Although the columns are m-vectors and the rows are n-vectors, it can be shown that, for any matrix, the column rank always equals the row rank; this common value is therefore simply known as the rank of the matrix. The subspace of $\mathbf{R}^m$ spanned by the columns of an $m \times n$ matrix A is called the **column space** of A, which we denote $CS(A)$. Since the rank is equal to the maximum number of linearly independent columns, the dimension of $CS(A)$ is equal to the rank of A. What characterizes the column space? That is, how do we decide whether or not a given m-vector is an element of $CS(A)$? Let $\mathbf{v}_1, \mathbf{v}_2, \ldots, \mathbf{v}_n$ denote the columns of A. If an m-vector $\mathbf{b}$ is in $CS(A)$, then there must be some linear combination of the columns of A that equals $\mathbf{b}$; that is, there must be scalars $k_1, k_2, \ldots, k_n$ such that:

$$k_1\mathbf{v}_1 + k_2\mathbf{v}_2 + \cdots + k_n\mathbf{v}_n = \mathbf{b}$$

But this equation can be written in matrix form as

$$\begin{pmatrix} | & | & & | \\ \mathbf{v}_1 & \mathbf{v}_2 & \cdots & \mathbf{v}_n \\ \downarrow & \downarrow & & \downarrow \end{pmatrix} \begin{pmatrix} k_1 \\ k_2 \\ \vdots \\ k_n \end{pmatrix} = \mathbf{b}$$

which is $A\mathbf{k} = \mathbf{b}$. So we see that an m-vector $\mathbf{b}$ is in $CS(A)$ if and only if the equation $A\mathbf{x} = \mathbf{b}$ has a solution.

The subspace of $\mathbf{R}^n$ spanned by the rows of an $m \times n$ matrix A is called the **row space** of A, which we denote $RS(A)$. Since the rank is equal to the maximum number of linearly independent rows, the dimension of $RS(A)$ is equal to the rank of A. How do we decide whether or not a given n-vector is an element of $RS(A)$? Perhaps the simplest way is to notice that:

$$RS(A) = CS(A^T)$$

which says that the row space of A is the column space of A^T. So, combining this observation with the criterion given above for membership in the column space, we conclude that an n-vector $\mathbf{b}$ is in $RS(A)$ if and only if the equation $A^T\mathbf{x} = \mathbf{b}$ has a solution.

By definition, the rows of A form a spanning set for $RS(A)$, but if the rows are not linearly independent, they do not form a basis for $RS(A)$. If we reduce the matrix A to echelon form by a sequence of elementary row operations, the nonzero rows that remain give a basis for $RS(A)$, and the number of these rows gives the rank of A. To find a basis for $CS(A)$, we notice that:

$$CS(A) = RS(A^T)$$

So, if we reduce A^T to echelon form and write the nonzero rows that remain as column vectors, we'll have a basis for $CS(A)$.

Example 5.12 For the following matrix, compute its rank, find a basis for its row space, and find a basis for its column space:

$$A = \begin{pmatrix} 1 & 1 & 1 \\ -1 & 1 & -1 \\ 2 & 0 & 2 \end{pmatrix}$$

Solution: Reducing A to echelon form, we get:

$$\begin{pmatrix} 1 & 1 & 1 \\ -1 & 1 & -1 \\ 2 & 0 & 2 \end{pmatrix} \xrightarrow[-2r_1+r_3]{r_1+r_2} \begin{pmatrix} 1 & 1 & 1 \\ 0 & 2 & 0 \\ 0 & -2 & 0 \end{pmatrix} \xrightarrow{r_2+r_3} \begin{pmatrix} 1 & 1 & 1 \\ 0 & 2 & 0 \\ 0 & 0 & 0 \end{pmatrix}$$

There are only two nonzero rows remaining, so the rank of the matrix is 2. As a basis for the row space of A, we can take the two nonzero rows in the echelon form:

$$\text{basis for } RS(A) = \big\{(1, 1, 1), (0, 2, 0)\big\}$$

(If it's desired to have basis vectors that were rows in the original matrix, we could take any two of the rows of A.) Notice that since the rank is 2, the number of vectors in a basis for the row space is two; thus, the row space is a 2-dimensional subspace of $\mathbf{R}^3$.

Now, a simple way to find a basis for the column space of A is to find a basis for the row space of A^T:

$$A^T = \begin{pmatrix} 1 & -1 & 2 \\ 1 & 1 & 0 \\ 1 & -1 & 2 \end{pmatrix} \xrightarrow[\substack{-r_1+r_2 \\ -r_1+r_3}]{} \begin{pmatrix} 1 & -1 & 2 \\ 0 & 2 & -2 \\ 0 & 0 & 0 \end{pmatrix}$$

By transposing the vectors in a basis for the row space of A^T, $\{(1, -1, 2), (0, 2, -2)\}$, we get a basis for the column space of A:

$$\text{basis for } CS(A) = \left\{ \begin{pmatrix} 1 \\ -1 \\ 2 \end{pmatrix}, \begin{pmatrix} 0 \\ 2 \\ -2 \end{pmatrix} \right\}$$

Notice that dim $CS(A)$ is also equal to 2. The dimension of the column space is always equal to the dimension of the row space; both are equal to the rank of the matrix.

OTHER VECTOR SPACES

Although we've been identifying and describing subspaces—namely, the nullspace, column space, and row space—that arise from matrices and matrix equations, several other vector spaces are commonly encountered.

Let n be a positive integer and consider the collection of all polynomials of degree $\leq n$. This set is closed under addition and scalar multiplication, so it's a vector space, denoted by P_n. The "vectors" in this space are polynomials. A basis for the polynomial space P_n is $\{1, x, x^2, \ldots, x^n\}$, which contains $n + 1$ elements, so dim $P_n = n + 1$. Other function spaces include the space of all bounded functions, all continuous functions, or all differentiable functions on a given interval; these spaces are infinite-dimensional.

The set of all $m \times n$ matrices with real entries is denoted $M_{m \times n}(\mathbf{R})$; it forms a vector space, since this set is closed under addition and scalar multiplication. The "vectors" here are $m \times n$ matrices. The dimension of $M_{m \times n}(\mathbf{R})$ is equal to mn. To illustrate this, notice that a basis for $M_{3 \times 2}(\mathbf{R})$ consists of these $(3)(2) = 6$ vectors:

$$\begin{pmatrix} 1 & 0 \\ 0 & 0 \\ 0 & 0 \end{pmatrix}, \begin{pmatrix} 0 & 1 \\ 0 & 0 \\ 0 & 0 \end{pmatrix}, \begin{pmatrix} 0 & 0 \\ 1 & 0 \\ 0 & 0 \end{pmatrix}, \begin{pmatrix} 0 & 0 \\ 0 & 1 \\ 0 & 0 \end{pmatrix}, \begin{pmatrix} 0 & 0 \\ 0 & 0 \\ 1 & 0 \end{pmatrix}, \begin{pmatrix} 0 & 0 \\ 0 & 0 \\ 0 & 1 \end{pmatrix}$$

DETERMINANTS

Let A be a square matrix. Then the **determinant** of A, denoted by $\det A$ or $|A|$, is a number associated with A that describes certain properties of A. First, we'll show how to evaluate the determinant of a matrix, then discuss its applications. The determinant is only defined for square matrices, so throughout this section all matrices are square. There are essentially two ways of computing the determinant. The first one defines the determinant by giving a specific formula for it, but using this formula is impractical for large matrices. The second way uses properties of the determinant function to provide a step-by-step method for its computation; this method is the one that's actually used in practice.

Consider the set **n** of integers from 1 to n. A **permutation** of **n** is a function from **n** to itself that is both one-to-one and onto. [Recall that a function f is **one-to-one** (or **injective**) if distinct elements in the domain are always mapped to distinct elements in the range, and f is **onto** (or **surjective**) if every element in the range has a pre-image in the domain.] For example, for the set **4** = {1, 2, 3, 4}, the function $\sigma: \mathbf{4} \to \mathbf{4}$ defined by the equations

$$\sigma(1) = 2, \quad \sigma(2) = 4, \quad \sigma(3) = 1, \quad \text{and} \quad \sigma(4) = 3$$

is a permutation of **4**. It maps the elements 1, 2, 3, 4 onto the elements 2, 4, 1, 3; essentially, then, a permutation of **n** is just some arrangement of the elements 1 through n.

Every permutation of **n** can be achieved by a sequence of transpositions; the **transposition** of two elements i, j is simply the same two elements in the reverse order: j, i. For the permutation given above, we can achieve the image of σ from the original order 1, 2, 3, 4 by the following sequence of transpositions:

$$1, 2, 3, 4 \quad \to \quad 2, 1, 3, 4 \quad \to \quad 2, 1, 4, 3 \quad \to \quad 2, 4, 1, 3$$

Since it took three transpositions and three is an odd number, the permutation σ is said to be **odd**. On the other hand, if the number of transpositions in the sequence were even, the permutation would be called **even**. The set of *all* permutations of **n** is denoted S_n. S_n contains $n!$ permutations, half of which are even and half of which are odd (if $n \geq 2$). The **sign** of a permutation σ, a number denoted sgn σ, is defined to be +1 if the permutation is even and –1 if it's odd.

Permutations of **n** are used to define the determinant of an $n \times n$ matrix. Recall that the entry in row i and column j of A is denoted a_{ij}. The determinant of A is defined to be the following sum

$$\det A = \sum_{\sigma \in S_n} (\text{sgn } \sigma) \, a_{1\sigma(1)} a_{2\sigma(2)} \cdots a_{n\sigma(n)}$$

where the sum is taken over all $n!$ permutations of **n**. It's easy to see why this formula is impractical for large matrices. For $n = 4$, there would be $4! = 24$ terms in this sum, for a 5×5 matrix, the sum would contain $5! = 120$ terms, and so on.

For a 2×2 matrix, however, the sum is easy to compute. There are only two permutations of the set **2** = {1, 2}, namely the even permutation 1, 2 and the odd permutation 2, 1. Therefore, the sum that defines the determinant of the 2×2 matrix

$$A = \begin{pmatrix} a_{11} & a_{12} \\ a_{21} & a_{22} \end{pmatrix}$$

is:

$$\det A = \sum_{\sigma \in S_2} (\text{sgn } \sigma) \, a_{1\sigma(1)} a_{2\sigma(2)}$$
$$= (+1)a_{11}a_{22} + (-1)a_{12}a_{21}$$
$$= a_{11}a_{22} - a_{12}a_{21}$$

This formula says that, to find the determinant of a 2×2 matrix, simply multiply "down" the main diagonal (to form the product $a_{11}a_{22}$), multiply "up" the off-diagonal (to form the product $a_{12}a_{21}$), and subtract:

$$\det A = \begin{pmatrix} a_{11} & a_{12} \\ a_{21} & a_{22} \end{pmatrix} = a_{11}a_{22} - a_{12}a_{21}$$

② minus this product

① this product

or, more simply, $\det \begin{pmatrix} a & b \\ c & d \end{pmatrix} = ad - bc$.

Memorize this formula!

The determinant of a 3×3 matrix can be computed using this formula, and the result isn't too intimidating; it's

$$\det A = \sum_{\sigma \in S_3} (\operatorname{sgn} \sigma)\, a_{1\sigma(1)} a_{2\sigma(2)} a_{3\sigma(3)}$$

$$= a_{11}a_{22}a_{33} + a_{12}a_{23}a_{31} + a_{13}a_{21}a_{32} - a_{13}a_{22}a_{31} - a_{11}a_{23}a_{32} - a_{12}a_{21}a_{33}$$

which can be remembered as follows: Copy the first two columns of A and place them to the right of A. Take the products formed by multiplying "down" and, from their sum, subtract the products formed by multiplying "up":

subtract these products

$$\begin{pmatrix} a_{11} & a_{12} & a_{13} \\ a_{21} & a_{22} & a_{23} \\ a_{31} & a_{32} & a_{33} \end{pmatrix} \begin{matrix} a_{11} & a_{12} \\ a_{21} & a_{22} \\ a_{31} & a_{32} \end{matrix}$$

add these products

This gives:

$$\det = a_{11}a_{22}a_{33} + a_{12}a_{23}a_{31} + a_{13}a_{21}a_{32} - a_{13}a_{22}a_{31} - a_{11}a_{23}a_{32} - a_{12}a_{21}a_{33}$$

A practical method for computing the determinant of large matrices (and which also can be used for 3×3 matrices) relies on the properties that actually *define* the determinant function:

1. The determinant is linear in each row, that is:

$$\det \begin{pmatrix} — & \mathbf{r}_1 & — \\ — & \mathbf{r}_2 & — \\ & \vdots & \\ — & \mathbf{r}_{i1} + \mathbf{r}_{i2} & — \\ & \vdots & \\ — & \mathbf{r}_m & — \end{pmatrix} = \det \begin{pmatrix} — & \mathbf{r}_1 & — \\ — & \mathbf{r}_2 & — \\ & \vdots & \\ — & \mathbf{r}_{i1} & — \\ & \vdots & \\ — & \mathbf{r}_m & — \end{pmatrix} + \det \begin{pmatrix} — & \mathbf{r}_1 & — \\ — & \mathbf{r}_2 & — \\ & \vdots & \\ — & \mathbf{r}_{i2} & — \\ & \vdots & \\ — & \mathbf{r}_m & — \end{pmatrix}$$

and

$$\det \begin{pmatrix} - & \mathbf{r}_1 & - \\ - & \mathbf{r}_2 & - \\ & \vdots & \\ - & k\mathbf{r}_i & - \\ & \vdots & \\ - & \mathbf{r}_m & - \end{pmatrix} = k \det \begin{pmatrix} - & \mathbf{r}_1 & - \\ - & \mathbf{r}_2 & - \\ & \vdots & \\ - & \mathbf{r}_i & - \\ & \vdots & \\ - & \mathbf{r}_m & - \end{pmatrix}$$

2. If two rows of a matrix are interchanged, the determinant changes sign.

3. The determinant of the identity matrix is equal to 1.

These properties can be used to describe the effect that the elementary row operations we studied earlier have on the value of the determinant:

4. If a row is multiplied by a constant, then the determinant is multiplied by that constant.

5. Adding a multiple of one row to another row leaves the determinant unchanged.

Remember that we used elementary row operations to reduce a matrix to echelon form. We now simply note the following additional facts about the determinant:

6. The determinant of a triangular matrix is equal to the product of the diagonal entries.

7. If a matrix has a zero row, the determinant is zero.

8. The determinant of the product of two square matrices of the same size is equal to the product of their determinants: $\det(AB) = (\det A)(\det B)$.

Using these properties, we can evaluate the determinant of a large matrix with much less computation than would be required by the formula given earlier involving permutations.

Example 5.13   What's the determinant of this matrix?

$$A = \begin{pmatrix} 4 & 4 & -1 \\ 2 & -3 & 0 \\ -1 & 2 & -1 \end{pmatrix}$$

Solution: Let's reduce A to upper-triangular form by a sequence of elementary row operations. First, switch rows 1 and 3, which changes the sign of the determinant:

$$\det A = -\det \begin{pmatrix} -1 & 2 & -1 \\ 2 & -3 & 0 \\ 4 & 4 & -1 \end{pmatrix}$$

Next, we add twice the first row to the second row and four times the first row to the third row; neither of these operations changes the determinant:

$$\det A = -\det \begin{pmatrix} -1 & 2 & -1 \\ 0 & 1 & -2 \\ 0 & 12 & -5 \end{pmatrix}$$

Adding –12 times the second row to the third row also doesn't change the determinant:

$$\det A = -\det \begin{pmatrix} -1 & 2 & -1 \\ 0 & 1 & -2 \\ 0 & 0 & 19 \end{pmatrix}$$

Since the determinant of a triangular matrix is equal to the product of the diagonal entries, we find that $\det A = -(-1)(1)(19) = 19$.

Example 5.14 If A is a 3×3 matrix whose determinant equals 5, what is the determinant of the matrix $2A$?

Solution: If only one row of A were multiplied by 2, the determinant would be multiplied by 2. However, the matrix $2A$ is formed by multiplying every row by 2. Since there are 3 rows, Property 4 states that we multiply the determinant by 2^3. Therefore:

$$\det(2A) = 2^3 \det A = 8(5) = 40$$

LAPLACE EXPANSIONS

Laplace expansion provides a method for computing an $n \times n$ determinant in terms of simpler, $(n-1) \times (n-1)$ determinants. Let A be an $n \times n$ matrix and choose any row, say row i. Let A_{ij} denote the $(n-1) \times (n-1)$ matrix obtained by deleting row i and column j from A. The determinant of A_{ij} is called the a_{ij} **minor**, and multiplying the a_{ij} minor by $(-1)^{i+j}$ gives the a_{ij} **cofactor**, denoted $\text{cof}(a_{ij})$:

$$\text{cof}(a_{ij}) = (-1)^{i+j} \, (a_{ij} \text{ minor})$$

The determinant of A is then equal to:

$$\det A = \sum_{j=1}^{n} a_{ij} \, \text{cof}(a_{ij})$$

This is called the **Laplace expansion** by row i. Let's illustrate this with the 3×3 matrix:

$$A = \begin{pmatrix} a_{11} & a_{12} & a_{13} \\ a_{21} & a_{22} & a_{23} \\ a_{31} & a_{32} & a_{33} \end{pmatrix}$$

The Laplace expansion by the first row is:

$$\det A = a_{11} \left(\begin{vmatrix} a_{22} & a_{23} \\ a_{32} & a_{33} \end{vmatrix} \right) + a_{12} \left(- \begin{vmatrix} a_{21} & a_{23} \\ a_{31} & a_{33} \end{vmatrix} \right) + a_{13} \left(\begin{vmatrix} a_{21} & a_{22} \\ a_{31} & a_{32} \end{vmatrix} \right)$$

The determinant of A can also be computed by finding the cofactors of the entries in any column from A; the Laplace expansion by column j is:

$$\det A = \sum_{i=1}^{n} a_{ij}\, \text{cof}(a_{ij})$$

For example, the cross product of a pair of 3-vectors, $\mathbf{u} = (u_1, u_2, u_3)$ and $\mathbf{v} = (v_1, v_2, v_3)$, is usually calculated by a Laplace expansion by the first row of the following symbolic 3×3 determinant:

$$\mathbf{u} \times \mathbf{v} = \begin{vmatrix} \hat{\mathbf{i}} & \hat{\mathbf{j}} & \hat{\mathbf{k}} \\ u_1 & u_2 & u_3 \\ v_1 & v_2 & v_3 \end{vmatrix} = \hat{\mathbf{i}} \begin{vmatrix} u_2 & u_3 \\ v_2 & v_3 \end{vmatrix} - \hat{\mathbf{j}} \begin{vmatrix} u_1 & u_3 \\ v_1 & v_3 \end{vmatrix} + \hat{\mathbf{k}} \begin{vmatrix} u_1 & u_2 \\ v_1 & v_2 \end{vmatrix}$$

Laplace expansions are especially useful when the matrix contains a row (or column) with zeros, since those terms drop out of the sum.

Example 5.15 Evaluate the determinant:

$$\begin{vmatrix} -1 & 0 & -2 & 1 \\ -2 & 3 & 0 & 0 \\ 1 & 1 & 0 & 1 \\ 0 & -1 & 0 & -3 \end{vmatrix}$$

Solution: The third column has only one nonzero entry, so we'll perform a Laplace expansion by the third column. The given determinant is equal to:

$$a_{13} \bullet (-1)^{1+3}\, \text{cof}(a_{13}) = (-2) \bullet (-1)^{1+3} \begin{vmatrix} -2 & 3 & 0 \\ 1 & 1 & 1 \\ 0 & -1 & -3 \end{vmatrix}$$

Now this 3×3 determinant can itself be computed by using the formula from p. 202 (add the downward-pointing products and subtract the upward-pointing products):

$$[6 + 0 + 0] - [0 + 2 + (-9)] = 6 - (-7) = 13$$

Therefore, the given 4×4 determinant is equal to:

$$(-2) \bullet (-1)^{1+3} \bullet 13 = -26$$

You can check that this determinant is correct using Gaussian elimination.

THE ADJUGATE MATRIX

Let A be an $n \times n$ matrix. Consider the $n \times n$ matrix whose (i, j) entry is the cofactor of the entry a_{ij} in A; the transpose of this cofactor matrix is called the **adjugate** (or **classical adjoint**) matrix of A, denoted $\text{Adj}\,A$:

$$\text{Adj}\,A = [\text{cof}(a_{ij})]^{\mathsf{T}}$$

Why form the adjugate matrix? Because if A is invertible, the following gives a formula for the inverse of A:

$$A^{-1} = \frac{\mathrm{Adj}\,A}{\det A}$$

This result establishes the following important theorem: *A square matrix, A, is invertible if and only if $\det A \neq 0$.*

Example 5.16   If A is an invertible $n \times n$ matrix with $\det A = k$, express the determinant of $\mathrm{Adj}\,A$ in terms of k.

Solution: From the equation for A^{-1} in terms of $\mathrm{Adj}\,A$, we can write:

$$\mathrm{Adj}\,A = (\det A)\,A^{-1} = kA^{-1}$$

Therefore, $\det(\mathrm{Adj}\,A) = \det(kA^{-1})$. Since $AA^{-1} = I$, we have $(\det A)(\det A^{-1}) = \det I = 1$, so $\det A^{-1} = (\det A)^{-1}$. Multiplying A^{-1} by k means multiplying every one of the n rows of A^{-1} by k, so the determinant of kA^{-1} is equal to k^n times the determinant of A^{-1}. We conclude that:

$$\det(\mathrm{Adj}\,A) = \det(kA^{-1}) = k^n \det(A^{-1}) = k^n(\det A)^{-1} = k^n(k^{-1}) = k^{n-1}$$

CRAMER'S RULE

Determinants can be used to give a formula—known as **Cramer's rule**—for the solutions of a square linear system. Let A be a square matrix and consider the system $A\mathbf{x} = \mathbf{b}$. Let A_j denote the matrix formed by replacing column j of A by the column vector $\mathbf{b}$. If $\det A \neq 0$, then the value of the unknown x_j is given by the equation:

$$x_j = \frac{\det A_j}{\det A}$$

Using Cramer's rule, we can establish the following result: If A is a square matrix, the linear system $A\mathbf{x} = \mathbf{b}$ has a unique solution for every $\mathbf{b}$ if and only if $\det A \neq 0$.

Example 5.17   Find the value of y if

$$2x - 3y + 4z = 1$$
$$4x + 9y = 0$$
$$7x - 2y + 5z = 0$$

Solution: Let's answer this using Cramer's rule. Since we want the value of the second unknown, y, we replace the second column of the coefficient matrix A with the column vector $\mathbf{b} = (1, 0, 0)^{\mathrm{T}}$ to form the matrix whose determinant is the numerator in the Cramer's rule expression:

$$y = \frac{\det A_2}{\det A} = \frac{\begin{vmatrix} 2 & 1 & 4 \\ 4 & 0 & 0 \\ 7 & 0 & 5 \end{vmatrix}}{\begin{vmatrix} 2 & -3 & 4 \\ 4 & 9 & 0 \\ 7 & -2 & 5 \end{vmatrix}} = \frac{-20}{-134} = \frac{10}{67}$$

LINEAR TRANSFORMATIONS

Let V and W be vector spaces. A **linear transformation** (or **linear map**) is a function $T: V \rightarrow W$ such that

$$T(\mathbf{x}_1 + \mathbf{x}_2) = T(\mathbf{x}_1) + T(\mathbf{x}_2) \quad \text{and} \quad T(k\mathbf{x}) = kT(\mathbf{x})$$

for any vectors $\mathbf{x}_1, \mathbf{x}_2, \mathbf{x}$ in V and any scalar k. If $W = V$, then a linear transformation T is also called a **linear operator**. Notice that a linear transformation always maps the zero vector in the domain space to the zero vector in the range space, because $T(\mathbf{0} + \mathbf{0}) = T(\mathbf{0}) + T(\mathbf{0})$ implies $T(\mathbf{0}) = T(\mathbf{0}) + T(\mathbf{0})$, so $T(\mathbf{0}) = \mathbf{0}$. Therefore, if a function T doesn't map the zero vector to the zero vector, it can't be a linear transformation.

There's a simple and elegant connection between linear transformations and matrices. Let A be an $m \times n$ matrix and define a function $T: \mathbf{R}^n \rightarrow \mathbf{R}^m$ by the equation $T(\mathbf{x}) = A\mathbf{x}$ for $\mathbf{x} \in \mathbf{R}^n$. Then T is a linear transformation, as you can verify. Conversely, if $T: \mathbf{R}^n \rightarrow \mathbf{R}^m$ is a linear transformation, then there's an $m \times n$ matrix A such that $T(\mathbf{x}) = A\mathbf{x}$ for all $\mathbf{x}$ in $\mathbf{R}^n$.

Let $T: \mathbf{R}^n \rightarrow \mathbf{R}^m$ be a linear transformation and let $B = \left\{ \mathbf{b}_1, \mathbf{b}_2, \ldots, \mathbf{b}_n \right\}$ be a basis for $\mathbf{R}^n$. Once the images of the basis vectors are known, the image of any vector in $\mathbf{R}^n$ is determined. To see why, notice that every vector $\mathbf{x}$ in $\mathbf{R}^n$ can be written as a unique linear combination of the basis vectors:

$$\mathbf{x} = k_1 \mathbf{b}_1 + k_2 \mathbf{b}_2 + \cdots + k_n \mathbf{b}_n$$

The column vector $\mathbf{k} = (k_1, k_2, \ldots, k_n)^{\mathrm{T}}$ is called the **component vector** of $\mathbf{x}$ relative to B, denoted $[\mathbf{x}]_B$. Using the linearity of T, we find that the image of $\mathbf{x}$ is:

$$\begin{aligned} T(\mathbf{x}) &= T(k_1 \mathbf{b}_1 + k_2 \mathbf{b}_2 + \cdots + k_n \mathbf{b}_n) \\ &= k_1 T(\mathbf{b}_1) + k_2 T(\mathbf{b}_2) + \cdots + k_n T(\mathbf{b}_n) \end{aligned}$$

So if we know $T(\mathbf{b}_i)$ for every i, we know $T(\mathbf{x})$ for any $\mathbf{x}$.

Example 5.18   If $T: \mathbf{R}^2 \rightarrow \mathbf{R}^2$ is the linear transformation that maps $(1, 1)$ to $(3, 4)$ and $(-1, 1)$ to $(2, 2)$, what's the image of $(3, 1)$?

Solution: Since the vectors $\mathbf{b}_1 = (1, 1)$ and $\mathbf{b}_2 = (-1, 1)$ are linearly independent and span $\mathbf{R}^2$, they form a basis for $\mathbf{R}^2$. Using the information given about the images of these basis vectors, we can find the image of $\mathbf{x} = (3, 1)$.

First, we need to find the components of $\mathbf{x}$ relative to this basis; that is, the scalars k_1 and k_2 such that $\mathbf{x} = k_1 \mathbf{b}_1 + k_2 \mathbf{b}_2$. This equation is equivalent to the system

$$k_1 - k_2 = 3$$
$$k_1 + k_2 = 1$$

which gives $k_1 = 2$ and $k_2 = -1$. Since $\mathbf{x} = 2\mathbf{b}_1 - \mathbf{b}_2$, linearity of T gives:

$$T(\mathbf{x}) = k_1 T(\mathbf{b}_1) + k_2 T(\mathbf{b}_2)$$
$$T(3,\ 1) = 2T(1,\ 1) - T(-1,\ 1)$$
$$= 2(3,\ 4) - (2,\ 2)$$
$$= (4,\ 6)$$

STANDARD MATRIX REPRESENTATIVE

If $\mathbf{R}^n$ and $\mathbf{R}^m$ are considered with their standard bases, that is, the bases composed of the standard basis vectors $\hat{\mathbf{e}}_i = (0,\ 0,\ \ldots 0,\ 1,\ 0,\ \ldots, 0)$, which have a 1 in the ith spot and 0's elsewhere, then finding a matrix representative, A, for $T: \mathbf{R}^n \to \mathbf{R}^m$ is easy: Column i of A is the image of $\hat{\mathbf{e}}_i$. The $m \times n$ matrix A is called the **standard matrix** for T, and $T(\mathbf{x}) = A\mathbf{x}$ for every $\mathbf{x}$ in $\mathbf{R}^n$.

Example 5.19   If $T: \mathbf{R}^3 \to \mathbf{R}^3$ is the linear operator that maps $(1, 0, 0)$ to $(1, 2, 3)$, $(0, 1, 0)$ to $(-1, 1, 1)$, and $(0, 0, 1)$ to $(1, -2, 0)$, find the standard matrix for T and use it to determine $T(3, 4, -5)$.

Solution: The vectors $\hat{\mathbf{e}}_1 = (1, 0, 0)$, $\hat{\mathbf{e}}_2 = (0, 1, 0)$, and $\hat{\mathbf{e}}_3 = (0, 0, 1)$ are the standard basis vectors for $\mathbf{R}^3$, so the standard matrix for T is formed by making the images of these basis vectors the columns of A:

$$A = \begin{pmatrix} 1 & -1 & 1 \\ 2 & 1 & -2 \\ 3 & 1 & 0 \end{pmatrix}$$

Therefore, writing $\mathbf{x} = (3, 4, -5)$ as a column vector, its image under T is computed by multiplying by A:

$$T(\mathbf{x}) = A\mathbf{x} = \begin{pmatrix} 1 & -1 & 1 \\ 2 & 1 & -2 \\ 3 & 1 & 0 \end{pmatrix} \begin{pmatrix} 3 \\ 4 \\ -5 \end{pmatrix} = \begin{pmatrix} -6 \\ 20 \\ 13 \end{pmatrix}$$

THE RANK PLUS NULLITY THEOREM

Let $T: \mathbf{R}^n \to \mathbf{R}^m$ by a linear transformation. The set of all vectors $\mathbf{x}$ in $\mathbf{R}^n$ that get mapped to $\mathbf{0}$ is called the **kernel** of T, denoted ker T:

$$\ker T = \{\mathbf{x}:\ T(\mathbf{x}) = \mathbf{0}\}$$

The kernel of T is a subspace of the domain space $\mathbf{R}^n$; its dimension is called the **nullity** of T. The set of all images of T is called the **range** of T, denoted $R(T)$:

$$R(T) = \{T(\mathbf{x}):\ \mathbf{x} \in \mathbf{R}^n\}$$

The range of T is a subspace of $\mathbf{R}^m$; its dimension is called the **rank** of T. Notice that if T is given by $T(\mathbf{x}) = A\mathbf{x}$, then the kernel of T is the same as the nullspace of A, and the range of T is the same as the column space of A.

The **Rank Plus Nullity S** states that:

$$\text{nullity}(T) + \text{rank}(T) = n = \dim (\text{domain } T)$$

If $T: \mathbf{R}^n \to \mathbf{R}^n$ is a linear *operator*, then the nullity of T is zero precisely when the rank of T is n. It can be shown that T is one-to-one when the nullity is zero, and that T is onto when the rank of T is n. Therefore, the linear operator T is one-to-one if and only if it's onto, and this happens when T has full rank. So, if $T(\mathbf{x}) = A\mathbf{x}$, then T is one-to-one and onto when the rank of A is n, that is, when $\det A \neq 0$.

Example 5.20   Determine the kernel, nullity, range, and rank of the linear transformation $T: \mathbf{R}^3 \to \mathbf{R}^2$ given by the equation $T(\mathbf{x}) = A\mathbf{x}$ where:

$$A = \begin{pmatrix} 1 & 2 & 3 \\ 4 & 5 & 6 \end{pmatrix}$$

Solution: The kernel of T is the nullspace of A, the set of the solutions to $A\mathbf{x} = \mathbf{0}$. Row-reducing A gives:

$$A = \begin{pmatrix} 1 & 2 & 3 \\ 4 & 5 & 6 \end{pmatrix} \xrightarrow{-4r_1 + r_2} \begin{pmatrix} 1 & 2 & 3 \\ 0 & -3 & -6 \end{pmatrix} \xrightarrow{-\frac{1}{3}r_2} \begin{pmatrix} 1 & 2 & 3 \\ 0 & 1 & 2 \end{pmatrix}$$

If $\mathbf{x} = (x, y, z)^T$, then we can take z as a free variable; let $z = t$. The bottom row of the final matrix implies that $y + 2t = 0$, so $y = -2t$. Substituting $y = -2t$ and $z = t$ into the equation corresponding to the first row, $x + 2(-2t) + 3t = 0$, gives $x = t$. Therefore,

$$\ker T = \{(1, -2, 1)t : t \in \mathbf{R}\}$$

Since $\ker T$ contains one parameter, it is one-dimensional, so the nullity of T is 1. By the Rank Plus Nullity theorem, the rank of T must be $3 - 1 = 2$. Since the range of T is a two-dimensional subspace of $\mathbf{R}^2$, it must actually be all of $\mathbf{R}^2$.

A NOTE ON INVERSES AND COMPOSITIONS

Let $T: \mathbf{R}^n \to \mathbf{R}^n$ be a linear operator. If T is both one-to-one and onto, then T has an inverse, T^{-1}, that's defined as follows: $T^{-1}(\mathbf{y}) = \mathbf{x}$ if $T(\mathbf{x}) = \mathbf{y}$. If A is the matrix representative for T, then A^{-1} is the matrix representative for T^{-1}.

Let $S: \mathbf{R}^m \to \mathbf{R}^n$ and $T: \mathbf{R}^n \to \mathbf{R}^p$ be linear transformations. If $[S]$ is the matrix representative for S, and $[T]$ is the matrix representative for T, then the matrix product $[T][S]$ is the matrix representative for the composition $T \circ S = TS$. In fact, the rather involved definition of matrix multiplication was motivated by this result.

EIGENVALUES AND EIGENVECTORS

If we multiply a square matrix A by a compatible nonzero column vector $\mathbf{x}$, the product $A\mathbf{x}$ is generally not a scalar multiple of $\mathbf{x}$. However, if $A\mathbf{x}$ *does* equal a scalar multiple of $\mathbf{x}$, that is, if $A\mathbf{x} = \lambda\mathbf{x}$ for some scalar

λ, then λ is called an **eigenvalue** (or **characteristic value**) of A, and the nonzero vector **x** is a corresponding **eigenvector** (or **characteristic vector**). If we interpret the product $A\mathbf{x}$ as the image of **x** by the linear transformation represented by A, then an eigenvector of A is a nonzero vector **x** that's transformed by A into a scalar multiple of itself (with the scalar giving the corresponding eigenvalue). Eigenvalues and eigenvectors are defined only for square matrices (or, equivalently, only for linear operators), so throughout this section, A will always represent a square matrix.

To find the eigenvalues and eigenvectors of a matrix A, we must find a nonzero vector **x** and a scalar λ that satisfy the equation $A\mathbf{x} = \lambda\mathbf{x}$. This equation can be rewritten in the form $(A - \lambda I)\mathbf{x} = \mathbf{0}$, which is homogeneous. As we've already seen, a homogeneous square system has a nonzero solution if and only if the coefficient matrix is noninvertible, which is true if and only if the determinant of the coefficient matrix is zero. In this case, the coefficient matrix is $A - \lambda I$, so the eigenvalues of A are the values of λ that satisfy the **characteristic equation**

$$\det(A - \lambda I) = 0$$

and the eigenvectors corresponding to each eigenvalue are the nonzero vectors **x** that satisfy $A\mathbf{x} = \lambda\mathbf{x}$.

> **Example 5.21** Find the eigenvalues and eigenvectors of the matrix:
>
> $$A = \begin{pmatrix} 1 & 2 \\ -1 & 4 \end{pmatrix}$$

Solution: First, we form the matrix $A - \lambda I$:

$$A - \lambda I = \begin{pmatrix} 1 & 2 \\ -1 & 4 \end{pmatrix} - \begin{pmatrix} \lambda & 0 \\ 0 & \lambda \end{pmatrix} = \begin{pmatrix} 1-\lambda & 2 \\ -1 & 4-\lambda \end{pmatrix}$$

The determinant of this matrix is the **characteristic polynomial** of A:

$$\begin{aligned} \det(A - \lambda I) &= \det \begin{pmatrix} 1-\lambda & 2 \\ -1 & 4-\lambda \end{pmatrix} \\ &= (1-\lambda)(4-\lambda) - (-2) \\ &= \lambda^2 - 5\lambda + 6 \end{aligned}$$

The characteristic equation, $\lambda^2 - 5\lambda + 6 = 0$, is equivalent to $(\lambda - 2)(\lambda - 3) = 0$, so we see that the eigenvalues of A are $\lambda = 2$ and $\lambda = 3$.

Now, to find the eigenvectors corresponding to $\lambda = 2$, we seek nonzero vectors **x** that satisfy $A\mathbf{x} = 2\mathbf{x}$, or, equivalently, that satisfy $(A - 2I)\mathbf{x} = \mathbf{0}$:

$$(A - 2I)\mathbf{x} = \mathbf{0} \quad \Rightarrow \quad \begin{pmatrix} -1 & 2 \\ -1 & 2 \end{pmatrix}\mathbf{x} = \mathbf{0} \quad \Rightarrow \quad \mathbf{x} = k\begin{pmatrix} 2 \\ 1 \end{pmatrix}$$

Since eigenvectors are nonzero by definition, the eigenvectors corresponding to the eigenvalue $\lambda = 2$ are all the nonzero multiples of $(2, 1)^{\mathrm{T}}$.

The eigenvectors corresponding to $\lambda = 3$ satisfy $(A - 3I)\mathbf{x} = \mathbf{0}$:

$$(A - 3I)\mathbf{x} = \mathbf{0} \implies \begin{pmatrix} -2 & 2 \\ -1 & 1 \end{pmatrix} \mathbf{x} = \mathbf{0} \implies \mathbf{x} = k \begin{pmatrix} 1 \\ 1 \end{pmatrix}$$

Thus an eigenvector corresponding to the eigenvalue $\lambda = 3$ is any nonzero multiple of $(1, 1)^T$.

Example 5.22   What can you say about a square matrix A that has zero as an eigenvalue?

Solution: If 0 is an eigenvalue of A, then the equation $A\mathbf{x} = 0\mathbf{x}$ must have a nonzero solution $\mathbf{x}$ (an eigenvector). Since $A\mathbf{x} = \mathbf{0}$ has nonzero solutions if and only if A is noninvertible, we can conclude that if 0 is an eigenvalue of A, then A is not invertible (or, $\det A = 0$).

Example 5.23   The **trace** of a square matrix is the sum of the diagonal entries; it's denoted $\text{tr}(A)$. Show that the characteristic polynomial for any 2×2 matrix A is:

$$\lambda^2 - [\text{tr}(A)]\,\lambda + (\det A)$$

Solution: Let

$$A = \begin{pmatrix} a & b \\ c & d \end{pmatrix}$$

be an arbitrary 2×2 matrix. Its characteristic polynomial is:

$$p(A) = \det \begin{pmatrix} a - \lambda & b \\ c & d - \lambda \end{pmatrix} = (a - \lambda)(d - \lambda) - bc$$

$$= \lambda^2 - (a + d)\lambda + (ad - bc)$$

$$= \lambda^2 - [\text{tr}(A)]\lambda + (\det A)$$

Recall that the sum of the roots of the monic polynomial equation

$$x^n + a_{n-1}x^{n-1} + \cdots + a_1 x + a_0 = 0$$

is equal to $-a_{n-1}$. Applying this to the characteristic equation of a 2×2 matrix A shows that the sum of the eigenvalues of A is equal to the trace of A. This result can be used to prove that the sum of the eigenvalues of A is equal to the trace of A for any size square matrix.

The product of the roots of the monic polynomial equation above is equal to a_0. Applying this to the characteristic equation of a 2×2 matrix A shows that the product of the eigenvalues of A is equal to the determinant of A. This result can be used to prove that the product of the eigenvalues of A is equal to the determinant of A for any size square matrix.

EIGENSPACES

Let λ be an eigenvalue of an $n \times n$ matrix A. If we adjoin the zero vector to the collection of all the eigenvectors corresponding to λ, the result is a subspace of $\mathbf{R}^n$ called the **eigenspace** of A corresponding to λ:

$$E_\lambda(A) = \left\{ \mathbf{x}: \; A\mathbf{x} = \lambda\mathbf{x} \right\}$$

Notice that $E_\lambda(A)$ is the nullspace of the matrix $A - \lambda I$.

Example 5.24   Without computing its characteristic polynomial, explain why the matrix A below has 0 as an eigenvalue, then find a basis for the corresponding eigenspace.

$$A = \begin{pmatrix} 1 & -1 & 1 \\ -1 & 1 & -1 \\ 1 & -1 & 1 \end{pmatrix}$$

Solution: Since the second row of the matrix is the opposite of the first row and the third row is equal to the first row, these rows are clearly not linearly independent, so the determinant of the matrix must be zero. Because the product of the eigenvalues always equals the determinant, the fact that $\det A = 0$ implies that A must have 0 as an eigenvalue.

The eigenspace corresponding to $\lambda = 0$ is the set of solutions to $A\mathbf{x} = \mathbf{0}$; reducing A to echelon form is easy:

$$\begin{pmatrix} 1 & -1 & 1 & 0 \\ -1 & 1 & -1 & 0 \\ 1 & -1 & 1 & 0 \end{pmatrix} \xrightarrow[\;-r_1 + r_3\;]{\;r_1 + r_2\;} \begin{pmatrix} 1 & -1 & 1 & 0 \\ 0 & 0 & 0 & 0 \\ 0 & 0 & 0 & 0 \end{pmatrix}$$

Since there's only one nonzero row remaining, there's only one constraint on the unknowns; therefore, $3 - 1 = 2$ of them are free variables. Let $\mathbf{x} = (x, y, z)^{\mathsf{T}}$, and take $y = t_1$ and $z = t_2$ as the free variables. Substituting these into the equation corresponding to the first row gives

$$x - t_1 + t_2 = 0 \;\; \Rightarrow \;\; x = t_1 - t_2$$

so the solutions of $A\mathbf{x} = \mathbf{0}$ can be expressed in the form

$$\mathbf{x} = \begin{pmatrix} t_1 - t_2 \\ t_1 \\ t_2 \end{pmatrix} = t_1 \begin{pmatrix} 1 \\ 1 \\ 0 \end{pmatrix} + t_2 \begin{pmatrix} -1 \\ 0 \\ 1 \end{pmatrix}$$

so $\left\{ (1,\, 1,\, 0)^{\mathsf{T}},\; (-1,\, 0,\, 1)^{\mathsf{T}} \right\}$ is a basis for the two-dimensional eigenspace $E_{\lambda=0}(A)$.

THE CAYLEY–HAMILTON THEOREM

The remarkable **Cayley–Hamilton theorem** states that every square matrix satisfies its own characteristic equation. That is, if $p(\lambda) = \det(A - \lambda I)$ is the characteristic polynomial of the matrix A, then $p(A) = 0$. This theorem can be used, for example, to express an integer power of A as a linear polynomial in A.

Example 5.25   If

$$A = \begin{pmatrix} 4 & -2 \\ 5 & -3 \end{pmatrix}$$

show that $A^4 = 5A + 6I$.

[handwritten annotations:]

$\begin{vmatrix} 4-\lambda & -2 \\ 5 & -3-\lambda \end{vmatrix} = \lambda^2 - \lambda - 2$

$A^2 = A + 2I$

$A^2 = \begin{bmatrix} 6 & -2 \\ 5 & -1 \end{bmatrix} = A + 2I \checkmark$

$A^3 = A + 2I + 2A = 3A + 2I$

$A^4 = 3A + 6I + 2A$

$= 5A + 6I$

Solution: The characteristic polynomial of A is

$$\det(A - \lambda I) = \begin{vmatrix} 4-\lambda & -2 \\ 5 & -3-\lambda \end{vmatrix} = \lambda^2 - \lambda - 2 = 0$$

so by the Cayley–Hamilton theorem, $A^2 - A - 2I = 0$. Therefore, $A^2 = A + 2I$. Multiplying both sides of this equation by A gives $A^3 = A^2 + 2A$, and using $A^2 = A + 2I$ again, we get $A^3 = 3A + 2I$. Multiplying by A again gives $A^4 = 3A^2 + 2A = 3(A + 2I) + 2A = 5A + 6I$, as desired.

CHAPTER 5 REVIEW QUESTIONS

Complete the following review questions using the techniques outlined in this chapter. Then, see Chapter 8 for answers and explanations.

1. Two distinct solutions, x_1 and x_2, can be found to the linear system $Ax = b$. Which of the following is necessarily true?

   (A) $b = 0$.

   (B) A is invertible.

   (C) A has more columns than rows.

   (D) $x_1 = -x_2$.

   (E) There exists a solution x such that $x \neq x_1$ and $x \neq x_2$.

---

2. The solution of the system

$$ax + ay - z = 1$$
$$x - ay - az = -1$$
$$ax - y + az = 1$$

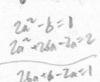 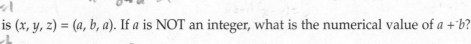

is $(x, y, z) = (a, b, a)$. If a is NOT an integer, what is the numerical value of $a + b$?

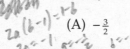

   (A) $-\frac{3}{2}$ (B) -1 (C) 0 (D) $\frac{1}{2}$ (E) 1

3. Let A, B, and C be real 2×2 matrices, and let 0 denote the 2×2 zero matrix. Which of the following statements is/are true?

   I. $A^2 = 0 \Rightarrow A = 0$

   II. $AB = AC \Rightarrow B = C$

   III. A is invertible and $A = A^{-1} \Rightarrow A = I$ or $A = -I$

   (A) I only   (B) I and III only   (C) II and III only

   (D) III only   (E) None of the above

---

4. If

$$\begin{pmatrix} 1 & 1 \\ 0 & 1 \end{pmatrix}^n - \begin{pmatrix} 1 & 0 \\ 1 & 1 \end{pmatrix}^n = \begin{pmatrix} 0 & 6 \\ -6 & 0 \end{pmatrix}$$

   then $n =$

   (A) -7 (B) -5 (C) 5 (D) 6 (E) 7

---

5. If the matrices

$$\begin{pmatrix} 3 & -2 & -2 \\ -1 & 1 & 1 \\ 3 & -1 & -2 \end{pmatrix} \quad \text{and} \quad \begin{pmatrix} 1 & a & 0 \\ -1 & b & 1 \\ 2 & c & -1 \end{pmatrix}$$

(handwritten: $3a-b-2c=0$, $-a-b+c=1$, $3a-2b-2c=0$, $b+c=3$, $-b=0$)

are inverses of each other, what is the value of c?

(A) –3   (B) –2   (C) 0   (D) 2   (E) 3

6. The vectors $\mathbf{v}_1 = (-1, 1, 1)$, $\mathbf{v}_2 = (1, 1, 1)$, and $\mathbf{v}_3 = (1, -1, k)$ form a basis for $\mathbf{R}^3$ for all real values of k EXCEPT $k =$

(handwritten: $-a+b=1$, $a+b=-1$, $a=-1$, $b=0$)

(A) –2   (B) –1   (C) 0   (D) 1   (E) 2

7. For the matrix

$$A = \begin{pmatrix} 1 & 2 & 3 \\ 4 & 5 & 6 \\ 7 & 8 & 9 \end{pmatrix}$$

(handwritten: $\begin{vmatrix} 1 & 2 & 3 \\ 0 & -3 & -6 \\ 3 & 0 & -3 \end{vmatrix} \rightarrow \begin{vmatrix} 0 & 2 & 4 \\ 0 & 1 & 2 \\ 1 & 0 & -1 \end{vmatrix}$ rank $= 2$; $45+84+12-8-72-105-78$; $-3+12-9=0$)

let r denote its rank and d denote its determinant. What is the value of $r - d$?

(A) –2   (B) –1   (C) 0   (D) 1   (E) 2

8. If

$$\det \begin{pmatrix} a & b & c \\ k & l & m \\ p & q & r \end{pmatrix} = d$$

then

$$\det \begin{pmatrix} k & 2(a-k) & p+k \\ l & 2(b-l) & q+l \\ m & 2(c-m) & r+m \end{pmatrix} =$$

(A) –8d   (B) –6d   (C) –2d   (D) 2d   (E) 8d

9. For what value of x will the following matrix be noninvertible?

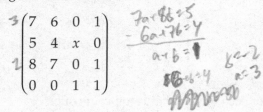

$$\begin{pmatrix} 7 & 6 & 0 & 1 \\ 5 & 4 & x & 0 \\ 8 & 7 & 0 & 1 \\ 0 & 0 & 1 & 1 \end{pmatrix}$$

(A) –1   (B) 0   (C) 1   (D) 3   (E) 9

10. For what value of d is the vector $\mathbf{b} = (12, 11, d)^{\mathrm{T}}$ in the column space of this matrix?

$$A = \begin{pmatrix} 1 & 2 & 3 \\ 4 & 5 & 6 \\ 7 & 8 & 9 \end{pmatrix}$$

(A) –26   (B) 10   (C) 13   (D) –10   (E) 26

11. What is the dimension of the following subspace of $\mathbf{R}^5$?

$$\mathrm{span}\left\{ \begin{pmatrix} 1 \\ 0 \\ -1 \\ 0 \\ 1 \end{pmatrix}, \begin{pmatrix} 0 \\ 1 \\ -1 \\ 1 \\ 0 \end{pmatrix}, \begin{pmatrix} 0 \\ 0 \\ 0 \\ 0 \\ 0 \end{pmatrix}, \begin{pmatrix} -1 \\ 0 \\ 1 \\ 0 \\ -1 \end{pmatrix}, \begin{pmatrix} 0 \\ 0 \\ 1 \\ 0 \\ -1 \end{pmatrix}, \begin{pmatrix} 0 \\ -1 \\ 1 \\ -1 \\ 0 \end{pmatrix} \right\}$$

(A) 1   (B) 2   (C) 3   (D) 4   (E) 5

12. A square matrix A is said to be **symmetric** if it equals its own transpose: $A = A^{\mathrm{T}}$. What is the dimension of the subspace $S_{n \times n}(\mathbf{R})$ of real symmetric $n \times n$ matrices in the space of all real $n \times n$ matrices, $M_{n \times n}(\mathbf{R})$?

(A) $\frac{1}{2}n$ (B) $\frac{1}{2}n(n-1)$ (C) $\frac{1}{2}n^2$ (D) $\frac{1}{2}n(n+1)$ (E) $\frac{1}{2}n!$

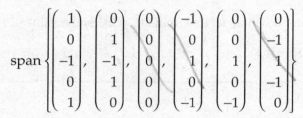

13. The set of all points (x, y) in $\mathbf{R}^2$ that satisfy the equation

$$\begin{vmatrix} x & y & 1 \\ 0 & y_1 & 1 \\ 1 & y_2 & 1 \end{vmatrix} = 0$$

forms

$xy_1 + y - y_1 - xy_2 = 0$

$x(y_1 - y_2) + y - y_1 = 0$

(A) an ellipse centered at the origin

(B) a line with slope $\dfrac{y_2}{y_1}$

(C) a circle with center $(0, y_1)$ and radius 1

(D) a line with slope $y_2 - y_1$

(E) a parabola with vertex $(1, y_2)$

14. The linear transformation $T: \mathbf{R}^2 \to \mathbf{R}^2$ that maps $(1, 2)$ to $(-1, 1)$ and $(0, -1)$ to $(2, -1)$ will map $(1, 1)$ to

(A) $(1, 2)$ (B) $(1, 0)$ (C) $(2, -1)$ (D) $(2, 1)$ (E) $(1, 1)$

15. Let $T: \mathbf{R}^5 \to \mathbf{R}^3$ be a linear transformation whose kernel is a three-dimensional subspace of $\mathbf{R}^5$. The set $\{T(\mathbf{x}): \mathbf{x} \in \mathbf{R}^5\}$ is

(A) the trivial subspace

(B) a line through the origin

(C) a plane through the origin

(D) all of $\mathbf{R}^3$

(E) Cannot be determined from the information given

16. Define linear operators S and T on the xy-plane ($\mathbf{R}^2$) as follows: S rotates each vector $90°$ counterclockwise, and T reflects each vector through the y-axis. If ST and TS denote the compositions $S \circ T$ and $T \circ S$, respectively, and I is the identity map, which of the following is true?

(A) $ST = I$ (B) $ST = -I$ (C) $TS = I$ (D) $ST = TS$ (E) $ST = -TS$

17. Choose a nonzero vector $\mathbf{v} = (a, b, c)^T$ in $\mathbf{R}^3$ and define a linear operator $T: \mathbf{R}^3 \to \mathbf{R}^3$ by the equation $T(\mathbf{x}) = \mathbf{v} \times \mathbf{x}$, the cross product of $\mathbf{v}$ and $\mathbf{x}$. Then $T(\mathbf{x}) = A\mathbf{x}$ for every $\mathbf{x}$ in $\mathbf{R}^3$ if $A =$

(A) $\begin{pmatrix} 0 & -c & b \\ c & 0 & -a \\ -b & a & 0 \end{pmatrix}$
$\checkmark$

(B) $\begin{pmatrix} 1 & -c & b \\ c & 1 & -a \\ -b & a & 1 \end{pmatrix}$

(C) $\begin{pmatrix} 0 & c & -b \\ -c & 0 & a \\ b & -a & 0 \end{pmatrix}$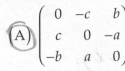

(D) $\begin{pmatrix} 1 & c & -b \\ -c & 1 & a \\ b & -a & 1 \end{pmatrix}$

(E) $\begin{pmatrix} 0 & a & b \\ a & 1 & c \\ b & c & 0 \end{pmatrix}$

$\langle a, b, c \rangle \times \langle x_1, x_2, x_3 \rangle$

---

18. If A is an invertible matrix with an eigenvalue of 3 corresponding to the eigenvector $\mathbf{x}$, which of the following statements must be true?

$A\mathbf{x} = 3\mathbf{x} \qquad \mathbf{x} = A^{-1} 3\mathbf{x}$

(A) The matrix A^{-1} has an eigenvalue of $\frac{1}{3}$ corresponding to the eigenvector $\mathbf{x}$. $A^{-1}\mathbf{x} = \frac{1}{3}\mathbf{x}$

(B) The matrix A^{-1} has an eigenvalue of $\frac{1}{3}$ corresponding to the eigenvector whose entries are the reciprocals of the entries of $\mathbf{x}$.

$\checkmark$

(C) The matrix A^2 has an eigenvalue of 3 corresponding to the eigenvector $\mathbf{x}$.

(D) The matrix A^2 has an eigenvalue of 6 corresponding to the eigenvector $2\mathbf{x}$.

(E) The matrix A^2 has an eigenvalue of 3 corresponding to the eigenvector $3\mathbf{x}$.

---

19. The eigenvalues of the matrix

$$A = \begin{pmatrix} 2 & b \\ 3 & -1 \end{pmatrix}$$

$\checkmark$

$|A - \lambda I| = 0$

$\begin{vmatrix} 2-\lambda & b \\ 3 & -1-\lambda \end{vmatrix} = -2 - \lambda + \lambda^2 - 3b = 0$

$(\lambda + 4)(\lambda - (b-1)) =$
$\lambda^2 \quad -^{+6} \quad b = 6$

are -4 and $b - 1$. Find b.

(A) 2   (B) 3   (C) 4   (D) 5   (E) 6

---

20. The complex matrix

$$A = \begin{pmatrix} 2 & 2+i \\ 2-i & 6 \end{pmatrix}$$

$\checkmark$

$12 - 8\lambda + \lambda^2 - 5$
$\lambda^2 - 8\lambda + 7$

has which one of the following as an eigenvalue?

(A) -1 (B) 3   (C) 7   (D) i (E) $1 + i$

6

Number Theory and Abstract Algebra

INTRODUCTION

In the first part of this chapter, we'll review some fundamental ideas in number theory; you'll need these not only for the few purely number-theoretic questions you might see on the GRE, but we'll also use these ideas in many of the examples in Part B, Abstract Algebra.

Since the abstract algebra on the GRE Math Subject Test concentrates on group theory, the bulk of this chapter will provide a review of groups and their structure. You'll also be required to know the definitions and fundamental properties of rings and fields, so we'll go over these as well. The area of abstract algebra is usually math majors' first contact with a subject in which the careful proof of theorems is an important part of the course. However, we won't bother with proofs of the theorems; knowing how to *use* them is much more important than is their derivation. Part B lists the many definitions and theorems that you'll need to know (and there are more than a few!); they're illustrated by an unusually large number of examples.

PART A: NUMBER THEORY

DIVISIBILITY

An important subdivision of number theory is the study of the divisibility properties of integers. Let a and b be integers (where $a \neq 0$); if $\frac{b}{a}$ is an integer—that is, if there exists an integer c such that $ac = b$—then we say that a **divides** b—or, equivalently, that b is **divisible** by a—and write $a|b$. For example $4|8$ and $-3|12$, but 4 does not divide 9 and -3 does not divide 13. If a divides b, then a is said to be a **divisor** or **factor** of b, and b is a **multiple** of a. There are a few well-known definitions that are based on divisibility: An integer n is said to be **even** if 2 divides n; otherwise, n is **odd**. Furthermore, an integer greater than 1 whose only positive divisors are 1 and itself is called a **prime number**; and an integer greater than 1 that's not prime is said to be **composite**. Prime numbers hold a prominent place in number theory, and we'll have more to say about them a little later.

There are a few ways of telling whether a given integer n is divisible by another integer m, some of which are undoubtedly very familiar.

An integer n is divisible:

- by 2, if and only if the units digit of n is 0, 2, 4, 6, or 8.

  For example, 1358 is divisible by 2, but 2467 is not.

- by 3, if and only if the sum of the digits of n is itself divisible by 3.

  For example, 28554 is divisible by 3 since $2 + 8 + 5 + 5 + 4 = 24$ is divisible by 3.

- by 4, if and only if the number formed by the last two digits of n is divisible by 4.

  For example, 139756 is divisible by 4 because 56 is divisible by 4.

- by 5, if and only if the units digit of n is 0 or 5.

  For example, 4085 is divisible by 5, but 5804 is not.

- by 6, if and only if n is divisible by both 2 and 3.

  For example, 6498 is divisible by 6 since it's even and $6 + 4 + 9 + 8 = 27$ is divisible by 3.

- by 8, if and only if the number formed by the last three digits of n is divisible by 8.

  For example, 4895064 is divisible by 8 since $064 = 64$ is divisible by 8.

- by 9, if and only if the sum of the digits of n is itself divisible by 9.

  For example, 4895064 is divisible by 9 since $4 + 8 + 9 + 5 + 0 + 6 + 4 = 36$ is divisible by 9.

- by 10, if and only if the units digit of n is 0.

  For example, 567890 is divisible by 0, but 98765 is not.

There is no simple test for divisibility by 7.

The rule for divisibility by 6 illustrates a basic result about divisibility in general:

> If n is divisible by a and b, where a and b are distinct primes, then n is divisible by ab.

Thus, if n is divisible by both 2 and 3, then n is divisible by $2 \cdot 3 = 6$. This result is true only if a and b have no common divisors (other than 1). For example, 20 is divisible by both 2 and 4, but 20 is not divisible by $2 \cdot 4 = 8$. The result quoted above can be generalized to any number of prime divisors (not just two), as well as to divisors that are relatively prime. Two nonzero integers are said to be **relatively prime** if the only positive divisor they have in common is 1. So, for example, 14 and 15 are relatively prime, but 14 and 16 are not. The generalized version of the result above can be expressed like this:

If n is divisible by $a, b, c, \ldots$, and these divisors are (pairwise) relatively prime, then n is divisible by the product of these divisors.

Example 6.1   Is 9876543210 divisible by 30?

Solution: Since $30 = 3 \cdot 10$, and 3 and 10 are relatively prime, n is divisible by 30 if and only if it's divisible by 3 and by 10. The integer 9876543210 is divisible by 10 since it ends in a zero. Furthermore, since $9 + 8 + 7 + 6 + 5 + 4 + 3 + 2 + 1 + 0 = 45$, which is divisible by 3, we can conclude that this integer is divisible by 3, and thus also by 30.

THE DIVISION ALGORITHM

If a and b are positive integers (and $a \neq 0$), then the **division algorithm** tells us that we can find unique integers q and r such that $b = qa + r$, with $0 \leq r < a$. We call q the **quotient** and r the **remainder**, when b is divided by a. This simple fact can be used to determine the greatest common divisor of two integers, in a process called the Euclidean algorithm. We'll return to this after the next section.

PRIMES

As we've said, a prime number has no positive divisors except 1 and itself, and the list of prime numbers begins: 2, 3, 5, 7, 11, 13, 17, 19, 23, 29, 31, ... The sequence of primes is infinite and rather mysterious. For example, there are arbitrarily large gaps in the sequence (for every integer k, we can find k consecutive integers all of which are composite), so we might suspect that primes are rather scarce. Nevertheless, for every integer $k > 1$, there's always at least one prime between k and $2k$, and the series

$$\sum_{k=1}^{\infty} \frac{1}{p_k}$$

where p_k is the kth prime, diverges. There's no formula for generating all the primes, but it is possible to estimate how many integers, less than or equal to a number x, are prime. Let $\pi(x)$ denote the number of primes that are less than or equal to x; then the prime number theorem says that $\pi(x) \approx x / \log x$, and the approximation gets better as x gets larger.

Every integer n greater than 1 can be expressed as a unique product of primes. If n is already a prime, then the "product" simply consists of one factor—the number itself. In addition, we don't consider a rearrangement of the prime factors as a different product; this is a statement of the **fundamental theorem of arithmetic**. For example, the prime factorization of 3960 is $2^3 \cdot 3^2 \cdot 5 \cdot 11$.

THE GREATEST COMMON DIVISOR AND THE LEAST COMMON MULTIPLE

To find the **greatest common divisor (gcd)** and the **least common multiple (lcm)** of two integers, a and b (both greater than 1), first express them in terms of their prime factorizations:

$$a = (p_1)^{a_1}(p_2)^{a_2}\cdots(p_k)^{a_k} \qquad \text{and} \qquad b = (p_1)^{b_1}(p_2)^{b_2}\cdots(p_k)^{b_k}$$

Notice that we've used the *same* list of primes—p_1 through p_k—in both factorizations; this can always be done for any two integers a and b if we allow for zero exponents. Now, for each i from 1 to k, let:

$$m_i = \min(a_i,\, b_i) \qquad \text{and} \qquad M_i = \max(a_i,\, b_i)$$

Then the greatest common divisor and least common multiple of a and b are given by:

$$\gcd(a,\, b) = (p_1)^{m_1}(p_2)^{m_2}\cdots(p_k)^{m_k} \qquad \text{and} \qquad \operatorname{lcm}(a,\, b) = (p_1)^{M_1}(p_2)^{M_2}\cdots(p_k)^{M_k}$$

It's also helpful to know that the equation $\gcd(a, b) \cdot \operatorname{lcm}(a, b) = ab$ is true for any two positive integers, a and b.

Example 6.2   What are the gcd and lcm of 3360 and 3960?

Solution: Since

$3360 = 2^5 \cdot 3 \cdot 5 \cdot 7 \cdot 11^0 \qquad$ and $\qquad 3960 = 2^3 \cdot 3^2 \cdot 5 \cdot 7^0 \cdot 11$

we can conclude that gcd(3360, 3960) = 23 • 3 • 5 • 70 • 110 = 120, and lcm(3360, 3960) = 25 • 32 • 5 • 7 • 11 = 110880.

THE EUCLIDEAN ALGORITHM

The **Euclidean algorithm** is a stepwise method to figure out the greatest common divisor of two integers. It's particularly convenient if the integers are large or if finding their prime factorizations is difficult. This algorithm makes repeated use of the division algorithm, and the following schematic—in which we find the greatest common divisor of 2002 and 315—illustrates the process:

$$\boxed{2002} = 6 \cdot \boxed{315} + 112$$
$$315 = 2 \cdot 112 + 91$$
$$112 = 1 \cdot 91 + 21$$
$$91 = 4 \cdot 21 + 7$$
$$21 = 3 \cdot 7 + \boxed{0} \longleftarrow \text{— this signals that the process STOPS}$$
$$\underset{\text{gcd}}{\uparrow}$$

Notice that each equation after the first one uses the remainder from the preceding equation as the new divisor. The last divisor that gives a remainder of 0 is the greatest common divisor of the two original numbers. Therefore, gcd(2002, 315) = 7.

Example 6.3   What are the greatest common divisor and the least common multiple of 1020 and 3234?

Solution: First, we'll use the Euclidean algorithm to find gcd(1020, 3234):

$$3234 = 3 \cdot 1020 + 174$$

$$1020 = 5 \cdot 174 + 150$$

$$174 = 1 \cdot 150 + 24$$

$$150 = 6 \cdot 24 + 6$$

$$24 = 4 \cdot 6 + \boxed{0} \longleftarrow \text{this signals that}$$
the process STOPS

gcd

This tells us that gcd(1020, 3234) = 6. Now, using the fact that the product of the greatest common divisor and the least common multiple of two integers is always equal to the product of the number themselves, we find that:

$$\text{lcm}(1020, 3234) = \frac{1020 \cdot 3234}{\text{gcd}(1020, 3234)} = \frac{1020 \cdot 3234}{6} = 549780$$

This example shows that it's possible to determine the greatest common divisor and the least common multiple of two integers even if we can't figure out the integers' prime factorizations.

THE DIOPHANTINE EQUATION $ax + by = c$

An equation that involves one or more variables is called a **Diophantine equation** if the solutions sought are restricted to a particular set of numbers, usually integers. To look at a very simple example, the equation $x + 2y = 3$ has infinitely many real solutions; but if we restrict x and y to be positive integers, the equation has only one solution, $(x, y) = (1, 1)$. If x and y simply need to be integers (not necessarily positive), then $x + 2y = 3$ has infinitely many solutions; and they're all of the form $x = 1 + 2t$, $y = 1 - t$, for any integer t. The most famous Diophantine equation of all time is $x^n + y^n = z^n$; Fermat's last theorem conjectured (without proof) that, if n is any integer greater than 2, then this equation has no solutions in nonzero integers x, y, and z. For over 350 years, proving (or disproving) this conjecture was one of the most outstanding unsolved problems in all of mathematics. The recent (1994) solution—a proof in the affirmative—by Andrew Wiles was front-page news around the world. But here our goal will be far more modest; we will look for a way to solve the linear Diophantine equation $ax + by = c$ in integers, where a, b, and c are themselves integers (with $ab \neq 0$).

First of all, the equation $ax + by = c$ will have no integral solutions if gcd(a, b) does not divide c. However, if gcd(a, b) *does* divide c, then the equation will have infinitely many integer solutions; if we can find even one—let's call it (x_1, y_1)—then all the solutions are given by the formulas

$$x = x_1 + (b/d)t \quad \text{and} \quad y = y_1 - (a/d)t$$

where $d = $ gcd(a, b), and t is any integer. The method for finding a solution follows directly from the Euclidean algorithm. By working backward with the list of equations generated by the algorithm, we can always write d, the greatest common divisor of a and b, as a linear combination of a and b; that is, we can always find integers, x_0 and y_0, such that:

$$ax_0 + by_0 = d$$

If $c = 0$, then all the integer solutions of $ax + by = c$ are given by $x = x_0 + bt$ and $y = y_0 - at$. If $c \neq 0$, we can multiply the equation above by $\dfrac{c}{d}$ (which will be an integer because d must divide c in order for the equation to have any solutions at all), and get

$$a\underbrace{\left(\tfrac{c}{d}x_0\right)}_{x_1} + b\underbrace{\left(\tfrac{c}{d}y_0\right)}_{y_1} = c$$

and the formulas given above will give us all the integer solutions.

Let's illustrate the method by finding all integer solutions to the equation

$$15x + 49y = 8$$

Since $\gcd(15, 49) = 1$, this equation will indeed have solutions. (In general, if a and b are relatively prime, then the equation $ax + by = c$ will have integer solutions.) The Euclidean algorithm would produce the following list of equations in search of the greatest common divisor of 15 and 49:

$$49 = 3 \bullet 15 + 4$$

$$15 = 3 \bullet 4 + 3$$

$$4 = 1 \bullet 3 + 1$$

$$3 = 3 \bullet 1 + 0$$

So, working from the second-line-from-the-bottom upwards, we can write:

$$\begin{aligned}
1 &= 4 - 3 \bullet 1 \\
&= 4 - (15 - 3 \bullet 4) \bullet 1 \\
&= 4 \bullet 4 - 15 \\
&= 4 \bullet (49 - 3 \bullet 15) - 15 \\
&= 15 \bullet (-13) + 49 \bullet (4)
\end{aligned}$$

We work our way back up by rewriting each step of the Euclidean algorithm above and substituting it into our expression. Therefore, the greatest common divisor of 15 and 49 can be written as a linear combination (with integer coefficients) of 15 and 49:

$$15 \bullet (-13) + 49 \bullet (4) = 1$$

Then, multiplying both sides by 8 gives us

$$15 \bullet (-104) + 49 \bullet (32) = 8$$

so one solution of our original equation is $x_1 = -104$ and $y_1 = 32$. Therefore, all the solutions of the equation are given by the formulas

$$x = -104 + 49t \quad \text{and} \quad y = 32 - 15t$$

for any integer t.

CONGRUENCES

Let a, b, and n be integers. If $n \neq 0$, we say that **a is congruent to b modulo n** if $a - b$ is divisible by n, which is written $a \equiv b \pmod{n}$. For example, $9 \equiv 1 \pmod 4$ and $-15 \equiv -3 \pmod 6$, but $21 \not\equiv 3 \pmod 5$. Congruences $(\bmod\, n)$ depend on the remainder that's obtained in the division algorithm when the divisor is n. For example, since $987 = 197 \cdot 5 + 2$, we know that $987 \equiv 2 \pmod 5$. Of course, it's also true that $987 \equiv 7 \pmod 5$ and that $987 \equiv -3 \pmod 5$, etc., but the idea of a congruence $(\bmod\, n)$ is that we throw out any multiple of n and keep only what's left over.

The list below gives several important rules that we can use when working with congruences. The first three of these are similar to the corresponding rules for equalities. Unless otherwise stated, all variables stand for integers, with n restricted to be a positive integer.

1. If $a \equiv b \pmod{n}$ and $b \equiv c \pmod{n}$, then $a \equiv c \pmod{n}$.

2. If $a \equiv b \pmod{n}$, then for any c,

   $$a \pm c \equiv b \pm c \pmod{n}$$

   $$ac \equiv bc \pmod{n}$$

3. If $a_1 \equiv b_1 \pmod{n}$ and $a_2 \equiv b_2 \pmod{n}$, then

   $$a_1 \pm a_2 \equiv b_1 \pm b_2 \pmod{n}$$

   $$a_1 a_2 \equiv b_1 b_2 \pmod{n}$$

4. For any positive integer c, the statement $a \equiv b \pmod{n}$ is equivalent to the congruences $a \equiv b$, $b + n$, $b + 2n$, $\ldots$, $b + (c-1)n \pmod{cn}$.

5. If $ab \equiv ac \pmod{n}$, then

   $$b \equiv c \pmod{n} \text{ if } \gcd(a, n) = 1$$

   $$b \equiv c \left(\bmod\, \frac{n}{d}\right) \text{ if } d = \gcd(a, n) > 1$$

6. **Fermat's Little theorem**. If p is a prime and a is an integer, then

   $$a^{p-1} \equiv 1 \pmod{p}, \text{ if } p \text{ does not divide } a$$

   $$a^p \equiv a \pmod{p}, \text{ for any integer } a$$

The rules above can be used to reduce a congruence and solve congruence equations. For example, let's figure out the remainder that results when 3^{10} is divided by 7. We could actually compute 3^{10}, divide by 7, and see what the remainder is, but that's quite a bit of work: Congruences will make this task a lot easier. We're asked to find the value of b such that $3^{10} \equiv b \pmod 7$, with $0 \leq b < 7$.

First, we notice that 3^2 is congruent to 2 $(\bmod\, 7)$. Since $3^{10} = (3^2)^5$, we can apply the third equation in rule 3 above and conclude that $3^{10} = (3^2)^5 \equiv 2^5 \pmod 7$. Now it's easy to figure out that $2^5 = 32 \equiv 4 \pmod 7$. Because $3^{10} \equiv 4 \pmod 7$, the remainder when 3^{10} is divided by 7 is 4.

Example 6.4 What's the remainder when 2^{345} is divided by 29?

Solution: Since 29 is a prime, Fermat's little theorem tells us that $2^{28} \equiv 1 \pmod{29}$.

Since $2^{345} = (2^{28})^{12} \cdot 2^9$, we can conclude that $2^{345} = (2^{28})^{12} \cdot 2^9 \equiv 1^{12} \cdot 2^9 \equiv 2^9 \pmod{29}$.

Now, since $2^5 \equiv 3 \pmod{29}$, we have $2^9 = 2^5 \cdot 2^4 \equiv 3 \cdot 2^4 = 48 \equiv 19 \pmod{29}$.

Therefore, when 2^{345} is divided by 29, the remainder will be 19.

THE CONGRUENCE EQUATION $ax \equiv b \pmod{n}$

Solving the ordinary equation $ax = b$ is easy; if $a \neq 0$, we just divide both sides by a and get $x = \dfrac{b}{a}$. Solving the congruence equation $ax \equiv b \pmod{n}$ is a little more complicated. First, in order for this congruence equation to have any solutions at all, it must be true that $\gcd(a, n)$ divides b. For example, if we tried to solve the equation $2x \equiv 5 \pmod 6$, our search would be hopeless. Since $2x$ is even for any integer x, it could not leave an odd remainder (like 5) when divided by the even number 6.

Let x_1 be a solution to the equation $ax \equiv b \pmod{n}$. Then $ax_1 \equiv b \pmod{n}$, which means that $ax_1 - b = nc$, or, equivalently, $ax_1 - nc = b$, for some integer c. Given a, n, and b, we already know how to find integer solutions (for x and c) of the equation $ax - nc = b$; this is the linear Diophantine equation that we studied earlier. So there are two methods for solving the congruence equation $ax \equiv b \pmod{n}$; we can either recast it in terms of a linear Diophantine equation, or use the rules for congruences given above. We'll complete our list of rules of congruences with the following:

7. The linear congruence equation $ax \equiv b \pmod{n}$ has a solution if and only if $d = \gcd(a, n)$ divides b, and

> if $d = 1$, then the solution is unique $\pmod{n}$
>
> if $d > 1$, then the solution is unique $\left(\bmod\ \dfrac{n}{d}\right)$

Let's do an example, solving the congruence equation $18x \equiv 5 \pmod 7$. Since $\gcd(18, 7) = 1$, we're assured that this equation will actually have solutions. Because $0 \equiv 7 \pmod 7$, adding these equations gives $18x \equiv 12 \pmod 7$. Dividing both sides by 6—which is permitted by rule 5 since $\gcd(6, 7) = 1$—gives us $3x \equiv 2 \pmod 7$. Adding this equation to $0 \equiv 7 \pmod 7$ gives $3x \equiv 9 \pmod 7$, and dividing both sides by 3, gives our final answer: $x \equiv 3 \pmod 7$. This tells us that any integer x that leaves a remainder of 3 when divided by 7 will have the property that $18x$ will leave a remainder of 5 when divided by 7. For example, $x = 3$ certainly satisfies $x \equiv 3 \pmod 7$; when we substitute $x = 3$ into the original congruence equation, we get $18 \cdot 3 \equiv 5 \pmod 7$, which is true, since $18 \cdot 3 - 5 = 54 - 5 = 49$, which is a multiple of 7.

Example 6.5   There's only one integer, x, between 100 and 200 such that $144x \equiv 22 \pmod{71}$. What's x?

Solution: Let's solve the linear congruence equation by the following steps:

$$144x \equiv 22 \pmod{71}$$

$$144x \equiv 93 \pmod{71} \qquad \text{[adding the congruence } 0 \equiv 71 \pmod{71}\text{]}$$

$$48x \equiv 31 \pmod{71} \qquad \text{[dividing both sides by 3]}$$

$$48x \equiv -40 \pmod{71} \qquad \text{[adding the congruence } 0 \equiv -71 \pmod{71}\text{]}$$

$$6x \equiv -5 \pmod{71} \qquad \text{[dividing both sides by 8]}$$

$$6x \equiv 66 \pmod{71} \qquad \text{[adding the congruence } 0 \equiv 71 \pmod{71}\text{]}$$

$$x \equiv 11 \pmod{71} \qquad \text{[dividing both sides by 6]}$$

Therefore, the positive values of x that satisfy the equation are:

$$11, \qquad 11 + 71 = 82, \qquad 11 + 2 \cdot 71 = 153, \qquad 11 + 3 \cdot 71 = 224, \ldots \text{etc.}$$

The only integer between 100 and 200 that satisfies this condition is $x = 153$. If we want, we can check our answer as follows: $144 \cdot 153 = 22032$, and 22032 divided by 71 gives 310 with remainder 22, as desired.

PART B: ABSTRACT ALGEBRA

Several standard sets will be used often throughout this section, so we'll list them here for reference:

$\mathbf{Z}$ = the set of all integers

$\mathbf{Q}$ = the set of all rational numbers (i.e., those real numbers of the form $\frac{a}{b}$, where a and b are integers and $b \neq 0$)

$\mathbf{R}$ = the set of all real numbers

$\mathbf{C}$ = the set of all complex numbers

$M_{m \times n}(S)$ = the set of all $m \times n$ matrices whose entries are in the set S

$M_n(S)$ = the set of all $n \times n$ (square) matrices whose entries are in the set S

Furthermore, a "+" superscript on a set of numbers indicates the subset of *positive* numbers in that set; so $\mathbf{Z}^+$ is the set of positive integers, $\mathbf{Q}^+$ is the set of positive rationals, and $\mathbf{R}^+$ is the set of positive reals. If the "+" superscript is accompanied by an overbar on the set—as in $\bar{\mathbf{Z}}^+$, $\bar{\mathbf{Q}}^+$, and $\bar{\mathbf{R}}^+$—this indicates the subset of all *nonnegative* numbers in that set. So, for example, $\bar{\mathbf{Z}}^+$ is the union of $\mathbf{Z}^+$ and {0}. And, finally, a "*" superscript on a set of numbers—such as $\mathbf{Z}^*$, $\mathbf{Q}^*$, $\mathbf{R}^*$, or $\mathbf{C}^*$—denotes the subset of all *nonzero* numbers in that set.

BINARY STRUCTURES AND THE DEFINITION OF A GROUP

Let S be a nonempty set; a function $f: S \times S \to S$, defined on every ordered pair of elements of S, to give a result that's also in S is called a **binary operation on S**. For example, let $S = \mathbf{Z}$, and $f(a, b) = a + b$. Addition is a binary operation on the set of integers. However, subtraction is not a binary operation on $\mathbf{Z}^+$, because the quantity $a - b$ is not a positive integer if $a \leq b$. (Another way of saying this is that $\mathbf{Z}^+$ is not **closed** under subtraction, since it's possible to subtract two elements of $\mathbf{Z}^+$ and get a result that isn't in $\mathbf{Z}^+$. Because $\mathbf{Z}^+$ is not closed under subtraction, subtraction cannot be a binary operation on $\mathbf{Z}^+$.) In abstract algebra, we don't usually write the result of the binary operation on the ordered pair (a, b) as $f(a, b)$. Instead, we invent some symbol, such as $*$, to denote the binary operation, and write $a * b$, rather than $*(a, b)$. A nonempty set S, together with a binary operation defined on it, is called a **binary structure**. For example, $(\mathbf{Z}, +)$ and $(\mathbf{Z}, -)$ are binary structures, but $(\mathbf{Z}^+, -)$ is not.

We'll now impose additional requirements on a binary structure. A binary operation, $*$, on S is said to be **associative**, if, for every a, b, and c in S, the following equation always holds:

$$a * (b * c) = (a * b) * c$$

A binary structure whose binary operation is associative is called a **semigroup**. For example, $(\mathbf{Z}, +)$ is a semigroup, since $a + (b + c)$ is always equal to $(a + b) + c$. However, the binary structure $(\mathbf{Z}, -)$ is not a semigroup, because subtraction is not associative; in general, $a - (b - c)$ does not equal $(a - b) - c$.

If we're given a binary structure, $(S, *)$, then an element e of S, with the property that

$$a * e = e * a = a$$

for every a in S is called the **identity**. We say *the* identity because if $(S, *)$ has an identity—not all do—then it's unique. (By the way, the use of the generic symbol e for the identity of a binary structure is quite common in abstract algebra, and should not be confused with the base of the natural logarithms, $e \approx 2.718\ldots$.) A semigroup that has an identity is called a **monoid**. For example, $(\mathbf{Z}, +)$ is a monoid, because it's a semigroup and its identity is zero; we know its identity is zero because $a + 0 = 0 + a = a$, for every a in **Z**. However, $(\mathbf{Z}^+, +)$ is a semigroup that's not a monoid, since it has no identity (remember that $\mathbf{Z}^+$ does not contain 0).

Let $(S, *)$ be a monoid, and let a be an element in S. If there's an element $\tilde{a}$ in S such that

$$a * \tilde{a} = \tilde{a} * a = e$$

where e is the identity, then we say that $\tilde{a}$ is the **inverse** of a. A monoid with the property that every element in S has an inverse is called a **group**. For example, $(\mathbf{Z}, +)$ is a group because it's a monoid and every element a in **Z** has an inverse (namely, $-a$). However, the binary structure $(\mathbf{Z}, \times)$, where $\times$ represents ordinary multiplication, is a monoid that's *not* a group. Why not? Because here the identity is the number 1, and it's easy to see that, under this operation, most elements of **Z** have no inverse (in **Z**) under this operation. For example, the multiplicative inverse of the number 2 (not to mention 0) is not in **Z**.

As we've seen, there are three requirements that a binary structure must meet before it is called a group. The choice of these three requirements was motivated by the desire to solve linear equations within such a structure. That is, if $(G, *)$ is a group, then for any elements a and b in G, the linear equation $a * x = b$ can be solved for x and the solution will be unique, and the equation $y * a = b$ can always be solved for y, and the solution will be unique. Neither of these statements would necessarily be true if we attempted to solve these equations in an arbitrary binary structure, semigroup, or even a monoid.

Let $(S, *)$ be a binary structure. If the equation $a * b = b * a$ holds for every two elements, a and b, in S, then we say the binary operation is **commutative**. A semigroup, monoid, or group whose binary operation is commutative is said to be **Abelian**. For example, $(\mathbf{Z}, +)$ and $(\mathbf{Q}^*, \times)$ are Abelian groups, but, if $n \geq 2$, the group of invertible n by n matrices under matrix multiplication is not Abelian (because, in general, matrix multiplication is not commutative).

Let $(S, *)$ be a group. If the set S contains precisely n elements for some positive integer n, then the group is **finite** and we say that the order of the group is n; otherwise, the group is **infinite.**

We'll finish up this first section by mentioning some abuses of notation that are common in group theory. Let G be a set, and let $*$ be a binary operation defined on G in such a way that $(G, *)$ satisfies the requirements to be a group. The group is often denoted simply by G, with the group operation omitted. Of course, it must be clear from context (or from a definition) what the operation actually is. Thus, G can denote either the underlying set or the group itself. The group operation is also usually suppressed when writing the result of applying the operation to a pair of elements; that is, we usually just write ab, instead of $a * b$, even if the operation isn't ordinary multiplication. Also, if the binary operation is commutative, it's common to see it denoted by $+$, even if the operation isn't ordinary addition.

EXAMPLES OF GROUPS

There are three things that must be true in order for a binary structure to be a group. First, the operation must be associative; second, there must be an identity element; and third, every element must have an inverse. So, if we're given a set and an operation, if the operation is not well defined (that is, if the set is not closed with respect to the operation), or if any of these three requirements are violated, we don't have a group. We've already given several examples of such structures.

Let's now look at a wider collection of binary structures that *are* groups. You'll need to be acquainted with all of these classic examples.

1. The following binary structures (where $+$ denotes ordinary addition and $\times$ denotes ordinary multiplication), are infinite, Abelian groups:

$$(\mathbf{Z}, +), \quad (\mathbf{Q}, +), \quad (\mathbf{R}, +), \quad (\mathbf{C}, +), \quad (\mathbf{Q}^*, \times), \quad (\mathbf{R}^*, \times), \quad (\mathbf{C}^*, \times)$$

2. If + denotes addition of matrices, then $(M_{m \times n}(S), +)$ and $(M_n(S), +)$ are infinite, Abelian groups, where S is $\mathbf{Z}, \mathbf{Q}, \mathbf{R}$, or $\mathbf{C}$.

3. Let $GL(n, \mathbf{R})$ denote the subset of $M_n(\mathbf{R})$ that consists of all invertible n by n matrices with entries in $\mathbf{R}$; these are the matrices whose determinant is not zero. Under the operation of matrix multiplication, $GL(n, \mathbf{R})$ is a group, called the **general linear group**. We can also replace $\mathbf{R}$ by $\mathbf{Q}$ or $\mathbf{C}$ and still have a group.

4. Let $SL(n, \mathbf{R})$ denote the subset of $GL(n, \mathbf{R})$, consisting of those matrices whose determinant is 1. Because of the formula $\det(AB) = (\det A)(\det B)$, the set $SL(n, \mathbf{R})$ is closed under matrix multiplication. In fact, $SL(n, \mathbf{R})$ is a group, called the **special linear group**. The set $\mathbf{R}$ can also be replaced by $\mathbf{Q}, \mathbf{C}$, or even $\mathbf{Z}$. [Notice that if we replace $\mathbf{R}$ by $\mathbf{Z}$ in $GL(n, \mathbf{R})$, we get a monoid but not a group, because the inverse of a nonsingular matrix with integer entries may not have integer entries. However, if the determinant of such a matrix is equal to 1, then the entries of the inverse will also be integers, which is why, for $n \geq 2$, $SL(n, \mathbf{Z})$ is a group but $GL(n, \mathbf{Z})$ is not.]

5. Let n be a positive integer, and consider the subset of $\mathbf{C}$

$$U_n = \left\{ z : z^n = 1 \right\}$$

consisting of the nth **roots of unity**. Under the operation of multiplication, U_n is a group. This is our first example of a finite group; the set U_n contains exactly n elements, so the order of U_n is n.

6. Let n be a positive integer, and consider the set, S_n, of all permutations (bijective functions) from the set $\mathbf{n} = \{1, 2, \ldots, n\}$ to itself. Under the operation of function composition, S_n is a group, called the **symmetric group on n letters**. This group is also finite, and its order is $(n!)$.

   Let $n = 3$, and consider the group S_3. Two of the permutations in this group are ϕ_1 and ϕ_3, where ϕ_1 sends 1 to itself and transposes 2 and 3, and ϕ_3 sends 3 to itself and transposes 1 and 2. Let's apply the group operation to this pair of permutations, looking at $\phi_1 \circ \phi_3$ and $\phi_3 \circ \phi_1$. The effect that $\phi_1 \circ \phi_3$ has on 1 is $(\phi_1 \circ \phi_3)(1) = \phi_1(\phi_3(1)) = \phi_1(2) = 3$, but the effect that $\phi_3 \circ \phi_1$ has on 1 is $(\phi_3 \circ \phi_1)(1) = \phi_3(\phi_1(1)) = \phi_3(1) = 2$. Since $(\phi_1 \circ \phi_3)(1) \neq (\phi_3 \circ \phi_1)(1)$, we conclude that $\phi_1 \circ \phi_3 \neq \phi_3 \circ \phi_1$. Therefore, S_3 is *not* Abelian (our first example of a group that's non-Abelian). In fact, it can be shown that S_n is non-Abelian for every $n \geq 3$, and that S_3 has the smallest order possible (namely, $3! = 6$) for a non-Abelian group.

7. Let P_n be a regular polygon with n sides ($n \geq 3$). So P_3 would be an equilateral triangle, P_4 a square, P_5 a regular pentagon, and so forth. Number its vertices consecutively (either clockwise or counterclockwise) from 1 to n, and make a copy of your numbered polygon. Imagine cutting out the polygon copy, and placing it on top of the first polygon, so that the vertices align in some order. Each such alignment ends up defining a permutation of the vertices; let D_n denote the collection of such permutations of the vertices of the polygon P_n. With the operation of function composition, D_n is a group, called the nth **dihedral group**. D_n is a finite group, and it can be shown that the order of D_n is $2n$. In fact, D_3 and S_3 are the same group!

8. A finite group can be defined by listing the elements in its underlying set and then giving a table (generically called a **multiplication table** or **group table**) that describes the group opera-

tion on every ordered pair of elements. For example, consider the set $\{e, a, b\}$, and let its multiplication table be:

•	e	a	b
e	e	a	b
a	a	b	e
b	b	e	a

The way you read a multiplication table is as follows: To find the value of $x \cdot y$, first find x in the far left column, then find y in the top row; the cell in the same row as x and the same column as y gives $x \cdot y$. So, for example, the table above would tell us that $a \cdot b = e$. This table could be used to check that all the requirements for a group are met (with e playing the role of identity) and that the group is Abelian. It's finite and its order is 3 (because it contains three elements).

9. Let n be an integer greater than or equal to 2, and consider the set $\mathbf{Z}_n = \{0, 1, 2, \ldots, n-1\}$. For any two integers a and b in $\mathbf{Z}_n$, define $a \oplus b$ to be the remainder when the usual sum, $a + b$, is divided by n. For example, in the set $\mathbf{Z}_6 = \{0, 1, 2, 3, 4, 5\}$, we would have $3 \oplus 4 = 1$, since 1 is the remainder when $3 + 4 = 7$ is divided by 6. Therefore, for every a and b in $\mathbf{Z}_n$, $a \oplus b$ is the unique integer in $\mathbf{Z}_n$ that's congruent to $a + b \pmod{n}$. With this operation, $(\mathbf{Z}_n, \oplus)$ is a finite, Abelian group of order n, called the **additive group of integers modulo** n. To illustrate, here's the group table for $(\mathbf{Z}_6, \oplus)$:

⊕	0	1	2	3	4	5
0	0	1	2	3	4	5
1	1	2	3	4	5	0
2	2	3	4	5	0	1
3	3	4	5	0	1	2
4	4	5	0	1	2	3
5	5	0	1	2	3	4

10. Let $\mathbf{Z}_n$ be the set $\{0, 1, 2, \ldots, n-1\}$ given above. Define another binary operation, $\otimes$, on this set by requiring that $a \otimes b$ equals the unique integer in $\mathbf{Z}_n$ that's congruent $(\bmod\ n)$ to the usual product ab. With this operation $(\mathbf{Z}_n, \otimes)$ is an Abelian monoid (with identity 1), but it's not a group, because not every element will have an inverse. Consider, for example, $(\mathbf{Z}_6, \otimes)$, whose multiplication table is shown below.

⊗	0	1	2	3	4	5
0	0	0	0	0	0	0
1	0	1	2	3	4	5
2	0	2	4	0	2	4
3	0	3	0	3	0	3
4	0	4	2	0	4	2
5	0	5	4	3	2	1

It's clear from this table that the elements 0, 2, 3, and 4 have no inverse. The number 0 would never have an inverse in any $(\mathbf{Z}_n, \otimes)$, but the reason that 2, 3, and 4 don't have an inverse in $(\mathbf{Z}_6, \otimes)$ is that they're not relatively prime to 6. One way to salvage a group out of this monoid is to restrict n to be a prime, p, and to omit 0. Therefore, if p is a prime, then $(\mathbf{Z}_p{}^*, \otimes)$ is a finite, Abelian group, of order $p - 1$, called the **multiplicative group of integers modulo p**. To illustrate this, the group table for $(\mathbf{Z}_5{}^*, \otimes)$ is given below:

$\otimes$	1	2	3	4
1	1	2	3	4
2	2	4	1	3
3	3	1	4	2
4	4	3	2	1

Look at the group table given for $(\mathbf{Z}_5{}^*, \otimes)$ and the multiplication table given for the monoid $(\mathbf{Z}_6, \otimes)$. In any *group* table, every element of its underlying set appears once, and only once, in every row and every column in the body of the table. If this criterion is not satisfied by a multiplication table, you'll know immediately that it cannot be a group table.

CYCLIC GROUPS

Let's look again at the multiplicative group U_n, consisting of the nth roots of unity. To be more specific, let's take $n = 4$. Then $U_4 = \{1, i, -1, -i\}$, where $i = \sqrt{-1}$. Notice that

$$i^0 = 1, \quad i^1 = i, \quad i^2 = -1, \quad i^3 = -i, i^4 = 1$$

and the cycle repeats when the exponent takes on the values 4, 5, 6, 7, and so on. This shows that every element in the group U_n can be generated by taking successive powers of one of its elements, namely i. A group G with the property that there's an element a in G such that

$$G = \{a^n : n = 0, 1, 2, \ldots\}$$

is said to be **cyclic**, and the element a is a **generator** of the group. The definition of a^n is what you'd expect: a^0 is defined as the identity of the group, a^1 is a, a^2 is $a \cdot a$, a^3 is $a^2 \cdot a$, and so on; in general, for $n \geq 1$, $a^n = a^{n-1} * a$, where $*$ is the group's binary operation. A cyclic group has, by definition, at least one generator, but this generator doesn't have to be unique. For example, the group U_4 is also generated by the element $-i$.

The group $(\mathbf{Z}_n, \oplus)$ is also cyclic, with 1 as a generator. In this case, the group operation is addition modulo n, so rather than writing the nth "power" of a as a^n, here it's common to write it as na, since $1 + 1 = 2 \cdot 1, 1 + 1 + 1 = 3 \cdot 1$, and so on. This group has other generators as well. In fact, it can be shown that:

The integer m is a generator of $(\mathbf{Z}_n, \oplus)$ if and only if m is relatively prime to n.

So, for example, $\mathbf{Z}_6$ is generated by 1 and 5, but not by 2, 3, or 4. This result can be generalized, as follows: Let G be a cyclic group with generator a, and let n be the smallest integer such that $a^n = e$. Then:

The element a^m is a generator of G if and only if m is relatively prime to n.

For example, the group U_4, which is generated by i, is also generated by $-i = i^3$, since 4 is the smallest positive integer n such that $i^n = 1$, and 3 is relatively prime to 4.

Let $(G, *)$ be a cyclic group, with generator a, and let a^m and a^n be any two elements in G. Since $a^m * a^n = a^{m+n} = a^{n+m} = a^n * a^m$, it's clear that every cyclic group is automatically Abelian, but the converse is not true. The simplest example of an Abelian group that's not cyclic is the **Klein four-group**, or **vier-gruppe**, V_4; this is the group of order 4 whose group table is:

	e	a	b	c
e	e	a	b	c
a	a	e	c	b
b	b	c	e	a
c	c	b	a	e

By checking the table, you can verify that V_4 is Abelian. But, because this group has order 4, in order for it to be cyclic, it would have to contain at least one element x such that the powers x^0, x^1, x^2, and x^3 would give, in some order, the four distinct elements e, a, b, and c. But this isn't the case here, since $x^2 = x^0 = e$ for every x in V_4.

SUBGROUPS

Let $(G, *)$ be a group. If there's a subset H of G such that $(H, *)$ is also a group, then we say that H is a **subgroup** of G, and write $H \leq G$. (If $H \neq G$, then we can write $H < G$ to denote that H is a **proper** subgroup of G.) Every group has at least two subgroups, namely, the **trivial subgroup**, $\{e\}$, that consists of just the identity, and G itself. The Klein four-group, V_4, also has three proper, nontrivial subgroups

$$\{e, a\}, \{e, b\}, \text{ and } \{e, c\}$$

as you can verify from its group table. In order for H to be a subgroup of G, you must check that (1) H is closed under the group operation (the same binary operation as G), (2) H contains the identity, and (3) the inverse of every element in H is also in H. For example, the subset $\{e, a, b\}$ of V_4 is not a subgroup of V_4 because it's not closed; the group table for V_4 says that $a * b = c$, and c isn't in $\{e, a, b\}$. For another example, let's find the subgroups of $\mathbf{Z}_6$. By looking back at the group table, we can verify that $\mathbf{Z}_6$ has exactly four subgroups:

$$\{0\}, \{0, 3\}, \{0, 2, 4\}, \text{ and } \mathbf{Z}_6$$

Example 6.6   Let G be a group. The set
$$Z(G) = \{z \in G: zg = gz \text{ for every } g \in G\}$$
which consists of all those elements in G that commute with every element in G is called the **center** of G. Show that $Z(G) \leq G$.

Solution: To show that $Z(G)$ is a subgroup of G, we must show that $Z(G)$ contains the identity, is closed under the group operation, and contains the inverse of z for every z in $Z(G)$. It's clear that $e \in Z(G)$, since $eg = ge$ is certainly true for every g in G. Next, let's assume that z_1 and z_2 are in $Z(G)$; then $z_1 g = g z_1$ and $z_2 g = g z_2$. Multiplying both sides of the equation $z_1 g = g z_1$ by z_2 on the right, we get $z_1 g z_2 = g z_1 z_2$. But, since $g z_2 = z_2 g$, this equation becomes $z_1 z_2 g = g z_1 z_2$, which shows that $z_1 z_2 \in Z(G)$. Finally, assume that $z \in Z(G)$, so z commutes with every element in G; it follows that $g^{-1} z = z g^{-1}$ for every g in G. Taking the inverse of both sides of this equation gives $(g^{-1}z)^{-1} = (zg^{-1})^{-1}$, which is equivalent to $z^{-1}g = gz^{-1}$, showing that z^{-1} commutes with every g in G, so $z^{-1} \in Z(G)$. (It's worth noticing that $(ab)^{-1} = b^{-1}a^{-1}$ for every pair of elements a and b in *any* group.) Thus, $Z(G)$ is a subgroup of G (and, in fact, it's clear from the definition that $Z(G)$ is Abelian).

CYCLIC SUBGROUPS

Let a be an element of a group G. With the binary operation of G, the set

$$\left\{a^n : n \in \mathbf{Z}\right\}$$

also denoted by $\langle a \rangle$, consisting of all integer powers of a, is a subgroup of G called the **cyclic subgroup generated by a**. If n is a negative integer, what does a^n mean? The notation a^{-1} is the traditional symbol for the inverse of a, and if n is a negative integer, then:

$$a^n = (a^{-1})^{-n} = \underbrace{a^{-1} \bullet a^{-1} \bullet \cdots \bullet a^{-1}}_{-n \text{ times}}$$

Earlier, we defined the order of a group as the number of elements in its underlying set, if it were finite. We can also define the **order** of an element of a group. The order of $a \in G$ is the order of $\langle a \rangle$, the cyclic subgroup generated by a, if it's finite; otherwise, the order of a is infinite. There's an equivalent way to define the order of an element of a group: The order of $a \in G$ is the smallest positive integer n such that $a^n = e$, where e is the identity (if such an n exists; otherwise, the order of a is infinite).

In $\mathbf{Z}_6$, the order of the element 4 is 3, since the cyclic subgroup generated by 4, $\langle 4 \rangle = \left\{0, 2, 4\right\}$, has order 3. In the Klein four-group, each element except the identity has order 2, since $x^2 = e$ for every $x \neq e$ in V_4. In the additive group $\mathbf{Z}$, every element m except the identity has infinite order, because the set

$$\langle m \rangle = \left\{\ldots, -2m, -m, 0, m, 2m, \ldots\right\}$$

is infinite for every $m \neq 0$.

If G is a group and $a \in G$, then the cyclic subgroup generated by a is the smallest subgroup of G that contains a. This subset contains all integer powers of a, and the definition can be generalized as follows. If $a_i \in G$ for every i in some indexing set I, then the subgroup generated by $\{a_i\}$ is the subgroup consisting of all finite products of terms of the form $a_i^{n_i}$, and is the smallest subgroup of G containing all the elements a_i.

If this subgroup is all of G, then we say that G is **generated by** $\{a_i\}$, and that the elements a_i are **generators** of G. A cyclic group is one that can be generated by a *one*-element set. To illustrate what we mean by "finite products of terms of the form $a_i^{n_i}$," consider the set $\{a, b, c\}$. The subgroup it generates would contain products such as these

$$a^2 b^{-3} c^0, \quad b^4 a c a^{-2} b^3, \quad c^5 b a^{-2} b^4 c^3 a^2, \text{ and so forth.}$$

For example, the Klein four-group, V_4, is not cyclic; it cannot be generated by any one-element set. But it *can* be generated by any of these two-element sets:

$$\left\{a, b\right\}, \quad \left\{a, c\right\}, \quad \text{or} \quad \left\{b, c\right\}$$

A group G that can be generated by a finite set is said to be **finitely generated**. We'll say more about finitely-generated *Abelian* groups later in this chapter.

GENERATORS AND RELATIONS

For some groups, particularly large ones, it's often more economical to specify a set of generators and a set of equations connecting them—called **relations**—that can be used to reconstruct the entire group table. Together, the set of generators and set of relations is called a **presentation** of the group.

For example, here's a presentation of the Klein four-group:

generating set: $\{a, b\}$, relations: $a^2 = e$, $b^2 = e$, $ab = ba$

Let's see how this presentation can be used to reconstruct the group table. First, we notice that the group must contain the elements e, a, b, and ab. Higher positive powers of a or b would give nothing new, since $a^2 = b^2 = e$. Furthermore, negative powers of a or b would also give nothing new since $a^2 = e$ implies that $a^{-1} = a$ (and, likewise, $b^2 = e$ implies that $b^{-1} = b$). Therefore, the group consists precisely of the four distinct elements e, a, b, and ab. The element ab is equal to the element c that appears in the group table for V_4 given earlier.

As another example,

generating set: $\{a\}$, relation: $a^6 = e$

is a presentation of the group $(\mathbf{Z}_6, \oplus)$.

SOME THEOREMS CONCERNING SUBGROUPS

The group V_4 has order 4, and the orders of its subgroups are 1, 2, and 4, all of which divide 4. Similarly, the group $\mathbf{Z}_6$ has order 6, and the orders of its subgroups are 1, 2, 3, and 6, all of which divide 6. These results illustrate an important fact about subgroups of a finite group, known as **Lagrange's theorem**:

> Let G be a finite group. If H is a subgroup of G, then the order of H divides the order of G.

Therefore, $\mathbf{Z}_6$, which has order 6, cannot have a subgroup of order 4 or 5, since neither 4 nor 5 divides 6. The Klein four-group, which has order 4, cannot have a subgroup of order 3. Is the converse of Lagrange's theorem also true? That is, *if* G *is finite and of order* n, *and* m *divides* n, *must* G *have a subgroup of order* m? If G is not Abelian, then, in general the answer is *no*. But if G *is* Abelian, the answer is *yes*:

> Let G be a finite, Abelian group of order n. Then G has at least one subgroup of order d for every (positive) divisor d of n.

If G is *cyclic*, the answer to the question above is again *yes*, and we can say even more:

> Let G be a finite, cyclic group of order n. Then G has exactly one subgroup—a cyclic subgroup—of order d for every (positive) divisor d of n. If G is generated by a, then the subgroup generated by the element $b = a^m$ has order $d = n/\gcd(m, n)$. [If $m = 0$, then we'll agree that $\gcd(m, n) = n$.]

This theorem is illustrated by the cyclic group $G = \mathbf{Z}_6$ and its four subgroups, listed earlier. The order of G is 6, whose positive integer divisors are 1, 2, 3, and 6. There's exactly one subgroup of order 1, $\{0\}$, generated by 0; there's exactly one subgroup of order 2, $\{0, 3\}$, generated by 3; there's exactly one subgroup of order 3, $\{0, 2, 4\}$, generated by 2 or by 4; and, of course, there's exactly one subgroup of order 6, $\mathbf{Z}_6$ itself, generated by 1 or 5.

Another result concerning the existence of subgroups of a finite group is known as **Cauchy's theorem**:

> Let G be a finite group of order n, and let p be a prime that divides n. Then G has at least one subgroup of order p.

Like Lagrange's theorem, this result applies to any finite group—not just to cyclic, finite groups. For example, Cauchy's theorem guarantees that the Klein four-group, V_4, has a subgroup of order 2; in fact, we know that it has three subgroups of order 2. Here's another example: If a group G is known to have a subgroup of order 5, but no subgroup of order 3, then the order of G could not be, say, 75.

We'll close this section with a generalization of Cauchy's theorem, known as **Sylow's first theorem**:

Let G be a finite group of order n, and let $n = p^k m$, where p is a prime that does not divide m. Then G has at least one subgroup of order p^i for every integer i from 0 to k.

For example, let G be a group of order 48. Since $48 = 2^4 \cdot 3$, G is guaranteed to have a subgroup of order $2^0 = 1$ (the trivial subgroup), a subgroup of order $2^1 = 2$, a subgroup of order $2^2 = 4$, a subgroup of order $2^3 = 8$, and a subgroup of order $2^4 = 16$. G must also have a subgroup of order 3. The fact that subgroups of orders 2 and 3 exist could have been predicted from Cauchy's theorem, but we'd need to invoke Sylow's first theorem to predict the existence of subgroups of orders 4, 8, and 16.

THE CONCEPT OF ISOMORPHISM

Let's write out a multiplication table for a group consisting of the three elements e, a, and b, where e is the identity. Since e is the identity, the table must begin as follows:

$\cdot$	e	a	b
e	e	a	b
a	a		
b	b		

Now, in order for a multiplication table to be a group table, every element of the group must appear once and only once, in every row and every column of the table. With this restriction, there's only one way to complete the missing entries:

$\cdot$	e	a	b
e	e	a	b
a	a	b	e
b	b	e	a

Let's now write out the table for the group $\mathbf{Z}_3$:

$\oplus$	0	1	2
0	0	1	2
1	1	2	0
2	2	0	1

If we place these group tables side by side,

$\cdot$	e	a	b
e	e	a	b
a	a	b	e
b	b	e	a

$\oplus$	0	1	2
0	0	1	2
1	1	2	0
2	2	0	1

it's easy to see that the names of the elements are different, but otherwise, the groups are structurally identical. The term in abstract algebra that means *structurally identical* is **isomorphic**, so we'd say that the group $(\{e, a, b\}, *)$ is isomorphic to $(\mathbf{Z}_3, \oplus)$. We denote the fact that G_1 and G_2 are isomorphic groups by writing $G_1 \cong G_2$. If a pair of groups are isomorphic, then all their structural properties are *identical*. Therefore, if there exists a structural property of one group that's not shared by another, then the groups can't be isomorphic. Structural properties include such things as: the order of the group; the number of subgroups of a particular order; the number of solutions of the equation $x * x = y$; whether the group is Abelian; whether it's cyclic, etc.

Let's look at an example. The Klein four-group, V_4, and the group $\mathbf{Z}_4$ both have order 4 and are Abelian, but nevertheless these groups are not isomorphic. We could give several reasons why: For instance, $\mathbf{Z}_4$ is cyclic, but V_4 is not; $\mathbf{Z}_4$ has only one subgroup of order 2, but V_4 has three distinct subgroups of order 2; $\mathbf{Z}_4$ has two elements of order 4, but V_4 has no elements of order 4. We couldn't say that V_4 and $\mathbf{Z}_4$ aren't isomorphic simply because the identity in V_4 is denoted by e and the identity in $\mathbf{Z}_4$ is 0, or that the binary operation in $\mathbf{Z}_4$ is called addition modulo 4 but the binary operation in V_4 isn't, because these are not structural properties. The condition of isomorphism isn't dependent on the names of the elements or the operations; only the group *structures* are important.

Consider the subgroup M of $(M_2(\mathbf{Z}), \times)$, consisting of the four matrices:

$$I = \begin{pmatrix} 1 & 0 \\ 0 & 1 \end{pmatrix}, \quad A = \begin{pmatrix} 1 & 0 \\ 0 & -1 \end{pmatrix}, \quad -A = \begin{pmatrix} -1 & 0 \\ 0 & 1 \end{pmatrix}, \quad \text{and} \quad -I = \begin{pmatrix} -1 & 0 \\ 0 & -1 \end{pmatrix}$$

The multiplication table for this group is:

$\times$	I	A	$-A$	$-I$
I	I	A	$-A$	$-I$
A	A	I	$-I$	$-A$
$-A$	$-A$	$-I$	I	A
$-I$	$-I$	$-A$	A	I

If we compare this to the group table for V_4,

	e	a	b	c
e	e	a	b	c
a	a	e	c	b
b	b	c	e	a
c	c	b	a	e

we notice that the names of the elements are different, but their group structures are identical! Therefore, $M \cong V_4$.

Here's another example: Consider the multiplicative group U_3 that consists of the cube roots of unity; to find the elements of U_3, we solve the equation $z^3 = 1$:

$$z^3 = 1 \quad \Rightarrow \quad (z-1)(z^2 + z + 1) = 0$$

$$\Rightarrow \quad z = 1 \quad \text{or} \quad z = \frac{-1 \pm \sqrt{-3}}{2} = -\tfrac{1}{2} \pm i\tfrac{\sqrt{3}}{2}$$

Therefore, $U_3 = \left\{1, -\frac{1}{2} + i\frac{\sqrt{3}}{2}, -\frac{1}{2} - i\frac{\sqrt{3}}{2}\right\}$. Although this group contains imaginary numbers, and the group operation is multiplication, it's isomorphic to the group, $\mathbf{Z}_3$, of integers, which has the group operation of addition (modulo 3): $U_3 \cong \mathbf{Z}_3$. Both of these groups have order 3, and we showed earlier that every group of order 3 is isomorphic to $\mathbf{Z}_3$. Since the group structure of U_3 is identical to that of $\mathbf{Z}_3$, we know that U_3 is cyclic, and is generated by either $\omega_1 = -\frac{1}{2} + i\frac{\sqrt{3}}{2}$ or $\omega_2 = -\frac{1}{2} - i\frac{\sqrt{3}}{2}$ (because $\mathbf{Z}_3$ is cyclic and generated by either one of *its* two nonidentity elements). Furthermore, without even working out the multiplication, we know that $\omega_1^2 = \omega_2$ and $\omega_2^2 = \omega_1$ because, in the group $\mathbf{Z}_3$, the corresponding equations are $1 \oplus 1 = 2$ and $2 \oplus 2 = 1$.

THE CLASSIFICATION OF FINITE ABELIAN GROUPS

In this section, we'll learn how to describe every finite Abelian group. First, let $(G_1, *_1)$ and $(G_2, *_2)$ be groups; on the set

$$G_1 \times G_2 = \left\{(a, b): a \in G_1 \text{ and } b \in G_2\right\}$$

define a binary operation, *, by the equation

$$(a_1, b_1) * (a_2, b_2) = (a_1 *_1 a_2, b_1 *_2 b_2)$$

Then $(G_1 \times G_2, *)$ is a group, called the **direct product** of the groups G_1 and G_2. If G_1 and G_2 are finite groups, and G_1 has order m and G_2 order n, then $G_1 \times G_2$ has order mn. If G_1 and G_2 are both Abelian, then the notation $G_1 \oplus G_2$ is sometimes used in place of $G_1 \times G_2$, and the resulting (Abelian) group is called the **direct sum** of the groups G_1 and G_2. Both the definition of a direct product (or direct sum) and the result about the order of the direct product can be generalized to any number of groups (not just two).

For example, let's consider the direct sum $\mathbf{Z}_2 \oplus \mathbf{Z}_4$. It consists of the following $2 \times 4 = 8$ elements:

$$(0, 0), \quad (0, 1), \quad (0, 2), \quad (0, 3), \quad \text{and} \quad (1, 0), \quad (1, 1), \quad (1, 2), \quad (1, 3)$$

Here's a question: Both $\mathbf{Z}_2$ and $\mathbf{Z}_4$ are cyclic; is their direct sum, $\mathbf{Z}_2 \oplus \mathbf{Z}_4$, also cyclic? Since $\mathbf{Z}_2 \oplus \mathbf{Z}_4$ has order 8, if this group were cyclic, there would have to be an element (a, b) with this property: The smallest integer n such that $n(a, b) = (0, 0)$ is $n = 8$. However, we can see that, here, this isn't the case. No matter which of the eight elements (a, b) we choose, we'll always have $4(a, b) = (0, 0)$; that is, the order of every element of this group is no greater than 4.

But what about the direct sum $\mathbf{Z}_2 \oplus \mathbf{Z}_3$? It consists of the following $2 \times 3 = 6$ elements:

$$(0, 0), \quad (0, 1), \quad (0, 2), \quad \text{and} \quad (1, 0), \quad (1, 1), \quad (1, 2)$$

Is $\mathbf{Z}_2 \oplus \mathbf{Z}_3$ cyclic? *Yes*; in fact, it's generated by the element $(1, 1)$, as we can check:

$$1(1, 1) = (1, 1)$$

$$2(1, 1) = (0, 2)$$

$$3(1, 1) = (1, 0)$$

$$4(1, 1) = (0, 1)$$

$$5(1, 1) = (1, 2)$$

$$6(1, 1) = (0, 0)$$

Why was $\mathbf{Z}_2 \oplus \mathbf{Z}_3$ cyclic, but not $\mathbf{Z}_2 \oplus \mathbf{Z}_4$? It is because 2 and 3 are relatively prime, but 2 and 4 are not. These examples illustrate the following theorem:

The direct sum $\mathbf{Z}_m \oplus \mathbf{Z}_n$ is cyclic if and only if $\gcd(m, n) = 1$. If this is the case, then, since $\mathbf{Z}_m \oplus \mathbf{Z}_n$ has order mn, $\mathbf{Z}_m \oplus \mathbf{Z}_n$ is isomorphic to $\mathbf{Z}_{mn}$.

We can generalize this result to any number of factors:

The direct sum $\mathbf{Z}_{m_1} \oplus \mathbf{Z}_{m_2} \oplus \cdots \oplus \mathbf{Z}_{m_k}$ is cyclic if and only if $\gcd(m_i, m_j) = 1$ for every distinct pair m_i and m_j. If this is the case, then $\mathbf{Z}_{m_1} \oplus \mathbf{Z}_{m_2} \oplus \cdots \oplus \mathbf{Z}_{m_k}$ is isomorphic to $\mathbf{Z}_{m_1 m_2 \cdots m_k}$.

For example, $\mathbf{Z}_8 \oplus \mathbf{Z}_3 \oplus \mathbf{Z}_{25}$ is cyclic and isomorphic to $\mathbf{Z}_{8 \cdot 3 \cdot 25} = \mathbf{Z}_{600}$, but the group $\mathbf{Z}_8 \oplus \mathbf{Z}_3 \oplus \mathbf{Z}_{10}$ is not cyclic, since $\gcd(8, 10) \neq 1$.

We're now ready to state the results of this section:

Every finite Abelian group G is isomorphic to a direct sum of the form

$$\mathbf{Z}_{(p_1)^{k_1}} \oplus \mathbf{Z}_{(p_2)^{k_2}} \oplus \cdots \oplus \mathbf{Z}_{(p_r)^{k_r}}$$

where the p_i are (not necessarily distinct) primes and the k_i are (not necessarily distinct) positive integers. The collection of prime powers, $(p_i)^{k_i}$, for a given representation of G, are known as the **elementary divisors** of G.

We can also write every finite Abelian group in another way:

Every finite Abelian group G is isomorphic to a direct sum of the form

$$\mathbf{Z}_{m_1} \oplus \mathbf{Z}_{m_2} \oplus \cdots \oplus \mathbf{Z}_{m_t}$$

where $m_1 \geq 2$, m_1 divides m_2, m_2 divides m_3, . . . , and m_{t-1} divides m_t. The integers m_1 through m_t are not necessarily distinct, but the list $m_1, \ldots, m_t$ is unique, and these integers are called the **invariant factors** of G.

Example 6.7	How many structurally distinct (that is, mutually nonisomorphic) Abelian groups are there of order 600?

Solution: Our first step is to find the prime factorization of 600:

$$600 = 2^3 \cdot 3 \cdot 5^2$$

Therefore, if G is an Abelian group of order 600, there are six possible collections of elementary divisors:

1) $2, 2, 2, 3, 5, 5$
2) $2, 2, 2, 3, 5^2$
3) $2, 2^2, 3, 5, 5$
4) $2, 2^2, 3, 5^2$
5) $2^3, 3, 5, 5$
6) $2^3, 3, 5^2$

Each of these lists of elementary divisors gives rise to an Abelian group, as follows:

1) $2, 2, 2, 3, 5, 5 \rightarrow \mathbf{Z}_2 \oplus \mathbf{Z}_2 \oplus \mathbf{Z}_2 \oplus \mathbf{Z}_3 \oplus \mathbf{Z}_5 \oplus \mathbf{Z}_5$

2) $2, 2, 2, 3, 5^2 \rightarrow \mathbf{Z}_2 \oplus \mathbf{Z}_2 \oplus \mathbf{Z}_2 \oplus \mathbf{Z}_3 \oplus \mathbf{Z}_{25}$

3) $2, 2^2, 3, 5, 5 \rightarrow \mathbf{Z}_2 \oplus \mathbf{Z}_4 \oplus \mathbf{Z}_3 \oplus \mathbf{Z}_5 \oplus \mathbf{Z}_5$

4) $2, 2^2, 3, 5^2 \rightarrow \mathbf{Z}_2 \oplus \mathbf{Z}_4 \oplus \mathbf{Z}_3 \oplus \mathbf{Z}_{25}$

5) $2^3, 3, 5, 5 \rightarrow \mathbf{Z}_8 \oplus \mathbf{Z}_3 \oplus \mathbf{Z}_5 \oplus \mathbf{Z}_5$

6) $2^3, 3, 5^2 \rightarrow \mathbf{Z}_8 \oplus \mathbf{Z}_3 \oplus \mathbf{Z}_{25}$

Therefore, there are six different Abelian groups (up to isomorphism) of order 600. We can also figure out the invariant factors of each of these six groups. In each case, we must express the group in the form $\mathbf{Z}_{m_1} \oplus \mathbf{Z}_{m_2} \oplus \cdots \oplus \mathbf{Z}_{m_t}$, where $m_1 \geq 2$ and m_i divides m_{i+1}. Notice the method we use to construct the invariant factors from the elementary divisors:

$2, 2, 3, 5, 5 \rightarrow$	2	2	2	$2, 2, 2, 3, 5^2 \rightarrow$	2	2	2
			3				3
		5	5				5^2
	↓	↓	↓		↓	↓	↓
	$\mathbf{Z}_2 \oplus \mathbf{Z}_{10} \oplus \mathbf{Z}_{30}$				$\mathbf{Z}_2 \oplus \mathbf{Z}_2 \oplus \mathbf{Z}_{150}$		

$2, 2^2, 3, 5, 5 \rightarrow$	2	2^2	$2, 2^2, 3, 5^2 \rightarrow$	2	2^2
		3			3
	5	5			5^2
	↓	↓		↓	↓
	$\mathbf{Z}_{10} \oplus \mathbf{Z}_{60}$			$\mathbf{Z}_2 \oplus \mathbf{Z}_{300}$	

$2^3, 3, 5, 5 \rightarrow$	2^3	$2^3, 3, 5^2 \rightarrow$	2^3
	3		3
5	5		5^2
↓	↓		↓
$\mathbf{Z}_5 \oplus \mathbf{Z}_{120}$		$\mathbf{Z}_{600}$	

Therefore, the six mutually nonisomorphic Abelian groups of order 600 can be expressed as follows, where in each case, we've written the representation of G in terms of the elementary divisors on the left, and the corresponding representation in terms of the invariant factors on the right:

1) $\mathbf{Z}_2 \oplus \mathbf{Z}_2 \oplus \mathbf{Z}_2 \oplus \mathbf{Z}_3 \oplus \mathbf{Z}_5 \oplus \mathbf{Z}_5 \cong \mathbf{Z}_2 \oplus \mathbf{Z}_{10} \oplus \mathbf{Z}_{30}$

2) $\mathbf{Z}_2 \oplus \mathbf{Z}_2 \oplus \mathbf{Z}_2 \oplus \mathbf{Z}_3 \oplus \mathbf{Z}_{25} \cong \mathbf{Z}_2 \oplus \mathbf{Z}_2 \oplus \mathbf{Z}_{150}$

3) $\mathbf{Z}_2 \oplus \mathbf{Z}_4 \oplus \mathbf{Z}_3 \oplus \mathbf{Z}_5 \oplus \mathbf{Z}_5 \cong \mathbf{Z}_{10} \oplus \mathbf{Z}_{60}$

4) $\mathbf{Z}_2 \oplus \mathbf{Z}_4 \oplus \mathbf{Z}_3 \oplus \mathbf{Z}_{25} \cong \mathbf{Z}_2 \oplus \mathbf{Z}_{300}$

5) $\mathbf{Z}_8 \oplus \mathbf{Z}_3 \oplus \mathbf{Z}_5 \oplus \mathbf{Z}_5 \cong \mathbf{Z}_5 \oplus \mathbf{Z}_{120}$

6) $\mathbf{Z}_8 \oplus \mathbf{Z}_3 \oplus \mathbf{Z}_{25} \cong \mathbf{Z}_{600}$

Example 6.8   Find the order of the element $(1, 6, 25)$ in the group $\mathbf{Z}_2 \oplus \mathbf{Z}_{10} \oplus \mathbf{Z}_{30}$.

Solution: By definition, the order of an element x is the smallest positive integer m such that $x^m = e$. In this case, since we're using additive notation for our Abelian groups, we want the smallest positive integer m such that $m(1, 6, 25) = (0, 0, 0)$. Clearly, the order of 1 in $\mathbf{Z}_2$ is $m_1 = 2$. Next, the order of 6 in $\mathbf{Z}_{10}$ is 5, because 5 is the smallest positive integer, m_2, such that $6 \cdot m_2$ is a multiple of 10. Finally, the order of 25 in $\mathbf{Z}_{30}$ is 6, because 6 is the smallest positive integer, m_3, such that $25 \cdot m_3$ is a multiple of 30. (It's worth noting that, in general, if $1 \le k < n$, then the order of k in $\mathbf{Z}_n$ is $n/[\gcd(k, n)]$, or, equivalently, $[\operatorname{lcm}(k, n)]/k$.) Therefore, in order for $m(1, 6, 25)$ to equal $(0, 0, 0)$, m must be a multiple of $m_1 = 2$, of $m_2 = 5$, and of $m_3 = 6$. Since we want the smallest positive integer m that has this property, we want the least common multiple (lcm) of 2, 5, and 6; this is $m = 30$.

GROUP HOMOMORPHISMS

Let $(G, \bullet)$ and $(G', *)$ be groups. A function $\phi: G \to G'$ with the property that

$$\phi(a \bullet b) = \phi(a) * \phi(b)$$

for all elements a and b in G, is called a group **homomorphism**. A homomorphism provides a direct relationship between the groups' structures. Why? Because we can operate on a and b in G (that is, form $a \bullet b$) and carry the result over to G' (in other words, apply ϕ to $a \bullet b$), or we could carry a and b over to G' first and then operate on them there; *the result will be the same*. This is precisely what the equation that defines a homomorphism says. A homomorphism that's one-to-one (injective) is called a **monomorphism**; if it's onto (surjective), it's called an **epimorphism**; and if it's one-to-one *and* onto (bijective), it's called an **isomorphism**. As we discussed earlier, two groups are said to be isomorphic if they're structurally identical. This is true if and only if there exists a bijective homomorphism, an isomorphism, between the groups. Finally, a homomorphism from a group to itself is called an **endomorphism**, and an isomorphism from a group to itself is called an **automorphism**.

The following is a list of some of the most important properties of homomorphisms. Each of the facts below applies to a homomorphism of groups, $\phi: G \to G'$:

1. If e is the identity in G, then $\phi(e)$ is the identity in G'.

2. If $g \in G$ has finite order m, then $\phi(g) \in G'$ also has order m.

3. If a^{-1} is the inverse of a in G, then $\phi(a^{-1})$ is the inverse of $\phi(a)$ in G'.

4. If H is a subgroup of G, then $\phi(H)$ is a subgroup of G', where:

$$\phi(H) = \big\{ \phi(h): h \in H \big\}$$

5. If G is finite, then the order of $\phi(G)$ divides the order of G; if G' is finite, then the order of $\phi(G)$ also divides the order of G'.

6. If H' is a subgroup of G', then $\phi^{-1}(H')$ is a subgroup of G, where

$$\phi^{-1}(H') = \big\{ h \in G: \phi(h) \in H' \big\}$$

If $\phi\colon G \to G'$ is a homomorphism of groups, then $\{e'\}$, where e' is the identity in G', is a subgroup—the trivial subgroup—of G'. By property 6, the inverse image of $\{e'\}$ is a subgroup of G. This subgroup is given a name: It's called the **kernel** of ϕ, denoted by $\ker\phi$:

$$\ker\phi = \left\{ g \in G \colon \phi(g) = e' \right\}$$

A homomorphism is a monomorphism if and only if its kernel is trivial.

Now, let's look at some examples on the following page.

Example 6.9 Let U_n be the multiplicative group of the nth roots of unity; this group is cyclic of order n and is generated by $\omega = \cos\frac{2\pi}{n} + i\sin\frac{2\pi}{n}$. If we define $\phi\colon (\mathbf{Z}, +) \to U_n$ by the equation $\phi(a) = \omega^a$, show that ϕ is a homomorphism. Is ϕ a monomorphism? an epimorphism? an isomorphism?

Solution: The function ϕ is a homomorphism, since:

$$\phi(a+b) = \omega^{a+b} = \omega^a\omega^b = \phi(a)\phi(b)$$

The kernel of this homomorphism is the subgroup:

$$\ker\phi = \left\{ a \in \mathbf{Z} \colon \omega^a = 1 \right\} = \left\{ mn \colon m \in \mathbf{Z} \right\}$$

The function ϕ is an epimorphism, but not a monomorphism (and thus not an isomorphism), since it's not one-to-one (its kernel is not trivial). We also know that ϕ is not an isomorphism, because an infinite group cannot be isomorphic to a finite group.

Example 6.10 Let $GL(n, \mathbf{R})$ be the multiplicative group of invertible n by n matrices with real entries. Show that the function $\phi\colon GL(n, \mathbf{R}) \to (\mathbf{R}^*, \times)$, given by $\phi(A) = \det A$, is a homomorphism, and find $\ker\phi$.

Solution: The function ϕ is a homomorphism because:

$$\phi(AB) = \det(AB) = (\det A)(\det B) = \phi(A)\phi(B)$$

The kernel of this homomorphism is the subgroup:

$$\ker\phi = \left\{ A \in GL(n, \mathbf{R}) \colon \det A = 1 \right\} = SL(n, \mathbf{R})$$

Example 6.11 If p is a prime and $\phi\colon \mathbf{Z}_p \to G'$ is a **nontrivial** homomorphism (that is, $\phi(n) \neq e'$ for every $n \neq 1$ in $\mathbf{Z}_p$), show that ϕ must be a monomorphism.

Solution: The kernel of a homomorphism is always a subgroup, so $\ker\phi$ must be a subgroup of $\mathbf{Z}_p$. Therefore, by Lagrange's theorem, the order of $\ker\phi$ must be a divisor of p. Because p is a prime, the order of $\ker\phi$ must be 1 or p. We've already ruled out the possibility that $\ker\phi$ has order p, by stating that ϕ is nontrivial. Therefore, the order of $\ker\phi$ is 1, so $\ker\phi$ must be the trivial subgroup of $\mathbf{Z}_p$; this shows that ϕ is one-to-one.

Example 6.12   Is there a nontrivial homomorphism $\phi: (\mathbf{Z}_8, +) \to (\mathbf{Z}_3, +)$?

Solution: If the answer is *yes*, then the homomorphic image of $\mathbf{Z}_8$ must be a subgroup of $\mathbf{Z}_3$. Since ϕ is nontrivial, the order of $\phi(\mathbf{Z}_8)$ is not 1. By Lagrange's theorem, then, the order of $\phi(\mathbf{Z}_8)$ must be 3. However, according to property 5 listed above, the order of $\phi(\mathbf{Z}_8)$ must divide the order of $\mathbf{Z}_8$. This is a contradiction, since 3 does not divide 8. Therefore, the answer to the question is *no*.

Example 6.13   Let $\phi: (\mathbf{Z}_4, +) \to (\mathbf{Z}_8, +)$ be a homomorphism such that $\phi(1) = 6$. Find $\phi(3)$. Is ϕ one-to-one?

Solution: First, it's worth noting that we know the image of every n in $\mathbf{Z}_4$ since we're told what ϕ does to 1. Once we know what a homomorphism of a cyclic group does to a generator of the group, we know what it does to *every* element in the group. In this case, $\phi(3) = \phi(3 \cdot 1) = \phi(1) = 3 \cdot 6 = 2$. Now, by definition,

$$\ker \phi = \left\{ n \in \mathbf{Z}_4 : \phi(n) = 0 \right\}$$

Since $\phi(n) = 6n$, $\ker\phi$ consists of those elements n in $\mathbf{Z}_4$ such that $6n$ is a multiple of 8. Only $n = 0$ satisfies this, so $\ker\phi$ is trivial, which implies that ϕ is one-to-one.

Example 6.14   Let $\phi: G \to G$ be a function such that $\phi(g) = g^{-1}$ for every g in G. Show that G is Abelian if and only if ϕ is an endomorphism.

Solution: First, let's assume that G is Abelian. Since the inverse of xy is $y^{-1}x^{-1}$ in any group (Abelian or not), we know that $\phi(xy) = (xy)^{-1} = y^{-1}x^{-1}$. Now, because G is Abelian, $y^{-1}x^{-1} = x^{-1}y^{-1}$, which is equal to $\phi(x)\phi(y)$. Since $\phi(xy) = \phi(x)\phi(y)$, ϕ is a homomorphism of G to itself.

   To complete the solution, let's now assume that ϕ is a homomorphism. Then $\phi(xy) = \phi(x)\phi(y)$, so $(xy)^{-1} = x^{-1}y^{-1}$, which implies $y^{-1}x^{-1} = x^{-1}y^{-1}$. Taking the inverse of both sides of this last equation, we get $(y^{-1}x^{-1})^{-1} = (x^{-1}y^{-1})^{-1}$, which is equivalent to $xy = yx$. This shows that G is Abelian.

Example 6.15   Is the group $(\mathbf{R}, +)$ isomorphic to the group $(\mathbf{R}^+, \times)$?

Solution: Define a function $\phi: (\mathbf{R}, +) \to (\mathbf{R}^+, \times)$ by the equation $\phi(x) = e^x$, where now e denotes the base of the natural logarithm. We'll show that ϕ is an isomorphism. First,

$$\phi(x + y) = e^{x+y} = e^x e^y = \phi(x)\phi(y)$$

so ϕ is a homomorphism. Next,

$$\phi(x) = 1 \;\Rightarrow\; e^x = 1 \;\Rightarrow\; x = 0 \;\Rightarrow\; \ker\phi = \{0\}$$

which shows that ϕ is one-to-one. Finally, for every x in $\mathbf{R}^+$, we have

$$\phi(\log x) = e^{\log x} = x$$

so ϕ is onto. Since ϕ is an isomorphism, we have $(\mathbf{R}, +) \cong (\mathbf{R}^+, \times)$.

Example 6.16 A subgroup N of G is said to be a **normal** subgroup if $xnx^{-1} \in N$ for every n in N and every x in G. If $\phi: G \to G'$ is a homomorphism of groups, show that $\ker\phi$ is a *normal* subgroup of G.

Solution: We already know that $\ker\phi$ is a subgroup of G; we're asked to show that it's actually a normal subgroup. Let g be any element in $\ker\phi$. Since $\phi(g) = e'$ and $\phi(x^{-1}) = [\phi(x)]^{-1}$, the following is true for every x in G:

$$\phi(xgx^{-1}) = \phi(x) \bullet \phi(g) \bullet \phi(x^{-1}) = \phi(x) \bullet e' \bullet \phi(x^{-1}) = \phi(x) \bullet [\phi(x)]^{-1} = e'$$

Therefore, $xgx^{-1} \in \ker\phi$. Since we've shown that $xgx^{-1} \in \ker\phi$ for every g in $\ker\phi$ and every x in G, we conclude that $\ker\phi$ is, by definition, a normal subgroup of G.

Example 6.17 Can an infinite group be isomorphic to one of its *proper* subgroups?

Solution: Consider the infinite, cyclic group $(\mathbf{Z}, +)$. For every integer $n \geq 2$, the group

$$n\mathbf{Z} = \{nk : k \in \mathbf{Z}\}$$

is an infinite, proper subgroup of $\mathbf{Z}$. We can define a function $\phi_n: \mathbf{Z} \to n\mathbf{Z}$ by the equation $\phi_n(k) = nk$, and show that ϕ_n is actually an isomorphism. First, because

$$\phi_n(k_1 + k_2) = n(k_1 + k_2) = nk_1 + nk_2 = \phi_n(k_1) + \phi_n(k_2),$$

we know that ϕ_n is a homomorphism. Next,

$$\ker\phi_n = \{k \in \mathbf{Z} : nk = 0\} = \{0\}$$

shows that ϕ_n is one-to-one. And finally, since every element of $n\mathbf{Z}$ is of the form nk for some integer k, and $\phi_n(k) = nk$, it's clear that ϕ_n is onto as well. Therefore, $(\mathbf{Z}, +) \cong (n\mathbf{Z}, +)$.

Example 6.18 Let G be a group. For a fixed element a in G, define a function $\phi_a: G \to G$ by the equation $\phi_a(g) = aga^{-1}$.
  (a) Show that ϕ_a is an automorphism. (It's called the **inner automorphism induced by** a.)
  (b) Let $\text{Aut}(G)$ denote the collection of all automorphisms of G. According to the operation of function composition, $(\text{Aut}(G), \circ)$ is a group. Show that the set of all inner automorphisms of G, $\text{Inn}(G) = \{\phi_a : a \in G\}$, is a subgroup of $\text{Aut}(G)$.
  (c) Describe $\text{Inn}(G)$ if G is Abelian.

Solution:

(a) First, the following equation establishes that ϕ_a is a homomorphism:

$$\phi_a(g_1 g_2) = ag_1 g_2 a^{-1} = ag_1 e g_2 a^{-1} = ag_1 a^{-1} ag_2 a^{-1} = (ag_1 a^{-1})(ag_2 a^{-1}) = \phi_a(g_1)\phi_a(g_2)$$

Next, we'll prove that ϕ_a is one-to-one. We can do this in two ways; we can either notice that

$$\phi_a(g_1) = \phi_a(g_2) \implies ag_1 a^{-1} = ag_2 a^{-1} \implies a^{-1}(ag_1 a^{-1})a = a^{-1}(ag_2 a^{-1})a \implies g_1 = g_2$$

or we can show that $\ker \phi_a = \{e\}$:

$$g \in \ker \phi_a \iff \phi_a(g) = e \iff aga^{-1} = e \iff ag = ea \iff g = e$$

Finally, we need to show that ϕ_a is onto G. Since G is a group, we know that $a^{-1}ga \in G$ for every a and g in G. Now, for every g in G, notice that the image of $a^{-1}ga$ is g:

$$\phi_a(a^{-1}ga) = a(a^{-1}ga)a^{-1} = (aa^{-1})g(aa^{-1}) = ege = g$$

Therefore, ϕ_a is onto, so we're able to conclude that it's an isomorphism of G to itself; that is, it's an automorphism of G.

(b) To show that $\mathrm{Inn}(G)$ is a subgroup of $\mathrm{Aut}(G)$, we need to show that $\mathrm{Inn}(G)$ is closed under the group operation, it contains the identity, and it contains the inverse of every element in $\mathrm{Inn}(G)$. Let's first establish closure. Let ϕ_a and ϕ_b be elements of $\mathrm{Inn}(G)$ then, since

$$\begin{aligned}(\phi_a \circ \phi_b)(g) = \phi_a(\phi_b(g)) = \phi_a(bgb^{-1}) &= a(bgb^{-1})a^{-1} \\ &= (ab)g(b^{-1}a^{-1}) \\ &= (ab)g(ab)^{-1} \\ &= \phi_{ab}(g)\end{aligned}$$

is true for every g in G, we know that $\phi_a \circ \phi_b = \phi_{ab}$, so $\mathrm{Inn}(G)$ is closed under function composition. Next, the identity of $\mathrm{Aut}(G)$ is clearly the identity map, $\mathrm{id}: G \to G$, where $\mathrm{id}(g) = g$ for all g in G. But if e is the identity of G, then the inner automorphism induced by e, ϕ_e, is the identity map, because

$$\phi_e(g) = ege^{-1} = ege = g$$

for every g in G. Therefore, $\mathrm{Inn}(G)$ contains the identity. Finally, we'll show that if a^{-1} is the inverse of a, then the map $\phi_{a^{-1}}$ is the inverse of ϕ_a. The calculation

$$aga^{-1} = g' \iff ga^{-1} = a^{-1}g' \iff g = a^{-1}g'a \iff g = a^{-1}g'(a^{-1})^{-1}$$

means that $\phi_a(g) = g' \iff g = \phi_{a^{-1}}(g')$, so $\phi_{a^{-1}}$ is indeed the inverse of ϕ_a. Thus, $\mathrm{Inn}(G) \leq \mathrm{Aut}(G)$.

(c) If G is Abelian, then for any a in G, $\phi_a(g) = aga^{-1} = aa^{-1}g = g$ for every g in G; so, for every a in G, the inner automorphism ϕ_a is just the identity map. Therefore, if G is Abelian, $\mathrm{Inn}(G)$ is the trivial subgroup of $\mathrm{Aut}(G)$.

RINGS

A group is a special binary structure with one binary operation; a ring is a special binary structure with *two* binary operations. To be more precise, a set R, together with two binary operations (we'll use addition, +, and multiplication, •), is called a **ring** if the following conditions are satisfied:

$(R, +)$ is an Abelian group;

$(R, •)$ is a semigroup (that is, multiplication is associative);

the distributive laws hold; that is, for every a, b, and c in R, we have:

$$a • (b + c) = a • b + a • c \quad \text{and} \quad (a + b) • c = a • c + b • c$$

This last requirement says that the two binary operations in the ring are compatible. A point of notation: We don't usually write the product of a and b as $a • b$; we just write ab.

If the multiplicative semigroup $(R, \bullet)$ is a monoid—that is, if there's a multiplicative identity—then R is called a **ring with unity**. The identity of the additive abelian group $(R, +)$ is usually denoted by 0 and, in a ring with unity, the identity of the multiplicative monoid $(R, \bullet)$ is usually denoted by 1. We typically require that these identities be distinct; that is, $0 \neq 1$. (Although this looks like an obvious statement concerning the numbers 0 and 1, remember that in a general ring, the additive identity is not necessarily the number 0, and the multiplicative identity is not necessarily the number 1.) If the operation of multiplication is commutative, then we call R a **commutative ring**. (The term *abelian* is generally *not* used to describe a ring in which multiplication is commutative.) If S is a subset of R, and S satisfies the ring requirements with the same operations as R, then we say that $(S, +, \bullet)$ is a **subring** of $(R, +, \bullet)$. As is the case with groups, it's common to refer to a ring $(R, +, \bullet)$ simply by R, if the two binary operations are understood.

Let R be a ring. The smallest positive integer n such that $na = 0$ for every a in R (if such an n exists) is called the **characteristic** of the ring, and we write char $R = n$. (Remember that if n is a positive integer, na means $a + a + \cdots + a$, where the sum contains exactly n summands.) If no such n exists (as, for example, in the infinite rings $\mathbf{Z}$, $\mathbf{Q}$, $\mathbf{R}$, and $\mathbf{C}$), then we say that R has characteristic **zero**. In the case that char $R > 0$, we don't need to check that $na = 0$ for every a in R; it is sufficient to find the smallest positive integer n such that $n \bullet 1 = 0$.

Here are some examples:

1. $(\mathbf{Z}, +, \bullet)$ is the simplest example of a ring; it's a commutative ring with unity, called the **ring of integers**. We mentioned earlier that $(\mathbf{Z}, \bullet)$ is not a group because most elements have no inverse; however, the definition of a ring doesn't require that $(R, \bullet)$ be a group, only a semigroup. If n is a positive integer and we let $n\mathbf{Z} = \{nk : k \in \mathbf{Z}\}$, then $(n\mathbf{Z}, +, \bullet)$ is a subring of $\mathbf{Z}$. Notice that, if $n > 1$, then $n\mathbf{Z}$ is also a commutative ring, but not a ring with unity.

2. The ring of integers is a subring of the rings $(\mathbf{Q}, +, \bullet)$, $(\mathbf{R}, +, \bullet)$, and $(\mathbf{C}, +, \bullet)$.

3. Since $(\mathbf{Z}_n, +)$ is an Abelian group and $(\mathbf{Z}_n, \bullet)$ is a semigroup, $(\mathbf{Z}_n, +, \bullet)$ is the **ring of integers modulo n**.

4. The set of n by n matrices with entries in $\mathbf{R}$, with the operations of matrix addition and multiplication, $(M_n(\mathbf{R}), +, \times)$, is a ring with unity, a noncommutative ring if $n > 1$. $M_n(\mathbf{Q})$ and $M_n(\mathbf{Z})$ are subrings.

5. The set $R = \left\{ a + b\sqrt{2} : a, b \in \mathbf{Z} \right\}$, together with the usual operations of addition and multiplication, is a commutative ring with unity. It's straightforward to check that R is closed under both addition and multiplication, since:

$$(a_1 + b_1\sqrt{2}) + (a_2 + b_2\sqrt{2}) = (a_1 + a_2) + (b_1 + b_2)\sqrt{2}$$

and

$$(a_1 + b_1\sqrt{2})(a_2 + b_2\sqrt{2}) = (a_1 a_2 + 2b_1 b_2) + (a_1 b_2 + a_2 b_1)\sqrt{2}$$

Notice, however, that the set $C = \left\{ a + b\sqrt[3]{2} : a, b \in \mathbf{Z} \right\}$ does not form a ring, since it's not closed under multiplication:

$$(a_1 + b_1\sqrt[3]{2})(a_2 + b_2\sqrt[3]{2}) = (a_1 a_2) + (a_1 b_2 + a_2 b_1)\sqrt[3]{2} + b_1 b_2\sqrt[3]{4} \notin C$$

6. With the operations of addition and multiplication in **C**, the set

$$\mathbf{Z}[i] = \left\{ a + bi : a,\ b \in \mathbf{Z} \text{ and } i = \sqrt{-1} \right\}$$

is a subring of **C**, called the **ring of Gaussian integers**.

7. Let R be a ring, and consider the collection of all polynomials—including the zero polynomial—in the variable (or **indeterminate**) x with coefficients in R:

$$R[x] = \left\{ r_0 + r_1 x + r_2 x^2 + \cdots + r_n x^n : r_i \in R \right\}$$

Then $R[x]$ is also a ring, called the **ring of polynomials in x over R**.

8. The collection of all functions $f : \mathbf{R} \to \mathbf{R}$ is denoted $\mathbf{R}^{\mathbf{R}}$. With the operations of addition—where $(f + g)(x) = f(x) + g(x)$—and pointwise multiplication—where $(fg)(x) = f(x)g(x)$—$\mathbf{R}^{\mathbf{R}}$ becomes a commutative ring with unity, called the **ring of real-valued functions on R**. The additive identity is the constant function 0, and the multiplicative identity is the constant function 1.

Example 6.19 Let R be a ring with unity, and let S be a subring with unity of R. Does the unity of S need to be the same as the unity of R?

Solution: Let R be the ring $\mathbf{Z}_{10}$ (whose unity is 1) and let S be the subset $\left\{ 0,\ 2,\ 4,\ 6,\ 8 \right\}$. It's straightforward to check that S satisfies the conditions to be a ring, but notice that the unity of S is the element 6, because:

$$0 \bullet 6 = 0, \quad 2 \bullet 6 = 2, \quad 4 \bullet 6 = 4, \quad 6 \bullet 6 = 6, \quad \text{and} \quad 8 \bullet 6 = 8$$

Therefore, S is a ring with unity 6 that's a subring of the ring R with unity 1.

Example 6.20 An element a of a ring R is said to be **nilpotent** if there's some positive integer, m, such that $a^m = 0$. If a and b are nilpotents in a commutative ring R, show that their sum, $a + b$, must be nilpotent, too. Is this result still true if R is not commutative?

Solution: Since a and b are nilpotent, there are positive integers, m and n, such that $a^m = 0$ and $b^n = 0$. (Notice that this automatically implies that $a^M = 0$ for every integer $M \geq m$ and that $b^N = 0$ for every integer $N \geq n$.) Let $k = 2 \bullet \max(m, n)$, and consider the binomial expansion $(a + b)^k$. Every term in the resulting polynomial consists of a numerical coefficient, c_{ij}, multiplied by $a^i b^j$, where i and j are nonnegative integers whose sum, $i + j$, is always equal to k. (We can write every term in the compact form $c_{ij} a^i b^j$, rather than leaving the mixed terms in the form $a^{i_1} b^{j_1} a^{i_2} b^{j_2} \ldots a^{i_k} b^{j_k}$, precisely because R is commutative.) Because of our choice of k, every term of this expansion will equal 0. To see why this is so, let's first answer this question: What if $i < m$? Then j cannot be less than n, since if it were, we'd have $i + j < m + n$, which contradicts the fact that $i + j = 2 \bullet \max(m, n)$. Since j must be at least equal to n, the term b^j will be 0, which makes the entire term $a^i b^j$ equal to 0. Similarly, if $j < n$, then it must be true that $i \geq m$, so the term a^i—and thus the term $a^i b^j$—will be 0. Therefore, for every term in the binomial expansion, we'll have $i \geq m$ or $j \geq n$, so every term will be 0. We've shown that $(a + b)^k$ is 0, so $a + b$ is nilpotent.

This result is not necessarily true if R isn't commutative. Consider the ring $M_2(\mathbf{Z})$, and take:

$$A = \begin{pmatrix} 0 & 0 \\ 1 & 0 \end{pmatrix} \quad \text{and} \quad B = \begin{pmatrix} 0 & 1 \\ 0 & 0 \end{pmatrix}$$

Then $A^2 = 0$ and $B^2 = 0$ (where 0 denotes the zero matrix here), so A and B are both nilpotent. However, their sum,

$$A + B = \begin{pmatrix} 0 & 1 \\ 1 & 0 \end{pmatrix}$$

is not nilpotent; $(A + B)^n$ is never equal to 0, since:

$$\begin{pmatrix} 0 & 1 \\ 1 & 0 \end{pmatrix}^n = \begin{cases} \begin{pmatrix} 1 & 0 \\ 0 & 1 \end{pmatrix} & \text{if } n \text{ is even} \\ \begin{pmatrix} 0 & 1 \\ 1 & 0 \end{pmatrix} & \text{if } n \text{ is odd} \end{cases}$$

Alternatively, we can simply note that $A + B$ is invertible (its determinant isn't zero). If an element is invertible, it can't be nilpotent. [Why not? Well, let's assume that c is invertible in a ring R; then c^{-1} exists and $cc^{-1} = 1$. This equation implies $(cc^{-1})^n = 1$ for every positive integer n, so $c^n(c^{-1})^n = 1$. Therefore, c^n cannot be 0 for any n; in other words, c can't be nilpotent.]

Example 6.21   What's char $\mathbf{Z}_n$?

Solution: The additive group $(\mathbf{Z}_n, +)$ is cyclic, with generator 1. Since $\mathbf{Z}_n$ contains exactly n elements—0, 1, 2, . . ., $n - 1$—we know that the smallest positive integer m, such that $m \bullet 1 = 0$ is $m = n$. Therefore, char $\mathbf{Z}_n = n$.

RING HOMOMORPHISMS

Let $(R, +, \times)$ and $(R', \oplus, \otimes)$ be rings. A function $\phi: R \to R'$ is called a **ring homomorphism** if both of the following conditions hold for every a and b in R:

$$\phi(a + b) = \phi(a) \oplus \phi(b)$$
$$\phi(a \times b) = \phi(a) \otimes \phi(b)$$

Notice that this is similar to the definition of a group homomorphism, except now that we're dealing with rings, we have two binary operations, so ϕ must preserve *both* operations. In the list below, we'll give several important facts for any ring homomorphism $\phi: R \to R'$:

1. The **kernel** of a ring homomorphism is the set $\ker \phi = \{a \in R: \phi(a) = 0'\}$, where $0'$ is the additive identity in R'. Just as the kernel of a group homomorphism $\phi: G \to G'$ is always a subgroup of G, the kernel of a ring homomorphism $\phi: R \to R'$ is always a subring of R.

2. The image of R, $\phi(R) = \{\phi(r): r \in R\}$, is a subring of R'.

3. The image of 0, the additive identity in R, must be $0'$, the additive identity in R'. It follows from this that $\phi(-r) = -\phi(r)$ for every r in R, where $-r$ is the additive inverse of r.

Now, we'll look at some examples that illustrate the concept of a homomorphism of rings:

1. The function $\phi: \mathbf{Z} \to \mathbf{Z}_n$ given by $\phi(k) =$ the unique integer in $\mathbf{Z}_n$ that's congruent to $k \pmod{n}$ is a ring homomorphism (actually, it's a ring epimorphism, since ϕ is onto). To show this, let $\phi(k_1) = m_1$ and $\phi(k_2) = m_2$. Then it must be true that $k_1 = a_1 n + m_1$ (where a_1 is an integer and $0 \le m_1 < n$) and, similarly, $k_2 = a_2 n + m_2$ (where a_2 is an integer and $0 \le m_2 < n$). Adding these two

equations gives $k_1 + k_2 = (a_1 + a_2)n + (m_1 + m_2)$, so $\phi(k_1 + k_2)$ is equal to either $m_1 + m_2$ (if $m_1 + m_2 < n$) or the unique integer in $\mathbf{Z}_n$ that's congruent to $(m_1 + m_2)$ (mod n). But $\phi(k_1) + \phi(k_2)$ also equals $m_1 + m_2$ (if $m_1 + m_2 < n$) or the unique integer in $\mathbf{Z}_n$ that's congruent to $(m_1 + m_2)$ (mod n). This shows that ϕ preserves the operation of addition. Now, by multiplying the equations $k_1 = a_1 n + m_1$ and $k_2 = a_2 n + m_2$, we get $k_1 k_2 = (a_1 a_2)n^2 + (a_1 m_2 + a_2 m_1)n + (m_1 m_2)$, so $\phi(k_1 k_2)$ is equal to $m_1 m_2$ (if $m_1 m_2 < n$) or to the unique integer in $\mathbf{Z}_n$ that's congruent to $m_1 m_2$ (mod n). But $\phi(k_1)\phi(k_2)$ also equals $m_1 m_2$ (if $m_1 m_2 < n$) or the unique integer in $\mathbf{Z}_n$ that's congruent to $m_1 m_2$ (mod n). This shows that ϕ also preserves the operation of multiplication. The kernel of this homomorphism is the subring $n\mathbf{Z} = \{nm : m \in \mathbf{Z}\}$ of $\mathbf{Z}$.

2. Let R be a ring and consider $R[x]$, the ring of polynomials in x over R. Every element in $R[x]$ is a polynomial, $p(x)$, with coefficients in R. For a fixed element a in R, define a function $\phi_a : R[x] \to R$ as follows:

$$\phi_a(p(x)) = p(a)$$

This says that in order to find the image of a polynomial, $p(x)$, under the map ϕ_a, substitute a for x in $p(x)$ and evaluate. The map ϕ_a is called the **evaluation** (or **substitution**) **homomorphism at** a. That ϕ_a actually is a ring homomorphism follows at once from the equations:

$$\phi_a(p(x) + q(x)) = p(a) + q(a) = \phi_a(p(x)) + \phi_a(q(x))$$

and

$$\phi_a(p(x)q(x)) = p(a)q(a) = \phi_a(p(x))\phi_a(q(x))$$

3. If R is a commutative ring with unity whose characteristic is a prime, p, then the function $\phi_p : R \to R$ given by $\phi(a) = a^p$ is a ring homomorphism (called the **Frobenius endomorphism**). To see why this is so, we need to show that ϕ_p preserves both addition and multiplication. The second part is easier, so we'll take care of that first. Since R is commutative, we have:

$$\phi_p(ab) = (ab)^p = \underbrace{(ab)(ab)\cdots(ab)}_{p \text{ factors}} = \underbrace{(aa\cdots a)}_{p \text{ factors}}\underbrace{(bb\cdots b)}_{p \text{ factors}} = a^p b^p = \phi_p(a)\phi_p(b)$$

Now, let's verify that $\phi_p(a + b) = \phi_p(a) + \phi_p(b)$, which is equivalent to the equation $(a + b)^p = a^p + b^p$. The binomial theorem says:

$$(a+b)^p = \sum_{k=0}^{p} \binom{p}{k} a^{p-k} b^k$$

where $\binom{p}{k}$ denotes the binomial coefficient:

$$\binom{p}{k} = \frac{p!}{k!(p-k)!} \quad (*)$$

But for $1 \le k \le p - 1$, the coefficient $\binom{p}{k}$ is divisible by p [since p is prime, there will always be a factor of p left in the numerator of (*) for $1 \le k \le p - 1$], so

$$(a+b)^p = a^p + \left(\sum_{k=1}^{p-1} (m_k p) a^{p-k} b^k \right) + b^p$$

where m_k is an integer. Every term of the form $(m_k p)a^{p-k}b^k$ is a multiple of p, so it's equal to 0 in R, because char $R = p$. This reduces the equation above to $(a + b)^p = a^p + b^p$. So, although beginning students sometimes make the mistake of writing, for example, $(a + b)^3 = a^3 + b^3$, this is actually correct in a ring of characteristic 3 (like $\mathbf{Z}_3$)!

4. Let $(R, +, \times)$ and $(R', \oplus, \otimes)$ be rings. It's possible for ϕ: $(R, +) \to (R', \oplus)$ to be a group homomorphism but not a ring homomorphism. Let $R = R' = \mathbf{Z}$, the ring of integers. Then the function ϕ: $(\mathbf{Z}, +) \to (\mathbf{Z}, +)$ given by $\phi(m) = 2m$ is a group homomorphism, but ϕ does not preserve the operation of multiplication, since $\phi(mn) = 2mn$, but $\phi(m)\phi(n) = (2m)(2n) = 4mn$.

5. Let $(R, +, \times)$ and $(R', \oplus, \otimes)$ be rings. It's possible for ϕ: $(R, \times) \to (R', \otimes)$ to be a group homomorphism but not a ring homomorphism. Let $R = GL(2, \mathbf{R})$, and let $R' = \mathbf{R}$; these are groups under matrix multiplication and ordinary multiplication, respectively. Then the function ϕ: $(R, \times) \to (\mathbf{R}, \bullet)$ given by $\phi(A) = \det A$ is a group homomorphism, but not a ring homomorphism since ϕ does not preserve the operation of addition: In general, $\det(A + B) \neq \det A + \det B$.

Example 6.22   Describe all the ring endomorphisms of **Z**.

Solution: For any rings R and R', the **zero map**, z: $R \to R'$, given by $z(r) = 0'$ for every r in R, is always a ring homomorphism (although certainly not a very interesting one). So now let's assume that f: $\mathbf{Z} \to \mathbf{Z}$ is a *nonzero* ring endomorphism. Since 1 generates the cyclic group **Z**, $\phi(1)$ cannot be equal to 0, because if it were, then $\phi(m)$ would equal 0 for every m in **Z** [because $\phi(m) = \phi(1 \bullet m) = \phi(1)\phi(m)$], contradicting our assumption that f is a nonzero map. Then $[\phi(1)]^2 = \phi(1)\phi(1) = \phi(1 \bullet 1) = \phi(1)$, but $\phi(1)$ is not equal to 0. The only nonzero integer n that satisfies $n^2 = n$ is $n = 1$, so we must have $\phi(1) = 1$. Now, if m is a positive integer, then $\phi(m) = \phi(1 + 1 + \ldots + 1)$, with m summands, which gives $\phi(m) = \phi(1) + \phi(1) + \ldots + \phi(1) = m\phi(1) = m \bullet 1 = m$; and $\phi(-m) = \phi(-1 + -1 + \ldots + -1)$, with m summands, which gives $\phi(-m) = \phi(-1) + \phi(-1) + \ldots + \phi(-1) = m(-\phi(1)) = -m$. And finally, if $m = 0$, then $\phi(0) = 0$, since any ring homomorphism maps the additive identity to the additive identity. Therefore, for every integer m, we have $\phi(m) = m$, so ϕ is the identity map. We conclude that there are only two ring homomorphisms from **Z** to itself: the zero homomorphism and the identity homomorphism.

Example 6.23   Let I be a subring of a ring R. If $rx \in I$ and $xr \in I$ both hold for every r in R and every x in I, then I is called an **ideal** in R. (This substructure of a ring is analogous to a normal subgroup, N, of a group G; see Example 6.16.)

(a) If n is a positive integer, verify that $n\mathbf{Z}$ is an ideal in **Z**.

(b) Show that $S = \left\{ \begin{pmatrix} a & b \\ 0 & c \end{pmatrix} : a, b, c \in \mathbf{Z} \right\}$ is a subring of $M_2(\mathbf{Z})$ but not an ideal.

(c) If ϕ: $R \to R'$ is a ring homomorphism, show that ker ϕ is an ideal in R'.

Solution:

(a) The subring $n\mathbf{Z}$ consists of all multiples of n, so every x in $n\mathbf{Z}$ is of the form mn for some integer m. Therefore, if r is any integer (that is, any element in $\mathbf{Z}$), we have:

$$r(mn) = (rm)n \quad \Rightarrow \quad r(mn) \in n\mathbf{Z} \quad \text{and} \quad (mn)r = (mr)n \quad \Rightarrow \quad (mn)r \in n\mathbf{Z}$$

By definition, then, $n\mathbf{Z}$ is an ideal in $\mathbf{Z}$.

(b) S contains the additive identity (the zero matrix, by taking $a = b = c = 0$) and the multiplicative identity (the identity matrix, by taking $a = c = 1$ and $b = 0$). It's closed under addition,

$$\begin{pmatrix} a_1 & b_1 \\ 0 & c_1 \end{pmatrix} + \begin{pmatrix} a_2 & b_2 \\ 0 & c_2 \end{pmatrix} = \begin{pmatrix} a_1 + a_2 & b_1 + b_2 \\ 0 & c_1 + c_2 \end{pmatrix} \in S$$

and under multiplication:

$$\begin{pmatrix} a_1 & b_1 \\ 0 & c_1 \end{pmatrix} \begin{pmatrix} a_2 & b_2 \\ 0 & c_2 \end{pmatrix} = \begin{pmatrix} a_1 a_2 & a_1 b_2 + b_1 c_2 \\ 0 & c_1 c_2 \end{pmatrix} \in S$$

Since $M_2(\mathbf{Z})$ is a ring with unity, it follows that S is a subring. But it's not an ideal. If $X \in S$, it's not true that $XA \in M_2(\mathbf{Z})$ for every A in $M_2(\mathbf{Z})$; for example:

$$XA = \underbrace{\begin{pmatrix} 1 & 1 \\ 0 & 1 \end{pmatrix}}_{X \in S} \underbrace{\begin{pmatrix} 0 & 0 \\ 1 & 0 \end{pmatrix}}_{A \in M_2(\mathbf{Z})} = \begin{pmatrix} 1 & 0 \\ 1 & 0 \end{pmatrix} \notin S$$

This shows that S is not an ideal.

(c) The kernel of a ring homomorphism is the following subring of R:

$$\ker \phi = \left\{ x \in R : \phi(x) = 0' \right\}$$

We want to show that rx and xr are both in $\ker \phi$ for every x in $\ker \phi$ and every r in R. The equations

$$\phi(rx) = \phi(r) \bullet (x) = \phi(r) \bullet 0 = 0 \quad \text{and} \quad \phi(xr) = \phi(x) \bullet \phi(r) = 0 \bullet \phi(r) = 0$$

verify that this is true.

INTEGRAL DOMAINS

Let's look again at $\mathbf{Z}_n$, the ring of integers modulo n, and take $n = 6$. Notice that it's possible to choose elements a and b, both of which are nonzero, for which $ab = 0$. For example, we could take $a = 3$ and $b = 4$; then $ab = 3 \bullet 4 = 12$, which is equal to 0 in $\mathbf{Z}_6$. The same thing can happen in a ring of matrices. For instance, in the commutative subring D of $M_2(\mathbf{Z})$ that consists of the diagonal matrices, if

$$A = \begin{pmatrix} 1 & 0 \\ 0 & 0 \end{pmatrix} \quad \text{and} \quad B = \begin{pmatrix} 0 & 0 \\ 0 & 1 \end{pmatrix}$$

then $AB = 0$ (where 0 is the additive identity of D, the zero matrix), even though neither A nor B is zero. A commutative ring with unity in which this type of behavior *cannot* happen is called an **integral domain**.

Normally, we accept the statement "$ab = 0$ if and only if $a = 0$ or $b = 0$," as self-evident, but that's only because we're used to working in the rings $\mathbf{C}$, $\mathbf{R}$, $\mathbf{Q}$, or $\mathbf{Z}$, all of which are integral domains. If a and b are both *nonzero* elements of a ring but the product ab is nevertheless equal to 0, then a is called a **left zero divisor** and b is called a **right zero divisor**. (If the ring is commutative, we don't need to specify left or right.) So, an integral domain is a commutative ring with unity $(1 \neq 0)$ that has no zero divisors.

Why is it desirable to work in an integral domain? Because the familiar **cancellation law**,

$$a \neq 0 \quad \text{and} \quad ab = ac \quad \Rightarrow \quad b = c$$

is only guaranteed when there are no zero divisors. To see why, notice that $ab = ac$ is equivalent to $a(b - c) = 0$, but this equation could hold if a and $b - c$ are zero divisors. In this case, $b - c$ would not be equal to zero, so b would not be equal to c. However, this situation wouldn't be possible if there were no zero divisors, that is, if a, b, and c were elements of an integral domain. For example, in $\mathbf{Z}_6$ (which is not an integral domain), it's true that $2 \bullet 1 = 2 \bullet 4$, but $1 \neq 4$. Also, notice that in the subring D of $M_2(\mathbf{Z})$ we considered above, if we choose

$$A = \begin{pmatrix} 1 & 0 \\ 0 & 0 \end{pmatrix}, \qquad B = \begin{pmatrix} 1 & 0 \\ 0 & 1 \end{pmatrix}, \qquad \text{and} \qquad C = \begin{pmatrix} 1 & 0 \\ 0 & 2 \end{pmatrix}$$

then $AB = AC$, but $B \neq C$. Making sure that the cancellation law does hold is the motivation behind the definition of an integral domain.

The reason that 3 and 4 were zero divisors in the ring $\mathbf{Z}_6$ is that neither of them is relatively prime to 6; the element 2 in $\mathbf{Z}_6$ is also a zero divisor (since $2 \bullet 3 = 0$). But the elements 1 and 5 are not zero divisors in $\mathbf{Z}_6$. In general, we can say that:

A nonzero element $m \in \mathbf{Z}_n$ is a zero divisor if and only if m and n are not relatively prime.

And this fact leads directly to the following important result:

If n is prime, then $\mathbf{Z}_n$ is an integral domain.

Example 6.24 Is the ring $\mathbf{R}^{\mathbf{R}}$ an integral domain?

Solution: Consider the functions $f \colon \mathbf{R} \to \mathbf{R}$ and $g \colon \mathbf{R} \to \mathbf{R}$ given by

$$f(x) = x - |x| \qquad \text{and} \qquad g(x) = x + |x|$$

The pointwise product function, fg, is the zero function—that is, $(fg)(x) = 0$ for every x in $\mathbf{R}$—even though neither f nor g is the zero function. Since $\mathbf{R}^{\mathbf{R}}$ contains zero divisors, it's not an integral domain.

FIELDS

Let a be a nonzero element of a ring R with unity. Since the multiplicative binary structure $(R, \bullet)$ isn't required to be a group, a may not have an inverse in R. However, if a *does* have a multiplicative inverse—that is, if it's **invertible**—then a is called a **unit**. (Don't confuse *unit* with *unity*: Unity is the unique multiplicative identity in R (a unit is a nonzero element with a multiplicative inverse.) For example, in the ring $\mathbf{Z}_6$, the element 5 is a unit since it has a multiplicative inverse (namely, itself, since $5 \bullet 5 = 1$ in $\mathbf{Z}_6$), but 2 is not a unit; there is no element b in $\mathbf{Z}_6$ such that $2 \bullet b = 1$. If every nonzero element in R is a unit—that is, if $(R^*, \bullet)$ is a group—then R is called a **division ring**. This name arises since in such a ring, every equation of the form $a \bullet x = c$ (with $a \neq 0$) can be solved for x by multiplying both sides by a^{-1}; that is, by "dividing by a." A commutative division ring is called a **field**. Let's look at some examples.

1. **Q**, **R**, and **C** are fields, but **Z** is not. **Z** is not a field since the only units in **Z** are 1 and –1.

2. The commutative ring with unity $\mathbf{Q}(\sqrt{2}) = \left\{a + b\sqrt{2}: a,\, b \in \mathbf{Q}\right\}$ is a field. All we need to show is that every nonzero element in $\mathbf{Q}(\sqrt{2})$ has an inverse in $\mathbf{Q}(\sqrt{2})$; if a and b are not both zero, then:

$$\frac{1}{a+b\sqrt{2}} = \frac{1}{a+b\sqrt{2}} \bullet \frac{a-b\sqrt{2}}{a-b\sqrt{2}} = \frac{a-b\sqrt{2}}{a^2-2b^2} = \frac{a}{a^2-2b^2} + \frac{-b}{a^2-2b^2}\sqrt{2} \in \mathbf{Q}(\sqrt{2})$$

3. It's not difficult to show that a *finite* integral domain must be a field. Using this result, it follows that if p is a prime, then $\mathbf{Z}_p$ is a field (our first example of a *finite* field). In particular, this means that every nonzero element in $\mathbf{Z}_p$ is a unit; this would not be true if p weren't prime.

4. Consider the subset K of $M_2(\mathbf{R})$ that consists of the following 2 by 2 matrices:

$$K = \left\{\begin{pmatrix} a & b \\ -b & a \end{pmatrix}: a,\, b \in \mathbf{R}\right\}$$

This set contains the additive identity (the zero matrix)—by taking $a = b = 0$—and the multiplicative identity (the 2 by 2 identity matrix)—by taking $a = 1$ and $b = 0$. Since K is closed under addition,

$$\begin{pmatrix} a & b \\ -b & a \end{pmatrix} + \begin{pmatrix} c & d \\ -d & c \end{pmatrix} = \begin{pmatrix} a+c & b+d \\ -(b+d) & a+c \end{pmatrix} \in K$$

and multiplication,

$$\begin{pmatrix} a & b \\ -b & a \end{pmatrix}\begin{pmatrix} c & d \\ -d & c \end{pmatrix} = \begin{pmatrix} ac-bd & ad+bc \\ -(ad+bc) & ac-bd \end{pmatrix} \in K$$

it follows that K is a subring with unity of $M_2(\mathbf{R})$. But although matrix multiplication is generally not commutative, multiplication in K *is* commutative, since:

$$\begin{pmatrix} a & b \\ -b & a \end{pmatrix}\begin{pmatrix} c & d \\ -d & c \end{pmatrix} = \begin{pmatrix} ac-bd & ad+bc \\ -(ad+bc) & ac-bd \end{pmatrix} = \begin{pmatrix} c & d \\ -d & c \end{pmatrix}\begin{pmatrix} a & b \\ -b & a \end{pmatrix}$$

Now, if a and b are not both zero, we have

$$\det\begin{pmatrix} a & b \\ -b & a \end{pmatrix} = a^2 + b^2 \neq 0 \quad\Rightarrow\quad \begin{pmatrix} a & b \\ -b & a \end{pmatrix} \text{ is invertible}$$

which shows that every nonzero element of K is a unit. Therefore, this set of matrices is a commutative division ring—it's a field! In fact, it can be shown that K is structurally identical—isomorphic—to **C**, the field of complex numbers.

5. Consider the subset H of $M_2(\mathbf{C})$ that consists of the following 2 by 2 matrices

$$H = \left\{ \begin{pmatrix} a & b \\ -\overline{b} & \overline{a} \end{pmatrix} : a,\, b \in \mathbf{C} \right\}$$

where $\overline{z}$ denotes the complex conjugate of z. Like the set K in the preceding example, we can show that H contains the additive identity and the multiplicative identity, and that H is closed under addition and multiplication. It follows that H is a subring (with unity) of $M_2(\mathbf{C})$. Furthermore, if a and b are not both zero, we have:

$$\det \begin{pmatrix} a & b \\ -\overline{b} & \overline{a} \end{pmatrix} = |a|^2 + |b|^2 \neq 0 \quad \Rightarrow \quad \begin{pmatrix} a & b \\ -\overline{b} & \overline{a} \end{pmatrix} \text{ is invertible}$$

Therefore, H is a division ring. However, matrix multiplication is not commutative in H, so H is not a field. It's a noncommutative division ring (also called a **strictly-skew field**); H is known as the division ring of **real quaternions**.

Example 6.25   An element a of a ring R is said to be **idempotent** if $a^2 = a$.

(a) Assume that R is a commutative ring with unity $1 \neq 0$. If T is the set of idempotent elements in R, show that T is closed under multiplication.

(b) If R is a division ring, how many idempotent elements does R have?

(c) Show that if every element of R is idempotent (whereupon we'd call R a **Boolean ring**), then R is commutative.

Solution:

(a) First, we notice that there are at least two elements in T, namely 0 and 1. [The fact that $1^2 = 1$ follows from the fact that 1 is the multiplicative identity, so $1 \bullet 1 = 1$. To show that $0^2 = 0$, we notice that $0^2 = 0 \bullet 0 = 0 \bullet (0 + 0) = 0 \bullet 0 + 0 \bullet 0$; adding $-(0 \bullet 0)$ to both sides gives $0 = 0 \bullet 0$.] Choose any two elements, a and b, in T; our goal is to show that ab is also in T. Consider the product $(ab)^2 = abab$. Because R is commutative, $ba = ab$, so $abab = aabb = a^2 b^2$. These equations imply that $(ab)^2 = a^2 b^2$. Now, because $a^2 = a$ and $b^2 = b$ (both a and b are idempotent), we get $(ab)^2 = ab$, which shows that ab is idempotent and thus in T.

(b) The equation $a^2 = a$ is certainly satisfied by $a = 0$, so we'll now assume that $a \neq 0$. Since R is a division ring, every nonzero element has an inverse. Multiplying both sides of $a^2 = a$ by a^{-1} gives $a = 1$. Therefore, the only nonzero element of R that's idempotent is 1. This tells us that a division ring has precisely two idempotents: 0 and 1.

(c) Although we're asked to prove something about the multiplicative structure of R, we can nevertheless exploit its additive structure and the fact that $(R, +)$ is a group. If x is any element in R, then $x + x$ is in R, so $x + x$ is idempotent, by hypothesis; thus, $(x + x)^2 = x + x$. This equation simplifies to $x^2 + 2x^2 + x^2 = x + x$, and since $x^2 = x$, canceling and substituting gives us $2x = 0$. Now, if a and b are any elements in R, then $a + b$ is in R, so $a + b$ is idempotent: $(a + b)^2 = a + b$, an equation that simplifies to $a^2 + ab + ba + b^2 = a + b$; since $a^2 = a$ and $b^2 = b$, we get $ab + ba = 0$. Because $2x = 0$ for any x in R, we can take $x = ab$ and write $2ab = 0$. Since $ab + ba = 0$ and $2ab = 0$, we conclude that $ab + ba = 2ab$. Adding $-ab$ to both sides gives $ba = ab$, which shows that R is commutative.

CHAPTER 6 REVIEW QUESTIONS

Complete the following review questions using the techniques outlined in this chapter. Then, see Chapter 8 for answers and explanations.

1. There is only one integer, x, between 100 and 200 such that integer pair (x, y) satisfies the equation $42x + 55y = 1$. What's the value of x in this integer pair?

    (A) 127   (B) 148   (C) 158   (D) 167   (E) 183

2. Let L be the least common multiple of 1001 and 10101. What's the sum of the digits of L? (All numbers are written in their usual decimal representation.)

    (A) 6   (B) 11   (C) 17   (D) 22   (E) 33

3. Let x_1 and x_2 be the two smallest positive integers for which the following statement is true: "$85x - 12$ is a multiple of 19." Then $x_1 + x_2 =$

    (A) 19   (B) 27   (C) 31   (D) 38   (E) 47

4. If x, y, and z are positive integers such that $4x - 5y + 2z$ is divisible by 13, then which one of the following must also be divisible by 13?

    (A) $x + 13y - z$ (B) $6x - 10y - z$ (C) $x - y - 2z$ (D) $-7x + 12y + 3z$ (E) $-5x + 3y - 4z$

5. When expressed in its usual decimal notation, the number 100! (that is, 100 factorial) ends in how many consecutive zeros?

    (A) 20   (B) 24   (C) 30   (D) 32   (E) 50

6. How many generators does the group $(\mathbf{Z}_{24}, +)$ have?

    (A) 2   (B) 6   (C) 8   (D) 10   (E) 12

7. Which one of the following groups is cyclic?

    (A) $\mathbf{Z}_2 \times \mathbf{Z}_4$ (B) $\mathbf{Z}_2 \times \mathbf{Z}_6$ (C) $\mathbf{Z}_3 \times \mathbf{Z}_4$ (D) $\mathbf{Z}_3 \times \mathbf{Z}_6$ (E) $\mathbf{Z}_4 \times \mathbf{Z}_6$

8. If G is a group of order 12, then G must have a subgroup of all of the following orders EXCEPT

    (A) 2   (B) 3   (C) 4   (D) 6   (E) 12

9. How many subgroups does the group $\mathbf{Z}_3 \oplus \mathbf{Z}_{16}$ have?

   (A) 6   (B) 10   (C) 12   (D) 20   (E) 24

10. If $S = \left\{ a \in \mathbf{R}^+ : a \neq 1 \right\}$, with the binary operation $\bullet$ defined by the equation $a \bullet b = a^{\log b}$ (where $\log b = \log_e b$), then $(S, \bullet)$ is a group. What is the inverse of $a \in S$?

   (A) $\dfrac{1}{e \log a}$ (B) $\dfrac{e}{\log a}$ (C) $e^{-\log a}$ (D) $e^{\log(1/a)}$ (E) $e^{1/\log a}$

11. Which of the following are subgroups of GL(2, $\mathbf{R}$), the group of invertible 2 by 2 matrices (with real entries) under matrix multiplication?

   I. $T = \left\{ A \in \mathrm{GL}(2,\mathbf{R}) : \det A = 2 \right\}$
   II. $U = \left\{ A \in \mathrm{GL}(2,\mathbf{R}) : A \text{ is upper triangular} \right\}$
   III. $V = \left\{ A \in \mathrm{GL}(2,\mathbf{R}) : \operatorname{tr}(A) = 0 \right\}$

   Note: $\operatorname{tr}(A)$ denotes the *trace* of A, which is the sum of the entries on the main diagonal.

   (A) I and II only   (B) II only   (C) II and III only   (D) III only   (E) I and III only

12. Let p and q be distinct primes. How many (mutually nonisomorphic) Abelian groups are there of order p^2q^4?

   (A) 6   (B) 8   (C) 10   (D) 12   (E) 16

13. Let G be the group generated by the elements x and y and subject to the following relations: $x^2 = y^3$, $y^6 = 1$, and $x^{-1}yx = y^{-1}$. Express in simplest form the inverse of the element $z = x^2yx^3y^3$.

   (A) $y^{-2}x^{-1}$ (B) xy^2 (C) xy (D) yx (E) y^2x

14. Let H be the set of all group homomorphisms $\phi : \mathbf{Z}_3 \to \mathbf{Z}_6$. How many functions does H contain?

   (A) 1   (B) 2   (C) 3   (D) 4   (E) 6

15. Let G be a group of order 9, and let e denote the identity of G. Which one of the following statements about G CANNOT be true?

   (A) There exists an element x in G such that $x \neq e$ and $x^{-1} = x$.
   (B) There exists an element x in G such that $x \neq e$ and $x^2 = x^5$.
   (C) There exists an element x in G such that $\langle x \rangle$ has order 3.
   (D) G is cyclic.
   (E) G is Abelian.

16. Let R be a ring; an element x in R is said to be idempotent if $x^2 = x$. How many idempotent elements does the ring $\mathbf{Z}_{20}$ contain?

(A) 2   (B) 4   (C) 5   (D) 8   (E) 10

___

17. Which of the following rings are integral domains?
   I. $\mathbf{Z} \oplus \mathbf{Z}$
   II. $\mathbf{Z}_p$, where p is a prime
   III. $\mathbf{Z}_{p^2}$, where p is a prime

(A) I and II only   (B) II only   (C) II and III only   (D) III only   (E) I and III only

___

18. Which one of the following rings does NOT have the same number of units as the other four?

(A) $\mathbf{Z} \oplus \mathbf{Z}$ (B) $\mathbf{Z} \oplus \mathbf{Z}_3$ (C) $\mathbf{Z} \oplus \mathbf{Z}_5$ (D) $\mathbf{Z} \oplus \mathbf{Z}_6$ (E) $\mathbf{Z}_3 \oplus \mathbf{Z}_3$

___

19. How many elements x in the field $\mathbf{Z}_{11}$ satisfy the equation $x^{12} - x^{10} = 2$?

(A) 1   (B) 2   (C) 3   (D) 4   (E) 5

___

20. Which of the following are subfields of $\mathbf{C}$?

   I. $K_1 = \left\{ a + b\sqrt{\tfrac{2}{3}} : a,\ b \in \mathbf{Q} \right\}$

   II. $K_2 = \left\{ a + b\sqrt{2} : a,\ b \in \mathbf{Q} \text{ and } ab < \sqrt{2} \right\}$

   III. $K_3 = \left\{ a + bi : a,\ b \in \mathbf{Z} \text{ and } i = \sqrt{-1} \right\}$

(A) I only   (B) I and II only   (C) III only
(D) I and III only   (E) None of the K_i are subfields of $\mathbf{C}$.

___

Additional Topics

INTRODUCTION

In this final chapter, we'll briefly review several other areas that may be covered on the GRE Math Subject Test. We'll look at some fundamental ideas of logic, set theory, combinatorics, graph theory, algorithms, probability and statistics, point-set topology, real analysis, complex variables, and numerical analysis.

LOGIC

In mathematics, logic refers to sentential calculus (also known as propositional calculus), which is a logical and well-defined system based on sentences. A **sentence** is a well-formed expression within a language and a syntax that can be evaluated as true or false using algebraic tools. The sentence "The ball is red," can be evaluated as either true or false, but the sentence "Red is the best color," cannot be.

The language of logic includes a set of variables and a set of **connectives** from which any sentence can be built according to the rules of syntax. On the GRE, capital letters, such as X or Y, are used to represent sentences. A list of connectives follows:

iff or $\leftrightarrow$	"if and only if"	
$\neg X$	the negation of X	
$X \wedge Y$	X and Y	
$X \vee Y$	X or Y	
$X \to Y$	If X, then Y	This conditional sentence is false only if X is true and Y is false.
$X \leftrightarrow Y$	X iff Y	This biconditional sentence says X is true iff Y is true. The two sentences, X and Y, are *logically equivalent*.

For sentences X, Y, and Z, the following theorems hold:

1. Double Negation: $\quad \neg\neg X \leftrightarrow X$

2. Commutativity: $\quad X \wedge Y \leftrightarrow Y \wedge X$ and $X \vee Y \leftrightarrow Y \vee X$

3. Associativity: $\quad X \wedge (Y \wedge Z) \leftrightarrow (X \wedge Y) \wedge Z$ and $X \vee (Y \vee Z) \leftrightarrow (X \vee Y) \vee Z$

4. Distribution: $\quad X \vee (Y \wedge Z) \leftrightarrow (X \vee Y) \wedge (X \vee Z)$ and $X \wedge (Y \vee Z) \leftrightarrow (X \wedge Y) \vee (X \wedge Z)$

5. de Morgan's Laws: $\quad \neg(X \wedge Y) \leftrightarrow \neg X \vee \neg Y$ and $\neg(X \vee Y) \leftrightarrow \neg X \wedge \neg Y$

6. Contradiction: $\quad X \to Y \leftrightarrow \neg Y \to \neg X$

Example 7.1   Prove the statement $X \to Y \leftrightarrow \neg Y \to \neg X$ using truth tables.

Solution: To prove this theorem, show that the truth table for $X \to Y$ is equivalent to that of $\neg Y \to \neg X$.

X	Y	$X \to Y$	$\neg X$	$\neg Y$	$\neg Y \to \neg X$
T	T	T	F	F	T
T	F	F	T	F	F
F	T	T	F	T	T
F	F	T	T	T	T

Since all values of the truth table are the same for $X \to Y$ and $\neg Y \to \neg X$, they are logically equivalent.

SET THEORY

The idea of a set is perhaps the most fundamental notion in mathematics and cannot be defined in terms of simpler concepts. A **set** is simply described as a collection of objects (called its **elements** or **members**) that can always be definitively defined either as belonging to the collection or not belonging. Let A be a set; if x is an element of A, then we write $x \in A$; if x is not an element of A, we write $x \notin A$. For example, the set A of positive even integers less than 10 is written:

$$A = \{2, 4, 6, 8\}$$

The braces enclose the elements of a set, which are separated by commas. Notice that for this set A, we have, for example, $6 \in A$, but $7 \notin A$. The set A can also be written as

$$A = \{x: x \text{ is a positive even integer less than } 10\}$$

which is read, "A is the set of all positive even integers x that are less than 10." The statement after the colon (which stands for *such that*) describes the condition that an object must satisfy in order to be considered an element of the set. Two sets are said to be **equal** if they contain exactly the same elements. The elements of a set can be anything—numbers, functions, matrices, etc. In fact, the elements of a set can themselves be sets; in this case, it's common to refer to a **collection** or **family** of sets, simply to avoid the phrase "a set of sets." Finally, it's very convenient to include the concept of the **empty set.** This is the set that contains no elements whatsoever; it's denoted $\varnothing$.

SUBSETS AND COMPLEMENTS

Let A and B be sets; if every element in A is also in B, then A is a **subset** of B (and B is said to be a **superset** of A), and we write $A \subseteq B$. Every set is a subset of itself, and it's agreed that the empty set is also a subset of every set. If A is a subset of B, and $A \neq B$, then A is said to be a **proper** subset of B, and we write $A \subset B$, (although some authors use this notation whether A is a proper subset of B or not). The standard way to prove that two sets are equal is to show that each is a subset of the other; that is:

$$A \subseteq B \text{ and } B \subseteq A \iff A = B$$

In many discussions involving sets, it's clear that all the sets are subsets of some **universal set**, U. For example, in calculus and real analysis, the domain and range of a function are implicitly assumed to be subsets of $\mathbf{R}$, the set of real numbers. When it's clear what the universal set is, we can define the **complement** of a set A—denoted by A^c or A'—as the set of all x in U that *aren't* in A:

$$A^c = \{x: x \in U \text{ and } x \notin A\}$$

We can also define the **difference of B from A**, also called the **complement of B relative to A**, as:

$$A - B = \{x: x \in A \text{ and } x \notin B\}$$

UNION AND INTERSECTION

Several other operations can be defined for sets. Given two sets, A and B, we can form their intersection and their union. The **intersection** of A and B, denoted $A \cap B$, is the set that contains all elements that are in both A and B:

$$A \cap B = \{x: x \in A \text{ and } x \in B\}$$

If $A \cap B = \varnothing$, then we say A and B are **disjoint**. The **union** of A and B, denoted $A \cup B$, is the set that contains all elements that are either in A or in B (or in both):

$$A \cup B = \{x: x \in A \text{ or } x \in B\}$$

The **symmetric difference** of two sets, A and B, is defined by the equation:

$$A \triangle B = (A - B) \cup (B - A)$$

A pair of laws relates the concepts of complement, intersection, and union; they're called **de Morgan's laws**. For two sets, A and B, they are:

$$(A \cap B)^c = A^c \cup B^c$$
$$(A \cup B)^c = A^c \cap B^c$$

Basically, de Morgan's laws say that the complement of an intersection is the union of the complements, and the complement of a union is the intersection of the complements. Both of these laws can be generalized to any number of sets, and we also have laws that concern set differences:

$$(A \cap B) - C = (A - C) \cap (B - C)$$
$$(A \cup B) - C = (A - C) \cup (B - C)$$

Another pair of laws can be used to simplify an expression involving both the intersection and the union of sets; they're known as the **distributive laws**:

$$A \cap (B \cup C) = (A \cap B) \cup (A \cap C)$$
$$A \cup (B \cap C) = (A \cup B) \cap (A \cup C)$$

The definitions of intersection and union can be generalized. Let I be some indexing set, and consider the family of sets $\{A_i\}_{i \in I}$. This notation means that there's a set A_i, associated with every $i \in I$. The intersection of the sets in this family is written:

$$\bigcap_{i \in I} A_i = \{x: x \in A_i \text{ for every } i \in I\}$$

Similarly, the union of the sets in this family is written:

$$\bigcup_{i \in I} A_i = \{x: x \in A_i \text{ for at least one } i \in I\}$$

Cartesian Products

If A and B are nonempty sets, we can form a set called their **cartesian product**, which is the set of ordered pairs given by:

$$A \times B = \{(a, b): a \in A \text{ and } b \in B\}$$

For example, $\mathbf{R} \times \mathbf{R}$ is the familiar xy-plane.

Intervals of the Real Line

The geometric interpretation of the set of real numbers, **R**, is a line (called the **number line** or the **real line**). The xy-plane is determined by two copies of the real line that are perpendicular to each other and intersect at the origin (the point corresponding to the number 0). Certain subsets of **R**, which are of fundamental importance, are called **intervals**. Let a and b be real numbers, with $a < b$; then the set of all x such that $a < x < b$ is called the **open interval** between a and b, and is denoted by (a, b):

$$(a, b) = \{x: a < x < b\}$$

Notice that (a, b) is also the notation for an ordered pair, which symbolizes a point in the xy-plane (the point at which $x = a$ and $y = b$). Contextually, it will be clear what (a, b) stands for, so no confusion should result. Other intervals of the real line are denoted as on the following page.

$$[a, b) = \{x: a \leq x < b\}$$
$$(a, b] = \{x: a < x \leq b\}$$
$$[a, b] = \{x: a \leq x \leq b\}$$

The first two are called **half-open** (or **half-closed**) intervals, and the third is called a **closed** interval. If the interval doesn't include one (or both) of its endpoints, we use a parenthesis, "(" or ")", for that endpoint, and if the interval does include one (or both) of its endpoints, we use a bracket, "[" or "]", for that endpoint.

The definition of an interval can be generalized to an infinite interval. Formally, we consider the set of **extended real numbers**, which is the set **R** with two elements, $-\infty$ (**minus infinity**) and ∞ (or $+\infty$, **plus infinity**)—adjoined: $\{-\infty\} \cup \mathbf{R} \cup \{\infty\}$, where by definition, $-\infty < x < \infty$ for every x in **R**. These symbols are introduced as a notational convenience for infinite intervals; if a and b are real numbers, then we have:

$$(-\infty, b) = \{x: -\infty < x < b\} = \{x: x < b\}$$
$$(-\infty, b] = \{x: -\infty < x \leq b\} = \{x: x \leq b\}$$
$$(a, \infty) = \{x: a < x < \infty\} = \{x: x > a\}$$
$$[a, \infty) = \{x: a \leq x < \infty\} = \{x: x \geq a\}$$
$$(-\infty, \infty) = \{x: -\infty < x < \infty\} = \mathbf{R}$$

Example 7.2   If $A = (-1, 2]$ and $B = (1, 3)$ are intervals of **R**, what are each of the following:

$$A \cap B$$
$$A \cup B$$
$$A - B$$
$$A \,\Delta\, B$$
$$A^c$$
$$B^c$$
$$A^c \cap B^c$$

Also, sketch the cartesian product $A \times B$.

Solution: It'll be helpful to sketch the intervals A and B:

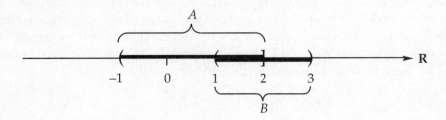

We can now see that:

$$A \cap B = (1, 2]$$
$$A \cup B = (-1, 3)$$
$$A - B = (-1, 1]$$
$$A \Delta B = (A - B) \cup (B - A) = (-1, 1] \cup (2, 3)$$
$$A^c = (-\infty, -1] \cup (2, \infty)$$
$$B^c = (-\infty, 1] \cup [3, \infty)$$
$$A^c \cap B^c = (-\infty, -1] \cup [3, \infty)$$

Notice that $A^c \cap B^c$ equals $(A \cup B)^c$, just as de Morgan's law says it should.

The cartesian product, $A \times B$, is sketched below; notice that the only points on the boundary of the rectangular region that are actually included in the cartesian product are the points of the form $(2, b)$, where $1 < b < 3$:

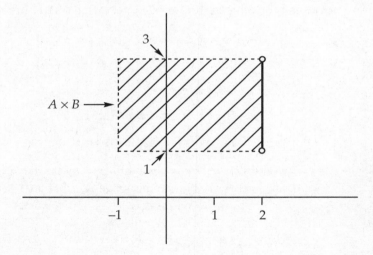

VENN DIAGRAMS

A **Venn diagram** is a way to illustrate operations on sets. Each set in a Venn diagram is depicted as the interior of some shape (a circle, ellipse, rectangle, etc.), and the result of some operation on the sets is shown by shading. Here are a couple of examples:

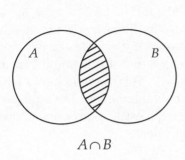

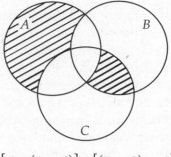

$$A \cap B$$

$$[A - (B \cup C)] \cup [(B \cap C) - A]$$

A Venn diagram can be very helpful in motivating the proof of a law that involves sets. For example, a Venn diagram involving two sets, A and B, like the one on the left on the previous page, can illustrate the following law:

$$A \, \Delta \, B = (A \cup B) - (A \cap B)$$

Example 7.3 For any three sets A, B, and C, let $D = A - (B - C)$ and $E = (A - B) - C$. Which one of the sets—D or E—is always a subset of the other?

Solution: A Venn diagram shows that E is always a subset of D:

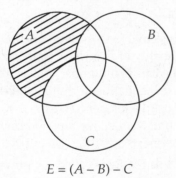

$$E = (A - B) - C$$

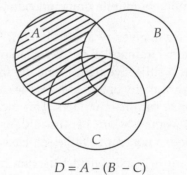

$$D = A - (B - C)$$

CARDINALITY

The **cardinal number** (or **cardinality**) of a set is the number of elements in the set. For a finite set, the notion of its cardinal number is straightforward. But for infinite sets, things get more complicated; after all, how do we talk about "the number of elements" in a set that contains infinitely many? To avoid this complication, we say that two sets, A and B, are **equivalent**—written $A \approx B$—if there's a bijective function (a one-to-one correspondence) between A and B. By definition, equivalent sets have the same cardinality.

Let n be a positive integer, and let $\mathbf{n} = \{1, 2, \ldots, n\}$; this is the set that contains the first n positive integers. If a set A is equivalent to some $\mathbf{n}$, we say that A is **finite** and contains precisely n elements. Thus, the cardinal number of A is n, which is written card $A = n$. If A is the empty set, then we still say that A is finite, but its cardinality is zero (card $A = 0$).

Now, let's consider a nonempty set A such that *no* one-to-one correspondence exists between A and any **n**. Then A is called an **infinite** set, and its cardinal number is infinite. There are actually different "levels" of infinity; that is, there's more than one infinite cardinal number. The prototype for the "first level" of infinity is the set of positive integers, $\mathbf{Z}^+$. If a set A is equivalent to $\mathbf{Z}^+$, then we say that A is **countably infinite**. The cardinal number of $\mathbf{Z}^+$—and therefore of any countably infinite set—is denoted $\aleph_0$ (aleph-null).

An important property that distinguishes finite sets from infinite sets is illustrated by the following example. Consider the set E of positive even integers. Despite the fact that E is a *proper* subset of $\mathbf{Z}^+$, we can nevertheless find a bijective function $f: \mathbf{Z}^+ \to E$, given by $f(n) = 2n$. Then, by definition, E has the same cardinality as $\mathbf{Z}^+$. This behavior cannot happen for a finite set; that is, if A is finite and B is a proper subset of A, there can be no one-to-one correspondence between A and B. But if A is infinite, there's always a one-to-one correspondence between A and a proper subset of itself. This example shows why the notion of "the number of elements" in a set gets fuzzy when we talk about infinite sets. The set E, being a proper subset of $\mathbf{Z}^+$, would seem to contain fewer elements than $\mathbf{Z}^+$, but the existence of a one-to-one correspondence between E and $\mathbf{Z}^+$ proves that these sets are actually equivalent.

Other sets that are countably infinite include:

- The set of all integers (positive, negative, and zero), $\mathbf{Z}$

- The set of all rational numbers, $\mathbf{Q}$

- The set of all algebraic numbers

  (A real number x is said to be **algebraic** if x is the root of a polynomial equation, $p(x) = 0$, with integer coefficients.)

- Any infinite subset of the integers, rationals, or algebraic numbers

- A finite cartesian product of countably infinite sets

- A finite union of countably infinite sets, $\bigcup\limits_{k=1}^{n} A_k$

- A countably infinite union of countably infinite sets, $\bigcup\limits_{k=1}^{\infty} A_k$

Let's say we're given two sets, A and B. If there exists an injective (one-to-one) function from A to B, then the cardinal number of A is less than or equal to the cardinality of B, and we write card $A \leq$ card B. If there exists a surjective (onto) function from A to B, then the cardinal number of A is greater than or equal to the cardinality of B, and we write card $A \geq$ card B. These inequalities are still valid even when we consider infinite cardinal numbers. This means that, for any positive integer n, we have $\aleph_0 > n$. We can use the strict inequality here because although we can always find a surjective function from a countably infinite set onto a nonempty, finite set, we can't find a bijective one; that is, $\aleph_0 \geq n$, but $\aleph_0 \neq n$.

Let A be any set, and consider the family of all its subsets; this family is called the **power set of A**:

$$\mathsf{P}(A) = \big\{B: B \subseteq A\big\}$$

If A is finite and contains precisely n elements, then the family $\mathsf{P}(A)$ contains 2^n sets. Therefore, if A is finite, the cardinality of $\mathsf{P}(A)$ is always greater than the cardinality of A, because for any integer n, 2^n is always greater than n. So there's always a surjective function from $\mathsf{P}(A)$ onto A, but never an injective one. In fact, it can be shown that the same thing happens even if A is infinite; therefore, the cardinal number of $\mathsf{P}(A)$ is always strictly greater than the cardinal number of A, for any set A, finite or infinite.

We'll finish this section with a look at the different "levels" of infinity, which we mentioned earlier. It can be proved that the set of all real numbers, $\mathbf{R}$, is equivalent to the power set of $\mathbf{Z}^+$. Accepting this fact, the cardinal number of **R** is strictly greater than the cardinal number of **Z**⁺; that is, card **R** $> \aleph_0$. Therefore, **R** is infinite but not countably infinite; it's said to be **uncountable**. The cardinality of **R** is denoted by $\mathfrak{c}$, which is called the **cardinal number of the continuum**. This provides the next "level" of infinity, which is greater than the infinity that describes the cardinality of the set of positive integers. Other sets that are uncountable include:

- The set of all irrational numbers, $\mathbf{Q}^c = \mathbf{R} - \mathbf{Q}$

- The set of all transcendental numbers

  (A real number is said to be **transcendental** if it's not algebraic. The two most familiar examples of transcendental numbers are π and e.)

- Any subset of **R** that contains a (nonempty) interval

By analogy with the expression for the cardinality of the power set of a finite set, the cardinality of the continuum, $\mathfrak{c}$, is also written as $2^{\aleph_0}$, because **R** is equivalent to $\mathbf{P}(\mathbf{Z}^+)$. Since the cardinality of the power set of A is always strictly greater than the cardinality of A, we can consider the cardinality of the power set of **R**, which represents the next "level" up in cardinality, and clearly the process can continue. We can now see that there are infinitely many cardinal numbers, which we can order as follows:

$$\underbrace{0 < 1 < 2 < \cdots}_{\substack{\text{finite} \\ \text{cardinal numbers}}} < \underbrace{\aleph_0 < \mathfrak{c} < 2^{\mathfrak{c}} < 2^{2^{\mathfrak{c}}} < \cdots}_{\substack{\text{infinite} \\ \text{cardinal numbers}}}$$

Example 7.4   Show that any open interval of the form (a, b), where a and b are real numbers and $a < b$, is uncountable.

Solution: Since **R** is uncountable, we'll show that (a, b) is uncountable by finding a bijection from (a, b) to **R**. First, the tangent function, $f(x) = \tan x$, is a bijective function from the interval $\left(\dfrac{-\pi}{2}, \dfrac{\pi}{2}\right)$ onto **R**. Next, the linear function

$$g(x) = \frac{\pi}{b-a}(x-a) - \frac{\pi}{2}$$

is a bijective function from (a, b) to $\left(\dfrac{-\pi}{2}, \dfrac{\pi}{2}\right)$. Therefore, the composite function $f \circ g$ is a bijection from (a, b) to **R**.

GRAPH THEORY

A **graph** consists of a finite collection of **vertices** and **edges** where each edge connects a distinct pair of vertices. We will only discuss simple graphs whose edges have no orientation; these graphs are called *undirected*. Let G be a graph; then we say $V(G)$ is the set of vertices and $E(G)$ is the set of edges. The order of a graph is $|V|$, the number of vertices; the size of the graph is $|E|$, the number of edges. If $a, b \in V(G)$ and are connected by the edge $\{a, b\}$, we say a and b are *adjacent* vertices. The **degree** of a vertex v is the number of vertices adjacent to v (or the number of edges at vertex v). A vertex with an odd degree is an *odd* vertex, and a vertex with an even degree is an *even* vertex. If every distinct pair of vertices is connected by an edge, the graph is *complete*.

Graphs F and G are **isomorphic** if there exists a function $f : V(F) \to V(G)$ that is both one-to-one and onto, and all adjacencies are preserved.

A **path** indicates movement from a start vertex to an end vertex. A path is a sequence of adjacent vertices and the connecting edges. A graph is *connected* if every pair of vertices can be connected by at least one path. A path that begins and ends at the same vertex is a **cycle**. A graph with no cycles is a *forest*, and if such a graph is connected, it is a **tree**. (Trees are the most widely used application of graph theory in applied mathematics.)

Let G be a graph with vertex and edge sets $V(G)$ and $E(G)$. H is a **subgraph** of G if

1. $V(H) \subseteq V(G)$

2. $E(H) \subseteq E(G)$

3.   every edge of H connects two vertices of H

This says that the vertices of H are a subset of the vertices of G, and every pair of adjacent vertices in H also appears in G.

If $V(H) = V(G)$, then H is a spanning subgraph of G. In addition, if H is a tree, then H is a **spanning tree** of G.

Example 7.5   Graphs X and Y are shown below.
   a.   Are the two graphs isomorphic?
   b.   What is the degree of vertex A?
   c.   What is the fewest number of edges you must add to each graph for it to be complete?

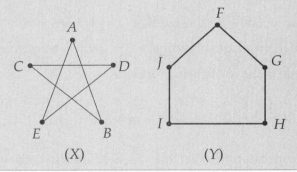

(X)   (Y)

Solution:

a.   First, note that each graph contains exactly five vertices. The function that maps A to F, B to G, C to H, D to I, and E to J is both one-to-one and onto.

   Next, list the edges for each graph. The first graph has edges $\{A, B\}$, $\{B, C\}$, $\{C, D\}$, $\{D, E\}$, and $\{E, A\}$. The second graph has edges $\{F, G\}$, $\{G, H\}$, $\{H, I\}$, $\{I, J\}$, and $\{J, F\}$. Since the function preserves every pair of adjacent vertices, the graphs are isomorphic.

b.   Since vertex A has exactly two adjacent vertices (B and E), A is an even vertex.

c.   Using the combination formula, 5 vertices can have $\dfrac{5!}{3!2!} = 10$ edges. Thus, each graph needs five more edges to be complete; for example, graph X needs $\{A, C\}$, $\{A, D\}$, $\{B, D\}$, $\{B, E\}$, and $\{C, E\}$.

ALGORITHMS

An **algorithm** is a finite sequence of well-defined and logical steps used to complete a task, usually to solve a problem. An algorithm has the following properties:

1. No instructions can be dependent on the user. All ambiguity in the process must be removed.

2. The process must end with a solution after a finite number of steps.

3. The process is deterministic; that is, each step unambiguously determines what the next step will be.

Simply stated, an algorithm must receive an input and through a finite process produce a solution. Using the same input value will always produce the same solution (unless a step incorporates randomizing).

An algorithm can have any sort of notation. An algorithm on the GRE could use any of the symbols commonly used in the section on Logic. Typically, ETS uses algorithms expressed in a programming language (or a flow chart). This language is designed to express the steps, or computations, that tell the computer how to behave. The syntax of a programming language used on the GRE should be simple enough to be understood by any test taker who has taken an undergraduate course in computer science.

Example 7.6   The following algorithm is used to prove the famous "$3x + 1$" problem.

```
input (a)
while a > 1
      begin
            if (a mod 2 = 0)
                a := a / 2
            else a := 3 • a + 1
            output (a)
      end
```

When the input value of the algorithm is 3, what is the sequence of outputs produced?

Solution: Interpret the steps of the algorithm. The input value is a, and a loop is created while a > 1. For each step, if a = 0 (mod 2), then divide a by 2. Otherwise multiply a by 3 and add 1. Finally, the algorithm will output the new value of *a* and reevaluate whether a > 1 before continuing.

The outputs of the algorithm will be the following:
10, 5, 16, 8, 4, 2, 1
Because a is not greater than 1, the process ends, and the sequence converges to a solution.

COMBINATORICS

Combinatorics is the branch of mathematics concerned with counting. (Although that may sound fairly easy, the methods of more advanced combinatorics are *far* from trivial.) Here's an example. Let's say we're trying to get from City *A* to City *C* via City *B*. If there are two roads between City *A* and City *B*, and three roads from City *B* to City *C*, how many different journeys are there from *A* to *B* to *C*? Since there are two choices for the first route, then three possible choices for the second, the total number of journeys is their product: $2 \times 3 = 6$. This illustrates a basic principle:

- If there are *a* possible choices for the first decision and *b* possible choices for the second decision, then the total number of possible ways these two independent decisions can be made is the product *ab*.

- If there's a third independent decision to be made (with, say, *c* choices), then the total number of ways to make all three decisions is the product *abc*, and so on.

Example 7.7   Let's say that the personal code for your ATM card consists of six characters, each of which can be any letter or numerical digit.
(a) How many possible personal codes are there?
(b) Suppose you want your personal ATM code to have no repeated characters; now how many possible codes are there?

Solution:

(a) There are twenty-six letters (A through Z) and ten digits (0 through 9), so there are 26 + 10 = 36 possible choices for each character. Since there are six decisions, any of which can use any of the 36 possible characters, the total number of ways the six decisions can be made is 36^6. (By the way, that's over two *billion* possible codes.)

(b) There are 36 ways to make the first decision, but only 35 for the second (because, to avoid a repeat, you can't use the same choice you made for the first character). Then there are only 34 possible choices for the third character, 33 for the fourth, 32 for the fifth, and 31 for the sixth. Thus, the total number of codes that don't have any repeated characters is $36 \times 35 \times 34 \times 33 \times 32 \times 31$. (This cuts down the total number of codes by roughly one-third.)

PERMUTATIONS AND COMBINATIONS

Let's say we're given a set of *n* objects; in how many different ways can we choose *k* of them? The answer depends on whether the order in which we select the objects makes a difference. For example, in a horse race that involves eight horses, how many win, place, and show possibilities are there? Well, we want to see how many ways we can choose three horses out of eight, but here order makes a difference; if horses *A*, *B*, and *C* are the ones that come in first (win), second (place), and third (show), it matters whether the finishing order is *A*, *B*, *C* or, say, *B*, *C*, *A*. On the other hand, if you're playing five-card draw poker, you receive five cards out of a standard deck of 52; the order in which they're dealt to you makes no difference. The number of possible poker hands is found by counting the number of ways we can choose five cards out of 52, without regard to order.

If the order in which the objects are chosen does make a difference, each complete selection of *k* objects from the original *n* is called a **permutation** (the variable *r* is often used in place of *k*). If the order is irrelevant, then each complete selection is called a **combination**. In general, there are always more permutations than there are combinations. To see why, let's go back to the example of the horse race. Each of the selections

$$A, B, C \quad A, C, B \quad B, A, C \quad B, C, A \quad C, A, B \quad \text{and} \quad C, B, A$$

is a different permutation, but they're all equivalent to a single combination.

Let's figure out the number of ways we can choose *k* things from *n*, with regard to order. For our first selection, we can choose any of the given *n* objects; for the second selection, we can choose any of the remaining *n* – 1 objects; this process continues until, for the kth selection, we can choose any of the remaining *n* – (*k* – 1) objects. Since these decisions are independent, the total number of **permutations of *n* things taken *k* at a time** is the product:

$$P(n, k) = n(n - 1)(n - 2) \ldots [n - (k - 1)]$$

Now, let's figure out the number of ways we can choose k things from n, without regard to order. Let's say we've chosen k objects from a group of n, with regard to order. That is, assume we have a permutation of n things taken k at a time. In how many ways can we permute these k objects? The answer is $k!$. For example, consider the example of the three horses—A, B, and C—given above. Let's say we selected them in the order A then B then C. Now that we have these three, we can arrange them in $3! = 6$ different orders; these orders are displayed above. Each of these six orders is a different permutation, but they collectively represent just one combination. In general, the number of **combinations of n things taken k at a time** is equal to the number of permutations of n things taken k at a time divided by $k!$:

$$C(n,k) = \frac{P(n,k)}{k!} = \frac{n(n-1)(n-2)\cdots[n-(k-1)]}{k!}$$

This expression for $C(n, k)$ can be written in another way:

$$C(n,k) = \frac{n!}{k!(n-k)!}$$

In this form, you should recognize it as the **binomial coefficient**:

$$\binom{n}{k} = \frac{n!}{k!(n-k)!}$$

It's called the binomial coefficient because it's precisely the coefficient that appears in the **binomial theorem**:

$$(a+b)^n = \sum_{k=0}^{n}\binom{n}{k}a^{n-k}b^k$$

Example 7.8   In a horse race consisting of 8 horses, how many different win-place-show (the top three) finishing orders are there?

Solution: The order in which the horses finish matters here, so we're looking for the number of permutations of 8 things taken 3 at a time; this number is:

$$P(8, 3) = 8 \cdot 7 \cdot 6 = 336$$

Example 7.9   How many 3-element subsets does a set containing 9 elements have?

Solution: The order in which the elements are arranged in a subset is irrelevant. The number of combinations of 9 things taken 3 at a time is:

$$C(9, 3) = \binom{9}{3} = \frac{9!}{3! \cdot 6!} = \frac{9 \cdot 8 \cdot 7}{3!} = \frac{9 \cdot 8 \cdot 7}{2 \cdot 3} = 3 \cdot 4 \cdot 7 = 84$$

With Repetitions Allowed

Imagine that you have a hat that contains 10 billiard balls, numbered 1 through 10. You're asked to choose three of the balls, but after each selection, you record the number and toss the ball back into the hat. So, for example, you could choose the 5 ball, then the 8 ball, then the 5 ball again. It's clear that the number of permutations and combinations of n things taken k at a time in a situation like this would be different than if repetitions weren't allowed. The formula for the number of permutations in this case is easy:

$$P(n, k) \text{ with repetitions allowed} = n^k$$

Determining a formula for the number of combinations is not as easy:

$$C(n, k) \text{ with repetitions allowed} = \binom{n+k-1}{k}$$

Example 7.10　In how many ways can we write the number 4 as the sum of 5 nonnegative integers?

Solution:　Consider the following set-up. You're given 4 balls and seated in front of 5 empty boxes, labeled 1, 2, 3, 4, and 5:

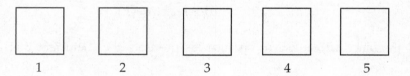

Your job is to place the 4 balls any way you want into the 5 boxes. You can place more than 1 ball into the same box, but you must drop in all 4 balls. After you've finished, there'll be k_1 balls in Box 1, k_2 balls in Box 2, etc., where each k_i is a nonnegative integer and $k_1 + k_2 + k_3 + k_4 + k_5 = 4$. The 5-tuple $(k_1, k_2, k_3, k_4, k_5)$ gives a way of writing 4 as the sum of 5 nonnegative integers. For example, let's say you placed the balls in the boxes as follows:

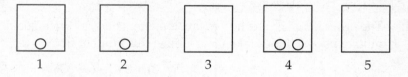

This would correspond to the 5-tuple (1, 1, 0, 2, 0), and $1 + 1 + 0 + 2 + 0$ is a way of writing the number 4 as the sum of 5 nonnegative integers. By placing 4 balls in these 5 boxes, you're choosing 4 objects from 5, with repetitions allowed (placing a ball in a box is your way of marking your choice of a box). Therefore, the total number of ways of writing 4 as the sum of 5 nonnegative integers, in which the order of the summands does matter, is the same as the number of ways of choosing 4 objects from 5, in which the order *doesn't* matter, with repetitions allowed. According to the formula given above, this number is:

$$\binom{5+4-1}{4} = \binom{8}{4} = \frac{8!}{4! \cdot 4!} = \frac{5 \cdot 6 \cdot 7 \cdot 8}{4!} = 70$$

THE PIGEONHOLE PRINCIPLE

This simple principle can be used in a variety of combinatorics and number theory problems. It states:

> If n objects are placed into k pigeonholes, and $n \geq k + 1$, then at least one pigeonhole must contain more than one object.

Imagine a mail carrier standing in front of five mailboxes. If he has six or more envelopes to place in these boxes, then at least one mailbox is going to get more than one envelope.

Here's a more generalized statement of the pigeonhole principle:

> Let's say you're given n objects, each of which is painted exactly one of c possible colors. Then for any integer k such that $k \leq [(n - 1)/c] + 1$, there must be k objects, all of which are painted the same color.

If this weren't true, then there'd be, at most, $k - 1$ different objects of each of the c colors, which would mean that $c(k - 1) \geq n$; or, equivalently, $n \leq c(k - 1)$. But this would contradict the assumption that $k \leq [(n - 1)/c] + 1$, which is equivalent to the statement $n \geq c(k - 1) + 1$.

Example 7.11   Let A be a set containing $n + 1$ integers. Show that it's always possible to choose two numbers, a and b, from A such that $a - b$ is divisible by n.

Solution: We can partition $\mathbf{Z}$ into n subsets $A_0, A_1, A_2, \ldots, A_{n-1}$ such that:

$$k \in A_i \text{ if and only if } k \equiv i \pmod{n}$$

Therefore, every integer is in exactly one of these subsets A_i. If we now place the $n + 1$ integers from A into these subsets, the pigeonhole principle tells us that at least one of the sets A_i—let's call it A_j—will contain at least 2 integers—call them a and b—from A. Since $a \equiv j \pmod{n}$ and $b \equiv j \pmod{n}$, we know that $a - b \equiv 0 \pmod{n}$, so $a - b$ is divisible by n.

Example 7.12   Imagine a set of 10 objects, each of which is painted one of 3 possible colors. Show that there exist 2 disjoint subsets of this set such that each subset consists of 3 objects all painted the same color.

Solution: Let $n_1 = 10$ and $c = 3$. Because $3 \leq [(n_1 - 1)/c] + 1$, our general statement of the pigeonhole principle assures us that there are at least 3 objects, all of which are painted the same color. Choosing exactly 3 of these objects, we get one 3-element subset that consists of objects all painted the same color. Now, removing these 3 objects from the original 10 leaves 7 objects, each of which is painted one of 3 possible colors. Now, let $n_2 = 7$ and $c = 3$; since $3 \leq [(n_2 - 1)/c] + 1$, again we know that there exist at least 3 objects, all of which are painted the same color. This gives us our second 3-element subset—which is clearly disjoint from the first—all of whose elements are painted the same color.

PROBABILITY AND STATISTICS

Consider rolling a fair die. It has six sides, all of which are equally likely to turn up. Since there are six possible outcomes, all equally likely, the probability of any one of them happening is $\frac{1}{6}$.

To find the probability of an event, simply divide the number of desired outcomes by the total number of possible outcomes.

Example 7.13   Each of the first ten positive integers is written on a slip of paper, and the ten slips are tossed into a hat. What's the probability that someone will pull out a prime number?

Solution: Assuming that all ten numbers are equally likely to be selected, we just divide the number of desired outcomes by the total number of possible outcomes. Among the first ten positive integers, there are only four primes: 2, 3, 5, and 7. Thus, the probability of selecting a prime from the hat is $\frac{4}{10} = \frac{2}{5}$.

Example 7.14   An ordinary deck of playing cards is shuffled, and a card is randomly chosen. What's the probability that the card selected is
(a) a heart?
(b) red?
(c) the jack of hearts?
(d) not a face card?

Solution: We'll use the fact that an ordinary deck contains 52 cards, with 4 suits of 13 cards each.
(a) Since there are 13 hearts, the probability that the card selected is a heart is $\frac{13}{52} = \frac{1}{4}$.
(b) Because two suits are red (hearts and diamonds), there are $13 + 13 = 26$ red cards, so the probability that a red card is selected is $\frac{26}{52} = \frac{1}{2}$.
(c) Since there's only one jack of hearts, the chances that this particular card is chosen is $\frac{1}{52}$.
(d) There are 3 face cards per suit: the jack, queen, and king. Since there are 4 suits (hearts, diamonds, spades, and clubs), there are $3 \times 4 = 12$ face cards. Therefore, $52 - 12 = 40$ of the cards are not face cards. We conclude that the probability of not selecting a face card is $\frac{40}{52} = \frac{10}{13}$.

Example 7.15   You deal 5 cards to yourself from a standard deck. The result is 4 diamonds and a club. You discard the club, and draw one more card from the deck. What's the probability of getting the flush (that is, of drawing a fifth diamond)?

Solution: After you deal yourself the original hand, the deck contains a total of 47 cards, $13 - 4 = 9$ of which are diamonds. Therefore, the probability of drawing one of the remaining 9 diamonds is $\frac{9}{47}$.

Example 7.16   Two points, x and y, are selected at random in the interval [0, 1]. What's the probability that the product xy will be less than $\frac{1}{2}$?

Solution: Selecting two points at random in the interval [0, 1] is equivalent to selecting a point (x, y) at random in the square $[0, 1] \times [0, 1]$. The following shows this square and the graph of the curve $xy = \frac{1}{2}$; the shaded region denotes those points (x, y) where $xy < \frac{1}{2}$.

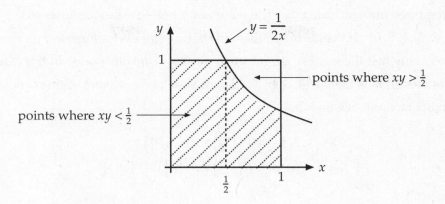

points where $xy < \frac{1}{2}$

points where $xy > \frac{1}{2}$

The area of the unshaded region is:

$$\int_{\frac{1}{2}}^{1}\left(1-\frac{1}{2x}\right)dx = \left[x - \tfrac{1}{2}\log x\right]_{\frac{1}{2}}^{1} = (1-0)-(\tfrac{1}{2}-\tfrac{1}{2}\log\tfrac{1}{2}) = \tfrac{1}{2}(1-\log 2)$$

Therefore, the area of the *shaded* region is $1-\left[\tfrac{1}{2}(1-\log 2)\right]=\tfrac{1}{2}(1+\log 2)$. Since the square has an area of 1, the ratio of this area to the area of the entire square is $\tfrac{1}{2}(1+\log 2)$, so this is the probability that $xy < \frac{1}{2}$.

PROBABILITY SPACES

We'll need to introduce some more formal terminology and techniques to continue our study of probability for the GRE Math Subject Test. Let S be a nonempty set, and consider $\mathsf{P}(S)$, the power set of S, which is the collection of all the subsets of S. A **Boolean algebra** (or simply an **algebra**) **of sets on** S is a nonempty subfamily of the power set of S, $\mathsf{E} \subseteq \mathsf{P}(S)$, that satisfies the following two conditions:

1. If A and B are sets in E, then so are $A \cup B$ and $A \cap B$.

2. If A is a set in E, then so is $A^c = S - A$.

Because E is nonempty, it contains some set, A. By the second condition, E must also contain $S - A$. Then, by condition 1, E must also contain $S = A \cup (S - A)$ and $\varnothing = S^c$. Therefore, every algebra of sets on S always contains the empty set and the universal set, S.

Now, let E be an algebra of sets on S. A function $P\colon \mathsf{E} \to [0, 1]$ is called a **probability measure on** E (or **on** S, if E is understood) if all of the following requirements are met:

1. $P(\varnothing) = 0$

2. $P(S) = 1$

3. $P(A \cup B) = P(A) + P(B)$ for every pair of *disjoint* sets A and B in E

A **probability space** is a set S, together with an algebra of sets on S and a probability measure on S. The set S is called the **sample space**, the elements of S are called **outcomes**, and the sets in E (which are subsets of S) are called **events**. With this terminology, $P(A)$ is the probability that event A occurs. Let's now look at some examples to illustrate all these definitions.

1. Consider throwing a six-sided die. The set of outcomes—the sample space—is $S = \{1, 2, 3, 4, 5, 6\}$. If the die is fair, then $P(\{n\}) = \dfrac{1}{6}$ for every number n on the die. What's the probability that the number we get when we throw the die is odd? In this case, the event we're interested in is the set $\{1, 3, 5\}$, which consists of 3 outcomes. Using condition 3 for a probability measure, we find that:

$$\begin{aligned} P(\{1, 3, 5\}) &= P(\{1\}) + P(\{3, 5\}) \\ &= P(\{1\}) + P(\{3\}) + P(\{5\}) \\ &= \tfrac{1}{6} + \tfrac{1}{6} + \tfrac{1}{6} \\ &= \tfrac{1}{2} \end{aligned}$$

2. Choose a card from a standard deck of 52. The set of outcomes—the sample space—is the set that consists of all 52 cards. If the selection is random, then $P(\{C\}) = \dfrac{1}{52}$, for every card C in the deck. What's the probability of drawing a club? In this case, the event we're interested in is the following subset of S

   ♣ = {2♣, 3♣, 4♣, 5♣, 6♣, 7♣, 8♣, 9♣, 10♣, J♣, Q♣, K♣, A♣}

   which consists of 13 outcomes. This tells us that $P(♣) = \dfrac{13}{52} = \dfrac{1}{4}$.

3. Imagine throwing three coins. If we let H denote "heads" and T "tails," then the set of possible outcomes is:

   $$S = \{\text{HHH, HHT, HTH, HTT, THH, THT, TTH, TTT}\}$$

   Since there are $2^3 = 8$ elements in S, if all the coins are fair, the probability that any of one of these outcomes will occur must be $\dfrac{1}{8}$. What's the probability of getting exactly 2 "heads"? In this case, the event is the following subset of S

   $$\mathsf{E} = \{\text{HHT, HTH, THH}\},$$

   which consists of 3 outcomes. Therefore, $P(\mathsf{E}) = \dfrac{3}{8}$.

Now that we're thinking of events as subsets of the sample space, we can state some important laws for computing probabilities. First, some definitions: If A and B are events in a probability space, then the statement "A or B" is equivalent to the event $A \cup B$, and the statement "A and B" is equivalent to the event $A \cap B$. Two events, A and B, are said to be **independent** if the occurrence of one does not influence (change the probability of) the occurrence of the other. Finally, two events, A and B, are **mutually exclusive** if the occurrence of one makes the occurrence of the other impossible; therefore, if A and B are mutually exclusive, then $P(A \cap B) = 0$.

1. $P(A \cup B) = P(A) + P(B) - P(A \cap B)$

2. A and B are independent if and only if $P(A \cap B) = P(A) \bullet P(B)$.

3. If A and B are mutually exclusive, then $P(A \cup B) = P(A) + P(B)$.

Example 7.17   A gambler throws two fair dice twice. Let A be the event that the first toss is a 7 or an 11, and let B be the event that the second toss is an 11. What's $P(A$ or $B)$?

Solution: The sample space, S, for each toss is the set of all ordered pairs (a, b) where a and b are any of the numbers 1 through 6, so S consists of $6^2 = 36$ possible outcomes, all of which are equally likely to occur. The event A is the subset of S that contains all ordered pairs (a, b) such that $a + b = 7$ or $a + b = 11$:

$$A = \{(1,6),\ (2,5),\ (3,4),\ (4,3),\ (5,2),\ (6,1),\ (5,6),\ (6,5)\},$$

which consists of 8 outcomes. This gives us $P(A) = \dfrac{8}{36}$. The event B is the subset of S that contains all ordered pairs (a, b) such that $a + b = 11$:

$$B = \{(5,6),\ (6,5)\},$$

which consists of 2 outcomes. This gives us $P(A) = \dfrac{2}{36}$. Since A and B are independent—contrary to popular belief, dice have no brains and therefore cannot store memories!—we know that $P(A$ and $B) = P(A) \cdot P(B)$. Therefore:

$$P(A \text{ or } B) = P(A) + P(B) - P(A \text{ and } B)$$

$$= \frac{8}{36} + \frac{2}{36} - \frac{8}{36} \cdot \frac{2}{36}$$

$$= \frac{43}{162}$$

Example 7.18   Let E be an algebra of sets on S that contains the sets A and B, on which a probability measure, P, is defined. Given that the events A and B^c are independent, where B^c represents the event that B does *not* occur, $P(A) = \dfrac{1}{4}$, and $P(B) = \dfrac{1}{3}$, what's $P(A$ or $B^c)$?

Solution: Because E is an algebra of sets that contains B, it also contains B^c. Since

$$1 = P(S) = P(B \cup B^c) = P(B) + P(B^c)$$

it must be true that $P(B^c) = 1 - P(B)$. Therefore:

$$P(A \text{ or } B^c) = P(A) + P(B^c) - P(A \text{ and } B^c)$$

$$= P(A) + P(B^c) - P(A) \cdot P(B^c)$$

$$= P(A) + [1 - P(B)] - P(A)[1 - P(B)]$$

$$= \frac{1}{4} + \frac{2}{3} - \frac{1}{4} \cdot \frac{2}{3}$$

$$= \frac{3}{4}$$

BERNOULLI TRIALS

Imagine flipping a coin five times. If the coin is fair, on every toss, the probability that the coin will come up heads ("H") is $p = \dfrac{1}{2}$, and the probability that it will come up tails ("T") is $q = 1 - p = \dfrac{1}{2}$. What's the probability that "heads" will come up exactly three times (and, therefore, "tails" exactly two times)? We'll first need to count how many ways we can get three heads (and two tails) in five tosses. This number is the binomial coefficient $\dbinom{5}{3}$. Therefore, the probability that we'll get three heads and two tails in our five tosses is:

$$\binom{5}{3} \bullet p^3 q^2 = \binom{5}{3} \bullet \left(\frac{1}{2}\right)^3 \left(\frac{1}{2}\right)^2 = \frac{5!}{3! \bullet 2!} \bullet \left(\frac{1}{2}\right)^5 = 10 \bullet \frac{1}{32} = \frac{5}{16}$$

This example illustrates the idea of a **sequence of Bernoulli trials**. A Bernoulli trial is an experiment in which there are only two possible outcomes, "success" and "failure," and for which one outcome does not affect the next outcome. For example, in the problem above, we thought of "H" as a success and "T" as a failure. The probability of a success is denoted by p, and the probability of a failure is denoted by q, which always equals $1 - p$. The probability of getting exactly k successes in n Bernoulli trials is given by the formula:

$$P(\text{exactly } k \text{ successes in } n \text{ trials}) = \binom{n}{k} \bullet p^k q^{n-k}$$

Example 7.19 A fair die is rolled 6 times. What's the probability of getting
  (a) exactly 2 fives?
  (b) no more than 2 fives?

Solution:

(a) The probability of a success (rolling a five) is $p = \dfrac{1}{6}$, and the probability of a failure (not rolling a five) is $q = \dfrac{5}{6}$. Therefore, the probability of getting exactly 2 fives in 6 rolls of the die is:

$$P(\text{exactly 2 successes in 6 trials}) = \binom{6}{2} \bullet p^2 q^{6-2} = \binom{6}{2} \bullet \left(\frac{1}{6}\right)^2 \left(\frac{5}{6}\right)^4$$

$$= \frac{6!}{2! \bullet 4!} \bullet \frac{5^4}{6^6} = 15 \bullet \frac{625}{46,656} \approx 0.16$$

(b) The probability of getting no more than 2 fives is equal to the sum of the probabilities of getting exactly 0 fives, 1 five, and 2 fives, which is:

$$\binom{6}{0} \bullet \left(\frac{1}{6}\right)^0 \left(\frac{5}{6}\right)^6 + \binom{6}{1} \bullet \left(\frac{1}{6}\right)^1 \left(\frac{5}{6}\right)^5 + \binom{6}{2} \bullet \left(\frac{1}{6}\right)^2 \left(\frac{5}{6}\right)^4$$

$$= \frac{5^6}{6^6} + 6 \bullet \frac{5^5}{6^6} + 15 \bullet \frac{5^4}{6^6}$$

$$= \frac{5^4 \left(5^2 + 6 \bullet 5 + 15\right)}{6^6}$$

$$= \frac{43,750}{46,656}$$

$$\approx 0.94$$

We'll mention that in a sequence of n Bernoulli trials (each with probability of success p), the most likely number of successes is $[p(n + 1)]$, the greatest integer less than or equal to $p(n + 1)$. If $p(n + 1)$ is actually an integer, then there are two most likely numbers of successes, $p(n + 1) - 1$ and $p(n + 1)$. For example, in 8 tosses of a fair die, the most likely number of fives is $[\frac{1}{6}(8 + 1)] = [\frac{3}{2}] = 1$.

RANDOM VARIABLES

Let $(S, \mathbf{E}, P)$ be a probability space with sample space S and probability measure P. We know that S consists of the possible outcomes of a trial (for example, the possible outcomes of throwing a die or a coin, selecting a card from a deck, etc.). A function $X: S \to \mathbf{R}$ is called a **random variable**. Therefore, to each outcome ω in S, the function X assigns some real number, $X(\omega)$.

Let t be a real number and consider the set:

$$\{\omega: X(\omega) \le t\}$$

This is a subset of S, and we'll assume that it's a member of the family $\mathbf{E}$; therefore, this subset is an event. We can associate a function, F_X, to the random variable X such that $F_X(t) = P(\{\omega: X(\omega) \le t\})$; this function F_X is called the **distribution function of X**. To simplify the notation, it's common to abbreviate the event $\{\omega: X(\omega) \le t\}$ by the statement $X(\omega) \le t$, or even just $X \le t$, so we'll usually write $F_X(t) = P(X \le t)$. By definition, the value of the distribution function at t gives the probability that the random variable will take on a value no greater than t, but the distribution function can also be used to give the probability that the random variable is bounded between two values, say t_1 and t_2. For example, notice that for any $t_1 < t_2$, the events $X \le t_1$ and $t_1 < X \le t_2$ are disjoint (after all, if $X(\omega) \le t_1$, then $X(\omega)$ can't be greater than t_1), and their union is the event $X \le t_2$. Therefore, $P(X \le t_2) = P(X \le t_1) + P(t_1 < X \le t_2)$, so:

$$P(t_1 < X \le t_2) = P(X \le t_2) - P(X \le t_1)$$

In terms of the distribution function, this equation translates into:

$$P(t_1 < X \le t_2) = F_X(t_2) - F_X(t_1)$$

[If we wanted to include the possibility that X can equal t_1, we'd simply add it on: $P(t_1 \le X \le t_2) = F_X(t_2) - F_X(t_1) + P(X = t_1)$, and if we wanted to exclude the possibility that X can equal t_2, we'd just subtract it: $P(t_1 < X < t_2) = F_X(t_2) - F_X(t_1) - P(X = t_2)$.] A necessary condition for a function F_X to be a distribution function is that $F_X(t) \to 0$ as $t \to -\infty$, and $F_X(t) \to 1$ as $t \to \infty$.

Example 7.20 Let X be a random variable whose distribution function is:

$$F_X(t) = \begin{cases} 0 & \text{for } t < 0 \\ 1 - e^{-2t} & \text{for } t \ge 0 \end{cases}$$

Find $P(X \le \frac{1}{2})$ and $P(\frac{1}{3} < X \le \frac{2}{3})$.

Solution: By definition, we know that $P(X \le \frac{1}{2}) = F_X(\frac{1}{2})$, so:

$$P(X \le \frac{1}{2}) = 1 - e^{-2(1/2)} = 1 - e^{-1} \approx 0.63$$

Next, since $P(\frac{1}{3} < X \le \frac{2}{3}) = P(X \le \frac{2}{3}) - P(X \le \frac{1}{3})$, we find that:

$$P(\frac{1}{3} < X \le \frac{2}{3}) = F_X(\frac{2}{3}) - F_X(\frac{1}{3}) = (1 - e^{-2(2/3)}) - (1 - e^{-2(1/3)}) = e^{-2/3} - e^{-4/3} \approx 0.25$$

In many cases, the random variable is defined so that the probability that X will equal any one particular number is zero; we'd only get nonzero probabilities by finding the probability that the value of X is in some interval. We call such a random variable (and its associated distribution function) **continuous**. The derivative of the distribution function, $f_X(t) = F'_X(t)$, is called the **probability density function of X** (or **of F_X**). The density function may be continuous, but we only really require it to be nonnegative and integrable, so that

$$F_X(t_2) - F_X(t_1) = \int_{t_1}^{t_2} f_X(t)dt$$

and that:

$$\int_{-\infty}^{\infty} f_X(t)dt = 1$$

Since $F_X(t) \to 0$ as $t \to -\infty$, we get the following important formula:

$$P(X \le t) = F_X(t) = \int_{-\infty}^{t} f_X(t)dt$$

In most problems, we're given the density function, $f_X(t)$, so it all comes down to this: To figure out the probability that the random variable, X, will be in some range of values, we integrate the density function over this range, since:

$$P(t_1 < X \le t_2) = \int_{t_1}^{t_2} f_X(t)dt$$

Notice that if X is continuous, the inequality signs on the left-hand side of this equation may be $<$ or $\le$, because the probability that X equals any one number is zero.

Example 7.21 A company hires a marketing consultant who determines that the length of time (in minutes) that a consumer spends on the company's Web site is a random variable, X, whose probability density function is:

$$f_X(t) = \begin{cases} 0 & \text{for } t < 0 \\ \frac{1}{6}e^{-t/6} & \text{for } t \ge 0 \end{cases}$$

What's the probability that a consumer will spend more than 10 minutes on the company's Web site?

Solution: The value of $P(X > 10)$ is equal to $1 - P(X \le 10)$, which we can figure out as follows:

$$P(X > 10) = 1 - P(X \le 10) = 1 - F_X(10) = 1 - \int_{-\infty}^{10} f_X(t)dt = 1 - \int_{0}^{10} \frac{1}{6}e^{-t/6}dt$$

$$= 1 - \left[-e^{-t/6}\right]_0^{10}$$

$$= e^{-10/6}$$

$$\approx 0.19$$

Expectation, Variance, and Standard Deviation

If X is a continuous random variable with probability density function f_X, we can define several quantities that are important in the statistical analysis of X. The **expectation** (or **mean**) of X, denoted by $E(X)$ or $\mu(X)$, is

$$E(X) = \mu(X) = \int_{-\infty}^{\infty} t f_X(t)\, dt$$

which gives us, intuitively, the average value of X. For example, if X is equal to the number rolled on a fair die—a discrete, rather than continuous random variable, but the idea's the same—the expectation of X is 3.5, which is just the average of the possible values—1, 2, 3, 4, 5, or 6—that X can have. The **variance** of X, denoted by either $\mathrm{Var}(X)$ or $\sigma^2(X)$, is:

$$\mathrm{Var}(X) = \sigma^2(X) = \int_{-\infty}^{\infty} [t - \mu(X)]^2 f_X(t)\, dt$$

The variance tells us about the spread of values of X from the mean (that is, from the expectation): The smaller the variance, the smaller the probability that the value of a random variable will stray far from its mean. Finally, another way to analyze the deviation of X from its mean is to compute the **standard deviation** of X. This is simply the (nonnegative) square root of the variance:

$$\text{standard deviation of } X\colon\ \sigma(X) = \sqrt{\sigma^2(X)}$$

This is the reason for the alternate notation, $\sigma^2(X)$, for the variance of X.

Example 7.22   Let X be a random variable whose probability density function is:

$$f(x) = \begin{cases} 0 & \text{if } x \le 0 \\ \frac{1}{4}x^3 & \text{if } 0 < x < 2 \\ 0 & \text{if } x \ge 2 \end{cases}$$

What's the standard deviation of X?

Solution: First, we'll need to figure out the mean of X:

$$\mu(X) = \int_{-\infty}^{\infty} t f(t)\, dt = \int_0^2 t \cdot \tfrac{1}{4} t^3\, dt = \tfrac{1}{4} \int_0^2 t^4\, dt = \tfrac{1}{4}\left[\tfrac{1}{5} t^5 \right]_0^2 = \tfrac{8}{5}$$

Now, we can find the variance:

$$\sigma^2(X) = \int_{-\infty}^{\infty} [t - \mu(X)]^2 f(t)\, dt$$

$$= \int_0^2 (t - \tfrac{8}{5})^2 \cdot \tfrac{1}{4} t^3\, dt$$

$$= \tfrac{1}{4} \int_0^2 (t^5 - \tfrac{16}{5} t^4 + \tfrac{64}{25} t^3)\, dt$$

$$= \tfrac{1}{4} \left[\tfrac{1}{6} t^6 - \tfrac{16}{25} t^5 + \tfrac{16}{25} t^4 \right]_0^2$$

$$= \tfrac{1}{4} \left[t^4 (\tfrac{1}{6} t^2 - \tfrac{16}{25} t + \tfrac{16}{25}) \right]_0^2$$

$$= \tfrac{1}{4} \cdot 16 \left[\tfrac{1}{6} \cdot 2^2 - \tfrac{16}{25} \cdot 2 + \tfrac{16}{25} \right]$$

$$= \tfrac{8}{75}$$

The standard deviation of X is the square root of the variance:

$$\sigma(X) = \sqrt{\sigma^2(X)} = \sqrt{\frac{8}{75}} = \frac{2\sqrt{2}}{5\sqrt{3}} = \frac{2\sqrt{2}}{5\sqrt{3}} \cdot \frac{\sqrt{3}}{\sqrt{3}} = \frac{2\sqrt{6}}{15}$$

The Normal Distribution

Statisticians analyze random variables that describe a variety of measurements—the length of long-distance phone calls, the lifetime of machine parts (and of people), the distribution of student grades in a large lecture, etc. Many such measurements obey a probability distribution known as the normal distribution; because of the wide range of applicability of normal distribution, it's the most important distribution function for a random variable.

A random variable, X, is said to be **normally distributed** if its probability density function has the form:

$$f_X(t) = \frac{1}{\sigma\sqrt{2\pi}} e^{-(t-\mu)^2/2\sigma^2}$$

The choice of parameters was no accident; σ is the standard deviation of X, and μ is its mean. The graph of f_X is the familiar "bell-curve."

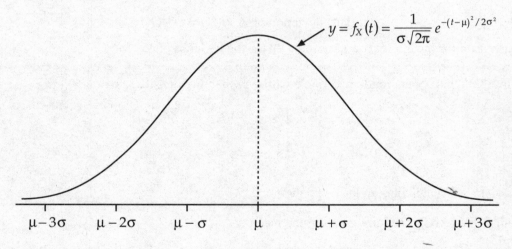

As is the case with any other density function, the total area under the graph is equal to 1. This graph is symmetric with respect to the vertical line $t = \mu$, so the line cuts the region below the graph exactly in half; the area to the left of $t = \mu$ is equal to $\frac{1}{2}$, and the area to the right of $t = \mu$ is also $\frac{1}{2}$. To figure out the probability that the value of a normally distributed random variable, X, will be in some range of values, we'd integrate the normal density function over the range:

$$P(t_1 < X \le t_2) = \int_{t_1}^{t_2} \frac{1}{\sigma\sqrt{2\pi}} e^{-(t-\mu)^2/2\sigma^2}\, dt$$

where t_1 and t_2 are any extended real numbers such that $t_1 < t_2$.

Since this integral cannot be expressed in closed form in terms of elementary functions, it must be integrated numerically. To put the general density function into a standard form—for which tables of values exist—we make the change of variable $u = (t - \mu)/\sigma$, and set $\sigma = 1$ to obtain the **standard normal probability density**:

$$f_Z(u) = \frac{1}{\sqrt{2\pi}} e^{-u^2/2}$$

for the standardized normal random variable, Z. This random variable is normally distributed with mean 0 and standard deviation 1, and it's related to the original random variable, X, by the equation:

$$P(t_1 < X \le t_2) = P\left(\frac{t_1 - \mu}{\sigma} < Z \le \frac{t_2 - \mu}{\sigma} \right)$$

The integral of $f_Z(u)$ gives the standard normal probability distribution, which is commonly denoted by Φ:

$$\Phi(z) = \int_{-\infty}^{z} \frac{1}{\sqrt{2\pi}} e^{-u^2/2} \, du$$

Then, if z_1 and z_2 are any two extended real numbers, with $z_1 < z_2$, we get:

$$P(z_1 < Z \le z_2) = \Phi(z_2) - \Phi(z_1)$$

Remember that since Z is a continuous random variable, the inequality signs on the left-hand side of this equation may be $<$ or $\le$, because the probability that X equals any one particular value is zero.

Example 7.23   The heights of the female employees in a large company are normally distributed, with mean 168 cm and standard deviation 7 cm. What's the probability that a female employee selected at random will be taller than 180 cm?

Solution: Let H be the random variable that measures the employees' heights. We'll transform this question about H into the corresponding question about the *standard* normal random variable, Z:

$$P(H > 180) = P\left(Z > \frac{180 - 168}{7} \right) = P(Z > 1.71) = 1 - P(Z \le 1.71) = 1 - \Phi(1.71)$$

A table of values for $\Phi(z)$ gives $\Phi(1.71) = 0.956$, so $P(H > 180) = 0.044 = 4.4\%$.

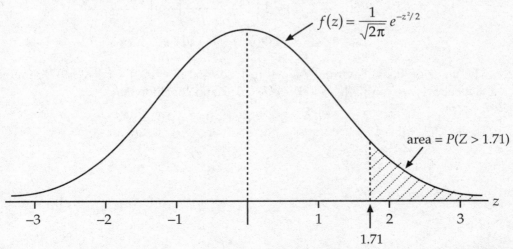

$$f(z) = \frac{1}{\sqrt{2\pi}} e^{-z^2/2}$$

area = $P(Z > 1.71)$

1.71

The Normal Approximation to the Binomial Distribution

In Example 7.19, we answered a question about a sequence of n Bernoulli trials. A random variable, X, used to describe such an experiment is said to have a **binomial distribution**; it's a **discrete** (rather than continuous) random variable and, in this case, if the probability of a success is p and the probability of a failure is $q = 1 - p$, then:

$$P(a_1 \le X \le a_2) = \sum_{k=a_1}^{a_2} \binom{n}{k} p^k q^{n-k}$$

If n is large, it can be quite difficult to evaluate the right-hand side of this equation. Instead, we can use the normal distribution to approximate it. The mean of X, μ, is np, and the standard deviation, σ, is $\sqrt{npq}$. It can be shown that:

$$P(a_1 \le X \le a_2) \approx \Phi\left(\frac{a_2 - \mu + \frac{1}{2}}{\sigma}\right) - \Phi\left(\frac{a_1 - \mu - \frac{1}{2}}{\sigma}\right)$$

Because it's helpful to memorize $\Phi(z)$ for various values of z, here's a brief table:

z	0	0.5	1	1.5	2	2.5	3 or more
$\Phi(z)$	0.5	0.69	0.84	0.93	0.97	0.99	≈ 1

To handle negative values of z, notice that, by the symmetry of the normal density function, it's always true that $\Phi(-z) = 1 - \Phi(z)$.

Example 7.24   A fair coin is flipped 100 times. What's the probability of getting between 60 and 70 "heads"?

Solution: We're asked to figure out $P(60 \le X \le 70)$, where X has a binomial distribution with $n = 100$ and $p = q = \dfrac{1}{2}$; this probability is equal to the value of the expression:

$$\sum_{k=60}^{70} \binom{100}{k} \left(\frac{1}{2}\right)^k \left(\frac{1}{2}\right)^{100-k}$$

We'll approximate this using the normal distribution. The mean of X is $\mu = (100)(\frac{1}{2}) = 50$, and its standard deviation is $\sigma = \sqrt{100(\frac{1}{2})(\frac{1}{2})} = 5$. Therefore:

$$P(60 \le X \le 70) \approx \Phi\left(\frac{70 - 50 + \frac{1}{2}}{5}\right) - \Phi\left(\frac{60 - 50 - \frac{1}{2}}{5}\right)$$
$$= \Phi(4.1) - \Phi(1.9)$$

The value of $\Phi(4.1)$ is virtually equal to 1, so $P(60 \le X \le 70) \approx 1 - \Phi(1.9)$. From our brief table above, we can write $\Phi(1.9) \approx \Phi(2) \approx 0.97$ and conclude that:

$$P(60 \le X \le 70) \approx 1 - 0.97 = 0.03 = 3\%$$

POINT-SET TOPOLOGY

INTRODUCTION

The subject of point-set topology provides a rigorous foundation for many of the advanced topics in mathematics. While proving theorems is an important part of most college courses in topology, the GRE doesn't expect you to provide proofs; instead, it will test you on your knowledge of many of the definitions in basic general topology and the statements of a few theorems. For this reason, we'll concentrate on stating the definitions and theorems and illustrating them with examples.

Let X be a nonempty set. A **topology on X**, denoted by T, is a family of subsets of X, for which the following three properties always hold true:

1. $\varnothing$ and X are in T.

2. If O_1 and O_2 are in T, so is their intersection, $O_1 \cap O_2$.

3. If $\{O_i\}_{i \in I}$ is any collection of sets from T, then their union, $\bigcup_{i \in I} O_i$, is also in T.

Conditions 2 and 3 say that a topology is always closed under finite intersections and arbitrary unions. The sets in T are known as **open sets**, and this is why we used the letter O to denote them. If $x \in X$ and N is a subset of X such that there exists an open set O with $x \in O \subseteq N$, then we say that N is a **neighborhood** of x. If O is an open set, then its complement, $O^c = X - O$, is called a **closed set**. (Note: In this section, we'll never use the alternate notation O' to denote the complement of O; this is because the use of a prime is a standard notation for something else in topology.) A set X together with a topology T on X, (X, T), is called a **topological space**. When the topology on X is understood, it's common to simply refer to "the topological space X," rather than "the topological space (X, T)." There's a rather weak condition that's usually imposed on topological spaces. We say that (X, T) is a **Hausdorff space** if for every pair of distinct points, x and y, in X, there exist *disjoint* open sets, O_x and O_y, such that $x \in O_x$ and $y \in O_y$.

If X is any nonempty set, then the collection $\{\varnothing, X\}$ is always a topology on X. It's called the **indiscrete** or **trivial topology**. At the other extreme, the power set of X, $\mathsf{P}(X)$, which consists of *all* subsets of X, is always a topology as well; it's called the **discrete topology**. If T_1 and T_2 are topologies on X, then we say that T_1 is **finer** than T_2 (or, equivalently, that T_2 is **coarser** than T_1) if $\mathsf{T}_1 \supseteq \mathsf{T}_2$. Therefore, the discrete topology is the finest topology a set X can have, and the trivial topology is the coarsest.

Here's an example. Let X be the set $\{a, b, c, d\}$, and let T_1 be the following collection of subsets of X:

$$\mathsf{T}_1 = \left\{\varnothing, \{a, b\}, \{c, d\}, X\right\}$$

Then T_1 is a topology on X. The collection

$$\mathsf{A} = \left\{\varnothing, \{a\}, \{a, b\}, \{c, d\}, X\right\}$$

is *not* a topology on X because, although $\{a\}$ and $\{c, d\}$ are in A, their union, $\{a, c, d\}$, is not. However, if we were to include this subset in A, the resulting collection,

$$\mathsf{T}_2 = \left\{\varnothing, \{a\}, \{a, b\}, \{c, d\}, \{a, c, d\}, X\right\}$$

is a topology on X, and one that's finer than T_1.

Let's now turn to a more interesting and useful example. In the set $X = \mathbf{R}$, the set of real numbers, let's declare a subset O of $\mathbf{R}$ to be open if, for every x in O, there exists some positive number, ε, such that every x' that satisfies the inequality $|x - x'| < \varepsilon$ is also in O. Then the resulting collection of open sets is a topology on $\mathbf{R}$. The empty set is open, since it satisfies the condition *vacuously* (that is, there's no x in $\varnothing$ that *doesn't* satisfy the condition), and the entire set $\mathbf{R}$ certainly satisfies the condition (since it contains every x in $\mathbf{R}$). Next, we'll check that this topology satisfies property 2. Let O_1 and O_2 be open sets, and consider the intersection, $O_1 \cap O_2$. If their intersection is empty, we're done; otherwise, let x be a point in $O_1 \cap O_2$. Then x is in O_1, which means that there exists some positive number, ε_1, such that $|x - x'| < \varepsilon_1$ for every x' in O_1; similarly, since x is also in O_2, there exists some positive number, ε_2, such that $|x - x'| < \varepsilon_2$ for every x' in O_2. Now, let ε be the smaller of ε_1 and ε_2; then all those points x' that satisfy $|x - x'| < \varepsilon$ will be in both O_1 and O_2 and thus in $O_1 \cap O_2$. This tells us that $O_1 \cap O_2$ is open. Finally, let's verify that property 3 is satisfied: If $\{O_i\}_{i \in I}$ is any collection of open sets, let x be a point in $\cup_{i \in I} O_i$. By definition, x must belong to at least one of the sets—let's call it O_x—in $\{O_i\}_{i \in I}$. Therefore, there exists some positive number, ε, such that every x' that satisfies the inequality $|x - x'| < \varepsilon$ is also in O_x, and, consequently, is also in $\cup_{i \in I} O_i$. With this topology, $\mathbf{R}$ is called the **real line**.

Earlier in this chapter, in the section on Set Theory, we mentioned that the set

$$(a, b) = \left\{ x \in \mathbf{R} : a < x < b \right\}$$

is called an *open* interval. We'll now see that it is indeed open in this topology on $\mathbf{R}$. Choose any point x in the interval (a, b), and let ε be the smaller of the numbers $x - a$ and $b - x$; then (a, b) contains every point x' that satisfies the inequality $|x - x'| < \varepsilon$, so (a, b) is open. In particular, the sets $(-\infty, a)$ and (b, ∞) are open sets, so their union, $(-\infty, a) \cup (b, \infty)$, is also open. The set $[a, b]$ is the complement of this union, so it's closed in this topology on $\mathbf{R}$, which agrees with our earlier statement that $[a, b]$ is called a closed interval.

THE SUBSPACE TOPOLOGY

If (X, T) is a topological space, we can use T to define a topology on any subset, S, of X as follows: A subset U of S is said to be **open in S** if U is equal to $O \cap S$, where O is open in X. This topology on S, denoted by T_S, is called the **subspace** (or **relative**) **topology**, and S is called a **subspace** of X. It's important to notice that a subset of S may be open in S (that is, a member of the subspace topology, T_S) but *not* open in X (that is, not a member of the topology T). For example, let $S = [0, 2)$ in $\mathbf{R}$. Then the set $U = [0, 1)$ is open in S, because, for example,

$$[0, 1) = (-1, 1) \cap [0, 2)$$

That is, $U = O \cap S$, where $O = (-1, 1)$ is an open set in $\mathbf{R}$. However, U is not open in $\mathbf{R}$ (with its standard topology), because $[0, 1)$ contains the point 0, and no matter how small we make the positive number ε, the set of all x' such that $|x' - 0| < \varepsilon$ is not contained in U. But we can say that if S is itself open in X, then every set that's open in S is also open in X.

THE INTERIOR, EXTERIOR, BOUNDARY, LIMIT POINTS, AND CLOSURE OF A SET

Let (X, T) be a topological space, and let A be a (not necessarily open) subset of X. The **interior of A**, denoted by int(A), is the union of all open sets contained within A, or, equivalently, it's the largest open set contained in A. The **exterior of A**, denoted by ext(A), is the union of all open sets that do not intersect A. (We say that a set U **intersects** A if $U \cap A \neq \varnothing$.) The exterior of A can also be described as the interior of the complement of A. The **boundary of A**, denoted by bd(A), is the set of all x in X such that every open set containing x intersects both A and the complement of A. A point x in X is called a **limit** (or **accumulation** or **cluster**) **point of** A if every open set that contains x also contains at least one point of A, other than x. The set of all the limit points of A is called the **derived set** of A and is denoted A' (not to be confused with the complement of A). Finally, the **closure of** A, denoted by cl(A), can be defined in two equivalent ways: It's equal to the union int(A) $\cup$ bd(A), and it's also equal to the union $A \cup A'$. The set A is closed if and only if it contains all of its boundary points and all of its limit points. Now, let's look at some examples to illustrate all these definitions.

1. Let A be the subset $(1, 2]$ in **R**:

Then we have:

$$\text{int}(A) = (1, 2)$$

$$\text{ext}(A) = (-\infty, 1) \cup (2, \infty)$$

$$\text{bd}(A) = \{1, 2\}$$

$$A' = [1, 2]$$

$$\text{cl}(A) = [1, 2]$$

2. Let A be the subset $(0, 1) \cup (1, 2)$ in **R**:

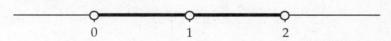

In this case:

$$\text{int}(A) = (0, 1) \cup (1, 2) = A$$

$$\text{ext}(A) = (-\infty, 0) \cup (2, \infty)$$

$$\text{bd}(A) = \{0, 1, 2\}$$

$$A' = [0, 2]$$

$$\text{cl}(A) = [0, 2]$$

3. Let **Z** be the set of integers in **R**:

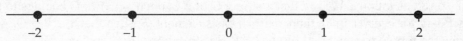

Then we have:

$$\text{int}(\mathbf{Z}) = \varnothing$$

$$\text{ext}(\mathbf{Z}) = \bigcup_{n \in \mathbf{Z}} (n-1, n)$$

$$\text{bd}(\mathbf{Z}) = \mathbf{Z}$$

$$\mathbf{Z}' = \varnothing$$

$$\text{cl}(\mathbf{Z}) = \mathbf{Z}$$

4. Let A be the subset $(0, 1) \cup \{2\} \cup [3, 4]$ in $\mathbf{R}$:

Then we have:

$$\text{int}(A) = (0, 1) \cup (3, 4)$$

$$\text{ext}(A) = (-\infty, 0) \cup (1, 2) \cup (2, 3) \cup (4, \infty)$$

$$\text{bd}(A) = \{0, 1, 2, 3, 4\}$$

$$A' = [0, 1] \cup [3, 4]$$

$$\text{cl}(A) = [0, 1] \cup \{2\} \cup [3, 4]$$

Notice here that 2 is a boundary point, but not a limit point, of A. In order for 2 to be a limit point of A, every open set containing 2 would need to contain a point of A other than 2 itself. But the open set $\left(\dfrac{3}{2}, \dfrac{5}{2}\right)$, for example, contains no point of A except 2.

BASIS FOR A TOPOLOGY

Let X be a nonempty set, and let B be a collection of subsets of X that satisfies the following properties:

1. For every x in X, there is at least one set B in B such that $x \in B$.

2. If B_1 and B_2 are sets in B and $x \in B_1 \cap B_2$, then there exists a set B_3 in B such that $x \in B_3 \subseteq B_1 \cap B_2$.

The collection B is called a **basis**, and the sets in B are known as **basis elements**. A basis is used to generate a topology, T, on X, as follows. We say that a subset O of X is open—that is, O belongs to the **topology generated by** B—if, for every x in O, there exists a basis element, B, such that $x \in B \subseteq O$. An equivalent way to describe the topology generated by the basis B is to say that the topology consists of all possible unions of basis elements.

For example, the collection $\mathsf{B} = \{(a, b) \subseteq \mathbf{R}: a < b\}$ of all open intervals of $\mathbf{R}$ is a basis for the **standard topology** on $\mathbf{R}$ (that is, the topology we described above). We can define another topology on $\mathbf{R}$ by using a different basis. Let:

$$\mathsf{B}' = \big\{[a, b): a,\ b \in \mathbf{R} \text{ and } a < b\big\}$$

The topology generated by this basis is called the **lower-limit topology** on $\mathbf{R}$. The interval $[0, 1)$ is open in the lower-limit topology, but not in the standard topology, on $\mathbf{R}$. Also, the lower-limit topology is finer than the standard topology; in fact, if we let T denote the standard topology on $\mathbf{R}$, and T_L the lower-limit topology, then $\mathsf{T}_\mathrm{L} \supseteq \mathsf{T}$, but $\mathsf{T}_\mathrm{L} \neq \mathsf{T}$, which shows that T_L is *strictly* finer than T. Every subset of $\mathbf{R}$ that's open in T is open in T_L, but not vice versa.

THE PRODUCT TOPOLOGY

If $(X,\ \mathsf{T}_X)$ and $(Y,\ \mathsf{T}_Y)$ are topological spaces, there's a standard way to define a topology on the cartesian product, $X \times Y$. If we let

$$\mathsf{B} = \big\{O_X \times O_Y: O_X \in \mathsf{T}_X \text{ and } O_Y \in \mathsf{T}_Y\big\}$$

then the topology generated by this basis B is called the **product topology** on $X \times Y$.

Example 7.25   Which of the following subsets of $\mathbf{R}^2 = \mathbf{R} \times \mathbf{R}$ are open in the product topology?
  (a) The interior of the unit circle (boundary not included)
  (b) The line $y = x$
  (c) The set $(1, 2] \times (1, 2)$

Solution: Notice that sets of the form $(x_a,\ x_b) \times (y_a,\ y_b)$—called **open rectangles**—are open in the product topology on $\mathbf{R}^2$.

(a)   The interior of the unit circle is open in $\mathbf{R}^2$; the following diagram shows a typical point contained within an open set:

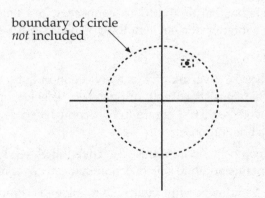

boundary of circle
not included

If the boundary of the circle *were* included, the region would be a closed set.

(b)   For no point p on the line can we find an open rectangle containing p that is a subset of the line. Therefore, the line is not an open set in $\mathbf{R}^2$.

(c)   Because the given set contains part of its boundary, the set cannot be open. (It's not closed either, because it doesn't contain *all* of its boundary points.)

CONNECTEDNESS

Let (X, T) be a topological space. If there exist disjoint, nonempty open sets, O_1 and O_2, such that $O_1 \cup O_2 = X$, then X is said to be **disconnected**. On the other hand, if T contains no pair of subsets of X that are disjoint and whose union is X, then X is said to be a **connected** space. If S is a subspace of X, then S is disconnected if it's possible to find two open subsets of X, A and B, such that $S \subseteq A \cup B$, and both $A \cap S$ and $B \cap S$ are disjoint and nonempty; otherwise, it's connected.

For example, the real line, **R**, is a connected space, and every interval in **R** is connected; in fact, the intervals are the *only* connected subspaces of **R**. Our intuition tells us that the subspace $S = (0, 1) \cup [2, 4]$ is disconnected, because it consists of two separate pieces. We can check that this is true by using the definition above. Let $A = (0, 1)$ and $B = \left(\dfrac{3}{2}, \dfrac{9}{2}\right)$, which are both open; then $S \subseteq A \cup B$, and both $A \cap S$ and $B \cap S$ are disjoint and nonempty. Here's a trickier example: Is $S = [2, 4)$ a connected subspace of **R** in the lower-limit topology? Well, the set S seems to be one piece and is connected as a subspace of **R** in its standard topology, but it's not connected as a subspace of **R** in the lower-limit topology. If we let $A = [2, 3)$ and $B = [3, 4)$, we notice that A and B are open and disjoint, and that their union is S.

The following can be used to identify connected spaces:

1. If A and B are connected and they intersect, then their union is also connected. (This result also holds true for any number of connected sets, as long as their intersection is nonempty.)

2. Let A be a connected set, and let B be any set such that $A \subseteq B \subseteq \mathrm{cl}(A)$. Then B is connected.

3. The cartesian product of connected spaces is connected.

4. Let X be a topological space with the property that any two points, x_1 and x_2, in X can be joined by a continuous path. This means that there exists a continuous function $p: [0, 1] \; X$ such that $p(0) = x_1$ and $p(1) = x_2$. Then X is said to be **path-connected**, and any path-connected space is connected. Interestingly, the converse is not true. There are connected spaces that are not path-connected.

Statement 3 can be used to show that $\mathbf{R}^2$ and $\mathbf{R}^3$ are connected, and statement 4 can be used to show that any convex set (such as the interior of a circle in $\mathbf{R}^2$ or a sphere in $\mathbf{R}^3$) is connected.

COMPACTNESS

Let (X, T) be a topological space. A **covering** of X is a collection of subsets of X whose union is X; an **open covering** is a covering that consists entirely of open sets. If every open covering of X contains a *finite* subcollection that also covers X, then X is said to be a **compact** space. Let's look at some examples to illuminate this rather abstract definition.

1. The real line, **R**, is not compact, because the open covering $\mathsf{A} = \left\{ A_n : n \in \mathbf{Z} \right\}$, where $A_n = (n-1, n+1)$, contains no finite subcollection that can cover all of **R**.

2. Any topological space X endowed with the trivial topology is compact, because the only open sets are $\varnothing$ and X, and the finite collection $\{X\}$ covers X.

3. The open interval $I = (0, 1)$ in **R** is not compact. Consider the collection of open subsets $\mathsf{A} = \left\{ A_n : n = 3, 4, \ldots \right\}$, where $A_n = (\frac{1}{n}, 1 - \frac{1}{n})$. Every point of I is in some A_n, so A is an open covering of I. However, no finite subcollection of A can also cover I. To see why this is, assume that there was a finite subcollection of A that covered I; of the intervals A_n in this finite subcollection, choose the one with the largest value of n; let's call it A_N. Then A_N contains all the other intervals A_n in this subcollection, but does not contain any of the points in the subinterval $(0, \frac{1}{N}]$ or in the subinterval $[1 - \frac{1}{N}, 1)$. This shows that the entire interval I cannot be covered by any finite subcollection of A.

4. In contrast to the preceding result, the *closed* interval $I = [0, 1]$ in **R** *is* compact. To see why, let $\{O_\alpha\}$ be an open covering of I, and define b as the largest number in I such that the interval $[0, b]$ can be covered by a finite subcollection of $\{O_\alpha\}$. (To be more precise, b should be defined as the least upper bound of the set of x's such that $[0, x]$ can be covered by a finite subcollection of $\{O_\alpha\}$.) If we can show that b is not less than 1, then we'll have shown that the entire interval $[0, 1]$ can be covered by a finite subcollection of $\{O_\alpha\}$, which would prove that $[0, 1]$ is compact. So, suppose that $b < 1$; now we'll derive a contradiction. Since $\{O_\alpha\}$ covers all of I, there must be at least one set in the covering that contains b; let's choose one and call it O_β. Since O_β is open, it must contain an open interval of the form $(b - \varepsilon, b + \varepsilon)$ for some positive number ε. Now, because we defined b as the largest x in $[0, 1]$ for which $[0, x]$ can be covered by a finite subcollection of $\{O_\alpha\}$, the number $b - \dfrac{\varepsilon}{2}$ is less than b, so the interval $[0, b - \dfrac{\varepsilon}{2}]$ can certainly be covered by a finite subcollection of $\{O_\alpha\}$. But then simply adjoining the set O_b to this finite subcollection gives us a finite subcollection that covers $[0, b + \dfrac{\varepsilon}{2}]$, which contradicts our definition of b.

The following can be used to identify compact spaces:

1. Let X be a compact topological space, and let S be a subset of X. If S is closed, then it's compact. The converse (compact subsets are closed) is true if X is Hausdorff.

2. The cartesian product of compact spaces is compact.

We'll close this section with what is perhaps the most commonly used result in identifying a compact set. First, a couple of definitions. We define the **norm** of a point $\mathbf{x} = (x_1, x_2, \ldots, x_n)$ in $\mathbf{R}^n$ as the real number:

$$\|\mathbf{x}\| = \sqrt{(x_1)^2 + (x_2)^2 + \cdots + (x_n)^2}$$

This is just the magnitude of the vector joining the origin, **O**, to the point **x**. A subset A of $\mathbf{R}^n$ is said to be **bounded** if there exists some positive number M such that the norm of every point in A is less than M. (This means that A is entirely contained within the sphere of radius M, centered at the origin.)

3. **Heine–Borel theorem:** A subset of $\mathbf{R}^n$ (in the standard topology) is compact if and only if it's both closed and bounded.

Notice that with this result, we could immediately say that the interval $(0, 1)$ is not compact (because it's not closed), but that the interval $[0, 1]$ is compact.

METRIC SPACES

Let X be a nonempty set, and let $d: X \times X \to \mathbf{R}$ be a real-valued function defined on ordered pairs of points in X. This function d is said to be a **metric on** X if the following properties hold true for all x, y, and z in X:

1. $d(x, y) \geq 0$, and $d(x, y) = 0$ if and only if $x = y$

2. $d(x, y) = d(y, x)$

3. $d(x, z) \leq d(x, y) + d(y, z)$

We call $d(x, y)$ the **distance** between x and y. A set X, together with a metric on X, is called a **metric space**. If ε is a positive number, then the set:

$$B_d(x, \varepsilon) = \left\{ x' \in X : d(x, x') < \varepsilon \right\}$$

is called an ε-**ball**, the (**open**) **ball of radius** ε **centered on** x.

Every metric space can be given the structure of a topological space. The collection of all ε-balls,

$$\mathsf{B} = \left\{ B_d(x, \varepsilon) : x \in X,\ \varepsilon > 0 \right\}$$

is a basis for a topology on X, called the **metric topology** (**induced by** d). In this topology, a subset O of X is open if and only if every point in O is the center of some ε-ball entirely contained within O; that is, O is open if for every x in O, there's some positive number, ε_x, such that $B_d(x, \varepsilon_x) \subseteq O$.

The euclidean spaces $\mathbf{R}$, $\mathbf{R}^2$, $\mathbf{R}^3$, etc. are all metric spaces. If we define the **euclidean metric** on $\mathbf{R}^n$ as

$$d(\mathbf{x}, \mathbf{x}') = \|\mathbf{x} - \mathbf{x}'\| = \sqrt{(x_1 - x_1')^2 + (x_2 - x_2')^2 + \cdots + (x_n - x_n')^2}$$

it can be shown that the metric topology induced by the euclidean metric, as well as by the simpler metric,

$$\sigma(\mathbf{x}, \mathbf{x}') = \max\left\{ |x_1 - x_1'|,\ |x_2 - x_2'|,\ \ldots,\ |x_n - x_n'| \right\}$$

(called the **square metric**, because the ε-balls $B_\sigma(\mathbf{x}, \varepsilon)$ in $\mathbf{R}^2$ are actually squares), gives the standard topology on $\mathbf{R}^n$.

CONTINUOUS FUNCTIONS

We've already discussed the idea of what it means for a function $f: \mathbf{R} \to \mathbf{R}$ to be continuous; in this section, we'll generalize the definition to functions between arbitrary topological spaces.

Let's first review the definition of continuity for a function $f: \mathbf{R} \to \mathbf{R}$. We say that f is continuous at the point x_0 if, for every $\varepsilon > 0$ (no matter how small), there exists a $\delta > 0$ such that:

$$|x - x_0| < \delta \quad \Rightarrow \quad |f(x) - f(x_0)| < \varepsilon$$

Now, let's generalize this to metric spaces. Let (X_1, d_1) and (X_2, d_2) be metric spaces. A function $f: X_1 \to X_2$ is said to be **continuous at the point** x_0 if, for every $\varepsilon > 0$ (no matter how small), there exists a $\delta > 0$ such that:

$$d_1(x, x_0) < \delta \quad \Rightarrow \quad d_2(f(x), f(x_0)) < \varepsilon$$

If f is continuous at every x_0 in X_1, then we simply say that f is **continuous**. Notice that in $\mathbf{R}$, the euclidean metric is $d(x, x') = |x - x'|$, so this definition is the same as the previous one, in the case of a function $f: \mathbf{R} \to \mathbf{R}$.

Based on our discussion of the metric topology, we can formulate the definition of a continuous function between metric spaces in another way. We can say that $f: X_1 \to X_2$ is **continuous at the point** x_0 if for every open set, O, containing $f(x_0)$, the inverse image, $f^{-1}(O)$, is an open set containing x_0. Now, let O be an open set in X_2 that contains $f(x_0)$, and choose an ε-ball, $B_{d_2}(f(x_0), \varepsilon)$, centered on $f(x_0)$ and contained in O. $f^{-1}\left(B_{d_2}(f(x_0), \varepsilon) \right)$ is open and contains x_0, so it must contain some open ball, $B_{d_1}(x_0, \delta)$, centered on x_0. Therefore, for any x such that $d_1(x, x_0) < \delta$, we have $d_2(f(x), f(x_0)) < \varepsilon$, which matches the condition for continuity given above.

We're now ready for the final generalization. Let (X_1, T_1) and (X_2, T_2) be topological spaces; we say that the function (or **map**) $f\colon X_1 \to X_2$ is **continuous** if, for every open set, O, in X_2 (that is, for every $O \in \mathsf{T}_2$), the inverse image, $f^{-1}(O)$, is open in X_1 (that is, $f^{-1}(O) \in \mathsf{T}_1$). In particular, f is **continuous at the point** x_0 if for every open set O in X_2 containing $f(x_0)$, there's an open set O_1 containing x_0 such that $f(O_1) \subseteq O$. If the topology of the range space, T_2, is generated by a basis, $\mathbf{B}$, then, to check whether $f\colon (X_1, \mathsf{T}_1) \to (X_2, \mathsf{T}_2)$ is continuous, it's sufficient to check that the inverse image of every basis element $B \in \mathbf{B}$ is open in X_1.

To illustrate this abstract definition, our first few examples will be of real-valued functions defined on $\mathbf{R}$, with which you're comfortable.

1. Let $f\colon \mathbf{R} \to \mathbf{R}$ be the function:

$$f(x) = \begin{cases} -2 & \text{if } x < 0 \\ +2 & \text{if } x \geq 0 \end{cases}$$

Consider the open set $O = (1, 3)$, which contains the point $f(0) = 2$. The inverse image of O is the set $[0, \infty)$, which is not open. Therefore, the topological definition tells us that f is not continuous at $x = 0$.

2. Let $f\colon \mathbf{R} \to \mathbf{R}$ be the function:

$$f(x) = \begin{cases} x & \text{if } x \neq 1 \\ 3 & \text{if } x = 1 \end{cases}$$

Consider the open set $O = (2, 4)$, which contains the point $f(1) = 3$. The inverse image of O is the set $f^{-1}(O) = \{1\} \cup (2, 4)$, which is not open. This tells us that f is not continuous at $x = 1$.

3. Let $f\colon \mathbf{R} \to \mathbf{R}$ be the function $f(x) = x^2$. If $y \geq 0$, then every basis element containing y is of the form $B = (y - \varepsilon_1, y + \varepsilon_2)$, where ε_1 and ε_2 are positive numbers. If $y - \varepsilon_1$ is positive, then

$$f^{-1}(B) = \left(-\sqrt{y + \varepsilon_2}, -\sqrt{y - \varepsilon_1}\right) \cup \left(\sqrt{y - \varepsilon_1}, \sqrt{y + \varepsilon_2}\right)$$

which is open. If $y - \varepsilon_1 \leq 0$, then

$$f^{-1}(B) = \left(-\sqrt{y + \varepsilon_2}, \sqrt{y + \varepsilon_2}\right)$$

which is also open. Therefore, f is continuous.

4. If X and Y are topological spaces and X is given the discrete topology, then *every* function $f\colon X \to Y$ is continuous. Given any open set O in Y, the inverse image $f^{-1}(O)$ is automatically open in X because *every* set is open in X. Similarly, if X and Y are topological spaces and Y is given the trivial (indiscrete) topology, then *every* function $f\colon X \to Y$ is continuous. The only sets that are open in Y are $\varnothing$ and Y itself, and $f^{-1}(\varnothing) = \varnothing$ and $f^{-1}(Y) = X$, both of which are open in X.

5. Let $i: (\mathbf{R}, \mathsf{T}) \to (\mathbf{R}, \mathsf{T}_L)$ be the identity function, $i(x) = x$ for all x, from $\mathbf{R}$ to itself, where the domain is $\mathbf{R}$, with its standard topology and the range is $\mathbf{R}$, with the lower-limit topology. Is i continuous? The set $O = [0, 1)$ is open in $\mathbf{R}$ with the lower-limit topology, but the inverse image, $f^{-1}(O) = O = [0, 1)$ is not open in $\mathbf{R}$ with the standard topology. Therefore, the function i is not continuous in this case.

These last two examples show that the continuity of a function depends on the topologies defined on the domain and range spaces.

How does the concept of continuity relate to some of the properties of sets and spaces that we've looked at? Well, each of the following important results applies to a continuous map between topological spaces, $f: (X_1, \mathsf{T}_1) \to (X_2, \mathsf{T}_2)$:

1. The set $f^{-1}(C)$ is closed in X_1 for every closed subset C of X_2.

2. If C is a connected subset of X_1, then $f(C)$ is a connected subset of X_2.

3. If C is a compact subset of X_1, then $f(C)$ is a compact subset of X_2.

4. Let $f: X \to \mathbf{R}$ be a continuous function, with X a compact space. Then there exist points a and b in X such that $f(a) \leq f(x) \leq f(b)$ for every x in X; the value of $f(a)$ is called the absolute minimum of $f(x)$ on X, and $f(b)$ is the absolute maximum of $f(x)$ on X. That is, any real-valued, continuous function defined on a compact space—in particular, on any closed and bounded subset of $\mathbf{R}^n$— must attain an absolute minimum at some point in X and an absolute maximum at some point in X.

Result 1 can be strengthened: The set $f^{-1}(C)$ is closed in X_1 for every closed subset C of X_2 if *and only if* the map $f: (X_1, \mathsf{T}_1) \to (X_2, \mathsf{T}_2)$ is continuous. Therefore, to decide whether f is continuous, you can either check that $f^{-1}(O)$ is open in X_1 for every open subset O of X_2, or that $f^{-1}(C)$ is closed in X_1 for every closed subset C of X_2.

Open Maps and Homeomorphisms

A map $f: X_1 \to X_2$ is said to be an **open** map if the image of every open set in X_1 is open in X_2. Notice that this is different from saying that f is continuous, which requires that the *inverse* image of every open set in X_2 is open in X_1. For example, although the identity map $i: (\mathbf{R}, \mathsf{T}) \to (\mathbf{R}, \mathsf{T}_L)$, where the domain is $\mathbf{R}$ with its standard topology and the range is $\mathbf{R}$ with the lower-limit topology, is not continuous, it is an open map, because every basis element for the standard topology on $\mathbf{R}$ is also open in the lower-limit topology. If $f: X_1 \to X_2$ is a bijection, and both f and f^{-1} are continuous (that last requirement is equivalent to saying that f is a continuous, open map), then f is called a **homeomorphism**. This is analogous to the concept of an isomorphism between groups (or rings). An isomorphism is a bijective function that preserves the algebraic structure, so that if two groups or rings are isomorphic, then they're algebraically identical. In the same way, if two topological spaces, X_1 and X_2, are **homeomorphic**, then a homeomorphism $f: X_1 \to X_2$ establishes a one-to-one correspondence between the points of X_1 and X_2, as well as between their open sets—so it preserves the topological structure. Therefore, the spaces are topologically identical; that is, every topological property of one space is automatically shared by the other. Examples of topological properties include the cardinal number of the topology, connectedness, and compactness (because each of these properties can be defined completely in terms of the open sets in the space). So, for example, the real line, $\mathbf{R}$, is not homeomorphic to the closed interval $[0, 1]$, because $[0, 1]$ is compact but $\mathbf{R}$ is not. However, $\mathbf{R}$ *is* homeomorphic to the open interval $(0, 1)$; a homeomorphism from $(0, 1)$ to $\mathbf{R}$ can be given by the composition $g \circ f$, where the functions f and g are given by:

$$(0, 1) \xrightarrow{\; f(x) = \pi\left(x - \frac{1}{2}\right) \;} \left(-\frac{\pi}{2}, \frac{\pi}{2}\right) \xrightarrow{\; g(y) = \tan y \;} \mathbf{R}$$

We'll close our section on topology with a result that includes many of the concepts we've reviewed and involves one of the most important classes of topological spaces—the compact Hausdorff spaces:

> Let $f: X_1 \to X_2$ be a bijective, continuous map of topological spaces. If X_1 is compact and X_2 is Hausdorff, then f is a homeomorphism.

REAL ANALYSIS

We've already reviewed many of the topics that fall under this heading (at the GRE Math Subject Test level) in Chapter 2. These topics include such items as limits, differentiation, Riemann integration, the intermediate- and mean-value theorems, the fundamental theorems of calculus, and sequences and series. In a first course in undergraduate real analysis, these topics—as well as others, particularly those in set theory and point-set topology—would be studied in depth, including analyses and methods for providing more careful definitions and proofs. But, as we said, the test doesn't expect you to provide proofs, so in this section, we'll review a basic property of the real numbers (the least upper bound axiom), and a topic in Real Analysis that the ETS specifically mentions in its description of the content of the test: Lebesgue integration.

THE COMPLETENESS OF THE REAL NUMBERS

Let X be a nonempty set of real numbers. Any number, u, such that $u \geq x$ for every x in X, is called an **upper bound** for X. If X has an upper bound, then X is said to be **bounded above**. Similarly, any number, l, such that $l \leq x$ for every x in X, is called a **lower bound** for X; if X has a lower bound, it's said to be **bounded below**. A set may have many upper bounds, because if X is bounded above and u is an upper bound, then any number, u', greater than u is also an upper bound. Similarly, a set may have many lower bounds.

Now, let X be a set of real numbers that's bounded above; if u is an upper bound for X and if no number smaller than u is an upper bound for X, then u is called the **least upper bound** of X. This is written $u = \text{lub } X$. The least upper bound is also called the **supremum** of X, denoted sup X, so lub $X \equiv$ sup X; the two notations are used interchangeably. If X is bounded below and l is a lower bound such that no number larger than l is also a lower bound for X, then l is called the **greatest lower bound** of X, written $l = \text{glb } X$. The greatest lower bound is also called the **infimum** of X, denoted inf X, so glb $X \equiv$ inf X. The following diagram illustrates these definitions:

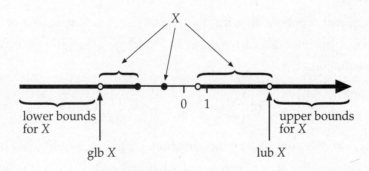

One of the axioms of the real number system, which is crucial for establishing many of the important theorems of calculus and real analysis, is called the:

> **Least Upper Bound Axiom:** If X is a set of real numbers that's bounded above, then there's exactly one real number u that is the least upper bound of X.

This property may seem obvious, but it's not; in fact, if *real* is replaced by *rational*, the statement is false. For example, the set

$$E = \left\{ 1,\ 1 + \tfrac{1}{1!},\ 1 + \tfrac{1}{1!} + \tfrac{1}{2!},\ 1 + \tfrac{1}{1!} + \tfrac{1}{2!} + \tfrac{1}{3!},\ 1 + \tfrac{1}{1!} + \tfrac{1}{2!} + \tfrac{1}{3!} + \tfrac{1}{4!}, \ldots \right\}$$

is a set of rational numbers. Since $n! > 2^{n-1}$ for every integer $n > 2$, we have:

$$1 + \tfrac{1}{1!} + \tfrac{1}{2!} + \tfrac{1}{3!} + \tfrac{1}{4!} + \cdots + \tfrac{1}{n!} < 1 + 1 + \tfrac{1}{2} + \tfrac{1}{4} + \tfrac{1}{8} + \cdots + \tfrac{1}{2^{n-1}}$$

$$< 1 + 1 + 1$$

$$= 3$$

This shows us that every element of E is bounded above by 3. Although this set of rational numbers is bounded above, there is no *rational* number that is the least upper bound of E. The least upper bound of E is the number e, which is irrational.

The least upper bound axiom can be used to prove the greatest lower bound theorem for **R**; that is:

> If X is a set of real numbers that's bounded below, then there's exactly one real number l that is the greatest lower bound of X.

These two results show that, intuitively, there are no "holes" in the set of real numbers—unlike in the set of rational numbers, for example. Loosely speaking, every sequence of real numbers that "wants" to converge can find a real number to converge to. To make this statement precise, we'll finish up this discussion with the definition of a Cauchy sequence. A sequence of real numbers, $(x_n)_{n=1}^{\infty}$, is called a **Cauchy sequence** if, for every $\varepsilon > 0$ (no matter how small), there exists an integer N such that for every pair of integers m and n (both greater than or equal to N), we have $|x_m - x_n| < \varepsilon$. This tells us that the terms of a Cauchy sequence become arbitrarily close together if we go far enough out in the sequence. For example, the sequence given above in the set E is an example of a Cauchy sequence. It seems like such a sequence *wants* to converge; that it *can* is the statement of the following theorem, which is an important consequence of the least upper bound axiom for **R**:

> Every Cauchy sequence of real numbers converges.

Any metric space in which every Cauchy sequence is guaranteed to converge (to a point in the space) is called a **complete space**. Therefore, **R** is complete—it has no holes!

LEBESGUE MEASURE

Let $\overline{\mathbf{R}}$ denote the set of real numbers, **R**, with ∞ adjoined. Let A be any subset of **R**, and find a countable, open covering of A by intervals of the form (a_i, b_i); thus, $A \subseteq \bigcup_{i=1}^{\infty} (a_i, b_i)$. We define a function $\mu^*: \mathsf{P}(\mathbf{R}) \to \overline{\mathbf{R}}$ by the equation

$$\mu^*(A) = \inf \left\{ \sum_{i=1}^{\infty} (b_i - a_i),\ \text{for } A \subseteq \bigcup_{i=1}^{\infty} (a_i, b_i) \right\}$$

where we allow $\mu^*(A) = \infty$. We now restrict this function, μ^*, to a subfamily, **M**, of $\mathsf{P}(\mathbf{R})$, where **M** is defined as follows: A subset M of **R** is a member of **M** if and only if $\mu^*(A) = \mu^*(A \cap M) + \mu^*(A \cap M^c)$ for every A in $\mathsf{P}(\mathbf{R})$. The sets in **M** are called (**Lebesgue**) **measurable sets**, and the restriction of μ^* to **M**, $\mu^*|\mathsf{M}$, is denoted by μ; this function is called **Lebesgue measure**. A measurable set M for which $\mu(M) = 0$ is said to be a set of **measure zero**.

The Lebesgue measurable sets include virtually every subset of **R** that will arise in practice. For example, every open set and every closed set in **R** is measurable, and every finite or countably infinite subset of **R** is also Lebesgue measurable. The complement of a measurable set is measurable, and a finite or countably infinite union—or intersection—of measurable sets is measurable. Nevertheless, nonmeasurable subsets of **R** *do* exist, but constructing an example of this takes quite a bit of work and the process is somewhat sophisticated. Therefore, we'll simply say that M is not all of P(**R**). Some properties of Lebesgue measurable sets and Lebesgue measure are summarized in the following list:

1. The empty set is measurable and has measure zero. If $M = \{m\}$ is a one-element subset of **R** (a **singleton**), then $\mu(M) = 0$. It also follows that if M is a finite or countably infinite subset of **R**, then $\mu(M) = 0$. For example, $\mu(\mathbf{Z}) = \mu(\mathbf{Q}) = 0$.

2. If $M = (a, b), [a, b), (a, b]$, or $[a, b]$, then $\mu(M)$ is just the length of the interval, $b - a$. If M is a finite union of disjoint, finite intervals, then $\mu(M)$ is the sum of the lengths of the intervals. For example, if $M = (-1, 2) \cup (6, 8]$, then $\mu(M) = [2 - (-1)] + (8 - 6) = 5$. If M is a measurable set that contains an infinite interval, then $\mu(M) = \infty$. In general, if $\{M_i\}$ is any countable collection of disjoint, measurable sets, then $\mu\left(\bigcup_{i=1}^{\infty} M_i\right) = \sum_{i=1}^{\infty} \mu(M_i)$.

3. If M_1 and M_2 are elements of M and $M_1 \subseteq M_2$, then $\mu(M_1) \leq \mu(M_2)$.

LEBESGUE MEASURABLE FUNCTIONS

A function $f: \mathbf{R} \to \mathbf{R}$ is said to be (**Lebesgue**) **measurable** if, for every open set O in **R**, the inverse image, $f^{-1}(O)$, is a Lebesgue measurable set. Since every open subset of **R** is measurable, it follows that every continuous function is measurable, but there do exist (some very important!) measurable, noncontinuous functions. The sum, difference, and product of measurable functions are also measurable. Furthermore, if f is measurable, then so is the function $|f|$, where, by definition, $|f|(x) = |f(x)|$.

If A is any subset of **R**, then we can define a function on **R**, denoted χ_A (where χ is the Greek letter *chi*), called the **characteristic function of** A, as:

$$\chi_A(x) = \begin{cases} 0 & \text{if } x \notin A \\ 1 & \text{if } x \in A \end{cases}$$

This function is measurable if and only if A is a measurable set. Using these functions, we can construct another important type of function, known as a **step** (or **simple**) **function**—a finite, linear combination (with real coefficients) of characteristic functions. A typical step function, s, has the form

$$s = \sum_{i=1}^{n} a_i \chi_{A_i} \quad \Rightarrow \quad s(x) = \sum_{i=1}^{n} a_i \chi_{A_i}(x)$$

where all the a_i's are real numbers. For example, the figure on the following page is the graph of the step function:

$$s = 2\chi_{(-3,-2)} - 3\chi_{[-1,2)} + 4\chi_{[4,6]}$$

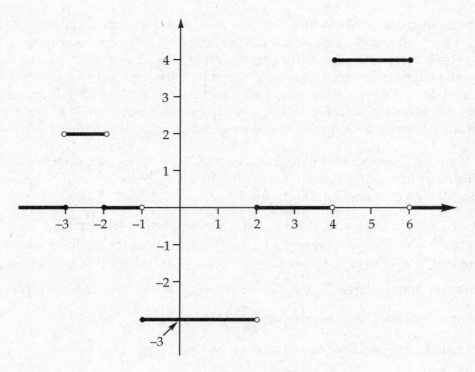

If every set A_i is measurable, then the step function $s = \sum_{i=1}^{n} a_i \chi_{A_i}$ is also measurable. This is our most important example of a measurable, noncontinuous function. It's essential to notice that the range of a step function is a *finite* subset of **R**. For instance, in the example above, the range of s is the set $\{-3,\ 0,\ 2,\ 4\}$.

Step functions provide the foundation for constructing the Lebesgue integral of a general function. With this goal in mind, we need the following theorem:

> Let f be a measurable function such that $f(x) \geq 0$ for every x in **R** (we abbreviate this by simply writing $f \geq 0$). Then there exists a sequence of step functions, $(s_1, s_2, \ldots)$, such that $0 \leq s_1 \leq s_2 \leq \ldots$ and for which $\lim_{n \to \infty} s_n = f$. [This last statement, $s_n \to f$, means that, for every x in **R**, the limit of the sequence $s_n(x)$ is $f(x)$.]

In general, if the function f_n is measurable for every positive integer n, and $f_n \to f$ **almost everywhere** (that is, $f_n(x) \to f(x)$ for all x in **R** except possibly for some x's, the set of which has measure zero), then the limit function, f, is also measurable.

LEBESGUE INTEGRABLE FUNCTIONS

Let $s = \sum_{i=1}^{n} a_i \chi_{A_i}$ be a step function such that every set A_i is measurable. Then s is a measurable function, and we say that s is **Lebesgue integrable** if:

$$a_i \neq 0 \quad \Rightarrow \quad \mu(A_i) < \infty$$

In this case, the **Lebesgue integral** of s is:

$$\int s \, d\mu = \sum_{i=1}^{n} a_i \mu(A_i)$$

[If $\mu(A_i) = \infty$ for some set A_i in the representation of s as a linear combination of characteristic functions, then, by our restriction above, it must be true that $a_i = 0$. In this case, we define $a_i \mu(A_i)$, which is $0 \cdot \infty$, to be zero.] For example, the Lebesgue integral of the step function sketched above, $s = 2\chi_{(-3, -2)} - 3\chi_{[-1, 2)} + 4\chi_{[4, 6]}$, is:

$$\int s \, d\mu = 2 \cdot \mu(-3, -2) - 3 \cdot \mu[-1, 2) + 4 \cdot \mu[4, 6]$$
$$= 2 \cdot (1) - 3 \cdot (3) + 4 \cdot (2)$$
$$= 1$$

Now that we've defined the Lebesgue integral of a step function, we're ready to show what it means for an arbitrary, measurable function to be Lebesgue integrable. First, let f be a measurable function such that $f \geq 0$. If every step function s, with $s \geq 0$ and $s \leq f$, is integrable and $\int s \, d\mu$ is finite, then we say that f is **Lebesgue integrable**. The value of the Lebesgue integral of f is

$$\int f \, d\mu = \sup \left\{ \int s \, d\mu \right\}$$

where the supremum is taken over all integrable, nonnegative step functions, s, such that $s \leq f$. Finally, to take care of the functions that are not everywhere nonnegative, we do the following. Every function f can be written as the difference of two nonnegative functions, $f = f^+ - f^-$, where $f^+ = \frac{1}{2}\left(|f| + f\right) = \max(f, 0)$ is the **positive part of** f and $f^- = \frac{1}{2}\left(|f| - f\right) = \max(-f, 0)$ is called the **negative part of** f (this last terminology can be a little confusing, since f^- is never negative). Therefore, an arbitrary measurable function, f, is Lebesgue integrable if both its positive and negative parts are Lebesgue integrable and, in this case:

$$\int f \, d\mu = \int f^+ \, d\mu - \int f^- \, d\mu$$

We've done a lot of work to lead up to a definition of the Lebesgue integral of a function. How does this integral differ from the Riemann integral that we studied in Chapter 2? To define the Riemann integral of f over some interval I, we split the domain of f into subintervals and construct vertical rectangles over these subintervals. The heights of these rectangles are taken to be close to the values of the function over each subinterval, so their total area approximates the area under the graph. Then, we take a limit—specifically, allow the lengths of all these subintervals, which are the bases of the rectangles, to approach zero. If the total area of these rectangles approaches a finite limiting value, this limit is called the Riemann integral of f over I. But things can go wrong. For example, if f is discontinuous at uncountably many points in I, then f is not Riemann integrable.

The Lebesgue integral takes a different approach. Rather than splitting the domain of f into subintervals, we split the *range* of f into subintervals, R_j, and form a step function, $s = \sum_j a_j \chi_{f^{-1}(R_j)}$, that approximates f, and then pass to the limit. Since $f^{-1}(R_j)$ doesn't have to be an interval—only a measurable set—this change in perspective enlarges the set of functions which can be called *integrable*.

For example, consider the function:

$$f(x) = \chi_{\mathbf{Q}}(x) = \begin{cases} 0 & \text{if } x \text{ is irrational} \\ 1 & \text{if } x \text{ is rational} \end{cases}$$

This function is not Riemann integrable on any interval, because it's discontinuous everywhere. However, this function *is* Lebesgue integrable; in fact, its integral is easy to figure out:

$$\int \chi_{\mathbf{Q}}\, d\mu = 1 \cdot \mu(\mathbf{Q}) + 0 \cdot \mu(\mathbf{Q}^c) = 1 \cdot 0 + 0 \cdot \infty = 0$$

The use of the Lebesgue integral also allows for stronger convergence theorems (the two most important are Levi's Monotone Convergence theorem and the Lebesgue Dominated Convergence theorem, which you may have studied already, but which you'll certainly study in graduate-level real analysis), which are used to establish important classical results, such as the fact that L^p, the space of measurable functions f such that $|f|^p$ is Lebesgue integrable, is a complete space if $p \geq 1$.

COMPLEX VARIABLES

INTRODUCTION

Just as irrational numbers were invented to provide solutions to equations such as $x^2 - 2 = 0$, complex numbers were invented to provide solutions to equations such as $x^2 + 2 = 0$. The **complex numbers**, denoted by $\mathbf{C}$, is the set of all ordered pairs of real numbers, (x, y), with the operations of addition and multiplication given by:

$$(x_1, y_1) + (x_2, y_2) = (x_1 + x_2, y_1 + y_2)$$

$$(x_1, y_1) \bullet (x_2, y_2) = (x_1 x_2 - y_1 y_2, x_1 y_2 + x_2 y_1)$$

With these operations, $\mathbf{C}$ is a field, with additive identity $(0, 0)$ and multiplicative identity $(1, 0)$. Because $(x_1, 0) + (x_2, 0) = (x_1 + x_2, 0)$ and $(x_1, 0)(x_2, 0) = (x_1 x_2, 0)$, the complex number $(x, 0)$ behaves just like the real number x, so we simply write x instead of $(x, 0)$, and think of $\mathbf{R}$ as a subfield of $\mathbf{C}$.

For the complex number $(0, 1)$, we notice that $(0, 1)(0, 1) = (-1, 0) = -1$. Therefore, the square of $(0, 1)$ is equal to -1; no real number has this property. This complex number is denoted by i, and is called the **imaginary unit**. Every complex number (x, y) can be written in the form $(x, 0) + (y, 0)(0, 1)$, or, equivalently, in the form $x + yi$—where x and y are real numbers—and this latter notation is the one we'll use. Also, it's customary to use z (or w) to denote an arbitrary complex variable. When we write $z = x + yi$, the real number x is called the **real part** of z (denoted by Re z), and the real number y is called the **imaginary part** of z (denoted by Im z). For every complex number expressed in standard form, $z = x + yi$, its (**complex**) **conjugate** is the number $\bar{z} = x - yi$. That is, if $\bar{z}$ is the conjugate of z, then Re $\bar{z}$ = Re z, but Im $\bar{z}$ = $-$Im z. (The conjugate of z is sometimes denoted by z^*.) Notice that z is real if and only if $z = \bar{z}$.

While $\mathbf{C}$ can be considered an extension of $\mathbf{R}$, there's an important property of $\mathbf{R}$ that doesn't carry over to $\mathbf{C}$. If a is a nonzero real number, then a is either positive or negative, but not both. One of the *order axioms* for $\mathbf{R}$ states that if $a > 0$, then $a^2 > 0$ also. If we wanted to extend these same axioms to $\mathbf{C}$, we'd run into a problem. Is i positive or is it negative? If it's positive, then i^2 must be positive, which is false. If i is negative, then $-i$ must be positive, which would imply that $(-i)^2$ is positive, which is also false. Therefore, we can't define an ordering of the complex numbers that's consistent with the order axioms of the real numbers. A statement such as $z_1 < z_2$ between complex numbers only makes sense if both z_1 and z_2 are actually real.

The arithmetic operations with complex numbers are performed by thinking of $x + yi$ as a binomial and replacing i^2 by -1 whenever it occurs. Higher powers of i are handled in the same way; for example, $i^{11} = (i^2)^5 i = (-1)^5 i = -i$. Here are some examples:

$$(2 - 3i) + (-5 + i) = (2 - 5) + (-3 + 1)i = -3 - 2i$$

$$(2 - 3i) - (-5 + i) = (2 + 5) + (-3 - 1)i = 7 - 4i$$

$$(2 - 3i)(-5 + i) = (2)(-5) + (-3i)(-5) + (2)(i) + (-3i)(i)$$
$$= -10 + 15i + 2i - 3i^2$$
$$= -7 + 17i$$

$$\frac{2 - 3i}{-5 + i} = \frac{2 - 3i}{-5 + i} \cdot \frac{-5 - i}{-5 - i} = \frac{-13 + 13i}{25 - i^2} = \frac{-13 + 13i}{26} = -\frac{1}{2} + \frac{1}{2}i$$

This last calculation shows the method for dividing one complex number by another: Multiply the numerator and denominator by the conjugate of the denominator.

Since a complex number is an ordered pair of real numbers, we can express complex numbers graphically as points in the xy-plane, so that $z = x + yi$ is associated with the point (x, y). When complex numbers are graphed in this way, we call the xy-plane the **complex plane**; the horizontal (x) axis is called the **real axis**, and the vertical (y) axis is called the **imaginary axis**. Real numbers are graphed on the real axis, and **pure imaginary** numbers (that is, complex numbers whose real part is zero) are graphed on the imaginary axis. Reflecting a point z in the complex plane across the real axis gives z's conjugate, $\overline{z}$.

THE POLAR FORM

The figure below shows a complex number $z = x + yi$ plotted in the complex plane. The distance from z to the origin is equal to $\sqrt{x^2 + y^2}$, which is called the **modulus** (or **magnitude** or **absolute value**) of z, denoted by $|z|$. The absolute value of z satisfies the equation $|z|^2 = z\overline{z}$:

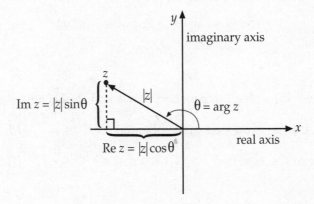

The angle θ that the vector (from the origin to z) makes with the positive real axis is called an **argument** of z, denoted by arg z. We can add any integer multiple of 2π to an argument of z, and the result is another argument of z. Therefore, we define the **principal argument** of z, denoted by Arg z (notice the capitalization), as the unique value of the argument that lies in the interval $-\pi < \theta \le \pi$. If we let $|z|$ equal r, then the modulus and argument of a complex number are simply the polar coordinates of its representative point in the plane. Since $x = r \cos \theta$ and $y = r \sin \theta$, we can therefore express z in the **polar form:**

$$z = r(\cos \theta + i \sin \theta)$$

Multiplying two complex numbers now has a simple geometric interpretation. Since

$$
\begin{aligned}
z_1 z_2 &= r_1(\cos\theta_1 + i\sin\theta_1) \bullet r_2(\cos\theta_2 + i\sin\theta_2) \\
&= r_1 r_2[(\cos\theta_1 \cos\theta_2 - \sin\theta_1 \sin\theta_2) + i(\sin\theta_1 \cos\theta_2 + \cos\theta_1 \sin\theta_2)] \\
&= r_1 r_2[\cos(\theta_1 + \theta_2) + i\sin(\theta_1 + \theta_2)]
\end{aligned}
$$

we can conclude that, in order to multiply two complex numbers, we simply multiply their moduli and *add* their arguments. It's also easy to show that, to divide two complex numbers, we divide their moduli and *subtract* their arguments.

THE EXPONENTIAL FORM

The Taylor series expansions for $\cos x$, $\sin x$, and e^x (from Chapter 2) provide us with a remarkable way to express complex numbers. If we write

$$
\cos\theta + i\sin\theta = \left(1 - \frac{\theta^2}{2!} + \frac{\theta^4}{4!} - \cdots\right) + i\left(\theta - \frac{\theta^3}{3!} + \frac{\theta^5}{5!} - \cdots\right)
$$

$$
= 1 + (i\theta) + \frac{(i\theta)^2}{2!} + \frac{(i\theta)^3}{3!} + \frac{(i\theta)^4}{4!} + \frac{(i\theta)^5}{5!} + \cdots
$$

we notice that this last expression is the Taylor series expansion for $e^{i\theta}$! The resulting equation,

$$e^{i\theta} = \cos \theta + i \sin \theta$$

is called **Euler's formula.** Since any complex number can be written in the form $z = r(\cos \theta + i \sin \theta)$, it follows from Euler's formula that any complex number can be written in the **exponential form** $z = re^{i\theta}$, where r is the absolute value of z and θ is an argument of z. A useful result that follows directly from Euler's formula is known as **de Moivre's formula**; since $(e^{i\theta})^n = e^{i(n\theta)}$, we can write:

$$(\cos \theta + i \sin \theta)^n = \cos n\theta + i \sin n\theta$$

COMPLEX ROOTS

If n is a positive integer, we can solve the equation $z^n = 1$ and the solutions are called the nth **roots of unity.** The real number 1 can be expressed in exponential form as $e^{i(2\pi k)}$, for any integer k. If we also write z in exponential form, the equation $z^n = 1$ becomes $r^n e^{i(n\theta)} = e^{i(2\pi k)}$. This implies that $r = 1$ and $\theta = \dfrac{2\pi k}{n}$, so $z = e^{i\left(\frac{2\pi k}{n}\right)}$. The set

$$
\left\{ e^{i\left(\frac{2\pi k}{n}\right)} = \cos\left(\frac{2\pi k}{n}\right) + i\sin\left(\frac{2\pi k}{n}\right) : k = 0, 1, \ldots, n-1 \right\}
$$

contains the n distinct n^{th} roots of unity. If we let k equal an integer greater than $n-1$, the value of $e^{i(2\pi k/n)}$ will be the same as a value that's already in the set above. Since $e^{i(2\pi k/n)} = [e^{i(2\pi/n)}]^k$, if we let $\omega_n = e^{i(2\pi/n)}$, then the nth roots of unity are equal to:

$$1,\ \omega_n,\ \omega_n^2,\ \dots,\ \omega_n^{n-1}$$

If they're plotted in the complex plane, the nth roots of unity all lie on the unit circle, $|z|=1$, and are equally spaced, with all the angles between the vectors that join any adjacent pair to the origin equal to $\dfrac{2\pi}{n}$.

The same method can be used to find the nth roots of any complex number, w. Writing w in exponential form as $Re^{i\Theta}$, or, more generally, as $Re^{i(\Theta + 2\pi k)}$, the equation $z^n = w$ becomes $r^n e^{i(n\theta)} = Re^{i(\Theta + 2\pi k)}$. This implies that $r = \sqrt[n]{R}$ and $\theta = (\Theta + 2\pi k)/n$. By the reasoning we used above, w has exactly n distinct n^{th} roots, the set of which is equal to:

$$\left\{ \sqrt[n]{R}\, e^{i[(\Theta + 2\pi k)/n]} \colon k = 0,\ 1,\ \dots,\ n-1 \right\}$$

Although any complex number w has n distinct n^{th} roots, we can define the **principal n^{th} root of w** as follows. First, we let Θ be the *principal* argument of w (the unique value of the argument such that $-\pi < \Theta \le \pi$); then, by choosing $k=0$ in the set above, we get $\sqrt[n]{R}\, e^{i(\Theta/n)}$, and call this the principal n^{th} root of w. If we denote the principal n^{th} root of w by the symbol $\sqrt[n]{w}$, then *all* the nth roots of w are equal to the products of the principal n^{th} root of w and the nth roots of unity:

$$w^{1/n} = \sqrt[n]{w},\ \omega_n \cdot \sqrt[n]{w},\ \omega_n^2 \cdot \sqrt[n]{w},\ \dots,\ \omega_n^{n-1} \cdot \sqrt[n]{w}$$

It follows that these roots are equally spaced around the circle $|z| = \sqrt[n]{R}$, in the complex plane.

Example 7.26   What are the fourth roots of $16i$?

Solution: First, we write $16i$ in exponential form as $16e^{i\pi/2}$. Then we get:

$$(16i)^{1/4} = \sqrt[4]{16} \cdot e^{i[(\pi/2) + 2k\pi]/4},\quad \text{for } k = 0,\ 1,\ 2,\ 3$$
$$= 2e^{i\pi/8},\ 2e^{i \cdot 5\pi/8},\ 2e^{i \cdot 9\pi/8},\ 2e^{i \cdot 13\pi/8}$$

These are the four fourth roots of $16i$. The *principal* fourth root is $2e^{i\pi/8}$, which can be expressed as $2\left(\cos\frac{\pi}{8} + i\sin\frac{\pi}{8}\right)$. If desired, we can simplify this by using the half-angle formulas for the cosine and sine. Since

$$\cos\frac{\pi}{8} = \cos\frac{1}{2}\left(\frac{\pi}{4}\right) = \sqrt{\frac{1 + \cos\frac{\pi}{4}}{2}} = \sqrt{\frac{1 + \frac{1}{\sqrt{2}}}{2}} = \frac{\sqrt{2 + \sqrt{2}}}{2}$$

$$\sin\frac{\pi}{8} = \sin\frac{1}{2}\left(\frac{\pi}{4}\right) = \sqrt{\frac{1 - \cos\frac{\pi}{4}}{2}} = \sqrt{\frac{1 - \frac{1}{\sqrt{2}}}{2}} = \frac{\sqrt{2 - \sqrt{2}}}{2}$$

we can write:

$$\sqrt[4]{16i} = 2(\cos\tfrac{\pi}{8} + i\sin\tfrac{\pi}{8}) = \sqrt{2 + \sqrt{2}} + i\sqrt{2 - \sqrt{2}}$$

COMPLEX LOGARITHMS

If x is a real number, then we've defined $\log x$ as the unique value of y such that $e^y = x$. In other words, the natural logarithm function is the inverse of the natural exponential function. The same idea motivates the definition of the logarithm of a complex number. So let's write z in exponential form, as $z = re^{i\theta}$. Taking the log of both sides, we get $\log z = \log r + i\theta$. However, we can add any integer multiple of 2π to θ in this last equation and the resulting expression will also give a logarithm of z, since $e^{\log r + i(\theta + 2\pi)} = e^{\log r} e^{i\theta} \cdot e^{2\pi} = re^{i\theta} \cdot 1 = re^{i\theta} = z$. Therefore, by contrast to the real logarithm, every nonzero complex number has infinitely many complex logarithms. If $z = re^{i\theta}$, then any complex number of the form $\log r + i(\theta + 2\pi k)$, where k is any integer, is a logarithm of z. The **principal logarithm** of z is defined to be the one value of $\log z$ whose argument falls in the range $-\pi < \arg(\log z) \leq \pi$. We use the notation $\mathrm{Log}\, z$ (notice the capitalization) to denote the unique, principal logarithm of z, and to distinguish it from $\log z$, which can represent any of the infinitely many different complex logarithms of z. Therefore, if $z \neq 0$,

$$\mathrm{Log}\, z = \log |z| + i\, \mathrm{Arg}\, z$$

where $\log |z|$ denotes the usual (real) logarithm of the positive real number .

Example 7.27   What's the principal logarithm of $-e^2 i$?

Solution: Because $\dfrac{-\pi}{2}$ is the principal argument of $-i$, we have $z = -e^2 i = e^2(-i) = e^2 \cdot e^{-i\pi/2}$.

Therefore, $\mathrm{Log}(-e^2 i) = \log(e^2) + i\left(-\frac{\pi}{2}\right) = 2 - \frac{\pi}{2} i$.

COMPLEX POWERS

If x and y are real numbers (and $x \neq 0$), the value of x^y is equal to $e^{y \log x}$. If we now want to generalize this definition and render it useful for expressions of the form z^w, where z and w are *complex* numbers, we need to realize that we'll get infinitely many values, because $\log z$ is infinitely valued. The values of z^w are given by $e^{w \log z}$, and the **principal value** of z^w is equal to $e^{w \,\mathrm{Log}\, z}$, where $\mathrm{Log}\, z$ denotes the principal value of $\log z$.

Example 7.28   What's the principal value of i^i?

Solution: Writing i^i as $e^{i \log i}$, we find that the principal value of i^i is

$$e^{i\,\mathrm{Log}\, i} = e^{i(0 + i\pi/2)} = e^{-\pi/2} = \frac{1}{\sqrt{e^\pi}}$$

which turns out to be a real number! The result of this example is a relationship between the numbers i, e, and π. What has been described as the most beautiful equation in mathematics relates not only these numbers, but also the numbers 0 and 1, thus providing a connection between the five most important constants in mathematics:

$$e^{\pi i} + 1 = 0$$

Now that we're working in the complex domain, it's important to be careful when using the familiar rules of radicals and exponents, since they may no longer be true. For instance, the equation $\sqrt{a}\sqrt{b} = \sqrt{ab}$, which is an identity when the quantities $\sqrt{a}$ and $\sqrt{b}$ are real, is not an identity if they're not real, as the following example shows:

$$\sqrt{-1}\sqrt{-1} = i \cdot i = -1 \qquad \text{but} \qquad \sqrt{(-1)(-1)} = \sqrt{1} = 1$$

THE TRIGONOMETRIC FUNCTIONS

The functions sine, cosine, tangent, cotangent, secant, and cosecant can also be defined for complex values of the argument. The motivation for their definition is Euler's formula, $e^{ix} = \cos x + i \sin x$, and the equation that results from taking the complex conjugate of both sides, $e^{-ix} = \cos x - i \sin x$. Combining these equations gives us $\cos x = (e^{ix} + e^{-ix})/2$ and $\sin x = (e^{ix} - e^{-ix})/2i$. We now allow x to be a complex variable, z, and define:

$$\cos z = \frac{e^{iz} + e^{-iz}}{2} \qquad \text{and} \qquad \sin z = \frac{e^{iz} - e^{-iz}}{2i}$$

Although the definitions of the sine and cosine of a complex number are quite different from their usual definitions for real numbers, it is nevertheless true that many of the familiar properties hold true. For example, $\cos 0 = \sin(\frac{1}{2}\pi) = 1$, and $\sin 0 = \cos(\frac{1}{2}\pi) = 0$. In addition, the trig identities that we reviewed, such as

$$\cos^2 z + \sin^2 z = 1$$
$$\cos(z_1 \pm z_2) = \cos z_1 \cos z_2 \mp \sin z_1 \sin z_2$$
$$\sin(z_1 \pm z_2) = \sin z_1 \cos z_2 \pm \cos z_1 \sin z_2$$
$$\sin(z + \tfrac{1}{2}\pi) = \cos z$$

continue to be valid. And, since e^z is periodic with period 2π (in stark contrast to the real exponential function, e^x, which is *not* periodic), the functions $\cos z$ and $\sin z$ are evidently periodic with period 2π; that is, $\cos(z + 2\pi) = \cos z$ and $\sin(z + 2\pi) = \sin z$. However, not all the properties of $\cos x$ and $\sin x$ (for real x) are the same as those of $\cos z$ and $\sin z$ (for complex z). One notable example is the fact that both $\cos x$ and $\sin x$ are bounded ($|\cos x| \leq 1$ and $|\sin x| \leq 1$ for every real x), but the functions $\cos z$ and $\sin z$ are unbounded (that is, $|\cos z|$ and $|\sin z|$ can assume *any* nonnegative real value).

The definitions of the other trig functions follow from those for $\cos z$ and $\sin z$:

$$\tan z = \frac{\sin z}{\cos z}, \quad \cot z = \frac{1}{\tan z} = \frac{\cos z}{\sin z}, \quad \sec z = \frac{1}{\cos z}, \quad \text{and} \quad \csc z = \frac{1}{\sin z}$$

Notice that these equations are just like their real counterparts.

Example 7.29   Does there exist a complex number z such that $\sin z = 2$?

Solution: Of course, there exists no *real* number x such that $\sin x = 2$, but there *does* exist a complex number z such that $\sin z = 2$—in fact, there are infinitely many. Using the definition of $\sin z$, the equation $\sin z = 2$ becomes:

$$\frac{e^{iz} - e^{-iz}}{2i} = 2$$

$$e^{iz} - e^{-iz} = 4i$$

$$e^{2iz} - 1 = 4ie^{iz}$$

$$(e^{iz})^2 - 4i(e^{iz}) - 1 = 0$$

Since this equation is quadratic in the quantity e^{iz}, the quadratic formula gives us:

$$e^{iz} = \frac{-(-4i) \pm \sqrt{(-4i)^2 + 4}}{2} = \frac{4i \pm i \cdot 2\sqrt{3}}{2} = (2 \pm \sqrt{3})i$$

Therefore, $iz = \log\left[(2 \pm \sqrt{3})i\right]$, which implies $z = -i\log\left[(2 \pm \sqrt{3})i\right]$, so:

$$
\begin{aligned}
z &= -i\log\left[(2 \pm \sqrt{3})i\right] \\
&= -i\left[\log(2 \pm \sqrt{3}) + i\left(\tfrac{\pi}{2} + 2k\pi\right)\right], \quad \text{for any } k \in \mathbf{Z} \\
&= \left(\tfrac{\pi}{2} + 2k\pi\right) - i\log(2 \pm \sqrt{3}), \quad \text{for any } k \in \mathbf{Z}
\end{aligned}
$$

THE HYPERBOLIC FUNCTIONS

The **hyperbolic cosine** (**cosh**, rhymes with *gosh*) and the **hyperbolic sine** (**sinh**, pronounced *sinch*) are defined for real x by the equations:

$$\cosh x = \frac{e^x + e^{-x}}{2} \quad \text{and} \quad \sinh x = \frac{e^x - e^{-x}}{2}$$

These functions have names similar to the trigonometric functions because they have many similar properties. For example, $\cosh 0 = 1$ and $\sinh 0 = 0$, just as $\cos 0 = 1$ and $\sin 0 = 0$; $\cosh(-x) = \cosh x$ and $\sinh(-x) = -\sinh x$, just as $\cos(-x) = \cos x$ and $\sin(-x) = -\sin x$; and the identity $\cosh^2 x - \sinh^2 x = 1$ is similar to the Pythagorean trig identity $\cos^2 x + \sin^2 x = 1$. One important difference between the hyperbolic functions and their "corresponding" trig functions is that, while $-1 \le \cos x \le 1$ for all real x, the hyperbolic cosine satisfies $\cosh x \ge 1$ for all real x; and although $-1 \le \sin x \le 1$ for all real x, the value of $\sinh x$ can be any real number. Thus, both $\cos x$ and $\sin x$ are bounded, but $\cosh x$ and $\sinh x$ are unbounded.

The definitions of the hyperbolic sine and cosine are exactly the same if x is allowed to be a complex variable, z. It's apparent that these definitions look remarkably like the definitions of $\cos z$ and $\sin z$ for complex z. The relationships between them are summarized in the following pairs of formulas:

$$
\begin{array}{ccc}
\cos(iz) = \cosh z & & \sin(iz) = i\sinh z \\
& \text{and} & \\
\cosh(iz) = \cos z & & \sinh(iz) = i\sin z
\end{array}
$$

With these formulas, we can derive equations that can be used to figure out the values of $\cos z$ and $\sin z$, where $z = x + yi$, in terms of x and y.

For example:

$$\cos z = \cos(x + yi) = \cos x \cos(yi) - \sin x \sin(yi)$$
$$= \cos x \cosh y - i(\sin x \sinh y)$$

and

$$\sin z = \sin(x + yi) = \sin x \cos(yi) + \cos x \sin(yi)$$
$$= \sin x \cosh y + i(\cos x \sinh y)$$

These equations can be used to derive the following (where we use the alternate notation, *, to denote complex conjugation):

$$\left|\cos z\right|^2 = (\cos z)(\cos z)*$$
$$= [\cos x \cosh y - i(\sin x \sinh y)][\cos x \cosh y + i(\sin x \sinh y)]$$
$$= \cos^2 x \cosh^2 y + \sin^2 x \sinh^2 y$$
$$= \cos^2 x(1 + \sinh^2 y) + (1 - \cos^2 x)(\sinh^2 y)$$
$$= \cos^2 x + \sinh^2 y$$

and

$$\left|\sin z\right|^2 = (\sin z)(\sin z)*$$
$$= [\sin x \cosh y + i(\cos x \sinh y)][\sin x \cosh y - i(\cos x \sinh y)]$$
$$= \sin^2 x \cosh^2 y + \cos^2 x \sinh^2 y$$
$$= \sin^2 x(1 + \sinh^2 y) + (1 - \sin^2 x)(\sinh^2 y)$$
$$= \sin^2 x + \sinh^2 y$$

Since $\sinh^2 y$ is unbounded, these equations verify our assertion in the last section that $\left|\cos z\right|$ and $\left|\sin z\right|$ are unbounded.

THE DERIVATIVE OF A FUNCTION OF A COMPLEX VARIABLE

A function $f(z)$, that accepts a complex number, z, as input is called a **function of a complex variable**. The function f can be expressed in terms of real-valued functions, as follows: Letting $z = x + yi$, we can write $f(z) = f(x + yi) = u(x, y) + iv(x, y)$. For example, the function $f(z) = z^2$ can be written as:

$$f(z) = (x + yi)^2 = \underbrace{(x^2 - y^2)}_{u(x,y)} + i\underbrace{(2xy)}_{v(x,y)}$$

A function $f(z)$ is said to be **differentiable at the point z_0** if

$$\lim_{h \to 0} \frac{f(z_0 + h) - f(z_0)}{h}$$

exists; if this is the case, the derivative of f at z_0 is denoted by $f'(z_0)$. It's important to understand that h is also a complex variable, so the statement "$h \to 0$" means that the complex number h approaches the origin. Because a nonzero complex number h can approach the origin from infinitely many directions, the existence of the limit above demands that the difference quotient approach a finite value regardless of the way that $h \to 0$. This is a very stringent requirement, much stronger than the corresponding statement that $h \to 0$ where h is a real variable (because in this latter case, h has only two avenues of approach to zero: from the right or from the left). Consequently, differentiability of a function of a complex variable has powerful repercussions (some of which we'll mention below), results that do not apply to functions of a real variable.

Let's look at a couple of examples. The function $f(z) = \bar{z}$ is not differentiable at the point $z = 0$, since

$$\frac{f(0+h) - f(0)}{h} = \frac{\bar{h}}{h}$$

and $\lim_{h \to 0} (\bar{h}/h)$ does not exist. To see why, notice that if h approaches the origin along the real axis, then $\bar{h} = h$, so $\lim_{h \to 0} (\bar{h}/h) = \lim_{h \to 0} (h/h) = \lim_{h \to 0} 1 = 1$; but, if h approaches the origin along the imaginary axis, then $\bar{h} = -h$, so $\lim_{h \to 0} (\bar{h}/h) = \lim_{h \to 0} (-h/h) = \lim_{h \to 0} (-1) = -1$.

However, we can show that the function $f(z) = z^2$ is differentiable everywhere; the difference quotient is:

$$\frac{f(z+h) - f(z)}{h} = \frac{(z+h)^2 - z^2}{h} = \frac{2zh + h^2}{h} = \frac{h(2z+h)}{h} = 2z + h$$

Therefore, no matter how h approaches 0, we have

$$\lim_{h \to 0} \frac{f(z+h) - f(z)}{h} = \lim_{h \to 0} (2z + h) = 2z$$

so $f'(z) = 2z$. Notice that the derivative of $f(z) = z^2$ is $f'(z) = 2z$, just as the derivative of the real-valued function $f(x) = x^2$ is $f'(x) = 2x$. In fact, all the differentiation formulas listed in Chapter 2 hold true in the case of a complex variable.

Example 7.30   If $f(z) = z - \arctan z$, solve the equation $f'(z) = \dfrac{4}{3}$.

Solution: Since $f'(z) = 1 - \left(\dfrac{1}{1+z^2} \right)$, we have:

$$1 - \frac{1}{1+z^2} = \frac{4}{3} \quad \Rightarrow \quad \frac{1}{1+z^2} = -\frac{1}{3} \quad \Rightarrow \quad z^2 = -4 \quad \Rightarrow \quad z = \pm 2i$$

THE CAUCHY–RIEMANN EQUATIONS

Let $f(z) = f(x + yi) = u(x, y) + iv(x, y)$. If f is differentiable at $z = x + yi$, then the limit

$$\lim_{h \to 0} \frac{f(z+h) - f(z)}{h} = \lim_{h \to 0} \frac{u(x + \operatorname{Re} h, y + \operatorname{Im} h) - u(x,y)}{\operatorname{Re} h + i \operatorname{Im} h} + \lim_{h \to 0} \frac{i[v(x + \operatorname{Re} h, y + \operatorname{Im} h) - v(x,y)]}{\operatorname{Re} h + i \operatorname{Im} h}$$

exists, regardless of how h approaches the origin. If we let h approach zero along the real axis, then $\operatorname{Im} h = 0$, and the right-hand side of the equation above becomes:

$$\lim_{\operatorname{Re} h \to 0} \frac{u(x + \operatorname{Re} h, y) - u(x,y)}{\operatorname{Re} h} + \lim_{\operatorname{Re} h \to 0} \frac{i[v(x + \operatorname{Re} h, y) - v(x,y)]}{\operatorname{Re} h} = \frac{\partial u}{\partial x} + i \frac{\partial v}{\partial x}$$

Alternatively, if we let h approach zero along the imaginary axis, then $\operatorname{Re} h = 0$, and the right-hand side of the equation that defines $f'(z)$ can be written as:

$$\lim_{\operatorname{Im} h \to 0} \frac{u(x, y + \operatorname{Im} h) - u(x, y)}{i \operatorname{Im} h} + \lim_{\operatorname{Im} h \to 0} \frac{i[v(x, y + \operatorname{Im} h) - v(x, y)]}{i \operatorname{Im} h} = \frac{1}{i}\frac{\partial u}{\partial y} + \frac{\partial v}{\partial y} = \frac{\partial v}{\partial y} - i\frac{\partial u}{\partial y}$$

The two expressions we've obtained must be identical, since they're both equal to $f'(z)$; therefore,

$$\frac{\partial u}{\partial x} + i\frac{\partial v}{\partial x} = \frac{\partial v}{\partial y} - i\frac{\partial u}{\partial y}$$

which implies that:

$$\frac{\partial u}{\partial x} = \frac{\partial v}{\partial y} \quad \text{and} \quad \frac{\partial v}{\partial x} = -\frac{\partial u}{\partial y}$$

These are called the **Cauchy–Riemann equations**, and both must be satisfied if $f(z)$ is to be differentiable. Conversely, if the Cauchy–Riemann equations are satisfied and the four partial derivatives are continuous throughout an open set containing z_0, then the function f is differentiable at the point z_0.

For example, we showed that the function $f(z) = \bar{z}$ is not differentiable at the origin. Using the Cauchy–Riemann equations, we could establish this result (and something more) with little effort. The equation $f(x + yi) = x - yi$ gives us $u(x, y) = x$ and $v(x, y) = -y$. Since

$$\frac{\partial u}{\partial x} = 1 \quad \text{but} \quad \frac{\partial v}{\partial y} = -1$$

the first of the Cauchy–Riemann equations, $u_x = v_y$, is never satisfied, so $f(z) = \bar{z}$ is differentiable *nowhere*.

If $f(z) = f(x + yi) = u(x, y) + iv(x, y)$ is differentiable throughout some open set O, then the Cauchy–Riemann equations hold true. Because $\partial u/\partial x = \partial v/\partial y$ and $\partial u/\partial y = -\partial v/\partial x$, we have

$$\frac{\partial^2 u}{\partial x^2} = \frac{\partial}{\partial x}\left(\frac{\partial u}{\partial x}\right) = \frac{\partial}{\partial x}\left(\frac{\partial v}{\partial y}\right) = \frac{\partial^2 v}{\partial x \partial y} \quad \text{and} \quad \frac{\partial^2 u}{\partial y^2} = \frac{\partial}{\partial y}\left(\frac{\partial u}{\partial y}\right) = \frac{\partial}{\partial y}\left(-\frac{\partial v}{\partial x}\right) = -\frac{\partial^2 v}{\partial y \partial x} = -\frac{\partial^2 v}{\partial x \partial y}$$

so:

$$\frac{\partial^2 u}{\partial x^2} + \frac{\partial^2 u}{\partial y^2} = 0$$

Any function of (x, y) that satisfies this equation (which is called **Laplace's equation**) throughout some open set O is said to be **harmonic** in O. Using the same method, we could use the Cauchy–Riemann equations to show that the function $v(x, y)$ also satisfies Laplace's equation; that is:

$$\frac{\partial^2 v}{\partial x^2} + \frac{\partial^2 v}{\partial y^2} = 0$$

Therefore, if $f(z)$ is differentiable throughout some open set, O, in the plane, then the real and imaginary parts of f—the functions $u(x, y)$ and $v(x, y)$, respectively—are harmonic in O.

ANALYTIC FUNCTIONS

If $f(z)$ is differentiable at z_0 and at every point throughout some open set in the complex plane containing z_0, then we say that $f(z)$ is **analytic at the point** z_0. In general, if $f(z)$ is differentiable throughout some open set O in the complex plane, then $f(z)$ is said to be **analytic in** O. If $f(z)$ is analytic *everywhere* in the complex plane, then $f(z)$ is said to be an **entire** function. Examples of entire functions include all polynomial functions, as well as the functions e^z, $\cos z$, and $\sin z$. A rational function of z—that is, a function of the form $f(z) = p(z)/q(z)$, where p and q are polynomials—is analytic at all points for which $q(z) \neq 0$.

If $f(z)$ is analytic, its component functions, $u(x, y)$ and $v(x, y)$, must have continuous partial derivatives of all orders. Furthermore, if $f(z)$ is analytic at some point z_0, then its derivative, $f'(z)$, is also analytic at z_0; this result immediately implies that the derivatives of *all* orders of $f(z)$ are analytic at z_0! There's no such result for functions of a real variable. For example, consider the real-valued function:

$$f(x) = \begin{cases} -\frac{1}{2}x^2 & \text{for } x < 0 \\ \frac{1}{2}x^2 & \text{for } x \geq 0 \end{cases}$$

Then $f(x)$ is differentiable everywhere, and

$$f'(x) = \begin{cases} -x & \text{for } x < 0 \\ x & \text{for } x \geq 0 \end{cases}$$

so $f'(x) = |x|$. However, the second derivative of $f(x)$ does not exist at $x = 0$, since we know that $f'(x) = |x|$ is not differentiable at $x = 0$.

Example 7.31   Let $f(z)$ be the function $f(z) = 2xy + i(x^2 + y^2)$. Show that there exist infinitely many points in the complex plane at which f is differentiable (and describe those points) but that f is analytic nowhere.

Solution: The component functions of $f(z)$ are $u(x, y) = 2xy$ and $v(x, y) = x^2 + y^2$. The partial derivatives of these functions are $u_x = 2y$, $u_y = 2x$, $v_x = 2x$, and $v_y = 2y$. We notice that the partial derivatives are continuous everywhere, so f will be differentiable wherever the Cauchy–Riemann equations are satisfied. The first Cauchy–Riemann equation, $u_x = v_y$, becomes $2y = 2y$, which is satisfied everywhere. The second Cauchy–Riemann equation, $u_y = -v_x$, becomes $2x = -2x$, which is satisfied if and only if $x = 0$. The line $x = 0$ is the imaginary axis, so f is differentiable at every point on the imaginary axis, and for these points we have:

$$f'(z) = u_x + iv_x = 2y + i(2x) = 2y$$

Despite the fact that f is differentiable at infinitely many points, it is analytic nowhere. By definition, f is analytic at a point z_0 if it's differentiable at every point throughout an open set containing z_0. However, every open set in the complex plane (for example, every open rectangle) that contains a point on the imaginary axis, contains points *not* on this axis. Because f is not differentiable throughout any open set in **C**, it's analytic nowhere.

COMPLEX LINE INTEGRALS

Let C be a smooth path in the complex plane, which is given parametrically by the equation $z(t) = x(t) + iy(t)$, from $t = a$ to $t = b$ (where t is real). If $f(z)$ is a continuous function along C, then we have:

$$\int_C f(z)\,dz = \int_a^b f(z(t)) \bullet z'(t)\,dt$$

For example, let's integrate the function $f(z) = z^2 - iz$ along the path $z(t) = x(t) + iy(t)$ that connects the origin to the point $1 + 2i$, given by:

$$\begin{cases} x = t \\ y = 2t^2 \end{cases} \quad \text{for } 0 \xrightarrow{\ t\ } 1$$

Since $f(x + yi) = (x + yi)^2 - i(x + yi) = (x^2 - y^2 + y) + (2xy - x)i$, we get:

$$\begin{aligned} \int_C f(z)\,dz &= \int_a^b f(z(t)) \bullet z'(t)\,dt \\ &= \int_0^1 f(t + 2t^2 i) \bullet \tfrac{d}{dt}(t + 2t^2 i)\,dt \\ &= \int_0^1 \left\{ [t^2 - (2t^2)^2 + 2t^2] + [2t(2t^2) - t]i \right\} \bullet (1 + 4ti)\,dt \\ &= \int_0^1 [(3t^2 - 4t^4) + (4t^3 - t)i](1 + 4ti)\,dt \\ &= \int_0^1 [(7t^2 - 20t^4) + i(16t^3 - t - 16t^5)]\,dt \\ &= \left[(\tfrac{7}{3}t^3 - 4t^5) + i(4t^4 - \tfrac{1}{2}t^2 - \tfrac{8}{3}t^6) \right]_0^1 \\ &= -\tfrac{5}{3} + \tfrac{5}{6}i \end{aligned}$$

Alternatively, we could have invoked the fundamental theorem of calculus and written

$$\int_C f(z)\,dz = \int_a^b f(z(t)) \bullet z'(t)\,dt = \int_a^b F'(z(t))\,dt = F(z(t)) \Big]_a^b = F(z(b)) - F(z(a))$$

where $F(z)$ is an antiderivative of $f(z)$. For $f(z) = z^2 - iz$, it's clear that we can take $F(z) = \tfrac{1}{3}z^3 - \tfrac{1}{2}iz^2$, so

$$\begin{aligned} \int_C f(z)\,dz &= \tfrac{1}{3}z^3 - \tfrac{1}{2}iz^2 \Big]_0^{1+2i} \\ &= \tfrac{1}{3}(1 + 2i)^3 - \tfrac{1}{2}i(1 + 2i)^2 \\ &= \tfrac{1}{6}(1 + 2i)^2 \left[2(1 + 2i) - 3i \right] \\ &= \tfrac{1}{6}(-3 + 4i)(2 + i) \\ &= \tfrac{1}{6}(-10 + 5i) \\ &= -\tfrac{5}{3} + \tfrac{5}{6}i \end{aligned}$$

which is the same result as before.

THEOREMS CONCERNING ANALYTIC FUNCTIONS

In this section, we'll list some of the most important results in complex analysis, which you should know for the GRE Math Subject Test.

1. **Cauchy's Theorem:** If $f(z)$ is analytic throughout a simply connected, open set, D, then for every *closed* path, C, in D, we have:

$$\oint_C f(z)\,dz = 0$$

   In particular, if $f(z)$ is an entire function, then $\oint_C f(z)\,dz$ is equal to 0 for *any* closed path in the plane.

2. **Morera's Theorem:** This result provides a sort of converse to Cauchy's theorem. If $f(z)$ is continuous throughout an open, connected set O in the complex plane, and $\oint_C f(z)\,dz = 0$ for every closed curve C in O, then $f(z)$ is analytic in O.

3. **Cauchy's Integral Formulas:** If $f(z)$ is analytic at all points within and on a simple, closed path, C, that surrounds the point z_0, then:

$$f(z_0) = \frac{1}{2\pi i} \oint_C \frac{f(z)}{z - z_0}\,dz$$

   Furthermore, the nth derivative, $f^{(n)}(z)$, is also analytic at z_0 for all positive integers n, and:

$$f^{(n)}(z_0) = \frac{n!}{2\pi i} \oint_C \frac{f(z)}{(z - z_0)^{n+1}}\,dz$$

   These formulas tell us that, if we know the values of an analytic function, $f(z)$, at all points on a simple, closed curve, then we know its value—and the values of all its derivatives—at any interior point.

4. **Cauchy's Derivative Estimates:** Let $f(z)$ be analytic on and within $|z - z_0| = r$, the circle of radius r centered at z_0. If M denotes the maximum value of $|f(z)|$ on the circle, then:

$$\left| f^{(n)}(z_0) \right| \le \frac{n!M}{r^n}$$

5. **Liouville's Theorem:** If $f(z)$ is an entire function that's bounded, then $f(z)$ must be a constant function.

6. **The Maximum Principle:** (also known as the **Maximum Modulus theorem**): Let O be an open, connected subset of the complex plane, and let $f(z)$ be a function that's analytic in O. If there's a point z_0 in O, such that $|f(z)| \le |f(z_0)|$ for every z in O, then $f(z)$ is a constant function. Said another way, if $f(z)$ is analytic and not constant in an open, connected subset of the plane, then $|f(z)|$ attains no maximum value in O. If O is bounded, then $|f(z)|$ *must* achieve a maximum value in cl(O), the closure of O. Since $|f(z)|$ cannot attain its maximum value at a point within the open set O, it must attain its maximum value at some point *on the boundary* of O.

TAYLOR SERIES FOR FUNCTIONS OF A COMPLEX VARIABLE

The Taylor series we reviewed at the end of Chapter 2 holds true if the real variable x is replaced by the complex variable z. However, the interval of convergence for a power series in the real variable x is now replaced by the idea of the **disk of convergence** for a power series in the complex variable z, since the inequality $|z - z_0| < R$ describes the interior of a disk of radius R, centered at the point z_0. The power series $\sum_{n=0}^{\infty} a_n z^n$ converges absolutely for all z that satisfy $|z| < R$, and diverges for all z such that $|z| > R$, where the **radius of convergence**, R, is given by:

$$R = \frac{1}{\lim_{n \to \infty} \sqrt[n]{|a_n|}}, \quad \text{if } \lim_{n \to \infty} \sqrt[n]{|a_n|} \text{ is nonzero and finite}$$

If $\lim_{n \to \infty} \sqrt[n]{|a_n|} = \infty$, then the power series converges only for $z = 0$, and if $\lim_{n \to \infty} \sqrt[n]{|a_n|} = 0$, then the series converges for every z. More generally, the power series $\sum_{n=0}^{\infty} a_n (z - z_0)^n$ converges absolutely for all z that satisfy $|z - z_0| < R$ and diverges for all z such that $|z - z_0| > R$, where R is given as above. If $\lim_{n \to \infty} \sqrt[n]{|a_n|} = \infty$, then the power series converges only for $z = z_0$, and if $\lim_{n \to \infty} \sqrt[n]{|a_n|} = 0$, then the series converges for every z.

Every function $f(z)$ that's analytic in an open, connected subset, O, of the complex plane can be expanded in a power series—its Taylor series—whose disk of convergence lies within O. That is, if z_0 is any point within O, and R is a positive number such that the disk of radius R centered at z_0 is contained in O, then

$$f(z) = \sum_{n=0}^{\infty} a_n (z - z_0)^n, \quad \text{where } a_n = \frac{f^{(n)}(z_0)}{n!}$$

is valid in the open disk $|z - z_0| < R$. Not only can every analytic function be expanded in a Taylor series; the converse is also true. That is, for every z in its disk of convergence, a Taylor series gives an analytic function.

SINGULARITIES, POLES, AND LAURENT SERIES

Let z_0 be a point in the complex plane, and R a positive number. The set of all z such that $0 < |z - z_0| < R$ is called the **punctured** open disk (of radius R) centered at z_0. If a function $f(z)$ is not analytic at a point z_0, but is analytic at *some* point in every punctured disk centered at z_0, then z_0 is said to be a **singularity** of $f(z)$. If z_0 is a singularity of $f(z)$, but $f(z)$ is analytic at *every* point in some punctured open disk centered at z_0, then we call z_0 an **isolated singularity** of $f(z)$.

Let's now assume that $f(z)$ has an isolated singularity at the point z_0. If there's a positive integer n such that

$$f(z) = \frac{g(z)}{(z - z_0)^n}$$

with $g(z)$ analytic in a nonpunctured open disk centered at z_0 and $g(z_0) \neq 0$, then the singularity z_0 is called a **pole of order** n. A pole of order 1 is called a **simple pole**, a pole of order 2 is called a **double pole**, and so forth. However, if we can't write $f(z)$ in this form, for any positive integer n, then z_0 is said to be an **essential singularity**.

If a function $f(z)$ has a singularity, it may not be possible to expand it in a Taylor series. For example, the function $f(z) = 1/(1-z)$ can be expanded in a Taylor series within the disk $|z| < 1$, but it can't be expanded in a Taylor series in the disk $|z| < 2$, because this larger disk contains the point $z = 1$, which is a singularity of $f(z)$, and the sum of a Taylor series is always an analytic function throughout its disk of convergence. To provide a valid series representation for functions that have singularities, we need to generalize the notion of a Taylor series.

An **annulus** is the region between two concentric circles; in the complex plane, an annulus centered at z_0 is described by a pair of inequalities of the form $R_1 < |z - z_0| < R_2$. (We'll allow R_1 to be zero, and we'll also allow R_2 to be ∞, so not only can an annulus be a finite ring, it could be a punctured disk of finite radius, the entire complex plane minus a closed disk, or the entire complex plane minus a single point, z_0.) If $f(z)$ is analytic in some annulus centered at z_0, then $f(z)$ can be expanded in a **Laurent series**, which is a series of the form:

$$\underbrace{\sum_{n=1}^{\infty} a_{-n}(z - z_0)^{-n}}_{\substack{\text{singular} \\ \text{(or principal)} \\ \text{part}}} + \underbrace{\sum_{n=0}^{\infty} a_n(z - z_0)^n}_{\substack{\text{analytic} \\ \text{part}}}$$

The coefficients of the nonnegative powers of $(z - z_0)$—those in the **analytic part**—are the usual Taylor coefficients, which can be calculated from the formula:

$$a_n = \frac{f^{(n)}(z_0)}{n!} \quad (n \geq 0)$$

The coefficients of the negative powers of $(z - z_0)$—those in the **singular** (or **principal**) **part**—are called **Laurent coefficients**. If C is a simple, closed, positively oriented curve in the annulus, then these coefficients can be computed using the equation:

$$a_{-n} = \frac{1}{2\pi i} \oint_C \frac{f(z)}{(z - z_0)^{-n+1}} \, dz \quad (n \geq 0)$$

In practice, we don't usually figure out the Laurent coefficients from this formula; instead, we derive them by algebraic manipulations of the Taylor series.

The Laurent series can be used to identify poles and essential singularities. If the singular part of the Laurent series contains at least one term, but only a finite number, then z_0 is a pole. In particular, if k is the largest integer such that $a_{-k} \neq 0$ but $a_{-n} = 0$ for all $n > k$, then z_0 is a pole of order k. On the other hand, if the singular part of the Laurent series contains infinitely many terms, then z_0 is an essential singularity.

Let's look at an example. The function $f(z) = 1/(1-z)$ has a singularity at $z = 1$, so it cannot be expanded in a Taylor series in, say, the disk $|z| < 2$. Within the disk $|z| < 1$, the Taylor series is valid, and we have

$$\frac{1}{1-z} = 1 + z + z^2 + z^3 + \cdots, \quad \text{for } |z| < 1$$

which is the well-known formula for the geometric series. Now, to avoid the singularity at $z = 1$, we expand $f(z) = 1/(1-z)$ in a *Laurent* series in the region $1 < |z| < \infty$. To do this, we first write:

$$\frac{1}{1-z} = \frac{1}{z\left(\frac{1}{z} - 1\right)} = -\frac{1}{z} \cdot \frac{1}{1 - \frac{1}{z}}$$

Now, we notice that, if $|z| > 1$, then $\left|\frac{1}{z}\right| < 1$, so the following expansion is valid:

$$\frac{1}{1-z} = -\frac{1}{z} \cdot \frac{1}{1-\frac{1}{z}} = -\frac{1}{z}\left[1 + \left(\frac{1}{z}\right) + \left(\frac{1}{z}\right)^2 + \cdots\right] = -\frac{1}{z} - \left(\frac{1}{z}\right)^2 - \left(\frac{1}{z}\right)^3 - \cdots, \quad \text{for } |z| > 1$$

Since there are infinitely many terms in the Laurent series, $z = 1$ is an essential singularity.

Example 7.32   Find the Laurent series expansions of the function

$$f(z) = \frac{4z}{(z-1)(z-3)^2}$$

that are valid in the annuli
(a) $1 < |z| < 3$
(b) $0 < |z-3| < 2$

Solution: The partial fraction decomposition of $f(z)$ is:

$$\frac{4z}{(z-1)(z-3)^2} = \frac{1}{z-1} + \frac{-1}{z-3} + \frac{6}{(z-3)^2}$$

(a) For $|z| > 1$, we can write:

$$\frac{1}{z-1} = \frac{1}{z\left(1-\frac{1}{z}\right)} = \frac{1}{z}\sum_{n=0}^{\infty}\left(\frac{1}{z}\right)^n = \sum_{n=1}^{\infty}\left(\frac{1}{z}\right)^n = \sum_{n=1}^{\infty} z^{-n}$$

Next, for $|z| < 3$, the following expansion is valid:

$$\frac{-1}{z-3} = \frac{1}{3\left(1-\frac{z}{3}\right)} = \frac{1}{3}\sum_{n=0}^{\infty}\left(\frac{z}{3}\right)^n = \sum_{n=0}^{\infty}\frac{1}{3^{n+1}} z^n$$

Finally, since $6(z-3)^{-2} = 6 \cdot (d/dz)[-(z-3)^{-1}]$, we get, for $|z| < 3$,

$$\frac{6}{(z-3)^2} = 6 \cdot \frac{d}{dz}\left[\frac{-1}{z-3}\right] = 6 \cdot \frac{d}{dz}\left[\sum_{n=0}^{\infty}\frac{1}{3^{n+1}} z^n\right] = \sum_{n=1}^{\infty}\frac{6n}{3^{n+1}} z^{n-1} = \sum_{n=0}^{\infty}\frac{6(n+1)}{3^{n+2}} z^n$$

Adding these three results gives the Laurent series expansion for $f(z)$ that's valid in the annulus $1 < |z| < 3$:

$$f(z) = \frac{1}{z-1} + \frac{-1}{z-3} + \frac{6}{(z-3)^2}$$

$$= \sum_{n=1}^{\infty} z^{-n} + \sum_{n=0}^{\infty}\frac{1}{3^{n+1}} z^n + \sum_{n=0}^{\infty}\frac{6(n+1)}{3^{n+2}} z^n$$

$$= \sum_{n=1}^{\infty} z^{-n} + \sum_{n=0}^{\infty}\frac{2n+3}{3^{n+1}} z^n, \quad \text{for } 1 < |z| < 3$$

(b) In the region $0 < |z-3| < 2$, we'll write:

$$\frac{1}{z-1} = \frac{1}{2+(z-3)} = \frac{1}{2\left(1+\frac{z-3}{2}\right)} = \frac{1}{2}\sum_{n=0}^{\infty}(-1)^n\left(\frac{z-3}{2}\right)^n = \sum_{n=0}^{\infty}\frac{(-1)^n}{2^{n+1}}(z-3)^n$$

Therefore, the Laurent series expansion of $f(z)$ in powers of $(z - 3)$ that's valid in the region $0 < |z-3| < 2$ is:

$$f(z) = \frac{6}{(z-3)^2} + \frac{-1}{z-3} + \frac{1}{z-1}$$

$$= 6(z-3)^{-2} - (z-3)^{-1} + \sum_{n=0}^{\infty} \frac{(-1)^n}{2^{n+1}}(z-3)^n, \quad \text{for } 0 < |z-3| < 2$$

Since the first two terms of the partial fraction decomposition have a pole at $z = 3$, the terms do not need Laurent series expansions.

Example 7.33   What's the Laurent series of the function $f(z) = ze^{1/z^2}$, for $|z| > 0$?

Solution: If we replace z by $1/z^2$ in the Taylor series for e^z, we get:

$$e^{1/z^2} = \sum_{n=0}^{\infty} \frac{1}{n!}\left(\frac{1}{z^2}\right)^n$$

This tells us that, for $0 < |z| < \infty$,

$$ze^{1/z^2} = z \cdot \sum_{n=0}^{\infty} \frac{1}{n!}\left(\frac{1}{z^2}\right)^n = z \cdot \left[1 + \sum_{n=1}^{\infty} \frac{1}{n!}\left(\frac{1}{z^2}\right)^n\right] = z \cdot \left[1 + \sum_{n=1}^{\infty} \frac{1}{n!}z^{-2n}\right] = \left[\sum_{n=1}^{\infty} \frac{1}{n!}z^{-2n+1}\right] + z$$

THE RESIDUE THEOREM

From the formula given above for the Laurent coefficients, we notice that if we take $n = -1$, we get:

$$a_{-1} = \frac{1}{2\pi i}\oint_C f(z)\,dz$$

C is a simple, closed, positively oriented curve in the annulus where the Laurent series expansion of $f(z)$ is valid. This implies that $\oint_C f(z)\,dz = 2\pi i \cdot a_{-1}$. The number a_{-1}, which is the coefficient of $(z - z_0)^{-1}$ in the Laurent series of $f(z)$, is called the **residue** of $f(z)$ at the singularity z_0; this is written $\text{Res}(z_0, f) = a_{-1}$. Therefore, if we can find the residue of $f(z)$ at z_0, we can easily compute the integral of $f(z)$ around any simple, closed curve C that surrounds z_0 (assuming, for now, that $f(z)$ has no other singularities within C).

For example, let's figure out the value of the integral

$$\oint_C \frac{4z}{(z-1)(z-3)^2}\,dz$$

where C is the circle $|z| = 2$, oriented counterclockwise. The Laurent series of the integrand is

$$f(z) = \frac{4z}{(z-1)(z-3)^2} = \sum_{n=1}^{\infty} z^{-n} + \sum_{n=0}^{\infty} \frac{2n+3}{3^{n+1}}z^n, \quad \text{for } 1 < |z| < 3$$

which is valid in an annulus that contains the circle C. If we expand this Laurent series as a polynomial, the coefficient of the z^{-1} term in this series is $a_{-1} = 1$, so:

$$\oint_C \frac{4z}{(z-1)(z-3)^2}\,dz = 2\pi i \cdot a_{-1} = 2\pi i$$

To find the residue of $f(z)$ at a singularity z_0, one option is to figure out its Laurent series and then simply read the coefficient of the $(z - z_0)^{-1}$ term. If the singularity is a pole, there's another way to find the residue; this alternate method is usually faster if the singularity is a pole of low order. Here's the formula: If z_0 is a pole of order k, then:

$$\text{Res}(z_0, f) = \frac{1}{(k-1)!} \cdot \lim_{z \to z_0} \frac{d^{k-1}}{dz^{k-1}} \Big[(z - z_0)^k f(z) \Big]$$

In particular,

$$z_0 \text{ is a simple pole} \quad \Rightarrow \quad \text{Res}(z_0, f) = \lim_{z \to z_0} \Big[(z - z_0) f(z) \Big]$$

$$z_0 \text{ is a double pole} \quad \Rightarrow \quad \text{Res}(z_0, f) = \lim_{z \to z_0} \frac{d}{dz} \Big[(z - z_0)^2 f(z) \Big]$$

Example 7.34   If C is the circle $|z - i| = \frac{1}{2}$, oriented counterclockwise, what's the value of the following integral?

$$\oint_C \frac{z+1}{z(z-i)^2} dz$$

Solution: The integrand has a double pole at $z = i$, and this is its only singularity within the circle C. The residue at $z = i$ is:

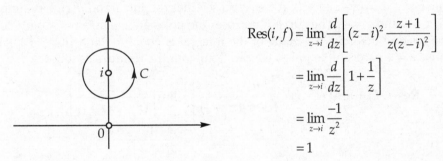

$$\text{Res}(i, f) = \lim_{z \to i} \frac{d}{dz} \left[(z - i)^2 \frac{z+1}{z(z-i)^2} \right]$$

$$= \lim_{z \to i} \frac{d}{dz} \left[1 + \frac{1}{z} \right]$$

$$= \lim_{z \to i} \frac{-1}{z^2}$$

$$= 1$$

Therefore,

$$\oint_C \frac{z+1}{z(z-i)^2} dz = 2\pi i \cdot \text{Res}(i, f) = 2\pi i \cdot 1 = 2\pi i$$

If the curve C surrounds more than one singularity of $f(z)$, we can still figure out the value of the integral $\oint_C f(z)\,dz$. We'll assume that $f(z)$ is analytic throughout the interior of C, except at a finite number of singularities—$z_1, z_2, \ldots, z_n$—inside C. In this case, the **residue theorem** says that *the integral is equal to $2\pi i$ times the sum of the residues*:

$$\oint_C f(z)\,dz = 2\pi i \cdot \sum_{m=1}^{n} \text{Res}(z_m, f)$$

Example 7.35   What's the value of the integral

$$\oint_C \frac{z}{(z-2)(z^2+1)}\,dz$$

where C is the curve shown below?

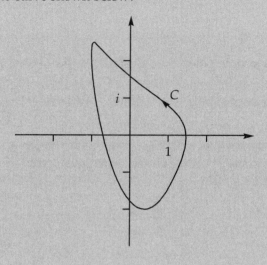

Solution: Because $z^2 + 1 = (z - i)(z + i)$, it's easy to see that the integrand, $f(z)$, has simple poles at $z = 2$, $z = i$, and $z = -i$. The curve C encloses the poles at $z = i$ and $z = -i$ only, so according to the residue theorem, the value of the integral is equal to $2\pi i \bullet [\text{Res}(i, f) + \text{Res}(-i, f)]$. Because $z = \pm i$ are simple poles, we can figure out the residues as follows:

$$\text{Res}(i, f) = \lim_{z \to i}\left[(z - i) \bullet \frac{z}{(z - 2)(z^2 + 1)}\right] = \lim_{z \to i}\left[\frac{z}{(z - 2)(z + i)}\right]$$

$$= \frac{1}{2(-2 + i)}$$

$$= \frac{1}{2(-2 + i)} \bullet \frac{-2 - i}{-2 - i}$$

$$= \frac{-2 - i}{10}$$

and

$$\text{Res}(-i, f) = \lim_{z \to -i}\left[(z + i) \bullet \frac{z}{(z - 2)(z^2 + 1)}\right] = \lim_{z \to -i}\left[\frac{z}{(z - 2)(z - i)}\right]$$

$$= \frac{1}{2(-2 - i)}$$

$$= \frac{1}{2(-2 - i)} \bullet \frac{-2 + i}{-2 + i}$$

$$= \frac{-2 + i}{10}$$

Therefore,

$$\oint_C \frac{z}{(z-2)(z^2+1)}\,dz = 2\pi i \cdot \left[\operatorname{Res}(i,f) + \operatorname{Res}(-i,f)\right]$$

$$= 2\pi i \cdot \left[\frac{-2-i}{10} + \frac{-2+i}{10}\right]$$

$$= -\tfrac{4}{5}\pi i$$

NUMERICAL ANALYSIS

Numerical analysis is the study of methods of computing numerical data. Often this analysis involves producing a sequence of approximations that converge towards a limit. A process that begins with an initial guess and finds successive approximations is an **iterative method**; the method is not expected to terminate in a finite number of iterations. Therefore, it is necessary to define a criterion for convergence, denoted ε, such that an approximation is sufficiently accurate when the measurement of error is less than ε. The speed at which a sequence approaches a limit is the **rate of convergence**. A particularly useful application of numerical analysis on the GRE is finding roots.

The simplest such method is the **bisection method**, which requires that the function f be continuous on an interval $[a, b]$ where $f(a)$ and $f(b)$ have opposite signs. By the Intermediate Value theorem, there must exist a root of f in the interval. With each step of the algorithm, the interval is divided in half:

$$c = a + \frac{a+b}{2}$$

Excluding the unlikely chance that $f(c)$ is a root, one of two options must be true: either $f(a)$ and $f(c)$ have opposite signs, or $f(b)$ and $f(c)$ do. We select the correct interval and repeat the process. This method converges linearly (slowly), but it is guaranteed to converge because a root must exist in this interval $[a, b]$.

Example 7.36 Let $P(x) = x^3 + \frac{4}{3}x^2 - \frac{59}{9}x + 2$. Perform two iterations of the bisection method to approximate the root closest to $x = 0$.

Solution: Since $P(x)$ does not appear to be factorable, we can use the bisection method to approximate the roots. Note that $P(-1)$ and $P(0)$ have the same sign, but $P(0) > 0$ and $P(1) < 0$. Since P is continuous everywhere, there must exist a zero in the interval $[0, 1]$. Calculate $P\left(\frac{1}{2}\right) = -\frac{39}{72} \neq 0$, so $\frac{1}{2}$ is not a root. Choose a new interval of $[0, \frac{1}{2}]$, since $P\left(\frac{1}{2}\right)$ and $P(0)$ have opposite signs. Now calculate $P\left(\frac{1}{4}\right) = \frac{265}{275}$, which is positive. We can now conclude that the root lies in the interval $[\frac{1}{4}, \frac{1}{2}]$, so a good approximation for the root is $x = \frac{3}{8}$. (The actual root is $x = \frac{1}{3}$, but it is likely that you will be able to eliminate several answer choices with your approximation.)

Newton's method is also used to find approximations for the zeros of a real-valued function. This method begins with an initial guess and calculates the x-intercept of the tangent line to the curve at the initial x-value, a process that can be iterated. Let f be a differentiable, real-valued function. Given an approximation x_n of a zero, the formula for the next best approximation, x_{n+1}, is:

$$x_{n+1} = x_n - \frac{f(x_n)}{f'(x_n)}$$

The choice of x_0 close to the root is important; otherwise, this method may converge slowly or not at all. A good initial guess will yield at least a quadratic rate of convergence, so Newton's method, while more complicated, converges faster than the bisection method.

CHAPTER 7 REVIEW QUESTIONS

Complete the following review questions using the techniques outlined in this chapter. Then, see Chapter 8 for answers and explanations.

1. For which of the following intervals does $P(x) = 4x^3 - 4x^2 - 33x + 45$ have a zero?

   (A) [−2, −1]   (B) [−1, 0]   (C) [0, 1]   (D) [2, 3]   (E) [3, 4]

2. Which of the following is the negation of the sentence $(S \vee T)$?

   (A) $\neg S \wedge \neg T$ (B) $\neg S \wedge T$ (C) $S \wedge \neg T$ (D) $\neg S \vee \neg T$ (E) $S \wedge T$

3. In a State Lottery, players choose 6 numbers from among the integers 1 through 51. The jackpot is awarded if the 6 numbers selected match the 6 numbers drawn. What's the minimum number of tickets someone would need to purchase in order to guarantee winning?

   (A) 720   (B) 18,009,460   (C) 377,149,517

   (D) 12,966,811,200   (E) 17,596,287,801

4. Using the undirected graph below, delete the edge DE. Which of the following must be true?

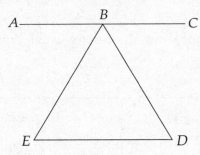

   I.   vertex D is even
   II. the graph is a spanning tree of the previous graph
   III. the graph is a forest

   (A) None of the above   (B) I and II only   (C) I and III only
   (D) II and III only   (E) I, II, and III

5. If a fair die is tossed twice, what is the expectation value for the number of times the die will show 3 or greater?

   (A) $\dfrac{8}{9}$ (B) $\dfrac{4}{3}$ (C) 1   (D) $\dfrac{2}{3}$ (E) 0

6. Suppose A is the set of all prime numbers, and B is the set of all odd integers. Then the relative complement $A - B$ is equivalent to the set of

(A) $\{x \mid x \text{ is even}\}$
(B) $\{x \mid x \text{ is positive and odd}\}$
(C) $\{x \mid x \text{ is a composite integer}\}$
(D) $\{2\}$
(E) $\{0\}$

7. Which of the following sets is NOT countably infinite?

(A) $\mathbb{Q}$, the set of rational numbers
(B) $\mathbb{Z}$, the set of all integers
(C) $\mathbb{Q}^c$, the set of all irrational numbers
(D) $\mathbb{Z}^+$, the set of positive integers
(E) $\mathbf{E}$, the set of positive even integers

8. A man forgot the combination to his safe. The combination consists of a sequence of four numbers, each from 1 to 60. The man only remembers the following pieces of information:

All the numbers are different.
The second number is twice the third number.
The third number is prime.

How many possible combinations must the man try to unlock his safe?

(A) 1377 (B) 33,060 (C) 34,220 (D) 35,400 (E) 11,703,240

9. What is the coefficient of the $(z - 2)^{-1}$ term in the Laurent series for $f(z) = \dfrac{1}{z-5}$ centered at $z = 2$?

(A) 81 (B) 27 (C) 9 (D) 3 (E) 1

10. Let $g(x)$ be a polynomial function whose derivative is continuous and nonzero on the interval $[a, b]$. Suppose there exists a y on this same interval such that $g(y) = 0$. Let x_0 be an arbitrary x-value in the interval. Then x_1 is the x-intercept of the line tangent to $g(x)$ at x_0. For each subsequent n, x_n is the x-intercept of the line tangent to $g(x)$ at x_{n-1}. Which formula best approximates the root of $g(x)$ using the method described above?

(A) $x_{n+1} = x_n - \dfrac{g(x)}{g^n(x)}$

(B) $x_{n+1} = x_n - \dfrac{g'(x)}{g''(x)}$

(C) $x_{n+1} = x_n + \dfrac{g(x)}{g'(x)}$

(D) $x_{n+1} = x_n - \dfrac{g(x)}{g'(x)}$

(E) $x_{n+1} = x_n - \dfrac{g'(x)}{g(x)}$

11. The steps below are used to compute Euclid's Algorithm to find the greatest common divisor of two integers. If the numbers 380 and 72 are input, how many iterations of the algorithm will it take to find the gcd?

```
input a;
input b;
while (b > 0)  {
      int r == a mod b;
      a == b;
      b == r;
}
int gcd == a;
output gcd;
```

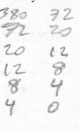

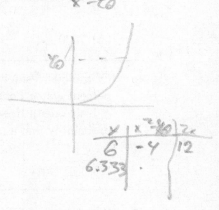

(A) 3   (B) 4   (C) 5   (D) 6   (E) 7

---

12. If $x^2 = 40$, use Newton's method twice to approximate the value of x to three decimal places.

(A) 6.223   (B) 6.225   (C) 6.320   (D) 6.323   (E) 6.325

---

13. Given the undirected graph below, what is the maximum number of edges that can be removed that still leaves a connected subgraph?

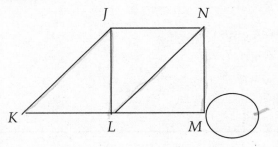

(A) 3   (B) 4   (C) 5   (D) 6   (E) 7

---

14. Find the Laurent series expansions of the function $f(z) = \dfrac{1}{z-3}$ that is valid in the annulus $|z-4| > 1$.

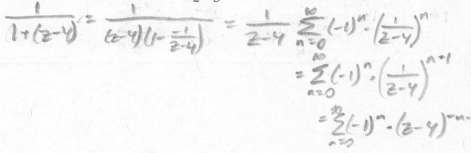

(A) $\displaystyle\sum_{n=1}^{\infty}(4-z)^{-n-1}$

(B) $\displaystyle\sum_{n=0}^{\infty}(-1)^{n}(z-4)^{-n}$

(C) $\displaystyle\sum_{n=1}^{\infty}(-1)^{n}(z-4)^{-n-1}$

(D) $\displaystyle\sum_{n=0}^{\infty}(-1)^{n}(z-4)^{-n-1}$

(E) $\displaystyle\sum_{n=1}^{\infty}(z-4)^{-n-1}$

6·5·4·$\binom{8}{2}$=

(4,1,1) $\binom{6}{4}$·6=90 (3,2,1) 6·$\binom{6}{3}$·3 = 360
(3,2,2) $\binom{6}{2}\binom{4}{2}$·6= 540 990

15. Suppose a teacher needs to divide up six students into three groups, each of which must contain at least one member. Each group will then be assigned uniquely to a different task. What is the total number of possible team and task assignments for the six students?

1   2   3

(A) 7200   (B) 720   (C) 540   (D) 90   (E) 65

   103-36=

16. Of the 600 residents of Clermontville, 35 percent watch the television show *Island Survival*, 40 percent watch *Lovelost Lawyers*, and 50 percent watch *Medical Emergency*. If all residents watch at least one of these three shows, and 18 percent watch exactly 2 of these shows, then what is the probability that a resident chosen at random watches all of the shows?

(A) $\dfrac{1}{4}$ (B) $\dfrac{1}{5}$ (C) $\dfrac{9}{50}$ (D) $\dfrac{7}{100}$ (E) $\dfrac{7}{200}$

17. Which of the following is the solution set of the inequality $x + \dfrac{6}{x} > 5$?

(A) $(0, 2) \cup (3, \infty)$
(B) $(0, 1) \cup (2, \infty)$
(C) $(-\infty, 2) \cup (3, \infty)$
(D) $(0, 2) \cap (3, \infty)$
(E) $(-\infty, 0)$

18. If the formula $A \vee B \rightarrow \neg C \vee D$ is true, which of the following statements is its contrapositive?

(A) $\neg C \wedge D \rightarrow A \wedge B$
(B) $C \wedge \neg D \rightarrow \neg A \wedge \neg B$
(C) $\neg C \wedge \neg D \rightarrow \neg A \wedge \neg B$
(D) $C \vee \neg D \rightarrow \neg A \vee \neg B$
(E) $A \vee B \rightarrow C \vee \neg D$

19. Which of the following sets in $\mathbb{R}^2$ is closed?

(A) $(2, 5) \times (1, 3)$ (B) $(2, 5] \times [1, 3)$ (C) $[2, 5] \times (1, 3)$ (D) $(2, 5) \times [1, 3]$ (E) $[2, 5] \times [1, 3]$

20. What is Log $(-e^3)$?

(A) -3 (B) 3 (C) $3 + \pi i$ (D) $3 - \pi i$ (E) $3 + 2\pi i$

21. Which of the following is NOT a tautology?

(A) $\neg(\neg A) \leftrightarrow A$

(B) $A \vee (\neg A)$

(C) $[(A \wedge B) \to C] \leftrightarrow [A \to (B \vee C)]$

(D) $\neg(C \wedge D) \leftrightarrow \neg C \vee \neg D$

(E) $A \vee (B \wedge C) \leftrightarrow (A \wedge B) \vee (A \wedge C)$

---

22. Which of the following graphs are isomorphic?

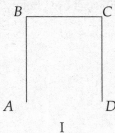 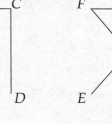 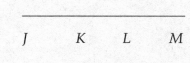

I   II   III

(A) None of the above   (B) I and II only   (C) I and III only

(D) II and III only   (E) I, II, and III

---

23. Given set $A = \{a, b\}$, set $B = \{c, d, e, f\}$, and set $C = \{g, h, i\}$. If set $D = P(C) \times B$, which of the following sets has the same cardinality as $P(D)$?

$2^3 \cdot 4$

$|P(D)| = 2^{32}$

(A) $P[P(A) \times P(C)]$

(B) $P[A \times C]$

(C) $P(A) \times P(C)$

(D) $[P(B) \times P(C)]$

(E) $P[P(A) \times P(B)]$

---

24. What are the complex roots of the equation $e^{2z} = i$?

(A) $\left(\dfrac{i}{2}\right)\left(-\dfrac{\pi}{2} + 2n\pi\right)$

(B) $(2i)\left(-\dfrac{\pi}{2} + n\pi\right)$

(C) $\left(\dfrac{i}{2}\right)\left(\dfrac{\pi}{2} + n\pi\right)$

(D) $(2i)\left(\dfrac{\pi}{2} + 2n\pi\right)$

(E) $\left(\dfrac{i}{2}\right)\left(\dfrac{\pi}{2} + 2n\pi\right)$

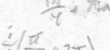

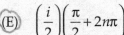

(handwritten at top) $(x+iy)^2 = (x-iy)^2$
$2xiy = -2xiy$

25. In the complex plane, the set of all points that satisfy the equation $(\bar{z})^2 = z^2$ is

    (A) a circle   (B) a point   (C) a ray   (D) a line   (E) two lines *(circled)*

---

26. Which of the following is a harmonic conjugate $u(x, y)$ of the harmonic function $v = x - 3x^{2y} + y^3$?

    (A) $x^3 - 3xy^2 + y$ (B) $-x^3 + 3xy^2 - y$ (C) $-y^3 + 3x^{2y} - x$

     (D) $y^3 - 3x^{2y} + x$ (E) $-x^3 + 3xy^2$

---

27. What's the value of the integral $\int_C \dfrac{z+1}{(z+3)(z^2+1)}\,dz$ where C is the curve shown below?

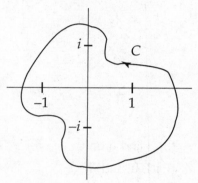

    (A) $\dfrac{4}{5}\pi i$

    (B) $\dfrac{2}{5}\pi i - \dfrac{1}{5}$

    (C) $\dfrac{4}{5}\pi i - \dfrac{1}{5}$

    (D) $\dfrac{2}{5}\pi i$

    (E) $-\dfrac{2}{5}\pi i$

---

28. Suppose X is a nonempty set for which $\delta : X \times X \to \mathbb{R}$ is a real-valued function defined on ordered pairs of points on X. Which of the following is NOT a property of the metric function δ?

    (A) $\delta(x, y) \geq 0$
    (B) $\delta(x, z) \leq \delta(x, y) + \delta(y, z)$
    (C) $\delta(x, y) = \delta(y, x)$
    (D) $\delta(x, y) = 0 \leftrightarrow x = y$
    (E) $\delta(x, z) = \delta(x, y) + \delta(y, z)$

---

29. A baseball team consists of 20 players, 5 of whom are pitchers and 15 of whom are position players. If the batting order consists of 8 different position players and 1 pitcher, and if the pitcher always bats last in the order, then which of the following expressions gives the number of possible different batting orders for this baseball team?

(A) $\dfrac{15!(5)}{8!}$ (B) $\dfrac{15!(5)}{7!}$ (C) $\dfrac{15!(5!)}{7!}$ (D) $15!(5)$ (E) $20!$

30. What is the polar form of a complex number equal to $(i - \sqrt{3})^6$?

(A) -2^6 (B) $2^6(-1 + i)$ (C) $2^6(1 - i)$ (D) $2^6\left(\dfrac{1}{2} - \sqrt{\dfrac{3}{2}}i\right) 2^6(\ )$ (E) 2^6

31. Which of the following sets in $\mathbb{R}^3$ is compact?

(A) $\{x, y, z \mid \mid x + y + z \mid < 5\}$

(B) $\{x, y, z \mid x < 2 \ \& \ y < 2 \ \& \ z < 2\}$

(C) $\{x, y, z \mid 0 \leq x \leq 3, 0 \leq y \leq 3, 0 \leq z \leq 3\}$

(D) $\{x, y, z \mid x \geq 0, y \geq 0, z \geq 0\}$

(E) $\{x, y, z \mid 2 < x^2 + y^2 + z^2 < 8\}$

32. If $f(x) = \begin{cases} \dfrac{x}{2} + c & \text{for } 0 \leq x \leq 8 \\ 0 & \text{otherwise} \end{cases}$, for what value of c is $f(x)$ the probability density function of a random variable X?

(A) $\dfrac{4}{3}$ (B) $\dfrac{15}{8}$ (C) $-\dfrac{15}{8}$ (D) $-\dfrac{4}{3}$

(E) No possible constant c will satisfy the conditions for a probability density function.

33. Which of the following represents the unoriented incidence matrix for the graph shown?

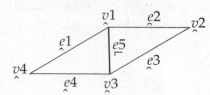

(A) $\begin{bmatrix} 1 & 1 & 0 & 0 & 1 \\ 1 & 0 & 1 & 0 & 0 \\ 0 & 0 & 1 & 1 & 1 \\ 0 & 1 & 0 & 1 & 0 \end{bmatrix}$

(B) $\begin{bmatrix} 1 & 1 & 0 & 0 & 1 \\ 0 & 1 & 1 & 0 & 0 \\ 0 & 0 & 1 & 1 & 1 \\ 1 & 0 & 0 & 1 & 0 \end{bmatrix}$

(C) $\begin{bmatrix} 0 & 0 & 1 & 1 & 0 \\ 1 & 0 & 0 & 1 & 1 \\ 1 & 1 & 0 & 0 & 0 \\ 0 & 1 & 1 & 0 & 1 \end{bmatrix}$

(D) $\begin{bmatrix} 1 & 0 & 1 & 0 & 1 \\ 0 & 1 & 1 & 0 & 0 \\ 0 & 1 & 0 & 1 & 1 \\ 1 & 0 & 0 & 1 & 0 \end{bmatrix}$

(E) $\begin{bmatrix} 1 & 1 & 0 & 1 & 0 \\ 0 & 1 & 1 & 0 & 0 \\ 0 & 0 & 1 & 1 & 1 \\ 1 & 0 & 0 & 0 & 1 \end{bmatrix}$

---

34. Let (X, T) be a topological space, and let A be the subset $(0, 1) \cup [4, 6)$ in $\mathbb{R}$. Find the exterior of A.

(A) $(-\infty, 0) \cup (2, 3) \cup (6, \infty)$
(B) $[0, 1] \cup [4, 6]$
(C) $(-\infty, 0) \cup (1, 4) \cup (6, \infty)$
(D) $(-\infty, 0] \cup [1, 4) \cup [6, \infty)$
(E) $(-\infty, 0) \cup (6, \infty)$

---

35. In how many ways can a company separate its 12 employees into 4 equally-sized committees?

(A) 369,600   (B) 184,800   (C) 61,600   (D) 384   (E) 48

---

36. Let C be the counterclockwise-oriented circle $|z| = 5$. If $h(a) = \int_C \dfrac{3z^2 + z - 4}{z - a}$, what is $h(3)$?

(A) $2\pi i$ (B) $16\pi i$ (C) $26\pi i$ (D) $52\pi i$ (E) $56\pi i$

---

37. If x is an element of the set $(A \cup B) \cap C$, which of the following must be true?
   I. $x \in (A \cap B) \cup C$
   II. $x \in (A \cup B)$
   III. $x \in (A \cap B) \cap C$

(A) I only
(B) II only
(C) III only
(D) I and II only
(E) II and III only

38. Let X be a random variable on $\mathbb{Z}^+$ whose distribution function is $F_X(t) = \dfrac{1}{3^t}$. Suppose that W is another random variable whose distribution function is $F_Y(t) = \dfrac{1}{4^t}$. What is the probability that at least one of the variables X and Y is greater than 2?

    (A) $\dfrac{5}{6}$ (B) $\dfrac{64}{81}$ (C) $\dfrac{1}{2}$ (D) $\dfrac{17}{81}$ (E) $\dfrac{1}{6}$

39. Which of the following sequences of vertices describes a circuit in the graph below?

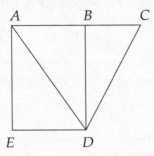

    (A) B, D, A, E, D, C, B
    (B) C, A, E, D, C
    (C) A, D, C, D, A
    (D) E, A, D, B
    (E) C, B, A, E, B, C

40. What is the order of the permutation $\sigma = \begin{pmatrix} 1 & 2 & 3 & 4 & 5 & 6 \\ 5 & 6 & 2 & 3 & 1 & 4 \end{pmatrix}$ on the set $S = \{1, 2, 3, 4, 5, 6\}$?

    (A) 1   (B) 2   (C) 3   (D) 4   (E) 6

41. Let A, B, C, and D be well-formed sentences. Suppose $A \to C$, $B \to D$, $\neg C \to \neg D$, and $\neg A \to \neg C$. Which of the following statements must be true?

    I. $A \to D$
    II. A and C are logically equivalent.
    III. $\neg A \to \neg B$

    (A) I only   (B) II only   (C) III only

    (D) I and II only   (E) II and III only

42. If $M = (-1, 3] \cup [7, 8)$, what is the Lebesgue measure of M?

    (A) -5 (B) -1 (C) 0   (D) 5   (E) 9

43. A florist is arranging flowers in centerpieces at each of four tables at an event. If he has 61 flowers total, which of the following statements are true?
    I   One table has no more than 13 flowers.
    II One table has at least 16 flowers.
    III Two of the tables have at least 31 flowers combined.

    (A) II only   (B) I and II only   (C) I and III only
    (D) II and III only   (E) I, II, and III

44. A fair coin is flipped 10 times. What's the probability of getting between 40 and 50 "heads"?

    (A) 10%   (B) 38%   (C) 41%   (D) 47%   (E) 53%

45. In how many different ways can four people sit around a restaurant table (not including rotations)?

    (A) 24   (B) 18   (C) 6   (D) 48   (E) 16

46. For what complex number z does $\cos z = 3$?

    (A) $i \log\left(3 \pm 2\sqrt{2i}\right) + 2k\pi$, for any $k \in \mathbb{Z}$

    (B) $2k\pi - i \log\left(3 \pm 2\sqrt{2i}\right)$, for any $k \in \mathbb{Z}$

    (C) $2k\pi - i \log\left(3 \pm 2\sqrt{2i}\right)$, for any $k \in \mathbb{Z}$

    (D) $i \log\left(3 \pm 2\sqrt{2i}\right) + 2k\pi$, for any $k \in \mathbb{Z}$

    (E) $i \log\left(3 \pm 2\sqrt{2i}\right) + 2k\pi$, for any $k \in \mathbb{Z}$

47. If $A \subseteq B$, which of the following conditions must be true?
    I. $A \cup B = B$
    II. $A - B = \varnothing$
    III. $C - B \subseteq C - A$

    (A) I only   (B) I and II only   (C) I and III only
    (D) II and III only   (E) I, II, and III

48. Let $f(z)$ be a complex analytic function such that $f(z) = (5x - 3y) + i\, v(x, y)$, where $v(x, y)$ is a real-valued function and $x, y, \in \mathbb{R}$. If $v(4, 1) = 7$, what is $v(3, 2)$?

    (A) –10   (B) –9   (C) 1   (D) 9   (E) 14

Use the algorithm for the "3x + 1" problem for exercises 49–50.

```
input (a)
while a > 1
      begin
            if (a mod 2 = 0)
                  a := a / 2
            else a := 3   a + 1
            output (a)
      end
```

49. Which of the following correctly represents the algorithm described above?

(A) $a_n = \begin{cases} \dfrac{1}{2}a_{n-1} & \text{for } a_{n-1} \text{ odd} \\ 3a_{n-1}+1 & \text{for } a_{n-1} \text{ even} \end{cases}$

(B) $a_n = \begin{cases} \dfrac{1}{2}a_{n-1} & \text{for } a_{n-1} \text{ even} \\ 3a_{n-1}+1 & \text{for } a_{n-1} \text{ odd} \end{cases}$

(C) $a_n = \begin{cases} \dfrac{1}{2}a_{n-1} & \text{for } a_{n-1} \text{ even} \\ \dfrac{1}{2}\left(3a_{n-1}+1\right) & \text{for } a_{n-1} \text{ odd} \end{cases}$

(D) $a_n = \begin{cases} \dfrac{1}{2}a_{n-1} & \text{for } a_n \text{ even} \\ 3a_{n-1}+1 & \text{for } a_n \text{ odd} \end{cases}$

(E) $a_n = \begin{cases} \dfrac{1}{2}a_{n-1} & \text{for } a_n \text{ odd} \\ 3a_{n-1}+1 & \text{for } a_n \text{ even} \end{cases}$

50. What is the sequence of outputs when the input value is 17?

(A) 17, 52, 28, 14, 7, 20, 10, 5, 16, 8, 4, 2, 1
(B) 52, 28, 14, 7, 20, 10, 5, 16, 8, 4, 2, 1
(C) 17, 52, 26, 13, 40, 20, 10, 5, 16, 8, 4, 2, 1
(D) 52, 26, 13, 40, 20, 10, 5, 16, 8, 4, 2, 1
(E) The sequence does not end.

8

Solutions to the Chapter Review Questions

CHAPTER 1 REVIEW QUESTIONS (PAGES 30–34)

1. **E** First, move the $\sqrt{2x-1}$ term to the right-hand side, then square both sides:

$$x-1 = x^2 - 2x\sqrt{2x-1} + (2x-1)$$
$$2x\sqrt{2x-1} = x^2 + x$$

Since $x = 0$ clearly does not satisfy the original equation, we can divide both sides of this equation by x, then square both sides again:

$$2\sqrt{2x-1} = x+1$$
$$4(2x-1) = x^2 + 2x + 1$$
$$x^2 - 6x + 5 = 0$$
$$(x-1)(x-5) = 0$$
$$x = 1,\ 5$$

Both of these values of x do satisfy the original equation (as you can verify), so the sum of the roots is $1 + 5 = 6$.

2. **A** Move the $1/(x-2)$ term to the left-hand side and combine the fractions:

$$\frac{1}{x} - \frac{1}{x-1} - \frac{1}{x-2} > 0 \quad (*)$$
$$\frac{(x-1)(x-2) - x(x-2) - x(x-1)}{x(x-1)(x-2)} > 0$$
$$\frac{2 - x^2}{x(x-1)(x-2)} > 0$$

Since this inequality is of the form $P(x)/Q(x) > 0$, the way we solve it is to first determine the values of x for which $P(x) = 0$ and the values of x for which $Q(x) = 0$. These values will partition the real line into intervals within which the sign of $P(x)/Q(x)$ does not change. The values of x for which $P(x) = 2 - x^2 = 0$ are $-\sqrt{2}$ and $\sqrt{2}$, and the values of x for which $Q(x) = x(x-1)(x-2) = 0$ are $x = 0$, 1, and 2. Therefore, the real line is partitioned into the following intervals:

Since we are asked only for the positive values of x that satisfy the given inequality, we need only consider the intervals for $x > 0$. On each of the these intervals, the signs of $P(x)$ and $Q(x)$ are shown:

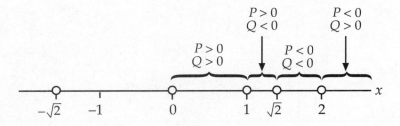

In order to satisfy $(*)$, the signs of P and Q must be the same; this occurs in the intervals $(0, 1)$ and $(\sqrt{2}, 2)$, so the solution set is given in choice A.

3.　**E**　We examine possible solutions in each of the four intervals $x \leq -1$, $-1 < x \leq 0$, $0 < x < 1$, and $x \geq 1$.

- In the interval $x \leq -1$, $|x+1| = -(x + 1)$, $|x| = -x$, and $2|x-1| = 2(1 - x)$, so the original equation becomes:

$$-(x + 1) - (-x) + 2(1 - x) = 2x - 1$$

This equation is satisfied by $x = \dfrac{1}{2}$, but since this is not in the interval under consideration here, we discard it.

- In the interval $-1 < x \leq 0$, $|x+1| = x + 1$, $|x| = -x$, and $2|x-1| = 2(1 - x)$, so the original equation becomes:

$$(x + 1) - (-x) + 2(1 - x) = 2x - 1$$

This equation is satisfied by $x = 2$, but since this is not in the interval under consideration here, we discard it.

- In the interval $0 < x < 1$, $|x+1| = x + 1$, $|x| = x$, and $2|x-1| = 2(1 - x)$, so the original equation becomes:

$$(x + 1) - (x) + 2(1 - x) = 2x - 1$$

This equation is satisfied by $x = 1$, but since this is not in the interval under consideration here, we discard it.

- Finally, in the interval $x \geq 1$, $|x+1| = x + 1$, $|x| = x$, and $2|x-1| = 2(x - 1)$, so the original equation becomes:

$$(x + 1) - (x) + 2(x - 1) = 2x - 1$$

This equation is an identity, satisfied by all x, so we conclude that the original equation is satisfied by all x in the interval under consideration here, that is, by all $x \geq 1$.

4.　**D**　Since $n + 2 = (n + 1) + 1$, we have:

$$f(n+2) = f[(n+1)+1] = 1 - [f(n+1)]^2$$

$$= 1 - \{1 - [f(n)]^2\}^2$$

$$= 1 - \{1 - 2[f(n)]^2 + [f(n)]^4\}$$

$$= 2[f(n)]^2 - [f(n)]^4$$

5. **C**   Since $f^{-1}(f(x)) = x$ for any x, we have $f(f^{-1}(f(2))) = f(2)$. Let $a = f(2)$; then $f^{-1}(a) = 2$. Using the formula given for $f^{-1}(x)$, we seek the real value of a that satisfies the equation $f^{-1}(a) = 2$:

$$a(1+a^2) + (1-a^2) = 2$$

$$a^3 - a^2 + a - 1 = 0$$

$$a^2(a-1) + (a-1) = 0$$

$$(a^2+1)(a-1) = 0$$

$$a = 1$$

6. **E**   Since $(f \circ g)(x) = f(g(x)) = f(\sqrt{x}) = \sqrt{x} + 1$ and $(g \circ h)(x) = g(h(x)) = \sqrt{h(x)}$, the given equation becomes $\sqrt{x} + 1 = \sqrt{h(x)}$. Squaring both sides gives:

$$h(x) = (\sqrt{x} + 1)^2 = x + 2\sqrt{x} + 1 = 1 + (\sqrt{x} + 2)\sqrt{x}$$

7. **B**   The set (or locus) of all points in the plane that are equidistant from two given fixed points is the perpendicular bisector of the segment joining the fixed points. Let $A = (-1, 4)$ and $B = (5, -2)$. The midpoint of the segment AB is the point:

$$C = \left(\frac{-1+5}{2}, \frac{4+(-2)}{2} \right) = (2, 1)$$

Since the slope of AB is

$$m_{AB} = \frac{-2-4}{5-(-1)} = -1$$

the slope of the perpendicular bisector of AB must be 1. The equation of the line with slope 1 that passes through the point C: $(2, 1)$ is $y - 1 = 1(x - 2)$, which can be written $x - y = 1$.

8. **E**   Take the given equation and complete the squares:

$$\left(x^2 - 2x + [\ \ ]\right) + \left(y^2 + 4y + [\ \ ]\right) = -5 + [\ \ ] + [\ \ ]$$

$$\left(x^2 - 2x + [1]\right) + \left(y^2 + 4y + [4]\right) = -5 + [1] + [4]$$

$$(x-1)^2 + (y+2)^2 = 0$$

The sum of two squares can equal 0 if and only if both numbers being added are 0 (since they're both real numbers). Therefore, only one point satisfies the given equation, $(x, y) = (1, -2)$.

9. **B**   Let x' and y' be the new coordinates. Then the transformation $(x, y) \mapsto (\frac{1}{2}x, y)$ means that $x' = \frac{1}{2}x$ and $y' = y$. Then $x = 2x'$, and the equation in x and y is transformed into the following equation in x' and y':

$$(2x')^2 + 4y'^2 = 16 \implies x'^2 + y'^2 = 4$$

This is a circle of radius $r = 2$, so the area it encloses is $\pi r^2 = 4\pi$.

10. **B** Perhaps the simplest way to answer this question is to choose a particular point P on the curve, determine its distance to the y-axis, then find the point $(p, 0)$ that is the same distance away from P. Choose the point $P = (1, 1)$. Its distance from the y-axis is 1, so its distance from $(p, 0)$ must also be 1. Therefore, $p = 1$.

11. **D** The foci of the hyperbola $\dfrac{y^2}{b^2} - \dfrac{x^2}{a^2} = 1$ are located at $(0, \pm c)$, where $c = \sqrt{a^2 + b^2}$. Since $c = \sqrt{2}$ and $b = 1$, the value of a is also 1.

12. **D** If $x = \sqrt{3} - \sqrt{2}$, then $x^2 = 3 - 2\sqrt{6} + 2 = 5 - 2\sqrt{6}$, so:

$$x^2 - 5 = -2\sqrt{6}$$

$$(x^2 - 5)^2 = (-2\sqrt{6})^2$$

$$x^4 - 10x^2 + 25 = 24$$

$$x^4 - 10x^2 + 1 = 0$$

13. **C** If $p(x)$ is divided by the second-degree divisor $x^2 - 1$, then the remainder could be 0 or at most a first-degree polynomial; call it $r(x) = ax + b$. Then:

$$p(x) = (x^2 - 1)q(x) + (ax + b) \quad (*)$$

Since $p(x)$ divided by $(x - 1)$ leaves a remainder of 1, the division algorithm assures us that for some polynomial $q_1(x)$:

$$p(x) = (x - 1)q_1(x) + 1 \quad (**)$$

And since $p(x)$ divided by $(x + 1)$ leaves a remainder of –1, we have for some polynomial $q_2(x)$:

$$p(x) = (x + 1)q_2(x) - 1 \quad (***)$$

Substituting $x = 1$ into (*) gives $p(1) = a + b$, and substituting $x = 1$ into (**) gives $p(1) = 1$; therefore, $a + b = 1$. Next, substituting $x = -1$ into (*) gives $p(-1) = -a + b$, and substituting $x = -1$ into (***) gives $p(-1) = -1$; therefore, $-a + b = -1$. Solving the simultaneous equations $a + b = 1$ and $-a + b = -1$ gives $a = 1$ and $b = 0$. Therefore, the remainder we seek, $r(x)$, is $ax + b = (1)x + 0 = x$.

14. **D** Consider the polynomial $p(x) - 5$; it's also of degree ≤ 4 (or the zero polynomial), so unless it's a zero, it can have at most four roots. Since we're told that one can find five distinct solutions to $p(x) = 5$, one can find at least five distinct roots of $p(x) - 5 = 0$. Therefore, $p(x) - 5$ must be identically 0, which means that $p(x)$ is also a constant polynomial, identically equal to 5.

15. **A** Let s and t be the roots of the equation $x^2 + bx + 1 = 0$. The sum of the squares of the roots of this equation is:

$$s^2 + t^2 = (s + t)^2 - 2st = (-b)^2 - 2(1) = b^2 - 2$$

Since the roots of the equation $x^2 + Bx + 1 = 0$ are s^2 and t^2, whose sum is $-B$, it must be true that $-B = b^2 - 2$, so $B = 2 - b^2$.

16. **C** Since every root of the equation is of the form $1 + bi$ (b real), we can conclude that $b = 0$ for one of the roots. Why? Because complex roots of a real polynomial must occur in conjugate pairs, a polynomial with real coefficient must have an even number of nonreal roots. Since the given polynomial has degree 3, it can have either 0 or 2 nonreal roots. In either case, there's at least one real root, so b must equal zero for at least one root, and thus 1 is a root. This implies that $x - 1$ is a factor of the given polynomial, and the given equation becomes:

$$(x - 1)(x^2 - 2x + 4) = 0$$

Applying the quadratic formula, we find the roots of $x^2 - 2x + 4 = 0$:

$$x = \frac{2 \pm \sqrt{(-2)^2 - 4 \cdot 4}}{2} = \frac{2 \pm \sqrt{-12}}{2} = 1 \pm i\sqrt{3}$$

Therefore, the roots of the given equation are $1 + 0i$, $1 + i\sqrt{3}$, and $1 + i(-\sqrt{3})$, so the largest value of b for which $1 + bi$ is a root is $b = \sqrt{3}$.

17. **E** Let $y = \log_a x$; then $a^y = x$. This equation implies $(a^2)^{y/2} = x$, which is the same as $A^{y/2} = x$, so $\log_A x = \frac{y}{2} = \left(\frac{1}{2}\right)\log_a x$. Therefore, $\log_a x + \log_A x = \log_a x + \left(\frac{1}{2}\right)\log_a x = \left(\frac{3}{2}\right)\log_a x = \log_a (x^{3/2})$, so:

$$a^{(\log_a x) + (\log_A x)} = a^{\log_a (x^{3/2})} = x^{3/2} = x\sqrt{x}$$

18. **C** Let $y = \log x$. Then the given equation is equivalent to $y^2 = 2y$. Solving this equation, we write $y^2 - 2y = 0$, so $y(y - 2) = 0$, which implies $y = 0$ or $y = 2$. If $y = 0$, then $\log x = 0$, so $x = 1$; if $y = 2$, then $\log x = 2$, so $x = e^2$. Thus, the roots of the equation are 1 and e^2.

19. **D** Given the equation $y = (e^x - e^{-x})/2$, we interchange x and y then solve for y:

$$x = \frac{e^y - e^{-y}}{2}$$

$$e^y - e^{-y} = 2x$$

$$e^{2y} - 1 = 2xe^y$$

$$(e^y)^2 - (2x)e^y - 1 = 0$$

$$e^y = \frac{2x \pm \sqrt{(-2x)^2 + 4}}{2}$$

$$= x \pm \sqrt{x^2 + 1}$$

Since e^y cannot be negative, we ignore the minus sign and conclude that:

$$e^y = x + \sqrt{x^2 + 1} \quad \Rightarrow \quad y = \log(x + \sqrt{x^2 + 1}) \quad \Rightarrow \quad \sinh^{-1} x = \log(x + \sqrt{x^2 + 1})$$

20. **E**   Using the definition of sinh x from the previous question, we have:

$$y = \tanh x = \frac{e^x - e^{-x}}{e^x + e^{-x}}$$

To find a formula for $\tanh^{-1} x$, we interchange x and y and solve for y:

$$x = \frac{e^y - e^{-y}}{e^y + e^{-y}}$$

$$xe^y + xe^{-y} = e^y - e^{-y}$$

$$xe^{2y} + x = e^{2y} - 1$$

$$e^{2y}(x-1) = -(x+1)$$

$$e^{2y}(1-x) = 1+x$$

$$e^{2y} = \frac{1+x}{1-x}$$

$$y = \frac{1}{2}\log\frac{1+x}{1-x}$$

(Note: From the definition of tanh x, we see that $-1 < \tanh x < 1$ for every x. Therefore, the domain of $\tanh^{-1} x$ is $-1 < x < 1$.)

21. **E**   First, since cosine is an even function, $\cos(-\sin x) = \cos(\sin x)$. Let $\theta = \sin x$. Because $0 < \theta < 1$, $\cos \theta$ is positive, so:

$$\cos\theta = \sqrt{1 - \sin^2\theta} = \sqrt{1 - (\sin\theta)^2} = \sqrt{1 - \left(\tfrac{1}{2}\right)^2} = \frac{\sqrt{3}}{2}$$

Or, even more simply, if $\sin(\sin x) = \dfrac{1}{2}$, then $\sin x = \dfrac{\pi}{6}$, so $\cos(\sin x) = \cos\left(\dfrac{\pi}{6}\right) = \dfrac{\sqrt{3}}{2}$.

22. **D**   In order for $f(x) = \log(\sin x)$ to be defined, $\sin x$ must be positive, so we seek the one value of x among the choices for which $\sin x > 0$ (if any). Dividing 11 by $\pi \approx 3.1$, we find that $11 \gtrsim (3.5)\pi$. Interpreting 3.5π as the radian measure of an angle in standard position (that is, its initial side is along the positive x-axis), the terminal side lies in one of the lower quadrants (it's just barely into the fourth quadrant), where the sine is negative. This rules out choice A. Next, $111 \gtrsim 10(11) \gtrsim 10(3.5\pi) = 35\pi$. An angle of measure $\gtrsim 35\pi$ radians is equal to 17 complete revolutions ($= 34\pi$) plus a little more than π, which again places it in one of the lower quadrants, where sine is negative; this eliminates choice B. Choice C is $1111 \gtrsim 353.64\pi$, and an angle of this magnitude is equal to 176 complete revolutions ($= 352\pi$) plus a little more than 1.64π, once again placing it in one of the lower quadrants, where sine is negative; this eliminates choice C. Finally, choice D is $11{,}111 \gtrsim 10(1111) \gtrsim 10(353.64\pi) = 3536.4\pi$, and an angle of this magnitude is equal to 1768 complete revolutions ($= 3536\pi$) plus a little more than 0.4π, placing it in the *first* quadrant, where sine is positive; thus, choice D is the answer.

23. **D**   Let $\theta = \arcsin\dfrac{1}{3}$. From the triangle below, we see that $\tan\theta = 1/(2\sqrt{2})$.

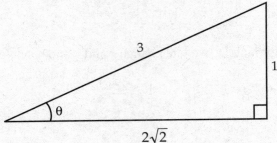

Therefore:

$$\tan 2\theta = \frac{2\tan\theta}{1-\tan^2\theta} = \frac{2 \cdot \frac{1}{2\sqrt{2}}}{1-\left(\frac{1}{2\sqrt{2}}\right)^2} = \frac{\frac{1}{\sqrt{2}}}{1-\frac{1}{8}} = \frac{\frac{1}{\sqrt{2}}}{\frac{7}{8}} = \frac{8}{7\sqrt{2}} = \frac{4\sqrt{2}}{7}$$

24. **D**   Let $\theta = \operatorname{arccot}\dfrac{\pi}{4}$. Using the trig identity $1 + \cot^2\theta = \csc^2\theta$, we can conclude that:

$$\sqrt{\csc^2\theta - 1} = \cot\theta = \cot(\operatorname{arccot}\frac{\pi}{4}) = \frac{\pi}{4}$$

25. **B**   First, notice that $\arctan 1$ is easy to compute; it equals $\dfrac{\pi}{4}$. Now, let $\alpha = \arctan 2$ and let $\beta = \arctan 3$; then $\tan\alpha = 2$ and $\tan\beta = 3$, so:

$$\tan(\alpha+\beta) = \frac{\tan\alpha + \tan\beta}{1 - \tan\alpha\tan\beta}$$

$$= \frac{2+3}{1-(2)(3)}$$

$$= -1$$

Since $0 < \alpha < \dfrac{\pi}{2}$ and $0 < \beta < \dfrac{\pi}{2}$, it must be true that $0 < \alpha + \beta < \pi$. Since $\tan(\alpha + \beta) = -1$, we must have $\alpha + \beta = \dfrac{3\pi}{4}$. Thus:

$$(\arctan 1) + (\arctan 2 + \arctan 3) = \frac{\pi}{4} + \frac{3\pi}{4} = \pi$$

CHAPTER 2 REVIEW QUESTIONS (PAGES 95–104)

1. **A** The term $\cos n\pi$ oscillates between –1 and 1, and the term $\sin^2 n$ is never greater than 1 in absolute value. Therefore,

$$-\frac{1}{n^{1/e}} \le \frac{(\cos n\pi)(\sin^2 n)}{\sqrt[e]{n}} \le \frac{1}{n^{1/e}}$$

is true for every $n \ge 1$. Since the sequences $\pm(\frac{1}{n^{1/e}})$ both converge to zero, the sandwich theorem guarantees that the given sequence will converge to zero also.

2. **B** Because the sequence converges, both x_n and x_{n-1} approach the same limit (let's call it x) as $n \to \infty$. Therefore, the equation $x_n = \sqrt{5x_{n-1}+6}$ becomes, in the limit, $x = \sqrt{5x+6}$ which implies:

$$x^2 = 5x+6 \;\Rightarrow\; x^2 - 5x - 6 = 0 \;\Rightarrow\; (x+1)(x-6) = 0 \;\Rightarrow\; x = -1,\, 6$$

Since all the terms of the sequence are positive, the limit cannot be negative. Therefore, $\lim x_n$ must be equal to 6.

3. **E** For $-(n+1) \le x < -n$, the value of $[x]$ is $-(n+1)$, so $\lim\limits_{x \to n-} [x] = -(n+1)$. For $n-1 \le x < n$, the value of $[x]$ is $n-1$, so $\lim\limits_{x \to n-} [x] = n-1$. Next, since $|x|$ is continuous for all x, it's easy to see that $\lim\limits_{x \to n-} |x| = \lim\limits_{x \to n-} |x| = n$. Therefore,

$$\lim_{x \to -n-}\big(|x|-[x]\big) - \lim_{x \to n-}\big(|x|-[x]\big) = \left\{ \lim_{x \to -n-}|x| - \lim_{x \to -n-}[x] \right\} - \left\{ \lim_{x \to n-}|x| - \lim_{x \to n-}[x] \right\}$$

$$= \big\{ n-(-(n+1)) \big\} - \big\{ n-(n-1) \big\}$$

$$= 2n$$

4. **B** The given limit gives the $\dfrac{0}{0}$ indeterminate form, so we apply L'Hôpital's rule

$$\lim_{x \to 0} \frac{\arcsin x - x}{x^3} = \lim_{x \to 0} \frac{\frac{1}{\sqrt{1-x^2}}-1}{3x^2} = \lim_{x \to 0} \frac{(1-x^2)^{-1/2}-1}{3x^2}$$

which also gives the $\dfrac{0}{0}$ indeterminate form. So, we apply L'Hôpital's rule again and find that:

$$\lim_{x \to 0} \frac{(1-x^2)^{-1/2}-1}{3x^2} = \lim_{x \to 0} \frac{x(1-x^2)^{-3/2}}{6x} = \lim_{x \to 0} \frac{(1-x^2)^{-3/2}}{6} = \frac{1}{6}$$

5. **D** Solve the given equation for y in terms of x:

$$2x^2 + 3x - 2xy - y = 6$$
$$2x^2 + 3x - 6 = y(2x+1)$$
$$y = \frac{2x^2 + 3x - 6}{2x+1}$$
$$\therefore y = (x+1) + \frac{-7}{2x+1}$$

Since $x = -\frac{1}{2}$ is excluded from the domain of this function, we know that $x = -\frac{1}{2}$ is a vertical asymptote. Furthermore, as $x \to \infty$, the term $-7/(2x+1)$ approaches zero, so $y = x+1$ is an asymptote also.

6. **D** Regardless of the value of k, the function f is continuous at all $x \neq 2$. In order for f to be continuous at 2, we must have $f(2) = \lim_{x \to 2} f(x)$; that is:

$$
\begin{aligned}
k &= \lim_{x \to 2} \frac{x^2 - 6x + 8}{x^3 - 2x^2 + 2x - 4} \\
&= \lim_{x \to 2} \frac{x^2 - 6x + 8}{x^2(x-2) + 2(x-2)} \\
&= \lim_{x \to 2} \frac{(x-4)(x-2)}{(x^2+2)(x-2)} \\
&= \lim_{x \to 2} \frac{x-4}{x^2+2} \\
&= -\frac{1}{3}
\end{aligned}
$$

7. **C** Since the integral equals 0 when $x = 0$, the limit is of the indeterminate form $\frac{0}{0}$, so we apply L'Hôpital's rule

$$\lim_{x \to 0} \frac{\displaystyle\int_0^x \frac{t+t^2}{1+\sin t}\, dt}{x^2} = \lim_{x \to 0} \frac{\frac{x+x^2}{1+\sin x}}{2x} = \lim_{x \to 0} \frac{x(1+x)}{2x(1+\sin x)} = \lim_{x \to 0} \frac{1+x}{2(1+\sin x)} = \frac{1}{2}$$

where the derivative of the integral in the first step follows from the fundamental theorem of calculus.

8. **D** First, the expression $\arcsin u$ is defined only for $-1 \leq u \leq 1$; therefore, we must have:

$$-1 \leq \log\sqrt{x} \leq 1$$

These inequalities imply that:

$$e^{-1} \leq \sqrt{x} \leq e^1 \quad \Rightarrow \quad e^{-2} \leq x \leq e^2$$

Therefore, the domain of f is the closed interval $[\frac{1}{e^2}, e^2]$.

9. **A** Using two applications of the chain rule, we find that:

$$\frac{d}{dx}\arcsin(\log\sqrt{x}) = \frac{1}{\sqrt{1-[\log(\sqrt{x})]^2}}\cdot\frac{d}{dx}(\log\sqrt{x})$$

$$= \frac{1}{\sqrt{1-[\log(\sqrt{x})]^2}}\cdot\frac{1}{\sqrt{x}}\cdot\frac{d}{dx}(\sqrt{x})$$

$$= \frac{1}{\sqrt{1-[\log(\sqrt{x})]^2}}\cdot\frac{1}{\sqrt{x}}\cdot\frac{1}{2\sqrt{x}}$$

$$= \frac{1}{2x\sqrt{1-[\log(\sqrt{x})]^2}}$$

Evaluating this at $x = e$ gives:

$$\left.\frac{1}{2x\sqrt{1-[\log(\sqrt{x})]^2}}\right|_{x=e} = \frac{1}{2e\sqrt{1-[\log(\sqrt{e})]^2}} = \frac{1}{2e\sqrt{1-[\frac{1}{2}]^2}} = \frac{1}{2e\frac{\sqrt{3}}{2}} = \frac{1}{e\sqrt{3}}$$

10. **E** Since the derivative of $x^2 + x - 3$ is $2x + 1$, and the derivative of $mx + b$ is m, we must have $2x + 1 = m$ at $x = 1$. Therefore, $m = 3$. Next, we use the fact that a differentiable function must be continuous; to ensure that f is continuous at 1, it must be true that $\lim_{x\to 1-}f(x)$ is equal to $\lim_{x\to 1+}f(x)$, so:

$$\lim_{x\to 1-}(x^2 + x - 3) = \lim_{x\to 1+}(mx + b)$$

$$-1 = m + b$$

Since $m = 3$, the value of b must be –4.

11. **B** This limit gives us the indeterminate form $\frac{0}{0}$, so we apply L'Hôpital's rule, differentiating with respect to h (*not* with respect to x):

$$\lim_{h\to 0}\frac{f(x+3h^2) - f(x-h^2)}{2h^2} = \lim_{h\to 0}\frac{6h\cdot f'(x+3h^2) - (-2h)\cdot f'(x-h^2)}{4h}$$

$$= \lim_{h\to 0}\frac{6f'(x+3h^2) + 2f'(x-h^2)}{4}$$

$$= \frac{6f'(x) + 2f'(x)}{4}$$

$$= 2f'(x)$$

12. **C**   Since $y' = 3x^2 - 6x + 4$, and $y'' = 6x - 6$, the curve could have an inflection point where $6x - 6 = 0$, that is, at $x = 1$. (Note that y' is negative for $x < 1$ and positive for $x > 1$, so $x = 1$ does indeed give an inflection point.) At $x = 1$, the value of y' is $3(1^2) - 6(1) + 4 = 1$, so this is the slope of the tangent line. Since $y = 1^3 - 3(1^2) + 4(1) = 2$ at $x = 1$, the tangent line has slope 1 and passes through the point $(1, 2)$. The equation of this line is $y = x + 1$.

13. **A**   First we find dy/dx by implicit differentiation:

$$xy(x + y) = x + y^4$$
$$x^2 y + xy^2 = x + y^4$$
$$\left(x^2 \frac{dy}{dx} + y \cdot 2x \right) + \left(x \cdot 2y \frac{dy}{dx} + y^2 \right) = 1 + 4y^3 \frac{dy}{dx}$$
$$\frac{dy}{dx}\left(x^2 + 2xy - 4y^3 \right) = 1 - 2xy - y^2$$
$$\frac{dy}{dx} = \frac{1 - 2xy - y^2}{x^2 + 2xy - 4y^3}$$

At the point $(1, 1)$, the value of dy/dx, which equals the slope of the tangent line, is:

$$\left. \frac{dy}{dx} \right|_{(1,1)} = \frac{1 - 2 \cdot 1 \cdot 1 - 1^2}{1^2 + 2 \cdot 1 \cdot 1 - 4 \cdot 1^3} = \frac{-2}{-1} = 2$$

14. **E**   For any $x < 1$, the value of $|x - 1|$ is $-(x - 1) = 1 - x$. Therefore, in a small interval containing $x = 0$, the function f can be written as $f(x) = 2(1 - x) + (x - 1)^2$, whose derivative is $f'(x) = -2 + 2(x - 1) = 2x - 4$. This gives $f'(0) = -4$. [Note: The given function f is differentiable for all $x \neq 1$; it is not differentiable at $x = 1$.]

15. **C**   The slope of the tangent line is the value of the derivative; the y-intercept of a curve is the point at which it crosses the y-axis, which occurs when $x = 0$. So, we're asked to evaluate $f'(0)$:

$$f(x) = \frac{e^x \arccos x}{\cos x} \quad \Rightarrow \quad f'(x) = \frac{(\cos x)\left[e^x \cdot \frac{-1}{\sqrt{1-x^2}} + (\arccos x) \cdot e^x \right] - (e^x \arccos x)(-\sin x)}{\cos^2 x}$$
$$\Rightarrow \quad f'(0) = \left[-1 + \arccos 0 \right]$$
$$\Rightarrow \quad f'(0) = \tfrac{\pi}{2} - 1$$

Note: The differentiation formula $\frac{d}{dx}(\arccos x) = -1 / \sqrt{1 - x^2}$ can be obtained in a couple of ways. One method is to rewrite $y = \arccos x$ as $x = \cos y$ and use implicit differentiation

$$x = \cos y \quad \Rightarrow \quad 1 = (-\sin y)\frac{dy}{dx} \quad \Rightarrow \quad \frac{dy}{dx} = -\frac{1}{\sin y} = -\frac{1}{\sin(\arccos x)} = -\frac{1}{\sqrt{1 - x^2}}$$

where the result used in the last step, $\sin(\arccos x) = \sqrt{1 - x^2}$, follows from the triangle:

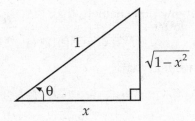

Another method is to notice that since $\arccos x + \arcsin x = \frac{\pi}{2}$ for all x, we have $\arccos x = \frac{\pi}{2} - \arcsin x$, so $\frac{d}{dx}(\arccos x) = -\frac{d}{dx}(\arcsin x) = \dfrac{-1}{\sqrt{1-x^2}}$.

16. **C** We use the expression $\Delta y \approx f'(x) \cdot \Delta x$. If $f(x) = \dfrac{1}{\sqrt{x^3+1}} = (x^3+1)^{-1/2}$, then

$f'(x) = -\frac{3}{2}x^2(x^3+1)^{-3/2}$. With $x = 2$ and $\Delta x = 2.09 - 2 = 0.09$, we find that:

$$\begin{aligned}
\Delta y &\approx f'(2) \cdot \Delta x \\
&= [-\tfrac{3}{2} \cdot 2^2(2^3+1)^{-3/2}] \cdot (0.09) \\
&= -6 \cdot \tfrac{1}{27} \cdot \tfrac{9}{100} \\
&= -\tfrac{1}{50} \\
&= -0.02
\end{aligned}$$

17. **D** By applying the quotient rule, chain rule, and product rule, we find that:

$$\begin{aligned}
\frac{d}{dx}\left[\frac{f(x^3)}{xf(x^2)}\right] &= \frac{xf(x^2) \cdot [f'(x^3) \cdot 3x^2] - f(x^3) \cdot [x \cdot f'(x^2) \cdot 2x + f(x^2)]}{x^2[f(x^2)]^2} \\
&= \frac{3x^3 f(x^2)f'(x^3) - 2x^2 f(x^3)f'(x^2) - f(x^3)f(x^2)}{x^2[f(x^2)]^2}
\end{aligned}$$

Substituting $x = 1$ gives:

$$\begin{aligned}
\frac{d}{dx}\left[\frac{f(x^3)}{xf(x^2)}\right]_{x=1} &= \frac{3f(1)f'(1) - 2f(1)f'(1) - f(1)f(1)}{[f(1)]^2} \\
&= \frac{3(1)(-1) - 2(1)(-1) - (1)(1)}{1^2} \\
&= -2
\end{aligned}$$

18. **B** The first few derivatives of $f(x) = (1-2x)^{-1}$ are:

$f'(x) = -(1-2x)^{-2} \cdot (-2) = 2(1-2x)^{-2}$

$f''(x) = 2(-2)(1-2x)^{-3} \cdot (-2) = 2 \cdot 2 \cdot (2) \cdot (1-2x)^{-3}$

$f'''(x) = 2 \cdot 2 \cdot 2 \cdot (-3) \cdot (1-2x)^{-4} \cdot (-2) = 2 \cdot 2 \cdot 2 \cdot (2 \cdot 3) \cdot (1-2x)^{-4}$

$f^{(iv)}(x) = 2 \cdot 2 \cdot 2 \cdot 2 \cdot 3 \cdot (-4) \cdot (1-2x)^{-5} \cdot (-2) = 2 \cdot 2 \cdot 2 \cdot 2 \cdot (2 \cdot 3 \cdot 4) \cdot (1-2x)^{-5}$

$\vdots$

We see a pattern emerging here; namely, that:

$$f^{(n)}(x) = 2^n(n!) \cdot (1-2x)^{-(n+1)} \quad (*)$$

Substituting $x = -\frac{1}{2}$, we find that:

$$f^{(n)}(-\tfrac{1}{2}) = 2^n(n!) \cdot [1-2(-\tfrac{1}{2})]^{-(n+1)}$$
$$= 2^n(n!) \cdot 2^{-(n+1)}$$
$$= \tfrac{1}{2}(n!)$$

[If desired, you can prove formula (*) by induction. It clearly holds for $n = 1$. Now, assuming that (*) is true, let's calculate $f^{(n+1)}(x)$:

$$f^{(n+1)}(x) = [f^{(n)}(x)]' = 2^n(n!) \cdot [-(n+1) \cdot (1-2x)^{-(n+1)-1} \cdot (-2)]$$
$$= 2^{n+1}(n+1)! \cdot (1-2x)^{-[(n+1)+1]}$$

This result establishes that (*) is indeed correct.]

19. **E**   The mean-value theorem (for derivatives) tells us that there is at least one point c between a and b at which the slope of the tangent line is equal to the slope of the chord connecting $(a, f(a))$ and $(b, f(b))$. That is, there is a point c, with $a < c < b$, such that:

$$f'(c) = \frac{f(b)-f(a)}{b-a} = \frac{3-1}{b-a} = \frac{2}{b-a} \quad \Rightarrow \quad (b-a)f'(c) = 2$$

20. **C**   Let the semicircle be the upper half ($y \geq 0$) of the circle whose equation is $x^2 + y^2 = a^2$:

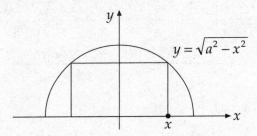

From the figure above, we see that the area of the inscribed rectangle is:

$$A = (2x)y = 2x\sqrt{a^2 - x^2}$$

To maximize $A(x) = 2x\sqrt{a^2 - x^2}$, we take the derivative,

$$A'(x) = 2x\left[\frac{1}{2\sqrt{a^2 - x^2}} \cdot (-2x)\right] + \sqrt{a^2 - x^2} \cdot 2 = \frac{2}{\sqrt{a^2 - x^2}}\left[-x^2 + (a^2 - x^2)\right]$$

set it equal to zero, and solve:

$$\frac{2}{\sqrt{a^2 - x^2}} \left[-x^2 + (a^2 - x^2) \right] \overset{\text{set}}{=} 0$$

$$-x^2 + (a^2 - x^2) = 0$$

$$-2x^2 = -a^2$$

$$x = \pm \tfrac{1}{\sqrt{2}} a$$

(It's clear from the geometry of this situation that a critical point will give a maximum, but you may verify this by checking that $A''(x)$ is negative at the critical points.) For $x = \frac{1}{\sqrt{2}} a$, we find that:

$$A(x) = 2x\sqrt{a^2 - x^2} \quad \Rightarrow \quad A(\tfrac{1}{\sqrt{2}} a) = 2(\tfrac{1}{\sqrt{2}} a) \cdot \sqrt{a^2 - (\tfrac{1}{\sqrt{2}} a)^2}$$

$$= (\sqrt{2} a) \cdot \frac{a}{\sqrt{2}}$$

$$\therefore \text{maximum area} = a^2$$

21. **B**   To find an extremum of f, we first take the derivative:

$$f(x) = \int_x^{2x} \frac{\sin t}{t} dt \quad \Rightarrow \quad f'(x) = \frac{\sin 2x}{2x} \cdot 2 - \frac{\sin x}{x} = \frac{\sin 2x - \sin x}{x}$$

This follows from the fundamental theorem of calculus and the chain rule (see the final result given in the solution of Example 2.18). Next, we set the derivative equal to zero and solve:

$$\frac{\sin 2x - \sin x}{x} \overset{\text{set}}{=} 0 \quad \Rightarrow \quad \sin 2x - \sin x = 0$$

$$\sin x(2\cos x - 1) = 0$$

$$\sin x = 0 \quad \text{or} \quad \cos x = \tfrac{1}{2}$$

$$\Rightarrow \quad x = \tfrac{\pi}{3} \quad \text{(because } 0 < x < \tfrac{3\pi}{2}\text{)}$$

Since f has only one critical point in the indicated interval, the statement of the question implies that $\frac{\pi}{3}$ must be the value of x at which $f(x)$ attains a local maximum. Note: We can verify that $x = \frac{\pi}{3}$ gives a local maximum by checking that $f''(\frac{\pi}{3})$ is negative:

$$f'(x) = \frac{\sin 2x - \sin x}{x} \quad \Rightarrow \quad f''(x) = \frac{x(2\cos 2x - \cos x) - (\sin 2x - \sin x)}{x^2}$$

$$\Rightarrow \quad f''(\tfrac{\pi}{3}) = \frac{\tfrac{\pi}{3}(2\cos \tfrac{2\pi}{3} - \cos \tfrac{\pi}{3}) - (\sin \tfrac{2\pi}{3} - \sin \tfrac{\pi}{3})}{(\tfrac{\pi}{3})^2}$$

$$= \frac{\tfrac{\pi}{3}(-1 - \tfrac{1}{2}) - (\sin \tfrac{2\pi}{3} - \sin \tfrac{\pi}{3})}{(\tfrac{\pi}{3})^2}$$

$$< 0$$

22. **E** Take the derivative of f,

$$f(x) = x^k e^{-x} \implies f'(x) = x^k(-e^{-x}) + e^{-x}(kx^{k-1}) = x^{k-1}e^{-x}(-x+k)$$

set it equal to zero, and solve:

$$x^{k-1}e^{-x}(-x+k) \overset{\text{set}}{=} 0 \implies -x+k=0 \implies x=k$$

The first implication follows from the fact that $x^{k-1} \neq 0$ (since we're told to maximize f for $x > 0$), and e^{-x} is never equal to zero. We can check that the critical point $x = k$ gives a maximum since:

$$f'(x) = x^{k-1}e^{-x}(-x+k) \implies f''(x) = x^{k-1}e^{-x}(-1) + (-x+k) \cdot \tfrac{d}{dx}(x^{k-1}e^{-x})$$
$$\implies f''(k) = -k^{k-1}e^{-k} < 0$$

Therefore, the maximum value attained by f is $f(k) = k^k e^{-k} = \left(\dfrac{k}{e}\right)^k$.

23. **A** The area of a circle of radius r is given by the formula $A(r) = \pi r^2$. Differentiating this with respect to time, we find that:

$$\frac{dA}{dt} = 2\pi r \frac{dr}{dt}$$

So, if $dr/dt = -0.5$ cm/sec, the value of dA/dt when $r = 4$ cm is:

$$\frac{dA}{dt} = 2\pi(4 \text{ cm})(-0.5 \text{ cm/sec}) = -4\pi \text{ cm}^2/\text{sec}$$

24. **B** Applying the final result quoted in the solution of Example 2.18, the fundamental theorem of calculus and the chain rule tell us that:

$$f(x) = \int_{e^x}^{e^{2x}} t \log t \, dt \implies f'(x) = [e^{2x}\log(e^{2x})] \cdot 2e^{2x} - [e^x \log(e^x)] \cdot e^x$$
$$= 4xe^{4x} - xe^{2x}$$
$$= xe^{2x}(4e^{2x} - 1)$$

Setting this equal to 0, we find the critical points:

$$f'(x) \overset{\text{set}}{=} 0 \implies xe^{2x}(4e^{2x}-1) = 0 \implies x=0 \text{ or } 4e^{2x}=1$$
$$\implies x=0 \text{ or } x=\tfrac{1}{2}\log\tfrac{1}{4} = \log\tfrac{1}{2} = -\log 2$$

The question tells us that f has an absolute minimum at $x = 0$, so we conclude that $x = -\log 2$ gives a local maximum. We could verify this by checking that $f''(x)$ is negative at $x = -\log 2$:

$$f'(x) = xe^{2x}(4e^{2x}-1) \implies f''(x) = (xe^{2x})(8e^{2x}) + (4e^{2x}-1) \cdot \tfrac{d}{dx}(xe^{2x})$$
$$\implies f''(-\log 2) = (-\log 2)(e^{-2\log 2})^2(8) + 0$$
$$= -\tfrac{1}{2}\log 2$$
$$< 0$$

[Note: An alternate solution would begin by actually evaluating the integral used to define $f(x)$. Using integration by parts, we would find that:

$$\int t \log t \, dt = \tfrac{1}{4}t^2(2\log t - 1)$$

This would give:

$$
\begin{aligned}
f(x) &= \int_{e^x}^{e^{2x}} t \log t \, dt \\
&= \left[\tfrac{1}{4}t^2(2\log t - 1) \right]_{e^x}^{e^{2x}} \\
&= \tfrac{1}{4}\left[(e^{2x})^2(2 \cdot 2x - 1) - (e^x)^2(2x - 1) \right] \\
&= \tfrac{1}{4}\left[e^{4x}(4x - 1) - e^{2x}(2x - 1) \right]
\end{aligned}
$$

We'd use this formula to determine $f'(x)$, and then proceed as before.]

25. **D**   We expand the integrand and integrate:

$$
\begin{aligned}
\int_{-1}^{0} x^2(x+1)^3 \, dx &= \int_{-1}^{0} x^2(x^3 + 3x^2 + 3x + 1)\, dx \\
&= \int_{-1}^{0} (x^5 + 3x^4 + 3x^3 + x^2)\, dx \\
&= \left[\tfrac{1}{6}x^6 + \tfrac{3}{5}x^5 + \tfrac{3}{4}x^4 + \tfrac{1}{3}x^3 \right]_{-1}^{0} \\
&= 0 - \left(\tfrac{1}{6} - \tfrac{3}{5} + \tfrac{3}{4} - \tfrac{1}{3} \right) \\
&= \tfrac{1}{60}
\end{aligned}
$$

26. **C**   A definite integral can be interpreted as an area, and this is precisely how we'll evaluate the given integral. The figure below shows the graph of the greatest integer function, $f(x) = [x]$, on the interval $[0, 4]$:

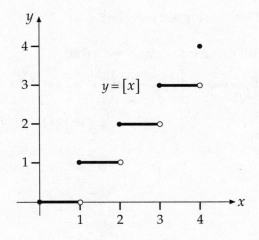

The integral $\int_0^{7/2} [x]\,dx$ is the area under this graph and above the x-axis from $x = 0$ to $x = \frac{7}{2}$; that is, it's equal to the total area of these shaded rectangles:

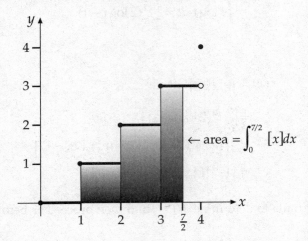

$$\leftarrow \text{area} = \int_0^{7/2} [x]\,dx$$

Since the total area of these shaded rectangles is $(1 \cdot 1) + (1 \cdot 2) + (\frac{1}{2} \cdot 3) = \frac{9}{2}$, we have:

$$\int_0^{7/2} [x]\,dx = \frac{9}{2}$$

27. **E** To evaluate the given integral, we first write it as a sum:

$$\int_{-1}^1 f(x)\,dx = \int_{-1}^0 f(x)\,dx + \int_0^1 f(x)\,dx$$

$$= \int_{-1}^0 -2(x+1)\,dx + \int_0^1 k(1-x^2)\,dx$$

$$= \left[-(x^2 + 2x)\right]_{-1}^0 + k\left[x - \tfrac{1}{3}x^3\right]_0^1$$

$$= -1 + \tfrac{2}{3}k$$

So, if this is to equal 1, the value of k must be 3.

28. **D** We make the trig substitution $x = \sin\theta$, $dx = \cos\theta\,d\theta$:

$$\int \frac{x^2\,dx}{\sqrt{1-x^2}} = \int \frac{\sin^2\theta(\cos\theta\,d\theta)}{\sqrt{1-(\sin\theta)^2}} = \int \sin^2\theta\,d\theta$$

$$= \int \tfrac{1}{2}(1 - \cos 2\theta)\,d\theta$$

$$= \tfrac{1}{2}(\theta - \tfrac{1}{2}\sin 2\theta) + c$$

$$= \tfrac{1}{2}(\theta - \sin\theta\cos\theta) + c$$

To change the variable back to x, we use the following triangle, which illustrates the original substitution, $x = \sin\theta$:

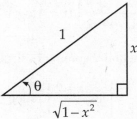

Thus,

$$\int \frac{x^2\,dx}{\sqrt{1-x^2}} = \tfrac{1}{2}(\theta - \sin\theta\cos\theta) + c = \tfrac{1}{2}\left(\arcsin x - x\sqrt{1-x^2}\right) + c$$

Of course, another solution is to differentiate each of the answer choices and stop once you've found the one whose derivative is $x^2/\sqrt{1-x^2}$!

29. **B**   The area we're looking for is given by the definite integral:

$$\int_0^1 (x\arctan x)\,dx$$

To determine $\int (x\arctan x)\,dx$, we use integration by parts, with $u = \arctan x$, $du = \left(\dfrac{1}{1+x^2}\right)dx$, and $v = \tfrac{1}{2}x^2$, $dv = x\,dx$:

$$\int (x\arctan x)\,dx = \tfrac{1}{2}x^2\arctan x - \tfrac{1}{2}\int \frac{x^2}{1+x^2}\,dx$$

$$= \tfrac{1}{2}x^2\arctan x - \tfrac{1}{2}\int\left(1 - \frac{1}{1+x^2}\right)dx$$

$$= \tfrac{1}{2}x^2\arctan x - \tfrac{1}{2}(x - \arctan x) + c$$

$$= \tfrac{1}{2}(x^2 + 1)\arctan x - \tfrac{1}{2}x + c$$

Therefore:

$$\int_0^1 (x\arctan x)\,dx = \left[\tfrac{1}{2}(x^2+1)\arctan x - \tfrac{1}{2}x\right]_0^1 = \arctan 1 - \tfrac{1}{2} = \tfrac{\pi}{4} - \tfrac{1}{2} = \tfrac{\pi-2}{4}$$

30. **D**   We first determine the integral

$$\int \frac{dx}{x^2 - 3x + 2}$$

by the method of partial fractions.
Since

$$\frac{1}{x^2 - 3x + 2} = \frac{1}{(x-1)(x-2)} = \frac{-1}{x-1} + \frac{1}{x-2}$$

we have:

$$\int \frac{dx}{x^2 - 3x + 2} = \int \left(\frac{-1}{x-1} + \frac{1}{x-2} \right) dx = -\log(x-1) + \log(x-2) + c = \log \frac{x-2}{x-1} + c$$

Therefore, by the fundamental theorem of calculus,

$$\int_3^5 \frac{dx}{x^2 - 3x + 2} = \left[\log \frac{x-2}{x-1} \right]_3^5 = \log \tfrac{3}{4} - \log \tfrac{1}{2} = \log \frac{\frac{3}{4}}{\frac{1}{2}} = \log \tfrac{3}{2}$$

so:

$$\exp \int_3^5 \frac{dx}{x^2 - 3x + 2} = \exp \left(\log \tfrac{3}{2} \right) \equiv e^{\log(3/2)} = \tfrac{3}{2}$$

31. **B**   According to the following figure,

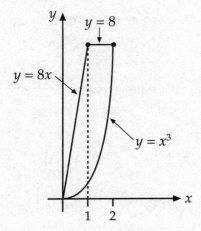

the area we're looking for is given by the sum of these two definite integrals:

$$\text{area of region} = \int_0^1 (8x - x^3)\,dx + \int_1^2 (8 - x^3)\,dx$$

$$= \left[4x^2 - \tfrac{1}{4}x^4 \right]_0^1 + \left[8x - \tfrac{1}{4}x^4 \right]_1^2$$

$$= \left[4 - \tfrac{1}{4} \right] + \left[(16 - 4) - \left(8 - \tfrac{1}{4} \right) \right]$$

$$= 4 - \tfrac{1}{4} + 4 + \tfrac{1}{4}$$

$$= 8$$

Alternatively, one could find the area of this region with a single integral by integrating with respect to y as follows:

$$\text{area of regions} = \int_0^8 \left(\sqrt[3]{y} - \frac{y}{8} \right) dy$$

$$= \left[\frac{3}{4} y^{4/3} - \frac{1}{16} y^2 \right]_0^8$$

$$= 12 - 4$$

$$= 8$$

32. **E** The circles intersect at the origin, and also when:

$$\sqrt{3} \sin\theta = 3\cos\theta \implies \tan\theta = \sqrt{3} \implies \theta = \frac{\pi}{3}$$

We now express the area of the shaded region,

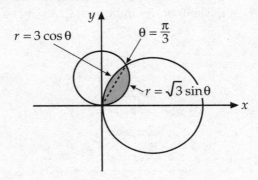

in polar coordinates, as the sum of these two definite integrals:

$$\text{area} = \int_0^{\pi/3} \tfrac{1}{2}(\sqrt{3}\sin\theta)^2 \, d\theta + \int_{\pi/3}^{\pi/2} \tfrac{1}{2}(3\cos\theta)^2 \, d\theta$$

33. **C** The parabola $y = ax^2$ and the line $y = -bx$ intersect at $x = 0$ and at $x = \dfrac{-b}{a}$. From the figure below,

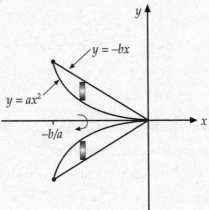

we see that the volume of the solid of revolution can be obtained by the washer method by evaluating the definite integral as on the following page.

$$\text{volume} = \int_{-b/a}^{0} \pi \left[(-bx)^2 - (ax^2)^2 \right] dx$$

$$= \pi \int_{-b/a}^{0} (b^2 x^2 - a^2 x^4) \, dx$$

$$= \pi \left[\tfrac{1}{3} b^2 x^3 - \tfrac{1}{5} a^2 x^5 \right]_{-b/a}^{0}$$

$$= \pi \left\{ 0 - \left[\tfrac{1}{3} b^2 \left(-\tfrac{b}{a} \right)^3 - \tfrac{1}{5} a^2 \left(-\tfrac{b}{a} \right)^5 \right] \right\}$$

$$= \tfrac{2}{15} \pi \cdot \tfrac{b^5}{a^3}$$

Now, if this result is to be a constant, independent of a and b, then the ratio b^5/a^3 must itself be a constant (necessarily positive, since we're told that both a and b are positive). That is, we must have $b^5 = ka^3$, for some positive constant k.

34. **A**   The parabola $y = x^2$ and the graph of $y = 6 - |x|$ intersect at $(\pm 2, 4)$. From the figure below, which includes the equations of the boundaries in the first quadrant solved for x explicitly in terms of y,

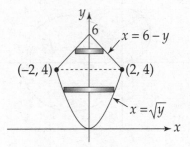

we see that the volume of the solid of revolution can be obtained by the disk method by evaluating the following pair of definite integrals:

$$\text{volume} = \int_{0}^{4} \pi \left[(\sqrt{y})^2 \right] dy + \int_{4}^{6} \pi \left[(6-y)^2 \right] dy$$

$$= \pi \int_{0}^{4} y \, dy + \pi \int_{4}^{6} (36 - 12y + y^2) \, dy$$

$$= \pi \left[\tfrac{1}{2} y^2 \right]_{0}^{4} + \pi \left[36y - 6y^2 + \tfrac{1}{3} y^3 \right]_{4}^{6}$$

$$= 8\pi + \tfrac{8}{3} \pi$$

$$= \tfrac{32}{3} \pi$$

Note: One way to avoid evaluating the second integral above (the more complicated of the two), and thus providing a short-cut to the answer, is to notice that the portion of the solid of revolution from $y = 4$ to $y = 6$ is a right circular cone with base radius $r = 2$ and height $h = 2$, so its volume is $V_{\text{cone}} = \tfrac{1}{3} \pi r^2 h = \tfrac{1}{3} \pi \cdot 2^2 \cdot 2 = \tfrac{8}{3} \pi$, just as we found above.

35. **A** First, we use the equation of the hypocycloid to find y':

$$x^{2/3} + y^{2/3} = 1 \quad \Rightarrow \quad y = (1 - x^{2/3})^{3/2}$$
$$\Rightarrow \quad y' = \tfrac{3}{2}(1 - x^{2/3})^{1/2} \cdot (-\tfrac{2}{3}x^{-1/3})$$
$$= -x^{-1/3}(1 - x^{2/3})^{1/2}$$

Then, using the formula for arc length, we get:

$$s = \int_{x=a}^{x=b} \sqrt{1 + (y')^2}\ dx = \int_{1/8}^{1} \sqrt{1 + \left[-x^{-1/3}(1 - x^{2/3})^{1/2}\right]^2}\ dx$$
$$= \int_{1/8}^{1} \sqrt{1 + x^{-2/3}(1 - x^{2/3})}\ dx$$
$$= \int_{1/8}^{1} \sqrt{x^{-2/3}}\ dx$$
$$= \int_{1/8}^{1} x^{-1/3}\ dx$$
$$= \left[\tfrac{3}{2}x^{2/3}\right]_{1/8}^{1}$$
$$= \tfrac{3}{2}\left[1 - (\tfrac{1}{8})^{2/3}\right]$$
$$= \tfrac{9}{8}$$

36. **D** Simplifying the left-hand side, we find that:

$$\int_{e}^{a^e} \frac{dx}{x \int_{a}^{ax} \frac{dy}{y}} = 1$$

$$\int_{e}^{a^e} \frac{dx}{x\,[\log y]_{a}^{ax}} = 1$$

$$\int_{e}^{a^e} \frac{dx}{x \log x} = 1$$

$$\log(\log x)\Big]_{e}^{a^e} = 1$$

$$\log(\log a^e) = 1$$

$$\log a^e = e$$

$$a = e$$

37. **B** The given limit is of the indeterminate form 1^∞. So we set $y = (\cos x)^{\cot^2 x}$, giving

$\log y = (\cot^2 x)\log(\cos x) = [\log(\cos x)]/(\tan^2 x)$, which is of the indeterminate form $\frac{0}{0}$. Applying

L'Hôpital's rule to this expression, we get:

$$\lim_{x \to 0} \frac{\log(\cos x)}{\tan^2 x} = \lim_{x \to 0} \frac{\dfrac{-\sin x}{\cos x}}{2\tan x \sec^2 x} = \lim_{x \to 0} \frac{\dfrac{-\sin x}{\cos x}}{2\dfrac{\sin x}{\cos x}\dfrac{1}{\cos^2 x}} = \lim_{x \to 0} \frac{-\cos^2 x}{2} = -\frac{1}{2}$$

Since $\log y \to -\dfrac{1}{2}$, we can conclude that $y \to e^{-1/2}$; that is:

$$\lim_{x \to 0} (\cos x)^{\cot^2 x} = e^{-1/2} = \frac{1}{\sqrt{e}}$$

38. **C** We can simplify the integral $\int dx/x(\log x)^n$ by making the substitution $u = \log x$, $du = dx/x$:

$$\int \frac{dx}{x(\log x)^n} = \int \frac{du}{u^n} = \begin{cases} \frac{1}{-n+1}u^{-n+1} & \text{if } n \neq -1 \\ \log u & \text{if } n = -1 \end{cases} = \begin{cases} \frac{1}{-n+1}(\log x)^{-n+1} & \text{if } n \neq -1 \\ \log(\log x) & \text{if } n = -1 \end{cases}$$

Since $\log x \to \infty$ as $x \to \infty$, we see that the improper integral converges if and only if $-n + 1 < 0$, that is, if and only if $n > 1$. In this case, we find that:

$$\int_e^\infty \frac{dx}{x(\log x)^n} = \lim_{b \to \infty} \left[\frac{1}{-n+1}(\log x)^{-n+1}\right]_e^b = \frac{1}{-n+1}\lim_{b \to \infty}\left[\frac{1}{(\log b)^{n-1}} - 1\right] = \frac{1}{-n+1}(0-1) = \frac{1}{n-1}$$

39. **E** Both of the integrals in this question are improper integrals of the second kind, since each integrand goes to infinity at the upper limit of integration, $x = a$. However, as we'll see, both integrals converge. The integral on the left-hand side of the given equation is simplified by making a trig substitution: $x = a\sin\theta$, $dx = a\cos\theta\,d\theta$:

$$\int \frac{dx}{\sqrt{a^2 - x^2}} = \int \frac{a\cos\theta\,d\theta}{\sqrt{a^2 - (a\sin\theta)^2}} = \int d\theta = \theta = \arcsin\left(\tfrac{1}{a}x\right)$$

The integral on the right-hand side of the given equation is simplified by making a simpler substitution: $u = a^2 - x^2$, $du = -2x\,dx$:

$$\int \frac{x\,dx}{\sqrt{a^2 - x^2}} = \int \frac{-\frac{1}{2}du}{\sqrt{u}} = \int \left(-\tfrac{1}{2}u^{-1/2}\right)du = -u^{1/2} = -\sqrt{a^2 - x^2}$$

Therefore, the equation

$$\int_0^a \frac{dx}{\sqrt{a^2 - x^2}} = \int_0^a \frac{x\,dx}{\sqrt{a^2 - x^2}}$$

simplifies to:

$$\left[\arcsin\left(\tfrac{1}{a}x\right)\right]_0^a = \left[-\sqrt{a^2-x^2}\right]_0^a$$
$$\arcsin 1 = |a|$$
$$a = \pm\tfrac{\pi}{2}$$

Since we're asked for the positive value of a that satisfies the equation, we take $a = \tfrac{\pi}{2}$.

40. **B** To evaluate the integral in I, make the substitution $x = \tan\theta$, $dx = \sec^2\theta\, d\theta$

$$\int \frac{dx}{(x^2+1)^2} = \int \frac{\sec^2\theta\, d\theta}{(\tan^2\theta+1)^2} = \int \frac{\sec^2\theta\, d\theta}{(\sec^2\theta)^2} = \int \frac{d\theta}{\sec^2\theta} = \int \cos^2\theta\, d\theta$$
$$= \int \tfrac{1}{2}(1+\cos 2\theta)\, d\theta$$
$$= \tfrac{1}{2}\theta + \tfrac{1}{4}\sin 2\theta$$
$$= \tfrac{1}{2}\theta + \tfrac{1}{2}\sin\theta\cos\theta$$
$$= \tfrac{1}{2}\arctan x + \frac{x}{2(x^2+1)}$$

where we've used the triangle

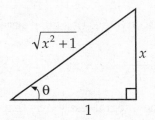

to calculate the product $\sin\theta\cos\theta = \left(x/\sqrt{x^2+1}\right)\left(1/\sqrt{x^2+1}\right) = x/(x^2+1)$. Now, since

$$\int_{-\infty}^{0} \frac{dx}{(x^2+1)^2} = \lim_{a\to-\infty}\left[\tfrac{1}{2}\arctan x + \frac{x}{2(x^2+1)}\right]_a^0 = \lim_{a\to-\infty}\left[-\tfrac{1}{2}\arctan a - \frac{a}{2(a^2+1)}\right] = -\tfrac{1}{2}\left(-\frac{\pi}{2}\right) - 0 = \frac{\pi}{4}$$

and

$$\int_{0}^{\infty} \frac{dx}{(x^2+1)^2} = \lim_{b\to\infty}\left[\tfrac{1}{2}\arctan x + \frac{x}{2(x^2+1)}\right]_0^b = \lim_{b\to\infty}\left[\tfrac{1}{2}\arctan b + \frac{b}{2(b^2+1)}\right] = \tfrac{1}{2}\left(\frac{\pi}{2}\right) + 0 = \frac{\pi}{4}$$

we conclude that the given integral converges, and, in fact, we have

$$\int_{-\infty}^{\infty} \frac{dx}{(x^2+1)^2} = \int_{-\infty}^{0} \frac{dx}{(x^2+1)^2} + \int_{0}^{\infty} \frac{dx}{(x^2+1)^2} = \frac{\pi}{4} + \frac{\pi}{4} = \frac{\pi}{2}$$

although for this question we're concerned only with the convergence of the improper integral, not its actual value.

To evaluate the integral in II, we use integration by parts, with $u = x$, $du = dx$, and $v = -e^{-x}$, $dv = e^{-x}\, dx$:

$$\int xe^{-x}dx = x(-e^{-x}) - \int(-e^{-x})\, dx = -xe^{-x} - e^{-x} = -e^{-x}(x+1) = -\frac{x+1}{e^x}$$

Therefore, the given improper integral converges, since

$$\int_1^\infty xe^{-x}dx = \lim_{b\to\infty}\left[-\frac{x+1}{e^x}\right]_1^b = \lim_{b\to\infty}\left[\frac{x+1}{e^x}\right]_b^1 = \lim_{b\to\infty}\left[\frac{2}{e}-\frac{b+1}{e^b}\right] = \frac{2}{e}$$

where we found $\lim_{b\to\infty}[(b+1)/e^b] = 0$ from one application of L'Hôpital's rule.

Finally, to evaluate the integral in III, we make the substitution $u = 2-x$, $du = -dx$:

$$\int\frac{dx}{(2-x)^2} = \int\frac{-du}{u^2} = \int\left(-u^{-2}\right)du = u^{-1} = \frac{1}{u} = \frac{1}{2-x}$$

We now see that the given improper integral diverges, because:

$$\int_0^2\frac{dx}{(2-x)^2} = \lim_{b\to2^-}\left[\frac{1}{2-x}\right]_0^b = \lim_{b\to2^-}\left[\frac{1}{2-b}-\frac{1}{2}\right] = \infty$$

Thus, only the integrals in I and II converge.

Alternatively, you can simply use estimates:

$$\frac{1}{\left(x^2+1\right)^2} = \frac{1}{x^4+2x^2+1} \simeq \frac{1}{x^4}$$

41. **A** Since the series $\displaystyle\sum_{n=1}^\infty\frac{1}{n^{5/4}}$ converges (it's the p-series, with $p = \frac{5}{4} > 1$):

$$\frac{\cos^4(\arctan n)}{n\sqrt[4]{n}} \leq \frac{1}{n^{5/4}} \text{ for every } n \implies \sum_{n=1}^\infty\frac{\cos^4(\arctan n)}{n\sqrt[4]{n}} \text{ converges}$$

As for the series in II, the integral test shows that it diverges, since:

$$\int\frac{dx}{x\log x} = \log(\log x) \implies \int_2^\infty\frac{dx}{x\log x} = \lim_{b\to\infty}\left[\log(\log x)\right]_2^b = \infty$$

The series in III also diverges, because the terms do not approach 0 as $n\to\infty$:

$$\lim_{n\to\infty}\frac{(n+1)^3}{5(n+2)(n+3)(n+4)} = \lim_{n\to\infty}\frac{n^3+3n^2+3n+1}{5n^3+45n^2+130n+120} = \frac{1}{5} \neq 0 \implies \sum_{n=0}^\infty\frac{(n+1)^3}{5(n+2)(n+3)(n+4)} = \infty$$

Therefore, the series in I is the only one among the three that converges.

42. **E** Let's apply the ratio test to the given series:

$$\lim_{n\to\infty}\frac{x_{n+1}}{x_n} = \lim_{n\to\infty}\left\{\frac{[(n+1)!]^2\,a^{n+1}}{[2(n+1)]!}\cdot\frac{(2n)!}{(n!)^2\,a^n}\right\}$$

$$= a\cdot\lim_{n\to\infty}\frac{(n+1)^2}{(2n+1)(2n+2)}$$

$$= a\cdot\lim_{n\to\infty}\frac{n^2+2n+1}{4n^2+6n+2}$$

$$= a\cdot\frac{1}{4}$$

In order for the series to converge, this limit must be less than 1; therefore, the series converges if $0 \le \frac{1}{4}a < 1$, that is, if $0 \le a < 4$. Thus, we take $b = 4$.

43. **D** The expression we're asked to simplify is the limit of a Riemann sum, which we can compute by evaluating its corresponding definite integral. Since

$$\frac{k}{n^2} - \frac{k^2}{n^3} = \frac{1}{n}\left[\left(\frac{k}{n}\right) - \left(\frac{k}{n}\right)^2\right]$$

we consider the function $f(x) = x - x^2$. The figure below shows the graph of this function on the interval [0, 1], with a collection of rectangles:

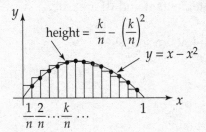

Each of these n rectangles has a base width of $\frac{1}{n}$, and the height of the kth rectangle is equal to $\frac{k}{n} - \left(\frac{k}{n}\right)^2$, the value of f at the right-hand endpoint of its base. Therefore, the sum of the areas of these rectangles is

$$\frac{1}{n}\left[\left(\frac{1}{n}\right) - \left(\frac{1}{n}\right)^2\right] + \frac{1}{n}\left[\left(\frac{2}{n}\right) - \left(\frac{2}{n}\right)^2\right] + \cdots + \frac{1}{n}\left[\left(\frac{n}{n}\right) - \left(\frac{n}{n}\right)^2\right] = \sum_{k=1}^{n} \frac{1}{n}\left[\left(\frac{k}{n}\right) - \left(\frac{k}{n}\right)^2\right]$$

which is precisely the sum whose limit we're asked to compute. Therefore, by definition of the definite integral, we have:

$$\lim_{n\to\infty} \sum_{k=1}^{n} \frac{1}{n}\left[\left(\frac{k}{n}\right) - \left(\frac{k}{n}\right)^2\right] = \int_0^1 (x - x^2)\, dx$$

Applying the fundamental theorem of calculus:

$$\int_0^1 (x - x^2)\, dx = \left[\tfrac{1}{2}x^2 - \tfrac{1}{3}x^3\right]_0^1 = \tfrac{1}{2} - \tfrac{1}{3} = \tfrac{1}{6}$$

Thus, we have shown that:

$$\lim_{n\to\infty} \sum_{k=1}^{n}\left[\frac{k}{n^2} - \frac{k^2}{n^3}\right] = \frac{1}{6}$$

44. **D**   Statement I is false, as the following counterexample shows. Let $a_n = 1/n^2$; then the series $\sum a_n$ converges (it's the p-series, with $p = 2 > 1$). However, since $\sqrt{a_n} = \frac{1}{n}$, the series $\sum \sqrt{a_n}$ is $\sum \frac{1}{n}$. This is the harmonic series, which is known to diverge.

Statement II is true, by the comparison test. Since for every $n \geq 1$, we have $0 \leq a_n \leq na_n$, the fact that $\sum na_n$ converges implies that $\sum a_n$ converges also.

Statement III is also true. The fact that $\sum a_n^2$ converges implies $a_n^2 \to 0$, which means that $a_n \to 0$. But the fact that the sequence (a_n) is decreasing and the terms have a limit of zero is sufficient to conclude, by the alternating series test, that the series $\sum (-1)^n a_n$ converges.

Therefore, only statements II and III are true.

45. **B**   Let's begin with this well-known series:

$$\sum_{n=0}^{\infty} x^n = \frac{1}{1-x}$$

Replacing x with x^2, we obtain:

$$\sum_{n=0}^{\infty} x^{2n} = \frac{1}{1-x^2}$$

Differentiating gives us:

$$\sum_{n=1}^{\infty} (2n)x^{2n-1} = \frac{d}{dx}\left(\frac{1}{1-x^2}\right)$$

Finally, by multiplying both sides by $\frac{x}{2}$, and simplifying, we get:

$$\sum_{n=1}^{\infty} nx^{2n} = \frac{x}{2} \cdot \frac{d}{dx}\left(\frac{1}{1-x^2}\right)$$

$$= \frac{x}{2} \cdot \frac{2x}{(1-x^2)^2}$$

$$= \frac{x^2}{(1-x^2)^2}$$

46. **C** Applying the ratio test, we have:

$$\lim_{n \to \infty} \left| \frac{a_{n+1}}{a_n} \right| = \lim_{n \to \infty} \left\{ \frac{[(n+1)!][2(n+1)]! \cdot |x^{n+1}|}{[3(n+1)]!} \cdot \frac{(3n)!}{n! \cdot (2n)! \cdot |x^n|} \right\}$$

$$= |x| \cdot \lim_{n \to \infty} \frac{(n+1)(2n+1)(2n+2)}{(3n+1)(3n+2)(3n+3)}$$

$$= |x| \cdot \tfrac{4}{27}$$

For the series to converge (absolutely), this limit must be less than 1. Therefore, the series converges if $|x| < \frac{27}{4} = 6\frac{3}{4}$ and diverges if $|x| > 6\frac{3}{4}$. Thus, the smallest positive integer x for which the given series does *not* converge is $x = 7$.

47. **C** The coefficient of x^3 in the Taylor series expansion of $f(x)$ is:

$$a_3 = \frac{f'''(0)}{3!}$$

If $f(x) = e^{x^2 - x}$, we have:

$$f'(x) = (2x - 1)e^{x^2 - x}$$
$$f''(x) = (2x - 1)^2 e^{x^2 - x} + 2e^{x^2 - x} = e^{x^2 - x}(4x^2 - 4x + 3)$$
$$f'''(x) = e^{x^2 - x}(8x - 4) + (4x^2 - 4x + 3)(2x - 1)e^{x^2 - x}$$

Therefore, $f'''(0) = (1)(-4) + (3)(-1)(1) = -7$, so:

$$a_3 = \frac{f'''(0)}{3!} = \frac{-7}{3!} = -\frac{7}{6}$$

Alternatively, from the known series for e^x, we can write

$$e^{x^2} = 1 + x^2 + x^4 + \cdots \qquad \text{and} \qquad e^{-x} = 1 - x + \tfrac{1}{2}x^2 - \tfrac{1}{6}x^3 + \cdots$$

so

$$e^{x^2 - x} = e^{x^2} e^{-x} = (1 + x^2 + \cdots)(1 - x + \tfrac{1}{2}x^2 - \tfrac{1}{6}x^3 + \cdots)$$

$$= 1(1 - x + \tfrac{1}{2}x^2 - \tfrac{1}{6}x^3 + \cdots) + x^2(1 - x + \tfrac{1}{2}x^2 - \tfrac{1}{6}x^3 + \cdots) + \cdots$$

$$= (1 - x + \tfrac{1}{2}x^2 - \tfrac{1}{6}x^3 + \cdots) + (x^2 - x^3 + \cdots) + \cdots$$

$$= 1 - x + \tfrac{3}{2}x^2 - \tfrac{7}{6}x^3 + \cdots$$

from which we can see directly that the coefficient of x^3 is $-\frac{7}{6}$.

48. **A** The right-hand side of the given equation is the Taylor expansion of the function $f(x) = x^4$ in powers of $(x + 1)$. The coefficient of $(x + 1)^3$ is therefore:

$$k_3 = \frac{f'''(-1)}{3!}$$

If $f(x) = x^4$, we have

$$f'(x) = 4x^3, \qquad f''(x) = 12x^2, \qquad f'''(x) = 24x, \quad \ldots$$

so $f'''(-1) = 24(-1) = -24$, which gives us:

$$k_3 = \frac{f'''(-1)}{3!} = \frac{-24}{3!} = \frac{-24}{6} = -4$$

49. **C** We're looking for the smallest integer, n, such that the nth-degree Taylor polynomial, $P_n(x)$, for $f(x) = e^x$ approximates $\sqrt[5]{e} = e^{0.2} = f(0.2)$ to within 10^{-6}. The difference between $f(0.2)$ and $P_n(0.2)$ is

$$f(0.2) - P_n(0.2) = \frac{f^{(n+1)}(c)}{(n+1)!}(0.2)^{n+1}$$

where c is some number between 0 and 0.2. Therefore, we want to find the smallest integer n such that:

$$\frac{f^{(n+1)}(c)}{(n+1)!}(0.2)^{n+1} < 10^{-6}$$

Because $f^{(n+1)}(x) = e^x$ for every n, we know that $f^{(n+1)}(c) = e^c$. Since $0 < c < 0.2$, we can confidently write $1 < e^c < 2$ (since $1 < e < 4$ and $0 < c < 0.5$, it must be true that $1 < e^c < 4^{0.5}$, and $4^{0.5} = 2$). Therefore, the above inequality becomes:

$$\frac{2}{(n+1)!}(0.2)^{n+1} < 10^{-6}$$

Here, the natural choice of n to try first is $n = 5$, because $(0.2)^{n+1} = \left(\frac{2}{10}\right)^{n+1}$, so if $n = 5$, we have $\left(\frac{2}{10}\right)^{n+1} = \frac{2^6}{10^6} = 2^6(10^{-6})$. So, with $n = 5$, we find that:

$$\frac{2}{(n+1)!}(0.2)^{n+1} = \frac{2}{(5+1)!}(0.2)^{5+1} = \frac{2}{6!} \cdot \frac{2^6}{10^6} = \frac{2^7}{6!} \cdot 10^{-6} < 10^{-6}$$

The choice of 5 for n is the smallest possible to ensure that the error is less than 10^{-6}, since if we try $n = 4$, we'd find that:

$$\frac{2}{(n+1)!}(0.2)^{n+1} = \frac{2}{(4+1)!}(0.2)^{4+1} = \frac{2}{5!} \cdot \frac{2^5}{10^5} = \frac{2^6}{5!} \cdot 10^{-5} \approx \tfrac{1}{2} \times 10^{-5} = 5 \times 10^{-6} \not< 10^{-6}$$

50. **D** Rather than use L'Hôpital's rule (which would get *very* complicated here), we try another method: Taylor expansions. From the known series for e^{x^2} (which we get by replacing x with x^2 in the expansion of e^x) and for $\cos x$, we can write:

$$\lim_{x \to 0} \frac{(e^{x^2} - x^2 - 1)(\cos x - 1)}{x^k}$$

$$= \lim_{x \to 0} \frac{[(1 + x^2 + \frac{1}{2}x^4 + \frac{1}{6}x^6 + \cdots) - x^2 - 1][(1 - \frac{1}{2}x^2 + \frac{1}{24}x^4 - \cdots) - 1]}{x^k}$$

$$= \lim_{x \to 0} \frac{[\frac{1}{2}x^4 + \frac{1}{6}x^6 + \cdots][-\frac{1}{2}x^2 + \frac{1}{24}x^4 - \cdots]}{x^k}$$

$$= \lim_{x \to 0} \frac{-\frac{1}{4}x^6 + \left(\frac{1}{48} - \frac{1}{12}\right)x^8 - \frac{7}{480}x^{10} + \cdots}{x^k}$$

Now, from this last expression, we can see that if $k > 6$, the limit will be infinite, and if $k < 6$, the limit will be zero. Therefore, only if $k = 6$ will the limit be finite and nonzero. If this is the case, then the limit, L, is:

$$\lim_{x \to 0} \frac{-\frac{1}{4}x^6 + \left(\frac{1}{48} - \frac{1}{12}\right)x^8 + \frac{7}{480}x^{10} + \cdots}{x^6} = \lim_{x \to 0}\left[-\frac{1}{4} + \left(\frac{1}{48} - \frac{1}{12}\right)x^2 + \frac{1}{144}x^4 - \cdots\right] = -\frac{1}{4}$$

CHAPTER 3 REVIEW QUESTIONS (PAGES 160–165)

1. **A** Place the cube in the first octant of xyz-space with the back, left-hand bottom corner at the origin. If each side of the cube has unit length, then the diagonals shown in the figure are the vectors $\mathbf{A} = (1, 0, 1)$ and $\mathbf{B} = (0, 1, 1)$. If θ is the angle between $\mathbf{A}$ and $\mathbf{B}$, then by definition of the dot product, we find that:

$$\cos\theta = \frac{\mathbf{A} \cdot \mathbf{B}}{AB} = \frac{(1,0,1) \cdot (0,1,1)}{\sqrt{1^2 + 0^2 + 1^2}\sqrt{0^2 + 1^2 + 1^2}} = \frac{1}{2} \quad \Rightarrow \quad \theta = 60°$$

2. **D** Every vector $\mathbf{w}$ that's orthogonal to $\mathbf{v}$ satisfies the equation $\mathbf{v} \cdot \mathbf{w} = 0$. All the vectors given as choices satisfy this equation except the one in (D). If $\mathbf{w} = \hat{\mathbf{i}} + 3\hat{\mathbf{j}} - \hat{\mathbf{k}}$, then:

$$\mathbf{v} \cdot \mathbf{w} = (2, -1, 3) \cdot (1, 3, -1) = (2)(1) + (-1)(3) + (3)(-1) = -4$$

Since $\mathbf{v} \cdot \mathbf{w} \neq 0$, $\mathbf{w}$ is not orthogonal to $\mathbf{v}$.

3. **B** The magnitude of the cross product of two vectors gives the area of the parallelogram they span, which is twice the area of the triangle they span. If $A = (0, 0, 1)$, $B = (0, 2, 0)$, and $C = (3, 0, 0)$, then:

$$\mathbf{CB} \times \mathbf{CA} = (-3, 2, 0) \times (-3, 0, 1)$$

$$= \begin{vmatrix} \hat{\mathbf{i}} & \hat{\mathbf{j}} & \hat{\mathbf{k}} \\ -3 & 2 & 0 \\ -3 & 0 & 1 \end{vmatrix}$$

$$= (2-0)\hat{\mathbf{i}} - (-3-0)\hat{\mathbf{j}} + [0-(-6)]\hat{\mathbf{k}}$$

$$= 2\hat{\mathbf{i}} + 3\hat{\mathbf{j}} + 6\hat{\mathbf{k}}$$

Therefore, the area of $\triangle ABC = \frac{1}{2}\|\mathbf{CB} \times \mathbf{CA}\| = \frac{1}{2}\|2\hat{\mathbf{i}} + 3\hat{\mathbf{j}} + 6\hat{\mathbf{k}}\| = \frac{1}{2}\sqrt{2^2 + 3^2 + 6^2} = \frac{7}{2}$.

4. **E** One way to answer this question is to try each of the choices to find the one that works. Let's start with choice (A). If $\mathbf{V} = \mathbf{B} + (\mathbf{A} \times \mathbf{B})$, then

$$\mathbf{A} \times \mathbf{V} = \mathbf{A} \times [\mathbf{B} + (\mathbf{A} \times \mathbf{B})]$$

$$= (\mathbf{A} \times \mathbf{B}) + \mathbf{A} \times (\mathbf{A} \times \mathbf{B})$$

$$= (\mathbf{A} \times \mathbf{B}) + (\mathbf{A} \cdot \mathbf{B})\mathbf{A} - (\mathbf{A} \cdot \mathbf{A})\mathbf{B}$$

$$= (\mathbf{A} \times \mathbf{B}) - \mathbf{B}$$

where we used the fact that $\mathbf{A} \cdot \mathbf{B} = 0$ (since $\mathbf{A} \perp \mathbf{B}$) and $\mathbf{A} \cdot \mathbf{A} = 1$ (since $\mathbf{A}$ is a unit vector). If we tried choice (B), the result would be the same as above except the minus sign would change to a plus sign. We can also rule out choice (C), since the calculation above showed that $\mathbf{A} \times (\mathbf{A} \times \mathbf{B}) = -\mathbf{B}$. [Note: If choice (C) had instead been $\mathbf{B} \times \mathbf{A}$ or its equivalent, $-(\mathbf{A} \times \mathbf{B})$, it would have satisfied the given equation.] As the calculation above showed, if $\mathbf{V}$ contains the term $+(\mathbf{A} \times \mathbf{B})$, the final result contains the term $-\mathbf{B}$. So, if we want $\mathbf{B}$, we should try a $\mathbf{V}$ containing the term $-(\mathbf{A} \times \mathbf{B})$; this observation leads us to choice (E). If $\mathbf{V} = \mathbf{A} - (\mathbf{A} \times \mathbf{B})$, then

$$\mathbf{A} \times \mathbf{V} = \mathbf{A} \times [\mathbf{A} - (\mathbf{A} \times \mathbf{B})]$$

$$= (\mathbf{A} \times \mathbf{A}) - \mathbf{A} \times (\mathbf{A} \times \mathbf{B})$$

$$= 0 - [(\mathbf{A} \cdot \mathbf{B})\mathbf{A} - (\mathbf{A} \cdot \mathbf{A})\mathbf{B}]$$

$$= \mathbf{B}$$

as desired. Notice that we used the fact that $\mathbf{A} \times \mathbf{A} = 0$.

5. **E** First, we notice that choice (A) cannot be correct since this point doesn't even lie on the given plane. Since the line L is parallel to the vector

$$\mathbf{PQ} = (4, 2, 1) - (-1, -2, 4) = (5, 4, -3)$$

parametric equations for L are:

$$L: \begin{cases} x = -1 + 5t \\ y = -2 + 4t \\ z = 4 - 3t \end{cases}$$

Therefore, L intersects the plane $x + y + 2z = 11$ when:

$$(-1+5t)+(-2+4t)+2(4-3t)=11$$
$$5+3t=11$$
$$t=2$$

When $t = 2$, the point on the line (and also on the plane) is $(9, 6, -2)$.

6. **B**   The line L containing P and Q is parallel to the vector

$$\mathbf{PQ} = (-3, 3, 3) - (1, -1, 1) = (-4, 4, 2)$$

so parametric equations for L are:

$$L: \begin{cases} x = 1 - 4t \\ y = -1 + 4t \\ z = 1 + 2t \end{cases}$$

When $t = 0$, we're at P, and when $t = 1$, we're at Q:

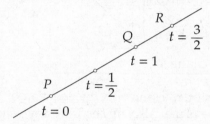

Now, when $t = \frac{3}{2}$, the figure shows that $RP = 3(RQ)$; that is, R is 3 times farther from P than it is from Q, so R is the point we're looking for. Thus:

$$R = (1 - 4 \bullet \tfrac{3}{2}, \ -1 + 4 \bullet \tfrac{3}{2}, \ 1 + 2 \bullet \tfrac{3}{2}) = (-5, 5, 4)$$

7. **D**   If the plane contains the line L, then it certainly contains the point A. This eliminates choices (A) and (C). Choice (B) is also eliminated since it's not satisfied by the point B. If the plane contains the points A and B, then it also contains the vector $\mathbf{AB} = (-2, 3, 1) - (3, 2, 1) = (-5, 1, 0)$. The cross product of $\mathbf{AB}$ and $\mathbf{v}$ will give a vector normal to the plane and allow us to find the equation of the plane. Since

$$\begin{aligned} \mathbf{AB} \times \mathbf{v} &= (-5, 1, 0) \times (-2, 1, 3) \\ &= \begin{vmatrix} \hat{\mathbf{i}} & \hat{\mathbf{j}} & \hat{\mathbf{k}} \\ -5 & 1 & 0 \\ -2 & 1 & 3 \end{vmatrix} \\ &= (3-0)\hat{\mathbf{i}} - (-15-0)\hat{\mathbf{j}} + [-5-(-2)]\hat{\mathbf{k}} \\ &= 3\hat{\mathbf{i}} + 15\hat{\mathbf{j}} - 3\hat{\mathbf{k}} \end{aligned}$$

we conclude that $\mathbf{n} = \hat{\mathbf{i}} + 5\hat{\mathbf{j}} - \hat{\mathbf{k}}$ is normal to the plane. (Notice that $\mathbf{n}$ is just $\frac{1}{3}$ times the cross product $\mathbf{AB} \times \mathbf{v}$. Any scalar multiple of a normal vector is also a normal vector.) Because $\mathbf{n} = \hat{\mathbf{i}} + 5\hat{\mathbf{j}} - \hat{\mathbf{k}}$ is normal to the plane, the equation of the plane must have the form $x + 5y - z = d$, for some constant d. Substituting the coordinates of either point A or B into this equation will give us the value of d. Using $A = (3, 2, 1)$, we find that $3 + 5(2) - 1 = d$, so $d = 12$. The equation of the plane is $x + 5y - z = 12$, which is choice (D).

8.   **C**   Let $\mathbf{n}$ be a nonzero vector normal to the plane, and let P be any point on the plane. If the vector $\mathbf{PO}$ is projected onto $\mathbf{n}$, the magnitude of the projection will give the perpendicular distance, d, from O to the plane:

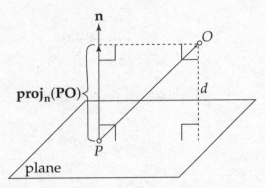

From the coefficients of x, y, and z in the equation of the given plane, we know that $\mathbf{n} = (1, 2, 2)$ is normal to the plane. Also, by choosing any values of x, y, and z that satisfy the equation, we'll obtain a point on the plane; let's choose $P = (6, 0, 0)$, so that the vector $\mathbf{PO}$ is $(-6, 0, 0)$. We now find that:

$$d = \left| \mathbf{proj}_{\mathbf{n}}(\mathbf{PO}) \right| = \left| \frac{\mathbf{n} \bullet \mathbf{PO}}{\|\mathbf{n}\|} \right| = \left| \frac{(1, 2, 2) \bullet (-6, 0, 0)}{\sqrt{1^2 + 2^2 + 2^2}} \right| = \left| \frac{-6}{3} \right| = 2$$

9.   **E**   If a curve in the xz-plane, whose equation contains only the variables x and z, is revolved around the x-axis, we replace z by $\pm\sqrt{y^2 + z^2}$ to obtain the equation of the surface of revolution. In this case, then, the equation for the curve, $z = f(x)$, becomes $\pm\sqrt{y^2 + z^2} = f(x)$, which implies $y^2 + z^2 = \left[f(x) \right]^2$.

10.   **C**   First, we rewrite the given equation in cartesian (rectangular) coordinates, x, y, and z:

$$z = r^2 \cos 2\theta = r^2 \left(\cos^2 \theta - \sin^2 \theta \right) = \left(r \cos \theta \right)^2 - \left(r \sin \theta \right)^2 = x^2 - y^2$$

Therefore, the general equation of the level curves is $x^2 - y^2 = c$. If $c = 0$, then these are the straight lines $x = \pm y$. If c is positive or negative, then $x^2 - y^2 = c$ are hyperbolas that have either x-intercepts (if $c > 0$) or y-intercepts (if $c < 0$). These curves are depicted in choice (C).

11. **D**   First, consider the function f_1. At any point on the line $y = 2x$, except the origin, the value of f_1 is:

$$f_1(x, y) = f_1(x, 2x) = \frac{x - 2x}{x + 2x} = -\frac{1}{3}$$

Therefore, if we approach the origin along this line, we would find that:

$$\lim_{\substack{(x, y) \to (0, 0) \\ \text{along } y = 2x}} f_1(x, y) = \lim_{x \to 0} f_1(x, 2x) = \lim_{x \to 0} \left(-\tfrac{1}{3} \right) = -\tfrac{1}{3}$$

Since the limit of f_1 as we approach $(0, 0)$ along this line is not equal to $f_1(0, 0) = 1$, we conclude that f_1 is not continuous at the origin. In order for any function to be continuous at the origin, the limit as we approach the origin must be the same regardless of how we approach this point (otherwise the limit does not exist), and the value of the limit must be equal to the value of the function at the origin.

Now consider the function f_2. At any point on the line $y = x$, except the origin, the value of f_2 is:

$$f_2(x, y) = f_2(x, x) = \frac{x^2}{x^2 + x^2} = \frac{1}{2}$$

Therefore, if we approach the origin along this line, we would find that:

$$\lim_{\substack{(x, y) \to (0, 0) \\ \text{along } y = x}} f_2(x, y) = \lim_{x \to 0} f_2(x, x) = \lim_{x \to 0} \left(\tfrac{1}{2} \right) = \tfrac{1}{2}$$

Since the limit of f_2 as we approach $(0, 0)$ does not equal $f_2(0, 0) = 0$, we conclude that f_2 is not continuous at the origin.

Finally, consider the function f_3. If we rewrite this function in polar coordinates, we get

$$f_3(x, y) = \begin{cases} \dfrac{(r\cos\theta)^3 - (r\sin\theta)^3}{r^2} & \text{if } (x, y) \neq (0, 0) \\ 0 & \text{if } (x, y) = (0, 0) \end{cases}$$

which simplifies to:

$$f_3(x, y) = \begin{cases} r(\cos^3\theta - \sin^3\theta) & \text{if } (x, y) \neq (0, 0) \\ 0 & \text{if } (x, y) = (0, 0) \end{cases}$$

Because for any θ, we have $\left|\cos^3\theta - \sin^3\theta\right| \leq \left|\cos^3\theta\right| + \left|\sin^3\theta\right| \leq 2$, as we approach the origin from any direction (that is, along any line or curve), the value of f_3 will approach 0, since:

$$\left| \lim_{(x, y) \to (0, 0)} f_3(x, y) \right| = \left| \lim_{r \to 0} f_3(x, y) \right| \leq \lim_{r \to 0} \left| f_3(x, y) \right| \leq \lim_{r \to 0} (2r) = 0$$

Since the limit of f_3 as we approach $(0, 0)$ is equal to $f_3(0, 0) = 0$, we conclude that f_3 is continuous at the origin. (Note: We could have investigated the continuity of f_1 and f_2 at the origin by rewriting the functions in polar coordinates; we would have noticed again that the "limit" at the origin would depend on the direction in which we approach. This means that there is *no* limit at the origin, so neither function is continuous at the origin.)

12. **C**   Since y is held constant along the curve C, the slope of the tangent line is equal to the value of $\partial z/\partial x$. Differentiating z with respect to x gives:

$$\frac{\partial z}{\partial x} = \frac{\partial}{\partial x}\left(\arctan\frac{x+y}{1-xy}\right) = \frac{\dfrac{(1-xy)(1)-(x+y)(-y)}{(1-xy)^2}}{1+\left(\dfrac{x+y}{1-xy}\right)^2}$$

$$= \frac{\dfrac{(1-xy)(1)-(x+y)(-y)}{(1-xy)^2}}{1+\left(\dfrac{x+y}{1-xy}\right)^2} \cdot \frac{(1-xy)^2}{(1-xy)^2}$$

$$= \frac{1+y^2}{1+x^2y^2+x^2+y^2}$$

Evaluating this expression at the point $(x, y) = (2, 1)$, we find that:

$$\text{slope} = \left.\frac{\partial z}{\partial x}\right|_{P=(2,1)} = \left.\frac{1+y^2}{1+x^2y^2+x^2+y^2}\right|_{P=(2,1)} = \frac{2}{10} = \frac{1}{5}$$

13. **A**   To find $\partial V/\partial T$, we first write V in terms of T:

$$V = \frac{nRT}{P} \quad\Rightarrow\quad \frac{\partial V}{\partial T} = \frac{nR}{P}$$

Similarly, to find $\partial T/\partial P$ and $\partial P/\partial V$, we write T in terms of P and then P in terms of V:

$$T = \frac{PV}{nR} \quad\Rightarrow\quad \frac{\partial T}{\partial P} = \frac{V}{nR} \qquad \text{and} \qquad P = \frac{nRT}{V} \quad\Rightarrow\quad \frac{\partial P}{\partial V} = -\frac{nRT}{V^2}$$

We now find that the product of these partial derivatives is:

$$\frac{\partial V}{\partial T} \cdot \frac{\partial T}{\partial P} \cdot \frac{\partial P}{\partial V} = \frac{nR}{P} \cdot \frac{V}{nR} \cdot \left(-\frac{nRT}{V^2}\right) = -\frac{nRT}{PV} = -1$$

(Note: The "numerators" and "denominators" of these partial derivatives cannot simply be canceled; doing so would have given 1 as the product.)

14. **A**   We appeal directly to the definition of a partial derivative to find $f_{xy}(0, 0)$. By definition of the partial derivative with respect to y, we have:

$$f_{xy}(0, 0) = \left.\frac{\partial(f_x)}{\partial y}\right|_{(0,0)} = \lim_{k \to 0}\frac{f_x(0, 0+k)-f_x(0,0)}{k} = \lim_{k \to 0}\frac{f_x(0, k)-f_x(0, 0)}{k}$$

We now need to find $f_x(0, k)$ and $f_x(0, 0)$. Let's first find $f_x(0, k)$. Since for any $(x, y) \neq (0, 0)$,

$$f_x = \frac{\partial}{\partial x}\left(xy\,\frac{x^2-y^2}{x^2+y^2}\right) = \frac{\partial}{\partial x}\left(\frac{x^3y-xy^3}{x^2+y^2}\right) = \frac{(x^2+y^2)(3x^2y-y^3)-(x^3y-xy^3)(2x)}{(x^2+y^2)^2}$$

we have, for $k \neq 0$:

$$f_x(0, k) = \frac{(x^2+y^2)(3x^2y-y^3)-(x^3y-xy^3)(2x)}{(x^2+y^2)^2}\bigg|_{(0, k)} = \frac{(k^2)(-k^3)-0}{(k^2)^2} = -k$$

Now, let's find $f_x(0, 0)$. By definition,

$$f_x(0, 0) = \frac{\partial f}{\partial x}\bigg|_{(0,0)} = \lim_{h\to 0}\frac{f(0+h, 0)-f(0, 0)}{h} = \lim_{h\to 0}\frac{f(h, 0)-0}{h} = \lim_{h\to 0}\frac{0-0}{h} = 0$$

since the formula given for $f(x, y)$ shows that $f(h, 0) = 0$ for all h. Substituting these last two results into our first equation gives:

$$f_{xy}(0, 0) = \frac{\partial(f_x)}{\partial y}\bigg|_{(0, 0)} = \lim_{k\to 0}\frac{f_x(0, k)-f_x(0, 0)}{k} = \lim_{k\to 0}\frac{-k-0}{k} = -1$$

15. **C**   The volume of the cylinder is given by the formula $V(r, h) = \pi r^2 h$. The question wants to know the value of the difference $V(101, 99) - V(100, 100)$. Let $P_0 = (r_0, h_0) = (100, 100)$ and let $P = (101, 99)$. We'll find the equation of the tangent plane to the surface $V = \pi r^2 h$ at P_0 in "rhV-space," and use this equation to give a linear approximation to V at P. Since

$$\frac{\partial V}{\partial r} = 2\pi rh \qquad \text{and} \qquad \frac{\partial V}{\partial h} = \pi r^2$$

we have

$$V - V_0 \approx \frac{\partial V}{\partial r}\bigg|_{P_0} \bullet (r - r_0) + \frac{\partial V}{\partial h}\bigg|_{P_0} \bullet (h - h_0)$$

$$= 2\pi rh\big|_{(100, 100)} \bullet (r - 100) + \pi r^2\big|_{(100, 100)} \bullet (h - 100)$$

$$V - V_0 \approx 2\pi(100^2)(r - 100) + \pi(100^2)(h - 100)$$

where $V_0 = \pi(100 \text{ cm})^3$ is the volume of the cylinder when $r = h = 100$ cm. So, when $r = 101$ and $h = 99$, we find that:

$$V - V_0 \approx 2\pi(100^2)(101 - 100) + \pi(100^2)(99 - 100)$$

$$= 2\pi(100^2) - \pi(100^2)$$

$$= \pi(100^2)$$

That is, the volume will increase (since $V - V_0$ is positive) by approximately $\pi(100^2)$ cubic cm.

16. **E** The given surface is the level surface of the function $f(x, y, z) = y^2z - 2xz^2 + 3x^2y$ that contains the point $Q = (1, 1, 1)$. The gradient of f at the point Q,

$$\nabla f\big|_Q = (f_x, f_y, f_z)\big|_Q$$
$$= (-2z^2 + 6xy, 2yz + 3x^2, y^2 - 4xz)\big|_{Q=(1,1,1)}$$
$$= (4, 5, -3)$$

is normal to the surface and to the tangent plane at Q. Therefore, the equation of the tangent plane has the form $4x + 5y - 3z = d$, for some constant d. Substituting the coordinates of the point $Q = (1, 1, 1)$ into this equation gives $d = 6$, so the equation of the tangent plane is $4x + 5y - 3z = 6$. Of the choices given, only the point in choice (E), $(-2, 4, 2)$, satisfies this equation.

17. **D** Holding x constant and differentiating the given equation with respect to y gives:

$$x^3z^5 - y^2z^3 - 3xy = 1$$
$$5x^3z^4 \frac{\partial z}{\partial y} - \left(3y^2z^2 \frac{\partial z}{\partial y} + 2yz^3\right) - 3x = 0$$
$$\frac{\partial z}{\partial y} = \frac{2yz^3 + 3x}{5x^3z^4 - 3y^2z^2}$$

Now, when $(x, y) = (-1, 1)$, the given equation becomes

$$x^3z^5 - y^2z^3 - 3xy = 1$$
$$-z^5 - z^3 + 3 = 1$$
$$z^5 + z^3 = 2$$

so by inspection, we see that $z = 1$. Substituting $x = -1$, $y = 1$, and $z = 1$ into the expression derived above for $\partial z/\partial y$ gives:

$$\frac{\partial z}{\partial y}\bigg|_{(-1,1,1)} = \frac{2yz^3 + 3x}{5x^3z^4 - 3y^2z^2}\bigg|_{(-1,1,1)} = \frac{2-3}{-5-3} = \frac{1}{8}$$

Another solution uses the chain rule. Let $w = F(x, y, z)$, where $z = f(x, y)$. If w is constant (that is, if $w = c$), then clearly $\partial w/\partial y = 0$. But the chain rule tells us that:

$$\frac{\partial w}{\partial y} = \left(\frac{\partial F}{\partial y}\right)_{x,z} + \left(\frac{\partial F}{\partial z}\right)_{x,y} \frac{\partial f}{\partial y}$$

Therefore,

$$\left(\frac{\partial F}{\partial y}\right)_{x,z} + \left(\frac{\partial F}{\partial z}\right)_{x,y} \frac{\partial f}{\partial y} = 0 \quad \Rightarrow \quad \frac{\partial f}{\partial y} = -\frac{(\partial F/\partial y)_{x,z}}{(\partial F/\partial z)_{x,y}}$$

So, to use this last formula, we differentiate F with respect to y (holding both x *and* z constant) and then with respect to z (holding x and y constant):

$$F(x, y, z) = x^3z^5 - y^2z^3 - 3xy \implies$$

$$\left(\frac{\partial F}{\partial y}\right)_{x,z} = -2yz^3 - 3x \quad \text{and} \quad \left(\frac{\partial F}{\partial z}\right)_{x,y} = 5x^3z^4 - 3y^2z^2$$

This gives

$$\frac{\partial f}{\partial y} = -\frac{(\partial F/\partial y)_{x,z}}{(\partial F/\partial z)_{x,y}} = -\frac{-2yz^3 - 3x}{5x^3z^4 - 3y^2z^2} = \frac{2yz^3 + 3x}{5x^3z^4 - 3y^2z^2}$$

just as we found before.

18. **B**   We recognize z as the dependent variable, x and y as intermediate variables, and u and v as the independent variables. According to the chain rule:

$$\frac{\partial z}{\partial v} = \frac{\partial z}{\partial x}\frac{\partial x}{\partial v} + \frac{\partial z}{\partial y}\frac{\partial y}{\partial v} = \frac{\partial f}{\partial x}\frac{\partial g}{\partial v} + \frac{\partial f}{\partial y}\frac{\partial h}{\partial v}$$

Therefore:

$$\left.\frac{\partial z}{\partial v}\right|_{P_0} = \left.\frac{\partial f}{\partial x}\right|_{Q_0} \cdot \left.\frac{\partial g}{\partial v}\right|_{P_0} + \left.\frac{\partial f}{\partial y}\right|_{Q_0} \cdot \left.\frac{\partial h}{\partial v}\right|_{P_0}$$

$$= (11)(2) + (-3)(2)$$

$$= 16$$

19. **A**   The gradient of a function f points in the direction in which the directional derivative is maximized; that is, the direction of ∇f gives the direction for the maximum rate of increase of f. Therefore, if the fly wants to move in the direction for the maximum rate of *decrease* of T, it must move in the direction of $-\nabla T$. Since $T(x, y, z) = 9x^2 - 3y^2 + 6xyz$, its gradient is:

$$\nabla T = (T_x, T_y, T_z) = (18x + 6yz, -6y + 6xz, 6xy)$$

At the point $P = (2, 2, 2)$, the gradient is:

$$\left.\nabla T\right|_P = (60, 12, 24) = 12(5, 1, 2)$$

This tells us that the vector $(5, 1, 2) = 5\hat{\mathbf{i}} + \hat{\mathbf{j}} + 2\hat{\mathbf{k}}$ points in the direction that will give the maximum rate of *increase* of T, so we conclude that the fly should move in the opposite direction; that is, in the direction of $-5\hat{\mathbf{i}} - \hat{\mathbf{j}} - 2\hat{\mathbf{k}}$.

20. **B**   Let $\mathbf{u}$ be the vector $\hat{\mathbf{i}} - \hat{\mathbf{j}}$, and let $\mathbf{v}$ be the vector $\hat{\mathbf{i}} + \hat{\mathbf{j}}$. We know that the directional derivatives of f at P in the directions of $\mathbf{u}$ and $\mathbf{v}$ are

$$\left.D_{\mathbf{u}}f\right|_P = \left.\nabla f\right|_P \cdot \hat{\mathbf{u}} \quad \text{and} \quad \left.D_{\mathbf{v}}f\right|_P = \left.\nabla f\right|_P \cdot \hat{\mathbf{v}}$$

respectively. The question tells us that:

$$D_{\mathbf{u}}f\Big|_P = \sqrt{2} \quad \Rightarrow \quad \nabla f\Big|_P \cdot \hat{\mathbf{u}} = \sqrt{2} \quad \Rightarrow \quad (f_x(P), f_y(P)) \cdot \frac{(1,-1)}{\sqrt{2}} = \sqrt{2} \quad \Rightarrow \quad f_x(P) - f_y(P) = 2$$

$$D_{\mathbf{v}}f\Big|_P = 3\sqrt{2} \quad \Rightarrow \quad \nabla f\Big|_P \cdot \hat{\mathbf{v}} = 3\sqrt{2} \quad \Rightarrow \quad (f_x(P), f_y(P)) \cdot \frac{(1,1)}{\sqrt{2}} = 3\sqrt{2} \quad \Rightarrow \quad f_x(P) + f_y(P) = 6$$

Solving these last two equations gives:

$$f_x(P) = 4 \quad \text{and} \quad f_y(P) = 2 \quad \Rightarrow \quad \nabla f\Big|_P = (4,2) = 4\hat{\mathbf{i}} + 2\hat{\mathbf{j}}$$

The maximum directional derivative of f at P is the magnitude of the gradient at P. Therefore, the max directional derivative of f at $P = \left\| \nabla f\big|_P \right\| = \left\| 4\hat{\mathbf{i}} + 2\hat{\mathbf{j}} \right\| = \sqrt{4^2 + 2^2} = \sqrt{20} = 2\sqrt{5}$.

21. **E**   The given surface is the level surface of the function $f(x, y, z) = \log(x + y^2 - z^3) - x$ that contains the point $P = (1, 8, 4)$. The gradient of f at the point P

$$\nabla f\Big|_P = (f_x, f_y, f_z)\Big|_P$$

$$= \left(\frac{1}{x + y^2 - z^3} - 1, \ \frac{2y}{x + y^2 - z^3}, \ \frac{-3z^2}{x + y^2 - z^3} \right)\Bigg|_{P = (1,8,4)}$$

$$= (0, 16, -48)$$

$$= 16(0, 1, -3)$$

is normal to the surface at P. Since $16(\hat{\mathbf{j}} - 3\hat{\mathbf{k}})$ is normal to the surface at P, we know that $\hat{\mathbf{j}} - 3\hat{\mathbf{k}}$ is also normal to the surface at P.

22. **D**   The critical points of f are found by setting both f_x and f_y equal to zero:

$$f_x = 3x^2 - 3y \overset{\text{set}}{=} 0 \quad \Rightarrow \quad x^2 = y$$

$$f_y = 3y^2 - 3x \overset{\text{set}}{=} 0 \quad \Rightarrow \quad y^2 = x$$

Substituting the first equation into the second equation gives:

$$(x^2)^2 = x \quad \Rightarrow \quad x^4 - x = 0 \quad \Rightarrow \quad x(x^3 - 1) = 0 \quad \Rightarrow \quad x = 0, 1$$

Since $y = x^2$, we know that there are two critical points: $P_1 = (0, 0)$, and $P_2 = (1, 1)$. We now use the second-derivative test to classify them. The Hessian of f is:

$$\Delta = \det \begin{bmatrix} f_{xx} & f_{xy} \\ f_{yx} & f_{yy} \end{bmatrix} = \det \begin{bmatrix} 6x & -3 \\ -3 & 6y \end{bmatrix} = 36xy - 9$$

The value of Δ at the first critical point, $P_1 = (0, 0)$, is negative, so it's a saddle point. Therefore, according to the statement of the problem, the other critical point, P_2, must be the location of the local minimum. [Note that the value of Δ at $P_2 = (1, 1)$ is positive and $f_{xx}\big|_{P_2} = 6x\big|_{(1,1)} = 6$ is positive, so P_2 does indeed give a minimum.] The value of $f(x, y) = x^3 + y^3 - 3xy$ at $P_2 = (1, 1)$ is $1^3 + 1^3 - 3(1)(1) = -1$.

23. C The distance from the origin to any point (x, y) in the plane is $d(x,y) = \sqrt{x^2 + y^2}$. To minimize d, it is sufficient (and less difficult computationally) to minimize the square of the distance:

$$D(x,y) = x^2 + y^2$$

So, we will minimize D subject to the constraint $g(x, y) = 20$, where

$$g(x,y) = 3x^2 + 4xy + 3y^2$$

by the Lagrange multiplier method, as follows:

$$\nabla D = \lambda \nabla g \quad \Rightarrow \quad (2x, 2y) = \lambda(6x + 4y, 4x + 6y) \quad \Rightarrow \quad \begin{cases} x = \lambda(3x + 2y) \\ y = \lambda(2x + 3y) \end{cases}$$

Subtracting the second equation from the first gives us $x - y = \lambda(x - y)$, so $\lambda = 1$ or $x = y$. If $\lambda = 1$, then the equation $x = \lambda(3x + 2y) = 3x + 2y$ implies that $x = -y$. So, we have two cases to check: $x = y$ and $x = -y$. In either case, the value of D will be $x^2 + (\pm x)^2 = 2x^2$. Substituting these cases into the constraint equation yields:

$$g(x,x) = 20 \quad \Rightarrow \quad 3x^2 + 4x^2 + 3x^2 = 20 \quad \Rightarrow \quad x^2 = 2$$
$$g(x,-x) = 20 \quad \Rightarrow \quad 3x^2 - 4x^2 + 3x^2 = 20 \quad \Rightarrow \quad x^2 = 10$$

We now see that the minimum value of D is $2x^2 = 2(2) = 4$, so the minimum value of d is $\sqrt{D} = \sqrt{4} = 2$.

24. D The area of the fence is equal to $\int_C f \, ds$, where $f(x, y) = x^3 - y^2 + 27$. To avoid fractional exponents, we can parametrize the base curve, C, as follows:

$$C: \begin{cases} x = t^2 \\ y = t^3 \end{cases} \quad \text{for } 0 \xrightarrow{t} 1$$

This parameterization, with t increasing in the positive direction of C, gives:

$$\frac{ds}{dt} = +\sqrt{\left(\frac{dx}{dt}\right)^2 + \left(\frac{dy}{dt}\right)^2} = \sqrt{(2t)^2 + (3t^2)^2} = t\sqrt{4 + 9t^2}$$

Therefore, the area of the fence is:

$$\int_C f \, ds = \int_0^1 [(t^2)^3 - (t^3)^2 + 27] \cdot t\sqrt{4 + 9t^2} \, dt$$
$$= 27 \int_0^1 t\sqrt{4 + 9t^2} \, dt$$
$$= 27 \cdot \left[\tfrac{1}{18} \cdot \tfrac{2}{3}(4 + 9t^2)^{3/2} \right]_0^1$$
$$= 13^{3/2} - 4^{3/2}$$
$$= 13\sqrt{13} - 8$$

25. **C** First, we parametrize the curve C:

$$C: \begin{cases} x = t \\ y = t^2 \end{cases} \quad \text{for} \quad -1 \xrightarrow{t} 0$$

We now evaluate the line integral as follows:

$$\begin{aligned}
\int_C \mathbf{F} \cdot d\mathbf{r} &= \int_C M\,dx + N\,dy \\
&= \int_C (3y - 2x)\,dx + (x^2 + y)\,dy \\
&= \int_{-1}^{0} [3(t^2) - 2t]\,dt + (t^2 + t^2)(2t\,dt) \\
&= \int_{-1}^{0} (3t^2 - 2t + 4t^3)\,dt \\
&= \left[t^3 - t^2 + t^4 \right]_{-1}^{0} \\
&= 0 - (-1 - 1 + 1) \\
&= 1
\end{aligned}$$

26. **E** The curve and the suggested parameterization are quite complicated, which is a clue that perhaps the path is actually irrelevant. This will be the case if the vector field being integrated is a gradient field. Because

$$\mathbf{F}(x, y) = (y \cos xy - 1,\ 1 + x \cos xy)$$

is defined and continuously differentiable throughout the entire plane, we simply need to check whether $M_y = N_x$ to see if it's a gradient field, and thus independent of path. Since

$$M_y = \frac{\partial}{\partial y}(y \cos xy - 1) = -xy \sin xy + \cos xy$$

is equal to

$$N_x = \frac{\partial}{\partial x}(1 + x \cos xy) = -xy \sin xy + \cos xy$$

we know that $\mathbf{F}$ is indeed a gradient field, and it's easy to figure out a potential function for $\mathbf{F}$:

$$f(x, y) = \sin xy - x + y \quad \Rightarrow \quad \nabla f = \mathbf{F}(x, y) = (y \cos xy - 1,\ 1 + x \cos xy)$$

Therefore, by the fundamental theorem of calculus for line integrals, we have:

$$\begin{aligned}
\int_C \mathbf{F} \cdot d\mathbf{r} = \int_{(1,0)}^{(0,1)} \nabla f \cdot d\mathbf{r} &= f(x, y) \Big]_{(1,0)}^{(0,1)} \\
&= (\sin xy - x + y) \Big]_{(1,0)}^{(0,1)} \\
&= (0 - 0 + 1) - (0 - 1 + 0) \\
&= 2
\end{aligned}$$

27.　**B**　The volume of the solid is equal to $\iint_R z\,dA$, where $z = f(x, y) = 8xy$ and R is the region shown below:

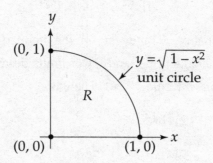

Setting up and evaluating this double integral gives:

$$\int_{x=0}^{x=1} \int_{y=0}^{y=\sqrt{1-x^2}} 8xy\,dy\,dx = \int_{x=0}^{x=1}\left(\int_{y=0}^{y=\sqrt{1-x^2}} 8xy\,dy\right)dx$$

$$= \int_{x=0}^{x=1}\left(\left[4xy^2\right]_{y=0}^{y=\sqrt{1-x^2}}\right)dx$$

$$= \int_0^1 4x(1-x^2)\,dx$$

$$= \int_0^1 (4x - 4x^3)\,dx$$

$$= \left[2x^2 - x^4\right]_0^1$$

$$= 1$$

28.　**E**　For any point (x, y) in the plane, let z_{top} denote the value of z on the paraboloid (the upper surface), and let z_{bottom} denote the value of z on the cone (the lower surface). Both of these surfaces intersect the xy-plane in the ellipse whose equation is $x^2 + \frac{1}{9}y^2 = 1$ (we can see this by setting $z = 0$ into both of the given equations), so the interior of this ellipse is the region R over which the double integral will be taken.

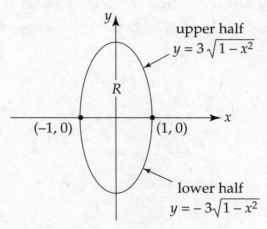

Thus, the volume of the solid described in this question is given by:

$$V = \iint_R (z_{top} - z_{bottom})\,dA$$

We now describe the region R and set up the iterated integrals. Solving the equation $x^2 + \frac{1}{9}y^2 = 1$ for y gives us the upper and lower limits describing the variable y, as shown in the figure above; the limits on x are –1 to 1. Therefore:

$$\begin{aligned} V &= \iint_R (z_{top} - z_{bottom})\,dA \\ &= \int_{x=-1}^{x=1} \int_{y=-3\sqrt{1-x^2}}^{y=3\sqrt{1-x^2}} (z_{top} - z_{bottom})\,dy\,dx \\ &= \int_{x=-1}^{x=1} \int_{y=-3\sqrt{1-x^2}}^{y=3\sqrt{1-x^2}} \left\{ \left[1 - (x^2 + \tfrac{1}{9}y^2)\right] - \left(\sqrt{x^2 + \tfrac{1}{9}y^2} - 1\right) \right\} dy\,dx \\ &= \int_{x=-1}^{x=1} \int_{y=-3\sqrt{1-x^2}}^{y=3\sqrt{1-x^2}} \left[2 - (x^2 + \tfrac{1}{9}y^2) - \sqrt{x^2 + \tfrac{1}{9}y^2} \right] dy\,dx \end{aligned}$$

29. **A** The fact that the integrand involves the quantity $x^2 + y^2$ implies that it might be advantageous to transform this double integral from rectangular coordinates to polar coordinates. The region over which the integral is taken is described by the equations $x = -\sqrt{2ay - y^2}$ to $x = 0$, with $y = 0$ to $y = 2a$. Let's rewrite the equation $x = -\sqrt{2ay - y^2}$:

$$\begin{aligned} x &= -\sqrt{2ay - y^2} \\ x^2 &= 2ay - y^2 \\ x^2 + y^2 - 2ay &= 0 \\ x^2 + (y^2 - 2ay + a^2) &= a^2 \\ x^2 + (y - a)^2 &= a^2 \end{aligned}$$

This last equation describes the circle of radius a centered at $(0, a)$. Since x extends from $x = -\sqrt{2ay - y^2}$ to $x = 0$, for $y = 0$ to $y = 2a$, the region of integration is as shown in the figure below:

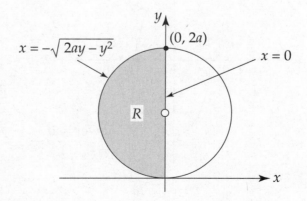

We recognize that the equation of this circle in polar coordinates is $r = 2a\sin\theta$, so when we change the double integral to polar coordinates, r will extend from 0 to $2a\sin\theta$, with θ running from $\frac{\pi}{2}$ to π. Therefore, we have:

$$\int_0^{2a}\int_{-\sqrt{2ay-y^2}}^0 \sqrt{x^2+y^2}\,dx\,dy = \int_{\theta=\pi/2}^{\theta=\pi}\int_{r=0}^{r=2a\sin\theta} r\,(r\,dr\,d\theta)$$

$$= \int_{\theta=\pi/2}^{\theta=\pi}\left(\int_{r=0}^{r=2a\sin\theta} r^2\,dr\right)d\theta$$

$$= \int_{\theta=\pi/2}^{\theta=\pi}\left[\tfrac{1}{3}r^3\right]_{r=0}^{r=2a\sin\theta} d\theta$$

$$= \tfrac{8}{3}a^3\int_{\pi/2}^{\pi}\sin^3\theta\,d\theta$$

$$= \tfrac{8}{3}a^3\int_{\pi/2}^{\pi}(1-\cos^2\theta)(\sin\theta)\,d\theta$$

$$= \tfrac{8}{3}a^3\int_{\pi/2}^{\pi}[\sin\theta + (\cos^2\theta)(-\sin\theta)]\,d\theta$$

$$= \tfrac{8}{3}a^3\left[-\cos\theta + \tfrac{1}{3}\cos^3\theta\right]_{\pi/2}^{\pi}$$

$$= \tfrac{8}{3}a^3[(1-\tfrac{1}{3})-(0+0)]$$

$$= \tfrac{16}{9}a^3$$

30. **C**   Apply Green's theorem:

$$\oint_{C^+=\partial R} M\,dx + N\,dy = \iint_R (N_x - M_y)\,dy\,dx$$

(The symbol ∂R means the boundary of R, and the + superscript on C reminds us that we must choose the positive orientation of C, which is the direction one would have to travel around the boundary to keep the region on the left. The boundary given in the figure with the question is oriented properly.) Since

$$N_x = \frac{\partial}{\partial x}(2x + y\sqrt{y}) = 2 \quad \text{and} \quad M_y = \frac{\partial}{\partial y}(e^{2x} - y) = -1$$

we can write:

$$\oint_C (e^{2x} - y)\,dx + (2x + y\sqrt{y})\,dy = \iint_R [2-(-1)]\,dy\,dx$$

$$= 3\iint_R dy\,dx$$

$$= 3 \cdot (\text{area of } R)$$

The area of the triangular region R is $\frac{1}{2}bh = \frac{1}{2}(2)(2) = 2$, so the value of the line integral is $3 \cdot 2 = 6$.

1. **E** We solve for y by integrating the right-hand side of the given equation:

$$y = \int \frac{x^2}{x^2+1}\,dx = \int \left(1 - \frac{1}{x^2+1}\right)dx = x - \arctan x + c$$

Since $y = 0$ when $x = 0$, the value of c must be 0, so $y = x - \arctan x$. Therefore, the value of $f(1)$ is $1 - \arctan 1 = 1 - \frac{1}{4}\pi = \frac{1}{4}(4 - \pi)$.

2. **C** To say that the population grows at a rate "proportional to the number present," means that

$$\frac{dN}{dt} = kN$$

for some positive constant k. Separating variables and integrating, we get:

$$\frac{dN}{N} = k\,dt \quad \Rightarrow \quad \int \frac{dN}{N} = \int k\,dt \quad \Rightarrow \quad \log N = kt + c \quad \Rightarrow \quad N = Ce^{kt}$$

If we let N_0 denote the number of bacteria present at time $t = 0$, then $C = N_0$, so the equation giving the number of bacteria at time t is $N = N_0 e^{kt}$. Next, using the given information that $N = 3N_0$ at $t = 2$, we find that $3 = e^{2k}$. Therefore, at $t = 4$, we have:

$$N = N_0 e^{4k} = N_0(e^{2k})^2 = N_0 \cdot 3^2 = 9N_0$$

Intuitively, one can also solve this problem by noting that if something triples in 2 hours, it will grow by a factor of 9 in 4 hours.

3. **D** Since the area of the rectangle is xy and the area bounded by the curve is equal to

$$\int_0^x f(t, c)\,dt$$

the statement given in the question becomes:

$$\int_0^x f(t, c)\,dt = \tfrac{1}{3}xy$$

Differentiate both sides with respect to x,

$$f(x, c) = (\tfrac{1}{3}xy)'$$
$$y = \tfrac{1}{3}xy' + \tfrac{1}{3}y$$
$$\tfrac{2}{3}y = \tfrac{1}{3}xy'$$
$$y' = \frac{2y}{x}$$

and solve the resulting separable equation:

$$\frac{dy}{dx} = \frac{2y}{x}$$

$$\int \frac{dy}{y} = \int \frac{2\,dx}{x}$$

$$\log y = 2\log x + \log c$$

$$\log y = \log cx^2$$

$$y = cx^2$$

4.   **C**   The given equation can be rewritten in the form

$$\left(\frac{dy}{dx}\right)^2 - \frac{2x}{y}\frac{dy}{dx} + \left(\frac{x}{y}\right)^2 = 0$$

$$\left(\frac{dy}{dx} - \frac{x}{y}\right)^2 = 0$$

which implies:

$$\frac{dy}{dx} = \frac{x}{y}$$

Separating variables and integrating gives:

$$\int y\,dy = \int x\,dx$$

$$\tfrac{1}{2}y^2 = \tfrac{1}{2}x^2 + \tfrac{1}{2}c$$

$$y^2 - x^2 = c$$

If $c = 0$, then this equation represents the pair of lines $y = x$ and $y = -x$. If $c \neq 0$, then we have a family of hyperbolas with this pair of lines as asymptotes:

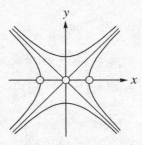

(Notice that we excluded the x-intercepts since the given differential equation implies that y cannot equal zero.)

5.   **A**   The auxiliary polynomial equation for the given homogeneous equation is

$$m^3 - am^2 + a^2m - a^3 = 0$$

whose roots can be determined by factoring the polynomial:

$$m^3 - am^2 + a^2m - a^3 = 0$$
$$m^2(m - a) + a^2(m - a) = 0$$
$$(m - a)(m^2 + a^2) = 0$$
$$\therefore m = a, \ \pm ai$$

We conclude that the general solution to the differential equation is:

$$y = c_1 e^{ax} + c_2 \cos ax + c_3 \sin ax$$

Now, we apply the initial conditions to evaluate the constants c_1, c_2, and c_3. Since

$$y(0) = 1 \ \Rightarrow \ c_1 + c_2 = 1$$
$$y'(0) = 0 \ \Rightarrow \ ac_1 + ac_3 = 0$$
$$y''(0) = a^2 \ \Rightarrow \ a^2 c_1 - a^2 c_2 = a^2$$

we find that $c_1 = 1$, $c_2 = 0$, and $c_3 = -1$. Therefore, the solution we're looking for is:

$$y = e^{ax} - \sin ax$$

If a is a positive constant, then for no positive values of x does e^{ax} equal $\sin ax$. One way to see this is to notice that the graphs of both $y = e^{ax}$ and $y = \sin ax$ have slope a at $x = 0$, but $y = e^{ax}$ crosses the y-axis at $(0, 1)$ and the ordinate is always greater than 1 afterwards, while $y = \sin ax$ crosses at $(0, 0)$ and its ordinate never becomes greater than 1.

6.   **D**   The given differential equation is exact since:

$$\frac{\partial M}{\partial y} = \frac{\partial}{\partial y}[y + g(x)] = 1 \quad \text{and} \quad \frac{\partial N}{\partial x} = \frac{\partial}{\partial x}[x - g(y)] = 1$$

Let G denote an antiderivative of g. Then:

$$\int M(x, y)\, dx = \int [y + g(x)]\, dx = xy + G(x)$$
$$\int N(x, y)\, dy = \int [x - g(y)]\, dy = xy - G(y)$$

These integrations imply that a function whose total differential is the left-hand side of the given differential equation is $f(x, y) = xy + G(x) - G(y)$, so the family of solutions are the curves:

$$xy + G(x) - G(y) = c$$

The curve in this family that passes through the point $(1, 1)$ has $c = 1$, since:

$$f(1, 1) = (1)(1) + G(1) - G(1) = 1$$

So, what other point is guaranteed to lie on the curve $xy + G(x) - G(y) = 1$? The point $(-1, -1)$, since $(-1)(-1) + G(-1) - G(-1) = 1$ also.

7. **B** The differential equation is first-order linear and has the following as an integrating factor:

$$\mu(x) = e^{\int P\,dx} = e^{\int (1/x)dx} = e^{\log x} = x$$

Multiplying both sides of the given equation by $\mu(x) = x$ gives

$$xy' + y = x\sin x \quad \Rightarrow \quad (xy)' = x\sin x$$

so integrating yields:

$$xy = \int x\sin x\,dx = -x\cos x + \sin x + c$$

We now apply the initial condition, $y(\pi) = 1$, to evaluate c:

$$\pi \cdot 1 = -\pi\cos\pi + \sin\pi + c \quad \Rightarrow \quad c = 0$$

The solution to the IVP is therefore

$$xy = -x\cos x + \sin x \quad \Rightarrow \quad y = -\cos x + \frac{\sin x}{x}$$

so the value at $x = \frac{1}{2}\pi$ is:

$$y(\tfrac{1}{2}\pi) = -\cos\tfrac{1}{2}\pi + \frac{\sin\frac{1}{2}\pi}{\frac{1}{2}\pi} = 0 + \frac{1}{\frac{1}{2}\pi} = \frac{2}{\pi}$$

8. **B** The differential equation can be written as $y^{(iv)} - y'' = 0$, so its auxiliary polynomial equation is $m^4 - m^2 = 0$. The roots of this equation are:

$$m^4 - m^2 = 0$$
$$m^2(m^2 - 1) = 0$$
$$m^2(m-1)(m+1) = 0$$
$$\therefore m = 0 \text{ (double root), } 1, -1$$

We conclude that the general solution is:

$$y = c_1 + c_2 x + c_3 e^x + c_4 e^{-x}$$

Applying the initial conditions determines the values of the arbitrary constants:

$$y(0) = 0 \quad \Rightarrow \quad c_1 + c_3 + c_4 = 0$$
$$y'(0) = 0 \quad \Rightarrow \quad c_2 + c_3 - c_4 = 0$$
$$y''(0) = 0 \quad \Rightarrow \quad c_3 + c_4 = 0$$
$$y'''(0) = -1 \quad \Rightarrow \quad c_3 - c_4 = -1$$

These equations give $c_1 = 0$, $c_2 = 1$, $c_3 = -\frac{1}{2}$, and $c_4 = \frac{1}{2}$, so the solution to the IVP is:

$$y = x - \tfrac{1}{2}e^x + \tfrac{1}{2}e^{-x} = x - \tfrac{1}{2}(e^x - e^{-x}) = x - \sinh x$$

9. **E** First, let's solve the corresponding homogeneous equation, $2\ddot{x} + 7\ddot{x} + 3\dot{x} = 0$, where each dot indicates a derivative with respect to t. We write down and solve the auxiliary polynomial equation:

$$2m^3 + 7m^2 + 3m = 0$$
$$m(2m^2 + 7m + 3) = 0$$
$$m(2m + 1)(m + 3) = 0$$
$$\therefore m = 0, \ -\tfrac{1}{2}, \ -3$$

Since we have distinct real roots, the general solution of the homogeneous equation is:

$$x_h = c_1 + c_2 e^{-t/2} + c_3 e^{-3t}$$

Recall that the general solution of a linear nonhomogeneous equation is given by $x = x_h + x_p$, where x_h is the general solution of the corresponding homogeneous equation and x_p is any particular solution of the nonhomogeneous equation. Based on the expression for x_h, we can eliminate choices (A), (B), (C), and (D). (Choice (E) is correct, since it's easy to notice that $x_p = 2t$ is a solution of the given nonhomogeneous equation.)

10. **D** Multiply both sides of the given differential equation by $\mu(x, y) = x^m y^n$:

$$(3x^{m+1}y^{n+2} - 5x^m y^{n+1})\, dx + (2x^{m+2}y^{n+1} - 3x^{m+1}y^n)\, dy = 0 \quad (*)$$

This equation is exact for some values of m and n. Since

$$\bar{M}_y = \frac{\partial}{\partial y}(3x^{m+1}y^{n+2} - 5x^m y^{n+1}) = 3(n+2)x^{m+1}y^{n+1} - 5(n+1)x^m y^n$$

$$\bar{N}_x = \frac{\partial}{\partial x}(2x^{m+2}y^{n+1} - 3x^{m+1}y^n) = 2(m+2)x^{m+1}y^{n+1} - 3(m+1)x^m y^n$$

the test for exactness, $\bar{M}_y = \bar{N}_x$, implies:

$$3(n+2) = 2(m+2) \qquad \text{and} \qquad 5(n+1) = 3(m+1)$$

These equations give $m = 4$ and $n = 2$, so equation (*) becomes:

$$(3x^5 y^4 - 5x^4 y^3)\, dx + (2x^6 y^3 - 3x^5 y^2)\, dy = 0$$

Now, we find the function $f(x, y)$ whose total differential is the left-hand side. Since

$$\int \bar{M}\, dx = \int (3x^5 y^4 - 5x^4 y^3)\, dx = \tfrac{1}{2}x^6 y^4 - x^5 y^3 + (\text{a function of } y \text{ alone})$$

$$\int \bar{N}\, dy = \int (2x^6 y^3 - 3x^5 y^2)\, dy = \tfrac{1}{2}x^6 y^4 - x^5 y^3 + (\text{a function of } x \text{ alone})$$

we can take $f(x, y) = \tfrac{1}{2}x^6 y^4 - x^5 y^3$. The general solution of the given equation is $\tfrac{1}{2}x^6 y^4 - x^5 y^3 = c$, which we can write in the form:

$$x^5 y^3 (\tfrac{1}{2}xy - 1) = c$$

11. **D** First, eliminate choice (E); it doesn't pass through the point (1, 1). Because the slope of the curve is equal to dy/dx, we need to solve the equation:

$$\frac{dy}{dx} = \frac{1 - 2xy}{x^2 + 3y^2 + 1}$$

Writing this in the form

$$(2xy - 1)\,dx + (x^2 + 3y^2 + 1)\,dy = 0$$

we notice that it's exact, since:

$$M_y = \frac{\partial}{\partial y}(2xy - 1) = 2x \qquad \text{and} \qquad N_x = \frac{\partial}{\partial x}(x^2 + 3y^2 + 1) = 2x$$

We therefore calculate

$$\int M\,dx = \int (2xy - 1)\,dx = x^2 y - x + (\text{a function of } y \text{ alone})$$
$$\int N\,dy = \int (x^2 + 3y^2 + 1)\,dy = x^2 y + y^3 + y + (\text{a function of } x \text{ alone})$$

and conclude that the general solution of the differential equation is the family of curves $x^2 y - x + y^3 + y = c$. The curve in this family that passes through the point (1, 1) has $c = 2$, so the particular solution we seek is:

$$x^2 y + y^3 - x + y = 2$$

12. **A** If we write the equation in the form

$$(x + y)\,dx - x\,dy = 0$$

we notice that the functions $M(x, y) = x + y$ and $N(x, y) = -x$ are both homogeneous of degree 1, so the differential equation is homogeneous. Therefore, substituting $y = xv$ and $dy = x\,dv + v\,dx$ should turn it into a separable equation in x and v:

$$(x + xv)\,dx - x\,dy = 0$$
$$dx = x\,dv$$
$$dv = \frac{dx}{x}$$
$$v = \int \frac{dx}{x}$$
$$v = \log x + \log c$$
$$v = \log cx$$
$$e^v = cx$$

Replacing v by y/x gives the general solution, $e^{y/x} = cx$.

13. D Two curves are orthogonal (perpendicular) if the product of their slopes is –1; that is, the value at the same point of dy/dx for one curve is the negative reciprocal of the value of dy/dx for the other curve. Therefore, we first find an expression for dy/dx for the given family; the negative reciprocal of this will give an expression for dy/dx for its orthogonal trajectories. Implicit differentiation gives:

$$(x-c)^2 + y^2 = c^2$$
$$2(x-c) + 2yy' = 0$$
$$y' = \frac{c-x}{y}$$

We now need to eliminate the constant c (notice that none of the choices contains c). The equation $(x - c)^2 + y^2 = c^2$ implies that $c = (x^2 + y^2)/2x$. Substituting this into the expression for y', we get:

$$y' = \frac{c-x}{y} = \frac{\frac{x^2+y^2}{2x} - x}{y} = \frac{y^2 - x^2}{2xy}$$

Therefore, the differential equation for the orthogonal trajectories is $y' = \dfrac{2xy}{x^2 - y^2}$.

14. B Since $g(0, y) = 0$ for all $y \neq 0$, it must certainly be true that $g(0, 1) = 0$. This observation eliminates choices (D) and (E). If the given equation is exact, then:

$$\frac{\partial}{\partial y}(\sin xy) = \frac{\partial}{\partial x} g(x, y)$$

We use this equation to find $g(x, y)$

$$\begin{aligned}
g(x, y) &= \int \left[\frac{\partial}{\partial y}(\sin xy) \right] dx \\
&= \int (x \cos xy)\, dx \\
&= x\left(\frac{1}{y}\sin xy \right) - \int \left(\frac{1}{y}\sin xy \right) dx \\
&= \frac{x}{y}\sin xy + \frac{1}{y^2}\cos xy + h(y)
\end{aligned}$$

where h is some arbitrary function of y. We now use the fact that $g(0, y) = 0$ for all $y \neq 0$:

$$g(0, y) = 0$$
$$\left[\frac{x}{y}\sin xy + \frac{1}{y^2}\cos xy + h(y) \right]_{x=0} = 0$$
$$\frac{1}{y^2} + h(y) = 0$$
$$\therefore h(y) = -\frac{1}{y^2}$$

Therefore, since

$$g(x, y) = \frac{x}{y} \sin xy + \frac{1}{y^2} \cos xy - \frac{1}{y^2}$$

we find that:

$$g(x, 1) = x \sin x + \cos x - 1$$

15. **C** One way to answer this question is to try all the choices until you hit the one that works. A little trial and error will help show that in order for $2w_x$ to equal $3w_y$, w must be a function of $3x + 2y$, so choice (C) is the answer. A method to approach this without trying the choices is to notice that the given PDE can be written as the dot product $(2, -3) \cdot (w_x, w_y) = 0$, which—by definition of the gradient of the function $w = f(x, y)$—is equivalent to $(2, -3) \cdot \nabla f = 0$. This equation says that ∇f is always orthogonal to the vector $(2, -3)$ in the plane. But we also know that ∇f is always orthogonal to the level curves of f, so the level curves of f must be parallel to the vector $(2, -3)$. That is, the level curves of f must be straight lines parallel to the line $2y = -3x$. If the level curves of f are given by the family of lines $3x + 2y = c$, then $f(x, y)$ is constant when $3x + 2y$ is constant. This implies that we can write $f(x, y) = g(3x + 2y)$ for some function g. Only choice (C) is a function of $(3x + 2y)$.

CHAPTER 5 REVIEW QUESTIONS (PAGES 214–218)

1. **E** A linear system can either have 0 solutions, 1 solution, or infinitely many solutions. Therefore, if a linear system has two distinct solutions, then it must have infinitely many.

2. **B** Substituting $(x, y, z) = (a, b, a)$ into the equations of the given system, we get:

$$a^2 + ab - a = 1$$
$$a - ab - a^2 = -1$$
$$2a^2 - b = 1$$

The last equation implies $b = 2a^2 - 1$, so substituting this into the first equation yields:

$$a^2 + (2a^3 - a) - a = 1$$
$$2a^3 + a^2 - 2a - 1 = 0$$
$$a^2(2a + 1) - (2a + 1) = 0$$
$$(a^2 - 1)(2a + 1) = 0$$

So $a = 1, -1,$ or $-\frac{1}{2}$. Since we're told that a is not an integer, it must be true that $a = -\frac{1}{2}$. Substituting this into the equation $b = 2a^2 - 1$ gives $b = -\frac{1}{2}$, so $a + b = -1$.

3. **E** None of the statements I, II, or III is true. A counterexample to statement I is provided by the matrix:

$$A = \begin{pmatrix} 0 & 1 \\ 0 & 0 \end{pmatrix}$$

For a counterexample to statement II, take A as above, $B = I$, and:

$$C = \begin{pmatrix} 0 & 0 \\ 0 & 1 \end{pmatrix}$$

A counterexample to statement III is provided by the matrix:

$$A = \begin{pmatrix} 0 & 1 \\ 1 & 0 \end{pmatrix}$$

4. **D** It's easy to see that

$$\begin{pmatrix} 1 & 1 \\ 0 & 1 \end{pmatrix}^n = \begin{pmatrix} 1 & n \\ 0 & 1 \end{pmatrix} \quad \text{and} \quad \begin{pmatrix} 1 & 0 \\ 1 & 1 \end{pmatrix}^n = \begin{pmatrix} 1 & 0 \\ n & 1 \end{pmatrix}$$

so the given equation becomes:

$$\begin{pmatrix} 0 & n \\ -n & 0 \end{pmatrix} = \begin{pmatrix} 0 & 6 \\ -6 & 0 \end{pmatrix} \quad \Rightarrow \quad n = 6$$

5. **E** The product of the matrices is:

$$\begin{pmatrix} 1 & 3a-2b-2c & 0 \\ 0 & -a+b+c & 0 \\ 0 & 3a-b-2c & 1 \end{pmatrix}$$

Since this equals the identity matrix I, it must be true that:

$$3a - 2b - 2c = 0$$
$$-a + b + c = 1$$
$$3a - b - 2c = 0$$

Solving this linear system, we find that $c = 3$.

6. **B** If $k = -1$, then the vector $\mathbf{v}_3$ will be a scalar multiple of $\mathbf{v}_1$, which would imply that the three given vectors could not be a basis for $\mathbf{R}^3$. More directly, form the matrix with $\mathbf{v}_1$, $\mathbf{v}_2$, and $\mathbf{v}_3$ as rows and reduce it to echelon form:

$$\begin{pmatrix} -1 & 1 & 1 \\ 0 & 2 & 2 \\ 0 & 0 & k+1 \end{pmatrix}$$

The rows will be linearly independent as long as $k + 1 \neq 0$; that is, if $k \neq -1$.

7. **E** The following row operations reduce A to echelon form:

$$A = \begin{pmatrix} 1 & 2 & 3 \\ 4 & 5 & 6 \\ 7 & 8 & 9 \end{pmatrix} \xrightarrow[-7r_1+r_3]{-4r_1+r_2} \begin{pmatrix} 1 & 2 & 3 \\ 0 & -3 & -6 \\ 0 & -6 & -12 \end{pmatrix} \xrightarrow{-2r_2+r_3} \begin{pmatrix} 1 & 2 & 3 \\ 0 & -3 & -6 \\ 0 & 0 & 0 \end{pmatrix}$$

Because only 2 nonzero rows remain, the rank of A is 2. Since the row operations performed on A do not change the determinant, and the determinant of the echelon matrix is zero (because there's a row of zeros), $\det A = 0$. Therefore, $r - d = 2 - 0 = 2$.

8. **C** The second matrix can be obtained from the first matrix by the following sequence of operations: (1) take the transpose (this doesn't affect the determinant); (2) switch columns 1 and 2 (this changes the sign of the determinant); (3) add the first column to the third column (this doesn't change the determinant); (4) multiply the second column by 2 (this multiplies the determinant by 2); and (5) subtract twice the first column from the second column (this doesn't change the determinant). Therefore, if the determinant of the first matrix is d, the determinant of the second matrix is $-2d$.

9. **A** The matrix is noninvertible if its determinant is zero. Compute the determinant by performing a Laplace expansion by the third column:

$$\begin{vmatrix} 7 & 6 & 0 & 1 \\ 5 & 4 & x & 0 \\ 8 & 7 & 0 & 1 \\ 0 & 0 & 1 & 1 \end{vmatrix} = -x \begin{vmatrix} 7 & 6 & 1 \\ 8 & 7 & 1 \\ 0 & 0 & 1 \end{vmatrix} - \begin{vmatrix} 7 & 6 & 1 \\ 5 & 4 & 0 \\ 8 & 7 & 1 \end{vmatrix}$$

$$= -x \begin{vmatrix} 7 & 6 \\ 8 & 7 \end{vmatrix} - \left(\begin{vmatrix} 5 & 4 \\ 8 & 7 \end{vmatrix} + \begin{vmatrix} 7 & 6 \\ 5 & 4 \end{vmatrix} \right)$$

$$= -x - 1$$

This equals 0 if $x = -1$.

10. **B** Augment the matrix A with the column vector **b** and reduce the augmented matrix to echelon form:

$$\begin{pmatrix} 1 & 2 & 3 & 12 \\ 4 & 5 & 6 & 11 \\ 7 & 8 & 9 & d \end{pmatrix} \xrightarrow[-7r_1+r_3]{-4r_1+r_2} \begin{pmatrix} 1 & 2 & 3 & 12 \\ 0 & -3 & -6 & -37 \\ 0 & -6 & -12 & d-84 \end{pmatrix} \xrightarrow{-2r_2+r_3} \begin{pmatrix} 1 & 2 & 3 & 12 \\ 0 & -3 & -6 & -37 \\ 0 & 0 & 0 & d-10 \end{pmatrix}$$

If $d - 10 \neq 0$, then the bottom row of the echelon matrix would signal an inconsistent system, so **b** would not be in the column space of A. Therefore, $d - 10$ must equal 0, so $d = 10$.

11. **C** Label the given vectors $\mathbf{v}_1$, $\mathbf{v}_2$, $\mathbf{v}_3$, $\mathbf{v}_4$, $\mathbf{v}_5$, $\mathbf{v}_6$ in the order in which they are listed. Notice that $\mathbf{v}_3 = 0$, $\mathbf{v}_4 = -\mathbf{v}_1$, and $\mathbf{v}_6 = -\mathbf{v}_2$. Therefore, $\mathbf{v}_3$, $\mathbf{v}_4$, and $\mathbf{v}_6$ can be thrown out without affecting the span. The remaining 3 vectors—$\mathbf{v}_1$, $\mathbf{v}_2$, and $\mathbf{v}_5$—are linearly independent, so the dimension of their span is 3.

12. **D**   The n^2 entries in an $n \times n$ symmetric matrix A cannot all be chosen independently. For example, once a_{12} is chosen, the entry a_{21} is automatically determined since $a_{21} = a_{12}$. You can see that we're free to choose the entries along and above the main diagonal, and once this is done, the rest of the matrix is set. So how many degrees of freedom do we have in choosing the entries? There are n choices for the first row, $n - 1$ for the second row, $n - 2$ for the third, . . . , down to 1 in the last row (row n). Therefore, the degrees of freedom total $n + (n - 1) + (n - 2) + \cdots + 1 = \frac{1}{2} n(n + 1)$. This gives dim $S_{n \times n}(\mathbf{R})$.

13. **D**   Expanding the given determinant using a Laplace expansion by the first column gives:

$$x \begin{vmatrix} y_1 & 1 \\ y_2 & 1 \end{vmatrix} + \begin{vmatrix} y & 1 \\ y_1 & 1 \end{vmatrix} = 0$$
$$x(y_1 - y_2) + y - y_1 = 0$$
$$y = (y_2 - y_1)x + y_1$$

This is the equation of a line with slope $y_2 - y_1$.

14. **B**   The vectors $\mathbf{b}_1 = (1, 2)$ and $\mathbf{b}_2 = (0, -1)$ form a basis for $\mathbf{R}^2$, so let's first write the vector $\mathbf{x} = (1, 1)$ in terms of $\mathbf{b}_1$ and $\mathbf{b}_2$. The equation $\mathbf{x} = k_1\mathbf{b}_1 + k_2\mathbf{b}_2$ becomes $(1, 1) = k_1(1, 2) + k_2(0, -1)$, so $k_1 = k_2 = 1$. Therefore, by linearity of T:

$$T(\mathbf{x}) = T(\mathbf{b}_1 + \mathbf{b}_2) = T(\mathbf{b}_1) + T(\mathbf{b}_2) = (-1, 1) + (2, -1) = (1, 0)$$

15. **C**   Since the nullity of T is 3, the rank plus nullity theorem tells us that the rank of T is $5 - 3 = 2$, so the range of T is two-dimensional. A two-dimensional subspace of $\mathbf{R}^3$ is a plane through the origin.

16. **E**   Let's find the standard matrix representatives for S and T. The columns of each matrix will be the images of the standard basis vectors, $\mathbf{e}_1 = (1, 0)^\mathrm{T}$ and $\mathbf{e}_2 = (0, 1)^\mathrm{T}$, under the action of the operator. Since $S(\mathbf{e}_1) = (0, 1)^\mathrm{T}$ and $S(\mathbf{e}_2) = (-1, 0)^\mathrm{T}$, the standard matrix for S is:

$$[S] = \begin{pmatrix} 0 & -1 \\ 1 & 0 \end{pmatrix}$$

Now, since $T(\mathbf{e}_1) = (-1, 0)^\mathrm{T}$ and $T(\mathbf{e}_2) = (0, 1)^\mathrm{T}$, the standard matrix for T is:

$$[T] = \begin{pmatrix} -1 & 0 \\ 0 & 1 \end{pmatrix}$$

Notice that the products $[S][T]$ and $[T][S]$ are

$$[S][T] = \begin{pmatrix} 0 & -1 \\ 1 & 0 \end{pmatrix}\begin{pmatrix} -1 & 0 \\ 0 & 1 \end{pmatrix} = \begin{pmatrix} 0 & -1 \\ -1 & 0 \end{pmatrix} \quad \text{and} \quad [T][S] = \begin{pmatrix} -1 & 0 \\ 0 & 1 \end{pmatrix}\begin{pmatrix} 0 & -1 \\ 1 & 0 \end{pmatrix} = \begin{pmatrix} 0 & 1 \\ 1 & 0 \end{pmatrix}$$

so only choice (E) is true.

17. **A** The columns of A are the images of the basis vectors, so the first column of A is the image of $\hat{\mathbf{i}} = (1, 0, 0)$:

$$T(\hat{\mathbf{i}}) = \mathbf{v} \times \hat{\mathbf{i}} = \begin{vmatrix} \hat{\mathbf{i}} & \hat{\mathbf{j}} & \hat{\mathbf{k}} \\ a & b & c \\ 1 & 0 & 0 \end{vmatrix} = -\hat{\mathbf{j}} \begin{vmatrix} a & c \\ 1 & 0 \end{vmatrix} + \hat{\mathbf{k}} \begin{vmatrix} a & b \\ 1 & 0 \end{vmatrix} = c\hat{\mathbf{j}} - b\hat{\mathbf{k}} = \begin{pmatrix} 0 \\ c \\ -b \end{pmatrix}$$

Therefore, the answer must be (A).

18. **A** If A is invertible and has eigenvalue λ with corresponding eigenvector $\mathbf{x}$, then $A\mathbf{x} = \lambda\mathbf{x}$. Multiplying both sides of this equation by A^{-1} gives $\mathbf{x} = A^{-1}(\lambda\mathbf{x})$, which is equivalent to $\lambda^{-1}\mathbf{x} = A^{-1}\mathbf{x}$. This equation shows that λ^{-1} is an eigenvalue of A^{-1} with corresponding eigenvector $\mathbf{x}$. [Note: Choice (E) would be true if "3" were replaced by "9" because, if λ has an eigenvalue of A, then λ^2 has an eigenvalue of A^2.]

19. **E** Recall that the sum of the eigenvalues is always equal to the trace of the matrix. Therefore, $-4 + (b - 1) = 2 + (-1)$, which gives $b = 6$.

20. **C** The characteristic equation for a 2×2 matrix A has the form:

$$\lambda^2 - [\text{tr}(A)]\lambda + (\det A) = 0$$

In this case, $\text{tr}(A) = 2 + 6 = 8$, and

$$\det A = (2)(6) - (2 - i)(2 + i) = 12 - (4 - i^2) = 12 - 5 = 7$$

so the characteristic equation is $\lambda^2 - 8\lambda + 7 = 0$, which is equivalent to $(\lambda - 1)(\lambda - 7) = 0$. The eigenvalues of this matrix are $\lambda = 1$ and $\lambda = 7$. [Note: The matrix A in this question is known as a **Hermitian** matrix (because it equals its own conjugate transpose). The eigenvalues of any Hermitian matrix are always real, an observation that would have eliminated choices (D) and (E) immediately.]

CHAPTER 6 REVIEW QUESTIONS (PAGES 254–256)

1. **B** Apply the Euclidean algorithm to find the greatest common divisor of 42 and 55:

$$55 = 1 \cdot 42 + 13$$
$$42 = 3 \cdot 13 + 3$$
$$13 = 4 \cdot 3 + 1$$
$$3 = 3 \cdot 1 + 0$$

Now, working from the second line from the bottom upwards, we write 1, the greatest common divisor of 42 and 55, as a linear combination (with integer coefficients) of 42 and 55:

$$1 = 13 - 4 \cdot 3$$
$$= 13 - 4 \cdot (42 - 3 \cdot 13)$$
$$= 42 \cdot (-4) + 13 \cdot 13$$
$$= 42 \cdot (-4) + (55 - 42) \cdot 13$$
$$= 42 \cdot (-17) + 55 \cdot (13)$$

Since $42 \cdot (-17) + 55 \cdot (13) = 1$, every solution in integers of $42x + 55y = 1$ can be written in the form

$$x = -17 + 55t, \quad y = 13 - 42t$$

where t is any integer. Therefore, the first few positive values of x that satisfy the equation are:

$$-17 + 55 = 38, \quad -17 + 2 \cdot 55 = 93, \quad -17 + 3 \cdot 55 = 148, \quad -17 + 4 \cdot 55 = 203, \text{ etc.}$$

Only $x = 148$ falls in the range $100 < x < 200$.

2. **A** Apply the Euclidean algorithm to find the greatest common divisor of 1001 and 10101:

$$10101 = 10 \cdot 1001 + 91$$
$$1001 = 11 \cdot 91 + 0$$

This shows us that $\gcd(1001, 10101) = 91$; therefore:

$$\mathrm{lcm}(1001, 10101) = \frac{1001 \cdot 10101}{\gcd(1001, 10101)} = \frac{1001 \cdot 10101}{91} = 11 \cdot 10101 = 111111$$

The sum of the digits of $L = 111111$ is $1 + 1 + 1 + 1 + 1 + 1 = 6$.

3. **E** We need to solve the congruence equation $85x \equiv 12 \pmod{19}$, which we can do as follows:

$$\begin{aligned}
85x &\equiv 12 \pmod{19} \\
85x &\equiv 50 \pmod{19} \quad &[\text{adding } 0 \equiv 38 \pmod{19}] \\
17x &\equiv 10 \pmod{19} \quad &[\text{dividing by 5}] \\
17x &\equiv -85 \pmod{19} \quad &[\text{adding } 0 \equiv -95 \pmod{19}] \\
x &\equiv -5 \pmod{19} \quad &[\text{dividing by 17}] \\
x &\equiv 14 \pmod{19} \quad &[\text{adding } 0 \equiv 19 \pmod{19}]
\end{aligned}$$

Therefore, the two smallest positive integers x that satisfy the congruence are 14 and $14 + 19 = 33$; the sum of $x_1 = 14$ and $x_2 = 33$ is $x_1 + x_2 = 47$.

4. **D** If $4x - 5y + 2z$ is divisible by 13, then $4x - 5y + 2z \equiv 0 \pmod{13}$. The following steps can now be applied to this congruence:

$$\begin{aligned}
4x - 5y + 2z &\equiv 0 \pmod{13} \\
-35x - 5y + 2z &\equiv 0 \pmod{13} \quad &[\text{adding } -39x \equiv 0 \pmod{13}] \\
-35x + 60y + 2z &\equiv 0 \pmod{13} \quad &[\text{adding } 65y \equiv 0 \pmod{13}] \\
-35x + 60y + 15z &\equiv 0 \pmod{13} \quad &[\text{adding } 13z \equiv 0 \pmod{13}] \\
-7x + 12y + 3z &\equiv 0 \pmod{13} \quad &[\text{dividing by 5}]
\end{aligned}$$

This proves that $-7x + 12y + 3z$ must also be divisible by 13.

An alternative solution would be to find—by trial and error—positive integers x, y, and z such that $4x - 5y + 2z$ is divisible by 13. For example, we could take $x = 4$, $y = 1$, and $z = 1$. Substituting these values into the answer choices would eliminate choices (A), (C), and (E). Another set of values—such as $x = 3$, $y = 1$, and $z = 3$—eliminates choice (B).

5. **B**   The number 100! can be expressed as the product $2^m 5^n c$, where c is relatively prime to both 2 and 5. Since there are more multiples of 2 than there are multiples of 5 (among the first 100 positive integers), the value of m will be greater than the value of n. Therefore, $100! = 2^{m-n} 2^n 5^n c = 2^{m-n} c (10^n)$, so n is the number of zeros at the end of 100!. The question then becomes, *How many factors of 5 will the first 100 positive integers contribute?* There are $\frac{100}{25} = 20$ multiples of 5, each of which contributes one factor of 5; and there are also $\frac{100}{25} = 4$ multiples of 25, each of which contributes one more factor of 5. Therefore, there are $20 + 4 = 24$ factors of 5 in 100!, so $n = 24$.

6. **C**   The cyclic group $\mathbf{Z}_{24}$ will be generated by any nonzero element $m \in \mathbf{Z}_{24}$ that's relatively prime to 24. There are exactly eight positive integers m less than 24 such that $\gcd(m, 24) = 1$; they are $m = 1, 5, 7, 11, 13, 17, 19$, and 23. Therefore, $\mathbf{Z}_{24}$ has eight generators.

7. **C**   The group $\mathbf{Z}_m \times \mathbf{Z}_n$ is cyclic if and only if $\gcd(m, n) = 1$. Therefore, of the choices given, only $\mathbf{Z}_3 \times \mathbf{Z}_4$ is cyclic. [Note: $\mathbf{Z}_m \times \mathbf{Z}_n$ is an alternate notation for $\mathbf{Z}_m \oplus \mathbf{Z}_n$.]

8. **D**   First, we'll write 12 in terms of its prime factorization: $12 = 2^2 \cdot 3$. According to Sylow's first theorem, G must have a subgroup of order $2^1 = 2$ and a subgroup of order $2^2 = 4$, as well as a subgroup of order 3. Every group is a subgroup of itself, so G has a subgroup of order 12. However, since we're not told that G is Abelian, there's no guarantee that G has a subgroup of order 6. [Note: The even permutations in S_n, the symmetric group on n letters, is a subgroup of S_n; this subgroup is called the **alternating group**, denoted A_n. This subgroup has exactly one-half as many elements as S_n has; therefore, the order of A_n is $(n!)/2$. The (non-Abelian) group A_4 has order $4!/2 = 12$, and it can be shown that A_n has no subgroup of order 6.]

9. **B**   The group $G = \mathbf{Z}_3 \oplus \mathbf{Z}_{16}$ is Abelian and has order $3 \times 16 = 48$ (in fact, since $\gcd(3, 16) = 1$, G is isomorphic to $\mathbf{Z}_{48}$). An Abelian group G or order n has exactly one subgroup of order d for every positive divisor d of n. Therefore, the number of subgroups of $\mathbf{Z}_3 \oplus \mathbf{Z}_{16}$ is equal to the number of positive divisors of 48. Since 48 has exactly ten positive divisors—they are $d = 1, 2, 3, 4, 6, 8, 12, 16, 24$, and 48—the group G has exactly ten subgroups.

10. **E**   First, we notice that e is the identity element in this group, since:

$$a \bullet e = a^{\log e} = a = e^{\log a} = e \bullet a$$

So, we want to find b such that $a \bullet b = e$ (because if this equation is satisfied, then $b = a^{-1}$). The equation $a \bullet b = e$ implies that:

$$a^{\log b} = e \quad \Rightarrow \quad \log(a^{\log b}) = 1 \quad \Rightarrow \quad \log b \log a = 1 \quad \Rightarrow \quad \log b = \frac{1}{\log a} \quad \Rightarrow \quad b = e^{1/\log a}$$

11. **B**   In order for a subset of a group to be a subgroup, the subset must contain the identity element of the group. Therefore, the subset V cannot be a subgroup, since the trace of the 2 by 2 identity matrix, I, is $1 + 1 = 2$, not 0. This observation rules out choices (C), (D), and (E). Next, the subset T is not closed under matrix multiplication; if A and B are matrices in T, then

$\det(AB) = (\det A)(\det B) = 2 \cdot 2 = 4$, so $AB \notin T$. This shows that T cannot be a subgroup of GL(2, **R**), eliminating choice (A). The answer is (B). Of the three subsets given, only U is a subgroup; it's closed under matrix multiplication (the product of two upper-triangular matrices is upper triangular), it contains the identity, and the inverse of an upper-triangular matrix in GL(n, **R**) is upper triangular.

12. **C**   If G is an Abelian group of order p^2q^4, where p and q are distinct primes, there are exactly ten sets of elementary divisors for G:

$\quad$ (1) p, p, q, q, q, q

$\quad$ (2) p^2, q, q, q, q

$\quad$ (3) p, p, q^2, q, q

$\quad$ (4) p^2, q^2, q, q

$\quad$ (5) p, p, q^2, q^2

$\quad$ (6) p^2, q^2, q^2

$\quad$ (7) p, p, q^3, q

$\quad$ (8) p^2, q^3, q

$\quad$ (9) p, p, q^4

$\quad$ (10) p^2, q^4

Each of these gives rise to a direct sum of cyclic groups, each of which is structurally distinct from the others. Therefore, there are ten mutually nonisomorphic Abelian groups of order p^2q^4.

13. **D**   Using the group relations, we can write:

$$z = x^{-2}yx^3y^3 = x^{-1}(x^{-1}yx)(x^2)y^3 = x^{-1}(y^{-1})(y^3)y^3 = x^{-1}y^{-1}y^6 = x^{-1}y^{-1} = (yx)^{-1}$$

The inverse of $z = (yx)^{-1}$ is $z^{-1} = yx$.

14. **C**   Because $\mathbf{Z}_3$ is cyclic, any homomorphism with $\mathbf{Z}_3$ as its domain is completely determined by the value of $\phi(1)$, since 1 generates $\mathbf{Z}_3$. Therefore, there are only six possible functions that could be homomorphisms from $\mathbf{Z}_3$ to $\mathbf{Z}_6$; namely, the functions ϕ_i ($i = 0$ to 5) such that $\phi_i(0) = 0$ for all i and:

$$\phi_0(1) = 0, \quad \phi_1(1) = 1, \quad \phi_2(1) = 2, \quad \phi_3(1) = 3, \quad \phi_4(1) = 4, \quad \text{or} \quad \phi_5(1) = 5$$

The zero map, ϕ_0, is always a homomorphism.

$\quad$ The map ϕ_1 is not a homomorphism from $\mathbf{Z}_3$ to $\mathbf{Z}_6$; since $\phi_1(2) = 2$, we have $\phi_1(\mathbf{Z}_3) = \{0, 1, 2\}$, which is not a subgroup of $\mathbf{Z}_6$. (Any subgroup of $\mathbf{Z}_6$ that contains the element 1 would be all of $\mathbf{Z}_6$.) If $\phi: G \to G'$ is any group homomorphism, then $\phi(H)$ must be a subgroup of G' for any subgroup H of G. In particular, $\phi(G)$ must be a subgroup of G'.

$\quad$ The map ϕ_2 is a homomorphism from $\mathbf{Z}_3$ to $\mathbf{Z}_6$; since $\phi_2(2) = 4$, it's easy to verify that $\phi_2(a + b) = \phi_2(a) + \phi_2(b)$ for every a and b in $\mathbf{Z}_3$ (there are only a few cases to check).

$\quad$ The map ϕ_3 is not a homomorphism; since $\phi_3(2) = 0$, we have $\phi_3(2 + 2) = \phi_3(1) = 3 \neq 0 = 0 + 0 = \phi_3(2) + \phi_3(2)$. This shows that the converse of the statement above is not true. Although $\phi_3(\mathbf{Z}_3) = \{0, 4, 5\}$, which is a subgroup of $\mathbf{Z}_6$, ϕ_3 is, nevertheless, not a group homomorphism.

The map ϕ_4 is a homomorphism from $\mathbf{Z}_3$ to $\mathbf{Z}_6$; since $\phi_4(2) = 2$, it's easy to verify that $\phi_4(a + b) = \phi_4(a) + \phi_4(b)$ for every a and b in $\mathbf{Z}_3$ (there are only a few cases to check).

Finally, the map ϕ_5 is not a homomorphism from $\mathbf{Z}_3$ to $\mathbf{Z}_6$; since $\phi_5(2) = 4$, we have $\phi_5(\mathbf{Z}_3) = \{0, 4, 5\}$, which is not a subgroup of $\mathbf{Z}_6$. (Any subgroup of $\mathbf{Z}_6$ that contains the element 5 would be all of $\mathbf{Z}_6$.)

Therefore, there are exactly three group homomorphisms—ϕ_0, ϕ_2, and ϕ_4—from $\mathbf{Z}_3$ to $\mathbf{Z}_6$.

15. **A**   If G has order 9, then it could be the additive group $\mathbf{Z}_9$. This group is cyclic, eliminating choice (D), and Abelian, eliminating choice (E). The group $\mathbf{Z}_9$ has a cyclic subgroup of order 3—namely, $\langle 3 \rangle = \{0, 3, 6\}$ —so choice (C) is ruled out. As for choice (B), if there exists an element $x \neq e$ such that $x^2 = x^5$, then $e = x^3$, where e is the identity of the group; therefore, if the statement in (C) can be true, then the statement in (B) can be true, too. [To illustrate the validity of (B) using our example of the group $\mathbf{Z}_9$, notice that since the operation in $\mathbf{Z}_9$ is addition, the equation $e = x^3$ becomes $0 = 3x$; the elements $x = 3$ and $x = 6$ satisfy this equation and the conditions of the statement in (B).] Therefore, choice (A) must be the answer. If there exists an element x in G such that $x \neq e$ and $x^{-1} = x$, then x generates a cyclic subgroup of order 2 (since $x^{-1} = x$ implies that $x^2 = e$). But by Lagrange's theorem, a group of order 9 cannot have a subgroup of order 2, because 2 does not divide 9.

16. **B**   The ring $\mathbf{Z}_{20}$ contains exactly four idempotent elements: $x = 0$, 1, 5, and 16, since these are the only elements in $\mathbf{Z}_{20}$ that satisfy $x^2 = x$. The following results show that no other elements of $\mathbf{Z}_{20}$ satisfy the equation $x^2 = x$:

$$2^2 = 8^2 = 12^2 = 18^2 = 4$$
$$3^2 = 7^2 = 13^2 = 17^2 = 9$$
$$4^2 = 6^2 = 14^2 = 16$$
$$9^2 = 11^2 = 19^2 = 1$$
$$10^2 = 0$$
$$15^2 = 5$$

17. **B**   An integral domain is a commutative ring with unity that contains no zero divisors. $\mathbf{Z} \oplus \mathbf{Z}$ is not an integral domain, since, for example $(1, 0) \cdot (0, 1) = (0, 0)$. The ring $\mathbf{Z}_p$, where p is a prime, is a field, so it's certainly an integral domain. However, $\mathbf{Z}_{p^2}$ is not an integral domain; for example, if we take $p = 2$, then $\mathbf{Z}_4$ contains a zero divisor, namely 2. (In fact, if p is a prime, then the element $x = p$ of $\mathbf{Z}_{p^2}$ will always be a zero divisor.)

18. **C**   Each of the rings $\mathbf{Z}$, $\mathbf{Z}_3$, and $\mathbf{Z}_6$ contains precisely 2 units (that is, precisely 2 invertible elements). In $\mathbf{Z}$, they are 1 and –1; in $\mathbf{Z}_3$, they are 1 and 2; and in $\mathbf{Z}_6$, the units are 1 and 5. Since each of the choices (A), (B), (D), and (E) is a direct sum of 2 of these groups, each of these groups contains $2 \times 2 = 4$ units. But since 5 is prime, the ring $\mathbf{Z}_5$ contains 4 units (1, 2, 3, and 4), so the ring $\mathbf{Z} \oplus \mathbf{Z}_5$ contains $2 \times 4 = 8$ units. For completeness, we'll list the units in each of the rings given as choices:

	Choice	Ring	Units
	(A)	$\mathbf{Z} \oplus \mathbf{Z}$	$(1, 1)$, $(1, -1)$, $(-1, 1)$, $(-1, -1)$
	(B)	$\mathbf{Z} \oplus \mathbf{Z}_3$	$(1, 1)$, $(1, 2)$, $(-1, 1)$, $(-1, 2)$
✓	(C)	$\mathbf{Z} \oplus \mathbf{Z}_5$	$(1, 1)$, $(1, 2)$, $(1, 3)$, $(1, 4)$, $(-1, 1)$, $(-1, 2)$, $(-1, 3)$, $(-1, 4)$
	(D)	$\mathbf{Z} \oplus \mathbf{Z}_6$	$(1, 1)$, $(1, 5)$, $(-1, 1)$, $(-1, 5)$
	(E)	$\mathbf{Z}_3 \oplus \mathbf{Z}_3$	$(1, 1)$, $(1, 2)$, $(2, 1)$, $(2, 2)$

19. **B**   We want to solve the congruence $x^{12} - x^{10} \equiv 2 \pmod{11}$. This congruence is equivalent to the congruence $x^{10}(x^2 - 1) \equiv 2 \pmod{11}$. Now, by Fermat's little theorem, we know that $x^{10} \equiv 1 \pmod{11}$ for every nonzero x in $\mathbf{Z}_{11}$. Therefore, the congruence we need to solve reduces to $x^2 - 1 \equiv 2 \pmod{11}$, or, equivalently, $x^2 \equiv 3 \pmod{11}$. Of the eleven elements in $\mathbf{Z}_{11}$, there are only two that satisfy this last congruence: $x = 5$ or $x = 6$.

20. **A**   First, it's worth noticing that every element in K_1 can be written in the form $a + b'\sqrt{6}$, for a and b' in $\mathbf{Q}$, since:

$$a + b\sqrt{\frac{2}{3}} = a + b\frac{\sqrt{2}}{\sqrt{3}} = a + b\frac{\sqrt{2}}{\sqrt{3}} \cdot \frac{\sqrt{3}}{\sqrt{3}} = a + \frac{b}{3}\sqrt{6} = a + b'\sqrt{6}$$

Therefore, K_1 is equivalent to the set:

$$K_1 = \left\{ a + b\sqrt{6} : a, b \in \mathbf{Q} \right\}$$

The set K_1 is closed under the operations of addition and multiplication, since

$$(a_1 + b_1\sqrt{6}) + (a_2 + b_2\sqrt{6}) = (a_1 + a_2) + (b_1 + b_2)\sqrt{6} \in K_1$$

and:

$$(a_1 + b_1\sqrt{6})(a_2 + b_2\sqrt{6}) = (a_1 a_2 + 6b_1 b_2) + (a_1 b_2 + a_2 b_1)\sqrt{6} \in K_1$$

It's now easy to see that K_1 is a commutative ring with unity. Furthermore, the inverse of every nonzero element in K_1 is also in K_1. If a and b are not both zero, then:

$$\frac{1}{a + b\sqrt{6}} = \frac{1}{a + b\sqrt{6}} \cdot \frac{a - b\sqrt{6}}{a - b\sqrt{6}} = \frac{a - b\sqrt{6}}{a^2 - 6b^2} = \frac{a}{a^2 - 6b^2} + \frac{-b}{a^2 - 6b^2}\sqrt{6} \in K_1$$

Therefore, we can conclude that K_1 is a field, a subfield of $\mathbf{C}$ (and of $\mathbf{R}$).

The set K_2 is not a field; in fact, $(K_2, +)$ isn't even a group, since it's not closed under addition. For example, $x = 1 + \sqrt{2}$ is in K_2, but $x + x = 2 + 2\sqrt{2}$ is not, since $2 \bullet 2 \nless \sqrt{2}$.

Finally, although K_3 is a commutative ring with unity (called the ring of **Gaussian integers**), it's not a field, because it doesn't contain the inverse of each nonzero element in K_3.

For example, K_3 contains $z = 1 + i$, but it doesn't contain its inverse:

$$\frac{1}{1+i} = \frac{1}{1+i} \cdot \frac{1-i}{1-i} = \frac{1-i}{1-(-1)} = \frac{1}{2} - \frac{1}{2}i \notin K_3$$

Therefore, of the choices given, only K_1 is a field. The correct choice is (A).

CHAPTER 7 REVIEW QUESTIONS (PAGES 319–329)

1. **D** $P(x)$ has a zero on an interval $[a, b]$ if $P(a)$ and $P(b)$ have opposite signs. Find $P(x)$ for the boundary of each interval. Since $P(-2)$, $P(-1)$, $P(0)$, $P(1)$, $P(3)$, and $P(4)$ are all positive, eliminate (A), (B), (C) and (E). $P(2)$ is negative, so $P(2)$ and $P(3)$ have opposite signs.

2. **A** By DeMorgan's Laws, $\neg(S \vee T) \leftrightarrow \neg S \wedge \neg T$

3. **B** The order in which the numbers are selected doesn't matter. Therefore, we want to figure out the number of combinations of 51 things taken 6 at a time: $C(52,6) = \binom{51}{6} = \frac{51!}{6! \cdot 45!} = \frac{51 \cdot 50 \cdot 49 \cdot 48 \cdot 47 \cdot 46}{6!} = \frac{51 \cdot 50 \cdot 49 \cdot 48 \cdot 47 \cdot 46}{2 \cdot 3 \cdot 4 \cdot 5 \cdot 6} = 17 \cdot 10 \cdot 49 \cdot 1 \cdot 47 \cdot 46 = 18,009,460$.

    Therefore, to guarantee a win, someone would have to buy more than eighteen million different tickets that cover all the possible combinations.

4. **D** After you delete edge DE, the subgraph has five vertices and four edges. Vertex D has exactly one adjacent edge, B, so D is odd. Eliminate (B), (C), and (E). III is the easier statement to evaluate. Since the graph no longer has any cycles without edge DE, this subgraph is a forest. (Because $|V| = |E| + 1$, the subgraph must be a tree, which makes it a spanning tree of the original graph.)

5. **B** The probability of a 3 or greater on a single roll is $\frac{2}{3}$ and of a 2 or less is $\frac{1}{3}$. Let L represent rolling a 2 or less and G represent rolling 3 or greater. The set of possible outcomes is $\{(L, L), (L, G), (G, L), (G, G)\}$. If X is the number of rolls that come up 3 or greater, then $P(X = 0) = P(L, L) = \frac{1}{9}$. $P(X = 1) = P(L, G) + P(G, L) = \frac{4}{9}$. Finally $P(X = 2) = P(G, G) = \frac{4}{9}$. Therefore, the probability distribution is
    $$f(x) = \begin{cases} \frac{1}{9}, \text{if } x = 0 \\ \frac{4}{9}, \text{if } x = 1 \text{ or } x = 2 \end{cases}$$
    so
    $$E(X) = \sum_{n=1}^{3} x_n f(x_n) = \frac{4}{3}. \text{ The correct answer choice is (B).}$$

6. **D** We are given $A = \{2, 3, 5, 7, 11, \ldots\}$ and $B = \{\ldots, -5, -3, -1, 1, 3, 5, \ldots\}$. To find the relative complement $A - B$, we find the set $C = \{ x \mid x \in A \wedge x \notin B \}$. The elements of C are all prime numbers that are not odd, and the only even prime number is 2.

7. **C** The prototype for the countably infinite sets is the set of natural numbers, $\mathbb{N}$. If there exists a bijective function between $B \to A$ and an infinite set A, then A is countably infinite. Every element in the set $\mathbb{Q}$ can be represented as $\frac{a}{b}$ and can be mapped to the set of ordered triples of natural numbers (a, b, c) where $c = 0$ if $\frac{a}{b}$ is positive and $c = 1$ otherwise. The set $\mathbb{Z}^+$ maps to $\mathbb{N}$ with the bijective function $f(x) = x - 1$. The set $\mathbb{Z}$ is a union of two countable sets, $\mathbb{Z}^+$ and $\mathbb{Z}^-$. The function $g(x) = 2x$ is a bijection from $\mathbb{Z}^+$ to E. By process of elimination, $\mathbb{Q}^c$ is the only set that is not countably infinite.

8. **B** To find the number of safe combinations, begin with the restriction. The man knows that the third number is prime, and the second number is twice the third number, so the third number must be a prime less than 30. There are 10 options for the third number. Once the third number is chosen, there is exactly 1 option for the second number. Finally, since all the numbers are different, there are 58 and 57 options for the first and fourth numbers respectively. Therefore, the number of safe combinations is $58 \cdot 1 \cdot 10 \cdot 57 = 33{,}060$.

9. **E** To find the Laurent series of $f(z)$, first manipulate the function:

$$f(z) = \frac{1}{z-5} = \frac{1}{z-2-3} = \frac{\frac{1}{z-2}}{1 - \frac{3}{z-2}} = \frac{1}{z-2} \sum_{n=0}^{\infty} \left(\frac{3}{z-2} \right)^n,$$ which is simply the sum of an

infinite geometric series. The coefficient of the $(z-2)^{-1}$ term corresponds to the $n = 0$ term of

the Laurent series, so the coefficient is 1.

10. **D** As Newton's method is described in the exercise, the slope of the line tangent to $g(x)$ at x_n is

given by $g'(x_n) = \dfrac{g(x)}{x_n - x_{n+1}}$, which is equivalent to choice (D).

11. **C** If the input values are $a = 380$ and $b = 72$, then the first iteration of the algorithm gives $a = 72$, $b = 20$, the second gives $a = 20$, $b = 12$, the third gives $a = 12$, $b = 8$, the fourth gives $a = 8$, $b = 4$, and the fifth and final iteration gives $a = 4$ and $b = 0$.

12. **E** If $x^2 = 40$, then define a function $f(x) = x^2 - 40$. Then $f'(x) = 2x$. Since 36 is the closest perfect square, guess $x_0 = 6$.

$$x_1 = 6 - \frac{-4}{12} = \frac{19}{3}$$

and

$$x_2 = \frac{\frac{19}{3} - \frac{1}{9}}{\frac{38}{3}} = \frac{721}{114}.$$ Using long division, $x_2 \approx 6.325$.

13. **B** A subgraph of this graph must also have five vertices, so we need at least four edges to ensure the subgraph is connected. Four edges can be deleted without making the graph disconnected. There are several ways to delete four edges, all of which include deleting loop M; for example, remove KL, JL, LN, and loop M. (This subgraph is also a spanning tree of the original graph.)

14. **C** The annulus is the entire complex plane minus a disk of radius 1 centered at $z_0 = 4$. For $|z| > 1$, we can write:

$$\frac{1}{z-3} = \frac{1}{1+z-4} = \frac{1}{(z-4)(1-\frac{-1}{z-4})} = \frac{1}{z-4}\sum_{n=0}^{\infty}\left(\frac{-1}{z-4}\right)^n = \sum_{n=0}^{\infty}(-1)^n\left(\frac{1}{z-4}\right)^{n+1} = \sum_{n=0}^{\infty}(-1)^n(z-4)^{-n-1}$$

Therefore, the correct Laurent series expansion is (D).

15. **B** The order in which students are assigned to teams is irrelevant, but the task order is not (the tasks are distinct). Hence the problem requires combines combinations (of the students to teams) and permutations (of teams to tasks). Moreover, there are three possible configurations of team sizes: (2,2,2), (3,2,1), and (4,1,1). Thus the total number of possible team and task assignments is the sum of the ways to assign the teams and tasks in each of the three team size combinations. For (2,2,2), that number is given by $\binom{6}{2} \cdot \binom{4}{2} \cdot \binom{2}{2} = 90$. For (3,2,1), it's $3\binom{6}{3} \cdot 2\binom{3}{2} \cdot 1\binom{1}{1} = 360$. For (4,1,1), the number of distinct team and task assignments is $3\binom{6}{4} \cdot \binom{2}{1} \cdot 1 = 90$. Thus the correct total should be $90 + 360 + 90 = 540$. (Choice C is correct.)

16. **E** Make a Venn Diagram for the residents:

Island   Lawyers

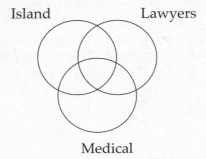

Medical

With three groups, we can make a formula to represent the total number of residents. If Group 1 is *Island*, Group 2 is *Lawyers*, and Group 3 is *Medical*, then the formula for these groups is:

Total = Group 1 + Group 2 + Group 3 – (number who watch 2 shows) – 2(number who watch 3 shows) + (number who watch no shows).

If someone is in all three groups, we need to subtract them twice to avoid double counting. The total is 600. Group 1 is 210, group 2 is 240, and group 3 is 300. There is no "0 shows" because everyone watches at least one show, and 108 people watch exactly 2 shows. Now just plug in: $600 = 210 + 240 + 300 - 108 - 2x + 0$ and solve for x to find how many people watch 3 shows: $x = 21$, and the probability is $\dfrac{21}{600} = \dfrac{7}{200}$, answer E.

17. **A** Simplify the inequality:

$$x + \frac{6}{x} > 5$$

$$x + \frac{6}{x} - 5 > 0$$

$$\frac{x + 6 - 5x}{x} > 0$$

$$\frac{(x-2)(x-3)}{x} > 0$$

The solution set of the inequality is equivalent to the set of x-values for which $\dfrac{(x-2)(x-3)}{x}$ is positive. The critical values are 0, 2, and 3. Eliminate (B) and (E). There are four important intervals which we must investigate: $(-\infty, 0)$, $(0, 2)$, $(2, 3)$, and $(3, \infty)$. The solution set is the two intervals for which $\dfrac{(x-2)(x-3)}{x} > 0$: $(0, 2)$ and $(2, 3)$.

18. **B** The given formula is an implication, and the contrapositive of an implication says that the negation of the conclusion implies the negation of the hypothesis. So, $\neg(\neg C \vee D) \to \neg(A \vee B)$. Using DeMorgan's Laws and double negation: $C \wedge \neg D \to \neg A \wedge \neg B$

19. **E** A set in $\mathbb{R}^2 = \mathbb{R} \times \mathbb{R}$ consists of a rectangle in the coordinate plane. If the set is closed, it contains every boundary point of the rectangle. The only answer choice that contains the boundary points along the lines $x = 2$, $x = 5$, $y = 1$, and $y = 3$ is choice (E).

20. **C** Since $\text{Log } z = \log|z| + i \text{ Arg } z$, we plug in $(-e^3)$ for z.

$$\text{Log }(-e^3) = \log\left|-e^3\right| + i \text{ Arg }(-e^3)$$

$$= \log(e^3) + i(\pi)$$

$$= 3 + \pi i$$

21. **C** A tautology is a formula in logic that is true for every possible truth value of its sentences. Choice (A) states that the double negation of a sentence A is logically equivalent to the sentence itself, which is always true. Choice (B) is a tautology called the law of the excluded middle because the sentence A and its negation $\neg A$ must have opposite truth-values. Choice (D) is one of DeMorgan's Laws, which proves it a tautology. Finally, choice (E) is the Distributive Property for sentential logic, so the statement is always true regardless of the values of sentences A, B, and C.

22. **C** Two graphs are isomorphic if there exists a function $f : V(G) \to V(H)$ that is bijective, and all adjacencies are preserved. Graph I has four vertices with the following edges: AB, BC, and CD. Although there exists a bijective function f such that $f(A) = E$, $f(B) = F$, $f(C) = G$, and $f(D) = H$, adjacencies are not preserved; for example, there is no edge EF. There also exists a bijective function g from Graph I to Graph III such that $g(A) = g(J)$, $g(B) = g(K)$, $g(C) = g(L)$, and $g(D) = g(M)$. Since the adjacent vertices are preserved for this function, Graphs I and III are isomorphic.

23. **A** First note that card $A = 2$, card $B = 4$, and card $C = 3$. Since card $P(C) = 2^{\text{card } C}$, then the cardinality of set D is $2^3 (4) = 32$. Thus card $P(D) = 2^{32}$. The only answer choice with cardinality 2^{32} is $P[P(A) \times P(C)]$. (Notice that the cardinality of the quantity in the brackets is $2^2(2^3) = 32$.)

24. **E** You can express the right side of the equation as a power of e and equate the exponents:
$$e^{2z} = e^{i(\pi/2 + 2n\pi)}$$

$$2z = i(\pi / 2 + 2n\pi)$$

$$z = \left(\frac{i}{2}\right)\left(\frac{\pi}{2} + 2n\pi\right), \text{ for } n \in \mathbb{Z}$$

25. **E** Let the arbitrary complex number $z = x + iy$. Then $\bar{z} = x - iy$, and
$$(x - iy)^2 = (x + iy)^2$$
$$x^2 - 2ixy - y^2 = x^2 + 2ixy - y^2$$
$$4ixy = 0$$
So the solution is either $x = 0$ or $y = 0$, two lines which represent the real and imaginary axes.

26. **B** To find the harmonic conjugate of $v = x - 3x^2y + y^3$, differentiate v with respect to y. $v_y = -3x^2 + 3y^2 = u_x$. Now we can integrate u_x to find the harmonic conjugate: $u = -x^3 + 3xy^2 + g(y)$. We still need to find $g(y)$, which we can do by differentiating our current function u with respect to y. So $u_y = 6xy + g'(y) = -v_x$, but we can also use our original function v to find an equivalent expression $-v_x = -1 + 6xy$. Setting $6xy + g'(y)$ equal to $-1 + 6xy$ says that $g'(y) = -1$, and so $g(y) = -y$. Therefore, the harmonic conjugate $u(x, y) = -x^3 + 3xy^2 - y$.

27. **D** Recall that $z^2 + 1 = (z - i)(z + i)$, so the integrand $f(z)$ has simple poles at $z = -3$, $z = i$, and $z = -i$. The curve C encloses only the poles at $z = i$ and $z = -i$, so the value of the integral (according to the residue theorem), is equal to $2\pi i * [\text{Res}(i, f) + \text{Res}(-i, f)]$. Because both poles are simple, we can easily find the residues using the formula:

$$\text{Res}(i, f) = \lim_{z \to i}\left[(z-i) \cdot \frac{z+1}{(z+3)(z^2+1)}\right] = \lim_{z \to i}\left[\frac{z+1}{(z+3)(z+i)}\right]$$

$$= \frac{i+1}{-2+6i}$$

$$= \frac{i+1}{-2+6i} \cdot \frac{-2-6i}{-2-6i}$$

$$= \frac{1-2i}{10}$$

$$\text{Res}\,(i, f) = \lim_{z \to -i}\left[(z-i) \cdot \frac{z+1}{(z+3)(z^2+1)}\right] = \lim_{z \to -i}\left[\frac{z+1}{(z+3)(z^2-i)}\right]$$

$$= \frac{1-i}{-2-6i}$$

$$= \frac{1-i}{-2-6i} \cdot \frac{-2+6i}{-2+6i}$$

$$= \frac{1+2i}{10}$$

Therefore,

$$\int_C \frac{z+1}{(z+3)(z^2+1)}\,dz = 2\pi i * \left[\text{Res}(i, f) + \text{Res}(-i, f)\right]$$

$$= 2\pi i * \left[\frac{1-2i}{10} + \frac{1+2i}{10}\right]$$

$$= \frac{2}{5}\pi i$$

28. **E** The function δ is essentially a distance function between two ordered pairs on the real-valued coordinate plane. Choice (A) says that distance cannot be negative, which is true. Choice (B) says the distance from x to z is either equal to or less than the sum of the distances from x to y and from y to z, which is also true. Choice (C) says that distance does not depend on the direction traveled, so the distance from x to y is equal to the distance from y to x. Choice (D) says that the distance between x and y is zero if x and y are the same point. Finally, choice (E) says that the distance from x to z is equal to the sum of the distances from x to y and from y to z. A quick counterexample will show that this is not true:

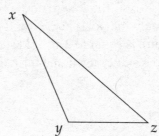

29. **B**   The order that the players are chosen matters, so the number of permutations of 8 out of the 15

position players is $\dfrac{15!}{(15-8)!} = \dfrac{15!}{7!}$. Since we then choose any 1 of the 5 pitchers, multiply the

result by 5 to get the answer.

30. **A**   Write the complex number $(-\sqrt{3}+1)$ in the form $z = re^{i\theta}$.

$$r = \sqrt{\left(\sqrt{3}\right)^2 + 1^2} = 2$$

$$\theta = \tan^{-1}\left(\frac{1}{-\sqrt{3}}\right)$$

So $-\sqrt{3}+1 = 2e^{i\frac{5\pi}{6}}$, and now we can find the sixth power of z.

$$\left(i-\sqrt{3}\right)^6 = \left(2e^{i\frac{5\pi}{6}}\right)^6 = 2^6 e^{5\pi i}$$

Now express z in the polar form: $z = r(\cos\theta + i\sin\theta)$

$$= 2^6(\cos 5\pi + i\sin 5\pi)$$
$$= -2^6$$

31. **C**   To identify which set is compact, first consider the Heine-Borel theorem says that a subset of $\mathbb{R}^n$ (in the standard topology) is compact if and only if it's both closed and bounded. Eliminate (B) and (D) because they are not bounded. Since answer choices (A) and (E) only use strictly less than or greater than symbols, neither of these sets is closed.

32. **E**   The correct answer will then be E, and the solution will then read thus: "By definition, we know that if f is a probability density function for X, then $\int_{-\infty}^{\infty} f(x)dx = 1$. Integrating $f(x)$, we have $\int_0^8 \frac{x}{2} + c = 1 \rightarrow \frac{x^2}{4} + cx\Big|_0^8 = 1 \rightarrow 15 = -8c \rightarrow c -\frac{15}{8}$. However, recall the additional condition for a probability density function that $f(x) \geq 0 \; \forall x$. Since in this case, $f(x) < 0$ for $0 \leq x < \frac{15}{4}$, the function as defined cannot be a probability density function (choice E is correct).

33. **B**   An unoriented incidence matrix is an organizational tool used to represent the relationships between the vertices and edges of an undirected graph. The dimensions of the matrix are $|V| \times |E|$, so there are four rows (for four vertices) and five columns (for five edges). An entry $b_{ij} = 1$ if vertex v_i and edge e_j are incident and equals 0 otherwise. Since e_1 is incident with v_1 and v_4, the first column should have 1's in the first and fourth rows only. Eliminate (A) and (C). e_2 is incident with v_1 and v_2, so the second column should have 1's in the first two rows only. Eliminate (D). e_5 is incident with v_1 and v_3, so the fourth column should have 1's in the first and third rows only. Eliminate (E).

34. **C**   The exterior of A, denoted by $\text{ext}(A)$, is the union of all open sets that do not intersect A. Eliminate (B) and (D) because they are not unions of open sets. $\text{ext}(A)$ is the union of three regions that constitute the complement of A: $(-\infty, 0)$, $(1, 4)$, and $(6, \infty)$.

35. **A**   The order that employees are placed into a committee is not important even though it matters what committee the employee is placed into. The number of combinations is

$$\binom{12}{3} \cdot \binom{9}{3} \cdot \binom{6}{3} \cdot \binom{3}{3} = 369{,}600 \text{ committees.}$$

36. **D**   The Cauchy integral formula says $f(z_0) = \frac{1}{2\pi i}\int_C \frac{f(z)}{z - z_0}\,dz$, for which z_0 is in the interior of C. We can apply this formula because $f(z) = 3z^2 + z - 4$ is analytic and $z_0 = 3$ is inside the circle $|z| = 5$. Then:

$$h(3) = \int_C \frac{f(z)}{z-3}\,dz = 2\pi i\, f(3) = 52\pi i$$

37. **D**   Represent the situation with a Venn diagram:

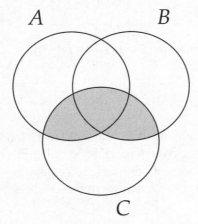

Since the set shown above is a subset of $(A \cap B) \cup C$, statement I is true. Eliminate (B), (C), and (E). Since statement III is not in any remaining answer choices, it must have been false. (The set in statement III is a subset of the one above, so it is not guaranteed that x will be an element of this smaller set.) Finally, notice that the set above is also a subset of $(A \cup B)$, so statement II is true.

38.   **E**   The problem asks for the probability that at least one of the variables is greater than 2. That's the same as 1 minus the probability that both variables are less than or equal to 2. Since X and Y are independent, we can multiply the complements of their individual probabilities.

So: $P(\text{at least one} > 2) = 1 - P(X \leq 2)\, P(Y \leq 2)$

$$= 1 - \left(\frac{3^2 - 1}{3^2}\right) \cdot \left(\frac{4^2 - 1}{4^2}\right)$$

$$= 1 - \frac{5}{6}$$

$$= \frac{1}{6}$$

39.   **A**   A circuit is a sequence of adjacent vertices that starts and ends at the same vertex and does not repeat any edges. Eliminate choice (D) because it does not begin and end with the same vertex. You can eliminate choice (B) because CA is not an edge of the graph. Choice (C) repeats the edges CD and AD. Finally, there is no edge connecting vertex E to vertex B, so eliminate (E). (The answer is only one of many cycles that exist in this graph.)

40.   **D**   The order of a permutation is the minimum value of n such that for every element $a \in S$, $\sigma^n(a) = a$ (that is, that applying the permutation n times returns the original element). First notice that $\sigma(1) = 5$, and $\sigma(5) = 1$, which says that the elements 1 and 5 both have order 2. Now apply the permutation to another element and iterate: $\sigma(2) = 6$, $\sigma(6) = 4$, $\sigma(4) = 3$, and $\sigma(3) = 2$. The order of these elements is 4. Thus, since $\sigma^4(a)$ for all elements in this set, and it is the least such value that will do so, the order of the permutation is 4.

41.   **E**   First, use the contrapositives of the last two statements so that you have four implications: $A \to C$, $B \to D$, $D \to C$, and $C \to A$. Now draw a diagram that represents these implications:

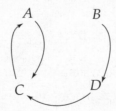

Statement I is true if we can follow a path from sentence A to sentence D. We can see from the diagram that $D \to A$, but not the other way around. Eliminate (A) and (D). Next, to prove statement II, we must show that $A \leftrightarrow C$. Since both $A \to C$ and $C \to A$, statement II is true. Before evaluating statement III, write the contrapositive of the statement: $B \to A$. Although there is no direct implication from sentence B to sentence A in the diagram above, we can see a transitive implication: $B \to D \to C \to A$. Thus statement III is true.

42.   **D**   If $M = (a, b)$, $[a, b)$, $(a, b]$, or $[a, b]$, then the Lebesque measure (denoted $\mu(M)$) is simply the length of the interval, $b - a$. In this case M is a finite union of disjoint, finite intervals, so then $\mu(M)$ is the sum of the interval lengths. $\mu(M) = [3 - (-1)] + (8 - 7) = 5$.

43. **D**   Suppose the four tables are W, X, Y, and Z. Since the question asks which must be true, we can quickly break Statement I with a counterexample. Let tables W, X, and Y have 15 flowers each; then table Z has 16 flowers, and no table has 13 or fewer flowers. Eliminate (B), (C), and (E). Since both answer choices include Statement II, we can assume it must be true. Looking at Statement III, suppose the florist only placed 30 flowers at tables W and X combined. Then 31 flowers are at tables Y and Z, so Statement III cannot be broken and must be true.

44. **D**   The question asks us to find $P(40 \leq X \leq 50)$, where X has a binomial distribution with $n = 100$ and $p = q = \dfrac{1}{2}$; this probability is equal to the expression:

$$\sum_{k=40}^{50} \binom{100}{k} \left(\frac{1}{2}\right)^k \left(\frac{1}{2}\right)^{100-k}$$

This expression is far too difficult to calculate on the GRE, so we will approximate using the binomial distribution. The mean of X is $\mu = np = 100\left(\dfrac{1}{2}\right) = 50$. The standard deviation is

$\sigma = \sqrt{npq} = \sqrt{100\left(\frac{1}{2}\right)\left(\frac{1}{2}\right)} = 5$. Therefore:

$$P(40 \leq X \leq 50) \approx \Phi\left(\frac{50 - 50 + \frac{1}{2}}{5}\right) - \Phi\left(\frac{40 - 50 - \frac{1}{2}}{5}\right)$$
$$= \Phi(0.1) - \Phi(0.1)$$

The table in the chapter shows the closest approximation of $\Phi(0.1)$ is $\Phi(0) \approx 0.5$.

We also know that $\Phi(-z) = 1 - \Phi(z)$, so $\Phi(-2.1) = 1 - \Phi(2.1)$, which is very close to 0.03.

Therefore:

$P(40 \leq X \leq 50) \approx 0.5 - 0.03 = 0.47 = 47\%$

45. **C**   At first this problem may seem like a simple permutation: $\dfrac{4!}{(4-4)!} = 24$ ways, but it's not. Since the arrangement into which you're placing the four people has no start or end (it's circular), then orientation should not matter. If we call our four customers A, B, C, and D, then these two arrangements should *not* be counted separately: $A\,B\,C\,D$ and $D\,A\,B\,C$.

As you can see from the diagram above, in both arrangements A is sitting with D to the left, B to the right, and C across. Therefore, we must divide our original computation by the number of possible locations for the first object placed (i.e., the number of seats!). There are $24 \div 4 = 6$ ways.

46. **C** We can rewrite $\cos z$ to solve this equation for z:

$$\frac{e^{iz}+e^{-iz}}{2}=3$$

$$e^{iz}+e^{-iz}=6$$

$$e^{2iz}+1=6e^{iz}$$

Now make a substitution $u=e^{iz}$ and apply the quadratic formula:

$$u^2-6u+1=0$$

$$u=\frac{6\pm\sqrt{36-4}}{2}$$

$$u=3\pm2\sqrt{2}=e^{iz}$$

Take the complex logarithm of each side to solve for z:

$$iz=\text{Log}\,(3\pm2\sqrt{2}\,)$$

$$z=-i\,\text{Log}\,(3\pm2\sqrt{2}\,)$$

$$z=-i\,[\log\,(3\pm2\sqrt{2}\,)+i(2k\pi\,)],\text{ for any }k\in\mathbb{Z}$$

$$z=2k\pi-i\log\,(3\pm2\sqrt{2}\,),\text{ for any }k\in\mathbb{Z}$$

47. **E** Begin by drawing a diagram of the relationship between sets A and B:

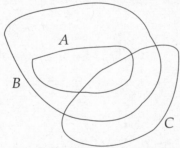

From this diagram, we can clearly see that the union of sets A and B is simply set B, so Statement I is true and eliminate (D). Statement II says that the set of all elements in A that are not in B is empty, and we can see that there cannot exist an element in A unless it is also an element of B. Eliminate (A) and (C). Finally, notice that the set $C-B$ is contained within the larger region created by $C-A$. Therefore, $C-B\subseteq C-A$, and the answer is (E).

48. **D** We are given that $f(z)$ is analytic, so $u(x,y)$ and $v(x,y)$ are harmonic conjugates. So $u_x=5=v_y$. Integrating with respect to y, we get $v(x,y)=5y+h(x)$, where v contains an unknown function in x. Now we turn to the other Cauchy-Riemann equation by evaluating $-v_x=-h'(x)=u_y$. But we already know that $u_y=-3$, so $h(x)=3x+c$.

At this point we know that $v(x,y)=5y+3x+c$, and we have an initial point to find c:

$$v(4,1)=7=5(1)+3(4)+c$$

$$c=-10$$

Therefore, $v(x,y)=5y+3x-10$. So $v(3,2)=9$.

49. **B**   While the value of the variable a is greater than 1, the first step of each iteration is to divide a by 2 if $a = 0$ (mod 2). This says that the value of a will be halved if a is even. Eliminate (A) and (E). Otherwise, if a is odd, multiply a by 3 and add 1. This eliminates choice (C). Finally, notice that a_n is determined by evaluating whether a_{n-1} is even or odd, which eliminates (D).

50. **D**   First, notice that the algorithm does not output until after the first iteration. Eliminate choices (A) and (C). Since 17 is odd, the first output will be $3(17) + 1 = 52$. The second output will be $52 \div 2 = 26$, so eliminate (B). The algorithm will converge to 1 eventually according to the sequence in choice (D).

9

Practice Test

MATHEMATICS TEST (RESCALED)
Time—170 Minutes
65 Questions

Directions: Each of the questions or incomplete statements below is followed by five suggested answers or completions. In each case, select the one that is the best of the choices offered and then mark the corresponding space on the answer sheet.

Computation and scratchwork may be done in this examination book. [***On the real exam, each left-hand page of the booklet will have test questions and each right-hand page will have a blank scratchwork area. For this practice test only, you may use separate scratch paper.***]

Note: In this examination:

(1) All logarithms with an unspecified base are natural logarithms, that is, with base e.

(2) The set of all x such that $a \leq x \leq b$ is denoted by $[a, b]$.

(3) The symbols $\mathbf{Z}$, $\mathbf{Q}$, $\mathbf{R}$, and $\mathbf{C}$ denote the sets of integers, rational numbers, real numbers, and complex numbers, respectively.

1. If $x^2 + x = 3$, then $x^4 + x =$

    (A) $x^2 + 3$ (B) $4(3 - x)$ (C) $3(x - 1)$ (D) $6(2 - x)$ (E) $3x$

2. $\dfrac{d}{dx}\left(\dfrac{1}{x} - \dfrac{1}{\log x} \right) =$

    (A) $\dfrac{x - (\log x)^2}{(x \log x)^2}$ (B) $\dfrac{x^2 - 2\log x}{2x^2 \log x}$ (C) $\dfrac{x - 1}{(x \log x)^2}$ (D) $\dfrac{2x - 1}{2x^2 \log x}$ (E) $\dfrac{2x - 1}{(x \log x)^2}$

3. $\displaystyle\lim_{x \to 0} \dfrac{\sqrt{x + 1} - 1}{x} =$

    (A) $-\dfrac{1}{2}$ (B) $\dfrac{1}{2}$ (C) 1 (D) 2 (E) ∞

4. Let $A = \{\varnothing, a\}$, where $\varnothing$ is the empty set. If B is the set of all subsets of A, what's the cardinality of the set $A \cup B$?

    (A) 4   (B) 5   (C) 6   (D) 7   (E) 8

GO ON TO THE NEXT PAGE.

$x < 0$

$4x^3 + 4x^2 + x = 0 \qquad 4x^2 + 4x + 1 = 0$

5. For how many values of a is the integral $\int_0^a (12x^2 + 8x + 1)\,dx$ equal to zero?

(A) 0   (B) 1   (C) 2   (D) 3   (E) 4

---

6. At how many points does the graph of the curve $y = x^5 + x^3 + x - 2000$ cross the x-axis?

$y' = 5x^4 + 3x^2 + 1 > 0$

(A) 1   (B) 2   (C) 3   (D) 4   (E) 5

---

7. Let $f(x, y) = xy(x - y)$, where $x(t, u) = t(t - u)$ and $y(t, u) = u(u - t)$. What is the value of $\dfrac{\partial f}{\partial t}$ at the point $(t, u) = (1, -1)$?

(A) -8 (B) -4 (C) 2   (D) 4   (E) 8

---

8. If $\int_0^b \tan x\,dx = 2$, then b could equal

$\left[\ln(\sec x)\right]_0^b \qquad \ln(\sec x) = 2 \qquad \sec x = e^2$

(A) arccos 2   (B) arccos$(2e)$ (C) arcsec 2   (D) arcsec$^2 e$ (E) arcsec(e^2)

---

9. Let a be the smallest positive value of x at which the function $f(x) = (\cos x^2)(\sin x^2)$ has a critical point. What is the value of $f(a)$?

(A) $\dfrac{\sqrt{2}}{4}$ (B) $\dfrac{1}{2}$ (C) $\dfrac{\sqrt{2}}{2}$ (D) 1   (E) $\sqrt{2}$

---

10. Find the equation of the integral curve that passes through the point $(2, 3)$ of the differential equation

$$y' = \frac{2x}{y^2 - 1}$$

$y^2 - 1 \; dy = 2x \; dx$

$\frac{1}{3}y^3 - y = x^2 + 2$

(A) $x^2 - 2 = \frac{1}{3}y^3 + y$ (B) $x^2 - 1 = \frac{1}{3}y^3 - 2y$ (C) $x^2 + 1 = \frac{1}{3}y^3 + y$

(D) $x^2 + 2 = \frac{1}{3}y^3 - y$ (E) $2(x^2 - 1) = \frac{1}{3}y^3 - y$

GO ON TO THE NEXT PAGE.

$a \cdot [a \times b + c \times b] = -30$ $a \cdot [a \times b + 12j - 6k] = -30$ $a \cdot (12j - 6k) = -30$

11. Let $\hat{i} = (1, 0, 0)$, $\hat{j} = (0, 1, 0)$, and $\hat{k} = (0, 0, 1)$. If $\mathbf{b}$ and $\mathbf{c}$ are vectors such that $\|\mathbf{b}\| = 3$, $\mathbf{b} \cdot \mathbf{c} = -3$, $\|\mathbf{c}\| = \sqrt{21}$, and $\mathbf{b} \times \mathbf{c} = -12\hat{j} + 6\hat{k}$, which of the following vectors satisfies the equation $\mathbf{a} \cdot [(\mathbf{a} + \mathbf{c}) \times \mathbf{b}] = -30$?

(A) $\mathbf{a} = 2\hat{i} + \hat{j} - 2\hat{k}$ (B) $\mathbf{a} = \hat{i} - \hat{j} + 2\hat{k}$ (C) $\mathbf{a} = \hat{i} - 2\hat{j} + \hat{k}$

(D) $\mathbf{a} = 2\hat{i} - \hat{j} + \hat{k}$ (E) $\mathbf{a} = \hat{i} + 2\hat{j} - 2\hat{k}$

---

12. If one arch of the curve $y = \sin x$ is revolved around the x-axis, what's the volume of the generated solid?

(A) $\dfrac{\pi^2}{4}$ (B) $\dfrac{\pi^2}{2}$ (C) 2π (D) π^2 (E) $2\pi^2$

---

13. If a is a positive constant, what is the maximum value of the following function?

$$f(x) = \frac{\log x}{x^a}$$

(A) $\dfrac{1}{ae}$ (B) a^{a-1} (C) a^e (D) e^a (E) $\dfrac{e^{a^2}}{a}$

---

14. Find the family of all nonzero solutions of the equation

$$\frac{d^2y}{dx^2} = \left(\frac{dy}{dx}\right)^2$$

$\dfrac{dy}{dx} = (-x - c)^{-1}$

$y = \ln(-x + c) + C_2$

(A) $y = \dfrac{1}{x + c_1} + c_2$ (B) $y = c_2 + \log(c_1 - x)$ (C) $y = c_2 - \log(c_1 - x^2)$

(D) $y = c_2 + \log(c_1 + x)$ (E) $y = c_2 - \log(c_1 + x)$

$\dfrac{dy}{dx} = \dfrac{-1}{x + c}$ $\dfrac{dy}{dx^2} = (x + c)^{-2}$

---

15. For each integer $n > 1$, let $a_n = 1/(\log n)$. Which of the following statements is/are true?

    I. The sequence (a_n) converges. ✓

$\dfrac{1}{\ln 2}$ $\dfrac{1}{\ln 3}$

    II. The series $\displaystyle\sum_{n=2}^{\infty} a_n$ converges. ✗

    III. The series $\displaystyle\sum_{n=2}^{\infty} (-1)^n a_n^2$ converges. ✓

(A) I only   (B) I and II only   (C) I and III only

(D) II and III only   (E) I, II, and III

GO ON TO THE NEXT PAGE.

16. Let $x = r \cos \theta$ and $y = r \sin \theta$. Which of the following expressions is equal to $\left(\dfrac{\partial \theta}{\partial r}\right)_x$, the partial derivative of θ with respect to r, keeping x constant?

(A) $r^{-1} \tan \theta$ (B) $-r^{-1} \tan \theta$ (C) $r^{-1} \cot \theta$ (D) $-r^{-1} \cot \theta$ (E) $-r^{-1} \csc \theta$

17. $1 + \cot^2 (\arcsin \dfrac{\pi}{4}) =$

(A) $\dfrac{3}{2}\pi$ (B) 2π (C) 3π (D) 5π (E) $\dfrac{16}{\pi^2}$

18. $\lim\limits_{x \to 0} (x + e^{3x})^{1/x} =$

(A) 0 (B) 1 (C) e^3 (D) $1 + e^3$ (E) e^4

19. If $y' = x - y$ and $y(0) = 1$, then $y(1) =$

(A) $\dfrac{1}{e}$ (B) $\left(\dfrac{1}{e}\right) + 1$ (C) $\dfrac{2}{e}$ (D) $\left(\dfrac{2}{e}\right) - 1$ (E) e

20. Let $f(x,y) = x^y$, for $x > 0$. Then $\left.\dfrac{\partial f}{\partial x}\right|_P = \left.\dfrac{\partial f}{\partial y}\right|_P$ at the point $P = (e, y_0)$, where $y_0 =$

(A) 1 (B) $\sqrt{e}$ (C) e (D) e^2 (E) e^e

21. For any real number x, let $[x]$ denote the unique integer, n, such that $n \le x < n + 1$. Evaluate the integral

$$\int_{-b}^{2b} (x - [x])\,dx$$

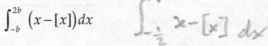

for $b = \dfrac{1}{2}$.

(A) $\dfrac{3}{4}$ (B) $\dfrac{7}{8}$ (C) $\dfrac{5}{4}$ (D) $\dfrac{9}{8}$ (E) does not exist

GO ON TO THE NEXT PAGE.

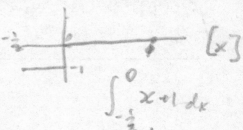

22. In SL(2, **Z**), the multiplicative group of all 2 by 2 matrices with integer entries whose determinant is 1, what is the order of the cyclic subgroup generated by the following element?

$$A = \begin{pmatrix} 0 & 1 \\ -1 & -1 \end{pmatrix}$$

(A) 2   (B) 3   (C) 4   (D) 6   (E) ∞

23. Determine the slope of the curve $y = x^\pi - \pi^x$ at the point $(\pi, 0)$.

(A) $\pi^\pi(1 - \log \pi)$ (B) $\pi^\pi(1 + \log \pi)$ (C) π^π

(D) 1   (E) 0

24. A six-sided die (whose faces are numbered 1 through 6, as usual) is known to be counterfeit: The probability of rolling any even number is twice the probability of rolling any odd number. What is the probability that if this die is thrown twice, the first roll will be a 5 and the second roll will be a 6?

(A) $\dfrac{2}{81}$ (B) $\dfrac{1}{18}$ (C) $\dfrac{2}{27}$

(D) $\dfrac{1}{9}$ (E) Cannot be determined from the information given

25. $\displaystyle\int_{-1/2}^{1/2} \dfrac{dx}{1-x^2} =$

(A) log 2   (B) log 3   (C) 3 log 2   (D) 2 log 3   (E) 3 log 3

26. Let C be the circle in the yz-plane whose equation is $(y - 3)^2 + z^2 = 1$. If C is revolved around the z-axis, the surface generated is a torus. What is the equation of this torus?

(A) $x^2 + y^2 + z^2 + 8 = 6y$

(B) $(x^2 + y^2 + z^2)^2 = 8 + 36(x^2 + z^2)$

(C) $(x^2 + y^2 + z^2 + 8)^2 = 36(x^2 + z^2)$

(D) $(x^2 + y^2 + z^2 + 8)^2 = 36(x^2 + y^2)$

(E) $(x^2 + y^2 + z^2 + 8)^2 = 36(y^2 + z^2)$

GO ON TO THE NEXT PAGE.

27. Find the general solution of the equation

$$\frac{d^4y}{dx^4} + 2\frac{d^3y}{dx^3} + 5\frac{d^2y}{dx^2} = 0$$

(A) $y = c_1 + c_2x + e^{2x}(c_3\cos x + c_4\sin x)$

(B) $y = c_1 + c_2x + e^{-2x}(c_3\cos x + c_4\sin x)$

(C) $y = c_1 + c_2x + e^{x}(c_3\cos 2x + c_4\sin 2x)$

(D) $y = c_1 + c_2x + e^{-x}(c_3\cos 2x + c_4\sin 2x)$

(E) $y = c_1 + e^{x}(c_2\cos 2x + c_3\sin 2x)$

28. Let $f : \mathbf{R}^3 \to \mathbf{R}^3$ be the function defined by the equation $f(\mathbf{x}) = A\mathbf{x}$, where

$$A = \begin{pmatrix} 1 & 2 & 3 \\ 4 & 5 & 6 \\ 7 & 8 & 9 \end{pmatrix}$$

Which of the following best describes the image of f?

(A) A point

(B) A line through the origin

(C) A plane through the origin

(D) The union of a plane through the origin and a line through the origin, with the line perpendicular to the plane

(E) All of $\mathbf{R}^3$

29. $\displaystyle\int_0^1 (x \log x)\, dx =$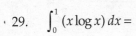

(A) -1 (B) $-\dfrac{1}{2}$ (C) $-\dfrac{1}{4}$ (D) 1 (E) does not exist

30. Define a binary operation on $\mathbf{Z}$, the set of integers, by the equation $m \bullet n = m + n + mn$. Which of the following statements is/are true about the binary structure $(\mathbf{Z}, \bullet)$?

   I. This structure is not a group since the operation is not associative.
   II. This structure is not a group since there is no identity element.
   III. This structure is not a group since not all elements have an inverse.
   IV. This structure is a group.

(A) I and II only   (B) I and III only   (C) II and III only
(D) III only   (E) IV only

GO ON TO THE NEXT PAGE.

31. Given that $\int_0^\infty e^{-x^2}\,dx = \frac{1}{2}\sqrt{\pi}$, what's the value of the following integral?

$$\int_0^\infty \frac{e^{-x}}{\sqrt{x}}\,dx \;=\; \int_0^\infty \frac{e^{-u^2}}{u}\cdot 2u\,du$$

(handwritten: $x=u^2$, $dx=2u\,du$)

(handwritten left: $54_m 23_s$)

(A) $\frac{1}{4}\sqrt{\pi}$ (B) $\frac{1}{2}\sqrt{\pi}$ (C) $\sqrt{\pi}$ (D) $2\sqrt{\pi}$ (E) $\frac{1}{4}\pi$

32. Let S be the surface whose equation is $x^2 - xy^2z + z^2 = 1$. The plane tangent to S at the point $(1, 1, 1)$ contains which of the following lines?

(handwritten: $\frac{\partial S}{\partial x} = 2x - y^2 z$, $\frac{\partial S}{\partial y} = -2xyz$, $\frac{\partial S}{\partial z} = -xy^2 + 2z$)

(A) $x = y = z$ (B) $x = y, z = 1$ (C) $x = z, y = 1$
(D) $y = z, x = 1$ (E) $x - 1 = 2(y - 1) = z - 1$

(handwritten: $L(1,1,1) = 1(x-1) - 2(y-1) + 1(z-1)$, $\langle 1, -2, 1 \rangle$)

33. Define a function $f(x)$ for all positive x by the equation

$$f(x) = \int_{x^2}^{x^3} (\log t)\,dt$$

Find the critical point(s) of this function.

(handwritten: $f'(x) = \log(x^3)\cdot 3x^2 - \log(x^2)\cdot 2x$, $x=0$ or $\log(x^2)\cdot 3x = 2\log(x^2)$, $x=1$, $9x=4$, $x=\frac{4}{9}$)

(A) $x = \frac{4}{9}, 1$ *(handwritten: answered originally)* (B) $x = 1$ (C) $x = \frac{3}{2}$ (D) $x = 1, \frac{3}{2}$ (E) $x = 1, \frac{9}{4}$

34. If $f(x) = \sum_{n=0}^{\infty} \frac{(n+1)^{n/2}}{(n!)^2}x^n$, what is true of the value of $f^{(4)}(0)$?

(handwritten: $n=4$)

(A) It is negative.
(B) It is positive and less than 1.
(C) It is equal to 1.
(D) It is greater than 1.
(E) It does not exist.   *(handwritten: Taylor series)*

(handwritten: $\frac{(n+1)^{n/2}\cdot n(n-1)(n-2)(n-3)}{(n!)^2}$, $\frac{5^2\cdot 5\cdot 4\cdot 3\cdot 2}{5!\,5!} = \frac{25}{120}$)

(handwritten: $f^{(n)}(0) = \frac{(n+1)^{n/2}}{n!}$, $n=4: f^{(4)}(0) = \frac{25}{24}$)

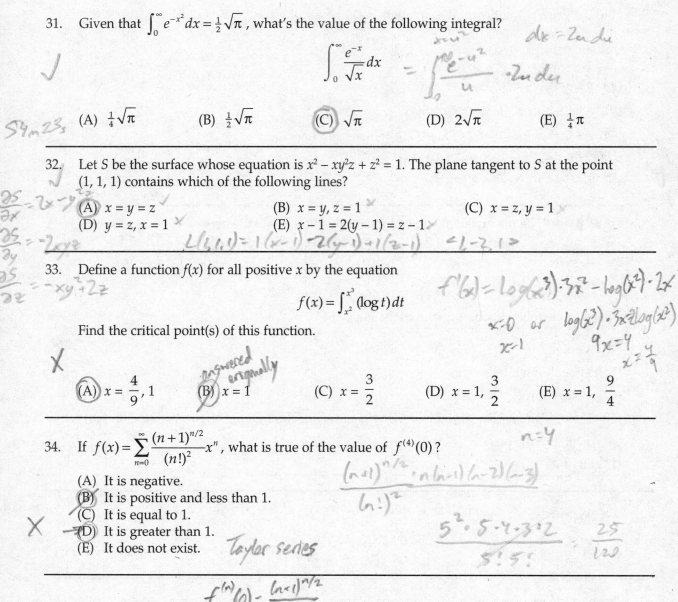

GO ON TO THE NEXT PAGE.

35. In a survey of 100 undergraduate math majors at a certain college, the following information is obtained about the courses they are taking during the Spring semester:

    41 are enrolled in real analysis,
    44 are enrolled in differential equations,
    48 are enrolled in linear algebra,
    11 are enrolled in both real analysis and linear algebra,
    14 are enrolled in both real analysis and differential equations,
    19 are enrolled in both differential equations and linear algebra, and
    10 are not enrolled in any of these three courses.

    How many of the students surveyed are enrolled in all three of these courses?

    (A) 1   (B) 2   (C) 3   (D) 4   (E) 5

36. Let $f(x)$ be a function whose graph passes through the origin. If $f(2n) = n^2 + f[2(n-1)]$ for every integer n, what is the value of $f(8)$?

    (A) 24   (B) 30   (C) 32
    (D) 36   (E) Cannot be determined from the information given

37. For how many values of the parameter, k, will the following system have *no* solutions?

$$kx + y + z = 1$$
$$x + ky + z = k$$
$$x + y + kz = k^2$$

    (A) 0   (B) 1   (C) 2   (D) 4   (E) Infinitely many

38. Consider the set X of all real-valued functions defined on the interval $[a, b]$, where $a < b$. Which of the following conditions, if true, would ensure that $f \in X$ is constant on $[a, b]$?

    I. The inverse of f is a constant function.

    II. The composite function $f \circ g$ is constant for every function g in X.

    III. $|f(x) - f(y)| \leq (x - y)^2$ for every x and y in $[a, b]$.

    (A) II only   (B) I and II only   (C) I and III only
    (D) II and III only   (E) I, II, and III

GO ON TO THE NEXT PAGE.

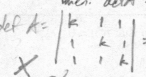

39. Let $g(x) = x^3 + x^2 + x + 1$ be defined for all real x. If $f(x) = \dfrac{1}{g^{-1}(x)}$, which of the following statements is true concerning the domain of f and the value of $f^{-1}(-2)$?

(A) The domain of f is the set of all real x such that $x \neq 0$ or 1, and $f^{-1}(-2) = -5$.

(B) The domain of f is the set of all real x such that $x \neq 0$ or 1, and $f^{-1}(-2) = -\dfrac{1}{5}$.

(C) The domain of f is the set of all real x such that $x \neq -1$, and $f^{-1}(-2) = -\dfrac{1}{5}$.

(D) The domain of f is the set of all real x such that $x \neq 1$, and $f^{-1}(-2) = -\dfrac{5}{8}$.

(E) The domain of f is the set of all real x such that $x \neq 1$, and $f^{-1}(-2) = \dfrac{5}{8}$.

---

40. The tangent line to the curve $y = x^{(e^x)}$ at the point $(1, 1)$ passes through the point $(2, y_0)$, where $y_0 =$

(A) $e - 1$ (B) e (C) $2e - 1$ (D) $e + 1$ (E) $2e$

---

41. Let $f(x)$ be a function that has derivatives of all orders at every real x, such that $f(0) = 0$. Assume the following about the values of the derivatives of f at $x = 0$:

I. $f'(0) = 1$

II. $f''(0) = 2$

III. $f^{(n)}(0) \leq \dfrac{n!}{2^{n-3}}$ for every integer $n \geq 3$

What is the smallest number m that makes the statement $f(1) \leq m$ true?

(A) 2   (B) 3   (C) 4   (D) 6   (E) 8

---

42. Find the dimension of the subspace of $\mathbf{R}^4$ that is the span of the following vectors:

$$\mathbf{v}_1 = \begin{pmatrix} 1 \\ -1 \\ 0 \\ 1 \end{pmatrix}, \quad \mathbf{v}_2 = \begin{pmatrix} -2 \\ 1 \\ 1 \\ 1 \end{pmatrix}, \quad \mathbf{v}_3 = \begin{pmatrix} 0 \\ 0 \\ 0 \\ 0 \end{pmatrix}, \quad \mathbf{v}_4 = \begin{pmatrix} -1 \\ 0 \\ 1 \\ 2 \end{pmatrix}, \quad \text{and} \quad \mathbf{v}_5 = \begin{pmatrix} 1 \\ 1 \\ -2 \\ -5 \end{pmatrix}$$

(A) 1   (B) 2   (C) 3   (D) 4   (E) 5

GO ON TO THE NEXT PAGE.

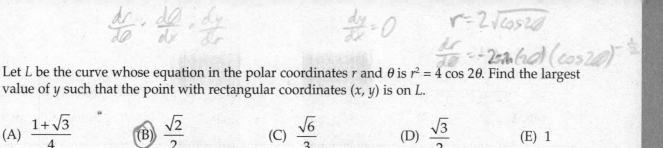

$\frac{dr}{d\theta} \cdot \frac{d\theta}{dx} \cdot \frac{dy}{dr}$ $\frac{dy}{dx} = 0$ $r = 2\sqrt{\cos 2\theta}$

$\frac{dr}{d\theta} = -2\sin(2\theta)(\cos 2\theta)^{-\frac{1}{2}}$

43. Let L be the curve whose equation in the polar coordinates r and θ is $r^2 = 4 \cos 2\theta$. Find the largest value of y such that the point with rectangular coordinates (x, y) is on L.

(A) $\dfrac{1+\sqrt{3}}{4}$ (B) $\dfrac{\sqrt{2}}{2}$ (C) $\dfrac{\sqrt{6}}{3}$ (D) $\dfrac{\sqrt{3}}{2}$ (E) 1

44. If the matrix $A = \begin{pmatrix} t & 1-t \\ 1 & 2t \end{pmatrix}$ has 1 as an eigenvalue, then another eigenvalue of A could be

(A) –3   (B) –2   (C) 2   (D) 3   (E) 4

45. Let C be the curve in the xy-plane given parametrically by the equations $x = te^{1-t}$ and $(0,0) \to (1, \frac{\pi}{2})$ $y = \arcsin t$, as the parameter t increases from 0 to 1. Evaluate the integral

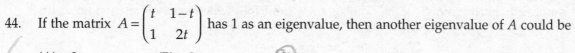

$$\int_C e^x(\sin y\, dx + \cos y\, dy)$$ path indep. use fund. thm line int.

$f(x,y) = e^x \sin y$ $f(1, \frac{\pi}{2}) - f(0,0)$

(A) 1   (B) e (left blank originally)   (C) $\dfrac{\pi e}{2}$ (D) $2e$ (E) πe $= e$

46. X is a finite set with the following property: The number of subsets of X that contain exactly 3 elements is 14 more than the number of subsets of X that contain exactly 2 elements. How many subsets of X contain exactly 4 elements?

(A) 24   (B) 25   (C) 28   (D) 32   (E) 35 $14 + \binom{X}{2} = \binom{X}{3}$

47. The curves $y = (\sin x + \cos x)^4$ and $y = (\sin x - \cos x)^4$ intersect at $x = 0$. If a is the smallest positive value of x at which these curves next intersect, determine the area between these curves from $x = 0$ to $x = a$.

(A) 2   (B) π (C) 4 (left blank originally)   (D) $\dfrac{3\pi}{2}$ (E) 2π

$(\sin x + \cos x)^2 = (\sin x - \cos x)^2$
$1 + 2\sin x \cos x = 1 - 2\sin x \cos x$
$4\sin x \cos x = 0$
$a = \frac{\pi}{2}$

$\int_0^{\frac{\pi}{2}} [(\sin x + \cos x)^2 + (\sin x - \cos x)^2]$
$[(\sin x + \cos x)^2 - (\sin x - \cos x)^2] dx$
$= \int_0^{\pi/2} 2[(1+\sin 2x) - (1-\sin(2x))] dx$
$= \int_0^{\pi/2} 4\sin(2x) dx$
$= [-2\cos(2x)]_0^{\pi/2} = -2(-1-1) = 4$

GO ON TO THE NEXT PAGE.

48. If m is an integer greater than 1, let $\mathbf{Z}_m$ denote the ring of integers modulo m. Determine the smallest value of n such that the set $A = \{\mathbf{Z}_n, \mathbf{Z}_{n+1}, \mathbf{Z}_{n+2}, \mathbf{Z}_{n+3}, \mathbf{Z}_{n+4}\}$ contains precisely one field.

   (A) 2   (B) 4   (C) 6   (D) 8   (E) None of the above

---

49. The value of the first term, x_1, of a sequence (x_n) of real numbers is unknown, but it *is* known that x_1 is not zero. Furthermore, for every integer $n \geq 1$, the following recursion relation holds true:

$$x_{n+1} = \frac{1}{2}\left(x_n + \frac{2}{x_n}\right)$$

   Which of the following statements is true about this sequence?

   (A) The sequence diverges if $x_1 < 0$ and converges to 1 if $x_1 > 0$.

   (B) The sequence diverges if $x_1 < 0$ and converges to $\sqrt{2}$ if $x_1 > 0$.

   (C) The sequence converges to -1 if $x_1 < 0$ and converges to $\sqrt{2}$ if $x_1 > 0$.

   (D) The sequence converges to $-\sqrt{2}$ if $x_1 < 0$ and converges to $\sqrt{2}$ if $x_1 > 0$.

   (E) The sequence diverges for any $x_1 \neq 0$.

---

50. How many structurally distinct Abelian groups have order 72?

   (A) 4   (B) 6   (C) 8   (D) 9   (E) 12

---

51. Let X be a random variable whose probability density function is

$$f(t) = \begin{cases} \frac{1}{2}e^{-(t-1)/2} & \text{if } 1 < t < \infty \\ 0 & \text{otherwise} \end{cases}$$

   What is the expectation (mean) of X?

   (A) 1   (B) 2   (C) 3   (D) 4   (E) 6

GO ON TO THE NEXT PAGE.

52. Let X be a topological space, and let A, B, and C be nonempty subsets of X such that $A \subset B \subset C$; that is, A is a proper subset of B, and B is a proper subset of C. Which of the following statements is/are true?

   I. If A and C are connected, then B is connected.
   II. If A and C are compact, then B is compact.
   III. If A and C are Hausdorff, then B is Hausdorff.

   (A) I and II only   (B) I and III only   (C) II and III only
   (D) III only   (E) I, II, and III

53. Let $T: \mathbf{R}^2 \to \mathbf{R}^2$ be the linear transformation that maps the point $(1, 2)$ to $(2, 3)$ and the point $(-1, 2)$ to $(2, -3)$. Then T maps the point $(2, 1)$ to

   (A) $(1, 6)$ (B) $(-1, 4)$ (C) $(3, 2)$ (D) $(-4, 3)$ (E) $(-3, 1)$

54. If C is the circle in the complex plane whose equation is $|z| = \pi$, oriented counterclockwise, find the value of the integral

$$\oint_C \left(\cos z - z \cos \frac{1}{z} \right) dz$$

   (A) $-2\pi i$ (B) $-\pi i$ (C) 0 (D) πi (E) $2\pi i$

55. Let A be the set of all ordered pairs of integers (m, n) such that $7m + 12n = 22$. What is the greatest negative number in the set $B = \{m + n : (m, n) \in A\}$?

   (A) -5 (B) -4 (C) -3 (D) -2 (E) -1

56. If k is a nonzero constant, find the critical point of the function

$$f(x, y) = \frac{k^2}{x} + \frac{k}{y} + xy$$

   (A) (k, k) (B) $(-1, -k)$ (C) $(1, k)$ (D) $(-k, -1)$ (E) $(k, 1)$

GO ON TO THE NEXT PAGE.

57. Cauchy's Mean-Value formula says that if f and g are two functions that are continuous on the nonempty, closed interval $[a, b]$ and differentiable on (a, b), then there exists at least one number c, with $a < c < b$, such that:

$$g'(c)[f(b) - f(a)] = f'(c)[g(b) - g(a)]$$

Consider the following argument:

(1) "The functions f and g in the result above satisfy the hypotheses of the Mean-Value theorem, so there exists a number c, with $a < c < b$, such that

$$f'(c) = \frac{f(b) - f(a)}{b - a} \quad \text{and} \quad g'(c) = \frac{g(b) - g(a)}{b - a}."$$

(2) "The equations in Step (1) imply that

$$b - a = \frac{f(b) - f(a)}{f'(c)} \quad \text{and} \quad b - a = \frac{g(b) - g(a)}{g'(c)}."$$

(3) "The equations in Step (2) imply that

$$\frac{f(b) - f(a)}{f'(c)} = \frac{g(b) - g(a)}{g'(c)}." \quad \checkmark$$

(4) "Cross multiplying, we get $g'(c)[f(b) - f(a)] = f'(c)[g(b) - g(a)]$."

Which of the following statements is/are true?

I. Step (1) is not valid. $\checkmark$
II. The conclusion of Step (1) does not imply the result of Step (2). $\checkmark$
III. The conclusion of Step (2) does not imply the result of Step (3).
IV. The conclusion of Step (3) does not imply the result of Step (4).

(A) I only

(B) II only

(C) I and II only

(D) IV only

(E) None are true; the argument is a valid proof of Cauchy's Mean-Value formula.

GO ON TO THE NEXT PAGE.

58. Define a topology, **T**, on the set of real numbers, **R**, as follows: **T** contains the empty set, ∅, and a nonempty subset O of **R** is in **T** if and only if O^c, the complement of O, is a finite set. Which of the following statements is/are true about **R** with this topology?

open sets have finite complements

   I. Every infinite subset of **R** is closed. ✗
   II. Every subset of **R** is compact. ✓
   III. **R** is Hausdorff. ✗ *can't have disjoint open sets*

(A) I only   (B) II only   (C) III only
(D) I and II only   (E) II and III only   *picked originally*

---

59. Let $\omega = e^{2\pi i/5}$ be a fifth root of 1. What is the value of the function $f(z) = z^2 + z$ at $z = \omega + \omega^{-1}$?

(A) –2   (B) –1   (C) 0   (D) 1   (E) 2 $\left(e^{2\pi i/5} + e^{8\pi i/5}\right)^2 +$

---

60. If **v** is an eigenvector of an invertible matrix A, then which of the following is/are necessarily true?

   I. **v** is also an eigenvector of $2A$. ✓
   II. **v** is also an eigenvector of A^2. ✓
   III. **v** is also an eigenvector of A^{-1}. ✓

(A) I only   (B) II only   (C) III only
(D) I and III only   (E) I, II, and III

$e^{6\pi i/5} + e^{4\pi i/5} + 2 + e^{2\pi i/5} + e^{8\pi i/5}$

---

61. Let C be the boundary, oriented counterclockwise, of the triangle in the xy-plane whose vertices are $(0, 1)$, $(1, 1)$, and $(1, 3)$. What is the value of the following integral?

$$\oint_C \sqrt{2x+1}\, dx + \left(2xy + \sqrt{y^2 - y}\right) dy$$

(A) 1   (B) $\dfrac{8}{3}$ (C) 3   (D) $\dfrac{10}{3}$ (E) 4

---

62. If $f : \mathbf{R} \to \mathbf{R}$ is a bounded function that is Lebesgue integrable, then which of the following must be true?

Take $f(x) = \begin{cases} 1 & \forall x \in \mathbf{Q} \\ 0 & \text{else} \end{cases}$

(A) f is Riemann integrable. ✗

(B) There does not exist a countably infinite E of **R** such that f is nondifferentiable at every $x \in E$. ✗

(C) There does not exist an uncountable subset E of **R** such that f is nondifferentiable at every $x \in E$. ✗

(D) There does not exist an uncountable subset E of **R** such that f is discontinuous at every $x \in E$. ✗

answered originally

(E) None of the above.

GO ON TO THE NEXT PAGE.

63. Find the largest number a that makes the following statement true:

> "The series $\displaystyle\sum_{n=0}^{\infty} \frac{(n!)^3}{(3n)!} x^{2n}$ converges for all x with $|x| < a$."

(A) 3   (B) $3\sqrt{3}$ (C) 6   (D) $6\sqrt{3}$ (E) 9

Want ratio <1

ratio = $\dfrac{(n+1)^3}{(3n+1)(3n+2)(3n+3)}a^2 \to \dfrac{a^2}{27}$

$a < \sqrt{27} = 3$

(slapped originally)

64. If A is the 2 by 2 matrix whose (i, j) entry is equal to $i + j$, and B is the 3 by 3 matrix whose (i, j) entry is equal to $i + j$, find the value of the sum $\det A + \det B$.

(A) –2   (B) –1   (C) 0   (D) 2   (E) 5

65. If $\mathbf{Z}_n$ denotes the ring of integers modulo n, for which of the pairs of rings $(\mathbf{Z}_m, \mathbf{Z}_n)$ given below does there exist a ring homomorphism $\phi: \mathbf{Z}_m \to \mathbf{Z}_n$ such that $\phi(1) = 1$?

(A) $(\mathbf{Z}_4, \mathbf{Z}_6)$ (B) $(\mathbf{Z}_6, \mathbf{Z}_4)$ (C) $(\mathbf{Z}_3, \mathbf{Z}_6)$
(D) $(\mathbf{Z}_6, \mathbf{Z}_3)$ (E) $(\mathbf{Z}_3, \mathbf{Z}_4)$

$$\begin{vmatrix} 2 & 3 \\ 3 & 4 \end{vmatrix} + \begin{vmatrix} 2 & 3 & 4 \\ 3 & 4 & 5 \\ 4 & 5 & 6 \end{vmatrix}$$

$-1 = 2(-1) - 3(-2) + 4(-1)$
$-1 - 2 + 6 - 4$

6 slapped

$\dfrac{49}{65}$

STOP

IF YOU FINISH BEFORE TIME IS CALLED, YOU MAY CHECK YOUR WORK.

10

Practice Test Answers and Explanations

1. **D** If $x^2 + x = 3$, then $x^2 = 3 - x$. This implies $x^4 = (x^2)^2 = (3 - x)^2 = 9 - 6x + x^2$. Now, since $x^2 = 3 - x$, we get $x^4 = 9 - 6x + (3 - x) = 12 - 7x$. Therefore, $x^4 + x = (12 - 7x) + x = 12 - 6x = 6(2 - x)$.

2. **A** We compute the given derivative as follows:

$$\frac{d}{dx}\left[x^{-1} - (\log x)^{-1}\right] = -x^{-2} + (\log x)^{-2} \bullet x^{-1}$$

$$= \frac{1}{x(\log x)^2} - \frac{1}{x^2}$$

$$= \frac{x - (\log x)^2}{(x \log x)^2}$$

3. **B** *Solution 1:* Multiply the given rational expression by the conjugate of the numerator over itself:

$$\lim_{x \to 0} \frac{\sqrt{x+1}-1}{x} = \lim_{x \to 0}\left(\frac{\sqrt{x+1}-1}{x} \bullet \frac{\sqrt{x+1}+1}{\sqrt{x+1}+1}\right) = \lim_{x \to 0} \frac{1}{\sqrt{x+1}+1} = \frac{1}{2}$$

Solution 2: Use L'Hôpital's rule:

$$\lim_{x \to 0} \frac{\sqrt{x+1}-1}{x} = \lim_{x \to 0} \frac{\frac{1}{2\sqrt{x+1}}}{1} = \frac{1}{2}$$

Solution 3: Recognize the given limit as the definition of $f'(1)$, where $f(x) = \sqrt{x}$. Therefore, the limit is equal to $f'(x) = \frac{1}{(2\sqrt{x})}$ evaluated at $x = 1$, which is $\frac{1}{2}$.

4. **B** Since B is the power set of A, we have:

$$B = \mathsf{P}(A) = \left\{\varnothing, \{\varnothing\}, \{a\}, \{\varnothing, a\}\right\}$$

Therefore, $A \cup B = \left\{\varnothing, a, \{\varnothing\}, \{a\}, \{\varnothing, a\}\right\}$, which contains 5 elements.

5. **C** Evaluating the integral, we get:

$$\int_0^a (12x^2 + 8x + 1)\,dx = \left[4x^3 + 4x^2 + x\right]_0^a$$

$$= 4a^3 + 4a^2 + a$$

$$= a(2a + 1)^2$$

This last expression is equal to 0 for only two values of a, namely $a = 0$ and $a = -\frac{1}{2}$.

6. **A** Every odd-degree polynomial, $p(x)$, with real coefficients has at least one zero. To see why this must be so, let the leading (highest-degree) term of $p(x)$ be $a_n x^n$, with n odd. Then as $x \to -\infty$, this term (and thus the value of the polynomial) also goes to $-\infty$. Similarly, as $x \to +\infty$, this term (and thus the value of the polynomial) also goes to $+\infty$. These observations imply that there's a positive number, M, such that $p(x) < 0$ for all $x < -M$ and $p(x) > 0$ for all $x > M$. By the Intermediate-Value theorem, there must be a point (between $-M$ and M) at which $p(x) = 0$. Therefore, this curve must cross the x-axis at least once. However, since $y' = 5x^4 + 3x^2 + 1$ is always positive, the curve is always increasing, so it can't cross the x-axis more than once.

7. **E** By the chain rule, we have:

$$\frac{\partial f}{\partial t} = \frac{\partial f}{\partial x}\frac{\partial x}{\partial t} + \frac{\partial f}{\partial y}\frac{\partial y}{\partial t} = (2xy - y^2)(2t - u) + (x^2 - 2xy)(-u)$$

Now when $(t, u) = (1, -1)$, the equations given for x and y tell us that $(x, y) = (2, 2)$. Therefore:

$$\left.\frac{\partial f}{\partial t}\right|_{(t,u)=(1,-1)} = (2 \cdot 2 \cdot 2 - 2^2)[2 \cdot 1 - (-1)] + (2^2 - 2 \cdot 2 \cdot 2)[-(-1)] = (4)(3) + (-4)(1) = 8$$

8. **E** Writing $\tan x$ as $(\sin x)/(\cos x)$, and making the substitution $u = \cos x$, $du = -\sin x\, dx$, we find that

$$\int \tan x\, dx = \int \frac{\sin x}{\cos x}\, dx = \int \frac{-du}{u} = -\log u = -\log(\cos x)$$

so $\int_0^b \tan x\, dx = \left[-\log(\cos x)\right]_0^b = -\log(\cos b)$. Therefore:

$$\int_0^b \tan x\, dx = 2 \quad \Rightarrow \quad -\log(\cos b) = 2$$
$$\log(\cos b) = -2$$
$$\cos b = e^{-2}$$
$$\sec b = e^{2}$$
$$b = \operatorname{arcsec}(e^2)$$

9. **B** Using the double-angle formula for the sine, we can write the given function in the form $f(x) = \frac{1}{2}\sin(2x^2)$. To find the critical points, we take the derivative, set it equal to zero, and solve:

$$f'(x) = \frac{1}{2}[\cos(2x^2)] \cdot 4x = 2x\cos(2x^2) \overset{\text{set}}{=} 0 \quad \Rightarrow \quad x = 0 \ \text{ or } \ \cos(2x^2) = 0$$

Since the question specifically asks for the smallest positive value of x that's a critical point, we ignore $x = 0$. We now notice that if a is the smallest positive number such that $\cos(2a^2) = 0$, then $\sin(2a^2) = 1$. Therefore, $f(a) = \frac{1}{2} \cdot 1 = \frac{1}{2}$.

10. **D** If we rewrite the equation in the form $M\, dx + N\, dy = 0$,

$$\frac{dy}{dx} = \frac{2x}{y^2 - 1} \quad \Rightarrow \quad (2x)\,dx = (y^2 - 1)\,dy \quad \Rightarrow \quad (2x)\,dx - (y^2 - 1)\,dy = 0$$

we notice that the equation is exact, since $M_y = N_x = 0$. Integrating both sides, we get $x^2 - \frac{1}{3}y^3 + y = c$ as the family of integral curves. To find the one integral curve that passes through the point $(2, 3)$, we evaluate c as follows:

$$2^2 - \frac{1}{3} \cdot 3^3 + 3 = c \quad \Rightarrow \quad -2 = c$$

Therefore, the integral curve we're looking for is $x^2 - \frac{1}{3}y^3 + y = -2$, which is equivalent to $x^2 + 2 = \frac{1}{3}y^3 - y$. [Choices (A) and (C) can be eliminated immediately since they don't pass through the given point, $(2, 3)$.]

11. **C** Both the cross product and the dot product are distributive over vector addition, so:

$$\mathbf{a} \cdot [(\mathbf{a}+\mathbf{c})\times\mathbf{b}] = \mathbf{a} \cdot [(\mathbf{a}\times\mathbf{b})+(\mathbf{c}\times\mathbf{b})]$$
$$= \mathbf{a} \cdot (\mathbf{a}\times\mathbf{b})+\mathbf{a} \cdot (\mathbf{c}\times\mathbf{b})$$

Now, because $\mathbf{a} \times \mathbf{b}$ is perpendicular to $\mathbf{a}$ by definition, the value of $\mathbf{a} \cdot (\mathbf{a} \times \mathbf{b})$ is zero, so the given equation reduces to $\mathbf{a} \cdot (\mathbf{c}\times\mathbf{b}) = -30$. Because $\mathbf{b}\times\mathbf{c} = -12\hat{\mathbf{j}} + 6\hat{\mathbf{k}}$ and cross-products are anticommutative, we know that $\mathbf{c}\times\mathbf{b} = -\mathbf{b}\times\mathbf{c} = 12\hat{\mathbf{j}} - 6\hat{\mathbf{k}}$. Therefore, if $\mathbf{a} = a_x\hat{\mathbf{i}} + a_y\hat{\mathbf{j}} + a_z\hat{\mathbf{k}}$, the equation $\mathbf{a} \cdot (\mathbf{c}\times\mathbf{b}) = -30$ becomes $12\,a_y - 6a_z = -30$. Of the choices given, only the vector $\mathbf{a} = \hat{\mathbf{i}} - 2\hat{\mathbf{j}} + \hat{\mathbf{k}}$ (choice (C)) satisfies this equation, since $12(-2) - 6(1) = -30$.

12. **B** As our one arch of the curve $y = \sin x$, we can take the portion of the curve from $x = 0$ to $x = \pi$. Revolving this portion of the curve around the x-axis generates a solid whose volume can be found by the disk method:

$$V = \int_0^\pi \pi(\sin x)^2\, dx$$
$$= \pi\int_0^\pi \tfrac{1}{2}(1 - \cos 2x)\, dx$$
$$= \tfrac{1}{2}\pi\left[x - \tfrac{1}{2}\sin 2x \right]_0^\pi$$
$$= \tfrac{1}{2}\pi^2$$

13. **A** Setting the derivative of $f(x)$ equal to zero and solving for x gives:

$$f'(x) = \frac{x^a \cdot x^{-1} - (\log x)(ax^{a-1})}{(x^a)^2} \overset{\text{set}}{=} 0$$
$$\frac{x^{a-1}(1 - a\log x)}{x^{2a}} = 0$$
$$\frac{1 - a\log x}{x^{a+1}} = 0$$
$$1 - a\log x = 0$$
$$x = e^{1/a}$$

The value of f at this critical point is:

$$f(e^{1/a}) = \frac{\log(e^{1/a})}{(e^{1/a})^a} = \frac{\dfrac{1}{a}}{e} = \frac{1}{ae}$$

[Checking that $f''(e^{1/a}) < 0$ would verify that $x = e^{1/a}$ does indeed give a maximum.]

14. **E**   Let $u = dy/dx$. Then the given equation becomes $du/dx = u^2$, which is separable:

$$\frac{du}{dx} = u^2 \quad \Rightarrow \quad \int \frac{du}{u^2} = \int dx \quad \Rightarrow \quad -\frac{1}{u} = x + c_1 \quad \Rightarrow \quad u = -\frac{1}{x+c_1}$$

(We ignore the solution $u \equiv 0$.) Integrating once more gives y:

$$y = \int dy = \int \frac{dy}{dx}\, dx = \int u\, dx = \int \left(-\frac{1}{x+c_1}\right) dx = -\log(x+c_1) + c_2$$

15. **C**   Since $\log n \to \infty$ as $n \to \infty$, we know that $a_n = 1/(\log n) \to 0$, so the sequence (a_n) converges (to 0). Eliminate (D). Applying the comparison test, the series $\sum a_n$ does not converge, since for all $n \geq 2$,

$$\log n < n \quad \Rightarrow \quad \frac{1}{\log n} > \frac{1}{n}$$

and the harmonic series, $\sum \frac{1}{n}$, diverges. Eliminate (B) and (E). Finally, the series $\sum (-1)^n a_n^2$ converges, because it's an alternating series and the terms

$$a_n^2 = \frac{1}{(\log n)^2}$$

decrease monotonically with a limit of 0.

16. **C**   If x is held constant, then $r \cos \theta = c$. Differentiating both sides of this equation with respect to r, we find that:

$$r \cos \theta = c$$

$$r \cdot \left[-\sin \theta \cdot \frac{\partial \theta}{\partial r}\right] + \cos \theta = 0$$

$$\frac{\partial \theta}{\partial r} = \frac{\cos \theta}{r \sin \theta} = r^{-1} \cot \theta$$

17. **E**   The Pythagorean identity $1 + \cot^2 \theta = \csc^2 \theta$ implies that

$$1 + \cot^2(\arcsin \tfrac{\pi}{4}) = \csc^2(\arcsin \tfrac{\pi}{4}) = \frac{1}{\sin^2(\arcsin \tfrac{\pi}{4})} = \frac{1}{(\tfrac{\pi}{4})^2} = \frac{16}{\pi^2}$$

18. **E**   Let $y = (x + e^{3x})^{1/x}$, so $\log y = \left(\dfrac{1}{x}\right) \log(x + e^{3x})$; we'll first find the limit of $(\log y)$ as x approaches 0 using L'Hôpital's rule:

$$\lim_{x \to 0} \frac{\log(x + e^{3x})}{x} = \lim_{x \to 0} \frac{\dfrac{1}{x+e^{3x}} \cdot (1 + 3e^{3x})}{1} = \lim_{x \to 0} \frac{1 + 3e^{3x}}{x + e^{3x}} = \frac{1+3}{0+1} = 4$$

Since $(\log y) \to 4$, we conclude that $y \to e^4$.

19. **C**   The equation $y' = x - y$ can be written in standard linear form as $y' + y = x$. The general solution of the associated homogeneous equation, $y' + y = 0$, is $y = ce^{-x}$. We can also see that $y = x - 1$ is a particular solution of the given nonhomogeneous equation. Therefore, the general solution of the nonhomogeneous equation is $y = ce^{-x} + x - 1$. To satisfy the initial condition $y(0) = 1$, we substitute $x = 0$ and $y = 1$, which gives $1 = c - 1$, so $c = 2$. Therefore, the solution of the IVP is $y = 2e^{-x} + x - 1$. This tells us that $y(1) = 2e^{-1} = \dfrac{2}{e}$.

20. **C**   If $f(x, y) = x^y$, then $\partial f / \partial x = yx^{y-1}$. Rewriting x^y as $e^{y \log x}$, we find that:

$$\frac{\partial f}{\partial y} = \frac{\partial}{\partial y}(e^{y \log x}) = e^{y \log x} \bullet \log x = x^y \log x$$

Therefore:

$$\left. \frac{\partial f}{\partial x} \right|_{(e, y_0)} = \left. \frac{\partial f}{\partial y} \right|_{(e, y_0)} \quad \Rightarrow \quad \left. yx^{y-1} \right|_{(e, y_0)} = \left. x^y \log x \right|_{(e, y_0)}$$

$$y_0 e^{y_0 - 1} = e^{y_0}$$
$$y_0 e^{-1} = 1$$
$$y_0 = e$$

21. **B**   The figure below shows the graph of the function $y = x - [x]$, and the area under this graph from $x = -\frac{1}{2}$ to $x = 1$ is shaded.

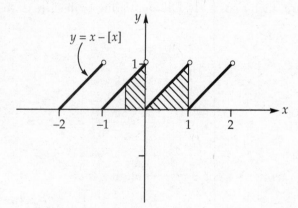

The area from $x = -\frac{1}{2}$ to $x = 0$ is equal to the area from $x = -1$ to $x = 0$, $(\frac{1}{2})(1)(1)$, minus the area from $x = -1$ to $x = -\frac{1}{2}$, $(\frac{1}{2})(\frac{1}{2})(\frac{1}{2})$; this gives $\frac{1}{2} - \frac{1}{8} = \frac{3}{8}$. Adding this to the area from $x = 0$ to $x = 1$, which is equal to $(\frac{1}{2})(1)(1) = \frac{1}{2}$, we get:

$$\int_{-1/2}^{1} (x - [x])\, dx = \frac{3}{8} + \frac{1}{2} = \frac{7}{8}$$

22. **B**   If a is an element of a group G, then the order of the cyclic subgroup generated by a is equal to the smallest positive integer n such that $a^n = e$, where e is the identity of the group (if such an n exists). The identity of SL(2, **Z**) is the 2 by 2 identity matrix I. Since

$$A^2 = \begin{pmatrix} 0 & 1 \\ -1 & -1 \end{pmatrix}\begin{pmatrix} 0 & 1 \\ -1 & -1 \end{pmatrix} = \begin{pmatrix} -1 & -1 \\ 1 & 0 \end{pmatrix}$$

$$A^3 = A^2 \cdot A = \begin{pmatrix} -1 & -1 \\ 1 & 0 \end{pmatrix}\begin{pmatrix} 0 & 1 \\ -1 & -1 \end{pmatrix} = \begin{pmatrix} 1 & 0 \\ 0 & 1 \end{pmatrix} = I$$

we see that $\langle A \rangle = 3$.

23. **A**   Since $\pi^x = e^{x \log \pi}$, we find that:

$$\frac{d}{dx}(\pi^x) = \frac{d}{dx}(e^{x\log\pi}) = e^{x\log\pi} \cdot (\log\pi) = \pi^x(\log\pi)$$

Therefore, if $y = x^\pi - \pi^x$, then $y' = \pi x^{\pi-1} - \pi^x(\log\pi)$. To find the slope of the curve $y = x^\pi - \pi^x$ at $(\pi, 0)$, we simply evaluate y' at $x = \pi$:

$$y'(\pi) = \pi \cdot \pi^{\pi-1} - \pi^\pi(\log\pi) = \pi^\pi(1 - \log\pi)$$

24. **A**   According to the information given in the question, the probability of rolling a 1, 2, 3, 4, 5, or 6 is p, $2p$, p, $2p$, p, or $2p$, respectively. Since one of these numbers must be rolled, it must be true that:

$$p + 2p + p + 2p + p + 2p = 1$$

Therefore, $9p = 1$, so $p = \dfrac{1}{9}$. The probability of rolling a 5 is $p = \dfrac{1}{9}$, and the probability of rolling a 6 is $2p = \dfrac{2}{9}$, so the probability of rolling a 5 then a 6 is $\left(\dfrac{1}{9}\right) \times \left(\dfrac{2}{9}\right) = \dfrac{2}{81}$.

25. **B**   First, find the partial-fraction decomposition of the integrand:

$$\frac{1}{1-x^2} = \frac{\frac{1}{2}}{1+x} + \frac{\frac{1}{2}}{1-x}$$

Integrating gives us:

$$\int \frac{1}{1-x^2}\,dx = \int \frac{\frac{1}{2}}{1+x}\,dx + \int \frac{\frac{1}{2}}{1-x}\,dx$$
$$= \tfrac{1}{2}\log(1+x) - \tfrac{1}{2}\log(1-x)$$
$$= \tfrac{1}{2}\log\frac{1+x}{1-x}$$

Therefore:

$$\int_{-1/2}^{1/2} \frac{1}{1-x^2}\,dx = \left[\tfrac{1}{2}\log\frac{1+x}{1-x}\right]_{-1/2}^{1/2} = \tfrac{1}{2}\left[\log\frac{\frac{3}{2}}{\frac{1}{2}} - \log\frac{\frac{1}{2}}{\frac{3}{2}}\right]$$
$$= \tfrac{1}{2}(\log 3 - \log\tfrac{1}{3})$$
$$= \tfrac{1}{2}(2\log 3)$$
$$= \log 3$$

26. **D** If a curve $f(y, z) = 0$ in the y-z plane is revolved around the z-axis, the equation for the resulting surface of revolution is obtained by replacing y with $\pm\sqrt{x^2 + y^2}$. In this case, $(y - 3)^2 + z^2 = 1$ becomes:

$$\left(\pm\sqrt{x^2 + y^2} - 3\right)^2 + z^2 = 1$$

$$[(x^2 + y^2) \pm 6\sqrt{x^2 + y^2} + 9] + z^2 = 1$$

$$x^2 + y^2 + z^2 + 8 = \pm 6\sqrt{x^2 + y^2}$$

$$(x^2 + y^2 + z^2 + 8)^2 = 36(x^2 + y^2)$$

27. **D** Replacing $d^n y / dx^n$ by m^n transforms the differential equation into the algebraic equation $m^4 + 2m^3 + 5m^2 = 0$, which we solve as follows:

$$m^4 + 2m^3 + 5m^2 = 0$$

$$m^2(m^2 + 2m + 5) = 0$$

$$m = 0, \quad \frac{-2 \pm \sqrt{2^2 - 4 \cdot 1 \cdot 5}}{2}$$

$$= 0 \text{ (double root)}, \ -1 \pm 2i$$

The part of the solution of the differential equation corresponding to the double root of 0 is $c_1 + c_2 x$, and the part corresponding to the conjugate complex roots $-1 \pm 2i$ is $e^{-x}(c_3 \cos 2x + c_4 \sin 2x)$. Therefore, the general solution of the given differential equation is:

$$y = c_1 + c_2 x + e^{-x}(c_3 \cos 2x + c_4 \sin 2x)$$

28. **C** The dimension of the image of f is equal to the rank of A. The following elementary row operations show that rank $A = 2$:

$$A = \begin{pmatrix} 1 & 2 & 3 \\ 4 & 5 & 6 \\ 7 & 8 & 9 \end{pmatrix} \xrightarrow[\substack{-4r_1 \text{ added to } r_2 \\ -7r_1 \text{ added to } r_3}]{} \begin{pmatrix} 1 & 2 & 3 \\ 0 & -3 & -6 \\ 0 & -6 & -12 \end{pmatrix} \xrightarrow[-2r_2 \text{ added to } r_3]{} \begin{pmatrix} 1 & 2 & 3 \\ 0 & -3 & -6 \\ 0 & 0 & 0 \end{pmatrix}$$

Since the image of f is a two-dimensional subspace of $\mathbf{R}^3$, it must be a plane through the origin.

29. **C** Integration by parts, with $u = \log x$, $du = \dfrac{1}{x}\,dx$, $v = \tfrac{1}{2}x^2$, and $dv = x\,dx$, yields:

$$\int (x \log x)\,dx = \tfrac{1}{2}x^2 \log x - \int \left(\tfrac{1}{2}x^2\right)\left(\frac{1}{x}\right)dx$$

$$= \tfrac{1}{2}x^2 \log x - \tfrac{1}{2}\int x\,dx$$

$$= \tfrac{1}{2}x^2 \log x - \tfrac{1}{4}x^2 + c$$

Therefore:

$$\int_0^1 (x \log x)\,dx = \left[\tfrac{1}{2}x^2 \log x - \tfrac{1}{4}x^2\right]_0^1$$

$$= \left(0 - \tfrac{1}{4}\right) - \left[\lim_{x \to 0}\left(\tfrac{1}{2}x^2 \log x\right) - 0\right]$$

To evaluate the limit, we use L'Hôpital's rule:

$$\lim_{x \to 0}\left(\tfrac{1}{2}x^2 \log x\right) = \lim_{x \to 0}\frac{\log x}{\frac{2}{x^2}} = \lim_{x \to 0}\left(\frac{\frac{1}{x}}{\frac{-4}{x^3}}\right) = \lim_{x \to 0}\left(-\frac{x^2}{4}\right) = 0$$

So we can now write:

$$\int_0^1 (x \log x)\,dx = \left(0 - \tfrac{1}{4}\right) - \left[\lim_{x \to 0}\left(\tfrac{1}{2}x^2 \log x\right) - 0\right]$$

$$= \left(0 - \tfrac{1}{4}\right) - \left[0 - 0\right]$$

$$= -\tfrac{1}{4}$$

30. **D** The binary operation is associative, as we can check:

$$(m \bullet n) \bullet q \overset{?}{=} m \bullet (n \bullet q)$$

$$(m + n + mn) \bullet q \overset{?}{=} m \bullet (n + q + nq)$$

$$(m + n + mn) + q + (m + n + mn)q = m + (n + q + nq) + m(n + q + nq) \ \checkmark$$

This binary structure does have an identity, namely 0, since

$$m \bullet 0 = m + 0 + m \bullet 0 = m \qquad \text{and} \qquad 0 \bullet m = 0 + m + 0 \bullet m = m$$

are true for all m. However, not all integers have an inverse with respect to this binary operation. For example, 1 has no inverse, for if we try to solve $1 \bullet n = 0$, we get

$$1 \bullet n = 0 \ \Rightarrow \ 1 + n + 1 \bullet n = 0 \ \Rightarrow \ 2n = -1$$

which is not satisfied by any integer n. Since not every element has an inverse, this binary structure is not a group. (It *is* a monoid, however. As an additional instructive exercise, show that the only elements in this binary structure that do have an inverse are 0 and –2.)

31. **C** Let $x = u^2$, so $dx = 2u\,du$. Applying this change of variable, we find that:

$$\int_0^\infty \frac{e^{-x}}{\sqrt{x}}\,dx = \int_0^\infty \frac{e^{-u^2}}{u}(2u\,du) = 2\int_0^\infty e^{-u^2}\,du = 2\left(\tfrac{1}{2}\sqrt{\pi}\right) = \sqrt{\pi}$$

32. **A** The surface S is a level surface of the function $f(x, y, z) = x^2 - xy^2z + z^2$. The gradient of this function, evaluated at the point P, will be normal to S, and, therefore, tangent to the plane at P. Since

$$\nabla f = \left(f_x, f_y, f_z\right)$$
$$= \left(2x - y^2z, -2xyz, -xy^2 + 2z\right)$$

we have $\nabla f\big|_{P=(1,1,1)} = (1, -2, 1)$. Since this is normal to the plane tangent to S at P, the equation of the tangent plane must have the form $x - 2y + z = d$, for some constant, d. Since this plane passes through the point $P = (1, 1, 1)$, the value of d must be 0, so the equation of the tangent plane is $x - 2y + z = 0$. Every point of the form $(t, t, t) = t(1, 1, 1)$ lies in this plane; but these points describe the line $x = y = z$, so this line lies in the plane.

33. **A** The critical points of f are found by determining the points at which the derivative is equal to 0. In this case, the fundamental theorem of calculus and the chain rule tell us that:

$$f'(x) = \frac{d}{dx}\int_{x^2}^{x^3} (\log t)\,dt$$
$$= [\log(x^3)] \cdot \tfrac{d}{dx}(x^3) - [\log(x^2)] \cdot \tfrac{d}{dx}(x^2)$$
$$= 9x^2 \log x - 4x \log x$$
$$= (x \log x)(9x - 4)$$

Setting this equal to 0, we get $x = 0$, $x = 1$, or $x = \dfrac{4}{9}$. Since f is defined only for positive x, we ignore $x = 0$, and conclude that the critical points occur at $x = \dfrac{4}{9}$ and $x = 1$.

34. **D** From the formula for the Taylor coefficients, we know that:

$$\frac{f^{(n)}(0)}{n!} = \frac{(n+1)^{n/2}}{(n!)^2}$$

Therefore:

$$f^{(4)}(0) = \frac{(4+1)^{4/2}}{4!} = \frac{5^2}{4!} = \frac{25}{24} > 1$$

35. **A**   We draw a Venn diagram with three circles, each one representing one of the three courses listed (R for real analysis, D for differential equations, and L for linear algebra). Letting n denote the number of students taking all three courses, we use the information given in the question to construct our diagram:

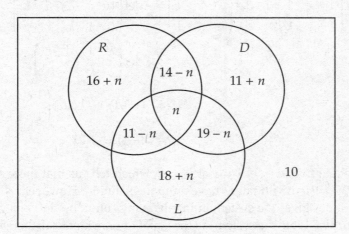

The sum of all the numbers listed (which are cardinalities) must be equal to 100, the number of students surveyed. Therefore:

$$10 + (16 + n) + (11 + n) + (18 + n) + (11 - n) + (14 - n) + (19 - n) + n = 100$$

Solving this equation for n, we get $99 + n = 100$, so $n = 1$.

36. **B**   Since the graph passes through the origin, we know $f(0) = 0$. Now, using the given recursion relation, we have:

$$f(2) = 1^2 + f(0) \;\Rightarrow\; f(2) = 1$$
$$f(4) = 2^2 + f(2) \;\Rightarrow\; f(4) = 5$$
$$f(6) = 3^2 + f(4) \;\Rightarrow\; f(6) = 14$$
$$f(8) = 4^2 + f(6) \;\Rightarrow\; f(8) = 30$$

Therefore, $f(8) = 30$.

37. **B** The linear system will not have a unique solution if the determinant of the coefficient matrix is zero, so we'll begin there:

$$\det\begin{pmatrix} k & 1 & 1 \\ 1 & k & 1 \\ 1 & 1 & k \end{pmatrix} = -\det\begin{pmatrix} 1 & 1 & k \\ 1 & k & 1 \\ k & 1 & 1 \end{pmatrix} = -\det\begin{pmatrix} 1 & 1 & k \\ 0 & k-1 & 1-k \\ 0 & 1-k & 1-k^2 \end{pmatrix}$$

$$= -\det\begin{pmatrix} k-1 & 1-k \\ 1-k & 1-k^2 \end{pmatrix}$$

$$= -(k-1)(1-k)\det\begin{pmatrix} 1 & -1 \\ 1 & 1+k \end{pmatrix}$$

$$= (k-1)^2(k+2)$$

Setting this equal to 0, we get $k = 1$ or $k = -2$, which tells us that there are only two values of k for which the system will fail to have a unique solution. However, as we'll see, one of these two special values gives the system infinitely many solutions, and one gives it no solutions. If we substitute $k = 1$ into the system, all the equations are identical; therefore, there are infinitely many solutions if $k = 1$. However, if we substitute $k = -2$ into the system, we get:

$$-2x + y + z = 1$$
$$x - 2y + z = -2$$
$$x + y - 2z = 4$$

The sum of the last two equations is $2x - y - z = 2$, or, equivalently, $-2x + y + z = -2$, which is clearly inconsistent with the first equation; this system has no solutions.

38. **D** If a function f in X has an inverse, that inverse can't be constant, so statement I is false. (If f^{-1} is constant, its graph is a horizontal line; say, $y = c$. The reflection of this graph across the line $y = x$ should give the graph of the inverse, which is $(f^{-1})^{-1} = f$. But the reflection of $y = c$ across the line $y = x$ is the vertical line $x = c$, which is not the graph of a function.) Eliminate (B), (C), and (E). Statement II is true; if we get a constant no matter what we substitute into f (because $g(x)$ is arbitrary), then f must be a constant. And, finally, statement III does guarantee that f is constant, since it implies that $f'(x) = 0$ for every x in $[a, b]$:

$$f'(x) = \lim_{x \to y} \frac{f(x) - f(y)}{x - y} \quad \Rightarrow \quad |f'(x)| = \lim_{x \to y} \left| \frac{f(x) - f(y)}{x - y} \right|$$

$$= \lim_{x \to y} \frac{|f(x) - f(y)|}{|x - y|}$$

$$\leq \lim_{x \to y} \frac{(x - y)^2}{|x - y|}$$

$$= \lim_{x \to y} |x - y|$$

$$= 0$$

39. E   From the formula given for $f(x)$, we know that the domain of f consists of all x for which $g^{-1}(x) \neq 0$. But $g^{-1}(x) = 0$ if and only if $g(0) = x$; substituting $x = 0$ into the equation for $g(x)$, we get $g(0) = 1$. Therefore, the domain of f consists of all real $x \neq 1$. That eliminates (A) and (B).

To figure out $f^{-1}(-2)$, we notice that $f^{-1}(-2) = a$ if and only if $f(a) = -2$. This equation is equivalent to $1/g^{-1}(a) = -2$, which implies $g^{-1}(a) = -\dfrac{1}{2}$. This last equation is true if and only if $g\left(-\dfrac{1}{2}\right) = a$. Therefore:

$$f^{-1}(-2) = g\left(-\frac{1}{2}\right) = \left(-\frac{1}{2}\right)^3 + \left(-\frac{1}{2}\right)^2 + \left(-\frac{1}{2}\right) + 1 = \frac{5}{8}$$

40. D   The slope of the line tangent to the graph is given by the derivative, so first we'll find y':

$$y = x^{(e^x)} = e^{e^x \log x} \quad \Rightarrow \quad y' = e^{e^x \log x}\left[e^x \cdot \tfrac{1}{x} + e^x \log x\right] = x^{(e^x)} e^x (\tfrac{1}{x} + \log x)$$

Evaluating this at $x = 1$, we get $y'(1) = e$; therefore, the equation of the line tangent to the graph of $y = x^{(e^x)}$ at the point $(1, 1)$ is $y - 1 = e(x - 1)$. Substituting $x = 2$, and solving for y, we get $y = e + 1$, so the tangent line passes through the point $(2, e + 1)$.

41. C   We use the Taylor formula:

$$f(x) = \sum_{n=0}^{\infty} \frac{f^{(n)}(0)}{n!} x^n$$

$$= f(0) + f'(0) \cdot x + \tfrac{1}{2} f''(0) \cdot x^2 + \sum_{n=3}^{\infty} \frac{f^{(n)}(0)}{n!} x^n$$

From the information given in the question about the values of the derivatives of f at zero, we can write:

$$f(x) = f(0) + f'(0) \cdot x + \tfrac{1}{2} f''(0) \cdot x^2 + \sum_{n=3}^{\infty} \frac{f^{(n)}(0)}{n!} x^n$$

$$\leq 0 + x + x^2 + \sum_{n=3}^{\infty} \frac{1}{2^{n-3}} x^n$$

Substituting $x = 1$ gives us

$$f(1) \leq 0 + 1 + 1^2 + \sum_{n=3}^{\infty} \frac{1}{2^{n-3}}$$

$$= 2 + \sum_{n=0}^{\infty} \frac{1}{2^n}$$

$$= 2 + 2$$

$$= 4 \qquad \text{(Answer (C).)}$$

where we've used the formula for the sum of a geometric series:

$$0 < x < 1 \quad \Rightarrow \quad \sum_{n=0}^{\infty} x^n = \frac{1}{1-x} \quad \Rightarrow \quad \sum_{n=0}^{\infty} \frac{1}{2^n} = \sum_{n=0}^{\infty} \left(\tfrac{1}{2}\right)^n = \frac{1}{1 - \frac{1}{2}} = 2$$

42. **B** First, eliminate choice (E); there is no five-dimensional subspace of $\mathbf{R}^4$. Next, ignore the vector $\mathbf{v}_3 = \mathbf{0}$; the zero vector adds nothing to the span of any collection of vectors. The span of $\mathbf{v}_1$, $\mathbf{v}_2$, $\mathbf{v}_4$, and $\mathbf{v}_5$ is equal to the column space of the matrix whose columns are these vectors, and the rank of this matrix gives the dimension of the column space:

$$A = \begin{pmatrix} 1 & -2 & -1 & 1 \\ -1 & 1 & 0 & 1 \\ 0 & 1 & 1 & -2 \\ 1 & 1 & 2 & -5 \end{pmatrix} \xrightarrow[\substack{r_1 \text{ added to } r_2 \\ -r_1 \text{ added to } r_4}]{} \begin{pmatrix} 1 & -2 & -1 & 1 \\ 0 & -1 & -1 & 2 \\ 0 & 1 & 1 & -2 \\ 0 & 3 & 3 & -6 \end{pmatrix}$$

$$\xrightarrow[\substack{r_2 \text{ added to } r_3 \\ 3r_2 \text{ added to } r_4}]{} \begin{pmatrix} 1 & -2 & -1 & 1 \\ 0 & -1 & -1 & 2 \\ 0 & 0 & 0 & 0 \\ 0 & 0 & 0 & 0 \end{pmatrix} \Rightarrow \operatorname{rank} A = 2$$

43. **B** This question asks us to maximize the value of $f(r,\theta) = r\sin\theta$ subject to the constraint $g(r,\theta) = r^2 - 4\cos 2\theta = 0$. This can be done by the Lagrange multiplier method, as follows:

$$\nabla f_\theta = \lambda \nabla g$$
$$(f_r, f_\theta) = \lambda(g_r, g_\theta)$$
$$(\sin\theta, \ r\cos\theta) = \lambda(2r, \ 8\sin 2\theta)$$

Eliminating λ from this last equation gives us

$$\frac{\sin\theta}{2r} = \frac{r\cos\theta}{8\sin 2\theta}$$

since both of these expressions are equal to λ. Cross multiplying, we get $2r^2\cos\theta = 8\sin\theta\sin 2\theta$. We can now use the constraint equation, $r^2 = 4\cos 2\theta$, to reduce this to $\cos 2\theta\cos\theta = \sin\theta\sin 2\theta$. and now solve this equation as follows:

$$\cos 2\theta\cos\theta = \sin\theta\sin 2\theta$$

$$\frac{1}{\tan\theta} = \tan 2\theta$$

$$\frac{1}{\tan\theta} = \frac{2\tan\theta}{1 - \tan^2\theta}$$

$$2\tan^2\theta = 1 - \tan^2\theta$$

$$\tan\theta = \pm\frac{1}{\sqrt 3}$$

From this last equation, we take $\theta = \dfrac{\pi}{6}$. Substituting this into the constraint equation gives $r^2 = 4\cos 2\dfrac{\pi}{6} = 2$, so $r = \sqrt 2$. We now conclude that the maximum value of $y = r\sin\theta$ is

$$y_{max} = \sqrt 2 \sin\frac{\pi}{6} = \frac{\sqrt 2}{2}.$$

44. **C**   A number λ is an eigenvalue of a matrix A if and only if $\det(A - \lambda I) = 0$. Therefore, if 1 is an eigenvalue of A, it must be true that:

$$\det(A - I) = \det\begin{pmatrix} t-1 & 1-t \\ 1 & 2t-1 \end{pmatrix} = 0$$

This equation implies that:

$$(t-1)(2t-1) - (1-t) = 0$$
$$(t-1)[(2t-1)+1] = 0$$
$$t = 0,\ 1$$

Since t can only equal 0 or 1, the given matrix must be:

$$A = \begin{pmatrix} 0 & 1 \\ 1 & 0 \end{pmatrix} \quad \text{or} \quad A = \begin{pmatrix} 1 & 0 \\ 1 & 2 \end{pmatrix}$$

In the first case, the eigenvalues are –1 and 1, while in the second case, the eigenvalues are 1 and 2. (An easy way to calculate the eigenvalues of a 2 by 2 matrix is to use the fact that the determinant of the matrix always gives the product of the eigenvalues, and the trace of the matrix—that is, the sum of the entries on the diagonal—always gives the sum of the eigenvalues. So, for the first possibility for the matrix A, the product of the eigenvalues must be –1 and their sum must be 0; therefore, the eigenvalues must be –1 and 1. We can figure out the eigenvalues of the second possibility for A in the same manner.) Therefore, another eigenvalue of A could be –1 or 2, but only 2 is listed among the choices.

45. **B**   If we let $M(x, y) = e^x \sin y$ and $N(x, y) = e^x \cos y$, then the integrand,

$$M\,dx + N\,dy = (e^x \sin y)\,dx + (e^x \cos y)\,dy$$

is an exact differential, since $M_y = e^x \cos y = N_x$. Therefore, $\mathbf{F} = (M_x, N_y)$ is equal to the gradient of some function, $f(x, y)$, and the line integral is independent of the path. In particular, a function f whose gradient is $(e^x \sin y,\ e^x \cos y)$ is $f(x, y) = e^x \sin y$.

Using the parametric equations (and the interval of the parameter, t) given in the question, we see that the curve C begins at the point $A = (0, 0)$ and ends at the point $B = (1, \frac{\pi}{2})$. Therefore:

$$\int_C M\,dx + N\,dy = \int_C \mathbf{F} \bullet d\mathbf{r} = \int_C \nabla f \bullet d\mathbf{r} = \int_A^B \nabla f \bullet d\mathbf{r}$$
$$= f(B) - f(A)$$
$$= \left[e^x \sin y \right]_{A=(0,0)}^{B=(1,\pi/2)}$$
$$= e$$

46. **E** Assume that X contains exactly n elements. Then the number of 2-element subsets is the binomial coefficient $\dbinom{n}{2}$, and the number of 3-element subsets is $\dbinom{n}{3}$. We first want to find the value of n such that $\dbinom{n}{3} = \dbinom{n}{2} + 14$. Perhaps the easiest way to do this is to write down Pascal's triangle, which is a triangular array of numbers such that the kth entry in the nth row (where we start counting from 0 in both cases) is equal to $\dbinom{n}{k}$. The rows always begin and end with 1, and every other entry is equal to the sum of the entries to its left and right in the row above.

$$
\begin{array}{ccccccccccccccc}
&&&&&&& 1 &&&&&&& \\
&&&&&& 1 && 1 &&&&&& \\
&&&&& 1 && 2 && 1 &&&&& \\
&&&& 1 && 3 && 3 && 1 &&&& \\
&&& 1 && 4 && 6 && 4 && 1 &&& \\
&& 1 && 5 && 10 && 10 && 5 && 1 && \\
& 1 && 6 && 15 && 20 && 15 && 6 && 1 & \\
1 && 7 && 21 && 35 && 35 && 21 && 7 && 1 \\
&&&&&&& \vdots &&&&&&&
\end{array}
$$

We're looking for the row in which the $\dbinom{n}{3}$ entry is 14 more than the $\dbinom{n}{2}$ entry. We see that this happens in the row for $n = 7$, since:

$$\binom{7}{2} = 21 \qquad \text{and} \qquad \binom{7}{3} = 35$$

Since X contains $n = 7$ elements, the number of 4-element subsets of X is:

$$\binom{7}{4} = 35$$

47. **C**   First, we'll find where the curves intersect:

$$(\sin x + \cos x)^4 = (\sin x - \cos x)^4$$
$$(\sin x + \cos x)^2 = (\sin x - \cos x)^2$$
$$2\sin x \cos x = -2\sin x \cos x$$
$$4\sin x \cos x = 0$$
$$2\sin 2x = 0$$

Since we want the smallest positive value of x at which the curves intersect, we take $2x = \pi$, so $x = \dfrac{\pi}{2}$; this is a. Therefore, the area between the curves from $x = 0$ to $x = a = \dfrac{\pi}{2}$ is:

$$A = \int_0^{\pi/2} [(\sin x + \cos x)^4 - (\sin x - \cos x)^4]\, dx$$
$$= \int_0^{\pi/2} [(\sin x + \cos x)^2 + (\sin x - \cos x)^2][(\sin x + \cos x)^2 - (\sin x - \cos x)^2]\, dx$$
$$= \int_0^{\pi/2} [2\sin^2 x + 2\cos^2 x][2\sin x \cos x - (-2\sin x \cos x)]\, dx$$
$$= 4\int_0^{\pi/2} (2\sin x \cos x)\, dx$$
$$= 4\left[\sin^2 x\right]_0^{\pi/2}$$
$$= 4$$

48. **C**   The ring $\mathbf{Z}_m$ is a field if and only if m is a prime. Choice (A) leads to the set containing $\mathbf{Z}_2$, $\mathbf{Z}_3$, $\mathbf{Z}_4$, $\mathbf{Z}_5$, and $\mathbf{Z}_6$, three of which are fields ($\mathbf{Z}_2$, $\mathbf{Z}_3$, and $\mathbf{Z}_5$). Choice (B) gives the rings $\mathbf{Z}_4$, $\mathbf{Z}_5$, $\mathbf{Z}_6$, $\mathbf{Z}_7$, and $\mathbf{Z}_8$, two of which are fields. Choice (C) gives the rings $\mathbf{Z}_6$, $\mathbf{Z}_7$, $\mathbf{Z}_8$, $\mathbf{Z}_9$, and $\mathbf{Z}_{10}$, exactly one of which ($\mathbf{Z}_7$) is a field, so this is our answer.

49. **D**   Assume that the sequence converges and let x denote its limit. Then both $x_n \to x$ and $x_{n+1} \to x$ as $n \to \infty$, so the recursion relation becomes, in the limit:

$$x = \frac{1}{2}\left(x + \frac{2}{x}\right)$$
$$x = \frac{x^2 + 2}{2x}$$
$$2x^2 = x^2 + 2$$
$$x^2 = 2$$
$$x = \pm\sqrt{2}$$

If x_1 is negative, the recursion relation implies that every term x_n is negative; on the other hand, if x_1 is positive, then every term x_n is positive. Therefore, we conclude that the sequence (x_n) converges to $-\sqrt{2}$ if $x_1 < 0$ and converges to $\sqrt{2}$ if $x_1 > 0$.

50. **B**   The prime factorization of 72 is $2 \times 2 \times 2 \times 3 \times 3$. Therefore, the list of possible elementary divisors for an Abelian group of order 72 reads:

1)   2, 2, 2, 3, 3

2) $2, 2, 2, 3^2$

3) $2, 2^2, 3, 3$

4) $2, 2^2, 3^2$

5) $2^3, 3, 3$

6) $2^3, 3^2$

This list implies that there are 6 nonisomorphic Abelian groups of order 72.

51. **C**   By definition, if the probability density function of a random variable, X, is $f_X(t)$, then the expectation (or mean) of X is $\mu(X) = \int_{-\infty}^{\infty} t \cdot f_X(t)\,dt$. In this case, then, we have $\mu(X) = \int_1^{\infty} t \cdot \frac{1}{2} e^{-(t-1)/2}\,dt$. We'll evaluate the integral $\int t \cdot e^{-(t-1)/2}\,dt$ using integration by parts, with $u = t$, $du = dt$, $v = -2\,e^{-(t-1)/2}$, and $dv = e^{-(t-1)/2}\,dt$:

$$\int t \cdot e^{-(t-1)/2}\,dt = -2te^{-(t-1)/2} - \int (-2)e^{-(t-1)/2}\,dt$$
$$= -2te^{-(t-1)/2} - 4e^{-(t-1)/2} + c$$

Therefore,

$$\mu(X) = \int_1^{\infty} t \cdot \tfrac{1}{2} e^{-(t-1)/2}\,dt$$
$$= \tfrac{1}{2}\left[-2te^{-(t-1)/2} - 4e^{-(t-1)/2} \right]_1^{\infty}$$
$$= \tfrac{1}{2}\left[(0-0) - (-2-4) \right]$$
$$= 3$$

where we've used the fact that $e^{-(t-1)/2} \to 0$ as $t \to \infty$, and also that $te^{-(t-1)/2} = t/e^{(t-1)/2} \to 0$ as $t \to \infty$, which can be proved in one step using L'Hôpital's rule.

52. **D** Statement I is false; consider the following counterexample for $X = \mathbf{R}^2$:

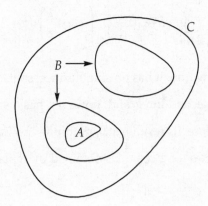

Then C is connected, and A is a connected subset of B, but the subset B of C is not connected. Statement II is also false. Let $X = \mathbf{R}^1$, and let $A = [0, 1]$, $B = (-1, 2)$, and $C = [-2, 3]$. Then $A \subset B \subset C$ and the closed intervals A and C are compact, but the open interval B is not. Once you eliminate (A), (B), and (E), you don't really need to check statement III, since it appears in both remaining choices. Statement III is true, since every subspace of a Hausdorff space is Hausdorff. To prove that C Hausdorff implies that a subset B of C is also Hausdorff, let x_1 and x_2 be distinct points in B; since x_1 and x_2 are also in C and C is Hausdorff, there exist disjoint open sets, O_1 and O_2, in C containing x_1 and x_2, respectively. Now, we simply notice that $O_1 \cap B$ and $O_2 \cap B$ are disjoint open sets in B containing x_1 and x_2, respectively.

53. **A** Because T is linear, $T(x\mathbf{a} + y\mathbf{b}) = xT(\mathbf{a}) + yT(\mathbf{b})$. Since we know where T maps $\mathbf{a} = (1, 2)$ and $\mathbf{b} = (-1, 2)$—which form a basis for $\mathbf{R}^2$—if we write the point $\mathbf{c} = (2, 1)$ as a linear combination of $\mathbf{a}$ and $\mathbf{b}$, we can use the equation above to find $T(\mathbf{c})$. Writing the points in $\mathbf{R}^2$ as column vectors, we want to find the scalars x and y such that:

$$x\mathbf{a} + y\mathbf{b} = \mathbf{c}$$

$$x\begin{pmatrix} 1 \\ 2 \end{pmatrix} + y\begin{pmatrix} -1 \\ 2 \end{pmatrix} = \begin{pmatrix} 2 \\ 1 \end{pmatrix}$$

This equation is equivalent to the system

$$x - y = 2$$
$$2x + 2y = 1$$

whose solution is $(x, y) = \left(\frac{5}{4}, -\frac{3}{4}\right)$. Therefore,

$$T(\mathbf{c}) = xT(\mathbf{a}) + yT(\mathbf{b})$$

$$T\begin{pmatrix} 2 \\ 1 \end{pmatrix} = \tfrac{5}{4} \cdot T\begin{pmatrix} 1 \\ 2 \end{pmatrix} - \tfrac{3}{4} \cdot T\begin{pmatrix} -1 \\ 2 \end{pmatrix}$$

$$= \tfrac{5}{4}\begin{pmatrix} 2 \\ 3 \end{pmatrix} - \tfrac{3}{4}\begin{pmatrix} 2 \\ -3 \end{pmatrix}$$

$$= \begin{pmatrix} 1 \\ 6 \end{pmatrix}$$

54. D The integral we're asked to evaluate is equal to:

$$\oint_C \cos z \, dz - \oint_C \left(z \cos \frac{1}{z} \right) dz$$

Since $\cos z$ is an entire function, it has no singularities, so its integral around any closed path is automatically zero. The second integrand, however, has a singularity at $z = 0$, which is inside the closed curve C; therefore, its residue at 0, multiplied by $2\pi i$, will give the value of the second integral. The Laurent series for $z \cos \frac{1}{z}$ is obtained by replacing z with $\frac{1}{z}$ in the well-known Taylor series for $\cos z$:

$$z \cos \frac{1}{z} = z \left[1 - \frac{1}{2!} \left(\frac{1}{z} \right)^2 + \frac{1}{4!} \left(\frac{1}{z} \right)^4 - \cdots \right]$$

$$= z - \frac{1}{2} \cdot \frac{1}{z} + \frac{1}{24} \cdot \frac{1}{z^3} - \cdots$$

Since the coefficient of $z^{-1} = \frac{1}{z}$ is $-\frac{1}{2}$, this is the residue of $(z \cos \frac{1}{z})$ at 0. Therefore:

$$\oint_C \left(\cos z - z \cos \frac{1}{z} \right) dz = \oint_C \cos z \, dz - \oint_C \left(z \cos \frac{1}{z} \right) dz$$

$$= 0 - \left[2\pi i \cdot \left(-\frac{1}{2} \right) \right]$$

$$= \pi i$$

55. B First, we'll find integers x and y such that $7x + 12y = 1$. Using the Euclidean algorithm, or by inspection, we get $x = -5$, $y = 3$. Multiplying each of these by 22 gives the solution $m = -110$, $n = 66$ to the equation $7m + 12n = 22$. This last result implies that *every* solution in integers to the equation $7m + 12n = 22$ is given by the equations

$$m = -110 + 12t \quad \text{and} \quad n = 66 - 7t$$

where t is any integer. Therefore, the sum of m and n is:

$$m + n = -44 + 5t$$

This sum is positive for every integer $t \geq 9$, so the greatest negative value for this sum is obtained by taking $t = 8$. This gives $m + n = -4$.

56. **E** The critical points of a function $f(x, y)$ are the solutions of the simultaneous equations $f_x = 0$ and $f_y = 0$. For $f(x, y) = \dfrac{k^2}{x} + \dfrac{k}{y} + xy$, we have:

$$f_x = \frac{\partial f}{\partial x} = -\frac{k^2}{x^2} + y \overset{\text{set}}{=} 0 \quad \Rightarrow \quad y = \frac{k^2}{x^2}$$

$$f_y = \frac{\partial f}{\partial y} = -\frac{k}{y^2} + x \overset{\text{set}}{=} 0 \quad \Rightarrow \quad x = \frac{k}{y^2}$$

Substituting the first equation into the second gives us:

$$x = \frac{k}{\left(k^2/x^2\right)^2}$$

$$x = \frac{x^4}{k^3}$$

$$1 = \frac{x^3}{k^3}$$

$$x = k$$

(We ignore $x = 0$, since the domain of f does not include $x = 0$.) Now, substituting $x = k$ into either of the equations above, we get $y = 1$. Therefore, the function $f(x, y)$ has a critical point at $(k, 1)$.

57. **C** Step (1) is not valid, because the point c that works for f is not necessarily the same c that works for g. All we *can* say is that there exists a point c_1, with $a < c_1 < b$ such that $f'(c_1) = \dfrac{f(b) - f(a)}{b - a}$ and a point c_2, with $a < c_2 < b$, such that $g'(c_2) = \dfrac{g(b) - g(a)}{b - a}$. Now it may turn out that $c_1 = c_2$ for a particular pair of functions f and g, but this would not be true in general.

    Furthermore, the conclusion of Step (1) does not imply the result of Step (2). If $f'(c) = 0$, or if $g'(c) = 0$, then we couldn't write the equations in Step (2) from the equations in Step (1). Therefore, statements I and II are true.

58. **B** Statement I is false. As a counterexample, consider the infinite set $(1, \infty)$; this set is closed if and only if its complement, $(-\infty, 1]$ is open. But $(-\infty, 1]$ is not open since its complement, $(1, \infty)$, is not finite. In fact, we can see that the only closed sets in this topology are the finite sets.

    Statement II is true. The nonempty sets in any open covering contain every point of $\mathbf{R}$ except a finite number, so every open covering of any set A in $\mathbf{R}$ will contain a finite collection that also covers A.

    Statement III is false. Let x_1 and x_2 be distinct points in $\mathbf{R}$. If O_1 is an open set containing x_1 and O_2 is an open set containing x_2, then the fact that both O_1 and O_2 contain every point of $\mathbf{R}$ except for a finite number, the intersection $O_1 \cap O_2$ can never be empty (in fact, it will be infinite).

59. **D** First, the expression we're trying to simplify is:

$$f(\omega + \omega^{-1}) = (\omega + \omega^{-1})^2 + (\omega + \omega^{-1})$$
$$= \omega^2 + 2 + \omega^{-2} + \omega + \omega^{-1}$$
$$= (\omega^2 + \omega + 1 + \omega^{-1} + \omega^{-2}) + 1 \quad (*)$$

Now, if $\omega^5 = 1$, then $\omega^5 - 1 = 0$. Since the polynomial $\omega^5 - 1$ can be factored as

$$\omega^5 - 1 = (\omega - 1)(\omega^4 + \omega^3 + \omega^2 + \omega + 1)$$

we have $(\omega - 1)(\omega^4 + \omega^3 + \omega^2 + \omega + 1) = 0$. Since $\omega \neq 1$, it must be true that:

$$\omega^4 + \omega^3 + \omega^2 + \omega + 1 = 0$$

Dividing both sides of this equation by ω^2 gives us:

$$\omega^2 + \omega + 1 + \omega^{-1} + \omega^{-2} = 0$$

Comparing this result with equation (*) above, we see that:

$$f(\omega + \omega^{-1}) = (\omega^2 + \omega + 1 + \omega^{-1} + \omega^{-2}) + 1$$
$$= 0 + 1$$
$$= 1$$

60. **E** If $\mathbf{v}$ is an eigenvector of A, then, by definition, $\mathbf{v}$ is a nonzero vector such that $A\mathbf{v} = \lambda\mathbf{v}$ for some scalar (eigenvalue) λ.

Multiplying both sides of $A\mathbf{v} = \lambda\mathbf{v}$ by 2 gives $(2A)\mathbf{v} = (2\lambda)\mathbf{v}$, so $\mathbf{v}$ is also an eigenvector of the matrix $2A$ (that corresponds to the eigenvalue 2λ). Therefore, statement I is true.

Multiplying both sides of $A\mathbf{v} = \lambda\mathbf{v}$ by A gives $(A^2)\mathbf{v} = (\lambda A)\mathbf{v}$, so $(A^2)\mathbf{v} = \lambda(A\mathbf{v})$. Since $A\mathbf{v} = \lambda\mathbf{v}$, this last result becomes $(A^2)\mathbf{v} = \lambda(\lambda\mathbf{v}) = \lambda^2\mathbf{v}$, so $\mathbf{v}$ is also an eigenvector of the matrix A^2 (that corresponds to the eigenvalue λ^2). Therefore, statement II is true.

Multiplying both sides of $A\mathbf{v} = \lambda\mathbf{v}$ by A^{-1} gives $\mathbf{v} = \lambda(A^{-1}\mathbf{v})$, which is equivalent to the equation $A^{-1}\mathbf{v} = \lambda^{-1}\mathbf{v}$. (Since A is invertible, it cannot have 0 as an eigenvalue. Why? Because the determinant of a matrix is equal to the product of its eigenvalues; so, if 0 were an eigenvalue, then the matrix would have determinant 0 and thus be noninvertible. This observation assures us that we can form λ^{-1}.) Therefore, $\mathbf{v}$ is also an eigenvector of the matrix A^{-1} (that corresponds to the eigenvalue λ^{-1}). Therefore, statement III is true.

61. **D** Let R be the triangular region whose boundary is C. Then by Green's theorem:

$$\oint_C \sqrt{2x+1}\, dx + \left(2xy + \sqrt{y^2 - y}\right) dy = \iint_R \left[\frac{\partial}{\partial x}\left(2xy + \sqrt{y^2 - y}\right) - \frac{\partial}{\partial y}\left(\sqrt{2x+1}\right)\right] dy\, dx$$
$$= \iint_R 2y\, dy\, dx$$

Using the figure below:

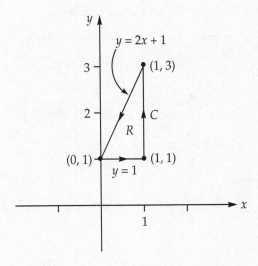

we can evaluate the double integral using iterated integrals:

$$\iint_R 2y\,dy\,dx = \int_0^1 \int_1^{2x+1} 2y\,dy\,dx$$
$$= \int_0^1 \left[y^2 \right]_1^{2x+1} dx$$
$$= \int_0^1 \left[(2x+1)^2 - 1 \right] dx$$
$$= \int_0^1 (4x^2 + 4x)\,dx$$
$$= \left[\tfrac{4}{3} x^3 + 2x^2 \right]_0^1$$
$$= \tfrac{10}{3}$$

62. **E**   We can show that choices (A), (B), (C), and (D) are all false with a single counterexample: Consider the characteristic function on **Q**, the set of rationals; this is the function defined by:

$$f(x) = \begin{cases} 1 & \text{if } x \in \mathbf{Q} \\ 0 & \text{if } x \notin \mathbf{Q} \end{cases}$$

This function is equal to zero almost everywhere; that is, the set of points at which the function is not zero (the set **Q**) has measure zero, because **Q** is a countable set. Therefore, this function is Lebesgue integrable (and the value of the integral is zero). This function is not Riemann integrable (so choice (A) is false). This function is discontinuous and nondifferentiable everywhere, so choices (C) and (D) are false; and since f is nondifferentiable on the entire real line, it's certainly nondifferentiable on every countably infinite of **R**, so choice (B) is false. The answer must be (E).

63. **B** The ratio test says that a series of positive terms, $\sum a_n$, will converge if $\lim_{n \to \infty}(a_{n+1}/a_n) < 1$. Applying the ratio test to the given series, we find that:

$$\lim_{n\to\infty}\frac{a_{n+1}}{a_n} = \lim_{n\to\infty}\left\{\frac{[(n+1)!]^3 x^{2(n+1)}}{[3(n+1)]!} \cdot \frac{(3n)!}{(n!)^3 x^{2n}}\right\}$$

$$= \lim_{n\to\infty}\left[\frac{(n+1)^3 x^2}{(3n+3)(3n+2)(3n+1)}\right]$$

$$= \frac{1}{27}x^2$$

From this, we find that:

$$\lim_{n\to\infty}\frac{a_{n+1}}{a_n} < 1 \quad \Leftrightarrow \quad \frac{1}{27}x^2 < 1 \quad \Leftrightarrow \quad x^2 < 27 \quad \Leftrightarrow \quad |x| < 3\sqrt{3}$$

64. **B** The 2 by 2 matrix whose (i, j) entry is $i + j$ is

$$A = \begin{pmatrix} a_{11} & a_{12} \\ a_{21} & a_{22} \end{pmatrix} = \begin{pmatrix} 1+1 & 1+2 \\ 2+1 & 2+2 \end{pmatrix} = \begin{pmatrix} 2 & 3 \\ 3 & 4 \end{pmatrix}$$

and the 3 by 3 matrix whose (i, j) entry is $i + j$ is:

$$B = \begin{pmatrix} b_{11} & b_{12} & b_{13} \\ b_{21} & b_{22} & b_{23} \\ b_{31} & b_{32} & b_{33} \end{pmatrix} = \begin{pmatrix} 1+1 & 1+2 & 1+3 \\ 2+1 & 2+2 & 2+3 \\ 3+1 & 3+2 & 3+3 \end{pmatrix} = \begin{pmatrix} 2 & 3 & 4 \\ 3 & 4 & 5 \\ 4 & 5 & 6 \end{pmatrix}$$

The determinant of A is easy to compute: $\det A = (2)(4) - (3)(3) = -1$. To find the determinant of B, we first subtract the second row from the third row and then subtract the first row from the second row. Since neither of these operations affects the determinant, we have:

$$\det\begin{pmatrix} 2 & 3 & 4 \\ 3 & 4 & 5 \\ 4 & 5 & 6 \end{pmatrix} = \det\begin{pmatrix} 2 & 3 & 4 \\ 1 & 1 & 1 \\ 1 & 1 & 1 \end{pmatrix}$$

The determinant of a matrix with two equal rows is zero, so $\det B = 0$. Therefore, $\det A + \det B = -1 + 0 = -1$.

65. **D** Let $\phi: \mathbf{Z}_m \to \mathbf{Z}_n$ be a ring homomorphism such that $\phi(1) = 1$. Since any ring homomorphism maps the additive identity to the additive identity, it must be true that $\phi(0) = 0$. In the ring $\mathbf{Z}_m$, we can write 0 as $m \bullet 1$, so:

$$\phi(0) = \phi(m \bullet 1) = m \bullet \phi(1) = m \bullet 1 = m$$

Because $\phi(0)$ must be equal to 0, the element m must be 0 in $\mathbf{Z}_n$. Therefore, it must be true that n divides m. The only pair of rings $(\mathbf{Z}_m, \mathbf{Z}_n)$ listed as a choice for which n divides m is choice (D), $(\mathbf{Z}_6, \mathbf{Z}_3)$.

GRE - SUBJECT TEST

SIDE 1

DO NOT USE INK

Use only a pencil with soft, black lead. (No. 2 or HB) to complete this answer sheet.
Be sure to fill in completely the space that corresponds to your answer choice.
Completely erase any errors or stray marks

1. NAME

Enter your last name, first name, initial (given name), and middle initial, if you have one.
Omit spaces, apostrophes, Jr., II., etc.

Last Name only (Family or Surname) - first 15 letters

First Name initial | Middle initial

BE SURE EACH MARK IS DARK AND COMPLETELY FILLS THE INTENDED SPACE AS ILLUSTRATED HERE.

The Princeton Review®

YOU MAY FIND MORE RESPONSE SPACES THAN YOU NEED. IF SO, PLEASE LEAVE THEM BLANK.

2. YOUR NAME:
(Print)

Last Name (Family or Surname)   First Name (Given)   M.I.

MAILING ADDRESS:

P.O. Box or Street Address

City   State or Province

Country   Zip or Postal Code

CENTER: City   State or Province

Country   Center Number   Room Number

SIGNATURE:

3. DATE OF BIRTH

Month	Day	Year
Jan.		
Feb.		
Mar.		
April		
May		
June		
July		
Aug.		
Sept.		
Oct.		
Nov.		
Dec.		

4. SOCIAL SECURITY NUMBER
(U.S.A. Only)

5. REGISTRATION NUMBER
(from your admission ticket)

6. TITLE CODE
(on back cover of your test book)

7. TEST NAME
(on back cover of your test book)

FORM CODE (on back cover of your test book)

8. TEST BOOK SERIAL NUMBER
(red number in upper right corner of front cover of your test book)

NOTES

NOTES

NOTES

NOTES

NOTES

NOTES

NOTES

More expert advice from
The Princeton Review

Give yourself the best chances for getting into the graduate school of your choice with **The Princeton Review**. We can help you get higher test scores, make the most informed choices, and make the most of your experience once you get there. We can also help you make the career move that will let you use your skills and education to their best advantage.